Lovingly,
Ione

John McMillan and Laureen Hemming

Lovingly, Ione

The Library of Congress has catalogued the paperback edition as follows:

Lovingly, Ione – 1st edition
ISBN: 978-1-944887-62-9
Library of Congress Control Number: 2020943044

Cover design by John McMillan.
Cover photo: Personal archive.
All photos used by permission.

Published by McMillan Design, Inc., 9816 Jacobsen Lane, Gig Harbor, WA 98332

Printed in the United States of America

www.ionemcmillan.com

February 3, 1942
Stanleyville, Congo Belge

Dearest Ones at Home,

"Hath God said, and shall He not do it? or hath He spoken and shall He not make it good?" Num. 23:19

I am writing this to send from Stanleyville when we shall arrive to-morrow, the Lord willing. My heart is full of praise and adoration for the One who has bro't us to very nearly the close of a wonderful journey. In two days we expect to arrive in Bongondza. The five weeks on the Ocean was truly a marvelous experience. It is true "a first ocean voyage holds more glamour than 100 succeeding ones." Outstanding were the salt breezes, the bright full moon over the crest of the waves, the brilliant phosphorus, the fellowship with other missionaries, the little French refugee girl who this year lost both father and lover in battle, the ship's officers who were kind and jolly, the most interesting of whom was the Chief Engineer, inclined at first to be gruff and then warming up to a friendly combat of words. The Chief's main ambition was to quit the sea and start a fur farm. I told him I tho't it would be quite a 'hair-raising' experience! He chuckled and from then on we were friends.

Jan. 19 - we sighted land and then started up the river toward Matadi. The first native I saw was a very little black boy with a very big white shirt on waving his arms from the shore. Then not satisfied that he had our attention, he pulled off the shirt and waved that; by that time I was half-way over the rail waving my own arms frantically and yodeling at him, much to the amusement of the older passengers.

Jan. 21 - stepped foot on shore, my right foot, as I remember. Temperature 97 degress. Boys on the dock were wearing varying degrees of clothing ranging from prisoners stripes on those who unloaded the mail, to tattered pants either moth-eaten or dog-bitten, and one boy with a coat, vest, tie, knee-length trousers, hat, hand-bag, and clothes brush! Before long we were surrounded by the black people and I was bewildered. Most all of the women were prettily dressed in long bright robes, carrying on their heads boxes, sacks, basins bottles(upright or on their sides, - the bottles, I mean!), pineapples, baskets, wood, and even an umbrella, long and black with a crook handle.

Jan. 23 - train ride from Matadi to Leopoldville, very hot and dirty trip on the "White Train" which is painted white. As soon as we came thru the first tunnel and emerged gasping for breath at the other end we discovered that neither we nor the train were any longer white. A missionary on this train told me, "Once you have been scorched by the African sun, you will never be satisfied anywhere else." Already I am freckled and tan and thoroughly scorched, but very happy and satisfied.

Jan. 24 - Aboard "Riene Astrid" beautiful Belgian river steamer for 12-day trip up the Congo. Two times I had a feeling of fear and helplessness - when we left and the drums down on the native's deck started to beat it was so forceful and strong and uncanny and increased in tempo until one's heart beat franticly. Then again when the white's up on the 'de luxe' deck started throwing money to little boys in the first village where we stopped for wood. Immediately about 75 little boys took off their trousers and plunged into the water and then came up and stretched out their hands and chanted a weird begging chant and clapped with an after-beat. It was amusing at first, then frightening. I turned away. This verse came to me, "I will trust and not be afraid -"

Jan. 28 - temperature 99 at 7:30 A.M. Noone looks at noon for it's too hot to look at anything. Past thru a village infested with sleeping sickness. Several said they saw tse-tse flies. Crocodiles and monkeys are seen occasionally. Here at Baloba the crocs ate 6 natives this year. When we stopped for wood we took on a parrot, two huge squealing pigs and a native murderer, all delivered on the lower deck, thank goodness.

Feb. 3 - still well and healthy, still able to keep my hair in curls and my nose powdered, tho' washing in yellow Congo water gives one a muddy complexion! Appetite good and have lots of pep. Hoping for some letters to-morrow - don't you fail me, now!

The letter from Ione McMillan to her family that colorfully describes her entrance into the Belgian Congo for the first time.

CONTENTS

AUTHORS' NOTE

This biography contains personal information that Ione and Hector McMillan intended only for recipients of their letters. The McMillan family feels, however, that their parents would have approved of sharing their life story with others.

Readers should also bear in mind that the letters were written during an earlier time in a Central African country with a history of colonial and racial injustice. As a historical document and teaching tool, it may include criticism of certain religious groups, strict disciplinary measures, mistreatment or killing of animals, and attitudes or comments that might be considered racial, offensive or inappropriate today.

Since hundreds of letters and documents needed condensing into a readable format, much effort and care was taken to publish only what was deemed essential to the story.

Letters and documents were compiled, transcribed, and digitized by John McMillan, fourth son of Hector and Ione. John also prepared the Epilogue, the Afterword, the cover art, the maps of Appendix A and B and the Chronology.

Cover photo of Ione and Hector was taken in New York shortly after they re-met having spent four years in a long-distance courtship. Front cover background is taken from a 1950s 15 centime Belgian Congo stamp.

Laureen (Walby) Hemming provided most of the text condensing and background commentary between the letters to blend the narrative together. Laureen is the eldest daughter of Alf and Eileen Walby, colleagues of Ione and Hector McMillan. The Walbys served as missionaries in the Belgian Congo until 1960. They led the work at Bongondza when the McMillans went back home for furlough, and lived in the houses Ione refers to. Laureen was the eldest girl resident in the Children's Home from 1955 until 1960. This biography is greatly enhanced by Laureen's medical experience and her in-depth knowledge of the mission and the political backdrop of the time.

Letters and other original documents are in italics and are largely unedited. They may contain explanatory text within brackets. Periodic footnotes provide background or further clarification.

Transitional material connecting the letters has been edited for American English; letters and other original documents maintain their original British or Canadian English.

PREFACE

The Hector and Ione McMillan story you are about to read spans the lives of two remarkable people and the family they raised in the heart of Africa. Although much material has been lost through the years, thankfully over 1,500 letters, news articles, and other documents were saved by Ione; her mother, Leone Reed; various family members; and fellow missionaries and friends. Some 35 years after their mother's death, David and John McMillan began chronologically compiling this complete collection of surviving correspondence. In so doing, they discovered a rich treasure trove of their parents' early days—love letters that brought Hector and Ione together, and photos and events they themselves knew little or nothing about. John accepted the enormous task of digitizing the material, energized by curiosity, anticipation, and inspiration. David and John felt privileged to be the first ones to read the story straight through. And what a story!

Although her husband, Hector, and her family play significant roles, Ione wrote most of the letters that make up the collection, so it seems fitting to view her as the subject of the story. Ione was a prolific letter writer who started writing at age 11 and continued right up to her death at age 63. All of the major events in her life are documented, often in detail. Six years before her death she trimmed her mailing list down to 1,350 names—an indication of the volume of newsletters that were mailed out at every major life transition. In addition, she dutifully and lovingly responded to all personal letters written to her throughout her life. Pen and paper and her worn-out typewriter were nearby at all times. She was a passionate writer, as you will see, filling the pages with personal anecdotes, humor, and interesting stories and accounts of people she worked with and met on her journeys. She wrote while on buses, trains, boats, and steamships on the Congo River and the Nile.

In 1959, while at the Children's Home at Kilometer 8, she wrote:

.....Last year Hector bought a desk file drawer for where I write letters, and it has been a useful remembrance of our years together. In it I have building project papers, children's records, staff records, books, household purchases, letters to answer, letters answered, visitor's book, valuable papers, stamps, envelopes, and a file for furlough addresses, etc. Also notes, diary, etc. for the book which will be written by someone someday, probably not me. I wonder if Mother will be too busy to take my 'collection' and do something with it. I have not said anything to her about it, but have carbons, etc. from when we first came to the field, and especially since the Children's Home project started.

We have let Ione tell most of the story through her own words even though the flow might often get broken. Gaps may be caused by wartime censorship, lost letters, termite damage or hasty departures. Hopefully the gift of her writing will soften the bumps. In an age of social networking where correspondence is easily and usually deleted, what a rare treat to have the lives of Hector and Ione McMillan, preserved to pass on to future generations.

ACKNOWLEDGEMENTS

by John McMillan

An enormous debt of gratitude from the McMillan family goes to Laureen Hemming for the many hours condensing the voluminous text into a readable format and for providing background commentary between the letters to blend the story together.

Were it not for all those who saved Ione's letters and documents, such as her mother, Leone Reed, the folks at the Unevangelized Fields Mission headquarters in the United States and Ione herself, we would not be enjoying this story.

A big thank you goes to David & Becky McMillan as well as Ginny McMillan (Ken's wife) for organizing over half of the letters and documents and making them available to me.

Compiling and transcribing (digitizing) the original documents took me the better part of a year starting in March of 2011. Much support throughout this project has come from my other brothers Ken, Paul, Steve and Tim.

And special thanks to Mary Manning, my partner, for her editing and patience during the years spent working on this project. Our collective gratitude goes to Alice Manning, Mary's mother, for the countless hours spent on editing the original, 1,000-page, digitized document. Additional proofreading by Vicki Nichelson, Mary Cloutier, Barbara Kline and David and Becky McMillan is much appreciated.

For all the letters, articles, notes and contributions that came from outside the McMillan family that shed light on this wonderful narrative, I would like to thank the following individuals or their living heirs on their behalf:

Laura Ambrose
Rev. Charles Baxter
Olive Bjerkseth
Doug Brock
Chester and Dolena Burk
Del and Lois Carper
Jim Carter
Chuck and Muriel Davis
Leslie Goodman
Sonia Grant
Pearl Hiles
Herb and Alice Jenkinson
Sid Katz

George Kerrigan
Al and Jean Larson
Bob and Alma McAllister
Ralph Odman
E.J. and Lilian Pudney
Mary Rutt
Charles Sarginson
Verna Schade
Betty Shultz
Florence Selden
Bill Snyder
Viola Walker
Dr. George Westcott

INTRODUCTION

Ione McMillan was an incredible Christian woman who lived a remarkable life of faith, strength and endurance. We know so much about her because she was a prolific letter writer. As a single woman, she had a good career, doing what she loved most – singing. She spent several years traveling with the Sunshine Gospel Trio throughout the eastern United States enjoying life on the road and always retaining her stylish appearance. She then committed her life to serving God in a foreign land and her first calling was to China. When that mission field closed due to World War II, the door to the Belgian Congo opened. Ione sailed across the Atlantic in the 1940s during the war years under blackout conditions, journeyed up the Congo River, and then for three years lived and worked as a single woman at a remote mission station in the center of colonial Belgian Congo's vast, dark forest.

Much of Ione's missionary story occurs under the umbrella of the Unevangelized Fields Mission (UFM), now called Crossworld. In the months leading up to her departure, Ione resided at the UFM headquarters in Toronto where she met Hector McMillan, who was hoping to do missionary work in Brazil.

Hector, who came from a humble Scottish farming family in Ontario, Canada, was a practical, inventive handy man with a humorous nature who was loved by those he lived and worked with. Early in his life, he also committed himself to the service of God and later became an ordained minister. The doors to Brazil closed as the war brought travel restrictions. Once Hector felt that God was leading him to missionary service in the Congo, he applied at the UFM. Hector took an instant liking to Ione when the two met at the UFM headquarters. One of many suitors Ione had, Hector sweetly finds his way into her heart over four romantic years of correspondence, most of which occurred while she was in the Congo and he was in Canada serving in the Canadian Airforce.

Through their letters, Ione and Hector became engaged to be married and their storybook wedding finally took place some 2,500 miles up the Nile at Juba in Anglo-Egyptian Sudan. Thus, they started their adventuresome lives together as a missionary couple in the Congo. They were both well suited to raising a large family of six boys, all born a year apart. They were devoted Christians who claimed verses from the Bible every day to guide them and their children through the maze of challenges they faced. As missionaries, they were always eager to share their love of God and the plan of salvation to those in need. Hector and Ione helped other missionaries so much that they were called "servants of the servants of God".

Before her life with Hector, Ione spent most of her time in the Congo looking after other missionaries and their children. Her desire to be a village evangelist was put on hold while she attended to the family of Dr. and Mrs. Westcott, missionaries at Bongondza, a remote hospital station. Ellen Westcott had a chronic health condition that often rendered her bedridden, so someone was needed to care for her and the children. Then there was the Children's Home which Hector and Ione established in order to care for all the UFM missionaries' children including their own, so that they could attend the Belgian school in Stanleyville. As station hosts, the task of caring for all traveling missionaries and several regional conferences also fell to them which included logistics, transportation, food preparation, accommodations, and even vehicle repair.

Ione had a keen sense for the natural world around her. Her descriptive writing brings to life what living in the center of Africa was really like. There was jungle life, listening to chimpanzees howling in the night, forest elephants, scorpions, finding a snake slithering under the bed, and having the home invaded by driver ants on a migratory raid, to say nothing of the physical impact—acquiring jiggers under the skin on toes and feet, being infested by filarial worms, and suffering amoebic dysentery and malaria.

Music was an important factor in their relationship. Ione was involved in music her whole life (singing, piano, autoharp, and accordion) and Hector learned to play the guitar and was enraptured with Ione's singing, as we all were. These two vibrant lives came together to form a single, rich tone, much like the tines of a tuning fork.

The Stanleyville area during the early 1960s was not a safe place to be as Congo gained independence. Many missionaries were unable to avoid the conflict and bloodshed of the Simba Rebellion including Hector McMillan who was killed on November 24, 1964, 8 kilometers outside of Stanleyville. A few days before this, Ione recalled of Hector:

.....He ate and drank normally, especially enjoying a cool drink of water. Sometimes he drank cup after cup before his thirst was quenched. Then he would give a shout, and say, "When I get to the River of Life, I'm going to drink and drink and drink." During the last few days, the other missionaries noticed and remarked about a happy other-worldly expression upon Hector's face, which never left, even after his spirit was gone.

The martyrdom of Hector and the incredible life he and Ione led together are all contained in their letters, the writing of which was a big part of their lives. They were both aware of their lasting impact. Hector wrote to Ione in the Congo during their long-distance courtship on September 28, 1942, from Toronto:

.....I can readily picture you and Pearl gleaning rich blessing from the Word as you sat under the lofty panoply, surrounded by the hum of forest life. But most of all the simile of the crickets—how do you think of such apt descriptions? I have listened to crickets for years but never before did it occur to me that it sounded like the winding of watches, which is the very truth of the matter. I think that I will not be satisfied until you write a book. Maybe that is why you want me for a right-hand man...so I can bring you bread and water, and paper and ink while you produce compositions of international fame.

Ione wrote to son, Ken, from Congo on January 28, 1971:

.....Today I tried getting up at 3 instead of 4 to get more supporters thanked. I love to write letters but do not like the cold, hasty way which only thanks but puts no interest & life into it. And this takes time & a clear mind. I want the dew of heaven to be in my letters as well as my life.

Chapter 1
IONE: THE EARLY YEARS

Ethel Leone Reed woke at five in the morning and knew instinctively that it was Sunday, the day that the Lord had given for rest and peaceful contemplation. This was possible, of course, for all the household chores had been done; her entire home was clean, neat, and tidy. Even the old laundry stove in the utility room, which not only heated water but kept the house warm in the winter, had been raked out and polished with black lead until it looked almost new. In this contented and carefree state of mind, Ethel, whom her family called Leone, reached out her hand through the bars of the baby's cot beside her to caress her little daughter. Immediately, she was wide awake as she realized that the cot was empty. In panic-stricken horror she thought that someone must have come through the door in the bedroom that opened onto the patio and yard and had stolen her baby. But when her husband, Arthur, in a similar state of panic checked on the door, he found it was still locked from the inside. An eerie silence lay over the house as together they began a frantic search through the whole house. They searched through the library, the living room, the parlor, the sewing room, on into the dining room and eventually into the kitchen. There, sitting atop the freshly cleaned stove was their beloved Ione, playing with the damper in the stove pipe with one hand while holding on to the cold chimney with the other hand to maintain her balance. Her excited little face and Dr. Denton sleepers were smeared with stove blacking and all her parents could do was clutch her in their arms in pure relief and joy. This voyage of discovery at such a tender age was the first indication of the remarkable spirit of adventure that was to become such a feature of Ione's long and eventful life.

It all began when Marguerite Ione Reed was born on August 17, 1913, in Grand Rapids, Michigan. It was a Sunday evening, 8.30 p.m. to be precise, and both her grandmothers were in attendance, excited and honored to be present at the arrival of a healthy 8-1/2–pound baby girl with long, straight black hair. Ione, the name she would always be known by, was the second daughter of four to be born to Arthur Stewart Reed and Ethel Leone Reed. In the years to come, Leone always maintained that the first few months of Ione's life, unless she was sleeping or feeding, had been spent crying lustily. She was not unhappy or in pain but merely exercising her vocal chords in readiness for a life that would be filled with song. This state of affairs did not last long and she soon displayed her sunny and loving disposition; another characteristic that would stay with her for the rest of her life. However, it was not always joy and happiness; there were lessons to be learned, as with all children. On one occasion, when Ione was not quite a year old, Leone took her daughters to visit their great-grandmother. Ione spent the day crawling around, making new discoveries, and reveling in all the lavish attention. When it came time to be fed, she

1

was given her bottle, but she was so intrigued with all the excitement that she refused to take it. Thus, began a battle of wills and, despite a spanking, Ione showed steely determination and continued to refuse the bottle. Leone was about to concede when her grandmother came into the room and cautioned her not to give in, as the battle would only have to be fought another day and, the older the child the more difficult that battle would be. And so, with both Leone and the wailing Ione, the conflict raged on until Ione finally gave in. Such were the guidelines in parenting at the beginning of the 20th century when adults didn't consider that their actions and attentions could cause hyperactivity in a child and subsequent overtiredness!

Ione with her mother, c1917

Attitudes toward disciplining small children have changed over the years, but it is perfectly clear that, for the rest of her life, Ione would always follow the instructions of those she perceived to be in a position of authority, be they human or divine. This would ultimately lead her into a unique missionary service using her special talents to care and provide for her own children and those of so many other missionaries.

Ione's entire life was spent traveling from place to place, creating one home after another. Her nomadic lifestyle began at an early age, moving with the family and her father's employment when she was three years old from Grand Rapids, Michigan, to Eire, Pennsylvania, and then on to Washington, DC, the following year. She sang wartime songs such as "Keep the Home Fires Burning" to small groups of soldiers and their families while her father was an instructor in the Navy yard and she seemed to enjoy "performing". Within two years, the family was on the move again to Pontiac, Michigan. There, she sang her first alto part in a duet with her sister during the Sunday morning church service. The years spent in Pontiac were settled for a while, and the friendships she forged there lasted her entire life. These friends and her city church played a huge part in her support system when she eventually became a missionary. Her recovery from a serious bout of pneumonia when she was eight years old, from which she almost died, was an early sign that the Lord had her life in His hands. More than that, He had the rest of her life planned out, should she choose to follow His calling. Happily, for the many people she would meet and help along the way, she was pleased to obey God's calling. Many years later she recalled:

.....Perhaps some of you remember when a group of us organized 'The Gospel Messengers', a little group who met regularly for prayer and then went out to meetings around Pontiac, and during evangelistic campaigns did personal work. I have just found in my diary for November 1931 an account of one of the first persons I dealt with; a man who sat near my mother and me in an evening

service. I spoke to him and he was very gruff in his reply and scared me so I cried and didn't want to talk to anybody after that. Then a few days later, I got up enough courage to go to the inquiry room and ask if I was needed there, and when they let me come in and help deal with those who came forward, lo and behold, I found there my 'gruff' man!! This was a real encouragement to me.

Ione Reed, c1935

While she was still in high school, she decided that in order to be a true Christian she needed to know more of God's word in the Bible and to distance herself from more worldly pursuits. The way to achieve this goal was to attend Moody Bible Institute (MBI) in Chicago, if the necessary funding could be found. As would happen so often during her life, the money for this undertaking came at the eleventh hour, and her ambitions began to be realized. Her connection with her parents and, by now, three sisters was strong and though she longed to be with them to rejoice in the good times and help out in the not so good, she committed herself to the Lord's service and, after joining MBI in 1932, sometimes found herself far from home and constantly on the move as a member of the singing group, The Sunshine Gospel Trio. Ione had a beautiful singing voice with a bell-like clarity and an instinct for harmony. Together with Genevieve Burns

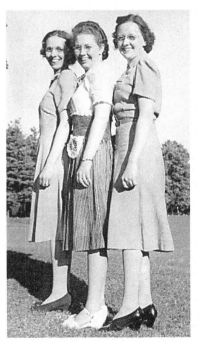

The Sunshine Gospel Trio: Otila (Tee) Mauch, Genevieve Burns and Ione Reed - c1937.

and Otila (Tee) Mauch, they traveled through thirty-three states as part of an outreach project, singing gospel songs, and giving talks and testimonies as to the effect of the Lord upon their lives. As befitted girl groups of the time, they were dressed in matching outfits that were both stylish and fashionable and which fulfilled Ione's notion of always looking as well as doing her best.

.....In a week or so I will be sending for some of my summer things, for we shall be quite far south in Ohio and it gets warm early. I'm planning to buy a new spring suit or coat. I'd like a tan and blue outfit. I'm tired of grey.

It was during these travels that her letter writing habit began whenever and wherever the opportunity arose to keep in touch with her beloved family and friends. Her trusty typewriter seemed always to be with her. She also included a line of Scripture that emphasized just what it was that she wanted to convey.

3

In September 1935, on her father's birthday, she wrote home and to him in particular:

..... 'Always in every prayer of mine for you all making request with joy' Phil. 1.4. With it comes all the love and tenderness that can come from a daughter to a father. I hope this may be the happiest birthday you have ever had and that as you are gathered around the supper table, having worship together, that your hearts may all be knit together in that bond of love. I will be there in spirit also. Will you turn over to Deuteronomy 8:2 and read it saying fifty years instead of forty?... 'And thou shalt remember all the way which the Lord thy God led thee these forty years in the wilderness to humble thee and to prove thee to know what was in thine heart whether thou wouldst keep his commandments or no'... How I thank my God for a Christian father and mother who are praying for me as I go from place to place.

She went on to ask after all the family and to say how much she missed them. She provided them with graphic information about a trip to the dentist and finished by suggesting that they might be able to hear some of her work with the Sunshine Gospel Trio if they listen to a particular radio station at 8:20 in the morning.

Her singing and good nature brought her compliments from many directions. She

"THEIR

Radiant Christian Spirit

SCATTERS SUNSHINE EVERYWHERE"

The

SUNSHINE GOSPEL TRIO

of

The Moody Bible Institute

of Chicago

Sunshine Gospel Trio

Graduates of

The Moody Bible Institute

Otila A. Mauch ....Second Alto
Genevieve M. Burns...First Alto
Ione M. Reed.........Soprano

Available for evangelistic meetings, Bible conferences, youth rallies, and other Christian gatherings.

One of the hopeful signs of the age is the response of young people to the leadership of Christ, but youth responds most quickly to youth. This has led The Moody Bible Institute of Chicago to put the Sunshine Gospel Trio into the field. Graduates of that Institute, they are not only ministers of music but also messengers of the Christian gospel.

These young women are on a youth crusade, and come to you with song winged with spiritual passion, and the stinging salt of witness-bearing speech.

They have toured twenty-eight states, giving their testimony to thousands of young people in colleges, high schools, churches, and over the radio.

Correspondence with the Extension Department concerning time and ministry is invited, and every effort will be made to arrange dates that will be mutually satisfactory.

Address correspondence to
The Moody Bible Institute of Chicago
Extension Department
153 Institute Place
Chicago, Ill.

The Trio in performance dress pictured on a promotional flier.

was working in Wilmore, Kentucky, when an unsolicited letter came addressed to Miss Reed from Reverend Clarence Baxter who desired to become Ione's pen pal!

.....May the sweet melody of your voice and your graceful poise, if nothing else, serve as an excuse for informally intruding upon the good nature of a young lady by addressing her without ever having been introduced to her. I sat in the auditorium of Ashbury College and listened to you sing. It so thrilled and enthralled me that if I ever had the privilege of hearing Jenny Lind[1] sing I could have praised her no more than I do you. Heaven was close the morning your sweet voice rang forth, as clear as a bell, in those sweet anthems. Your speech also was delivered in a superb way and it carried a thought that made me desire your friendship... I would count it a great joy to meet you someday. May I at least receive a response to this letter and I shall not feel disappointed.

It was indeed an era when letter writing was something of an art form, and that particular demonstration of unrequited love had come from a reverend! Ione was not short of suitors to whom she would write back at first, but she soon found that absence did not always make the heart grow fonder.

.....When I saw him at Founder's Week Conference I loved him, or thought I did. Then when he left, I found out I got along nicely without him.

Of another she wrote to her sister:

.....The one young man here who likes me and is nice looking asks me continually for dates and was over to the house the other night after the service but I just don't dare date him. If I did all the young women would go back on me, for they all like him. He is real tall, dark curly hair . . . an Englishman. But I know he will be bald one day and he is not dependable nor a good provider: besides I don't care for him.

And thus, another suitor fell by the wayside. The irony is that when she did fall in love, the man would himself be bald! If Ione ever felt confused by her emotions, she would ask her mother's advice and would be answered by return post and, on one occasion, with short shrift:

.....She reprimanded me for continuing Bob's friendship when I would never marry him. She said 'I would rather see you go to China'.

This last comment was a reference to Ione's decision to be a missionary in China. The martyrdom of John and Betty Stam, murdered by Communist Chinese soldiers in 1934, had fueled her enthusiasm and she was hoping to persuade her family to approve. Her mother most certainly did not, but her mother's comment was the tip of the wedge that Ione needed to get her family on her side. Ione learned that the folks in her church, including her family, had obtained a real vision of the SCBM (South China Boat Mission) through Helen Western, who had recently returned from there.

.....They were willing for me to go to China, provided I go with her [Helen]. So, I am now about to fill out my application blank. I do it prayerfully and with much consideration for although I have looked forward to it for two years, it is too big

---

[1] The acclaimed Swedish opera singer of the late 1800s who toured America with P. T. Barnum.

a step to take lightly. And in doing so I say, as did Spencer Walton's: 'I desire
nothing but the will of God; nothing more, nothing less and nothing else.'

But China and her missionary work were still some time away. In the meantime, she
continued traveling, singing, and witnessing, all the while missing her family and
wishing that she could do more to help them back home. Sitting in the Wacker Hotel
in Chicago in February, 1938 she wrote:

.....We finished our work at Olney [Illinois] Sunday night with a packed house.
The Lord blessed us much while there, but there were few visible results. I know
of six who accepted Christ, and about a dozen who re-consecrated their lives to
the Lord. The work was mostly among the young people and many came to us
individually and said they had given up worldly amusements. On the last Sunday
afternoon we took full charge of a young people's meeting and afterward people
came to us and said they wished that we had had full charge all through the two
weeks. I know there would have been more results. The people gave us a fine
offering ($171), and a cordial invitation to come back.

Monday night we held a service in Martinsville, Illinois, the place where our
trio was three years ago when little Esther was born. You remember? We had a
wonderful time. Two hands raised. Offering was $30. I guess the Lord knows
that Tee needs money. The money I am enclosing is to begin straightening my
debts at home. The $10 money order is tithe money for Marcellyn's [Ione's
younger sister] Moody fund, to be put in [the] bank. The 5 is to go on my loan
from Mother and Papa, leaving $65 yet, I believe.

.....Bob [Arthur] writes me very regularly. He told me when he wrote to mother
that he had a hard time writing it. Just tell Bob to wait for a number of months
or until our Trio work finishes. Tee says that will be a year from April. But I have
told Tee that if the China situation clears up before then, I would feel constrained
to go to China. I think that Bob and I can continue writing without definite plans
for the future. I don't know why I always rush into things so and am so
inconsistent. I just let my feelings rule me. And the worst of it is that my feelings
for Bob have not changed in the three weeks since I saw him. I think you should
write him soon, if you have not already. And please forgive me for causing you
heart aches. I'll be in a steady grind of meetings from now on and perhaps I'll
reach a more sober point of view.

.....I hope this letter finds things better at home.

Ione, from the very beginning of her writings, had deep emotional feelings for her
mother and sisters, especially when she heard of their health, financial and
housekeeping problems on the home front.

.....Mother shouldn't have to do a thing about the house, but plan the meals, the
budget, clothes, perhaps mend and <u>write letters to me!!</u> I think it's a pity for
Mother to have to worry about all the details of the house.......And Lucille [Ione's
older sister] shouldn't have to bear it either. She has enough. If I felt that it
weren't possible for you to get along at home, I would quit the Trio and come
home, but it wouldn't be right and I don't think it's necessary.

.....I guess I shouldn't be so blue about everything, but I couldn't help it, knowing that [my absence] was causing extra heart aches. But I know that everything will come out all right, for Romans 8:28 is still in the Bible! 'All things work together for good, to them that love the Lord.'

.....I want you to know that I love you all as much as a daughter can, and I am always longing to see you. My prayers go up for you continually. I want God's best in my life and that I'll never disappoint you. May the Lord bless you and keep you while we are absent one from the other! - - Lovingly, Ione.

Phil. 1:3-6 'I thank my God upon every remembrance of you.

Always in every prayer of mine for you all making request with joy,
For your fellowship in the gospel from the first day until now;

Being confident of this very thing, that he which hath begun a good work in you, will perform it until the day of Jesus Christ.'

Ione's ministry with the sunshine Trio lasted for seven years, until 1939. All the meetings she took part in, the broadcasts, and the work with children were, without a doubt, the Lord's preparation for her eventual work as a missionary. Constantly traveling from state to state, she missed her family desperately but was still able to visit home intermittently. When her mother fell ill, she felt that she ought to go home and help but learned another valuable lesson, that her family could manage quite well without her, as many other families did at times. When letters did not arrive from them, it was good training for having to wait far longer at the mercy of foreign postal services. In her personal life, she was also learning where her priorities lay. Though she chastised herself often for her indecision regarding her would-be partner and the pressures of leaving the work at home to her mother and sisters, she held fast waiting for the will of God and did not bow to the pressure she was subjected to.

Ione's letters home were full of the love that she had for her family. The following was written on Mother's Day, May 8, 1938:

.....How I long to be home! 'Tis there I know I'd find the dearest Mother in all the world. There are so many things I'd like to have given you, Mother, but I know all you want is our love. And I do love you very much, Mother.

And when I think of Mother I always think too of Papa, for he means so much to me. Nothing makes me happier than to know that I have a Christian father. I look forward to the day when there will be no more separations, but we'll all be together in Heaven, - or on Earth if He comes soon.

On October 20, 1938, Ione's father died and she wrote a poem for him in his memory. (Of the many archived poems that she wrote, this is an example.)

ONLY A DAD with a tired face
Coming from the daily race
Bringing the little of gold or fame
To show how well he has played the game;
But glad in his heart that his own rejoice
To see him come and hear his voice.

ONLY A DAD with brood of four
One of ten million men or more,
Plodding along in the daily strife,
Bearing the whips and scorns of life
With never a whimper of pain or hate,
For the sake of those who at home wait.
ONLY A DAD, neither rich nor proud,
Merely one of the surging Crowd,
Toiling, striving from day to day,
Facing whatever may come his way.
Silent, whenever the harsh condemn
And bearing it all for the love of them.
ONLY A DAD but he gave his all
To smooth the way for his children small.
Doing with courage stern and grim,
The deeds which meant sacrifice for him,
This is the line that for him we pen
ONLY A DAD, but the best of men.

At the same time, Leone needed an operation, which was also a cause of concern for Ione; should she go home to be with her or send the money to pay for a special nurse for a day?

.....I am trusting the Lord for this operation. I believe He will see you through, Mother. It takes courage, but 'He doeth all things well'. Dr Horulett is a good doctor and I have confidence in him.

Her confidence was well placed and the operation was a success.

In April 1939, Ione was at the National Bible Institute in New York. With her adventurous spirit, she found the big city exciting and full of possibilities.

.....The subways are the most used and they are crowded! You have to run like everything and push if you get in one. And when you get into the car you've got to sit immediately if there's a seat. I stopped to straighten my coat and sat on a Jew! Getting the last seat in the car is like Grandpa Snazzy with eleven forks in his hand!

.....We had meetings every night last week but in the daytime saw many places of interest. One day we saw Harry Emerson Fosdick's Riverside Church. He is America's leading modernist preacher. The church has a high carillon tower with the largest bells in the world. One bell weighs 20 tons. We also saw Columbia University, Union Theological Seminary, and National Jewish Theological. Another day we took a nickel ferry to Staten Island, which passed the Statue of Liberty, Ellis Island, Battery Park. We happened to pass the huge ocean liner 'Queen Mary', one of the two largest in the world. It was thrilling.... Today we are going to take a bus and ride through Harlem. Maybe we'll see some black people! [If only she had known what the future held for her.]

Nevertheless, the work of singing, taking services, and broadcasting on the radio was always more important to her. She constantly asked to be remembered in her family's prayers that there would be a continuous program of places to go and people to minister to. There was still time to indulge in some retail therapy, though.

> .....We went shopping and found some cute dresses—a shade of purple and rose combination. I had to get some $1.98 patent leather pumps to go with the dress! We had an important meeting that night.... We wore our new dresses. Mr Olsen [Vice President of the Fitch Investment Company] announced from the platform that we looked just as sweet as we sang!

The suitors were still there in abundance, and one called Ernie:

> .....he sent me a deluge of letters the last few days and his letter this morning asks me whether I have decided I want to marry him. I'm not ready for such a question for I hardly know him but if I can't stall him off until I know him better and if he won't wait for his answer I'll just have to say 'No' – as much as I like him. I wish you could meet him, Mother, and tell me what you think. In the meantime, pray for me.

Two weeks later, the poor young man was in hospital with appendicitis and still desired an answer to his proposal. Ione wrote to her mother:

> .....Pray for 'E' now in the hospital, and for our friendship. I think it won't work.... He isn't as refined as I'd like him to be!

In the meantime, there were places to go and new experiences to try out. One day in May of 1939, the girls all went to the World's Fair. There, having paid 75 cents to get in, they happened upon the Bell Telephone exhibit and as they entered the building were asked if they would like to sign up for a demonstration of a long-distance call. Ione, of course, rang her mother and sister and could have talked all day. But more than a long-distant call took place:

> .....After this exciting time we strolled around the building and came to a room where they asked us if we would like to record our voice on a steel tape and hear it again. We said 'Sure', so we stepped up in line. We told the man we were a trio and he said, 'Oh fine, we'll see that you get in!' This too was supposed to be just certain ones to get to do it but we got it right away and when our group of five came out we were instructed what to say by a man. The other two were students at Columbia University, young men. We had two minutes all together. The man would ask questions about what we did and what we were interested in. Then he asked us to sing and we sang 'Every day with Jesus'; when we finished he said, 'Fine, sing another, there is time!' So we sang 'In my heart there rings a melody'. There were about 150 people listening then, and when we finished, the tape was reversed and we sat down with the audience and heard it repeated. So, we really sang four times and gave the Gospel message to that many people!! I can't tell you all the wonderful things and buildings and exhibits we saw after that, but it was well worth the money. It cost me a dollar all together.

The cost of the day out was a bargain given the experiences they had, but money was regularly a subject for some concern. Everyday living in New York was more expensive than they had thought, especially all the traveling on the subway. They walked as much as possible:

> .....*I wear out about a pair of stockings a week. We have to go such long distances to our meetings ... and it takes so much walking that my sox are gone before I know it. And I have to have my hair set oftener. I had to borrow $17 of Tee by the time I got my check, which, by the way, came late. The $17 was for our new uniforms ($7), patent leather pumps to go with it ($2), hair sets twice ($2), stockings about $2.50, $1 at the Fair and the other $2.50 for little things such as powder, both talcum and face, etc.*

Ione would have liked to send money home to help out the family and also to fund her sister's hope of going to Moody, but New York was so much more expensive and the girls felt they needed to maintain their appearance in order to do better work as a trio. Ione once again felt cut off from her family and complained to them for not writing to her, prompting them with a tirade of questions about life at home.

> .....*How does Marcellyn like her job and does she work steady? Is Flora* [a boarder] *still staying with us? How much does she pay? Do you have the garden in yet? And did Doris get her new coat and hat?*

She shows her genuine concern for them but was soon telling them of more adventures in the city:

> .....*Tuesday night we again had a free night so a returned missionary whom we met before in Pana, Illinois, took us to Chinatown and the Bowery. We wouldn't have gone without him, for it would be very dangerous. It's the worst section of town. We went in the Midnight Mission where so many wonderful Christian leaders were saved and saw how it was transformed from an opium den. There were still the three arched passageways which led out formerly to various places in the city where the elite of N.Y. went through to keep from being known. A Chinese woman always prepared the opium for the society people, for if they prepared it themselves they might take too much.*
>
> *The man who was explaining said these passageways were rat-infested and very terrible to see. As he was talking, we heard an awful scratching sound. It was about a foot from me where I was sitting, in a box beside me. I jumped about two feet in the air it scared me so; I thought a rat was coming out. I didn't land in the same seat when I came down but made sure I was sitting further away, on a seat on the other side of the missionary! I peeked around at it and lo! ... a scrawny, dirty old cat crawled out!*
>
> *When we were out again a drunk man harassed us until we had to call a policeman to steer him off; he was begging for money. Then, when we had seen a Chinese temple, the quaint shops, the ugly filthy grocery stores, we went to the Bowery. Nothing happened there for we hurried through, passing terrible looking men with beady eyes, slinking in the shadows. When we got within a block of home we were complementing ourselves on getting through Chinatown and the Bowery without seeing anything so terrible, when all of a sudden, we looked just ahead of us and a man was laying on his face right in front of the*

gutter which had about an inch of water. His head was just under the curve of the back wheel of an auto. Three men were looking at him and debating what to do; they wanted to move their car but didn't dare touch him until a policeman came. We were waiting a few minutes when another man came and said, 'I know him; he's an epileptic; has those spells often; don't worry about him.' He turned to go and so did we, but just then a policeman came. He dragged him up on the walk, more like an animal than a man. We drew closer and looked at him just as the cop turned him over and when we saw his face we were shocked. It was all bashed in and bloody and he was dead! The cop took his pulse and shook his head, but said, 'I'll call an ambulance anyway.' So he went to the drugstore and took one man with him for a witness as to how the man was found. That's all we saw but that was enough to haunt us in our sleep! We had to come all the way back from the slums to have that happen.

I hope this letter doesn't make you have bad dreams. I really must close and get the other 23 letters I owe! Have you heard from Lucille lately? I don't think I've heard from her since March!

I'm feeling fine but all the running around has taken my weight down a little.....We eat most of our meals in the Horn and Hardart Automat. Maybe you've heard of the automatic cafeterias in N.Y. You get your money changed into nickels and dimes and put them in the slots in the wall and open a little door and out comes what you want. They have wall after wall of doors about the size of a dinner plate, with one section for all kinds of sandwiches, salads, hot dishes, breads, etc. You even put a nickel in for coffee or other drinks, put your cup or glass under a faucet and out comes exactly as much as you're supposed to get! All the little doors are glassed so you can see what you get. Of course, they have steam table for the meat and vegetable dinners but even there you have to put money in the slot before they give it to you. When you finish eating, you just get up and walk out; your dinner is all paid for and consumed. Best of all, there's no smoking or drinking allowed.

They were exciting times indeed. In June, they finally left New York and headed south to Decatur, Alabama. Ione was delighted with a letter from home at last and wrote back immediately, admonishing her mother to take more care of herself, to make sure Doris did all the heavy work in the garden, and not to take on so many outside activities for the church.

Having worried everyone about her weight loss, she reassured them that her weight was going back up again and she had a new position:

.....Your honourable daughter, Ione, is Directress of the Bible School here! Is it ever a job! About 200 or 300 kiddies each day. Pray lots for me.

It was not only the work that was exhausting; the weather in Decatur took some getting used to:

.....Everything has been going well, except that one feels tired easily here with the humid, heavy atmosphere. I can easily understand why everyone appears to be lazy. We have not had extremely hot weather but so damp! A rainstorm comes

up in a minute and everything you wear droops and wrinkles. We stay in a two-room apartment with bath. It is an old house and we are on one side of the first floor with our own side porch. It is not a very clean place and we have killed four different kinds of bugs. The second night I chased down two cockroaches the size of small mice. They scared us terribly at first for we didn't expect to see them. I thought they were elephant Junebugs and was going to sweep them outside with a broom. When I got the broom a foot away, they ran like horses and me after them. Got them both. Since then we have killed a couple every night when we come home. The second kind is a centipede about three inches long; we've killed two. Then there are hundreds of ordinary cockroaches of the half inch variety; we just don't bother to chase them. And yesterday we came in and met a big fat green worm waddling across the linoleum. Last night we laughed and laughed at Gen. She went to put on her bedroom slipper and there was a great big roach; she almost put her foot right on it. Now we shake our shoes before putting them on.

.....We all three have been having colitis or malaria or something. We were told that most everyone is that way for a while when they come down here. Our only trouble is having to run to the bathroom all the while. Mrs Britton, the pastor's assistant's wife, gave us some Paregoric but we haven't used it yet. Think I will today.

All this is another example of good missionary training but of a slightly different nature. The Daily Vacation Bible School (DVBS) work continued moving on to Chattanooga, Tennessee, and then on to Chicago, although Ione was still convinced that she was destined to be a missionary in China. She was aware that this could cause difficulties in any relationship but she was convinced that she must do the right thing and follow her calling. She found that one of her former suitors, Bob Arthur, had given up his application to China for health reasons, prompting Ione to wonder if he had only applied in order to be with her. The next suitor who declared his unwillingness to go to China was pressing for an answer to his proposal of marriage.

.....It'll have to be 'no' for I can't marry him when the Lord wants me in China. Pray for me ... Lovingly in Him, Ione

The traveling and long hours working began to take a toll on the girls' health, and on Tee in particular, who had been suffering with tonsillitis and had been told she was anemic. They were not working as well as a team, as Tee and Genevieve were not getting along well, which left Ione in the middle. Ione was also disappointed that her breakup with Ernie was quite bitter and she wondered if she made an error in judgment with Bob Arthur, but she realized that she was just feeling sorry for herself and a bit lonesome. It is around this time that the girls meet a woman with a passion for sewing who taught them how to make clothes out of remnants of material bought cheaply in sales. This skill would stand Ione in good stead in years to come, but at this point she was unaware of how important it was. She threw herself into the work, and in a moment of genius came up with "Tony the Monkey," a hand puppet that would work with her and travel with her for many years to come. It was not all bad; when they arrived in Grand Rapids, they found that they have been booked into the Morton Hotel.

> .....We found a gorgeous suite of rooms awaiting us; two bedrooms, one with twin beds and one with a double bed; a reception hall between; two bathrooms with shower and tubs, etc.; two closets; lovely draperies of contrasting shades in each room; telephones in both rooms; even two spittoons!

It was a lovely change but short-lived and the girls kept moving on. Ione wrote to her mother:

> .....I'm praying much for our future. As yet I don't know what I'll do, but with so many ways to turn, I'm deathly afraid of running ahead of the Lord.

There was talk of replacing Tee in the trio, which caused upset and some uncertainty as to whether MBI would keep the girls on for much longer. Ione wrote to the family on April 28, 1940, informing them of a conversation she had with Dr. Hockman at Moody about her call to China. He suggested that she take some courses in missionary work at the college, though she felt that if the opportunity arose, she would just go to the mission field as soon as possible.

While on this visit to Moody, Ione wrote to the family about another man she had recently met, the father of Betty Stam, the martyred missionary to China, and Ione became more convinced than ever that this was the right move for her. Not only that, but a church in Milwaukee had promised to fund her $150 a year for the seven-year term of service and a family had offered to buy her a cine camera to record all her travels. The church had no other missionaries to support and so Ione's visit to them had been a timely one.

> .....It gave me the courage to believe that if He wants me to go He will supply the needs for every cent of our debts to be paid by the time I sail!

She believed that her family's finances would be settled and that they would be able to cope, even if she were 10,000 miles away. She wrote to a friend:

> .....The China matter increases more and more and even now, dear old China stands before me in her huge bulk as an insurmountable, impassable burden. There is no turning aside from her. I must go ... [missionary] Leona Ross is sailing July 22. How I would love to go with her! But perhaps God has some very special lesson for me yet, or a definite work here yet!

On November 15, 1940, a news article appeared in the *This and That*, a Kentucky-based paper:

> While there's no place like home to most of us; while war strikes at plagued Europe, I have just learned that Miss Ione Reed, of Pontiac, Michigan, will at last realize her remarkable ambition to go to China as a missionary. She will sail November 29 from San Francisco on the steamer 'President Coolidge' for Canton, China as a missionary to the South China Boat Mission.
>
> She is a graduate of Moody Bible Institute, Chicago, and in spite of her youth, has traveled extensively, including Kentucky, for a number of years with the 'Sunshine Gospel Trio'.

Several months ago, while visiting me here, she delighted those present at a prayer meeting at the First Presbyterian Church with her characteristically inspirational talk, and a vocal solo.

A small monkey called 'Tony' will accompany her on her trip to China.

But it was not all to be plain sailing. When Ione's visa and passport for China were recalled because of the Second World War, she worked for a time in the office of the First Baptist Church in Pontiac, where she learned from Bessie Savage (wife of Rev. Bob Savage) of the need for a nurse and helper for Dr. Westcott, a missionary with the Unevangelized Fields Mission (UFM) in the Belgian Congo. As one door closed, another opened, and Ione embarked on a new phase of her life.

The UFM was a relatively small faith-based missionary society set up in England in 1931. It was formed largely by missionaries working with the World Evangelistic Crusade (WEC) and members of the Interdenominational Missionary Training College.

She was invited to join a "boot camp" for would-be missionaries at the mission headquarters for North America, which at the time was at 18 Howland Avenue, Toronto. Later, another office would be established in Philadelphia, but for the time being, Ione had to cross the border into Canada. The mission directors, Rev. Edwin J. Pudney and his wife, Lilian, had been missionaries in the Congo in the early 1930s and had come from England specifically to set up and manage a headquarters in Canada for the newly formed missionary society. The Pudneys invited Ione to join them with six other applicants who all hoped to be accepted to serve in Brazil. She recognized God's plan for her in this work and she heeded the call:

.....So, I came to Toronto in May 1941 from Pontiac, for my month-long candidate period and arrived by train at the Union Station. Mrs Pudney sent a young man to meet me ... I telephoned from the station and Mrs Pudney told me, 'There will be a young man to meet you, tall, thin, with glasses and carrying a magazine.' She meant the U.F.M. magazine, though she had not said this!

Sometime later I telephoned again and said, 'Mrs Pudney, I looked for the young man, but there are MANY tall young men with glasses, and they are all carrying magazines!' 'Well, never mind' she said. 'If you do not see him, you had better take a taxicab.' My taxi pulled up in front of 18 Howland just behind the Pudney's car. The tall, thin young man was returning a bit bewildered from the wrong station. This was the first time I ever saw him and I decided that if I ever had anything to do with that fellow's cooking, I would fatten him up a bit!

The tall, thin young man with glasses was Hector McMillan.

Chapter 2
HECTOR: THE EARLY YEARS

Hector McMillan was born July 16, 1915 in a modest framed farmhouse a half-mile west of Avonmore, Ontario. He was the sixth child of Daniel Lochiel (DL) McMillan, a Scotch Canadian farmer and Jane McElheran McMillan. DL and Jane married in 1903 when DL was 34 and she was 28, and their first son, Archie, was born two years later. Archie's birth was followed by the birth of four girls, Florence, Irene, Alice, and Jean. Three years after the girls, Hector was born, after which the McMillans had another girl, Eleanor. Despite being part of a large family, Hector was shy and reluctant to leave his mother's side in large gatherings.

Avonmore Farm

In the terrible Spanish Flu epidemic in 1918, the entire family was ill, except for Jane, who nursed the rest of the family. While Jane survived this epidemic, she later developed tuberculosis and died when Hector was only five. Hector recalled:

.....My mother loved the Lord, when she knew she was dying with tuberculosis and would not live to raise her family, she trusted God to look after us. Her verse was from Psalm 138:8 – "The Lord will perfect that which concerneth me."

DL managed his grief by keeping busy, and the family had daily devotions every day after breakfast. Everybody in the family had their chores, Florence looked after the younger ones but could not really manage the youngest, two-year-old Eleanor, who was sent to live with relatives in Montreal, a two-hour drive away.

Hector was not fond of school, although he was a quick learner and loved to be busy. Florence recalled that after their mother died, Hector decided to be a dog, and he crawled around the floor refusing to sit at the table for mealtimes and refusing to speak. His food was placed on a plate on the floor. He kept this up for several days before giving up.

Another example of his vivid imagination was his explanation of thunder as "God moving furniture upstairs." He was also a fairly pragmatic child: One day on a visit to the fairground his father gave him 25 cents. At the end of the outing, the family was unable to find Hector, but upon returning home found him there. When questioned, Hector explained that since he had spent his money, he decided to go home because there was no longer anything of interest to him.

The years after World War I on the farm were hard, as DL could not get help. His solution was to take Archie out of school, a move he always regretted but one that made him determined to ensure that the other children had a good education. The children walked a half-mile to school four times a day in all weather, prompting them to debate whether the wind was colder from the north or from the east. Alice made the best use of school and graduated from high school at the age of 15.

DL's sister Marjorie was a great support and comfort, and she helped the family by mending clothes and having them around on Sunday mornings after church, a treat the entire family enjoyed.

Although not keen on academic learning, Hector had an inquisitive mind and he would take things apart only to rebuild them, like a watch he purchased from Eaton's mail-order catalog for $2.50. Unfortunately, his rebuilding was not always successful. The resourceful Hector returned the watch to Eaton's, indicated it was unsatisfactory, and requested a pair of roller skates instead. He enclosed an extra 50 cents to cover the extra expense. Hector then tried to roller skate from home to town in two minutes, a feat he never managed to achieve. When given a guitar, Hector taught himself to play and annotated a hymn book with all the chords he would need.

He loved carpentry and making things, and the family recalled how he made a device to open the gate for the cows. The family maintained a herd of cows and hauled the milk to Avonmore each day where it was shipped to Montreal by train. Each evening, Hector had to drive the old horse, Minnie, down to the station to collect the milk cans, and his friends would join him for the trip home on the cart.

His cousin Howard McMillan recalled that one time, Hector took an eight-day clock (one that needs winding only once a week) and somehow adapted it so that it would ring every 35 minutes. This was to ensure that his teachers ended class on time.

The young Hector was also a good shot with a rifle. One story goes that no sooner had DL planted a four-acre field with corn, when the crows descended. Hector borrowed a rifle and, leaning out from a small upstairs window, proceeded to shoot at the crows. To his amazement, he was successful. He rushed out across the field, retrieved the dead crow, and strung it up on a post so everyone could see.

As a teenager, Hector had access to the Essex, the family car. Sometimes he would arrive home late at night, much to his father's consternation. Hector got around this problem through a little experimentation. He ascertained his traveling speed in the Essex to the point that he could cut off the motor a safe distance down the road and drive into the garage adjoining the home without detection.

Cousins from western Canada visited the McMillan farm from time to time, many of them either proceeding on to the foreign mission fields or returning therefrom. In 1936, the year he graduated from Avonmore High School, a seed was planted in Hector's heart after a visit from Rev. and Mrs. Elmer V. Thompson, who had stopped by on the way back from Cuba. Hector soon decided to enroll in the

Prairie Bible Institute (PBI) at Three Hills, Alberta, a school that had been born out of the religious zeal of his aunt in western Canada.

Hector as a first-year student at PBI, 1937.

Having felt all along that a God of love would surely take him to heaven, he was surprised as a new student in that western school on the prairies to learn that, "Except a man be born again, he cannot see the kingdom of God" (John 3:3). Two days before school commenced, Hector took Christ as his Savior and was thus set free from the wrath of God. Later he recalled, "I was filled with joy to realize the answer to my mother's prayer."

In February 1940, while at the PBI, Hector wrote to his sister Florence:

.....I'll be reading Acts tonight. What a sermon Stephen preached just before his death! In fact, it caused his death. I trust I shall also be faithful even unto death, and I shall have a crown of life. I know you are joining in prayer that the rest of the family might be saved.

Hector knew that his father really wanted him on the farm, and he wrote to Florence:

.....I cannot content myself with anything less than preaching the unsearchable riches of Christ. The task before me is mountainous and many have turned back. No earthly syndicate pays dividends like the Lord and Master who sends us into this spiritual warfare. He equips us, protects us, encourages and corrects us and finally, rewards us with a crown of Glory just for being faithful for a few short years.

Oh, Florence, I love Him and want to be His bond slave, even though my heart and flesh cringe and tug the other way. Do pray that I may fit God's uniform of righteousness.

At the end of his four years of training at the Bible Institute he was convinced that his mission in life was to work in Brazil. The Unevangelized Fields Mission considered him a candidate for missionary service, and he spent a year at the Mission Medical Institute in Toronto, where he gained valuable experience in caring for the ill. While at the mission headquarters in Toronto, he was invited to join a handful of other candidates who also wanted to work in Brazil. He was also asked to go to the railway station to meet another candidate and bring her back to the headquarters, a young woman named Ione Reed.

Chapter 3
18 HOWLAND ROAD, TORONTO

Rev. Edwin and Lilian Pudney had served as missionaries in the Belgian Congo between 1923 and 1931 with the World Evangelistic Crusade (WEC) mission.[2] Their return to England from the Congo was principally for a furlough or break, however, Lilian's father was not well and the Pudneys did not envisage going back to Africa at this time. Rev. George Kerrigan, a colleague of the Pudneys in the Congo, was also home in England in 1931. There was a great deal of discussion both in Africa and England, with differences of opinion between the missionaries in the field (principally the Congo and Brazil) and the organizational leaders in the home countries. This resulted in the formation of a new mission society—the Unevangelized Fields Mission (UFM), which was to be interdenominational as well as international. The politics and drivers for this change are not pertinent to Ione and Hector's story, but suffice it to say, the mission was established in 1931, with Rev. Len Harris as the home secretary in London.

Rev. W. F. Roadhouse, the North America leader for both the WEC and the UFM, resigned his position due to ill health and the UFM leaders requested that the Pudneys consider taking on the North American leadership, to be based in Toronto, Canada. Lilian Pudney had suffered a great deal of ill health while in the Congo and the couple felt that they could not return there. This request, however, would allow them to continue their mission work in another way and they accepted the invitation and moved to Toronto in September 1931.

First based in a small, three-room apartment, they moved to a bigger apartment and then finally, to 18 Howland Road as they became more established. The mission, besides being international and interdenominational, was also a faith mission. They believed that God would provide all their needs and guide them in the direction they should go; support came from many sources. In the early days, Lilian stayed at home, maintained the office, and managed all the letters, while Edwin took every opportunity to visit churches interested in mission work to spread the word about the mission.

With all their experience working in the tropics, the Pudneys were well equipped to prepare and guide would-be missionaries. The headquarters at 18 Howland Avenue meant that several candidates, who were expected to stay for at least a month, could be resident, live as a family, and share chores as well as the worship. This would prepare them for communal living and collaborative work that would be part of being a missionary. Hector arrived first, with plans to go to Brazil. Six others

---

[2] The Pudneys, rarely referred to as Edwin and Lilian, were affectionately called Pudu and Ma Pudu.

joined him, with Ione the last to arrive in May 1941. The day Hector was supposed to meet her at the station, he went to the wrong station and missed her, forcing Ione to take a taxi to Howland Avenue.

In May, Ione described her first day at the UFM home to her mother:

.....*It's a good deal as I expected, a private dwelling, and the candidates help do the work. It's as deeply spiritual as I expected and very sensible and not fanatic. So far, every contact has been a real blessing and I feel as the Lord has truly "called me apart" for not only a change and a rest, but to show me His will for my life. I arrived in time for "tea" Monday, helped with the dishes, spent awhile in my room writing letters (cards) and then had a cozy chat with Mrs Pudney, who is a very lovable person. It's been a little difficult to get used to her talk and her expressions and I have to ask her sometimes several times, but I found it paid to find out first rather than do the wrong thing* [while America and the UK share English as a common language, Ione is beginning to realize that there are nuances and differences that affect meaning]. *Yesterday I slept until almost noon—under orders, and I have a good bed—got a bit of breakfast for myself at 11:30, washed the breakfast dishes, helped get dinner, and washed dishes. I did a few little extra things (squeezed out dirty dish towels, etc.) which she commended me for, and then went to my room for a while. She let me get supper (tea) all alone and I served it out in the garden, which is a fenced-in grassy plot with flowers around a lilac bush, etc. Hector, the young man candidate, washed the dishes, as is the drill in the evening for the men. I made a hospital call with Mrs P. Ironed a cotton blouse for her upon return; she was pleased. We sang at the piano and went to bed.*

.....*Tomorrow I'm to sleep late again and then help her get a room ready for some more candidates. She calls them her "candid dates". We sang again tonight. We have prayer both at dinner & supper. Read from Daily Light some scripture passages and one prays for some definite need.*[3]

.....*At any rate, I feel grand, have good food, lots of rest, and time to actually* think*. Pray much that the Lord will help me when candidate study begins— tomorrow afternoon I think.*

Candidate study started in earnest, initially led by Lilian Pudney, and their focus was on a book, *Ambassadors for Christ* by Mildred Cable and Francesca French, which Ione had already read. This was followed by a two-hour prayer and intercession period:

.....*This morning we spent an equally long time and now I know this is the secret of their success in the field. There is a regular prayer meeting like this each Tuesday (I spoke at the last one) and while candidates are here it's each day.*

---

[3] The *Daily Light* is a Christian devotional book first published in 1845; it is a grouping of biblical verses apportioned for each day of the year that can be read morning and evening. There is no additional commentary, as the verses speak for themselves with the intention of being supportive and inspirational. The book is still published and used today.

*I'm learning some real lessons. These British folk have something that we
don't have. The more I read here and see what a missionary must face, the less
courage I have…. Oh Mother, I don't see how we have gotten along heretofore
with so little prayer. So many weighty things to decide, and we've spent so little
time in prayer; now I know this is the secret of their success in the field.*

There were opportunities to socialize with other missionary hopefuls, which Ione
found especially uplifting, as she explained to her mother:

*…..Today is Empire Day, a national holiday (in Canada) so we had an outing—
went to what they call 'The Island'—a ferry ride and three-mile hike around the
island, interspersed with baseball. We went with the eleven candidates at the
China Inland Mission Home, which is just a few blocks away. It was wonderful
to be with these all afternoon. Imagine! Sixteen young men, nine women, ready
to sail for China, Brazil and Africa.*

Lilian had several issues with Ione that she felt should be addressed. One was that
she wanted Ione to be less interested in the style and fashion of the day and to fit in
more with the style of the other applicants. Ione could see Lilian's point—every
other woman seeking to be a missionary that Ione met at this time had their hair
pulled back and secured with pins. Not only that, but their hemlines were noticeably
longer. However, Ione appreciated the simplicity of their dress and decided that by
mismatching her outfits she could achieve a more homely appearance.

The other problem was her relationship with George Kissinger, who was
interested in Ione. Lilian had noticed that Ione was being deluged with letters from
him, and although she felt he was a good Christian with good intentions, unless he
was destined to be a missionary, he was not suitable for Ione. Having a relationship
based on letters might eventually make Ione want to give up her calling and go
home. Once again, Ione saw the wisdom of Lilian's words and reluctantly realized
that the relationship was doomed. This was hard for Ione, but she was so focused on
her mission to Africa now that she was able to break the relationship off. At the
same time, she had noticed Hector's laughing eyes, and she described seeing him in
a mirror in the mission dining room:

*…..[He has] a pair of large hazel-brown eyes studying me. But I never met them
with my own blue eyes. He was applying for Brazil, while my field was to be the
Congo.*

Besides noting the color of his eyes, Ione noted Hector's wicked sense of humor.
One time, after Ione made a batch of muffins that were inedible and had to be thrown
away. Hector, much to her consternation, kept asking where the muffins were, as he
had seen her preparing a batch. He thus forced Ione to come clean to everyone and
own up to the food that had been wasted.

As it turned out, her pathway to Africa was hampered for a while when a ship
carrying missionaries with the Sudan Inland Mission was sunk and the passengers
taken prisoners by the Germans.

*…..The sinking of this ship may make it harder to get a passport for Africa, but
Mrs Pudney says that a boat may be available by September. The Lord knows*

about that. He may not want me to go to Africa, and if so, I believe He'll tell me. 'A man's heart deviseth his way: but the Lord directeth his steps'.

Ione admired Lilian Pudney enormously; she soon became accustomed to her different way of speaking and was able to have some cozy and personal chats. As Ione wrote to her family:

.....I'm very happy here and the adjustment has been good for me. We're used to so much at home and I'm trying to learn how to conform. If anyone is careful of mission funds, it's the UFM, for they are so very frugal here and every penny goes to the field.... Every speck of food is used but we have the best of everything, fresh vegetables, fruits, etc., and always our nightcap of milk before we go to bed. We are so busy, but I'm enjoying it very much. How I praise the Lord for letting me be here.... I am becoming more and more sure that the Lord wants me in Africa. The Scripture has opened up to me in a wonderful way; and the hours with the Lord bring me so vividly in touch with the great need there. There is every opportunity to change plans and not go, as the Pudneys have in no way forced it upon me. But I do believe the Lord wants me there. One thing they have both made plain to me is that if I'm sure the Lord wants me in Africa, I must be willing to leave 'home' although they have said that it would be very possible to still help (you) in a financial way. And I must be willing to leave all the comforts of this land.... I have faced this all along with other things which must be laid aside in order for me to carry the Gospel message so far. And I do believe I am willing. Tonight we're going to see some films on South America that will be interesting, and we take notes and will be questioned later. There's plenty to study, besides getting meals, scrubbing, washing dishes, laundry etc. And we're required to walk two miles a day. And we must have our lights out by 10:30. Discipline!!

Finally, the evening came when the candidates appeared before the UFM Board in order to be accepted by the mission. The seven young people stood in the kitchen, their hearts skipping beats, until they were called one by one. Hector and the others were accepted for Brazil. Ione was accepted for the Congo.

In July, Ione, from her home in Pontiac, Michigan, wrote to the passport office in Washington, DC, for permission to travel to Africa, after having tentatively booked passage to sail in September. Permission entailed submitting a letter from the missionary society indicating why it was necessary for her to travel to the Belgian Congo for missionary work, a letter which Rev. Pudney supplied the following month. He indicated that Pearl Hiles, a nurse, was urgently needed to assist Dr. Westcott, and Ione was needed to assist the ailing Mrs. Westcott and to take care of the Westcott children.

The announcement about Ione's missionary assignment reached home in Pontiac and the First Baptist Church published the following in the autumn issue of its magazine, *Gospel Echoes*:

New Recruits for the Mission Field

In this issue we present two more missionaries who plan to sail for Africa October 30th. They are going to assist in the work at the hospital at Bongondza[4] [bon-GON-dza], where Dr. George Westcott is located.

Miss Ione Reed is one of our own young people. She had hoped to go out to China last Fall but was unable to obtain a passport. She has been assisting in the Church Office in the capacity of Membership Secretary. Ione will assist in the care of Mrs. Westcott and the children until they are able to return home. She will then assist in the hospital and general missionary work at Bongondza. The Board of Missions had been praying for some time for a Nurse to go out and assist Dr. Westcott in the work at the hospital and to take over the work while he was home on furlough.

The name of Pearl Hiles was brought to their attention—a nurse who had just recently graduated from the Moody Bible Institute. A letter was sent to her and at the time the letter was delivered she was on her knees asking the Lord where He would have her serve Him. For the past several months Pearl has been taking special Tropical Medicine training in a hospital in New Orleans, awaiting the first possible sailing for Africa.

Ione and Pearl plan to sail on October 30th in company with Misses Schade and Walker of the Unevangelized Fields Mission who are returning to Bongondza. Pray for these young women as they go out.

In the autumn, some of the candidates gathered at the newly established UFM headquarters in Philadelphia. Ione was surprised to find Hector there, and Lilian Pudney took them all to dinner at the apartment of a dear Christian friend of hers, Mrs. Evans. Ione wrote:

.....Hector sat writing in the well-furnished living room in a chair next to mine. Hector's chair was beautiful but somewhat frail, even slightly unsteady on its legs, so he concentrated his thoughts on it as he tested the strength of each leg in turn while sitting in an upright position. Then, with an overwhelming desire to see what was wrong with that chair underneath, he

Left, Pearl Hiles, a nurse, and Ione Reed; and *right,* Hector McMillan, in Philadelphia in April, 1941.

shocked everyone by jumping up and turning the chair upside down. Satisfied that he could do the job, he reached in his pocket for a small tool and tightened the loosened parts. Mrs Evans came to call us for dinner just as Hector finished

---

[4] Bongondza is a mission station (see map in Appendix A) of the Unevangelized Fields Mission in Belgian Congo (Democratic Republic of Congo).

the repair of the chair. She was surprised to find her chair turned over, but exceedingly pleased to find that it was now steady on its legs. As we walked to the table, Hector quoted in my ear from Proverbs 18:16 'A man's gift maketh room for him'. I decided that Hector's gift would make room for him anywhere he went.

Despite expecting to go to Brazil, Hector's future took a sudden turn when he was required to serve his country for at least two years, after which he would be free to apply for a missionary assignment with UFM. The Pudneys hoped to send Hector to the Congo. Ione wrote at that time:

.....This was the first time that I knew Hector might be going to my field of service. Mrs Pudney was quick to notice my surprised pleasure. 'Does this interest you?' she asked and then went on to say 'and if it does, you might be glad to know that he likes the way you cock your head on one side like a robin!'. And Mrs Pudney laughed in high girlish glee. 'If he writes to you, would you answer?' was her next pertinent question, 'for if you are not interested, we will not make him miserable by sending him to your field. That fellow is too much in love to be put through such pain'. I told her that I was interested, and would answer a letter if Hector wrote.

Miss Ione Reed

THE WILL OF GOD:
NOTHING MORE!
NOTHING LESS!
NOTHING ELSE!

ADDRESS:
Bongondza,
Kole via Stanleyville,
Congo Belge, Africa

"Praying also for us. that God would open unto us a door of utterance." . . . Col. 4:3.

THE SUPREME NEED — YOUR PRAYER

Ione's prayer card

However, Lilian decided to play a waiting game and did not reveal to Hector that Ione would look favorably on him, should he wish to correspond with her.

While waiting for her sailing date, Ione found herself making curtains for the rooms and helping out in the kitchen preparing meals. Ione also took meetings and sang in the services. She wrote home:

.....We are going to pay $4 a week board here. We'll learn more French and some of the native language, too. And Pearl has to be inoculated yet, too. There is so much more to be done and learned before we go. Pray much that the visas will come soon. Also, that the gov't will extend our passports when they run out Nov. 20th and 24th respectively. The devil is making it as hard as he can, but we have a great God, don't we?

After receiving her passport, Ione then learned that all passports would be revoked due to America entering the war in Europe. This necessitated trips to Washington, DC, and in-person appeals at the passport office, which finally gave Ione, Pearl, and others permission to leave. But the additional costs meant letters to her mother with requests for postal orders and bank transfers. Ione felt the responsibility of leaving home and tried to ensure that her sisters would support their mother in her absence. Ione finally saw her family one last time before she departed in mid-December, 1941.

23

Chapter 4
IONE IN AFRICA

On December 17, 1941, after all her preparations, Ione finally sets sail from New York for the Belgian Congo on a cargo ship called the SS *West Lashaway*. She was accompanied by the nurse Pearl Hiles and Viola Walker, a returning missionary.

The journey to Matadi (ma-TA-di), the Congolese port, was expected to take four weeks, with a stopover in Trinidad. Permission to sail was given one week after America joined World War II, the impact of which, unlike Europe, had yet to be felt in the United States. The reality of war, however, became apparent to the passengers when the threat of torpedoes and minesweepers became real and blackouts were enforced. Part of the travel route was to keep close to the American coast toward the Caribbean until they could take the shortest route possible to Africa, thus avoiding the usual shipping channels. While navigating, the ship used a zigzag course as a contingency against being caught by German U-boats patrolling the Atlantic and the American coastline, which

Ione and Pearl on the SS *West Lashaway*.

meant that they crossed the equator more than once. The ship was evidently part of the war effort, as its cargo consisted of truck parts to be reassembled in Léopoldville and then driven to the warfront in North Africa. The captain felt that by plotting an unpredictable course for his ship, it would be safer. Ione, not wishing to worry her family focused on other things when she wrote:

> .....It was so thrilling to walk up to the pier and see the boat that was to be our home for many weeks. But I must confess I was disappointed, for I tho't it was going to be a majestic impressive hulk. It was so small I could hardly see it over the stack of merchandise to go on board! I tried to think how I would feel when the waves got high, and the tho't came to me "well, when I asked the Lord for a boat I forgot to tell him I wanted a big one, so this is no doubt the one He tho't best for me", and I must say I have been satisfied. It has already proved itself very seaworthy.

Besides Ione and her two friends, the others onboard included the crew, two American freelance writers, three Baptist missionaries, and a French woman with whom Ione practiced French conversation. Most were good sailors, but Viola suffered from seasickness and was quite ill. When stormy, the waves were huge and dark, flooding over the ship, which Ione described as black mountains with a phosphorescent gleam at night. The chief engineer assured them that all was well and they should only worry if the swell covers the smoke stack. When calm, everyone enjoyed the sea breezes, the pink clouds at sunset, and the moon's reflection. The days aboard soon took on a routine: breakfast at 7:30 a.m., lunch at 11:30 a.m., and supper at 5 p.m. The food was so good that Ione found herself gaining weight, so she and Pearl devised ways of getting exercise; they started by trotting around the deck, then played a game of "rooster fights." Their other option was to scramble and climb over the cargo. Ione devised squat and thrust exercises holding onto the deck rails, which she did when no one was looking.

Time was spent writing letters, learning Bangala (bang-A-la, the African dialect used on several UFM mission stations in Congo) and French (Ione was determined to arrive "useful"), and playing games such as Chinese checkers and Lexicon.[5] Porpoises and flying fish offered another distraction, and when one fish landed on deck, Ione promptly retrieved it and gave it to the captain. That evening she was presented with it for her supper, beautifully cooked.

Evenings were spent on deck talking and, in the run-up to Christmas, singing carols. Ione and Pearl busied themselves making cards and small Christmas presents for everyone, and everyone got drawn into the Christmas preparations, although the ladies were not too complimentary about the steward's efforts, when she wrote that "the tinsel was wound around the tree in such a manner as to look like fur necklaces on each limb."

Pearl found tree lights in her belongings and added them to the tree, and once everyone put their little gifts for each other underneath, it looked festive. Mr. Armstrong, one of the Baptist missionaries, played Father Christmas and distributed the gifts. Ione received stockings, carbon paper, Bible games, hankies, and candy. Back in the privacy of the cabin, Ione opened the gifts from her family, which included cold cream, toilet water, a Precious Promise New Testament, a box containing scrolls of Bible verses that one can select at random, from her mother. She was unable to open other gifts, which were in her trunk in the ship's hold, so Ione had those to look forward to after her arrival. She managed to find a fine Victrola[6] needle, which meant she could hear the recorded messages from home; this brought home so much closer to her and made her cry a little.

Christmas lunch consisted of cream of spinach soup, celery and olives, roast turkey, giblet gravy, cranberry sauce, candied yams, asparagus, homemade bread, mince pie, plum pudding, fruit cake, nuts, raisins, candy, apples—another appreciated meal. There must have been time for reflection on the journey about the enormity of the step Ione was taking because she dipped into her "promise box" and extracted the following text:

---

[5] Lexicon was a card game first introduced in 1932. It was later called Lexicon-Go and is also an online role-playing game.

[6] An upright or console model phonograph from the early 1900s, usually with a wooden cabinet body, that plays 78 rpm records using a steel needle.

..... *"Now thanks be unto God which always causeth us to triumph in Christ, and maketh manifest the saver of His knowledge by us in every place." II Cor. 2:14*

Ione wrote home:

.....*It is such a joy to know that we are in the centre of His Will. The ship moves rapidly along and each hour we are nearer the place of His Choosing. How thrilling to be really 'on the way!'*

The Atlantic Ocean was perilous, with the threat of mines and German U-boats, especially near the American coastline. Indeed, a ship following them was torpedoed, and as they neared the coast of Africa more danger was in store, this time from the dangerous waters where the enormous Congo River pours into the sea. The passengers watched silently as the ship navigated the narrow passage and the whirlpools of the Devil's Cauldron, edging toward the docks at Matadi.[7]

ARRIVAL AT MATADI

Ione did not dwell on the maritime dangers. Her letters were full of the excitement of reaching Africa. On January 21, 1942, she wrote:

.....*I saw my first black boy with a white shirt on. He first waved his arms and that being insufficient; he took off his shirt and waved that. By that time I was almost out of mine, hanging over the rail, yelling and waving at him.*

In a diary excerpt, she remembered the temperature as being 97 degrees Fahrenheit, men wearing a variety of clothes, from prison stripes to rags, and women wearing colorful robes and carrying all manner of things on their heads: boxes, sacks, basins, bottles (upright or on their sides), pineapples, baskets, wood, and even a long, black umbrella with a crook handle.

They disembarked around midday and had to stand around at the hottest time of the day while they were processed through customs. The older, returning missionaries took care of the novice ones and ushered them through together, ensuring that there were no problems; they ensured the girls went with them to the Swedish mission house at the top of a hill, which afforded them fresh cooling breezes as well as panoramic vistas, which Ione documented:

.....*Pearl and I are typing at a table in a lovely room with two nice beds with a canopy of dainty netting with attractive cotton frill. The canopy is of course to keep out the mosquitoes but looks like old-fashioned beds. We had a lovely three-course dinner, and Oh, I forgot, Coca Cola this afternoon! You would be so happy, Mother, to see how the Lord has given so many friends to look out for our welfare, and every piece of baggage is here and in good condition.*

They spent two days at the Swedish mission in Matadi before embarking on the next part of their journey. During that time, Ione accepted a lunch invitation from the ship's third mate, Max, who had helped her to fashion deck quoits (rings) out of old bits of rope during the voyage for a game of hopscotch. Max was described as tall, handsome, with brown curly hair, and "not at all forward." During the voyage, they

---

[7] These details were extracted from a letter written by Pearl Hiles in 1991.

had several conversations about Christianity; like the captain, Max was an unbeliever, but unlike the captain, he was sufficiently interested to raise the subject time and time again, and Ione took every opportunity to "witness" to him. Ione spoke better French than Max, which pleased her enormously, as they were able to get a table in the hotel. The enjoyable lunch on the veranda consisted of seven courses, washed down with lemonade. They spent the afternoon resting in chairs in the shade, regaled by a purported magician with extraordinary tales of escape from 36 lions and a rogue elephant. Ione's letters made no further references to Max, but she obviously had an impact on him—when Viola met up with him while sorting out her luggage, he gave her a $50 check for Ione.

The next part of the journey was by train to Léopoldville (Congo's capital) on what was called the "white train," but as Ione stated, neither she nor the train were white after they emerged from the first tunnel. They hoped to get to Léopoldville in time to board a Belgian boat, the *Reine Astrid*, which would take them to Stanleyville, many miles up the Congo River and the main town near Ione's final destination. Their departure from Matadi was delayed however, as they completed formalities at the bank and cleared the last of their possessions through customs. Once in Léopoldville, they met yet another customs official, who initially wanted to charge them 3,000 francs to clear all their baggage, but after some negotiations, he dropped the fee considerably. As they departed, he wished that they all meet "beautiful husbands!" The three ladies—Ione, Pearl, and Viola—boarded the *Reine Astrid* with a mere half an hour to spare. Had they missed the boat, they would have had to spend a month in Léopoldville waiting for the next opportunity. In a letter home in April 1942, Ione itemized her expenses for the voyage—a total of $607.24. Ione was ever mindful that she was spending donations from churches as well as family and friends and wanted to be seen as spending the money wisely.

The *Reine Astrid* was a Belgian-owned steamer, considered the best of the fleet that plied up and down the Congo River between Léopoldville and Stanleyville. The steamer was not as comfortable as the *West Lashaway*, but it was to be their home for the next 12 days. The Africans on the lower decks beat out a rhythm on drums called *gudu-gudus*, pigs and chickens squeaked and squawked, and the odor of burning wood permeated

The Congo River boat *Reine Astrid*, c1949

throughout. One passenger was described as a "pest," as he tried to sell pith helmets, English magazines, and ivory canes to the ladies, and they did their best to avoid his attentions. The layout of the steamer took some getting used to, and Ione and Viola had a taxing time on the first day locating a toilet; neither of them had sufficient French language to get them where they wanted to go. At their first inquiry for a "bain" they were shown a bathtub; next, they asked a cabin boy for a "douche" and were shown the shower room. They accidentally stumbled on a door marked WC, which Viola explained to Ione was a term the English use for a "water closet"! Language acquisition speeded up, as Ione explained:

.....*We were in French territory from then on and ate, slept, and tried to talk French.*

As on the *Lashaway*, life on the *Reine Astrid* took on a daily pattern punctuated by mealtimes. Breakfasts consisted of fresh fruit, tangerines, and *pai pai* (papaya) doused in lime juice; lunch fried bananas or plantain and pineapple fritters; and dinner four or five courses, each place setting a stack of plates that dwindled as each course was served. Two or three courses consisted of meat that was cooked rare. Ione remarked, "I never find more than one cockroach during a meal!"—obviously not part of the "meat" course.

More problematic than food was water, which was available as carbonated water at 12 centimes a bottle. Had they not been teetotalers, the ladies could have had any kind of liquor imaginable.

Ione spent an hour a day in private devotions and she, Pearl, and Viola got together after each meal for further prayer and Bible reading. Their beds were covered with a mosquito tent and they sat inside writing letters home. Thoughts of family were never far away, and Ione remembered to write a "birthday" letter to her mother assuring her that she was well cared for. The *Reine Astrid* stopped at villages and towns along the way, taking on pigs and fresh supplies of fruit; at one stop a murderer was taken aboard and ensconced on one of the lower decks.

The river boat was often met with vendors from riverside villages.

The river trip allowed the ladies time to acclimatize to the tropical Congo heat and humidity, in which the temperatures rose to 99 degrees Fahrenheit by 7:30 a.m., and for occasional forays onshore to buy gifts of ivory from the local markets. The Africans purchased butterworms (palm grubs), dried fish, manioc (cassava, a potato-like tuber), smelly pieces of dried meat, and fruit—bananas, tangerines, limes, and lemons—which formed their diet onboard. They saw monkeys, parrots, and crocodiles, and Ione recounted how in the village of Boloba, six people had been eaten by "crocs" that year.

On one excursion ashore, the ship's photographer got rid of a group of children trailing after him by announcing that Ione, Pearl, and Viola had money. Fortunately, as a returning missionary, Viola was able to converse with the children, and she persuaded them that they had been misinformed and that no money would be forthcoming—the band dissipated.

Ione took time to maintain her appearance, her hair still curled, and despite the heat, she powdered her nose, but she quipped that her complexion was "muddy" from washing in the yellow river water.

All these inconveniences paled into insignificance when Ione described the "romantic beauties of the Congo scenery":

....*The yellow sun, blue sky, green trees, shifting as we moved gracefully along, while natives fished, played, or washed their children. The moonlight was exquisite over the waving palms, the arching flat leaves of the elephant trees, the broad flat banana leaves overshadowed by the slender shoots of plantain. Most lovely of all were the lacy tropical ferns with huge hibiscus or a white lily peeking thru.*

Ione taking in the scenery of the Congo River.

However, one aspect deeply disturbed Ione, and she referred to it more than once in letters home to her family and friends. At first, she delighted in the African children jumping into the river around the boat, and on one occasion there were about a hundred boys clapping, chanting, and begging for money, which upper-class passengers on the top deck encouraged by throwing them money. Ione described the syncopated beat as "hypnotizing" and she felt "the power of Satan behind it all." Ione turned her back to the scene unfolding in front of her, as she felt the need to physically distance herself from this.

Eventually, after five weeks of travel, they reached Stanleyville. They spent one more night aboard before moving into a hotel for one night. The final leg of their trip was a two-day truck ride to their final destination, Bongondza, arriving on February 7. This meant that they spent one night "sleeping" in the truck, listening to chimpanzees howling in the forest! Ione found the ride bumpy and suffered motion sickness, which she in part attributed to the heat and not drinking enough water. Although honest enough to tell her mother about her minor ailments, she reassured her that she was well and fit.

BONGONDZA: A NEW BEGINNING

Bongondza, at 1,700-ft altitude and just 2 degrees north of the equator in the very middle of Africa, was the central point of the UFM mission in the Belgian Congo. Ekoko (ee-KO-ko) was 200 miles in one direction and Boyulu (bo-YU-lu), 200 miles in the other. Stanleyville, on the Congo River, was 150 miles south. The hospital established at Bongondza was operated by Dr. George Westcott, an American missionary. The hospital became fully operational in 1941 and was a huge success, with people traveling over 400 miles from the north and at least 150 miles from the south to receive treatment.

In a May letter, Pearl described the hospital:

.....The little hospital here far surpasses anything that I had ever hoped to find in Africa, because of the inventive ability of Dr Westcott. He takes a little bit of something that most people would throw away and makes it into an instrument or piece of equipment that will meet the immediate need, and then it outlasts in durability the same thing which in the homeland would cost a great deal of money. When I see the practicability of the whole set-up and realize that he has made most of the hospital equipment, I just stand in amazement and wonder what he will tackle next.

The hospital proper consists of a vestibule for receiving patients, a dispensary, a pharmacy, a laboratory, an examining room, an office, an operating room, an X-ray fluoroscopy room, a dental department, an X-ray developing room, a battery room which is connected electrically with a generator in the workshop and also with the hydro-electric water wheel.

Dr. Westcott recorded that he was swamped with work and needed more help. He estimated that he needed another four qualified nurses. The mission leaders decided to base Pearl, Ione, and Viola there; Pearl would nurse alongside Dr. Westcott and Ione would care for Dr. Westcott's wife, Ellen, and their three children. Ellen had been ill and needed care until she was well enough to make the journey back to America, but the outbreak of war had delayed their plans. Viola Walker of Grimsby, Ontario, was to resume her work at Bongondza with classes for women, boys and girls, Kibua language studies, Bible translation and area village evangelism (trekking).

The doctor and his wife had already served one term (usually a period of five years) in the Belgian Congo. Being a practical man, Dr. Westcott started building a church, hospital, and houses at Bongondza, some of which were made of bricks created two at a time in a brick-making press before they were fired and used. Their second term of service was bedeviled with illness: Dr. Westcott suffered from blackwater fever and several bouts of malaria, the children had amebic dysentery, and Ellen had tuberculosis and mastoiditis. Dr. Westcott and the children recovered well from their various illnesses but not Ellen. Anne, the eldest child also contracted tuberculosis but recovered better than her mother.

Ione's appearance was most welcome, and Dr. Westcott wrote that the children were "100% sold on Aunty Ione" and he couldn't have wished for a better companion/nurse for his wife. Ellen managed to leave her bed for two hours in the afternoon with Ione's help, something she had not managed to accomplish for a while.

The doctor's house was set at the top of a hill (see Map of Bongondza in Appendix A) and the hospital was at the bottom. It seems that Ellen designed the house layout and was responsible for where fruit trees were planted and where the tennis court was sited. It was a large house and, being built on a hill, had a lower ground floor. The veranda at the front faced out toward the hospital and was one story up so that it benefited from any blowing breezes.

Ione's first house at Bongondza.

Ione and Pearl shared a house and their day soon achieved a routine where they breakfasted together and then went their separate ways—Pearl to the hospital and Ione to the Westcott house. Ione's duties included organizing and supervising "house boys"[8] for both homes (effectively managing five people working for her), planning meals, and supervising the three Westcott children, Anne, Bobbie and Charlotte. Among her activities with the children were "cookie making" sessions.

According to Ione's description, the Westcotts had a nice home, which included a piano that satisfied Ione's passion for music; after dinner the doctor would play while Ione sang for anywhere from one to three hours. It would seem that music was therapeutic for everyone; Ellen stayed in the living room longer and the doctor relaxed and rested more. Ione wrote home that she was very happy and despite not having all her possessions (which were on their way from Matadi), she was managing well. Despite the food shortages, everyone on the mission station coped.

In letters home, Ione maintained a positive attitude and viewed her time managing two households as an opportunity to acquire more language skills. She did not appear envious of her friend Pearl being stuck in the nitty-gritty reality of mission work that included delivering babies and removing tumors. Ellen asked Ione to accompany them back to the States when they went, and even though Ione had only just arrived, she did not let the disappointment show. She told Ellen she would be happy to travel with her; only to her mother, in her first letter home after arriving at Bongondza, did she confide that she hoped it would not be necessary.

In Ione's first two months in the Congo, she did not receive any mail, and her longing for contact was evident, although she played it down. Eventually, the first letter arrived on March 6 and Ione wept for joy! She wrote back to her sister, "The news was licked up, every bit!"

In the letter to her sister, Ione recounted more about her life at Bongondza, graphically describing a storm that lifted the corrugated tin roof off their kitchen and how she and Pearl struggled to reorganize their belongings to protect them from the rain seeping in through the leaf roof. Eventually, they sought sanctuary at the Jenkinson's house and dried off in front of their warm fire.

Herbert Jenkinson, an English missionary who ran the school and was a founding resident at Bongondza, had been the field leader since 1935. Everyone affectionately called him Kinso and his wife Ma Kinso. The "Kinsos," became surrogate parents to all the missionaries and the most loved surrogate "grandparents."

---

[8] Special note to readers: Whereas this phrase was commonly used to refer to staff hired to perform household duties and yard chores, in the interest of appropriateness in this biography, it will be replaced with "helper" or "staff".

Herbert and Mrs. Jenkinson, the "Kinsos."

Kinso had served in the Coldstream Guards during the First World War; after he was demobilized, he undertook missionary training and set sail for the Belgian Congo in 1920 with his wife, Alice, a gentle diminutive lady. They worked together caring, serving, and supervising all the missionaries working with them. Their house was situated at the top of the drive into the mission station and, like the doctor's house, was of brick construction.

Ione and Pearl, having lived in their house with no roof for a few days, moved into a vacated house which Ione described in a letter:

.....It is surrounded by gorgeous flowers and trees and has pineapple, bananas, plantain, and citrus fruit trees in the back yard. At night the air is pungent with perfume.

And in a later letter, she added:

.....We're against the forest and hear the chimps but no leopards as yet, altho' the Doctor treated a man yesterday near here after he had been attacked [by a chimp].

Ione described the incident better in a letter written in May:

.....[The man] *had a broken arm and back, and many bruises. He is a very quiet, patient sufferer and we didn't know until this day that the way he was hurt was at the time so many of the natives were out after rubber* [to meet quotas required by the often-brutal Belgian authorities]. *There was a big chimpanzee in one of the trees and the 'capita' or head man ordered him to climb the tree and get* [the chimp] *out. The man did climb the tree. He attacked the animal which put up a terrific fight...and threw the man several feet clear of the tree and he crashed to the ground. His legs are paralyzed; the fluoroscope will fully tell the damage done.*

Descriptions of life in Africa included the story of Viola killing a snake in her house, Dr. Westcott dispatching a huge hairy spider, and scorpions and poisonous centipedes. Ione had her first encounter with "driver ants," but these had not attacked.[9] The Westcott children appropriated two birds, a praying mantis, and what Ione described as "a tiny bear-like creature which cried like a kitten and would eat chickens when he got big," which she bottle-fed when the children went on a short trip to Buta (BOO-ta).

Ione also recounted how Ellen was responding and eating well, sitting out of bed for three hours a day, and managed an outing to the Kinsos' house. Ione was pleased

---

[9] Dorylus, also known as siafu or army ants, migrate as an army searching for food and eat everything in their path. The Africans vacate their homes during this migration and return knowing all vermin will be cleared and their homes clean. They can pick the bones clean of large animals and have been reported to kill humans.

with the progress, as it would herald her way to being involved more in "mission work," such as teaching "black children and trekking." She went out to the villages with the Kinsos, but this only whetted her appetite to do more. The two ladies seem to enjoy each other's company and had a good rapport.

By March, Ione became acquainted with the reality of living in a hot, dusty climate and acquired "jiggers" in her toes.[10] Foot hygiene was extremely important and just another lesson for novice missionaries.

Besides working at the hospital, Pearl looked after a starving black baby boy who was brought in after his mother died. Caring as ever, Ione wrote home that they needed diapers and clothes for the little boy and in true Ione style, she stipulated "good medium flannel". As a result of this incident, Pearl began child care clinics once a week. These occurred in the local villages or at the hospital when more detailed care was needed.

After seven weeks, Ione's main baggage had still not arrived, but all the missionaries pooled their belongings so Ione and Pearl managed and could even host visitors. The sharing of what they all had was again evidenced when Ione gave Ellen her vitamin pills. Having a doctor at the mission station meant that everyone who needed medical care came to Bongondza; the Africans camped out on the hospital grounds, but all other visitors were accommodated as guests in the mission houses. Through her letters, it emerged that Ione was usually in charge of catering to their needs and feeding them during their recovery. This would become important experience later on in attending to the food and lodging needs of many visiting missionaries.

All the letters from home were censored, but fortunately for Ione the family did not include anything that was seen as a threat to the war, so most letters arrived without pieces cut out.

As in all letters that Ione wrote to her family, the following one included concern for her mother's well-being and reassurance that she was well. She also voiced concern about her family:

> .....Did Marcellyn have to give 14% of her income in war tax? I have been concerned, and if you have any doubt that you can maintain the home, let me know, for I would never want the home broken up. I'm sure I could do something about it.

Ione also detailed housekeeping news, such as setting up her bank account in Stanleyville and a request for the home and garden magazine, as someone else was supplying her with the *Moody Monthly*.

---

[10] Jiggers (*tunga penetrans*; alternatively, *chiggers*) are small fleas that burrow into the skin; the males suck blood and fall off, but the females embed themselves and lay eggs. The site of infestation is itchy and marked by a small white spot, and the egg sack has a black center, which are the legs of the flea protruding for its exit once the egg sack ruptures. Jiggers are removed with a sterilized needle. If the sack grows large. it leaves an open wound that needs to be kept clean and free from infection. However, if caught early enough, all that remains is a small puncture mark.

Her next letter, written later in March continued with the housekeeping theme and listed items she wanted the family to send her. The doctor had told her these items would take a long time to reach her, so she was shopping in anticipation of a long wait. The list consisted of the following:

White shoes—leather oxford with rubber or crepe soles, size 8AAAA

Flashlight bulbs—10 standard size

Flashlight batteries—10A (they deteriorate very quickly)

Bedroom slippers—any kind in leather—low heels

Cretonne fabric—bright colours, backgrounds—several patterns—about 10 yards—not expensive

Bright kitchen curtains—2 pairs

5 padlocks and hasps

Bubble gum for novelty for kiddies—Beeches—a few 10-cent store prizes—small knives & forks

Some Crisco, Spam and canned vegetables would be good—no milk

Victrola needles

Ione also offered the following advice:

.....Home canned things will not come in very good shape, nor candy, except melt-proof, or if wrapped very, very well from the heat. Gum is OK.

If you line the packing box in oilcloth it will be good and I can use it. Do not pack too tight, but securely. Not one thing was broken or chipped that you packed for me, but the aluminium was squashed a little.

For all these items, Ione wanted her mother to collect two months of her salary from her sponsoring church rather than have the money sent to her, and she requested that if any money was left over, her mother should retain it to buy birthday presents for her nieces and nephews back home.

The tone of this letter was more businesslike, and Ione reported that Ellen seemed to have relapsed and was unable to sit up, which was disappointing for all, especially Ellen who made an effort to help herself. It was disappointing for Ione too in that she could not be released to do more of what she perceived as "missionary work." Ione detailed the nutritious drinks she made Ellen, who appeared unable to eat normal food. The doctor himself ate all the food prepared for him and complimented Ione on her efforts.

The missionaries employed staff to help with cooking and menial chores, and a letter written on April 1, explained that they paid the Belgian government an annual head tax of one and a half dollars for each staff member employed. The staff members earned the equivalent of 15 cents a week. Ione recounted that one helper built himself a bed in the kitchen, and so slept on the job. He had also been caught stealing coffee so had his pay reduced. She also indicated that Pearl was more masterful in getting the staff to work quicker and do as she bid. It was evident that Pearl had a reputation; she was characterized as *azi mabe* (is bad) or *kusala noki-noki* (works quickly).

Having staff could be frustrating. Ione left one making a chocolate cake and came back to find him rolling the dough out for a pie crust. Another time, he put coffee where the water should go in the coffee percolator. This was seen as wanton waste, especially when food was scarce and there were no local shops. Ione wrote:

> .....*Vegetables are so scarce, the only thing we can get in tins is peas and carrots, but there are some fresh vegetables like spinach, tomatoes and native potatoes available daily. I was able to buy Klim [milk, spelled backward, which is powdered whole milk] at Stan[leyville] and as cheaply as at home. We buy eggs here for about a penny apiece, but they are small and often rotten. Meat is very scarce, but we have plenty of cans. The Spam is a real treat.*

Ione was ecstatic when her belongings finally reached her from Matadi. She was much amused to find tins wrapped in red and green paper—gifts from a church at home that envisaged her opening them at Christmastime.

Her letters returned to a recurrent theme—animals:

> .....*Bobbie Westcott brought in a beetle tonight as big as your fist. Its pinchers work like a jig saw and he looks like he's lacquered. He has him on a leash in his bedroom. I went in to make Bob's bed after his nap the other day and stepped on four lizard eggs and kicked over a bottle with ten worms and two cocoons.*

Ellen was having a good spell of health, which enabled Ione to visit a leper colony with the Jenkinsons. It was evident that these early days were taxing for Ione and Pearl, as Ione requested that the family pray for them as they struggled with the climate, the language, and the people; her frustrations were evident in finishing one letter to supporters:

> .....*These dear missionaries are working their heads off from dawn till late at night, the Jenkinsons [are] 'way over furlough, Ludwig's just about sick (Verna has a bad sore on her leg and Fred looks so tired—they were here a week), Doctor seldom takes his clothes off. And some of you folk could help so much. There's no reason why the Lord's work should stagnate in Wartime is there? God has his best things for the few who dare to stand the test.*
> *He has His second choice for those who will not have His best.*

A letter home from Ione two weeks later had a different tone, starting with:

> *"I will cause the shower to come down in His season; there shall be showers of blessing." Ezekiel 34:26*
> *Trials make the promise sweet;*
> *Trials give new life to prayer;*
> *Trials bring me to His feet,*
> *Lay me low, and keep me there.*

In the first letter from Hector, written on February 16, it was clear that he saw Ione as a "special" friend, and there was no proclamation of love at this point. He wrote:

> .....*Would that I were accompanying this letter. I have just looked up the verse in Daily Light for this evening and the one that best applies is, "Lord, all my desire is before Thee; and my groaning is not hid from Thee." Ps. 38:9.*

Hector had felt that he was called to serve the Lord in Brazil, but problems in that region meant the mission leaders had to reconsider the deployment of missionaries. Early in 1942, Hector was asked to reconsider his options and think of going to the Belgian Congo instead. The Pudneys were aware of the emerging feelings Hector and Ione had for each other and they stressed to Hector that his choice must be for the right reason and not a "secondary" one, that is, Ione. While getting his passport changed for a new destination, Hector discovered that being Canadian meant he was required to do military service. He was told he may be exempt under special circumstances, but working as a missionary in African did not appear to be one of them.

In a letter Ione received from Lilian Pudney, written April 11, she learns more about Hector:

.....Now my dear Ione, I must give you a wee line which is private, just for your sweet self. I did not feel that I should write your message to Hector, it all seemed to happen so quickly, I hesitated to bring anything about which was not of the Lord. Without any word to Hector about you, we knew of his desire to go to Congo if the way to Brazil closed, the matter was discussed at a Council meeting concerning his desire to go to Congo, but there was no mention of you in the matter at all, but solely from the standpoint of the opportunity and the open door, as it seemed then. The Council advised that a letter should be sent to Hector asking him to consider the Congo field. He did not hurry about any reply but waited before the Lord. Eventually he felt that the Lord would have him go to Congo as the door to Brazil was closed. All this development without any message from me, regarding you. Thus, that has not been the influence in his decision. Once he made the decision, he took steps to get his passport, in the meantime he has become of military age, it complicates matters, and we yet await the decision of the military Council with regard to his case. We are hoping that he will get ordained, in which case he could get exemption. He has no desire to escape military service, in fact it is a Mission Field in itself, but only the odd one goes out to the spiritual battle on the Mission Field and we know that for victory anywhere that will be lasting, there must be the propagation of the precious Gospel.

.....It so happened that Hector had come to the Toronto home for a time, he did some papering and painting, and he wanted to see us also about the future. The night before we left, I took him into the office and gave him your message verbally. I think he was filled with awe, to have such a precious message from you. But we talked over other possibilities, that you might meet someone else and he might meet someone else, so that until you two are definitely sure that your friendship should develop there is nothing binding between the two of you. If you both feel that the Lord is leading you together, then that must be settled between you in your correspondence. If it is nothing more than just a friendship, then no harm has been done. I have waited for four months before even mentioning the matter. The only persons who know about this are the four of us, you, Hector,

Mr Pudney and I. Others have teased you both, but there is nothing authentic. Others have not spoken of you together at all, so it is now between you and Hector. If you wish matters to drop, this is the time, before anyone knows anything about the friendship. If you want things to develop, the way is open. There are many things to consider, let not mere loneliness decide for you, a life-time together is a serious matter. We love both of you and desire only God's will for you.

Meanwhile, Ione's next letter eloquently describes life at Bongondza for her and her friend Pearl.

.....Our recent experiences could hardly be classified as 'trials', altho' we would not have chosen them for ourselves. Pearl is adapting herself more quickly to this strange new life; in fact, she says she feels just like she was in New Orleans, only it is cooler! Some days have been 120 degrees, but most of the time it is very pleasant and we often are real chilly. I think I notice the heat more because my busiest part of the day is thru the noon hour when I am concentrating my activities in the Westcott kitchen. However, I am gaining in weight and feeling fine all the time. I think the biggest jogs to me have been in the way of <u>ants</u>, millions of them, they appear in everything from your soup to your clothes; <u>roaches and crickets</u>; my pink and blue rayon dress has all the blue flowers eaten out already, and the edges of the bindings on all of my books are chewed; <u>mould</u>, especially in my typewriter, but in anything not exposed to the open; <u>jiggers</u>, in toes and fingers occasionally; <u>food</u>, swell, if you want to live out of cans all the while, but it's a good idea to spread out the supplies and after all there are lovely things here to eat, tho' they come rather sporadically, and when fresh meat arrives it must be eaten in one or two days or it will spoil like a nice chicken we had only eaten the wings from! One has to watch carefully to keep a well-balanced diet. But it is altogether possible, and we enjoy the finest I am sure. If one can get the house helper to prepare what you want, when you want it and how, everything is lovely.

.....At the moment, we are without a cook. Our baby-faced water and wood fellow has been pinch-hitting, but the poor chap is in line for an operation and we hate to work him too hard. He's so afraid of Pearl he jumps when she looks at him, and he's so afraid of the dishes that you can hear them rattle when he carries them. He's not used to knives and forks and we have to teach him every little wee step in cooking, dish-washing, etc. His name is Camille (Ca-MEEL-ie). The word we use the most with him is "asili?" (finished?) but he never is! He fooled me the other day. I said, "Asili, Ca-meel-ie?" And he answered, "Malamu, Madamu!" "It is well, Madame". But what tickled me was that it rhymed so perfectly. He arrived to prepare supper the other night at 7 P.M. I was battling away trying to get the wood fire to burn, my eyes streaming with tears from the smoke, when he arrived. He strolled in and I tried to use all my vocabulary on him, which is more now than when I last wrote, and when I finished, he said words to the effect of, "Well, a fellow has to get a haircut, doesn't he?" And I

looked and sure enough, he'd had somebody cut his hair, all but a spot as big as your fist on top!

.....It has been great fun getting settled in our four-room mud house. The house is old, but Doctor and Mr Jenkinson have been having the workers fix it up with new plaster and now a lovely new plaster-paint on the walls, with a mixture of mud and clay and water which makes a creamy tan. We have been washing the wood-work and putting on linseed oil, which gives a lustre and brings out the beautiful grain of the solid wood. Two of our floors will be laid with bricks soon, which will be an improvement over mud with a mat rug covering.

We have a light in each of the four rooms, all a part of the Doctor's electric system, the latter which by the way runs a good deal of the time directly by water power from the stream and his water wheel [turbine]. He is going to fix us a sink and faucet in the kitchen which will be an improvement over the old basin and pitcher or combination. We'll also have a desk lamp. Now we're trying to figure out what we can sew together to cover eight windows! We bro't about ten yards of cretonne apiece, but have odds and ends that can be stitched together for more. I am using little embroidered dish towels for kitchen curtains.

.....I was happy to learn that two souls accepted Christ yesterday at the hospital. They have enrolled at the baptism. Viola Walker just returned from two weeks of trekking, tired from walking about 3 hours each day, but happy that souls were saved and many Christians encouraged. How I long to go trekking. I shall when I have more of the language and learn better how to live among the natives. It is surprising how safe one is here to walk places alone. No gunmen, kidnappers, highway robbers, and the wild animals run if they see you first. The only things that don't get out of your way are the driver ants. I saw the first ones tonight, not many feet from our house. They were going in the other direction, but we must be prepared to quickly evacuate the house if they decide to come this way. They eat everything in sight and cover all the furniture. Time out—I just saw a big rat make a dash for our washroom. I was scared to look out there for fear I'd see him again, so I just woke Pearl (it's 10:30) and asked what I should do, "Go ahead and kill him," she mumbled and turned over and went back to sleep again. I tho't sure she'd be wide-eyed like I am. She has enough of the language now that she talks it in her sleep. I caught myself praying in Bangala unconsciously the other day. I think I shall quit now before I get more scared. I think there's a cockroach after that rat out in the washroom.

Please be assured that I am very happy out here. I may sound like I am frightened to bits, but it is surprising how little these little things do disturb one. I come from a line of scaredy-cats. My aunt tho't she saw a mouse in the kitchen and in turning to run she stubbed her toe and fell down; she didn't wait to get up but crawled as fast as she could on her hands and knees!

.....I have never seen such darkness as here, and I have never seen Christ in a brighter clearer truer way than since I came. He is so real and in giving me a passion for souls he has given me a passion for Himself that I have never before

experienced. How I wish there were more I could do for Him! "For every drop of crimson blood thus shed to make me live, O wherefore, wherefore have not I a thousand lives to give!

Hector penned the following to Ione on April 16, after a conversation with Lilian Pudney:

My Dear Ione:

Words almost fail me but I will see what I can find on this typewriter that will convey something across the dark waters of the Atlantic. I had the courage to inquire about air mail; and although it appears costly, it is quicker and surer.

I would just love to see you trying to study the language, and then tell Tony [Ione's hand puppet] *all that you have learned. At least you can make him consent that you are right. His little fur coat must be pretty warm.*

It will soon be a year ago that you came to Toronto for the candidate period. I am sure of one thing now, that I would not miss you again when I was supposed to meet you at the station. It has been a source of pleasant memories to think back on that sweet fellowship that we had with the Lord and with one another. And then there is more recent but not less interesting candidate period down in Phila. at 1162. Days and evenings that we can never forget. What a privilege we had of seeing the Lord's hand manifested on the behalf of His servants! The reception day is of course the outstanding event, and intermingled with that is the loss of ½ dozen doughnuts. [A prank was played on Hector while he was staying at the mission headquarters in Philadelphia—doughnuts went missing and no one owned up to taking them. Periodically, Hector refers to these, as he has always suspected that Ione was the instigator, which she always denied.] *Do I still hear you trying to evade the issue as to the guilty party? But there is yet one thing that I consider of probable serious consequence......The Wissahickon hike. And one incident in particular; when I had the supreme and gratifying task of helping you down the hill. A trifling matter and yet what longings, aspirations, hopes, ambitions, reflections and even anticipations have coursed through my heart; the future now and then dark; now and then bright, until I must needs put down on paper, that there is a distinctiveness about you that I believe the Lord has allowed me to observe and discern.*

As present this is the situation. I am without a passport. Dr Smith of the People's Church has been used of God to suggest a plan. I am just entering a pastorate which is without a leader. I will be ordained D.V. (God willing) shortly into this ministry; then I can reapply for my passport; then a visa for the Belgian Congo; then a boat or an airplane; then Stanleyville; then Bongondza; then Ione. I better turn over the paper and change the subject.

On April 27, Ione responded to a letter from her friend Agnes Sturman (Agnes was an active member of Ione's church) in which she gave more details about life at Bongondza and the Wesctcott family she served:

.....[Remarking about the papaya fruit] we have a huge one split for our breakfast every morning and do love them very much. At first I didn't when they served us

our first at the Swed. Mission at Matadi, but now we can't get enough. Whenever someone goes to Kole [KO-le is the Belgian administrative post nearest to Bongondza; it is a small outpost with shops and government buildings], *we have a new supply of a dozen or more, serve them halved with salt on, or mashed as mayonnaise in salad, or mixed with pineapple, bananas and orange juice. I tried a new recipe for cabbage salad today using the ends of the pineapple stalks cut small; is crispy like celery and tastes like cabbage.*

.....My curtains are made of five dish towels, red, green, yellow, blue and pink. Embroidered on each are the names, Virginia Reese, Edith Eastham, Helen Newhouse, Louise Goodsell, and with the fifth I have made a valance in red with Nellie Miles written across the right hand corner.[11] I'll bet you can't guess where they all came from! I have them arranged in stripes to match my fiesta china and colored enamel pots and pans. Colour cannot be too bright out here. Pearl says it hurts her eyes when she goes into the kitchen! She has made rose and green draperies for the three windows in the bedroom. We have a veranda all the way around the house, and the place is almost covered with vines and large bushes. Since we came the jungle has crept up about two feet on us! One must constantly fight it back, for vegetation grows so rapidly. We don't want to get snowed under so shall engage a gardener to cut us out soon. You know, the closer the jungle comes, the louder do we hear the chimps at night!

I am so happy here, Agnes. I gave my first testimony the other night and could hardly sleep that night. It's so hard not to be able to praise the Lord adequately in the native language when He means just everything to me. Pray that I may speak better soon.

I wrote to Kenneth Hempstead [at UFM headquarters in Philadelphia] *last night and at that time felt a bit discouraged about Ellen, but she is much better today. It seems she sleeps good one night and then can scarcely sleep at all the next. You know how that is! And then she has no appetite the next day and its liquids again. She is recovering now from a form of epidemic that has been going around. Pearl had a bit of it for a few days. It causes severe vomiting but no fever. At that time Ellen's heart seemed very weak but her pulse is normal now. If the present vaccine treatments work, she will be more resistant to the constant colds and epidemics and can maybe try sitting up and walking again. I love to take care of her for she is so patient and always thinks of the family first, and insists on my getting sufficient rest. She is highly intelligent and possesses a beautiful vocabulary and is conversant on all the latest issues. She has her finger tips on the activity of every member of the family, including all the staff. She sews much and makes lovely doll clothes for the kiddies as well as clothes for themselves and her. She has everything under control except her husband, who simply adores her, but won't get the proper rest and won't wear pajamas to bed,*

---

[11] Friends from the First Baptist Church in Pontiac, Michigan.

in fact sometimes doesn't go to bed. She's crazy about him, too, and takes an active interest in every little thing he is interested in.

The kiddies are well disciplined by both parents, but have lacked Mother's help at the table and in a few small things which I think I can help with. They are so loving and appreciative of every little thing. Missing regular school has been a handicap, for they have learned to amuse themselves in outdoor things, animals and bugs, they spend hours dissecting a fish head and cutting the eyes open, watching a lizard hatch, or teaching a goat to pull a wagon, but it is hard to knuckle down to long periods of study. Anne loves to paint and plans her own settings, maybe picks a bouquet of lovely flowers, arranges them beautifully in a rose glass vase, sketches it in pencil and then uses water colours. She reads well and knows simple arithmetic. Bob can read some but is so far ahead of the baby stuff that he must do to get the practice and is not able to read the stories advanced enough for his mind, so that it discourages him and he looks at the pictures and can tell the story just as well as tho' he'd read it. He's going to be a genius like his father, for he's a stickler for details, preoccupied to the nth degree, and as smart as anything. He looks like Bob Savage [minister at the First Baptist Church] *used to look only has dark eyes. Charlotte is a beautiful child with honey-colored hair and brown eyes, so warm and cosy and everybody loves her. She is getting brave like the others about pain, and today hardly struggled at all when a jigger was removed. Now Anne is 9, Bob just turned 8, and Charlotte 4.*

.....Will you kindly share this letter with the Savages and any others who are interested? I would like so much to know how they are and Helen, too. Give Norma a hug for me. Tell her I've had three letters from old boyfriends, so I don't feel I am so far away at that! G. Kissinger has written once, was quite put out that I left so suddenly without letting him come to the boat. It was best, tho'. He has left his churches now and is Dean of the Norfolk Bible Institute—Va. Tell you more later.

Love, Ione

Ione wrote her first letter to Hector from Bongondza on May 17th. She supplied him with news of Tony:

Dear Hector,

Greetings in Jesus' precious Name!

Your letter was very welcome indeed, and arrived on the 15th, which proves that Airmail service is really the best, altho' some have taken three months even by Airmail. I'm so glad you did write. I have been wanting to, but didn't know whether I should. When one is many miles away, it is easy to run ahead of the Lord in what one says in letters. It's nice to know that you want to write and I shall do my best to give you all the information you wish.

Tony the Monkey sends his regards and appreciates honourable mention from you. He is becoming decidedly dusky in complexion and a bit oily from being petted by little brown hands. But he is very happy, tho' not half so happy as his owner! My greatest thrill came a few weeks ago when I endeavoured to give my first testimony in an informal gathering; the speech was stumbling and punctuated with a few tears, but I believe they understood.

She candidly explained her hesitancy in writing to Hector, as she did not want to influence him unduly. However, her delight in hearing from him was evident as they continued to banter about the disappearing doughnuts. She was encouraging as she pointed out ways in which Hector could contribute to the mission work:

.....And there is a real field of service right here for you immediately, for the building and mechanical end is a real burden to the two men, who would love to be freer for their respective tasks, medical and preaching, teaching. You could step into a very big job the day you arrive without more than a word or two of the language. There is the work shop, where boards are cut and prepared for finishing the Doctor's house, the guest house, which is nearing completion, the new church, which is the Doctor's latest vision, etc., then, the water wheel which bursts out each heavy rain; the generator needs constant repairs; the brick kiln, etc. I have itemized in my mind a hundred jobs to 'let Hector do'. Please hurry and come!

.....You will be thrilled at the many opportunities to make something out of nothing. Doctor was quite pleased with your refrigerator idea on the closet door, and the porch light shade out of a bread tin. Any odd things you can bring for such inventions will be a source of real joy to the two men. And bring plenty of films. Flashlight batteries deteriorate in about a week, I don't know why. Maybe you can do something about that! By the way, my motion picture camera is at Phila., for your specific use on the way out and at any time. I was afraid it would be taken at the coast, but it wasn't such a danger after all.

.....Now I must close and let Pearl know that I am something more than a silent image at the typewriter. Be assured that we shall be praying much for your departure. It is truly in God's Hands.

"God holds the key to all unknown, and I am glad:
If other hands should hold the key,
Or if He trusted it to me,
I might be sad."

And to her sisters, Ione playfully wrote:

Hi, you old chuckleheads, you snuffy old drones, you with the bare faces hanging out, you with the ruby lips flapping in the breeze and the big splay feet! (I've been reading 'Robin hood')

I know that no matter when I write I'm just a season behind you, so maybe I had better tell you now what I want for my birthday—see if you can guess what it is—'tall dark and handsome and drives a crocodile V-8'

Mental Picture #1 for you: Me, taking my first bath in my collapsible tub. First getting it so as it won't collapse. Next filling it from two pails, a hot one and a cold one. Next, draping the cracks in the door with a canvas sheet. It falls down, put it up three times and then try my raincoat over the corner of it. Success using both together. Look around for other cracks. Window is of parchment; O.K. Place soap, washcloth, towel, and powder on stool; Skid on a thousand-legged worm on the way into the tub. Scrape my foot off on the chair leg. Water too hot, put in more cold; fish out a roach and two May flies. Wash cloth is sour; get a clean one. Step gingerly into tub, its legs wobble, but safe. Sit down, but look around furtively to make sure no one is peeking in. See a hole in the parchment in the window; try to reach it by stretching from tub; feet slip, big splash, no harm done to the tub. Give up the hole. Stand up, reach for the light and turn it out. Settle down again and take a bath in the dark!

Mental Picture #2: On writing a letter. Take typewriter down from top of clothes cupboard where it's supposed to stay dry. It is covered with mould ¼ inch thick. Wipe it off. Bring paper & envelopes. Also carbon, but roaches have chewed holes in it! Find a solid enough place to use. Feet hurt, look for bedroom slippers; shake two cockroaches out of one and one out of the other; feel funny after putting them on; shake out one more. Turn my ankle, look down at heel and something has eaten away one side of heel of slipper. Proceed with letter. Swarm of flying ants sweep in at the light under which I'm sitting. Stick in my hair and every crevise of typewriter. Clean out typewriter; find ants have left their wings all over my paper; blow it off (these are the edible ants that the natives eat). Finish letter. Envelope flaps have stuck shut, steam them open with semi-hot water; glue them shut. Stamps have stuck to paper which I put between them. Steam them off; paste them on. Letter goes on its way, once a week.

Mental Picture #3: My Day. Arise when it gets light, sometimes 5:30 or as late as 7; it gets light all at once and gets dark all at once twelve hours later. Nothing happens if it's dark or rainy. Whistle blows, then a bugle. Morning devotions at three points, we take turns going to each—Mr Jenkinson's workmen, Viola Walker's girls, and at the hospital. Before we leave we set out coffee, oatmeal, and bread sliced for toast for the helper; also beat up our Klim with water for milk. Eat breakfast, have devotions, go to hospital and doctor's respectively (Pearl and I) at 9 A.M. or later if it's rainy. Inspection at Doctor's to see if kiddies have eaten breakfast, washed, cleaned teeth, straightened rooms. Give Ellen breakfast and try to cheer her up for the day; help her out in the living if she's able. School from about 10 to 11:30. A romp outside; help cook finish up dinner in time to eat at 12:30. Read a chapter of 'Robinhood' (Doctor has devotions with the kiddies before he leaves in the morning) and they take their naps. I spend the time with Ellen or do a thousand and one jobs around the house I have been waiting all day to do, bake, sew, sort clothing, check on silverware, china and linens. Go home at about 4, if the Doctor stops in for awhile, or leave all with the cook if tho't wise. Go home to clean up, rest, set out supper for cook at my house. Go back to see about chocolate milk and a cookie for kiddies and Ellen. Plan supper which they eat at about 7. When Doctor comes, I leave. Some afternoons I stop in at the women's meeting or have Viola's little girls over. I have engaged a native to give me further instruction in the language. After Pearl and I eat supper we take a stroll to the village and gab with the women, or oil furniture, or sew draperies or write letters or visit the other missionaries. An interesting life.

To make your eyes pop; today a snake was killed on the station 8 feet 4 inches, a type of boa constrictor [a python] *which squeezes you to death. Its head as big as a saucer and body as big as a cup.*

Please write me soon. I long for news. Love, Ione

Three days later, Ione wrote home again informing them that the dampness affected her curls so she had changed her way of combing her hair. She thanks them all for the card, photos, and small gifts she had received; Christmas, Valentine, and Easter cards arrived out of sequence but no matter, each was valuable to her. Again, Ione captured in her descriptive narrative what life was like:

.....If you would like to picture us here you may imagine 7 adults and three children, the only whites for many miles, living in a little slit of cleared land with the jungle pressing on both sides. A highway runs alongside, but that is a narrow road and impassable in rainy season. We are shut off from the world, but the people to whom we are sent are here and that is the great satisfaction. Tragedies are common. Another attempted suicide on the part of a fine native Christian, but he has come back to the Lord and has a wonderful victory. The rhythmic shouting and chanting of a heathen dance was heard just two nights ago for a dead baby. They brought it to the hospital, but it died immediately. The women wore grass skirts and hunched up their backs to dance for the departed. So many are brought when it is too late and they die here. Dr is intending with his frequent visits to train them to bring them in before they've tried the witchdoctor. Only 7 adults to stand between these people and the blackness of heathendom. I think often of the 7 loaves that Christ broke to minister to the people, and the 'few small fishes'—the Westcott kiddies who have their part also in drawing people to Christ. Little Anne, age 9, said the other day she was not satisfied because she hasn't been doing missionary work. She wants to go down to the village with me one evening a week and tell the women and children about Christ. One cannot help feeling the impulse to snatch these people from their darkness. Much prayer is needed for us that we may have wisdom and strength.

This is the rainy season and Pearl and I just finished planting ten beds of vegetables. Ma Kinso's chickens were following close behind us but I think we managed to save some that we planted. Pearl threw the rake at one old cock and said, "If you don't go to roost, I'll see that you roast!"

The birds are most harmonious at this time, reminding one of the beautiful songs heard in a large conservatory in the tropical bird section. The high flutelike tones, the calls, the chatter, the sad croon of one similar to a mourning dove and in the same rhythm as the native drums; strange that even the birds sing in syncopation! It is most fascinating.

A dozen women cleared away our jungle in back and we discovered we have more bananas than we can ever use, a very large patch of pineapple, a grove of slender pai-pai trees, and much manioc, a starchy potato-like vegetable. The sunset is beautiful from this little hill when one looks thru the broad leaves of a banana tree across the black-green tops of elephant and giant trees to the pearly-rose sky. It is a veritable fairy land.

I have not wearied of my work, but am more and more interested in making a real success of caring for the Westcotts. They have all gained in weight, in fact, I have myself. And my arms are getting big and strong. I feel fine. Mrs Westcott's physical condition is best yet and she started playing the piano a few days ago, which gave her a new lease on life.

Ione finally received Lilian Pudney's April letter and responded on May 19, saying:

.....I have written Hector a letter expressing my joy at his plans for coming out. I wanted to write sooner, but did not want to be at all responsible for his decision and when I left, I had not heard for sure yet. He seems quite satisfied to turn his eyes in this direction, and I am thrilled that it is really settled. Of course, there are many obstacles, but I am confident God can open the way if it is His Will. If the Lord shall lead him out here, he'll find a great work waiting. There are a hundred and one jobs to 'let Hector do', and I'm sure he can do them very acceptably! There are some lovely single girls here and it may be that he would find another that he would like better than me. There may be someone else who would be better suited and I feel that our contacts should be only casual until he comes. It's hard to be casual, tho', when one is so far away! And it takes a letter so long to go back and forth. It's true, too, that much depends upon what is said and done now. I know I would be very happy with Hector; he would make any girl happy. The question is whether he would be provoked with my queer ways, and our backgrounds are somewhat different. Yet, Dr Westcott came from the city and Ellen from the country and they are very happy. I must pray more about this and have the assurance from Him that it is all right. "Perfect love casteth out fear", when the love is God's and the fear ours, but I am sure it can be true also in a friendship ordained by God.

This clearly showed that Ione was a level-headed young woman. She had experienced many advances from men during her singing career and she wanted to be sure not only that Hector was the right partner for her but that she would also complement Hector and be the right partner for him.

Rev. Pudney received a more factual letter from Ione:

.....After having sent an answer to Mrs Pudney's recent letter I learned from Mr Jenkinson that you have certain gifts for me in the Mission account which require disposal. I would appreciate it very much if you would send the entire amount, $40.00, to my Mother. I shall write the Thendara S.S., thanking them for the $30.00; The Church of the Open Door, Louisville, KY, for $5.00; and Mrs H.C. Bliss, Cleveland, for $5.00.

Would it trouble you greatly to send my Mother the equivalent of about $5.00 per month, should gifts come in to equal that? You may feel free to take it from any amount so long as I know which it is.

You may be sure we are all well cared for here. There is no difficulty in keeping the wolf away from the door! (Only leopards!) Food is very high and scarce, but one can manage for quite a length of time with native things. However, there comes often a craving for more fresh vegetables and meats. Pearl and I have been taking Vitamin tablets that seem to make up for some of the deficiency. It is great fun discovering what one can do with native foods.

Our contacts with Kinsos are always refreshing and helpful. They are never too busy to stop and hear of our problems and give such good advice. It is so good to know that there are two such as them on this end of the line and two such as you and Mrs Pudney at the other end! There have been many problems in caring for Mrs Westcott, and they, as well as the Doctor, have been very sympathetic. I love Mrs Westcott and shall be so happy when we shall see her able to conduct herself normally. The three little children are very cooperative and make "Auntie Ione" feel very important. They love stories and have many

Botiki (Dr Wescott's assistant), and his wife, Maria.

good books which we explore together occasionally. My work is very confining, as you may know, and I have been limited in getting the language as I should, but am studying Welles Grammar, and Machini[12] has agreed to come over to the Doctor's in the afternoon to give me a lift which will enable me to progress better and still 'hold the fort' at their house. I still remember your remarks at the table, Mr Pudney, "Yes, I know you have it on paper, but it is better in your head!'

I am happy to observe how the Lord is blessing here. Everything is so progressive, from the building of Kinso's new garage, which looks like a cathedral; to the guest house, a very attractive place for white patients; and now Doctor is cutting 40-foot timber for a new church building. The waterwheel is a real success; the hospital is very well organized and Pearl has everything at her fingertips.

.....Doctor is spending an hour every evening with a score or more men getting some choir numbers ready. He does well with them. He has arranged for me to take their wives and do some group work with them. Botiki's wife is going to write on paper the names of all the women interested; then we'll get started. I laughed when Doctor called his group his 'paid choir', but he explained that each boy had to pay ten francs to get in. This to be refunded if they make good. Quite an incentive!

---

[12] Machini was an African teacher, who received his name because his mother saw her first bicycle (machine) at his birth. Later, after becoming a Christian, he was called Machini Philippe.

Pearl and I have enjoyed setting up housekeeping together. The natives call us the Mademoiselles long and short! We have a garden in now with ten beds of vegetables. The manioc stalks make a nice fence [when stuck in the ground] *to keep the Kinsos' chickens out! We are next the K's* [Kinsos']. *Our garden is hard against the jungle and low. Then as one walks up the hill there is a pineapple patch to the left, and pai-pai trees to the right. On up the hill one passes beneath stately banana and plantain trees with leaves twice Pearl's length. Then perched on the ridge is a large orange tree and the beginning of a tropical flower garden with palms and cactus. The cook's house to one side, then our 4-room manse spread across the front. We are at the head of a broad road that leads down to the main highway, and we love to come up the road and see our cottage snuggled against the hilltop with its bougainvillea blossoms waving from the leaf-roof.*

How I wish you and Mrs Pudney were here! All you told us was true, and more beside, and I know I shall never be happy elsewhere. All here are praying for the next party to come out. I am happy to learn that Hector has set his face in this direction. I trust the matter of his responsibility to country will be cared for with his ordination. Although, I'm sure he would be pleased to serve the Lord in any capacity. It is true that when one is in the place of God's choice, one is willing to do <u>anything</u>. I would not be satisfied to serve as housekeeper and governess in any other place but Africa! Hector wrote me a real nice letter with some of the typical comments which Mrs Pudney would have said were 'not necessary'!!

May the Lord richly bless you as you not only 'hold the ropes' but endeavour to propagate the Gospel and make known the need of foreign missions.

Yours for Souls, Ione Reed

By the end of May, Ione experienced her first change in an African season as they moved into the "wet" season. She explained this in a letter sent to various people at one time (the family and the girls who were in the trio with her). This letter would not be sent by airmail, so she started with Christmas greetings in an attempt to send greetings at the right time of year for everyone. She wrote:

.....Your seasons change from time to time, but our only changes are from rain to sun to rain; always balmy, refreshing, tropical days, sometimes so humid one's head aches with the pressure, sometimes so hot one feels as tho' the sun were burning a hole thru the head, but always pleasant during some part of the day. The storms are terrific. I was alone with Bobby Westcott two days ago and the rain and wind was so strong that a river made its way straight thru the house before we could roll back the 9 by 12 rug on the living room floor, and that with the door closed. Enough water dropped in two minutes to make a pool with high waves in the back yard. A few days before that their brick flower house went down on one side. Also this week the dam at the water wheel burst thru. It seems what the bugs leave the storms finish. Our little cottage is quite secure, however, for we are between Jenkinson's and Viola Walker, on a hill, yet sheltered by the

other two. Our first little one-room house was first in line, that's why we lost our roof.

In another letter written to her family, Ione expanded on the impact of the rainy season:

.....We have had so much rain (and I mean RAIN) that I can scarcely battle my way down to the garden. And the pole beans are 'way above my head. But the jungle—I never in my life saw the like! The vines hang in curtains, and when a path has been forced thru, it must be a tunnel thru which one walks. I followed the Doctor's house helper thru one with the kiddies to look for a kombo-kombo tree which is good to make toys out of, and the path underfoot was all of vines, damp and green, one could not see more than a few feet thru the vegetation, not far ahead, for there were kinks and turns frequently. One could almost rub elbows with a hippo and not know it.

And the ferns, as high as trees, growing right on the trees, the waving palm branches pressing tight upon them from above; and the cry of insects and birds, day and night has grown to a shrill chorus. One big bee buzzes so loudly that I can never tell whether it's a car coming or not. He is as big as a sparrow. I almost stepped on a snail in the path last night, I thought it was a stone; it stood up about a foot high. I can see it's no wonder the natives, as well as the Westcott kiddies, place such an importance on the value of insects and animals in their lives.

The letter written on May 31 demonstrated that Ione had a dilemma in caring for the Westcotts; it was not her perception of "missionary work". The following letter in which she described her walk with Anna supports this view:

.....I have not led a soul to Christ yet, but opportunities are coming and more and more I can understand them and can talk. A native woman, Anna, walked with me to the stream this week. She helped me dig up a pretty fern and transplant it in a bowl for the house, then carried it for me and talked all the way. One part of what she said I understand quite clearly. "You are a great chief or king, you know all about the book of God". I said, "I know not all; God in Heaven is the Great Chief. I love Him much." "Solo?" [Truly?] she said. Just a weak attempt at a testimony, but it thrilled me. Anna is not a Christian. She and her cousin, Leone, both are unbelievers.

Ione then graphically described a social event she and Pearl organized:

.....Pearl had invited the nurses up; there are four, plus Botiki, the Doctor's right-hand man. Three have wives.

It rained Friday and no one came. I had made fritters, whole lot of them, and when they didn't show up, tried to eat them all myself and got plenty sick. Well, last night here they all came, and I had eaten up the refreshments! There were about 14 in all and they seemed to have a good time. I tried to teach them how to play spin the platter and the game of dropping clothespins in a bottle, and they surely took to it in a great way. It was so strange to spend a social evening with all black people, but they were so nice, and Botiki's wife is a large woman, and everyone laughs at her. When she got up to drop the clothes pins in the bottle, her tummy was so big she never could get them in; of course, it was funny to all, and they have such an acute sense of humor. Then I let Tony, the Monkey perform and Alphonse, the 'baby' nurse (age 15) fell right over in his chair laughing. We sang hymns with the autoharp and Botiki led in prayer; then served each a bit of peppermint candy stick. They all examined them closely and remarked that they tasted like 'dawa' (medicine).

Ione must have felt the tensions of the war to some degree, as she ended her May 31 letter home to her family by saying:

.....Oh how I wish I could have a chat with each of you. You are all so near and dear to me. Between us lie terrible battles on the Atlantic, threatening north of us in Libya, we are no more secure here than are you, but God is over all and how I do praise Him. Write soon, Mother, sometime I'd like a stapler for holding papers together, some cockroach powder and more films for 620 camera. Don't be afraid to write or send things; they come, eventually, I think! Loads of love, Ione

Not long after this letter, Ione wrote two letters. One which appears to be on behalf of Ellen Westcott, and the second letter, written to Hector, was honest in depicting the difficulties and illnesses that were part of living in Africa. Despite only the briefest encounters before sailing to Africa, Ione felt confident enough in Hector to write about things she did not share with her family or George Kissinger. Ellen's condition had deteriorated and her demands on Ione meant that the children got little schooling or attention. At this time, Dr. Westcott made a trip to Stanleyville and Bobbie developed cerebral malaria. Ione wrote:

.....I turned aside from the many duties for a few moments and read from "Streams in the Desert", the words, 'Make thy petition deep'.[13] And I surely did, which time was followed by days and nights of wondering, and then a real sign of progress, praise God. I know God answers prayer. Now, tonight, I find a new condition to refer to Him. Dr went to Stanleyville for two days and just a few hours after he left, little Bobbie, age 8, was taken with an attack of cerebral malaria. Perhaps you know the nature of this form of malaria, quite serious immediately, with nervous twitching, dizziness, a semi-delirious state, seeing things in the room, and nausea. Bobbie's temperature went soaring and his vomiting was violent; after a few hours I had Pearl come up from the hospital and give him a quinine shot. He was quite ill for a while but now I think the shot has taken affect.

The doctor returned from his trip ill, his wife had a heart attack, and it seemed that everyone at the mission, except for Ione and the two Westcott girls, was ill. Ione realized how little she knew of Hector:

---

[13] L. B. Cowman, *Streams in the Desert* (Los Angeles: Oriental Missionary Society, 1925), 174.

.....I wish you would write me a great deal about what you are doing, both at home and when you are away. Tell me something about your father and brothers; I remember the sister whose picture you showed me. She was so pretty; I should like to meet her. I have forgotten her name. I suppose by now you have put away your green hat and green topcoat for the hot summer days (or were they blue?). You're probably ready to take a good swim in some lake. Last summer you were bicycling at the Pudneys cottage, weren't you? That must have been fun. Is there a lake near your farm?

And then Ione's frustrations bubbled up again:

.....I am at a standstill with language at present. Night and day with the sick has been the extent of activities of late, it is unfortunate too, for I must contact the natives so much and I feel so limited. I can 'get by', but I am not satisfied and it is so hard to not be able to carry on the language study of the normal missionary, but I realize I am sent first of all to remedy the Westcott situation, and then to be a normal missionary. Will you pray for real patience in this regard!

In June Ione wrote to her friend Inez Slater, another person she could honestly share some of her struggles and frustrations. Her letter started thus:

My dear Inez,

"When the moon has curved a thousand times across the velvet dark,
Who will remember these bursting bombs, their futile flare and spark,
Or the pigmy rulers who strut and fume? Shadows will cover them –
But across the night will glow, unchanged, the Star of Bethlehem!"
L.S. Clark—"King's Business"

What a blessing my "King's Business" has been to me, 'way out here around the corner from nowhere! I cannot thank you enough for your thoughtfulness in having this magazine sent to me. You always have been a real peach to me and have helped me in so many ways. I think the greatest gift of all was when I wanted so badly to help my little sister thru Moody and you came along just at the right time. I praise Him for your willingness to be used of Him in so many ways.

.....It seems so odd seeing so many black faces all of the time. My work with Ellen and the kiddies keeps me from having very much contact with them, but often Pearl goes from morn till night and doesn't see a white person until she sees mine at night, (and that's not so white always either!) for she works with five native nurses besides Botiki. You would be amazed at the work Pearl puts out and the neat way she keeps the hospital. Doctor has given her things to do that a surgeon studies for a long while; I can't think of their technical spelling, but she does some delicate needle business on the lungs, deflates big tummies, cuts off big lumps, cuts people open, sews them up, gets blood all over her and pulls teeth. I have been watching some and would like to be a little help to her later on. She sent me for a bandage to tie up a little new baby the other night and after she told me four times where it was, finally left the baby and came for it herself. I 'helped' another time, too, - I held a light. At first I got sick every time Doctor removed one of the kiddies' jiggers, or pulled a tooth, but I can do

it myself, now. And when Bobbie had cerebral malaria while Dr. was away I was quite proud to be able to 'special' him night and day.

Ione explained how everything they had brought out with them was used, even the packaging, and how much she enjoyed her friend, Pearl:

.....It is marvellous how the Lord supplies one's needs. My bandages were wrapped in waxed paper, so now we have a supply of that. And my dishes were packed in newspaper and excelsior and waterproof paper, so we have a stack of that for use. And Pearl's oilcloth in her barrels and boxes is on our shelves already; I had not tho't of that. Funny how one cherishes little bits of paper, string, etc. here, for you just can't get more. We're just about all settled; today Pearl took hammer in hand and put her wooden boxes together for a cupboard; then she hunted up an electric cord and rigged up a light over our study table. Because I am the tall one (the long one, the natives say) it fell my lot to stand on top of a box which stood on top of the flour drum and pound the nails and screws in the ceiling. Pearl says that her father was a carpenter so she made herself a cupboard, her brother is an electrician so she decided to do some wiring. I told her my great-great grandfather might have been a monkey, so I suppose that's why I was climbing up to pound for her! Honestly, I think she could get work out of a stump. While we were eating the other day, a little ant dropped in her food, so she picked it up gently, brushed it off, and said, "Akei malamu" (go well, or good-bye). Another fell in her tea and died, so she lifted his still form carefully and stretched him on the table cloth, four legs pointing north, and two south, and said, "Akufi malamu" (died well). A lizard was busily engaged on one side of our wall and when we looked closely, we discovered thousands of tiny baby spiders; the wall was simply speckled with them. After we took a big cloth and wiped them all off and stepped on those that fell on the floor, Pearl remarked drily, "Do you suppose they all had the same Mother? Well, anyway, the kids all look alike." Life doesn't get dull here at all, with the ants and spiders and lizards and cockroaches and snakes — and Pearl.

In June, Hector responded to Ione's letter:

My Own,[14]

I am not so fearful and uncertain now when I sit down to write to you. I was so glad to get that letter.

.....Now to tell you a few of the personal things that have happened in the past two months. I was so glad to be able to write to you and time alone will tell how much the letters I get from you will mean. I certainly need an anchor and I am glad it is in the mission field in the Belgian Congo. I know that you have counted the cost before you went. After all we have to be willing to face the future alone. It is just a pleasant surprise along the way if the Lord leads someone across our path. Since I first met you outside of 18 Howland Ave., there has been some inner attraction that has grown to be more than mere friendship. It was no accident

---

[14] This is one of Hector's poetic salutations, the full phrase being, 'My Own Ione'.

that you found me down at the home in Phila. Altho' I pulled no wires, yet I was so grateful for the further acquaintance that those few weeks afforded. Even when I said goodbye at the station that Sunday evening, it didn't seem as though it would be for long. Some of these . . . shall we call them "spiritual inklings" . . . are apparently given to prepare us for what lies in the veiled future. It means that in the intervening time I shall be kept from any attachments in this country which could easily cause me to miss the will of God for my life.

The rest of the letter was devoted to Hector's activities and offered an explanation of how he finally decided not to strive for ordination in the ministry but to enlist in the Air Force as a radio technician:

.....One evening as Mr Pudney and I were walking home from People's Church, we discussed a little of the plans for ordination and decided that since the government is rather unfavourable to so many getting ordained that it might be just as well to enquire into the possibilities in the air force for some training that would be valuable. We later heard that all the ordinations that have taken place since some time last summer are not valid, altho' there may still be loop holes. So I went down to the air force headquarters and was told that since I have the necessary educational requirements that I should consider a course as a radio technician. Then the next morning in Mission prayers Mr. Thomas prayed that I might have the voice of the Lord and not of men. Going later to my room I asked the Lord to direct me by His Word; the Still Small Voice; circumstances or even another Christian, but I wanted to know that it was His voice. As I waited before Him, a portion of a verse came to mind, "Go in this thy might . . ." I remembered that it was in connection with Gideon and so turning up to Judges 6, it was the first verse that caught my eye. The latter part of it was very definite, "Have not I sent thee." All that was left for me to do was to put in my application.

Hector ended his letter with:

.....Well, Ione, I would rather take the place of this letter; but when I do it will be with a greater knowledge of radio work. Who knows but there will yet be a broadcasting station on the Field. So you keep faithfully at the language, because you may be speaking and singing to thousands of darkened hearts, for Him who died for them and us.

In Christ . . . Hector

Ione's ability to work as a missionary in the Belgian Congo depended on support from churches back in America. Mindful of this, she wrote regularly to her sponsors, giving them news and descriptions of her life. In the following letter, Ione focused more on life beyond the mission compound:

.....At 4:30 we heard the gudu-gudu [drums] beating its tattoo [rhythm], so I went out to see where the afternoon meeting would be. Jenkinsons and Viola Walker were out in meetings with the car and Pearl was busy, so I went alone with the natives, about a half hour's walk down the road. At every little village the head man stood from his seat on his little hillock and waited for the white lady to 'sene' (greet) him, which I did—after Libona, the native teacher

reminded me about it. I learned how to say, 'walk down the hill' and 'cause to enter into your heart' on the way. No village seems to have more than a half dozen people in it, but many goats, chickens, and dogs. Some houses are round, but most are very small and square, made of small poles criss-crossed in squares and hand-fulls of mud thrown into the openings. The village we stopped at had a semi-circle of huts and we were led to the middle and a chair brought to me. The headman was very gracious and spoke to me in French. I heard a wheezy accordion being played and asked about it and they brought it. The head man put it in my lap and I slid my hands into either end and endeavoured to play the base notes. They were not [working]—and someone suggested that they had 'akufied'—(died). I found one octave in the treble that would play and pulled the thing apart for a good push of air and brought it together again vigorously. Every puff of air that I squeezed out of it blew bugs and dust in my face but I played, "Everything's All right in My Father's House"!! A hum of appreciation swept over my congregation and I laid aside the instrument lest it should fall apart on a second selection.

She also took time to recount how she used the gifts the church gave her:

.....I wish you could know how I have put to use every little thing that you gave. The dresses are a real source of comfort and the careful workmanship of each is proving itself under the strain of constant wear. Our house helper must wash twice a week as things mould so quickly; we have taught him to put the pembi (white) things in the moi (sun) and the langi (colored) things on the libandu (veranda) which runs all the way around our cottage. He had his own ideas about using the charcoal iron on the full-skirt gathered dresses; when I came to inspect them he had made all the little gathers into accordion pleats! And it had taken him one hour to do each dress. He was rather relieved when I told him they need not be pleated. It was such a happy surprise to find the canned goods you had put in my trunk all wrapped in red and green tissue. And you rascals— you remembered the three favourite foods of mine. We have surely been enjoying them. And I am happy to know that we are able to get more of all three here, for we can grind our own peanut butter from native-grown peanuts and sweet potatoes and baked beans are not so difficult to manage. Martha Johnson's pole beans, corn, peas, carrots and lettuce which she bought for Pearl are growing magnificently and we have already had some lettuce. Without our own garden we should have to be satisfied with plantain and native spinach.

Ione wrote a letter similar to the one above to another group of friends; here Ione offered another aspect of life—bugs:

.....The drab brown walls of our four-room mud house have been painted a cheery cream colour with a clay-starch-water mixture. Since then we have been noticing little brown tunnels where white ants were starting to come, so we dropped arsenic in them and they left—we thought! A short time ago we observed that all at once great holes were eaten in the walls and that the same ants were making nests which perforated both the sides and floor of one room. When we

put arsenic in these immediately, and an evacuation took place which spread them throughout the house by the hundreds. We ran for the insect spray, but with the first spray of insecticide, a swarm of flying black ants hurled themselves into our faces, coming from the very holes of the white species! The wings fell off the black ones and they soon died, but their white friends still remain to give us new surprises weekly. The spiders are good to us and eat the smaller bugs; there are the big slow ones the size of one's fist, the big running ones, slight, fat ones, and tiny nervous ones. We have grasshoppers, black lacquered fellows, also green and gold ones, some of them streamlined like the latest Model Pontiac car, some are sluggish and square, like a Ford Model T. We have crickets which enjoy our cotton things, roaches that enjoy the silks, and a cunning little praying mantis which cocks his head on one side as if to say, "have You prayed yet today?" Nurse Hiles, with whom I live, says she is going to write a new poem, taken from Edgar Allan Poe's, "Bells, Bells, Bells," and call it, Bugs, Bugs, Bugs.

Another facet of African life was given to Ione's young nephew Lawrence Peterson in July. In a birthday letter, she wrote:

I have not forgotten that this month you have a birthday, and since I cannot send you something yet because of the war, I will write you a letter. I am saving up things for you, though, and will give them to you when I come home again. I will bring you some elephants and big crocodiles if you like.

.....There are no other little white children here except Anne, Bob, and Charlotte. All the rest are black. And some of them are very nice. But they do not like to wear any clothes. They just wear strings of beads or a little raggedy pair of panties. As soon as a tiny baby is born, they put beads around its stomach, and sometimes their stomachs get very fat and the beads break, or else it hurts their stomachs. One little boy came to the hospital with a very bad sick leg which hurt him very much. It was caused by the tight beads. The leg grew bigger and bigger until it looked like it would burst; then the Doctor cut it open and it bled very much and the little boy cried. His leg felt better then, but he grew littler and littler until he died. Another little boy came to the hospital just a week after he was born. His mother had died and his father didn't give him anything to eat. He was very hungry. Then Nurse Hiles fed him some milk and bananas. He didn't have a name, so Nurse called him 'My Dollie', so now his name is Midoli in their language. He has big brown eyes and long eyelashes and curly black hair. He laughs if you rub the back of your finger on his cheek. His cheek feels like velvet.

.....Would you be afraid, Lawrence, if you were out in Africa and met a big black snake? Would you be afraid if a tiger came to your back door? Would you be afraid if an elephant stuck his big old trunk in your window? Would you be afraid if a hundred ants started to crawl up your legs? No, I know you wouldn't, would you—for you would ask Jesus to take care of you, just like I do. And maybe when you are a big man Jesus will want you to come out here, too. But you must be a very big boy now and very brave and do as Mother and Daddy say. You must

pray, too, that Jesus will help Auntie Ione to tell many black girls and boys about Him.

.....Lovingly, Auntie Ione

Dr Westcott insisted Ione carry a flashlight at night to look out for driver ants and snakes saying a gray snake was killed in his flower house recently. In addition, Viola had an encounter with a big black snake in her house one night while finishing her bath. She ran out of the house and in her haste, remembered needing her dressing gown and courageously ran back inside. She then fetched the house helper to investigate but by then the snake was missing. It made her a bit nervous to sleep there alone, so she had one of her little girls stay the rest of the evening and night with her.

.....Dr. has been telling me what to do if drivers come in the night. I haven't had any yet, but last night a tremendous swarm of little black ants made a raid on about 15 pounds of sugar. It was 10 P.M. and I was ready for bed, but soon put on some speed and put soapy water on them and rescued the sugar.

Enough on bugs. You will be happy with me to know that after five long months I have finally succeeded in praying and witnessing in public. I should have done this much sooner, but my work has been rather confined to white folk, you know. It has been a real sorrow to me that I could not say enough to win a soul to Christ, but just yesterday I was able to pray spontaneously, praise the Lord. Then a young man came to inquire about I Cor. 7 and his responsibility toward a wayward heathen wife, and I felt that what I said to him over our open Bibles was of some help; we had prayer together then, and to my great joy, I discovered our bad, fiery-tempered helper, sitting on the veranda listening. He drinks, he smokes, won't go to church, won't listen to hymns, and his wife killed herself because of his meanness. Won't you pray that old Zaze will be saved; he will be a real trophy for Christ.

Ione received two letters from Hector; in one he again refers to her as "My Ione." In these, he updated her about the birth of a baby boy to their mutual friends the Goodmans and a holiday spent with the Pudneys. Lilian Pudney also wrote to Ione. It was evident she had yet to receive a letter from Ione and was unsure of Ione's feelings for Hector, but she continued to sing his praises and offered support for an alliance between them. She also wrote to Ma Kinso enlisting her support in encouraging the romance.

Hector wrote in August informing Ione that he had received his call-up papers. While waiting for these to arrive, he spent time at Howland Avenue in Toronto and built a bookcase from two planks of wood that he planed and polished, thus offering Ione an insight into what she could expect in the way of home improvements when he finally reached the Congo. This letter was signed "Lovingly Hector."

In the following letter, Ione's concern for her mother's welfare was to the fore. It seemed that her mother's lodgers who helped with the house bills both left at the same time, and Ione was concerned about her mother coping financially. She wrote on August 15, 1942:

.....Remember I will be coming back in just two and one-half years, or before, if it is decided that I accompany Mrs Westcott. Don't feel that I am so far away that I am not interested in home affairs. I want to hear so much. I have wondered what the rent is now, how many pupils Mother has, what Marcellyn makes now, how much more you need, and what bills have been paid. How much more is there on the funeral bill, doctor, by Wheaton, life insurance, etc.? On an average, how much extra a month do you need? Don't hesitate to tell me, for extra funds do reach me and it may be possible to transfer them.

And then there was the description of life, the highs and the lows:

.....Life does not cease to be interesting—and fascinating. One can watch the process of clay turning into brick houses and guest homes, sturdy trees falling and becoming attractive cupboards in our bedroom, coffee on bushes thru the roasting and grinding to the table, flour and yeast to golden loaves of bread, everything must come out of a sack, a can, or the jungle. Today Pearl and I watched peacocks [Great Blue Turacos] *in the top of a fifty-foot tree, flitting, preening, and screeching. A big chimp lazily swung from limb to limb one sunny afternoon in the back of the Doctor's house. I have been alone in the house for about two weeks again since Pearl has been* [nursing] *a Belgian lady in the guest house down the hill by the hospital. I went to my kitchen at 10 P.M. one night and took a banana off the lower shelf and proceeded to step over to the table where I peeled and ate it. As I finished my eyes fell on the lower shelf again where, about 3 inches from where I had reached for the banana a slimy head poked out and a red tongue flashed. I looked under and saw a creature about a foot long, but I know it wasn't a snake for it had millions of legs and two long fins on the end of its tail. I didn't know what it was, but I knew I couldn't call the house helper and Pearl wasn't there, so it was up to me to kill it. I took the machete (big knife) and went after it. I wounded it in the back of the neck, but didn't cut it off. It lay still for a while until I tried to slide a white paper under it to get a better look, and then it started performing, so I retreated for a better aim, and knocked him out this time, but left him still intact to have a further study of his anatomy. I put him in a can and saved him until morning when I learned that he was a centipede, very poisonous. Now I feel brave enough to tackle a hippo!*

.....I have been a real Martha these past two weeks, spending much time in the kitchen.[15] I have been sending trays for all meals to both Pearl and her patient, as well as the patient's relatives, also to a Greek who is staying in another little brick house after an operation, besides feeding my own little family of five! Ellen has to have special things, as well as pretty close attention, and I've been trying to give the kiddies about an hour of schooling every morning.

---

[15] Not a reference to the twenty-first-century Martha Stewart, but more likely to Martha, sister of Lazarus and Mary and friend of Jesus (Luke 10:40), who was a woman who kept herself busy with domestic affairs.

.....There has been a deluge of white patients, five and six a day, and if they have a meal here it must be prepared by myself. Viola is overwhelmed with both the boys' and girls' school and women's meetings, and Pearl must give anaesthetics, etc. So, I set my trays out at night and write up my menus in the morning when I find out what they can eat that day. It is not easy, for I have so little food to do with.

.....It is a real experience for me, but I know the Lord is helping and I am much better able to be a leader than before. And I am realizing more and more what it means to keep house and care for a family. My work is not hard and my hands do not show any traces of dishwater or scrubbing, but it takes a lot of mental energy to keep the helpers going. When we got tied up for help, we got in a group of helpers and I had charge of three on the ironing and two in the kitchen, besides the two in the yard and two at my own house.

I enjoy Pearl so much; her funny jokes are so refreshing and she is so energetic and vigorous and does things so well. We have quite a system in the house here. We have divided up our work; she keeps the washroom tidy and I the kitchen, and both do the other two rooms. She kills the congoli worms and the spiders and the hornets; I kill the roaches, white ants and lizards, if any lizards get obstreperous or are the poisonous kind. Last Sunday Pearl knocked down nine blue hornet nests and got stung by one. The centipede was really in Pearl's class for it had many legs, but since she wasn't there, I had to do it.

.....I have a new way of fixing my hair so I don't have to plaster it down with pins—roll it over a bandana and tie it over my noble brow. I have worn out one pair of shoes and half dozen cotton dresses are too tight for my fat mid-line!
Love, Ione

Ione wrote to Hector on the same day, August 15, where she related news that might interest him more than how she fixed her hair:

.....I watched Dr's brick machine which makes two bricks at once. All he uses is good smooth dirt, grease the moulds with palm fat and a big lever comes down and compresses it hard. He has a long shed which accommodates thousands of bricks, then he builds them up and builds a fire inside, which is the kiln. And they look fine, too. He has some forty-foot timbers, ready now and sliced four inches thick for the beams of the new church. Beautiful dark hardwood, exquisitely marked. He has built some 60 houses for the operatives on his waiting list. There is a new road which we call 'Stump Street', well-named for the stumps that yet remain. The jungle is so thick and dense it takes many men, or women, as the case may be, to cut even a path thru.

And added:

.....It surely will be a fine experience if you are called up as a radio technician. Doctor was happy to know that, altho' he had hoped you would be soon on your way out. He feels your interests will surely fit in with the need on this station. I am sure the Lord will guide you very definitely. He will not let you run ahead nor lag behind. "God's way is the best way"

.....Tony [the monkey] *spoke in Bangala to the evangelists who convened last week for the yearly Matondo (harvest). They were a lively bunch and doubled up in laughter over him. I am happy to know that the native church here has been able to support fully all of the outstation churches and their evangelists this year. Many of them have suffered real persecutions, but they have radiant testimonies and are on fire for the Lord.*

Although incredibly busy, Ione and Pearl had a way of unwinding and feeding the spirit:

.....This afternoon Pearl and I took the ground sheet and started down a path behind the girl's dormitory, walked 'way down that hill to a level spot beside a stream, in a circle of giant trees. It was a delightful spot and there we spent over two hours studying Hebrews and James together. It was a precious time. We stayed there until we just had to come back, and as we folded up the sheet we hear the crickets winding up their watches for the night.

Ione's sense of fun broke through in her ending to this letter to Hector:

.....Sincerely in Him, Ione

P.S. I baked you a cake today, but the rest of the folk ate it all up!

She celebrated her twenty-ninth birthday on August 17ᵗʰ and on the 30ᵗʰ, she wrote home:

Dear little sisters,

Your letters of March and May respectively were so welcome. And just last week I received letters from both Mother and Lucille; they had mailed them in July 17 & 15. I have received four letters now from Mother.

My Birthday was such a happy occasion. Early in the morning, while Pearl and I were having devotions, Viola sent her little girls over; they gathered so quietly that we did not hear them, and then all started to sing, "Happy Birthday" first in English, "Happy Burseday, Mademoiselley," and then in their tribal tongue, Libua. Then one of them stepped forward and presented me with a gorgeous bouquet of huge pink, wax like flowers, with honeysuckles all around them. Another followed her with a dainty little colored native basket with a big bow on it (from Vee). Another had a gift wrapped in tissue from Ma Kinso (Mrs Jenkinson) who is away for 3 mo. Her gift was an ivory letter opener and a set of cellophane lids for dishes. The day was busy, as usual, but pleasant, as Ellen usually sees to that. I went home for a little while during nap time and when I came back the kiddies had been working hard to make presents for me. Anne drew a picture of a horse on a little tray cloth which she had hemmed by hand; she also gave me some other pretty drawings; Bobbie had attempted a tray cloth also and succeeded pretty well, even washed and ironed it after his rather grimy little hands had finished it. All had made pretty colored blotter pads of different shapes, and Pearl had made little poems typed in. At 4 P.M. I made some chocolate cupcakes for a birthday cake and we had a tea party. When I went home at 7 Pearl had a lovely supper all ready and had baked some tasty little cinnamon buns. My plate was surrounded with gifts from her, each wrapped separately; a mirror, hairpins, darning cotton, hair-oil, ivory butter knife, and shoe-trees. Each gift had the cutest little poem on it. Then under my plate was the loveliest letter to me. She is so good to me and a real pal.

The same letter told that Ellen could fly back to the United States and that the American consul had cleared Ione to travel with Ellen. However, the mission was reluctant for Ellen to go without her family and the doctor did not want Ellen to return at the start of "cold weather" in the States. Ione asked her family to pray that the right decision would be made.

While the Jenkinsons had a break from Bongondza, the mission was managed by George Kerrigan, who was normally stationed at Maganga (ma-GANG-a). Like Kinso, he was affectionately called Keri and his wife was referred to as Ma Keri. The Kerrigans came originally from Scotland and were seasoned campaigners like the Jenkinsons. George first arrived in the Belgian Congo in 1922 and later met Dora, his future wife, who arrived in 1926. The two were married in 1928 and it was perhaps their experiences which colored the rules that were set out for future missionaries who met in "the field." George originally set up a mission station at Boyulu as a single man before moving to Maganga and setting up an establishment there. He was Kinso's second in command.

Keri could appear a "dour" Scotsman, but he was kindness itself, especially with children, as he missed his own children growing up, who were raised in Scotland by family members. Keri went to Buta and fetched back supplies, which included a treat—a bottle of Grenadine (pomegranate syrup), which the girls mixed with Klim (milk) to make a "cherry soda." A typical "caring" touch from Keri.

In her next letter, Ione described an invasion of driver ants:

.....The big feature of the week was DRIVER ANTS. We had our first initiation two nights ago at 10 P.M. A few days before they had visited the Westcott chicken coop where some tiny ducks were trying to hatch; as fast as the little things pecked the egg open the ants poured in. Two ducks had succeeded in getting on their two feet, but they were black with ants and were peeping miserably, soon to die if not helped. The kiddies found them and Anne engineered the work of dashing into the box for an egg or a duck and picking furiously, shaking the ants off her fingers before they could bite. I was afraid to try, for I'd already felt a number of times the bad pinch they can give with their big front pinchers while they stand on their hind legs. But Anne said, "Well, do you want them to DIE!" So, I swallowed hard and made a plunge and found it not so hard, but one must work fast and watch both hands as well as the little duck. We got their box outside and hopped on one foot and then the other to keep them from climbing our legs, but at last all were freed that had hatched and we cleaned the pen out.

That was in the daytime and they were not raiding, but Friday night they really raided our house. We were just nicely resting in bed with the light out when the two chickens we had under a crate on the back porch began squawking and kicking their cup over. We tho't it might be a snake and took a light out. But no sooner had we stepped outside the door when we felt some pinchers and looked down and we were in a black pool of ants; then we started hopping and dashed in and picked them off. We made another attempt to go out, this time overturning the crate but the chickens were so dopey they didn't know enough to move; (in the morning one's tail was missing) we shooed them, and then stamped out to the cook house. The ground was black all the way and the cook house was covered with them. We tried pouring hot water on them but as soon as the water cooled, they proceeded. By the time we got back they had started in two doors and were coming down the walls over the places where we do not yet have board ceilings. We put our clothes on, grabbed a blanket and light and went out the one remaining door and by that time they had surrounded three sides of the house. We have been told it takes them about 2-1/2 or 3 hours to raid one house, depending upon how much food is open and how many roaches one has.

We didn't wait to watch, however, but begged Viola for a nail to hang on [a bed] for the night and she graciously made us comfortable where we slept until nearly 6 A.M. There were still some there in drawers and various spots which showed us they had not missed many inches of the place. I crawled back into bed for a few extra winks and came out with a bound with one hanging on me; they were in our clothes and during breakfast one bit me in a very bad spot to get at quickly.

.....I don't think I shall ever forget the sight of these millions of ants taking possession of everything we owned!

On September 6, Ione wrote to Hector:

"Let us lift up our hearts with our hands unto God in the heavens." – Daily Light today. Also,

"Because thy loving kindness is better than life, my lips shall praise thee. Thus will I bless thee while I live; I will lift up my hands in thy name…

Whatsoever ye shall ask in my name, that will I do."

Your two letters of July 14 and 28 reached me Aug. 18, and I do thank you very much. I have placed the picture beside our map of Africa where I may be continually reminded of Africa—and you—together.

Now take care of yourself Hector. You must be quite stout when you come to the field. I'm writing this letter in red to tell you that it will be a red letter day when I see you once more.

In Christ, Ione

On September 14, Hector shared with Ione how he constantly thought of her when at work:

.....You may wonder sometimes how much time I spend thinking about you. Here is the answer; there is a rule in electrical work: the current passing through a wire, when <u>multiplied</u> by the resistance that it encounters (such as electrical light bulbs or motors) is equal to the force that is behind it — for instance a battery or dynamo. The letter for current is "I" standing for intensity or amount; the letter for resistance is "R" while the other letter is "E" for Electro Motive Force. Probably you have guessed it already. "I"one "R"eed equals "E"verything. You

may be sure that I find it always on the tip of my tongue when we have to work out any equations, and that is usually several times a day. Thinkest thou not that this adds a little spice to inanimate objects?

When Hector was home for Labor Day at his family home in Avonmore, he let his father read one of Ione's letters. His father realized the impact Ione was having on his son and he gave his blessing to their friendship. Hector heard that American forces reached the Belgian Congo and wished he were part of the expedition. He wrote to his sister Florence:

.....I had a letter from Ione this week. It was about a month coming over. She is a lovely character, and I can never thank the Lord enough for leading us together. When one thinks of all the people that we meet and yet there is one who is definitely the Lord's choice for us. What an advantage the Christian has over an unsaved person; they chose whom they will and take the bad with the good; while the Lord knows just how to mould two lives so that they will glorify Him. I do trust that it will not be too long before I will be able to get to the Field; but that too is in the Lord's hands.

Hector's letter of September 28 to Ione contained a great deal of banter and teasing:

.....Do you mean to tell me that you are more heartless than Pearl? Almost anyone can venture to kill an ugly creature, but to dispose of the <u>shapely</u> ones, needs a well-qualified criminal. Of course, I must make allowances for self-defence. I better take note of all these things since someday I might be the victim.

Throughout all the letters, it was evident that both Ione and Hector relied on God's word to lead them, and in this letter, Hector thanked Ione for the excerpt she had sent him, saying:

.....Thanks so much for the promise that you drew for me. Indeed, the Lord's hand is not shortened. I heard something quite good some time ago. Someone began to complain that the Lord did not show much interest since He made so little manifestation. The answer was that God's clock struck but once or twice in a thousand years, but the wheels were moving all the time. So, it is now, with me. It may seem to be rather inconvenient, not to be able to go out right away, but His plans do not necessarily run by our calendar.

Hector's admiration and love for Ione was not overtly stated but were nonetheless clear in this paragraph:

.....I can readily picture you and Pearl gleaning rich blessing from the Word as you sat under the lofty panoply, surrounded by the hum of forest life. But most of all the simile of the crickets—how do you think of such apt descriptions, I have listened to crickets for years but never before did it occur to me that it sounded like the winding of watches, which is the very truth of the matter. I think that I will not be satisfied until you write a book. Maybe that is why you want me for a right-hand man . . . so I can bring you bread and water, and paper and ink while you produce compositions of international fame. But you better wait until you change your name before you become too widely known. About all McMillans

*are famous for up until now is that of being Scotchmen. Maybe they will have a
break yet.*

*.....Thanks once more for writing. I think this is <u>one</u> way at least of becoming
better acquainted. I never forget to pray for you that the Lord's guardian angels
may be around and about you; that your life may show forth the glories of Him
who has called you out of darkness into His marvellous light; and that you may
be given the health and strength and patience and faithfulness for your tasks.*

*"He bore on the tree
The sentence for me
And now both the Surety and sinner are free:
And this I shall find,
For such is His mind,
He'll not be in glory and leave me behind."*

Thanks for the cake. Love, Hector

On October 10, Ione penned a letter to her sister Doris, sending her birthday wishes.
Ione was missing key moments in family life such as Doris and Marcellyn's
graduation. It was now almost a year since she had last seen them, yet while she
regretted not being there, she was convinced that the decision to be a missionary had
been the right one. While it may not be an easy path, it was the one Ione believed
she must undertake.

Ione included funny stories about lizards dropping on a pile of nurses' uniforms
Pearl was carrying and then running down her back, at which point she dropped
everything and screamed. A lizard dropped on Ione's head and "scared me half to
death." Finally, a lizard dropped on the table and fell to the floor, leaving his tail
behind. Ione asked the helper to clear the tail away, and while he was doing that, the
head end bit his toe.

Language continued to be a problem, although Ione felt she was getting better,
as she explained to Doris:

*.....I am working on an object lesson, translating it into Bangala to give in one
of Viola Walker's children's meetings. I will soon be able to give real messages.
Up to now I have been saying things very simply but am learning how to describe
things. Instead of saying, "Ok<u>a</u>ngi mo<u>n</u>oko na yo" (shut your mouth!), I can say
more politely, "Otik<u>a</u>li bi" (Be quiet). Give (Opisi) and do (Osali) were my chief
words at first, but now I can say, "Okamati mosala na yo" (Begin your work)
which sounds better.*

Food was another preoccupation, and when a local teacher killed an animal, such as
a goat, they had fresh meat, which was a change from Spam. Ione wrote:

*.....We can get sugar here, grown in Africa; it is coarser, but otherwise just like
ours at home. There is a native seed that pops like popcorn but only swells up
and is very tender and crunchy like peanuts. I put some in some fudge tonight. It
is called cocoliko. We are learning more and more what is good here.*

Life did sometimes prove too much and Ione shared her problems with Ma Kinso,
whom she described as "motherly"; in another letter, Ione described Ma Kinso and

her husband as "pillows of comfort." Ma Kinso was the epitome of an "English rose"—she had a genteel demeanor that hid a true pioneering core, a matronly figure, and the most wonderful smile. Kinso was the most patient of men—tall, pensive, always thinking before speaking. In sharing with her sister Doris, Ione said:

.....I get discouraged sometimes, because Mrs Westcott has had about twelve relapses since I came, gets back into bed and stays there for days and can't eat.

Viola Walker with her sewing class.

But she has walked off a pair of shoes, so I have much for which to be thankful. Pearl is studying French hard, so that she can go to Stanleyville for a month of special training which will give her a paper to conduct the medical work of the station when the Doctor leaves. She does some hospital work, too. Viola has been conducting both girls' and boys' school as well as the women's sewing class and will be glad of a lift when the Kinsos get back. Dr is working from early morning till late at night. He came to dinner today at 3; he operates about twice a day, besides making bricks, building houses, a new church, running the waterpower which makes the electricity, clears the jungle back, has directed the building of some 60 native houses for pre-operatives, goes to the forest, marks trees, has them cut into boards for furniture and window frames, etc. He never stops and none of us can keep up with him. I tried to yesterday, holding down the household affairs with two house helpers, a gardener, their three kiddies plus two Greek kiddies whose Daddy has had an operation, and Mrs W. vomiting every two jerks. Dr came strolling in at 8 bells for his supper, just thirteen hours since I came on the job, he looked a little tired but was quite peppy, and I was all dragged out, went home and lost my dinner.

I find I can take eleven hours of it without a rest, but out here there is no limit and one has to sort of test one's endurance to see how much you can stand according to the weather. I did come home for a little afternoon nap at first, but I have a woman sewing at the Westcott house from 2 to 5 which is a great help with a big family mending, but I must be there with her. I think I could manage the family all right with all of the help I have, but it's the extra things, white patients continually who need trays, meals, teas, lunches, and whose kiddies like to play with ours and stay all day. It's ever so much fun and I meet such interesting people, but my head often buzzes trying to think in every direction at once.

.....Maybe this sounds like I am not going to stand the big task I have undertaken, but really, I am very healthy and continue to have a big appetite and am fairly

bursting out of my clothes. It's true the continual starchy diet does make one get quite fat, but the heat takes you down, so I don't try to curb the appetite.

.....How I long to be cheered up by you. Loads of love to my little honey-bunny-boo.

In Him, Ione

In a letter to Dr. Savage written at the end of October, Ione restated that the Kinsos seemed to absorb and suppress difficulties as they arose, which must have provided her with a confidential refuge when looking after Ellen proved far more challenging than she expected. As well as "loving" others, Ione received "love."

Around the same time, she wrote to Lilian Pudney:

.....I had another good letter from Hector last evening. I had one also from the other young man who came to your house (tho' I have not written him since I left America he has sent four letters), and there was no comparison in the two letters. Hector's was miles ahead. He said I was the apple of his eye and he signed the letter with love and I do believe he meant it! I'm so happy that he feels that way.

.....I have never been sorry, Mrs Pudney, for your good work in behalf of Hector and myself. His letters do mean a great deal and help to bridge the gap while waiting for him to come out. I am so glad he is having this special training, too.

Interestingly, Hector also mentioned Lilian's "good work" in a letter he wrote to Ione on the same day Ione wrote to Lilian about Hector. He recounted how nervous he felt when Lilian approached him, wishing to have a "quiet word". He said he feared the worst at that point: "My heart was at a loss to know whether to go to my shoes or my throat." Since the conversation enlightened him as to Ione's feelings, he felt he could bear anything:

.....I feel that there is no price too great for me to pay, that I may be counted worthy of your affection; in other words, a Christian gentleman. And so I press on. The other evening in prayer I just had to thank the Lord that you are the most precious thing on earth to me.

He shared with Ione a passage from *The Upper Currents* that he believed summed up his vision of Ione:

"Wherever she moves she leaves a benediction. Her sweet patience is never disturbed by the sharp words that fall about her. The children love her because she never tires of them. She helps them with their lessons, listens to their frets and worries, mends their broken toys, makes dolls' dresses for them, straightens out their tangles, settles their little quarrels, and finds time to play with them. When there is sickness in the home she is the angel of comfort. Her face is always bright with the outshining of love. Her voice has music in it as it falls in cheerful tenderness on a sufferer's ear. Her hands are wondrously gentle as the soothing touch rests on the aching head, or as they minister in countless ways about the bed of pain."[16]

---

[16] James Russell Miller, *The Upper Currents* (London: Hodder & Stoughton, 1902), 177.

Yet there was so much he did not know about Ione; he didn't know her birthdate, and the only picture he had of her was one printed in a magazine called *Light and Life*, published by the mission society:

> .....*Speaking of pictures, you should see the dresser in this room. There is one of my home; another of my Mother and Dad taken on their wedding day (this is about the only picture we have of mother); one of each of my four sisters, and a small snap of the fifth; and then in the midst of all, the magazine, "Light & Life", of last December, is folded so as to present to view a smiling Princess. Do you know what I have in my mind? I intend to write to your mother after this set of exams are over, which will probably be next week; and in a roundabout way I'll ask if she has any stray pictures of her daughter that she could <u>loan</u> to me.*

In a letter Ione wrote on October 29, she described the month of June as being a turning point and that Ellen's condition had worsened:

> .....*I didn't think I could go on, and I couldn't by myself. Ellen's spells were so bad and I was entirely incapable to cope with the situation.*

Ione genuinely cared for and admired Ellen and it would appear that Ione was tasked with more than being a "nurse" to her. With the doctor away and Bob developing cerebral malaria, Ione was stretched. One sleepless night, she turned to reading *Streams in the Desert* and found these words of comfort:

> *"Make thy petition deep, O heart of mine,*
> *Thy God can do much more*
> *Than thou canst ask;*
> *Launch out on the Divine,*
> *Draw from His love-filled store.*
> *Trust Him with everything;*
> *Begin today,*
> *And find the joy that comes*
> *When Jesus has His way!"*
>
> *I bowed my head and committed to Him the large petition. . . Then I had peace.*

It was hardly surprising that Ione pleaded for letters from those back home, as they had always been a bedrock of strength. But now she was so far from them and her need was so great, however, it made her turn and rely more on her faith than ever before. While she referred to "hardships," she was not explicit, and it seems like the task had become a test of her strength. Letter writing freed her from focusing on what she really had to deal with and was filled with colorful descriptions of life at Bongondza.

On the theme of communication, Ione described in a letter home how time was marked at the mission station: Kinso blew a whistle for the afternoon meeting, while Machini sent messages via the talking drum:

> .....*Immediately the drum took up the call and is now beating a tattoo vigorously under the nimble manipulations of Machini, station evangelist. I cannot see him from my desk, but I have many times watched him, bending over the big hollow*

tree-trunk, his white teeth glistening in the sun. In half an hour he'll beat the drum again and then start off with Libona, station teacher, a trail of school children behind, for a nearby village. Later this evening perhaps we'll hear another drum beating down near the hospital, a wild erratic staccato for the death of a village headman; this will be accompanied by weird cries and perhaps the women will put on leaf skirts and dance; this has been going on for several weeks and they seem to get no satisfaction from it and there seems to be no end of noise and palaver. But the old headman was a heathen and refused Christ many times.

There are souls being saved continually, but it seems impossible to reach them all with the present staff. The backwoods people or 'basenjies' never come out and must be reached by treks to their own villages on foot thru the forest path. If there is a path or cutting one's way if not. These paths resemble tunnels, closed in overhead by the jungle thickness, vegetation many feet thick underfoot. It is in these dark damp places that numerous orchids are found, free of charge! These 'basenji' folk do not all speak Bangala so it is necessary to take an evangelist along who speaks Babua, their own tribal tongue. Bangala seems to be the trade language among many people, and that is what we speak, but few missionaries have learned very many words of the difficult Babuan language. It sounds to me like a series of ba's and kwi's. The staff speak it among themselves.

There are few Bangala words that I cannot recognize now, altho' my speaking vocabulary is limited yet. I learned three new words this morning in church. Mr Jenkinson was telling the story of Joseph and his dreaming (kuluta). He said that because Joseph was willing to eat (kulia) much sorrow (mawa mingi), God used him to cause many people to live (kubikisa batu mingi). In spite of the fact that his friends (abungaki) forgot him, God remembered and helped him (asalisaki ye). It is strange to be opening the 'mouth' of the house and to be 'hearing' pain. Their language uses common words in so many interesting ways.

As with most letters home, Ione described life in the forest:

Nurse Hiles killed a scorpion in our house the other day; he was a big fellow waving his stinger high in the air; I guess I told you about the centipede I found. I put mine in a can, but Pearl just left her animal's carcass lying on the floor and when she went back to it, it was gone—it had revived! Well, there's only one thing worse than having a scorpion in the house, and that's having an injured one. So, we turned everything upside down until we found it again, walking bravely along. Pearl killed it again and then we went to supper. After supper we tho't we'd put him on the table for further scrutiny and dissection possibly, but he was gone again! About that time, I felt like telling Pearl she wasn't a very good steward of the things the Lord had sent her, but we found it again, this time it was being helped along by a drove of black ants. We killed it the third time and this time it stayed dead.

This is a strange buggy land, and our discomforts do not cease with the visible variety either! There are any number of the tiny invisible kind that Doctor calls 'damnosiums' that leave big welts on the skin. Little Anne Westcott had a filarial [worm] removed as it was crossing inside her eye last week; that's the only place they come closely enough to the surface to remove. They keep constantly moving and cause large swellings and pain. But here I am talking about bugs all of the time.

A typical street scene in Stanleyville with Hotel Des Chutes in the background, c1940.

.....I am alone in the house again, with Pearl away in Stanleyville meeting the requirements for a medical permit. I haven't heard anything worse at night than a chimpanzee's wheezy squeal and a growl in the cook house. I saw two beautiful parrots in a tall giant tree and they were talking, but I couldn't understand their language—it wasn't even Bangala. But the way they tossed their heads and glanced sidelong at me, I have a feeling they were saying, "Pooh, what good is that missionary to our forest people. She has scarcely been off the station since she arrived!" But I looked at them squarely and said, "Just you wait until Mrs Westcott is better and she and Dr and the kiddies are safely at home for their rest—then you'll see me pack a dunnage bag and beat down the trail into the backwoods! You'll hear a shout that will drive you both to the topmost limb of your big tree, and you'll hear hot fast words bearing the message that has been burning in my heart for nearly a year. Even you birds up there will know that Christ was born in Bethlehem, and died on the cross for all of those backwoods basenjies!"

Loads of love in Him, Ione

It must have been hard for Ione to be tied to the station and the doctor's house, and it evidently was not what she felt she had been called to do. So, it was unsurprising that her letter of November 9 carried so much detail about an opportunity to leave the station:

.....It will be Christmas time or past when you receive this, but whether late or not, let me wish you one and all a very happy Christmas. I trust Christ will be made real to you at this time. He is truly a wonderful Saviour. We have in the Bangala language words to the Gospel song, "Down From His Glory" (tune: O Solo Mio). The chorus is especially expressive: "How is the Creator, He is a Saviour, God Himself, Jesus Christ." If you care to sing it—"Na-lingi Yesu! Nan-dimi Ye, Kulika solo kula nyo-so. Ye Moja_lisa, Na Mo-bi-ki-sa, N-zam-be pin-za, Yesu Kristu."

Yesterday at tea time Mr Jenkinson came to my little mud house and asked if I were free to accompany him and Mrs Jenkinson to an evening gathering which he had called out on a little by-path named the Bagara Road. There were folk out there who were out of reach of the Gospel message. I went in his station

67

wagon with Miss Walker, six of her little girls, a native woman and her little fat crying baby, a man who begged a ride, and a station teacher. Not a bad crowd at all. We arrived in good time and immediately the big bass gudu-gudu boomed out the news that we had arrived. While Mr Jenkinson was preparing for lantern slides which he manipulated by light from his car battery, Miss Walker and I took a flashlight and crept thru the passage ways from one hut to another, discovering their fires behind them and women who were putting their pots away to come to the meeting. One must bend nearly double to enter some of the doorways.

We stumbled over a few dogs but were met in every case by a cheery greeting. These folk do not even speak our Bangala, but their own tribal tongue, Babua. I learned their form of greeting then and felt their warmth and appreciation for our coming. They were fascinated by the pictures of the life of Christ, and as Miss Walker's little girls sang, "All for Jesus" when the picture of Christ was shown on the cross, there was not a sound. All were silently watching Christ dying on the cross. Afterward a number came close to us, and one young man spoke to me in Bangala, "O, Mademoiselle, we are greatly desiring a teacher. We have had none; only one day was Mademoiselle Walker with us when she passed thru on her bicycle. May we not have someone to tell us more about believing?" I said, "Do you believe in Jesus? Has he washed your sins away?" "O, yes, Madame, but there are many here who do not know of Him."

It was the first native heart-cry I have heard since coming here, and I cannot forget it. I am hoping soon to go to just such people with the glad news of Jesus. The hour was late, but the people still pressed close to the automobile; it was with difficulty that Mr Jenkinson turned the car around so that we could make our departure.

.....I would like to acknowledge your gifts received to date. .....May the Lord bless every man, woman and little child who makes missionary work possible.

Please write me and tell about what you are doing. I can pray more intelligently if I have just a word, you know. Yours in His Service, Ione

On November 12, Hector wrote to Ione's mother, Leone Reed. Since Ione and Hector were having an unconventional courtship, and Ione could hardly take him home to meet her mother, Hector had to do this for himself:

Dear Mrs Reed:

You will doubtless wonder who this letter could be from. However I feel that I should write and tell you a few matters that concern you and yours.

Probably Ione has intimated, at some point or other, that she has made my acquaintance. But since we have been corresponding quite regularly of late, it is time that you should be informed about the present state of affairs, and just who this person is, that dares to solicit the affection of your daughter.

It might be well if I related a little of my early life, so that we will be on the ground of common knowledge. Perhaps I should start with an incident that happened a little more than twenty years ago. As a result of the flu epidemic after *the last war, my mother was taken to the hospital, having contracted T.B. I have heard since that three relatives and friends, went to have prayer with her and for her. As is natural they asked the Lord to restore her to health and her family, if it were His will. But mother seemed to <u>know</u> the truth. She was not long for this world. She was ready to meet her Saviour, face to face; but what of those she was leaving. Praying as only mothers can, she committed her five daughters and two sons into the hands of One who hears and answers prayer. And so she passed into the presence of the Lord of Glory.*

Years have come and gone. Until I was 21, I travelled the broad road that leads to destruction. In some strange way I was restrained from going very far into open sin; but yet I was in spiritual darkness. It was at a Bible School out in Alberta, 2500 miles from our little home in Eastern Ontario, that I was saved. There I settled accounts with God; whose gentle and tender dealings I had so long neglected. The past was forgiven and forgotten; as I stood on the threshold of a new life in Christ Jesus. Prayer had been answered. Furthermore, I have had the joy of leading my eldest sister to the Lord and we are trusting for the others.

I might say that since my conversion I have never been vitally interested in anyone as a life partner, until — Well, this is the beginning of another story.

I suppose you recall sending your daughter to Toronto, for the candidate period of the Mission, about a year and a half ago. It was a time of rich spiritual fellowship as we studied the constitution of the Mission, and were taught by Mr and Mrs Pudney what they expect of their candidates. Of course, we as young people got to know each other better. From the very first I found Ione to be quite congenial; willing to share in the joys and sorrows of others. Her open-hearted testimony for Christ was a blessing to all with whom she came in contact. So, the three weeks ended and we all separated.

There was no thought in my mind of anything further. I was preparing to go to Brazil. Due to gov't restrictions down there, they could not grant us visas. It meant a period of waiting. The opening of the new mission home in Philadelphia afforded an avenue for some of my repairing ability; and I was glad to be able to help the Pudneys in fixing up their new home. After a few days, word came through that the two girls were coming from Pontiac. That must have been a time of deep heart searching for you as you parted with one who was very dear to you. But when it is a matter of the Lord's will, I know you would not have it otherwise. I imagine you look upon the whole affair much like Moses, "For he had respect unto the recompense of the reward." I believe the Lord must have a special place in His kingdom, for those who give of their own flesh and blood, that the Gospel of Saving Grace might be carried to the dark corners of this earth.

Thus, it was my privilege to renew friendship with Ione. There was some inference that if the way did not open to Brazil, the Congo might be the next consideration, but it did not look like anything serious. It happened that I had to *come back to Toronto, as my passport time had elapsed; but I do thank the Lord for the happy time we had, as a <u>family</u>.*

Hector spoke of the way to Brazil being closed after which he applied for Africa. He also mentioned his need to maintain his military service, and his enlisting in the Canadian Air Force.

.....I am enclosing a little snap that was taken this past summer. I have also sent one to Ione. Air mail letters allow about one sheet of paper and a picture; so I expect that she may be sending the odd one from the Field. However, if there is one around the home that you could spare, I would appreciate having one <u>to adorn the mantel piece</u>.

It seems that this letter has grown to quite a volume, and I promise that the next ones will be kept to one or two pages. If you have time to drop a line some time, I would be only too glad to hear from you.

Sincerely yours in Christ, Hector McMillan

Lilian wrote to Ione on November 17. While not breaching confidences, Ma Kinso had brought to Lilian's attention that both Pearl and Ione were having trying times, which prompted Lilian to write:

.....I want to hear from you girls. Ma Kinso has written and she hoped that you would write frankly to me about your situation and this is what we asked also before you left. We knew that there would be problems and we praise God for the grace and strength given to you.

No task is easy, and yours has not been but you have faithfully ministered to those dear ones and the Lord will undertake for you. There is no doubt that the Westcott family must come home and only a miracle will bring them. We are just afraid that you and Pearl are doing far too much and that was another of our warnings, but I suppose it is easy for us to talk but when you have so much to do, it is another matter. However, provision should be made for time for yourselves and for the study of the language. I am sure that you and Pearl have grand times together and I am so thankful that you have each other as companions. I am sure too that you are a real blessing to Mrs Westcott and the family. Hector writes about each month and of course always mentions his 'Princess', he sure is—IN LOVE! I am so glad for you both, may the Lord bring you together in His own good time. Hector will make a real missionary and be all the more seasoned through his present experience in the army.

While life was trying, Ione found comfort in Biblical readings, as seen in this letter she wrote home on November 21:

Dearest Mother and Family,

"The Lord, He it is that doth go before thee; He will be with thee, He will not fail thee, neither forsake thee." Deut. 31:8

"In quietness and in confidence shall be your strength." Isa. 30:15

.....This may reach you when the New Year is far spent and Christmas is past history, but know that I am thinking about you and loving you no matter what the season. It has been a long time since I have written anyone. It takes a lot of

living, you know, to write down a very little! Just living, in Africa, sometimes is a real struggle. Every time one comes to an exasperating discovery, such as when all of the flour becomes mouldy; someone says, "Oh, that's the Congo for you!" As we step over the threshold of another New Year, how very comforting out here to remind ourselves that come what may on any day of the year, all is known to our Father-God. What He has promised, He is able to perform, even during the uncertain and eventful days before us!!

We are safe here from danger of the War and what a comfort! I am well cared-for, thanks to the gifts of real Christians who love the Lord sincerely. And greatest joy of all, souls are being saved. Our little wood and water fellow, Andre, accepted Christ after coming to the hospital meetings. There will be a baptismal service tomorrow, Lord willing, in Goa's village, one of the out-stations nearby, where Mrs Jenkinson has been all week questioning the candidates for baptism. These people have all been won to the Lord, probably 8 or 10, by Goa, native evangelist. I visited his village last Sunday, a beautiful white sand compound immaculately cleaned, with a quaint two-room mud house for white people to stay. I have had dinner twice there. Goa's wife, Juliana, dimpled and smiling, made us very welcome.

I attended the dedication of a new church, built entirely by the natives themselves, in a village just beyond Goa's. The congregation of 50 could scarcely squeeze into the little building, decked gaily with palms, flowers and two Belgian flags. It was made of poles covered with mud, open on three sides, with a leaf roof. Scarcely had the service begun when a little hairy dog set up a howl to the tune of the first hymn. He was a second cousin to an Airedale and an offspring of a Scotch terrer, I think, I mean terrier! He was only one of four in church, so it was decided that all must leave on his account. Mr Jenkinson took the opportunity to present a platitude. He said if they would chase the sins out of their bodies like they chased dogs out of church, the Lord could use them. After that, during the service, whenever a dog jumped in a window, he was treated like sin itself. When the service was finished, we sat in a leafy shelter for a while before starting the journey back and ate some delicious corn roasted in a native fire.

Life at the Westcott home continues to be interesting, yes, and complicated too, at times, when the frequent white patients need attention and there are many mouths to feed. But the kiddies are real pioneers and all turn out to make any newcomer welcome. Every time a patient leaves, little Charlotte sheds a few tears and says, "Bad news! They've gone, too." When there are no other white children around, she has imaginary ones that she makes dolls and toys for. The other day they held a 'ceremony' for two little Greek children and then cornered them in the bedroom and told them they must become Christians. The Lord is quite real to Anne, Bob, and Charlotte. The other night after all were in bed, I heard Bobbie call out to Anne and say, "Anne, what are you doing?" She answered, "Oh, just sticking my foot out from under the covers and thinking about the coming of the Lord!" When Charlotte asks the blessing, she strings it out as long as she can until Bob reminds her (in a heavy whisper) — "Don't forget to bless about the food!" Then if she doesn't catch the hint, Anne says, quite decisively for her, "For Jesus sake, Amen."

.....Yes, we take 4 grains of quinine each day. I had my first attack of malaria two weeks ago when I stopped for a few days (the gov't warned us to cut down a bit on account of shortage), so I guess it is quite necessary. I still have a great many of the supply we bro't out and am so glad we bro't them. You might put that down on your list for me. The capsules I bro't have 5 grains and are quinine sulfate. They are a bit stronger than the gov't has been providing and not quite so quick acting but will do. The Salvation Harbour Missionary ladies' flannel gowns & diapers will be very helpful. Any time they would want to start on children's dresses and suits they may, too! I expect to go to Ekoko in the spring and will need ever so many little clothes. Verna Ludwig has several hundred school children and all must have clothes, if they are to be dressed at all! They're made very simple and of any cheap material. All sizes. Bandages are so needed, too, as well as simple medicines to put on them. Boric acid, sulphur, iodine, mercurochrome, adhesive tape. By the way, adhesive tape is very handy for keeping ants out of things. We use a lot. I will need lots of school supplies for Ekoko, too, just everything. How I long to get started there! Tell the ladies, prayer is mostly needed.

Loads of love in Him, Ione

Despite taking time to write this long letter home, Ione continued with another long letter, this time to Hector:

Dear Hector,

What a joy your letters have been, tho' I've neglected you so badly for two months!! I have read and reread and looked at the pictures, but it seems to have taken three cups of strong tea and a great desire to write to get this one off at 1:30 A.M. These have been strange months, and especially so these past few weeks, with their busy hours, the click, click of heels on cement or mud, going to and from sick folk, first one, then two, then three, then four and five, there seemed no end, not too wearying for a new missionary, but leaving no time for the needed letters.

The promise for the New Year is Deut. 31:8 – "The Lord He it is that doth go before thee; He will be with thee, He will not fail thee, neither forsake thee." As we step onto the threshold, how very comforting to remind ourselves that come what may on any day of the year, all is known to our Father-God. What he has promised, He is able to perform, even during the uncertain and eventful days before us.

I am wondering what you are doing, if your training will soon end, if you will be actively engaged (I mean in the way—perhaps otherwise also, when the War is ended and you come to the field.) I wish I were a little flea in some of your classes. I wouldn't bother to bite, I'd just look and listen. I'm so glad you received a 92%. It makes me so proud of you. I know how difficult the work must be and I am praying that you make a real success of this period of training. Wish I could see you in your English-made suit. Anything from England always seems to be better, doesn't it? I have always felt that way, perhaps because my grandmother came from England.

The Field Council seems quite definitely inclined to send me to Ekoko in the spring, which matter I have been praying about for some time. It seems my heart will jump right out of my throat when I think of it, for that was the church's first desire also, and I have felt that I have been marking time so far as the Lord's work is concerned. But I must know also that this work which I am now doing is of Him, too, and "for this cause came I unto this hour". Pray much for this new step in my life.

Pearl has been in Stanleyville for her month and is due back this coming week. I shall shout hurrah for I have been terribly lonely. I never have been alone, tho' often I wished I could be. Well, I've had a chance and don't like it so well after all. I think the main difficulty is that I don't have anyone to talk to, and it's so dull talking to oneself! Of course, when I say I am alone, I mean from 9 P.M. to 7 A.M. for I'm at Dr's a good deal of the rest of the time. But when I come home, I hate to find the house empty. I wish you could do something about conditions like this!

I have five letters to acknowledge from you, beginning with your letter of August 13 which arrived Sept. 8, just after I sent my last letter to you. The other four came in less than a month in every case. Thanks so much for all, especially the pictures. I don't know which to talk about first. I'm glad my name could be of some help to you in remembering your I, R, and E's. I am happy you were at your own home for Labour Day. How I would love to meet your Dad and sisters and brother. How I would love also to hear you say, 'dear, and 'apple of my eye' out loud!

Well, it has been a hour well-spent, talking to you this way. I'll promise not to stay up so late again if you'll just keep a steady line of letters coming.

"The Lord bless thee, and keep thee; the Lord make His face to shine upon thee, and be gracious unto thee; the Lord lift up His countenance upon thee, and give thee peace."

Yours in Him, Ione

If Ione was struggling with work that she had not expected, Hector had his own frustrations, but realized he also was doing the Lord's work, even if that also was not exactly as he had imagined. He wrote to Ione on November 28, starting with a verse:

"For God is not unrighteous to forget your work and labour of love, which ye have showed toward His name, in that ye have ministered to the saints, and do minister." Heb. 6:10.

He then wrote that Lilian Pudney had invited him to spend Christmas with them, but as he only had three days leave, he declined and opted to visit his own family.

Lilian had also offered him a small room at the top of mission headquarters as a permanent base, and they joked about decorating the walls with mud to prepare him for living conditions in the Belgian Congo.

The following paragraph shows that it was evident Hector felt his mission work was beginning:

.....There is a group of young people in Toronto who have taken upon themselves the task of supplying the Christian boys in the armed forces with gospel tracts. They call their group the Christian Commandos Committee, and they sort of supply us with ammunition. I wrote to them about two weeks ago and received a lovely letter back with a fine selection of tracts. They promise to pray for us and make contacts in Christian homes where we are made one of the family, when we have leave. Already I have had some good opportunity to use this literature. As you might know, it is necessary to have someone in the supply room at the technical school. There are two such shops where they keep tools, meters, and all sorts of radio equipment, which we get out for an hour or two on "checks". Each student takes a turn at this. So as the Lord opens the way I am able to have a word with them and leave a tract.

He then recounted experiencing an electric shock when testing a transformer, the force of which violently threw his hand away, and he was fortunate that both hands had not been involved:

.....I was not long in recognizing the Lord's presence. There are certainly just as many dangers right here at home, as there are in the dense jungle.

Hector also copied the response he had from his letter to Ione's mother. He had obviously made an impact communicating directly with her. Ione's mother wrote to Hector:

.....It was just grand of you to write to me and I do appreciate your interesting letter so much.

It is so hard to wait upon God when one's heart is longing so much for the thing you know God has called you to do. One of the lessons that I have been so surprised to learn, is that after the Lord speaks to one about a certain work and puts a great love in one's heart for that work, or in other words, prepares the heart first that we may be willing, then He prepares the way; and oh, how hard that in between is for the servant of the Lord.

You will be included in our prayers and I hope that whatever the Lord has for yours and Ione's life will be revealed; for I feel sure that you both are so worthy of His best, and you both deserve your hearts desires. May His pattern be unfolded and His plan be fulfilled. As Ione so often has quoted, "God has His best for those who stand the test. His second best for those who will not have His best.

In response to this letter, Hector made plans to visit Leone Reed in person in the New Year. He routinely wrote to Ione once a fortnight regardless of whether or not he had heard from her. He recalled events of an earlier year in a letter written on December 14:

.....A year ago next Wednesday will be a memory of one thing in particular; your last glimpse of the shores of America. I suppose you are quite a seasoned missionary by now, at least in the physical realm. It is so good that your health has stood up, especially when you have such a great responsibility. Remember those two ladies that we sat with in the restaurant in New York. How interested they were in your going out to the field, and so surprised that you were not afraid!

At this point, while living at the mission house in Toronto, Hector mentioned to Ione all the wonderful contacts that the Lord was giving him. One was a chance encounter at a railway station while a few of the soldiers attending the radio class awaited a train. One started cursing and swearing, so one of the boys mentioned to him that Hector was a minister. The rude soldier was not deterred and continued his tirade. As soon as he stopped for a breath, Hector told him that there was a cure for that kind of talk, but that didn't seem to interest him. So, Hector left the crowd and walked leisurely away, and in a short while, met a Christian soldier. They sat together on the train and had a grand time. Hector later recalled the verse admonishing believers to "part company with those that are despisers of the Lord's mercy". Hector thought how richly the Lord rewarded him – much like when Christian met Faithful in *Pilgrim's Progress* and was accompanied by him on his journey.

Hector again ended the letter with "Lovingly yours, Hector."

In her next letter home, Ione wrote that she would finally be doing the missionary work she had signed up for, even though she had been busy serving the Lord:

.....What a time we have had these past two months! Every member of the Westcott family was ill at once. November is the hardest month here and one after the other had colds and Ellen had a bad relapse of pneumonia. She is just recovering now. A few days after the last child was out of bed we had guests for over the holidays; all of the missionaries from Boyulu and Maganga (U.F.M. stations) were here, in fact, everyone but the Ludwigs. Pearl and I entertained two girls at our house, and I was hostess at Dr's for two there. Then the various families and groups rotated for meals. It kept me hopping, keeping things going in two places, and Ellen was quite ill all of the while. I was so weary toward the end of the ten days that one night when I prayed I almost fell asleep and caught myself saying, in the presence of the three other girls here, "And dear Lord, take us all to California" – I guess Doris was unconsciously on my mind. The girls laughed at me, for two of them are from England and said they hoped the Lord did not answer that prayer since they want to go home soon. It was a precious time for all of us, for we see so few white people and real Christians are scarce. Many of the whites who come here for treatment or operations have black wives and have terrible diseases.

As she looked forward to the coming year, Ione hoped that the Westcotts would be traveling home so that she would be released to go to the Ekoko mission station to help with the boys' school established there. She wrote on December 28th:

.....I want to be in the centre of His Will. He has given me peace while being a Martha for a year, so I shall be happy wherever He sends me. I count this year as my wilderness experience. It has taken just that to bring me to the place of real service for Him. I have been battered and knocked about a bit, so to speak, but "A bruised reed shall He not break" and I believe out of it will come a field of service heretofore yet unknown. I have come to the place where I feel that I shall die if I cannot win souls for Christ."

Ione ended with descriptions of Thanksgiving and Christmas:

.....I tried to make a real Christmas for the kiddies here. They had a paper tree – a nice size and we made decorations from bits of wrapping paper and parts of Christmas cards, little baskets, candles, etc. They had tinsel, and that with the home-made chains and little imitation icicles, it looked quite nice. A big tinsel star was at the top. We put it on a wicker table beside the stone fireplace. We mended some velvet poinsettias and pinned them on the curtains, tied red bows around candles, and made a huge wreath from African holly for over the fireplace. The three children hung up their stockings and I worked until midnight making popcorn balls, roasting peanuts, making fudge, for you know we could not run down to the store for anything. We had a few tins of walnut meats. Then we filled in the empty with small combs, perfume, etc. The kiddies were quite happy on Christmas morn. Ellen was quite ill but tried to be cheery for their sake. We served tea to 17 that evening.[17] For the Christmas dinner at Jenkinsons we had roast duck and dressing, cabbage, potatoes, other vegetables, a real English pudding and mince pie—not bad!

Did I tell you that on Thanksgiving I made pumpkin pie for the Westcotts out of pai-pai—it tasted nearly like it. I was happy on Christmas because I had made the children happy, but there was a little sadness that I had not heard from home and could send nothing. There is nothing out here that I could send except ivory, and that is so heavily dutied or banned entirely that folk have discouraged me from sending stuff. I have a nice collection for you all, however, of knives, forks, spoons, salad sets, pickle forks, napkin rings, little elephants, etc. I trust you will accept my love. I cannot be stopped from sending that—nor can it be censored! Take good care of our family.

Lovingly in Christ, Ione XXXXXXX

Hector wrote to Ione on December 30. He had hoped to visit Ione's family, but his leave had been canceled so he had to make do with a phone call to Ione's mother and sisters. Hector described Christmas with his family:

.....It was nice to be down on the farm again for a few days. There is always plenty of fun, or at least we seem to have a good time. It was nice to be able to

---

[17] Missionaries from two other mission stations joined the team at Bongondza; Ione and Pearl had two guests and the doctor accommodated a married couple. One of the adults dressed as Santa and distributed gifts to everyone. A letter to Lucille in January 1943 revealed that Ione herself played Santa! While Pearl looked after their guests, Ione managed the Westcott household and their guests.

repair the radio; put a ventilator in the kitchen; sit down to help eat a 15 lb. turkey; conduct family worship; help with the chores around the stables etc & etc. Then I went down to see some more of my sisters in Montreal. One of them has her first little girl, named Barbara. Of course, it isn't hard to convince a mother that her baby is the very best in the universe. But really this one is quite charming. I was able to get her a little play suit and there happened to be three booties with it. I guess the extra one is to serve as a spare tire, in case of rationing.

He also pondered what the new year would bring:

.....This New Year is fortunately shrouded in mystery. The very thought of its uncertainty makes us draw closer to the Lord.

HE measures it out to us in minute little things; each one furnished with 60 wings;

they fly along on an unseen track, and never a moment ever comes back.

Yet every one that goes by makes me happier that I am a Christian. As one person said, "If the Lord failed, I would be bankrupt". That seems to indicate a whole-hearted dependence on Him, who keeps us by the power of God.

Hector was also disappointed with the lack of mail from Ione:

.....The mail coming from Africa must have been placed in a rocket plane that has missed the earth altogether. Three months without news from you seems quite a while but it will be more precious when it gets here.

Thus, ended Ione's first year in Africa. It had been exciting yet testing and, as she put it, her wilderness experience, referring to the forty days and nights Jesus spent in the wilderness. She graphically described aspects of her life—the vegetation, the animals, the language—yet some aspects were given scant words, like Ellen's illness. Ione often felt at a loss about what to do. Pearl and Ma Kinso provided her with the support she needed, but it was evident that her faith and reliance on God's would give her the peace and strength to continue. Her newfound friendship with Hector and the letters from home were of great solace, but she never knew when they might arrive.

Chapter 5
THE LONG-DISTANCE COURTSHIP

The letters between Ione and Hector in 1943 begin to show more creative ways of expressing their love and growing devotion for each other.

But Ione's first letters of the year were to the family. She heard from Marcellyn that Doris had moved to California and married a young man named Lloyd on November 7. Doris's marriage had caused some degree of consternation among the Reed family, and Ione tried to remain positive and supportive from a distance. She had an inkling all was not well, as she had not heard from Doris. To Lucille she wrote:

> .....I have many questions to ask, but I have committed her and Lloyd to the Lord, and trust they will be guided aright. I am happy to have a new brother. I am so proud of Maurice [Lucille's husband] and so glad he is in full-time Christian service. I do not want to be disappointed in Doris' husband, and perhaps I shall not. If he is a good man, and honourable, he will want to give his heart to the Lord. Then he will make a fine husband, too.

As Ione thanked her sister for the Christmas card sent, she confessed to not having sent any, which reflected just how pressured she was in November 1942. It was also evident in this letter that communication and transport had worsened as the war progressed and caused issues for the Westcotts, who had started packing for a flight home. In Lucille's letter, written on January 24, 1943, Ione elaborated on services she had been involved with:

> .....The highlight of recent weeks has been my taking Gospel services myself. It is such a thrill, and I find it not hard at all. The messages are already in my heart, the fire has been burning these many months and now the words come tumbling out. I can hardly speak without weeping. I have waited so long to tell them the Good News. This morning I spoke on the word, "Go", and found that the 81 references to it in Acts were quite appropriate here. The group was a Christian group and it seemed to me they just must go and tell their friends and relatives.

Ione appeared to have a close bond with Lucille and was able to share some of her frustrations, as she wrote:

> .....I am anxious to hear from you again. You seem just to understand so many things that we face, the farness from home, and the great effort it takes to do the very smallest thing. One cannot compare values here with those at home, results, work accomplished, etc. The language is such a barrier, customs, trying to "think black", etc. It seems so simple to do one's work with so much help, but it's another thing to get that 'help' to work! Then insects and wild animals are

an obstacle, deterioration of everything you cherish. Fear becomes impossible, except in a sense of surprise at the next thing.

.....Tomorrow I expect to take Tony the Monkey down thru the native village and invite all women and children to the first 5 P.M. meeting. I know they'll come if Tony invites them—they all just love him—he's like the Pied Piper of Hamlin, and there are scores of kiddies around. It will be possible as long as Ellen is well enough to take an interest and if the Westcott children can come along. But if Ellen is ill, I will have to be with her. Pray much that these meetings will provide the way for many souls to be saved.

She confided to Lucille that Hector had sent a cable to her. As air mail letters were banned, and while that allowed some news to reach her, it also caused consternation, as she worried that all was not well. She begged Lucille to give her some information on everyone, her mother, Marcellyn, as well as her own news. Perhaps this indicated how much Ione was feeling the physical distance between herself and the family and how inept she felt about influencing things from such a distance.

In a shocking letter to her mother written January 24th, Ione tells of the sinking of the *Lashaway*, the ship they had sailed on just a year earlier:

.....Just today we learned that a ship was sunk a few months ago and the description sounds like our very ship. There were five little missionaries' children on it, one was lost and the mother and father, leaving two of their children alone; the other two children were with their mother. The account spoke of the bravery of the children, singing hymns on the raft while they were floating until they were rescued. The Captain became crazy, it said with the heat, but we believe because he was a drinking man, and not a Christian. The article said he raved and ranted before he died, and after his body was thrown into the water the sharks followed close behind. We went thru that same water a year ago. How marvellously God spared us and brought us here. We had many talks with the Captain about his soul, but he only laughed at us and said we were foolishly throwing our lives away. Now he knows better.

On a more positive note, Ione continues:

.....My greatest joy is that now I can witness and conduct meetings. I have been having morning meetings for three weeks for women. This is only the beginning, but I have found that it is so easy! I can use my same messages with few exceptions. In fact, I have been following the same outlines and just jotting down the words that I am not yet familiar with. I make some mistakes, but Botiki's wife, Maria, helps me when I say the wrong thing. You can't imagine how strange it is, trying to think black, trying to understand their problems, which are ever so many more than ours. If a woman's husband doesn't beat her, he is not a real husband; she carries the huge loads of wood, cotton, plantain; he goes ahead, with a little knife or spear, looking noble, but doing little. She carries the baby, too.

Ellen's health, once again seemed to improve. Ione wrote again to her mother on January 27, a letter that took her a few days to complete but which indicated much more freedom to do the missionary work she most wanted to do:

.....*My tongue has been loosed and I can speak Bangala freely and best of all, I can tell the Good News so that they understand it. Even the little children seem to comprehend and words that I have only heard from time to time are mine now and I can unburden my heart in prayer publicly and it is such a relief. And the methods are the same, souls are won in the same manner as back home. Now all I lack is time, and even that does not stop me, for I have been able to have meetings mornings or night or talk any time of day in the daily routine.*

It is great, winning souls. Jeremiah said the fire burned hotter on the inside than the fire of opposition on the outside, and he HAD to speak to relieve himself. Oh, that I could go, go, go, to all of them, all around and tell them. I shall; you wait and see! My wilderness experience has been good for me and it may not be ended yet for a while, but it is doing something for me I know. I have learned what hard work means, what it means to be really tired, to have patience beyond all I tho't I could endure, and to come out on top every time. But it's just the Lord. He had this lesson yet for me. And then—real service for Him!

The Victrola is doing fine. The needles started to rust so I have put them in talcum. I will need some more needles soon if you think of it sometime. Both fine and coarse. And how I wish I had more records. But you will begin to think I do nothing but beg. Anything you buy, will you always please keep an account and let it come out of my salary, for I cannot buy much here and if I have it at all, it will need to come from the home end and be paid for there. It's a strange life.

Well, I had a grand children's meeting yesterday at 5 P.M. The Westcott kiddies went along and helped. Tony was the big feature. At first the village kiddies said he was a devil and was going to hell. They were afraid, but I told them he would sing hymns for them, so they followed along, and were so cute. They asked him questions as we went, one little girl, a Christian already, who attends Viola's school, said: "Tony, you are a Christian, aren't you?" I nodded his head. "You are on your way to heaven?" "Yes". "You have come to teach the children about Jesus?" "Yes". Then we come to the village next to the hospital (a group of about a dozen houses, all attached to one another), and there they put bricks in a circle. Tony sang, "Be Careful Little Eyes" "Osinziri bamisu", and then "Oh, How I Love Jesus", "Ngai alingi Yesu". Then I taught them a new chorus which I made up from the little prayer song, "We all rise up together", which finally ends in "We all kneel down together", "Osemami sikomoko", and they were very quiet while little Allietta prayed a long prayer (I had to suggest its close gently). Then we had the story of the little lost sheep, and Charlotte was that sheep, baa-ing plaintifully behind a tuft of sugar-cane. They all cheered when the good shepherd found her. Then when asked who was the Good Shepherd they agreed that it was Jesus. I prayed then and asked the Lord to save any little lost sheep there. Then Tony sang again and invited them to come again next Monday for three days a week. I'm looking forward so much to the next time.

Lovingly in Christ, Ione

On January 31, Ione sent a cablegram to Hector, congratulating him on passing his examinations. Using a Bible quotation to say how thrilled she was at his success, she wrote:

CABLE RECEIVED. GRADUATION CONGRATULATIONS. DANIEL NINE TWENTY TWO TWENTY THREE. KEEP LOOKING UP, IONE

The Bible quotation had to be explained at the post office in America, as officials thought Ione was sending a secret code; fortunately, Hector persuaded them otherwise. Daniel 9:22-23 reads:

He instructed me and said to me, "Daniel, I have now come to give you insight and understanding. 23) As soon as you began to pray, a word went out, which I have come to tell you, for you are highly esteemed. Therefore, consider the word and understand the vision.

On February 14, Ione wrote to Rev. Pudney. She and Pearl had celebrated their first year at Bongondza and her letter started with this:

.....Last week we celebrated our first anniversary on the field. Viola spoke in church and at the close of her message I sang, "Speak, My Lord!" a new translation of Vee's. I remember our first Sunday here, when the three of us sang the song, "His Love is Wonderful to Me", in Bangala and we read our testimonies from a sheet of paper. I tho't I would never be able to pray freely and give a testimony, but the time did come, and while Vee was away this past month, I took all of her women's meetings; also started a regular tri-weekly children's meeting at the hospital. I was thrilled to find that the methods of conducting a children's meeting were much the same as in America.

However, there were a few other aspects causing concern, and Mrs. Westcott remained her prime preoccupation. Ione spoke of having been very weary of late, but had been promised a two-week vacation soon. The likelihood of that occurring was remote. Besides Mrs Westcott, there were two missionaries from Ekoko: Verna Ludwig and Mrs Faulkner waiting to give birth, and the doctor had operated on his own daughter, Anne, who had appendicitis. Added to this, Pearl had bronchial pneumonia with heart complications and was confined to bed. Ione recognized that she was fortunate not to have been ill herself:

.....I have not been ill a day, and I do praise the Lord, for there are so many sick people to take care of. My heart's desire is to be winning souls and there are some opportunities along with my other duties. But I am longing for the day when I shall be a real missionary. Won't you pray that these present difficulties may be stepping stones rather than stumbling blocks in the Lord's service. I tho't surely after a year of this it would be possible for me to enter into missionary activities.

It also seems highly unlikely that the Westcotts would return home in the spring as anticipated, as the increased activity of the German U-boats and their success had made sea travel untenable and air travel was also incredibly difficult. It would be possible to fly Ellen Westcott home, but Ellen felt she could not be separated from her family. There had been some debate regarding Verna Ludwig accompanying Ellen, however, she too did not want to leave children behind. It was hardly surprising that Ione wrote:

.....*I cannot help being a bit discouraged about it all, but I'm also sure I'm in the Lord's will, and He makes me happy.*

The decision not to fly was not ruled out entirely, as seen from part of a letter Ione wrote to her dear friend and fellow singer from the Gospel Trio, Genevieve Burns, on February 23:

.....*When I come home (and it MAY be soon! sh sh) I shall make a bee-line to you and just bask in all of the new stuff you can give me. All of the music I have is two years old now.*

Speaking of coming home, there is a vague possibility of a plane journey with the Dr's wife. She must get home [for further medical attention], and I may be the only one to bring her. If I don't come now, I will be coming at the end of three years, two more, the Lord willing. I am due for a vacation of some kind now, but don't know when or how or where yet.

The following paragraph revealed more of the "girlie" side of Ione's character:

.....*It's been a hard year, tho' I look pretty much the same, last year's dresses you know, and the same hair only it's straight and priggish looking. The permanents in Stanleyville are very bad, they say. How I wish someone would take pity on me and send me some hair and dress styles! Out here no one knows and no one cares, much, but I do. I still have one pair of Nylon hose. But I wear sox nearly all of the time. And cotton dresses the year around. I have a new order supposedly on its way from America and will get a new vision of what things look like at home when it arrives. It is fun, living in our mud house, having a house helper fix one's breakfast, sweep the floor, serving the native papaya (like melon) with lemon juice; some toast made from bread baked in an outdoor stone stove; oatmeal from a tin, perhaps an egg if the hen is in a generous mood. Meat comes once a week now by courier and is very welcome.*

And Ione revealed more about the state of her heart. She confessed:

.....*Hector seems to have wound himself around my heart these days. He's in military service, having graduated from a course in radio technique last month—sent me a cable. But he hopes to get out when he's released. He's a dear and so much fun. He said I was the apple of his eye and that seems to go a long way with me!*

On February 24, Hector could once again write to Ione and not rely on cablegrams. The cablegram from Ione arrived just before he sat for his final exams and it seemed to have spurred him on to do well, making his teacher proud. Hector was planning to visit Ione's mother, as he had some leave coming up and was looking forward to the visit:

.....I'm really looking forward to meeting your mother; she must be a wonderful woman to have a daughter like you!!!!!

He fantasized about things he might be able to do once in Africa:

.....These days of training are proving of real value in a physical sense. I have seldom felt better than I do now. I can almost picture myself out in the Congo training the natives to fall into line; march on the incline; break into quick time; salute to the front and retire; form flight on the right; etc, etc. I enjoy it immensely, even though we do come in at the end of the day feeling a little weary.

.....It is great fun shining buttons and shoes. Likely you will have plenty of silverware etc. ready for me to work on when I get out to the field.

Hector during his RCAF days.

The next letter from Hector was dated March 9 and indicated he had finally made contact with Ione's family:

.....Well, finally it (the train) pulled into the big city and my heart was all trembling with joy and excitement. Your mother said she would try and meet me at the station. So, when I alighted, I looked for someone who might fill the bill. I noticed an interesting young lady there but walked on over towards the station. When I turned around this same girl walked up and asked me if I were Hector McMillan. Receiving an affirmative answer, she said she was Ione's sister, Of course her voice gave away the case. I hadn't heard of her directly. I knew there was a younger sister and one older but of Marcellyn I was ignorant. How much I have been missing. She is almost as charming as her next oldest sister.

As we journeyed home on the bus, she said it was like having Ione home again, and for my part it was just like visiting Ione.

And then I met your mother. Now I know why you are what you are. Words can't express how happy my heart was to enjoy such rich fellowship in natural things and spiritual. The table was bountifully laden with all sorts of good things. But before we started, we had reading and prayer. While we ate she told me how it originated and how finally your dad became interested once more in spiritual things. She said the verse that helped her start family worship was the one on <u>faith cometh by hearing</u>. She used to pray out in the kitchen that the Lord would strengthen her, especially when visitors were in. She even told one lady what to say when her turn for prayer came.

After supper Marcellyn and I talked and did the dishes in between times. What good laughs we had! Your mother said she has just grown up with her daughters; and she is still so youthful in spirit and appearance. I think it was about 10:30 when we put the last dish away.

The front room was the scene of a picture review. Someone brought down the pictures that they had shown at the farewell for you. Childhood with its usual cuteness; school days with their carefreeness; than the most interesting time in any girl's life when boys fill the hours of sunset and twilight; then the section on consecration, with pictures of the trio. What an interesting life you have had! Of course, Marcellyn had to supplement many details which were most enlightening. Thus, the evening passed quickly away.

Hector spent the next day in Ione's home town, visiting the church and meeting Dr. Savage; then he visited Marcellyn at her place of work and helped with filing. After supper, they went to the church and Hector was allowed to say a few words. He met the Missionary Committee, which offered to support him and Ione once he got to the mission field. Hector left the next day for a posting in a town near Port Huron and Simcoe to undertake a short radio course.

On March 21, 1943, Ione wrote a newsletter intended for those who supported her work as a missionary; she described the rainy season and how a tornado came:

.....The storm came, gathering leaves, limbs, followed by a driving rain, the kind one can scarcely stand under. After one tremendous twist of the wind, the side and roof of the [work]shop was wrenched and fell to the ground. The tribunal and post office at Kole also fell. Our roof was pulled partly off the house. A few days past and Doctor cleared away the wreckage and started repairs. Then another storm came which tore away the entire front gable. I wish you could see a tornado such as we have had—a cone shaped spiral which carries everything straight up and away. I don't see how the Doctor had the heart to start on it again, but today I saw him climbing to the top of the roof to see that it was getting on straight again. Perhaps this week another tornado will come; but he'll begin again and keep on until it stays. It's been that way with his water wheel, too.

Ione had additional children to care for in addition to the Westcotts', namely the Ludwig and Faulkner children, whose mothers were due to give birth:

.....We use the big front porch for a school room and have tables [in] three sizes. I am satisfied if the wee ones just sew a picture card or make flower designs on the cane seats of the chairs, but the older ones have readin', writin' and 'rithmetic, as well as piano and handwork. Then they all have lessons in cooking at least once a week. Little Freddie and Marilee Ludwig, ages 3 and 4, as well as Charlotte Westcott, 5, can combine all the ingredients for muffins as well as put them into pans for baking. And how they love it! Bobbie is just as interested, tho he's a boy and 9 (just had a birthday), and can make nice fudge and gingerbread men. There is a nice sand pile at the side of the house and lots and lots of clover lawn to play in. The children have charge of all the chickens, 3 goats, 2 rabbits, several ducks, 2 cats, and of late a tiny motherless chick named "Rubberneck".

Ione then continued with an interesting visitor:

I must tell you about Fataki, the trained chimpanzee who visited us a short time ago. Miss Hiles and I were eating supper when a car drove in front of the door. A gentleman came to the door and spoke in English, introducing himself as Mr Putman. We invited him in and asked if there were others in the party, and he said, "Only my pet chimp." "Well, have him in, too," I said, rather jokingly. So he said, "Fataki!!" And in walked a huge black monkey with a long protruding chin and ugly teeth. He proceeded to the nearest chair and climbed onto it and sat down. After a bit of conversing we gave the man a cup of tea; and then the ape, leaving his chair went out into our dining room and explored, lifting various lids, until I served him some supper (on our best china!), and then bro't in the teapot and he poured his own tea onto the cup, served himself sugar, stirred it and drank it. He ate with a fork also. Well, it was a surprise. All he could say was "Oomph, oomph" He wanted more sausage for breakfast & grabbed my hand & squeezed it until I gave them to him. It hurt for a long time.

Ione added that she did not get much time to work with the "natives," however, she did attend early morning meetings, often having to round up people who were:

.....brushing their teeth with the ends of long fibrous sticks, or braiding their funny, fuzzy pigtails. One little fat naked boy follows me everywhere I go and is always there. I let him be the little black sheep when I told the story of the lost sheep.

Three days later, in a March 24 letter to her sister Lucille, Ione expanded on the subject of the morning meetings at the hospital:

.....My morning meetings at the hospital are at 6:30 and sometimes there are over 100 there. Souls are being saved & they start in baptism training classes once a week. After about a year they are admitted to membership in the native church. One must be so careful here of backsliders and they really do backslide! Polygamy is so common. The headman & chief of villages have 20 or 30 wives. So it's easy to break the rules of the church. The leading teacher here just had to be dismissed for seeking a second wife. It was a heartache for the missionaries who had trained him.

Ione ended the letter with questions about the family:

.....I have not heard from Mother since Doris was married and do not know how she felt. I rec'd Marcellyn's letter of Dec. Have you heard from Doris? I want so badly to know about her. Did you get over your sick spell? And how are the children and Maurice? Nearly half of my term is past and it doesn't seem long until I shall see you again. I don't think it will be necessary to accompany the W's home, but one cannot tell yet. Arrangements are being made for some sort of plane passage in June or before. Pray for Mrs Westcott. She gets very discouraged at times.

Please write soon—and often. The Lord is good to give me such a nice family. I dreamed the other night you were helping me on with my wedding dress! Maybe it'll come true someday.

Load of love, Ione XXXXX M.L.E.L.R. (Maurice, Lucille, Esther, Lawrence, and Ruth)

On March 27, Ione responded to Hector's letter of March 9. She was pleased he managed to fix her mother's clock and wished he were available to mend hers, which was no longer keeping time. Ione apologized for not writing sooner, claiming that there had been increased sickness (mentioning no names) and the doctor had been working long hours:

> .....*I never seem to have a chance to have someone take care of me—I guess I'm just disgustingly healthy—but there's been a variety of things I have found I could do for the sick. Wish I had gone to MMI* [Mission Medical Institute]. *There's only one more baby yet to come, but I think I will have a little vacation before Mrs Carter comes.*

Jim and Mary Carter, missionaries based at the Boyulu station, were expecting their baby at the end of May or beginning of June. They had been missionaries in the Congo since 1935, both arriving separately at Léopoldville (Mary on November 22, 1934, and Jim on December 11, 1934) and both completed a boat journey similar to Ione's to Stanleyville. In some ways, Jim and Mary's story was similar to Ione and Hector's: They had met in England (Jim had come from Australia to complete missionary preparation) in Keswick in July 1934 and became engaged in October 1934, after Jim had undertaken a course in Tropical Medicine in Belgium. Mary had started at Bongondza like Ione, while Jim worked at Boyulu. Eventually, they were officially married at Bafwasende (ba-fwa-SEND-e), a Belgian government post, and had a church wedding at Boyulu on April 11, 1936. Mary didn't meet her Australian family until 1940, when the Carters had a year's furlough (that included spreading the news of their work in the Belgian Congo and mustering financial support for their next term). Ione suspected that when Hector arrived in the Congo that they too, like Jim and Mary, would work at different stations.

Hector wrote to Ione on March 28, the letters being what he called a "hobby" rather than a task:

> .....*You have no idea the comfort it gives me to have someone so precious to think about, write to and pray for. It is like the quieting of a troubled sea. Continuing the theme; just a few days ago I came across the passage in Galatians 4 where the heir and servant are compared. The work of the servant is planned merely because the work has to be done. But the life of the heir is planned since he has a reputation to live up to; and some day will inherit a throne and responsibility. People of the world have a hit and miss existence. Some are fortunate in finding a worthy partner, but how many other lives are wrecked due to mismatches. We who are heirs of God through Christ have the daily assurance of His guiding hand. If we trust Him, we can be sure that He will not let us make a mistake. We are preserved unto a Heavenly Kingdom; and besides He chooses our inheritance for us. It has been a relief to me to realize that I do not have to flirt around until I find someone that suits my fancy. There is only one right one, and so I can rightly afford to be completely faithful to her; (even though separated by land and sea). I believe the Lord is far more interested in these matters than we think. How far could some Christian men have gotten without their better half of 51%? A man is either made or broken on this score. I do thank the Lord for this beginning of a friendship that shall last on and on into Eternity; where our inheritance will be consummated.*

Hector wrote that he had been promoted to Leading Aircraftsman and was engaged in work that was "secret," but he did not expand on that aspect. The ending of this letter is very romantic:

> .....Sometimes I waken early in the morning in the barracks, just when the dawn is beginning to show through the window. Everything is so quiet, and it is a real joy to engage in prayer for you especially. I know that you are in His care and so for another fortnight I commit you to the One that "called you out of darkness into His marvellous light."[18]
>
> Yours by His Grace, Hector

Two weeks later, on April 11, Hector again wrote to Ione; this time he seemed entirely sure whom he wanted to marry, but it seems he only came to this conclusion after having supper with Harry and Jean Titcombe, a young couple who opened up their home to servicemen to give them some respite from barrack life. Jean had asked some poignant questions. He also received advice from senior staff at UFM. He wrote to Ione:

> .....This is a letter of good tidings and I just must express my heart's desire. I've had a talk with Mrs Goodman [wife of the Canadian General Secretary of the UFM] and am writing Mrs Pudney. I believe that your mother would be agreeable, so all I need now is your consent, or in other words, 'voluntary agreement'.
>
> As far as I am concerned, I need no further persuasion. Maybe my letters haven't been able to show it, but my heart is fixed. It would probably be best to ask you to pray about this step and I will do the same. I think you know me as well as anyone does, but if there are any further questions you would like answered, be really frank. Life is too short to be filled with misunderstandings. This relationship is the _most_ intimate, but it is also the most blessed when it has Heaven's blessing.
>
> Now that you know the situation, I will await further plans as regards the jewelry. You may as well know this (since it would be known later) that there is a diamond ring in the mission property that someone gave as a gift. Mrs Pudney has mentioned to me that I could buy it and have it put in a new setting, which would be quite the thing. I have been wondering if your finger is the same size as Marcellyn's; but you can tell me all the details when you write, and advance any suggestions. I imagine it could be sent out airmail, but if not then I'll have to let Verna [Schade] take it with her.
>
> I would like to get the matter settled before I get posted out of Canada. Affairs move quickly these days, so we must always be prepared. If it should happen that I am to leave in a few weeks, I will get someone here to look after the business. Thus, my dear, the matter, is in your hands for better or for worse.
>
> .....It is a glorious thing to feel secure;
>
> In solitude, or 'mid the world's rude din,

---

[18] 1 Peter 2:9

Against all fears to be sustained within.[19]

Lovingly yours in Christ, Hector

While Hector maintained his "hobby" of writing to Ione once a fortnight, Ione neglected responding to each letter, but on April 12, finally wrote to Hector:

The weeks and months have passed and you have been so faithful. I have before me five letters and a cable, all unacknowledged. Each one has been a real joy and comfort and has made me know and appreciate you better……Every month makes me realize more what you really mean to me.

The Christmas gift which you mentioned in your Nov. 14 letter arrived safely and I was so happy to have two such lovely handkerchiefs. Thank you so much for them. Your sister's choice was very good. I shall save them for a very special occasion.

.....Your cables were so thrilling and helpful during the times I might not have otherwise heard. In my cable to you I meant it to convey to you by the Bible verse, "thou art a man greatly beloved"[20]—that you were—by me! But maybe you'd rather I'd just tell you instead of hiding it in a scripture verse. I like your way of signing your name in your Feb. letter! To think you were at my house and met my people—it was great.

Two weeks after writing and telling Ione he wanted to marry her, and without waiting for a reply, Hector wrote again on April 25. They were celebrating Easter in Toronto, and Lilian Pudney arrived with the ring that had been donated to the mission, which she allowed Hector to buy. Verna Schade, the missionary who had been biding her time working at a jewelry store before being sent to the mission field, had the ring reset; she and Lilian guessed Ione's ring size, hoping she had average-size fingers. Full of confidence, Hector wrote:

.....Last night when I came in from Clinton [Ontario] *on special leave, we sat in the living room for quite a while and then she [Mrs Pudney] took me upstairs; got out a little white box and let me open it. What a charming surprise! There is nestled, in between two little folds of white cloth. My breath was almost taken away with its beauty. I really hadn't expected to see anything quite so lovely. I had written her asking about the possibilities of getting it fixed up; and here she gets Verna to take it down to the jewelry shop and brings it up here all ready. She took her own and Verna's fingers as average sizes so I hope it will be alright. Not having held your hand I have no accurate idea of the size. I spent plenty of time holding it up to the light and seeing the colours. It goes down to a point underneath, and the setting shows it off well; how much more when it gets on your finger. It seems that they are quite sure of Verna's getting out so she will be my substitute. I'm sure you will love it.*

Hector was given an extended course in radio work and a chance of getting commissioned as an officer and given a new posting in Canada. Exam marks, past

---

[19] M. J. Chapman, "Sonnets," *Blackwood's Edinburgh Magazine* 42 (Oct. 1837), 549.

[20] Daniel 9:23

history, and administrative ability were considerations for such promotions. Also, at this time he applied for special leave to see the Pudneys. One of his superior officers heard his story, had seen Ione's picture and wanted to know more about Hector's going to Africa and all about the Belgian Congo. It must have melted his heart since within a half hour, he had Hector through the red tape and granted his request!

The next day, Hector added more to his letter; he had been in contact with Ione's mother and hoped to make another visit.

On May 2, Ione wrote to her friend Agnes Sturman. She had respite from caring for the Westcotts, as they had gone to Stanleyville for a weekend break, their first trip all together for many years. However, Ione still had duties:

.....I am helping take care of the 33 chickens, 3 goats, several ducks, Blackie, the father cat, Midnight, the mother, and her four little ones.

.....We have been enjoying our orange tree so much. I knocked off fifty the other morning, and they are so huge and juicy. They are a great help to Pearl at this time. When I go to the Doctor's in the morning I fix her the juice of one in a glass and she drinks it mid-morning; I set out the food for the cook to fix at noon and for night and try to send her juice during the afternoon. Then when I come at night she has already eaten and I snatch a bite, too. Doctor usually gets a box of fresh meat by courier each Thurs. This time they were not here, so the rest of us had a feast. We invited the Jenkinsons and Viola over and made steak smothered in onions, and a native woman came by with two tender ears of corn, so we had even corn on the cob! And best of all mulberry shortcake, and the berries from Dr's bush are huge. It was fun. Pearl made some cute little place cards and sat in a reclining chair during supper. She put the most familiar saying of each person on the card and each had to find his place by that saying. Mine was, "Think of that", Kinso's—"Righto" (he's English, you know), Ma Kinso—"Quite", Viola "for the umpteenth time" and Pearl's—"Golly Neds". Last night we had another get together, a ping-pong match between Kinso and myself (I lost every game!) followed by sandwiches and tea in the garden back of our house. The flying ants bombarded us, but they lent atmosphere.

Hector's next letter to Ione spanned four days starting on May 8, which included time on a 48-hour pass to see Ione's mother. During these four days, he finally received the response he had been waiting for—Ione sent a cablegram:

DLT. RECEIVED APRIL 11 LETTER. ANSWER IS YES. RING IDEA GOOD. RUTH ONE SIXTEEN. IONE

Ruth 1:16–17 reads:

And Ruth said, Intreat me not to leave thee, or to return from following after thee: for whither thou goest, I will go; and where thou lodgest, I will lodge: thy people shall be my people, and thy God my God:

Where thou diest, will I die, and there will I be buried: the Lord do so to me, and more also, if ought but death part thee and me.

Hector was delighted:

.....Words fail to express what I want to say! So you really are my beloved; XX That, with a great big hug ! ! That cablegram reached me in record time. I just stood at the window of the barrack room and thanked the Lord with all my heart, for one so precious as you are. Believe me, the boys are really jealous, since they have heard so much about you, and especially that verse in Ruth. How did you ever find that one? I doubt if there is any other single verse that says so much. May the Lord bless it to both our hearts. To think that we are going to be married; I guess no one is quite as happy as I am. I phoned Pontiac tonight and Marcellyn was so excited about it all, and she said mother would be so glad. But my main ambition is to make you happy which I have already found out is not a very hard task.

Hector ended this letter with greater detail of his stay at Ione's family home:

.....It is more home to me now than Avonmore. I just love being with your mother, since she gives such wise counsel, and has such a big heart; I know that she will fill a real vacancy in my life. When I was leaving, her eyes were full of deep expression as we shook hands. I too can say, ".....thy people shall be my people......"

It is almost time to go back to the barracks again. I would just love to kneel beside you and talk the whole matter over with the One who has arranged all these things for us. It will be so nice to tell folks what a fortunate man I am. It has a telling effect on the other lads when I tell them how happy the Lord makes us in choosing His plan for our lives.

.....I've told ever so many people about our engagement and nobody has said I've done wrong. Of course, I wouldn't believe them anyway. Love is not blind but has a third eye. My whole soul goes out to you and I only wait for the day when I can press you close to me,

My own BELOVED. X X X Yours, Hector

Hector was not the only one in this partnership who could problem solve; Ione explained in a letter to her family on May 22 how she mended her typewriter:

.....Perhaps I should explain the uneven lines I have just finished. Well, just as I started the letter, I heard a whirring sound and a bang, and the typewriter stopped. I discovered that the spring had broken, the one that automatically carries the roller back and forth. My heart sank, for it will be months and months before I can get a replacement. I tried tying the little string that broke when the spring sprang, but it still didn't work. Then I found that by pulling the roller with one hand and typing with the other I could still go on, but that was killing, it was going to take me ages to finish. Then Pearl offered to pull it for me, but soon I saw she was getting a little pale around the gills, so I tho't of fixing a string to the roll and tying it on the screen door which has a spring on it. Then I realized that the hornets would be thick in here if the screen was held open, so now I have a better idea, AND IT WORKS! Picture me sitting on our cushioned davenport (made of dark wood forest tree; cushions stuffed with local cotton) with my typewriter in my lap; my blue enamel kitchen chair by my knees; a string running

from the roller of the typewriter to the handle of a red enamel kitchen pan, which acts as a pulley and keeps the roller going while I type! It works fine, only the pan clangs against the metal of the chair and makes a sound like a life buoy in a fog. Pearl said it sounded like a cowbell on the farm. I might explain the greasy spots, too, —they are specks of chocolate cake. Pearl make a sour milk chocolate cake yesterday, the first she has felt like making in a long while; while I was examining the interior of this machine, she presented me with a piece, and I attribute my bright idea to the additional nourishment the cake gave.

Her news from the mission station was that Ellen was enjoying better health and had been able to assist her husband as an anesthetic nurse when their daughter needed an appendectomy. Freed from caring for Ellen, Ione had been tasked with mending nurses' uniforms and furnishing the guest house for white patients, which entailed making curtains, bedding, and mattresses. Doing less in the Westcott home meant Ione could do other things that she enjoyed:

.....I get out to a good many Sunday afternoon village meetings, and speak occasionally. My Monday and Friday hospital meetings are very well attended. The porch of the hospital is full and they spread out into the yard and road in front. I visit the wards either before or after the service and pray with the bed patients. It is so sad when there is a death. A woman had a huge tumour removed the other day and died shortly after. Her daughter just couldn't believe it, and kept shaking her, and pulling at her hands and her feet and head.

.....My latest effort in conducting meetings has been a boys' Sunday school, conducted each Sunday afternoon. The schoolboys and those in nearby villages who cannot come to school are my clients. They're a great bunch; we meet in the classroom that Verna Schade [the woman at Mission Headquarters in the States who facilitated the resizing of Ione's engagement ring] *built while she was here. They always pray that Miss Schade will soon come back. She may be able, soon, too, war conditions permitting. She had a large boys' work, the kind I hope to have some day at Ekoko. Pearl will have a girls' Sunday school when she is well enough. I wish you would pray for this group of boys. Some of them will be evangelists someday.*

Technically, Ione and Hector got engaged on May 12, 1943 by mail; however, Ione suggested that it was not a foregone conclusion and continued:

.....Now about Hector - Well, he has proposed! At least that's what it looked like in his letter. He is the type that says you're the apple of his eye instead of telling you he loves you. He doesn't write in flowery words, or say he wants to walk down life's pathway with you. He just says he thinks my mother would be agreeable to it, and he just needs my consent now! He didn't say to what—but I just guessed that. He says, "Maybe my letters haven't been able to show it, but my heart is fixed. This is a letter of good tidings and I just must express my heart's desire." He wants to send a diamond out. I believe the reason he is sort of pushing this thing is that he will be leaving the country soon; perhaps to go to England, and just wanted to know something definite before leaving. At any

rate, I have known him now for two years, been writing for one, and there doesn't seem to be any doubt in my mind but that he's my missionary. Sooo, I sent him a cable that it may reach him before he leaves, and told him the answer is yes.

Now that doesn't mean I'm engaged, for I don't know whether the cable reached him, nor if he changed his mind in the meantime, nor whether he will really get out here yet. But I've 'done my part'—! He's not very handsome, unless a uniform has improved him, nor is he a brilliant speaker, but he's good natured, handy about the house, a real homemaker and missionary,—and best of all, he can lay down like a dog! He turns around three times in his long, lanky fashion, puts out his paws, and rolls his eyes like a cocker spaniel for all the world!! [Hector often played dog as a child. See Chapter 2.] *He comes from a wholesome farm atmosphere and eats anything and everything. He's partly bald and has at least one plate of false teeth. And he really loves the Lord. Even tho' I'm nearing thirty years I feel I need my family's advice. I trust this step will not be a disappointment to you all.*

Other news for the family was that Ione had finally heard from Doris, which reassured her, but Ione was worried about her sister Lucille, from whom she had not received a letter, although she knew that Lucille's daughter, Ruthie, had been unwell. As ever, she had concerns for her mother:

.....Mother, if you are thinking now that if I am married, I cannot help you, it will not be that way. For should I marry, my salary will remain the same, the Lord willing, and the combined salaries in one home should make additional help at home possible. By the way, how much more a month do you need to get along? I do not want you to work yourself sick anymore trying to make ends meet. Is the public school teaching too hard for you? If so, I can arrange to have my entire salary sent to you (it isn't much, tho', you know, but we have been promised an increase for this year) and I can manage on the special gifts that the Lord seems to liberally send each month. Please tell me how you feel and if you are worried about anything. I haven't heard from you in so long and I really am concerned.

The greatest impact of the war on Ione was the effect on communications; this letter was largely written in response to a letter from Marcellyn dated on March 9, which didn't reach Ione until April 29. The other aspect was that the Westcotts couldn't travel back to America, as neither planes nor boats wanted to transport children through areas affected by war. This meant that Ione couldn't leave Bongondza to work at Ekoko, her long-term goal. Ione ended this letter with a list of things to pray for:

That the Ludwig's will be able to go home soon.

That the Westcott's may be able also to go home.

Pearl's recovery.

That Hector may come out.

That I may go to Ekoko, if it be His will.

That I may become adjusted to this strange land, pioneer methods, rough life.

That Doris may stay true to Christ.

That Marcellyn may be in Christian service all her life.

That Lucille and Maurice may be geographically in His Will; if the Lord wishes a change that He will lead.

That Mother may be able to continue Christian services.

That their relationships between the U.F.M. and the Church may continue to be good.

Our old house helper's conversion (Zaze).

That Amiazi (a teacher) may come back to the Lord and his first wife.

The safe arrival of two new missionaries from England.

All of these are uppermost in my mind. Perhaps I am a bit out of date on some items and you can put me right. But won't you join me in prayer?

I love you all so much. May the Lord richly bless. Lovingly, Ione

At the end of May, Ione wrote to church friends who knew the Westcotts well. With her eye for detail, Ione starts the letter by describing the doctor and his wife:

.....The Doctor—continues to be rather on the heavy side in weight. He looks well, tho' very tired at times, maintains a merry twinkle. This morning Ellen and all three of the children managed to hold him down and tie his hands for calling them 'woggle-boggles' or some endearing term. He wears his pockets out carrying nails, and tools of all kinds. I reinforced one set of trousers twice and finally made new pockets of double thickness then, much to my sad dismay, the trousers went to pieces! I forgot about that scripture about putting new cloth on old garments! I am glad to report that he comes to his meals more regularly than when I first arrived. I don't think I have to send for him more than three times now. And the other day he said he would have come much sooner if he had known we were having pie! He has a tremendous sweet tooth and shortcakes, pies, candy all are past history before they get cold. In order to keep a tin of fudge, I have to put a skull and cross-bones on it with the words, "Beware!" He never gets thru' making his rounds, for the circle is never ending. To us, he seems never to stop working.

Next, Ellen—she walks well now; I can hardly remember those early days when she was always in bed. We do many things together; have many things in common, the love of pretty flowers, music, children, ideals for them, etc. We have done much sewing for the hospital and guest house, curtains, spreads, mattresses, and now baby things for the latest additions and to-be's of the mission families. You no doubt know that she gave Anne's anesthetic in February when her appendix was removed. She has been trying to do many things which help her to keep an even keel. She has a good sense of humor and that helps when she might be very discouraged. The other day she was speaking about the 16 operations that she has had and referred to the Scripture verse, "When thou passest through the waters, I will be with thee; and through the rivers, they shall not overflow thee." She smiled and said, "That is very true, but a person has to do a jolly good lot of kicking, too!"

93

Anne is getting taller every day. She is chubby and has a good appetite. She thinks she is not good-looking and worries about her eyes. But I told her those were the kind of eyes I always wanted—wide blue eyes with an interesting tilt above high cheek bones and important pug nose! And what little girl shouldn't be happy if she looks just exactly like her mother!

.....Bob is getting straight and tall, but no thinner, I think. I think he is going to be a great figure-outer someday, he figures out so many things. He gets so preoccupied figuring out that he just doesn't hear anything or anyone. He was threading the bobbin on the sewing machine for me and I left for some reason and when I came back I waited for awhile and then seeing he was deeply engrossed, I asked him why, and he looked up dreamy-eyed and said, "Do you know that the sun has gone around the earth six times while you were gone?" He was watching the two little gadgets that go around each other on the machine. Ellen dropped a clock and the little spring came loose. Bobbie fixed it together and it works fine now. This pleased Ellen, for she says she believes Bob has something that her Dad had and that Dr has. I don't know exactly what it is, but I think you all do!

Charlotte, or Shally, as we call her, is more beautiful than ever, and her hair persists in curling, even tho' it gets so little attention. She has determination written all over her face and her eyes just snap when things are all wrong. She is quite tall now, but is broader than the rest for their size, more like her Daddy. She is very affectionate.

This is just a wee resume, but trust it will help until you see them. I wish to send my best regards to you all. Be assured that we are praying for you every day. In Christ, Ione

On May 31, Hector wrote a more passionate letter than he had ever dared before:

Dearest:

The heart of your lover is hungry for your presence this evening. No one knows how many times a day I think of you; wondering what you are busy at; how your health is standing the climate; if you are making someone laugh at your capers; and if you are making a long list of things that we will want in our little home; but most of all I love to think of looking once more into those deep eyes so full of expression. I'm glad I sat across from you at the table in Phila. for those three weeks. The Pudneys have mentioned the times that they noticed those sly glances, but they didn't see them all. ha! ha!

Hector devised that if he had recordings duplicated of Ione singing when she was in the trio, he would be able to have her with him all the time:

.....It will almost make me feel like putting my arms around the gramophone. I know all my sisters will be so glad to hear your voice and especially my Dad, since he does love to <u>listen</u>. When I tell folks about you and show them your picture and all that has happened recently, I usually end up by wondering why you said "yes". Someday it will be all made clear.

He wrote that the boat departure Verna Schade was supposed to take to Africa had been canceled, which meant Ione had a longer wait for her engagement ring:

.....How am I ever to get that ring out to you! Mrs Pudney just won't let me send it by post. What do you think of the matter? I've been threatening to build me a boat just for that one purpose. Poor Verna!! If you two could change places for about a week.

Despite not getting any mail from Ione for six months, Hector continued to write once a fortnight. This one, written on June 16, includes how he pasted a tiny photo of Ione on the face of his watch:

"I rejoice therefore that I have confidence in you in all things." II Corin. 7:16.

There is only one thing that I cannot understand, Ione; that is; how one young woman away out in Africa can make a young man so <u>happy</u>. The past two weeks have almost been a heaven here below. Your ears must have been burning most all the time, even while you were asleep.

It happens that I am now in Montreal visiting some of my sisters. Tomorrow morning I'll be leaving for Phila. to visit Mrs Pudney until Sunday. Then comes our posting to the East Coast of Canada. So that is where the next letter will be written. It may be that you'll have to employ an interpreter, from then on, as I'll likely have to write long hand. It has been so handy to use the typewriter but probably it lacks the personal touch. However, it can make XXs in copious quantities.

.....Just now I am looking at a lovely picture on the mantle in Irene's living room, a big 8 x 10 folder. I wonder if you remember that large picture you had taken in Dallas. When your mother showed us some of your pictures and then brought out this one; I knew once and for all that this was the one. I took it down town and got a small negative made. In Toronto I was able to get a whole supply, seven large ones and a dozen of the size I'm enclosing. Besides that, there was a little picture of the trio; and your face is just the right size for the top part of my wrist watch. It covers number 12, so you're right at the top. Usually I have to look about three times before I see the time. It's so lovely to have you with me all the time. [See photo in Chapter 6 of Hector's revised design on the face of his new watch.]

.....But most of all I love to hear you sing. On Monday evening Doris was there and we all went over to Stricklins. They too had some records, even one of the Choir from First Baptist. I have just two discs; one has "My Faith Looks Up to Thee", and "When they ring the golden bells <u>for you and me</u>." The other one we made up that night, "Grace greater than our sin" with Marcellyn and Doris and on the opposite side, "Family worship and the Lights of Home". So now I have the whole family along. Everybody loves your two solos.

My sister Irene wants to have some space to write to her new "sister". So while I am down town she is going to continue on this same letter. Lovingly, yours in Christ, X Hector

Irene added:

> *Dear Ione: This is a grand opportunity for me to tell you how happy I am to hear that you and Hector have become engaged. I wish you both abundant happiness. Hector has been telling me a great deal about you and I am most anxious to meet you in person and give you a personal welcome into our family.*
>
> *We want you to know that by increasing Hector's happiness, you are also making our family very, very happy. He has always been of a happy disposition, but this visit it is very apparent that his cup is overflowing. I always dread seeing him leave here—he is such wonderful company—we just never stop talking about our interests in life.*
>
> *He was telling me about his visit to your home in Michigan—just what a wonderful mother-in-law he is going to have. Being so young when his own mother died, you will agree that he has been robbed of mother-love to a great extent and that sharing your mother with you will fill that gap in his life. He is a very precious member of our family, and we are so proud of the path he has chosen in life, and now he has chosen a girl whose path follows along with his, makes us doubly proud.*
>
> *I enjoy so much listening to your records. I will look forward to hearing from you—I know you must have a big correspondence, but I will be very patient, I promise you.*
>
> *Sincere regards, Irene*

With letters taking so long to cross the Atlantic, it was inevitable that there would be cross-postings. While Hector bemoaned not hearing from Ione, she was actually writing to him. On June 20, she wrote:

> *.....Your April 25 letter arrived June 10 and I was glad to know about the ring. It sounds very interesting. I promise you shall hold my hand with it on!—some day. When I think of the future—with you it spells satisfaction, peace of mind, comfort, laughs, real companionship with someone who will always understand. Most of all it means a consummation of God's will for me. He said He would bring 'it' to pass; He said He would not withhold one good thing from me; also that 'all things work together for good to them that love God, to them who are called'; and He knows that I can never do all this work by myself. He promised me that I would abound to every good work, but when He found that I wasn't big enough to do the work, He provided someone to do it so that I could just help. I came out here as a 'helper', you remember. By His grace I would like to continue as such, provided I can be your 'helper'!! Have I ever told you that I love you?*
> *.....You no doubt notice how badly my typewriter is working. It is because you are not here.*

Ione summarized how she dealt with the problem, however, not in as much detail as in an earlier letter to the family:

> *.....Maybe you could send a spring to me with Verna—and the ring—that would make me think you were fixing it for me anyway. I don't know what kind it is, but it's a Remington Rand and it's the spring that pulls the roller back as one types.*

Have you heard about the new Carter twins? Gordon and Rosemary arrived last week and are both doing well, also their Mother and Father. This adds four new missionaries to our list. The Lord seems to be adding to our staff even in wartime![21]

.....We are all anxiously looking for the arrival of the two new English girls. They are due in Stanleyville July 4. We do praise the Lord for their safe journey across the Ocean. They will come here for a short time, and then it is thought the nurse will go to Boyulu. I think Jim Carter will feel the need of a nurse to help with the twins!

I can't think of any questions, Hector. I know I should have some, but you see, I never was married and I don't know what I should ask ahead of time. Anything you want to tell me about yourself I will be glad to know. Right now I'm mostly concerned that you take care of yourself until you get here.

Greet the Mission friends when you see them. Lovingly in Christ, Ione

About a year after starting to correspond with Ione, Hector wrote on June 25:

My Beloved & Longed for: To my Love with All my Love

It is almost a year to the day since I started writing to you and how precious these past months have been. No one is more fortunate than I am. You, my dear, have fulfilled every ideal of your mother & every dream I've had. Distance apart shouldn't mean much to us when we're sure of God's will; nevertheless, you need protection & companionship & I need a girl just like you. X

One of the lads tonight was asking me if I were not worried when I didn't hear from you. So I had a good chance to tell him the difference between worry and concern. How much better to pray than to worry. I read something the other day from a worm-eaten book Mr Goodman took from Brazil, called "Life's Dusty Way".[22] *Two buckets were used to take water from a well. As they met one complained, "No matter how full I go up, I always come down empty"; The next time they met the other optimistically replied, "No matter how empty I go down I always come up full". So just believe me that I do enjoy writing to you because I'm sure of your affection, tho' occasionally expressed. Someday a nice "full" letter will reach me.*

Once again, Hector went to Philadelphia and stayed with the Pudneys:

.....Of course, you must hear something of the visit to Philadelphia. I was delayed for about 10 hrs. in Montreal, due to border regulations, and had to wire Mrs Pudney for $13. But the disappointment was smoothed over when I had the joy of seeing Madam Chang Kai Chek [sic] at the station. She evidently was on her way to Washington & had a special coach on the same train as I went in.

New York was a welcome sight once more. Sweet Memories!!! I got in to Phila in time for dinner on Friday. Mrs Pudney was glad to see the lovely big

---

[21] So, the one baby Ione had written about earlier in the year turned out to be two who arrived on June 8, 1943.

[22] William Y. Fullerton, *Life's Dusty Way: Old Failures and New Ideals* (London: Morgan & Scott, 1919).

photo of you & was she full of questions! In the afternoon we went to the Zoo, then home for supper. Since we were down town Mrs Pudney & I walked over to the "Trans-Lux" where they have a news film which is quite educational. It was still quite light when we came out & it was good to see more of the city. She enjoyed seeing me salute some of the American Officers.

.....You may be sure I spent plenty of time looking around Wissahickon for familiar spots, but was surprised to recall so few. I guess I must have been looking at you most of the time. It was a good thing Pearl was with us that day or we might never have returned. I was in special search of that rather steep decent where after a few faltering moments, I even dared to hold your arm. I can still appreciate its delicate warmth & tender dependence.

.....Do you know what Mrs Dean said when Mrs Pudney introduced me to her & told her that I was interested in Ione Reed?. . . Her face brightened up & very spontaneously she said, "She is such a lovely girl!" Mrs Pudney just had to break in with the remark that I enjoyed hearing comments like that.

.....That front room on the third floor has the loveliest furniture in it now. The bed is a brown finish with very dainty corner posts. The dressing table has a <u>heavy</u> marble top and a large mirror that <u>has</u> framed the most pleasing of all gracious women. Surely you understand that they have moved this furniture from its original setting in the middle room. I used to like to be assigned duties <u>there</u>, <u>because it was Ione's room</u>. Why didn't I tell you then that I loved you? X?

Then in July, Hector sent a short letter to accompany his birthday gifts for her:

Dearest Ione,

"For we have not a high priest which cannot be touched with the feeling of our infirmities, but was in all points tempted like as we are yet without sin." Heb. 4:5

Just a short letter this time along with these birthday gifts. One side of the bracelet has 28+27 links on one side, and 28+28 on the other (our ages between July 16 & Aug 17). Now <u>you count</u> them.

I wonder where you are tonight. I imagine you must be rather weary sometimes, so I ask the Lord several times a day to strengthen you.

.....The sun is down; the air is still, the birds are farewelling, the ¾ moon is up; so I better leave this cozy nook in the forest and get back to camp. May your heart beats remind you of the Lord's continued Mercy and my constant Love,

Hector X multiplied by 29 (one for each year!)

Also, in July, Ione finally got her 3-week vacation. After resting a week, she and Viola Walker went on a "trek" through the jungle to meet the Basali (ba-SA-lee) people and preach the gospel. Ione wrote a graphic and detailed letter home to her church friends:

Dear Friends in Christ:

Beside a Congo mud house, the Lord is very near. The birds call in rich, clear tones, the black children are playing around the fires; the men and women are working in their peanut gardens; a one-legged hen and her five chicks are standing and staring at me in the same manner as did the black forest farmers when we arrived. I have just finished praying for the 60 former Moody students

on my prayer list for today; I found a promise for them: "The wilderness and the solitary place shall be glad for them and the desert shall rejoice, and they shall see the glory of the Lord, and the excellency of our God. Strengthen ye the weak hands, and confirm the feeble knees. Say to them that are of a fearful heart, Be strong, your God . . . will come and save you."

This is the wet season, not too good a time to be walking through these woods, but Miss Walker and I have a great time climbing, sliding, and splashing along the trail. Only twice has my foot slipped and let me down, but it was more fun after my feet were wet than before, for I stopped wondering whether they would get wet! We spent two nights at Bate's

Ione walking in the forest.

village, the first of our Basali itinerary. The leading Christian's name sounds like Varsity. He made us very welcome, generating a warm 'alma mater' spirit. On the journey to Dunda's village we stopped at a tiny house with a bleached pole fence in front. An old lady ran out clapping her hands and I noticed one thumb was gone. We went in and met her son who was ill. She told us smiling that they were both Christians and had moved to this present house during his illness so that they could be near Dunda's village. The Christians would help them, she added. It was refreshing to stop with them a few moments.

Dunda met us when we were nearly there. He was dressed in grey trousers and a spotless white shirt; he was barefoot, and his dimpled, effeminate, refined, beaming face reflected the sunlight rays spreckling down from the tall trees. He waited quietly at the bend of the path and then stretched out his hands to greet us. It was a thrill to discover that I could understand Bangala so easily, but I should know it somewhat after being in Africa 1-1/2 years. I have learned to recognize a few words of their Libua vernacular.

At Anziembo's village the moon had grown to a full moon in all of its shimmering whiteness. The song-birds reluctantly went to sleep, but the natives had planned an all-night festival. Ignace and his wife were celebrating the terminus of a long year's mourning. A relation of his wife had died and she had shaved her head and put on 'peli' or dark, drab clothes. On this occasion of her putting on bright clothing and combing her hair, which among pagans would have been an orgy of drinking and sin, they had successfully arranged a night of prayer for the Christians. There were 125 guests present and among them were two neighbouring chieftains. During the afternoon the men of the village had gone hunting. We saw them pass our door with their picturesque spears and nets, heard their shouts and the barking of the dogs; then later they passed again with their prey, two sad-faced antelopes and a spotted cat. Their feast was a sight indeed—no rationing, except perhaps in sugar for their coffee! They ate roasted corn, spinach, plantain, manioc, peanuts, rice, onions, pineapple, and chicken, in addition to the wild animals they had caught. They built a dozen or more fires and a booth of palm branches and then sat about in little groups to eat, the women and men separately, the little children carrying the food to the men. As we stepped from our doorway we beheld a colourful sight: red fires, grey logs, brown faces with bright eyes and teeth, green plantain leaves blending into the black forest silhouette, and then the great white light of the moon. They sang hymns, laughed at Tony, the puppet monkey, listened quietly as Miss Walker talked about Lulu, the Hen, who died in a fire in order to save her ten chickens; then our little house helper Kibibi, age about 12, one of Miss Walker's school girls, explained the story in Libua. We saw real understanding in their eyes as they realized by means of the feltograph just what it cost Christ to die on the Cross for us.

The two chieftains manifested a keen interest, one had said earlier in the day that he wished to accept Christ. I do not think he will yet, however, for seven reasons—his seven wives. The multiplicity of wives seems to be a great drawback in accepting Christ. One of these seven wives accepted Christ the morning that Miss Walker went to that village, but even if this one happened to be his latest and best beloved wife, and he abandoned the other six, what would become of them? One old man solved the problem. He wanted to be a Christian and had many years ago asked a missionary to baptize him. The missionary refused because he had two wives. Time went on and he said he prayed much about this matter. And the Lord answered his prayer, too, he said for one wife died!!

We have come four days into the deep forest to what is known as the End Village, the last village on the beaten path. As you may guess, white people are a rarity here and every inch of peeking is reserved at almost any hour of the day. Perhaps you will be interested to read a bit from yesterday's diary:

5:00 A.M.—The sound of the drum. Beaten by Ngambo, visiting teacher (he always beats it SO early!). After a little quiet time, we entered the open-air chapel made of poles bound together by vines. I spoke this morning on "The Colored Church," an object lesson prepared by Rev. Arnold Carl Westphal, Children's Shepherd, 1st Baptist Church, Michigan City, Ind., it was easily adapted to this language. Five people were among the little group, the five who had been saved the night before I sang a trio with Anziambo and Kibibi. We sang, "His Love is Wonderful to Me".

7:00 A.M.—Breakfast—'pai-pai', rice porridge, eggs and some bits of mbengi, a red animal. After breakfast we packed our bed sacks; in mine I put my folding bed and mattress, table, chair, bedding, pillow, extra shoes, literature, some extra tins of food, and wash basins. We put our writing materials and *changes of clothes in a small tin trunk, our dishes and general groceries in a wooden box called the 'chop box'. We had eight carriers—two of them fastened my bed sack to a stout pole, two others took Miss Walker's sack; two the trunk, and two the chop box. Six little children ran along and carried the lamp and oil can alternatively. We cut up a pineapple and shared it all around to cheer the carriers. At various places people came out with food to sell. We bought 12 eggs and some tomatoes on this stretch. Upon arrival we bought two chickens, some more pineapple, some onions, and a baby pig, the latter we traded for a Bangala Bible. The pig wasn't such a good bargain after all, for he died the next day.*

1:00 P.M.—Arrived at the End Village and met Amundu, a strange-looking fellow, hardly bearing the dignity of a pedagogue. He greeted us amiably in ragged khaki shorts and a black vest, which matched his hairy arms and chest and moustache. He ushered us into our present house in a manner befitting the occasion. The house was new and he had made it with his own hands; he had also built a sturdy bed and a pretty redwood table. He moved out his and his wife's belongings, leaving only a few things which I felt he thought would lend atmosphere to our stay,—some reading cards hanging on a nail, a perfectly whole white china cup, a locked tin box, and a pair of brilliant purple trousers! We set up our beds and had a dinner of nice fried eggs and fresh pineapple. While the fire was hot, I made some biscuits.

.....5:00 P.M.—Miss Walker gave a feltograph message about the Cross, telling the story of Christ's death and resurrection. I sang a duet with Kibibi, "All for Jesus."

6:00 P.M.—Dinner—roast chicken, hot biscuits, and fresh wild honey (the latter tasted excellent in the twilight, but not so good in the morning when we could see the clay and baby bees in it!).

7:00 P.M.—A pleasant walk through the village, receiving a greeting from the chief, squatting among the wives back of the house, sitting on logs in front with the men while they munched their supper, then looking out into the dark forest to the darkness which still possessed the secret of what was beyond the End Village.

We are half-way through the trek now and tomorrow we'll wind our way out of the woods. We'll say good bye to these people with funny names, such as Knee, Rain, Profit, Will-Come-Tomorrow, Made-Room-for-Another, Her-Mother-Died-When-She-Was-Born, Thanksgiving, and their dogs with equally funny names, He-Clutters-Up-The-Village, Money-Spoils-Friends, and Box,— stopping but a short time at each place again, we'll walk nearly to Buta where we'll be met by an automobile. There have been 11 souls saved thus far and I do praise the Lord. When I return to the station it will be with muchly-tanned skin and many strange insect bites, but with a heart full of rejoicing. May the Lord bless you all abundantly,

Yours for Souls, Ione Reed

This is what Ione had traveled all the way to Africa to do; no wonder she sounded so happy!

On July 28, Hector wrote to Ione, and on this day had the luxury of a whole evening. He started by saying he would love to write every day because Ione is worthy of such attention, but then added that as the mail was not collected daily, he'd stick to his twice-a-month routine. He added that duty carried out regularly always got done as opposed to when there are no fixed time limits. That is why, he said, God dedicated one day a week to be set apart for worship.

Hector wrote that his father has promised him some financial help with the wedding; his sisters had received 200 dollars and Hector wondered what a son would get! The news that was uppermost in Hector's mind concerned a colleague named Doug Brock to whom he had given a Gideon New Testament:

.....*Tonight, before I came over to my woody nook in Sunshine Corner he said, "See what I've been reading today." And he had Matt. 11:28 underlined & some in chapter 12, such as, "He that is not with me is against me." Isn't it wonderful to see a soul growing. He loves to read it consecutively & get everything in context. I told him I was going to write to you tonight & tell you about our Bible Study. He wrote home to his wife & tells her what we've been reading. I would rather keep on writing to you dear but I must keep some space for sending my love. Shall I express it this way, "I am yours alone." X Hector*

Hector's next letter, on August 11 from Scoudouc, New Brunswick (where he was posted), was to Ione's mother:

Your kindly gift finally caught up with me. I was away from here for a week on temporary duty so that explains the delay. You may be sure it is greatly appreciated. I can almost picture you choosing it. The title is quite outstanding. As soon as I got into the barrack room the boys wanted to know what it was, so I told them it was a book on "Prayer – Asking and Receiving".[23] I heard this John Rice when he was at People's Church in Toronto, and enjoyed his straight-forward, heart-searching messages. I know this book will be a real blessing in these days of so much unbelief. I have already gotten well started in it.

I'll be writing to Ione on the week end, so I can tell her about it. I'm still longing to hear from her. Every so often I read over some of the old letters to see if I can find any shade of meaning previously over-looked, and that seems to smooth over the yearning feeling. How I long for the day to look once more into that lovely face! I trust, that will not be too far distant.

.....Well, Mrs Reed, I must close for this time. I can never tell you all that your friendship means to me. It puts a new meaning in my life. Thanks once more for your remembrance of my birthday. Love and Prayer, Hector

Keeping to his fortnightly routine, Hector wrote to Ione on August 15:

---

[23] John R. Rice, *Prayer: Asking and Receiving* (Wheaton, IL: Sword of the Lord Publishers, 1942).

.....There are quite a few interesting things to tell this time. One is about the strong wind up the coast of Canada. A guard was outside the building on duty when a storm started. The wind backed him up against the wall & held him there until he froze to death. What a country!

.....Last Sunday evening I had a two hour talk with a fellow very much addicted to drink. He's been in Christian Science most of his life & it took a lot of Truth to bring him down to facts. In his own words he finally said, "Well, I'll admit my way is screwy." He naturally hates talking about spiritual things, but since he has been with me over a year now he has seen a new side of a Christian's life & told me he has never seen anyone else live what they believe. So, he too, is becoming honest with the Lord.

.....I'm up to about page 60 now [of the John Rice book given by Ione's mother] *and already it has begun to revolutionize my communication with God. He says most praying people are like the ladies going out to "window shop". They spend hours doing it and bring nothing home. Whereas a man goes into a shoe store, gives the clerk the size, number and colour, tries them on, gets the old ones wrapped up, pays the bill & comes home—10 minutes.*

We say so many nice things to God; but ask for nothing and get just that.

.....I promised to tell you about a week end trip I had last month. There is a family in Moncton and one of the boys married my sister Irene. I was in there at the home on my 48-hour pass. We got two bicycles and Stan & I went out of town about 6 miles to see the "Magnetic Hill". It's a rare phenomenon. From one spot near a house you look down into an apparent valley where a white post stands by the road side. Stan told me that the white post was higher than the house. So we started down the hill but strangely enough we had to pedal. I notice water in the ditch flowing toward us. And then we looked back, saw the house down below our eye level & coasted down or up, I don't yet know which. It is an optical illusion! Maybe we'll go there on our honeymoon, if you come home before I go out to Africa.

So this Tuesday is your birthday. Wouldn't I just love to be at your party. I'd help you blow out all those candles. Do you know dear, I like to look at people on the streets of the various cities, and I often try to pick out someone that looks & acts like you, but there is no one. "Many daughters have done virtuously, but thou excellest them all." Prov. 31:29. And to know that you are my own.

Now about the farmer. His son went to the city and got a job with a shoemaker. Now the farmer makes hay while the son shines! Your Lover X Hector

To celebrate Ione's Birthday, Hector sent a cablegram on August 16:

HAPPY BIRTHDAY GREETINGS. LETTERS GOING REGULARLY. HOPING FOR ANSWER. ROMANS ONE NINE TO TWELVE. LOVE—MCMILLAN

Romans 1:9-12 reads:

God, whom I serve in my spirit in preaching the gospel of his Son, is my witness how constantly I remember you in my prayers at all times; and I pray that now at last by God's will the way may be opened for me to come to you.

I long to see you so that I may impart to you some spiritual gift to make you strong—that is, that you and I may be mutually encouraged by each other's faith.

Besides writing to Ione, Hector corresponded regularly with his own family, his sister Florence in particular. In a letter to her, Hector retells Ione's joke that had reminded her of his army life:

Sentry—Halt, who goes there?

Voice in the dark—Cook, with doughnuts for breakfast.

Sentry—Pass, cook. Halt, doughnuts.

.....She is full of fun that I long to be with her again. Pray for the Lord's undertaking. She asks us to "Pray the Lord of the harvest to send forth labourers into His harvest."

Despite Hector's efforts to write letters regularly, it was evident the letters did not arrive that way. Ione's letter of August 20 confirmed this, as she stated:

Dearest Hector,

Nearly three months passed before any of your letters came through; then they came in twos every week until yesterday when your cable arrived. How thoughtful you are, and how happy you made me on my birthday. Your picture and the bracelet and handkerchief arrived the mail day before my birthday and the cable the mail day just after; it made me feel as tho' my birthday lasted one week instead of one day. You must have planned very carefully and I am not deserving of it, for your birthday was not even remembered. I'm so sorry.

The bracelet is lovely and I wear it all of the time. Whenever I look at it, which is often, I find myself thinking of you and longing to see you. I wear the kiss side down because that side is closest to me. I try to make Pearl think I am in need of identification all of the time; she asked me if I intended to wear it even when I go to the Doctor's house to work. "Of course," I said, "One never knows—I might drop dead on the way and need identifying!" She laughed, but I think she knows WHY I wear it. The hankie is so pretty. You may see me wearing it on my hair or some place when I get married. Did you know I was going to get married? Your picture is the best present of all; it is so good of you, the nicest you have sent me yet. Thank you so much for giving me such a Happy Birthday.

.....Oh, I must tell you that according to my figures, I am really 30 and not 29. I was born in 1913, so it must be true, I think now I shall just stay 30 for at least five years; women do that sometimes, you know! It helps when you're nearing forty.

There are so many things about what you do from time to time that thrill me so. Your contacts with my family are so satisfying to hear about. I know Mother must be very happy, for you're just the son-in-law that she's longed and longed for (me, too). And your frequent visits help them I am sure.

Thank you for sending me the picture of myself. It's rather refreshing to see myself as I used to look. You should see me now! You know, my hair is really quite straight after all, and there is a handful of white (1-1/2 yrs. growth!) which I shall someday pull out and label, "Because I needed Hector", but perhaps you will recognize me.

I was so glad to have a note from your sister Irene. I want to meet her; she seems such an interesting person. I like to hear a sister talk that way about her brother. I will try to send her a letter soon. Do you have any spare snapshots of your family?

Perhaps you have recalled my mentioning Charlotte, the smallest Westcott girl. She is 5, now. She says such cute things and when she heard you and I were engaged, she sang a funny little song. It was supposed to be sung, "Needles and pins, needles and pins, when a man's married his trouble begins," but she graciously changed it to, "Needles and pins, needles and pins, when Hector's married his fun begins." I think she must know that you'd have fun wherever you go and whatever you do, if you can lay down like a dog, as I told her.

Yesterday as I was walking up our hill to our house after the early morning village meeting (I have one every morning now!) I tho't our little cottage looked so nice and secretly wished it were ours.

.....To give you an account of what I have been doing: I have conducted over 100 meetings since Jan. and am happy to have my missionary schedule constantly increased and the house work diminished, as Mrs Westcott is more able to take over her own family duties. They gave me three weeks' vacation in July; I rested one week, and then went trekking for two with Viola Walker, a most delightful experience. My increased missionary schedule includes a daily singing class for the evangelists' class as well as one day a week teaching them methods in giving messages. I have hospital meetings and visitation twice a week and a boys' Sunday school. I have inserted a Saturday ping-pong round with Joan Pengilly as a very necessary part of my program, too. We're hoping to hold a championship meet with Dr and Kinso tomorrow. This week I have had the happy privilege of leading two souls to Christ. I tell you there is no greater joy.

We watched the eclipse of the moon last Sunday. It was interesting to hear the native's comments; some said something was eating the moon; others said it was just hiding. Dr's house helper volunteered the information that when the moon acts that way it is a sign that a great man will die. I asked him whom he meant by a great man. He said, "Someone who has, say – about 20 wives!"

Ione's letter of June 20 finally reached Hector on August 19. Hector, completely in love, responded on August 27 as follows:

My dearest:

Can God furnish a table in the wilderness?

Indeed, He can. Your priceless letter of June 20th arrived Aug 18. The time, up until then, was much like a wilderness, but what a feast of good things I could hardly read it I was so thrilled. Everyone rejoiced with me. I wrote and told your *mother I would like to send your letter along but that I didn't have it <u>all</u> memorized. It is <u>so</u> precious. I've had it with me ever since, in my New Testament. Now to answer it.*

.....The question of my getting out to the field is full of "whens" and "hows". It seems so like a dream to think of someday actually being on my way to Stanleyville and yet who knows how soon.

Your reference to the cablegram recalls the day and hour I received it. <u>Never</u> shall it be forgotten. I've quoted Ruth 1:16 to more people. Bless your heart for such tender love so sweetly expressed. How I long to see once again the wondrous depths of your <u>eyes</u>, the perfect oval of your face, the sensitive lips. These are the things which charm me. There is no one like Ione Reed X.

Thanks for the <u>permission</u> to (someday) hold your hand. It's a remote temptation. And how strong men fall for it.

.....I spent a lot of time thinking up all sorts of things that will make you happy and incidentally to show you that I <u>love</u> you. A perfect love casts out fear. A courtship without jealousy is a rarity, but you need never entertain a thought of my affections wandering. The searchlight beam of love is pencilled in <u>one</u> direction <u>only</u>. Right to a little hut in Africa and nestles right down beside <u>your</u> <u>heart</u>.

Spurgeon said, "I'll give my heart to my lady's keeping and ever her strength on mine shall lean; and the stars shall fall and the angels be weeping, ere I cease to love her, my queen, my queen. If my son were called to be a missionary, I should not want him to descend to the throne of a king.[24]" So that's one better than being a queen. But I still like to call you Princess.

No doubt you'll be glad when I take my nice new typewriter to the field. Having two in the family will mean that we can repair one while using the other.

Must close now beloved, committing you to Him. (Acts. 20:32) X Much love, Hector

On August 30, Ione wrote to her friend Marjorie Baker who is told of some African critters:

.....I am keeping well; have had only one attack of malaria and one filaria,[25] a little worm that enters the body by means of a Likinga fly and the worm moves about causing swellings and itching. It is only visible when it crosses the eyeball and can be removed then by a delicate operation, but most folk prefer the worm. There are very few missionaries who do not get them from time to time as the flies are common. We have screens which help some. The station school teacher who lives next door found a huge snake in her chicken house two days ago. Her native helper killed it, but he could not use a knife, for it jumped so high and

---

[24] Charles Spurgeon, English Baptist preacher and author.

[25] Filariasis is the medical term for this parasitic disease, of which there are three types. The subcutaneous type is caused by the loa loa, or eye worm, which is deposited into the skin by mosquitos. Lymphatic filariasis is known as elephantiasis. In an earlier letter, Ione described how the doctor removes one from his daughter Anne's eye.

swelled to immense proportions. He used a long stick and beat it to death while it was cornered in the chicken house. It took a long time to kill it. We watched, not too closely, as you may well imagine! It measured 7 ft. 6 in.

On September 12 while stationed at Fox River, Gaspe Peninsula, Quebec, Hector creatively wrote to Ione about being seasick:

My Dearest:

Isn't it grand to have the typewriter again? . . . Last evening I gave it an overhaul and it is really in ship-shape now.

Do you know my dear that I was part way out to see you last week? [Hector had spent time in Cape Breton, the far eastern edge of Canada.] It was grand to be so near Africa. It must have been the thought of not being able to go all the way that made me seasick. Regardless of the cause I was still a victim of the result. This is the story.

It was necessary that we had to stay in a private home in Glace Bay, so we had quite a lot of liberty. The corporal that I was with is a great lad and since we often have to work in the evening, he felt inclined to give me the day off to go out with the men who catch swordfish. There is quite a fleet at the Bay and the day previous I walked up town with an old fisherman that asked me to come along if I could. He had been the operator of a boat since he was 18 and at present has the biggest boat of the lot. He was practically brought up on the sea and told me the amazing fact that he gets land sick if he is on it for more than a week. They walk along the street as if they expect any minute that it is going to start rocking from side to side.

So at 7 o'clock I was down at the dock and looked up the boat by the name of George Beulah (his two children). After a time it was our turn to edge our way out of the forest of masts and head out to sea. I was going to be a real sea man. Right up at the prow I stood for a while, then I sat down and watched the waves roll and tumble. The sea had now settled down from the wind of the day before. These boats have a long catwalk projecting out in front where the captain stands with the harpoon at hand. Three or four men are up in the crow's nest scanning the sea for the sight of a projecting sword. A lad in Airforce uniform searches his mind to find from his knowledge of medical science the cause of the unbalance of his internal anatomy. He doesn't feel quite so well. Probably a prostrate position would alleviate the distress. Deep breathing gave some comfort, but. . . . Would the inevitable come? It is common knowledge that people have lost their dental plates, in sympathy with fish who are not able to afford a dental appointment. Picture the ocean floor strewn with dentures that are fit for neither man nor beast.

And so the teeth are slyly removed and placed in a safer pocket. Without any warning to either the man or the fish; they gain what he loses.

It were but one attack it would be worth the struggle. But to have the same procedure with no results. The old cook comes up from the hold and offers the lad a sort of cushion. He still knows enough to put it under his head. Time, space, friends, even the sweetheart is forgotten, just groaning petitions for the Lord's mercy. But death stands aloof, disdaining to seize the helpless victim. What a burden it has become to be forced to live. Hours pass. The men occasionally draw near, cast a glance and pass on. Twenty miles out to sea the boat makes wide circle and begins the search for . . . [censored for war-time security reasons].

Finally, a last vicious spouting ends the blockade; land is in sight and I got well as quickly as I got sick. It seemed like a nightmare. Of course, the sea was quieter now. I even dared to walk out where the captain had been standing all day. As we came into port the people lined the wharf to see the luck that the various boats had had. But none of them knew what I passed through between the hours of dawn and dusk. But like every great affliction, I too can say that I wouldn't have missed it for anything. This took place on Friday.

.....The only other news is that soon I will be tired of travelling and will be content to sit by your side and eat out of your hand. Abundance of love and kisses, Hector

On September 17, Ione wrote to her friend Tee. The letter marked Tee's birthday and put Ione in a reflective mood:

Dearest Tee,

Many Happy Returns of the Day! Many seasons of joy be given! May the Lord in His mercy prepare you on earth, For a beautiful Birthday in Heaven!

Ten years ago today we were getting ready for our first extensive tour thru Michigan. We were planning what style we wanted those long-sleeved black dresses, weren't we? And what collars we'd wear with them. We were practicing with Lois Guither (who now has another baby according to "Moody Monthly"!)

Nine years ago today we had recently returned from our 'most ambitious tour' and were relaxing; went to the World's Fair. Nine years ago yesterday we took charge of the music at the Berwin Branch of the Cicero Church. We sang, "Pray Till Light Breaks Through", "God Leads His Dear Children Along", "Precious Hiding Place", "Why Should I Not Love Him?" and "Hallelujah" (whatever was that last one? I have forgotten).

Eight years ago today we were travelling in full time service for the Institute. Seven years ago today we started Wheaton College. Pauline was married.

Six years ago today you were recuperating from your operation. Somewhere along this time in September I came from Cleveland to see you and was accepted by the South China Boat Mission. Remember the ambulance ride to the train, and the train ride home?

Five years ago today we finished our vacation period and started working for the Institute again. A month later my father died.

Four years ago today you and Gen [illegible text and burn marks]. *And you were writing to Frank, weren't you? I can't remember whom I was writing to.*

Three years ago today you and Gen were both married and I was working for the Pontiac Church, hoping to sail for China in November.

Two years ago today I was packed ready for Africa.

One year ago today some babies were on their way to certain homes and I was writing to Hector.

Today—everything is changed. The years show tell-tale marks on our faces. But what a joy each year has been and what a privilege we have had and are having to service the Lord in so many places. How I do thank Him for giving me your friendship and companionship. It meant so much and I am sure was instrumental in directing me the right way. You and Pauline were an inspiration right from the start, you were so courageous and trusted the Lord for every need. How I thank Him for the Trio! Many of our old friends still write and I try to send the pastors and some of the people my form letters. These contacts will always be a blessing to all of us I am sure. Someday we'll get together and sing, "A Mighty Redeemer Is Jesus our Lord", again as we did in our earliest days. And then we'll sing some of the pretty arrangements with Gen like the Cross medley. I had a letter from Mrs Brook and she mentioned that one especially. Your message, "Stop, Look and Listen", I have translated into Bangala and use it quite frequently. There have been souls saved as a result. I have thirty of my Westphal object lessons translated and use them. And you remember, "Come Over, Come Over, Over on the Sunny Side." Well, thirty boys sang it two Sundays ago while I played a little accordion I have recently acquired. And do you remember, "We All Rise Up Together, We All Sit Down Together?". Well, they do that, too. It's—"Osemami sikamoko; Otikali sikamoko; soko bisu ba Christu, osemami sikamoko!" I use the "Little Lost Sheep", too, with actions, choosing one littlest one and having the sheep go into the pasture and eat grass, etc. I am sure you use ever so many trio things in your work, too. Tony the Monkey is just about worn out. But he doesn't lack for popularity. I am known now as Tony's mama. A very dignified title! I think I use everything of the Trio except the high heeled shoes.

What would you like to know about Hector? He's thin, medium tall, kind of bald, big kind eyes, is ever so funny in everything he says, and is good natured. I've had letters from two of his sisters and they seem quite nice, too. Hector was a candidate for Brazil while I was at the Toronto Mission Home in May, '41. I spent about a month there and had lots of fun with him but he was always going in a different direction. Then the summer passed and when I was ready to sail I spent about seven weeks at the Philadelphia Mission Home and he was there visiting. Had been all ready to sail for Brazil with equipment packed, etc., but couldn't for some government restrictions. Well, he didn't say he might go to Africa then, but I know quite well, very well, that he liked me.

.....[In] May I gave Hector his ['proposal'] answer by cable. When he got it he called up my mother long distance. He finished at the Officer's Training School, but I do not know exactly what he is doing now. He is either in active service or waiting to be sent from somewhere in eastern Canada. He is in the R.C.A.F. He sent me a lovely bracelet in an Airmail letter, several hankies at other times, and

today his sister sent me a pretty piece of lace. I have no idea when Hector will get out here. And I can't see my ring until he finds a safe way of getting it out. Such is a missionary's life!

.....Well, does this give you enough news? Oh yes, you asked if I was fat. Just about 125# most of the time, same as Gen, I believe. I had a blood test yesterday and Dr. says I am anaemic, the blood count is down 20 points from when I came, but he gave me iron to take and outside of that I am fine. The girl I came out with and have been living with for nearly two years had the TB clinic here and contracted the disease. I have been with her during about 8 months of her illness, but haven't any symptoms yet. I had a TB test this week. She has gone to the mountains now. And Mrs Westcott, too, still has traces of it, but I seem to have a good resistance. I think having my tonsils & appendix out before I came helped. The Lord does take care of us always. Love, Ione

In Tee's letter, Ione talked of translating songs into Bangala, however, her grasp of the language enabled her to do more than just translate songs, as she described in a letter to her friend Norma in September, 1943:

.....I just finished teaching Elementary Notation and Sight Reading to my evangelists' class. They give good messages but they need to know more about Music. I teach them singing every morning but this weekly lesson helps them to read and write notes. I translated, "My Sins are Gone", from Glad Gospel Songs into words fitting for a Christmas hymn and call it "Noel", pronounced the same in Bangala as in English. They are learning it in notes and syllables. Their textbook is a large Time Magazine envelope with carbon copies inside! I have also a class in Methods which I think is interesting. I am introducing object lesson work that I think will be practical in their village meetings. I have taught them how to cut with knives or tear crosses and stars out of large leaves. We have made wordless books out of scrap pieces of colored papers from Christmas cards, illustrating the black heart of sin, the red for Jesus' blood, etc. There are ever so many children's talks that they can use.

I have been carrying on classwork since I returned from trekking in August. Mrs Westcott is trying to supervise her own children's schoolwork during the mornings. Then I go over in the afternoon and direct Botiki's wife in her sewing, the children's afternoon activities, help Ellen with whatever sewing she feels able to do, and plan supper and 'some special dessert'. I try to see that the cook has a few things lined up for next day's dinner, too. Planning the meals is so hard for Ellen, because she rarely has an appetite.

Isn't it good that I love to fuss and work about the kitchen? There has been so much of that to do these past eighteen months. I found a little poem one day which made me feel that my job as a Martha rather than a Mary wasn't so bad after all;

"A kitchen is a valiant room-
Melting pot of stove and broom,
Of homely tasks, of dreams and plans

Nurtured over pots and pans—
Life's richness other rooms adorn
But in the kitchen home is born!"[26]

—*War Cry*

I led my first soul to the Lord on my birthday one month ago. Since then there have been ten more. Many of them have been in the early morning meetings that I conduct at the hospital. There are generally about 100 percent. Five accepted Christ in the boys' meeting that I have every Sunday afternoon. Two boys gave over their lives to Christian service and have offered to go on my next trek with me.

What do you think of my cable engagement? Agnes said it was rather remote control! And I guess it is, with the emphasis on the 'remote'.

Ione wrote to Hector on September 25th:

My dearest Husband (2 B),

I haven't had any letters since I wrote to you last on Aug. 20, but I know that is not your fault. When they do come, they come in pairs, or threes and then my joy is bubbling over. I did have a birthday card from your sister Jean and a lovely tiny lacy doily. That was so good of her, and it made me very happy. She gave me some helpful information about you, too. I won't tell you, tho', because your hat might not fit afterward!

How does it feel to be called a husband? I thought I'd try and see if you will get used to it. But maybe it's a little too soon. A fellow has to be called that a long time after he's married. I wonder what it would have been like to be married for a hundred years or so like Abraham and Methuselah, etc. Maybe it was that long time that constrained Moses to grant a bill of divorcement! There really should be no excuse now since folk don't live nearly that long. And if all the girls had husbands like I'm to have they could well wish it would be for hundreds of years, don't you think?

Last night we had a Social Evening at Jenkinsons' house, the second or third such occasion we've had since being here, when all gather just for a good laugh. It was good for everyone. We were required to come dressed to represent some well-known song. I'll tell you what they all were:

Ma Kinso had a daily schedule pinned on the front of her dress; she was "My Task".

Kinso a cartoon of people outside the home of Goering (General) shouting "We want Goering" (this was like an announcement on the radio that people had assembled before his house and sang, "The Beer-Barrel Polka" or "Roll out the Barrel").

Mrs Westcott was there with two white carnations in her hair, her song being, "Mighty Like a Rose".

---

[26] Constance V. Frazier, "To a Kitchen." During the 1930s and 1940s, Constance Frazier published a column in *Home Arts-Needlecraft* magazine called "Party Lines."

Doctor wore a tie, which he <u>never</u> does, illustrating, "Blest Be the Tie that Binds".

The Westcott children were the "Three Blind Mice" with little cloth ears and long tails, and I was the farmer's wife who cut off their tails (someone said I would make a good farmer's wife and I agreed that it would be quite agreeable were that farmer from Avondale [sic]).

Oh, yes, Viola was in green with her autoharp as, "The Harp that Once in Terra's Hall", or something like that.

And Joan Pengilly was the bride of "Lohengrin's Wedding March".

Mr and Mrs Percy Moules of the Heart of Africa Mission were present and Mr Moules wore a violin with no strings on it, "The Lost Chord".

And Mrs Moules had drawn an excellent figure of Goering, also representing, "The Beer Barrel Polka."

This group comprised the entire white assembly of Bongondza.

Pearl is gone, did you know? She went two weeks ago to Ruwenzori to live in the mountains. This should speed her recovery. And it also frees the Doctor from her weekly treatments as she will now be under Dr. Becker's care. Dr Westcott and family (maybe me) will probably get off in about three weeks for a long trip. Pray that Pearl may soon be able to resume her nursing work.

I am still on half-time schedule. Today at Doctor's house I baked two loaves of banana nut bread; two days ago, I baked four dozen raisin-filled cookies and another loaf of banana nut bread. I can't seem to keep them filled up over there! But how I do love to work in the kitchen! I like to have about six things going at once. This week I made tomato chutney and Cape plum jelly. I enjoy experimenting about and using up all of the leftovers.

.....Besides wishing and wishing that you were here to cook and plan for, I find myself actually getting provoked that you aren't here. When Pearl went, I tried to get my little clock to work again and thought if I could just unscrew a few screws—you know, or maybe put in a little oil—or boil it like the Doctor does! But somehow, I unscrewed one thing too many and there came a loud whirring sound and the clock collapsed. After that I couldn't get anything back in and there were ever so many parts lying about. I stacked them up in four piles and put them back on my table, hoping that some kind soul seeing them would help me. But today there was a bad wind storm and when I came home there was disorder everywhere and curtains and draperies had blown down and my clock parts were scattered all over the floor. I don't mind doing without a time piece, but I just can't do without you. It doesn't help for me to tell you, but I surely feel helpless about a lot of things. If I just know WHEN you could come--But I'm sure you don't know that yourself, and we can't expect the Lord to arrange world conditions to fit our needs. But we know that "He shall give thee the desires of thy heart."[27]

[27] Psalm 37:4

Marcellyn's most recent letter tells me that since her conversation with you about Africa, she has been praying and thinking much about it, and feels that the Lord is speaking to her definitely about that land. She is especially interested in Ekoko. She said she'd like someday to come out and work with you and me! I am happy that she has given her life to the Lord for fulltime service if He so desires. I remember the time when Doris publicly offered her life for foreign missions. But somehow, she has been side-tracked, maybe for just awhile. I trust so. "All things are possible." Marcellyn also said she and Mother plan to break up our home and go south. Has this taken place, do you know? It seems I shall have many changes to face when I return home. That is one of our 'losses' I guess. But His gains overbalance them all.

Mother and Marcellyn surely have fallen in love with you. I am so happy that there is such a glad relationship. No doubt you have had to be very patient with my family; we are noisy and talkative at times. Most women are I guess. Doris would not seem to you like she did to me before I left, for no doubt she has become more serious. She was a funny frolicsome girl when I left and I was trying to teach her manners. Now there must be a strained feeling when she is at home. I am sorry about that. Doris used to cheer everyone up, but now that she is away, you seem to have accomplished that job.

It's about 10:30 P.M. and I am listening to the night sounds. A hyrax crying in a nearby tree; he is a little animal something like a big chipmunk and he cries as he climbs the tree, his call becoming more shrill and higher in pitch as he ascends. A frog is croaking like a xylophone out in the trench that surrounds my house. Many crickets are chirping. Left-over rain is dripping from the leaf roof. But otherwise it's quiet, very quiet. I'll take another promise for you, "The people that do know their God shall be strong and do exploits." Dan. 11:32. Above my desk is a little card that says, "Be Still." Underneath that is, "Be quiet, fear not." Isa. 7:4. Then,

> *"Lord, how I need the quiet heart, Thy still, small voice to hear;*
> *The Voice that speaketh truth and hope and husheth all our fear.*
> *The quiet mind, Lord, give it me, subdue my thoughts and will,*
> *Above the warring sounds of earth, Breath Thou Thy, Peace be still."*
> *–A.G. Fisher*

I am praying, 'Dear Lord, bless him, and keep him always true.'
With love in Him, Ione

Keeping to his routine, Hector wrote to Ione on September 28. Excerpts follow:
Dearest:

A verse that has been made precious to me is in II Peter 1:4, "...Partakers of the divine nature, having escaped the corruption that is in the world through lust." This present war is a result of lust but we have escaped the corruption of it because we are now, as Christians, of another nature.

Most fellows are glad for the middle and end of each month, because it brings pay day; but I enjoy a far greater benefit, that of writing to the loveliest girl under God's heaven. It's rather a shame that the world steals all the nice expressions of love and gives them a frivolous meaning. But that does not keep me from saying that I love you for your loveliness of spirit, soul and body. Memory is a wonderful thing when it enables me to bring to mind the pleasing bird-like tilt of your head; the mischief in your eyes and the coy manner of speech. It is too bad that we cannot think into the future with the same clarity. Then what an account I could write . . . just to hold you in my arms, dear, for one long minute . . . !! A few nights ago I told the Lord that I never expected as lovely a gift as you are, when I started out to live the Christian life. First, I live for Christ and then for Ione.

.....While up at Fox River I was amazed to find myself playing an old guitar that they borrowed from someone. My best effort was, "Shall we gather at the river", so it soon became the favourite. I didn't know all the words, so since I have come back, I was able to get a hymn book with that song in, so I sent the whole thing up. I trust that in this way the gospel will find an entrance into their hearts. I also had the privilege of preaching there one evening. Romans 5:1-10 seemed to be the Lord's choice and it was a fresh blessing to my own heart while preparing it.

.....I must not forget to tell you that my savings account is reaching quite a figure; so pay day does mean a little bit after all. By the end of the month the total should be around $150. It seems quite a lot when some fellows haven't saved a nickel. It is quite nice to be on a salary. In fact, it is the first time in my life that I've had a regular income. Still, I know you will have plenty to teach me about money matters. I remember that evening down in Phila. when we were at that prayer meeting. I remember a man told of his special need. Afterwards when we "two" were walking along the street and I told you that I had given him $5, you were rather amazed. I guess maybe I am a little too liberal, but it shouldn't be very hard to strike a balance.

.....Goodbye for now, dearie. Keep still hoping and trusting for that sweet day when we shall be together once more. It can't be too far distant. Your mother sent me some little extra signs which evidently mean a hug. I will send you one for a sample and you can tell me what they mean. XXO   Only yours . . . in Christ, Hector

On September 30, Ione again wrote to her supporters, this time referring to them as "the Loyals," and alluded again to the trek she undertook with Viola in July:

.....I am working half-time in the native evangelists' school, villages, etc., and half-time over at the Westcotts. I go out early in the morning for the village meetings, one week I go north and one week south. Have helped the women prepare palm-nuts, sat inside their tiny houses on rainy mornings around the fire, played their funny musical instruments, and chatted comfortably with them. I have wanted so long to really get to know them, and opportunities are unlimited this way. I could go farther if I had a bicycle, but it will take me some time to

make the acquaintance of all the people within walking distance around Bongondza.

I would like to acknowledge the gifts of money you have been continually sending to me. Since coming to the field I have received salaries for 1 year and 4 months @ $25 per month ($10 retained at home for savings and return transportation fund), plus 2 months' salary at $30 per month. I received a gift from the Loyals at Christmas of $11, for which I thank you very much. I know many of you are giving sacrificially these days and I do appreciate it. I do not want to ever be a disappointment to you all.

The Westcotts plan to leave for vacation in two weeks; they will go to the mountains. I am not sure yet whether I am to accompany them.

.....I am teaching every day in the evangelists' school. This is a class just recently started; Mrs Jenkinson has charge of them, and will keep them here for two years before they will be sent out into villages as regular teachers. There are six pupils; they receive the regular school course, but in a way that they will be able to teach it later to others. I have two types of music classes, both Class Singing and Elementary Notation and Sight Reading; then once a week I have a class in Methods in which they prepare object lessons and messages to give. It was with great rejoicing this week-end that we saw them going out with flannel graph boards and envelopes of object lessons tucked under their Bibles; this was their first experience of going out for a week-end in this way. Mr Jenkinson said he has waited years to see this.

I would love to hear from you all again. And don't forget to pray. Oh, did you all know that I have become engaged in May to a Canadian fellow, Hector McMillan? Of course, he can't come out until after the war, but it's kind of nice looking forward to it.

Love to you all, Ione

At the beginning of October, Hector wrote to Ione's mother, whom he addressed as "Mother":

.....And how is the moving business! Wouldn't I love to be with you in these days. So often I think of you; and how fortunate I am to be "son"! I can hear your voice and see your face even now; and I do long for another visit. If you even know how much that book on Prayer is meaning to my Christian life you'd feel well repaid for sending it. I'm about ½ way through and it's still getting better. It gives me real "talking" material when I discuss spiritual things with the staff. Just this afternoon I was with quite a group and one fellow plainly confessed that he was bordering on Atheism because he had never seen a real genuine life of true faith. After some minutes I was able to bring it down to a quotation from your book and it was this, "A man is unsaved for one of two reasons. Either he wants to find some other way because he doesn't like the <u>truth</u> or he doesn't know of God's plan of salvation." So after today, he can't plead ignorance. It's a wonderful experience the Lord has granted me to live among the fellows. I love to find out <u>what</u> they believe and then by the Scriptures try to help them out of

their trouble. And they do really appreciate it. It will be invaluable training for the mission field as it drives me deeper into the Word to find God's mind on these matters.

Of course, we have our times of witty joking together. I laughed at one chap today who knows me quite well. We were talking about Ione and he was saying how little she really knows about me since she has been away so long. He said she might have changed a lot in her ideas and to quote him, "When she gets you, for all she knows she's just like buying a pig in a bag." It surely sounded funny. However, I showed him a few sentences of her last letter and everything was straightened out.

.....Well, dear, I better close for now as it is getting late. I know prayer will soon be answered for you because you are yielded to His will. That alone is more consolation than any other blessing.

The will of God. Nothing More. Nothing Less. Nothing Else.

Your loving Son, Hector

Hector then wrote to Ione on October 13:

I'm just getting this letter written in time; in fact, as it looks now it may be written in sections. However, I must not fail my dear little sweetheart over in the Lord's vineyard. I know He is answering prayer for you and His presence will bring such real joy to your heart. Just to think that He sees both of us and is planning some wonderful union, not too far in the future. In my own mind I have it planned out several times a day, just what it will look like, but I know it will be ever better than that.

.....Last Sunday I started asking the Lord for something definite. There are so many people to meet every day that there must be someone in spiritual need. I often testify that there is scarcely a day passes but that I am able to speak to some soul. But now I have asked the Lord to make one contact each day that I know is of Him.

Hector goes on to write of daily experiences of sharing his testimony of the Lord's saving grace.

He wrote to Mrs. Reed on October 24, revealing more of his activities but also giving insight into her new home:

Dear Mother:

Your lovely big letter was waiting for me when I returned from Halifax on Thursday. I would have answered it the next day but as usual there was something to cause a delay. I was only in Scoudouc for about 12 hrs. when I was sent out on another job; all the way back to Halifax and about 100 miles beyond that. So at last, on a nice quiet Sunday morning I can sit down and write to you. It is a very pretty spot here and I will enjoy a few days of such surroundings.

Before I begin to answer your letter, I must give you a wonderful promise from the "Word of Life". "Behold, I send an Angel before thee, to keep thee in the way, and to bring thee into the place which I have prepared." Ex 23:20. How is that for protection and direction! And to think that your letter of how

116

graciously the Lord has fulfilled that already in your life recently. You can just picture how happy I was to read of the plans for the next few weeks. This reunion will mean so much to both of you. I know you will be all thrilled, just like when you were 16. How like the Lord to take you both right back to the place where the devil caused all the misunderstanding. This enemy is so subtle and determined to upset God's plans.

So you have settled right down in Pontiac. I was afraid you might be going farther away and I might not see you for a <u>long</u> time. It will be grand for you to have more spare time to use for other things besides washing dishes and doing housework, (although it is nice to get acquainted with people right in their own kitchen). That seems to be where we had the most laughs. I'm quite sure we could never carry on like that in a restaurant.

.....Sun. evening 8:45 - I've been away all day in town and just arrived back in barracks. I was wishing Ione was with me for the nice chicken dinner. I'm afraid I can't get along without her very much longer. In fact, I'll let you in on a little secret.

As you know, ordained men [as opposed to a mere missionary] *are exempt from military service. Well, I'm planning on applying for a discharge from the Air Force through* [a recommendation from] *the padre* [military chaplain] *which may be quite a task but then who knows. Then I can get ordained and start out for Africa even if I have to take the "Jonah" transport* [boat]. *This could all take place in a few weeks or it may take months. I enjoy my present work but there are plenty more to replace me. We are fighting for freedom to worship in all countries, (including the Belgian Congo). But you know how impossible it is for the natural man to see spiritual realities.*

.....By the way the ring is in Mrs Pudney's safe keeping in Philadelphia. Thanks so much for enclosing those two folders. It's grand to know you have included my name on your missionary list, along with your precious Princess. And that picture you enclosed is already in a folder I have. Really you should see the way folks look at her face. And then utter some expression of admiration. What would they say if they could see the original [Ione herself]*! That's what I'm interested in.*

.....Well my dearest it is about time to close. I'll have to start Ione's letter in a day or two. It's such a privilege to carry on a correspondence with both of you. Thanks so much for writing.

Great things are ahead for you so keep me informed.

Yours in Calvary's Love, Hector X

Hector's next recorded letter was sent to Ione on October 27:

Beloved:

Something rather unique I read the other day . . . "The man I marry must be brave as a lion but not forward; handsome as Apollo but not conceited; wise as Solomon, but meek as a lamb; a man who is kind to every woman, but loves <u>only</u> me."

.....This little gift [a white silk hankie] *was purchased on a train and it is something I've always wanted to get for you. It is somewhat like our crest & has the RCAF letters interwoven. The man said it could be washed but I don't know how often.*

Do you remember being down at the Bapt. church in Cleveland, Ohio for a month while one member of your trio was convalescing from an operation? Well your mother found a bulletin with your picture in & sent it to me in her last letter. How thrilling to hear what other people think of you.

"The voice of Miss Ione Reed has been heard on many Radio Network Programs & has won the hearts of thousands by her interpretation of Gospel songs. For several years as a member of a youth crusade, she has contacted many young people in heart to heart talks or from the platform in 28 states of the Union."

What a lively life you've had! Is there any place you haven't been? I like that reference about heart to heart talks.

Your mother has gone into full time Christian Service with the Faith Gospel Mission in Pontiac. She seems very happy about it, altho' it is quite a change to not have to do her own housework. I still write her every other week but this last time I couldn't stop short of ten pages. I was telling your mother in the last letter that I can't do without you very much longer. After being near Halifax for about a week we went back to Scoudouc and I hardly had time to get a breath when another lad & I were sent down to another station about a 300-mile trip. He has gone back but I have to stay on for a few days.

Really, Ione, all this travelling makes me feel like the two men out in a fishing boat. Being of German extraction they got their w's and v's mixed up. They finally had to admit they could not find their way back to land. Said one, "Ev only our vives knew vhere ver ve." Feeling the situation a little more keenly, the other chap replied, "Ev only ve knew vhere ve vere ourselves.

And then about the two morons [more jokes]. *One had just come down from a mountain when he discovered he had lost his watch, but he didn't go back after it because he knew it would run down. The other put a chair in his uncle's coffin for Rigormortis to set in.*

Someone has his radio on in the barracks and the song is, "My Faith Looks Up to Thee."

I had an interesting time yesterday going thro' a plant where they make yeast cakes. They have a new process now for dehydrating it so that one pound is reduced to 6 oz. Thus, it requires no cold storage. The foreman was very kind to me, and before I left, I gave him a tract and told him something of the Lord's blessing in my life. Then I had a visit with the local blacksmith. I guess you've never heard of oxen having steel shoes. I saw him making enough for two oxen. I know the folks at home would be interested so I got two old shoes to send home as a souvenir.

In the evening I went to a prayer meeting and heard an elderly saint of 96 winters give a wonderful witness. He's just waiting to cross Jordan.

I hope I can think up a suitable cable for Christmas. There are two promises recently given. Is. 49:16; Ex. 23:20

Lovingly as Ever, Hector X

As Ione mentioned earlier, she and the Westcotts took time off from their duties and traveled to the mountains. They reached Butembo (boo-TEM-bo, a town at 4,531 ft altitude in Eastern Congo's North Kivu) where she wrote to the family on November 16:

Dearest Mother and Marcellyn,   Greetings in Christ from 'way up in the mountains!

I have received your letters of May 28 and July 12 with Mother's note attached and was surely thrilled with them. The greatest joy I believe was to hear that Marcellyn might come out here. I am praying that someday, not too far distant, we might be working together. And what would hinder Mother from coming, too? There are many missionary mothers that I have met here, all enjoying good health and very happy to be working with their children. If you felt you could not come out under any mission, we could maybe save up enough money to help you come and be with us. There's much you could do for the Lord out here.

.....I am glad you could make some records and that I will be able to hear them before very long. I may come home before Hector gets out, and if so, we might have the real people sing, "Because" and "I Love You Truly" at our wedding. I have told Hector that if he suddenly finds he can come to wait until he finds out for sure that I'm not already on the way home, for the Westcotts are thinking they may need me to help them get home. It would be rather a shame for us to find that we were going in the opposite directions at the same time!

This vacation has not exactly been a success thus far, for there has been so much sickness. Mrs Westcott has spent 5 out of the first 14 days in bed, and we've all been in bed part of the time with a bad cold that came this week. It took weeks and weeks to help them get ready & for Dr to leave his work and during that time Ellen had two severe sick spells & Dr had one, but finally we started off Mon. Nov. 1 to Stanleyville where we stayed in the hotel three days. I did some shopping for the children and Ellen & I got permanents, very nice ones, but they cost $10. I let them cut my hair to the length it was when I left home. It had grown 'way down my back. I bought a pretty blue & rose flowered shanting dress & some blue & white sandals. We drove on Thursday to Maganga, one of the U.F.M. stations & stopped for tea; went on to a lovely forest hotel where there were many animals like goats, antelope, etc. We had a little brick house to ourselves with a shower bath; no electric lights, slept in two rooms—Anne is my sleeping pal. Then on Friday we stopped at Boyulu, another of the U.F.M. stations, and went on to Nia Nia to another hotel, with huge rooms with life-size palms painted on the wall. The bath tub was like a horse trough & right in the *most conspicuous part of the room. They give one towel to a family & it is as big as a blanket. Ellen laughed heartily when I spread in on a chair so that I could get at a corner of it to wipe Charlotte's face.*

There are as many dogs & cats as people in some of the hotels & often they eat on the table with the people. Saturday we went on to Lolwa, an A.I.M. station where we were royally entertained by the Deans. Their station is in the Ituri Forest and among the Pygmies. We saw many of them and heard them sing. The babies are the size of other native babies, but at the age of about 10 they stop growing. Some say it's because they seldom are in the sunlight. They cannot stand it out of the forest. They are nomadic & never stay in one place longer than 3 weeks.

Mrs Westcott had a severe heart attack on the way here & we stopped & all got out & let her stretch out & rest. She could not be moved from the Deans for 3 days.

On Thursday we left and went to Oicha [o-EE-tcha], another mission station, where Dr Becker is, the man who gives Pearl her weekly treatments. But we did not see Pearl for she lives right on Ruwenzori Mountain, some 50 kilometres away. We had planned to go to Ruwenzori, but the people had gone away who were to have entertained us, so we only saw that beautiful mountain from the distance, but we clearly saw the snow on two of its glacier peaks. Imagine, snow a few miles south of the Equator! We went to a little hotel at Beni, on Wednesday, where we could see Mt. Ruwenzori all the time when it was clear. Here Mrs Westcott had a severe ill spell & we all got colds & Charlotte dysentery. We could not leave until yesterday, Monday. It was a miserable hotel, very unclean & the proprietress & her daughter were carrying on some kind of funny business with different men every night. However, the food all along has been better than we have at Bongondza; fresh vegetables & meat & even strawberries!

We just had to leave Beni yesterday as a great group of soldiers had spoken for our rooms. So both Charlotte & Ellen got out of their beds & managed to make the journey here. We climbed all the way and have come to a delightful, cool spot where we can look down on the clouds. It is called the Butembo Guest House & we have two cozy rooms right on the top of the mountain, a back door looking down over clouds, a riot of beautiful wild flowers & hills, our front door opening out on gorgeous European & American flowers, dahlias, all colours, iris, calla lilies, nasturtiums, verbenas, painted daisies, roses all colours, and carnations. It is most restful & Mrs Westcott is able to walk again. The colds persist, but I think this cool climate will help. The food is very good. We may stay here as long as 16 days. If we do, it will cost me 1,000 francs ($25), but it is worth it.

The rest of the journey is the most promising, barring illness. We are now only a short distance from real volcanoes, a crater lake where we can swim, springs with boiling water, the great wild animal reservation where we'll see 100 or more hippos at once, buffaloes, hyenas, lions, tigers, elephants, etc., then we'll come to an elephant farm where they train elephants to pull & push loads. The older elephants teach the younger & when they don't mind, they spank them with their trunks!

I have much for which to praise the Lord. Many missionaries live their entire years of service in the Congo without seeing this most beautiful part & I am seeing it already. It is not like a real rest, as I have much to do for Ellen & the children, but the change is fine & a real opportunity. It is improving my French also. I must supervise the children entirely most of the time & going to these French places I have to say something you know!

I am going to try to buy a cheap imitation diamond ring, for I have always one of two difficulties, I'm either taken for Dr's wife, or else tho't to be footloose & free. So I want these French soldiers & whatnots to know that Hector has me spoken for me. My own diamond may not come out for a long time.

There is a Greek refugee camp where we were where those people are staying during the war. I had the joy of dealing with a Greek merchant about his soul. Well, I expect we'll be travelling for about two months unless Ellen gets too sick. I do not know where I'll be at Christmas. I have an invitation to spend it with the Ludwigs at Ekoko. I would like that very much, but don't expect I'll be back.

.....I am trusting Him for all of my needs—and yours. Loving you very much,
Ione

An ecstatic Hector wrote to his prospective mother-in-law on November 22, although it took three months to arrive. He had heard from Ione that she had received all his gifts and was wearing the bracelet he had sent with the kiss next to her skin:

.....There are so many more things that I would like to tell you but most of all is that she loves me with ALL her heart. Her constant prayer for me is that I will always keep true. Bless her little heart! How could I help myself! The Lord has made me so thankful that his grace is well able to keep the sanctuary of my heart for Himself and Ione.

I'd just love to see you now and tell you all that the Lord has done in recent days since I last wrote you. Your prayers for me must be answered every day. Just to be God's mouthpiece for a few minutes each day fills my soul with his glory and presence. What a preparation for the mission field!

On November 25, Ione wrote a letter to her sister Marcellyn from the guest house at Butembo wishing her a happy birthday. Elaborating on the 6-week vacation with the Westcotts, Ione described leaving Bongondza in the pouring rain in Kinso's Ford delivery truck. The doctor fashioned a bench in the rear of the truck to accommodate the children, while Ione, Ellen, and the doctor sat in the cab. The party left Butembo on November 20 and went to Nyankunde (nyan-KUN-di) because Ellen's condition had deteriorated and the doctor felt they needed to be somewhere warmer. Ione wrote:

.....This is a mission station where two brothers and their wives live. We have been here four days now and Ellen is walking again. But today Bob is ill. Dr. & Anne have taken a two-day journey up north to Rethy, [RE-thee] an A.I.M.

station. We have wonderful food here; fresh pork, tomatoes, parsnips, lettuce, celery, beets, strawberries. I am putting on a few pounds I know. I heard from Hector along the way & have a picture of him in uniform. Don't forget that wherever I am I still love you all. In Christ, Ione

In a buoyant mood, Hector wrote to Ione on November 28 and described the barrack room scene:

.....This is two o'clock Sunday afternoon. I am sitting in the end bed in the barrack room. Butterfield is just about ten feet away ironing his shirts (imagine - and him a Presbyterian). I helped him do his washing last evening and we had a good talk besides. He has done most of his Christmas shopping and did he ever make me envious. He got the grandest dresser set for his fiancée, something like $22. The mirror is especially nice. Oh, if your address were anywhere on this continent, I would surely make use of the baggage facilities. But this one thing I can send you Ione, and that is the love out of a heart that is devoted to you alone. Probably this is of more value than any material gift. After getting those two letters, I've been so happy to tell you that the Lord is continually answering your prayers that I will be kept true.

Hector responded to the top points Ione had raised in a previous letter—the fact she was a year older than she thought did not cause him concern, and he stated:

.....The change in your age is of no great consequence, except as it relates to other precious things that improve with age. Strange as it may be, the little picture that I have in my watch is evidently being slightly affected by the sunlight and you hair is turning white. Shall I say that it makes you more charming! ! ! One of the lads down in Yarmouth barely refrained himself when he saw this set up on my wrist, from repeating the usual associations of a face and a clock. At least mine is still going [a reference to Ione's broken clock].

.....Your lover, Hector PS: Honey! Did the bees make you? X

On December 13, Ione again received a letter from Hector:

Dear Miss Reed:

Not that my heart is saying that but just to have something different. I better start in this time by answering your letter in case I might not have enough room at the end. But first I must tell you that I love you more and more and more all the time. You must really be praying that something will happen as there seems to be something astir. Oh! how I long to be in your presence, in fact your absence is painful. But I guess it must needs be that way for a time.

.....Needless to say I read your letter over several times, and finally I awakened to the fact that 2B was intended for to be. I suppose it is because it is not accompanied by that cute little side tilt of your head. I'll have to go a long way before I am worthy of the title Mrs Pudney used so much, "My wonderful Husband." But I give you my promise that I will try to be the best husband possible. I'm certainly looking forward to happy times together . . . maybe even a hundred years.

.....Your kitchen activity assures me that I shall never go hungry. And I will admit you need someone to help you fix clocks. Poor dear Ione; all by herself. Someday we'll be glad to forget all about a time piece, except to let us know the time of the wedding.

The other day I was able to go shopping so I thought it would be only the right thing to do, to get something for this Reed family. I got a cute little blue sweater for Marcellyn and a silver serviette ring with 'Mother' engraved in it for our mother. I know she will like it.

On December 18, after six weeks of traveling, Ione was back at Bongondza, and wrote to her mother. During that time, plans had frequently changed, and instead of an early return to America or visiting the Ludwigs at Ekoko for Christmas, Ione was again spending 10 hours a day at the doctor's house. She also rose early to squeeze in what she regarded as "true" missionary work. The trip had given her a new perspective and possibilities, and Ione clutched at the thought of her mother joining her in Africa. She seemed to be heading for a Christmas quite different from the previous one; her home had been damaged by a leaking roof, her best friend was miles away, and her current house companion was about to relocate to the mission station she had hoped to be posted. No wonder she hankered for her mother and wished she and her sister could join her.

Hector's year ended with him spending Christmas at Avonmore with his family:

.....My brother was at the station with the car and of course he asked me if I wanted to drive it home ... which I did. What a turkey dinner ! ! Then we opened our gifts. Dad got so many things! I was able to get him a pair of sheepskin lined shoes. They are worth $6, but I knew they would give him a lot of comfort. Ken and Irene gave me a billfold, Jean a diary and picture folder; Archie a subscription to the "Reader's Digest", Alice sent a nice pair of Airforce Blue socks, etc....

He and Florence had talked about the plan of salvation and a decision one way or another. Hector also took the opportunity to have Bible readings and prayer with his relatives. His biggest hurdle came when Jean became confused and stubborn one afternoon and Hector closed in prayer. He went outside on the porch and wept his heart out. He just couldn't let her go.

For Hector, it was a real burden that his family did not convert to Christianity, as he would have liked. He said that one's own loved ones are sometimes the hardest to talk to.

Chapter 6
WINDS OF CHANGE AND SHIFTING SANDS

On January 9, 1944, Ione wrote to her good friend Evie telling of her recent trip to the mountains and that, although Mrs Westcott has not fully recovered, the mission leader, Mr Jenkinson recognized Ione's need for something that would fulfill her. She wrote that he offered her:

> .....*full charge of the boys' school next term and this gives me a real thrill, for I have been very interested in them. I expect there will be at least fifty, and I hope to make it 100.*

In this letter, the plan was still for Ione to accompany the Westcotts back to America, with the hope that she and Hector would get married before returning to Africa; otherwise, Hector would have to spend some time apart from Ione. The other reason for wanting to see Ione and Hector married before Hector reached the Congo was that the Jenkinsons had not been back to England for a long time and were due a break. If the McMillans came back as a couple, they could relieve the Jenkinsons and both stay at Bongondza.

Ione's home circumstances had also changed:

> .....*So much for news. I have been thinking how long it has been since I heard from you, and how little I've been writing. I expected to write while on the journey, but every moment was occupied with children and sick folk. I think I should qualify for nurse or governess soon! Now I am taking care of a little mulatto child;[28] she is asleep in the next room at the moment, about 2 years old. I keep her all day and she sleeps with a responsible native lady at night. Her father was a Greek and he was brought here unconscious, and after an illness of several weeks, died. I stayed some nights with him, and helped to feed his brother—who took care of him. He had nephritis, and then contracted a disease that everyone in the station had been calling Dengue Fever. It only is fatal with infants and the infirm, but it was fatal to him. When he died, Doctor had spent so many nights and days over him that he himself contracted it, and I had to take charge of the burial, the making of the coffin, digging the grave, etc. We didn't know about his native wife until the cousins and brother came bringing this little girl for us to take care of. There was a baby boy, too, but that is still with the mother. But the [Greek] relatives want little Katherine to be cared for as a white person. Mrs Jenkinson has been supervising this, but she is away just now. Katherine is a dear little girl, and it is so much fun to arrange the dark ringlets*

---

[28] Mulatto children were often abandoned in the forest in the Congo at that time, as neither black nor white society wanted them; the lucky ones were rescued.

in little curls. When she is old enough, she will go to a mulatto school at Katwa in the mountains.

The impact of living in such a humid country was further revealed with regard to Ione's home:

.....You would laugh at my little mud house, now, for it is in need of a new roof. It leaks in every room and a tropical shower is no small trickle either! The mud walls are crumbling on the outside, and the cream colored plaster is peeling off inside. But the little one-room brick house where Pearl and I first stayed has been remodelled and has now four rooms and [a] bath and in a few weeks I may move there while a new roof goes on this one. The natives will gather leaves from the forest, split their stems and tie them on to poles. They fit on like petals of flowers, very pretty while green and prettier still when brown with a huge purple bougainvillea bush flowering over it. Where leaves have rotted on the roof sometimes plants and vines start to grow. In the front yard are yellow and pink roses in bloom now. We have some unusual flowers and vegetables we bro't back from the mountains to start in Mrs Westcott's flower house. There are strawberries, rhubarb, carnations, and Easter lilies among them. May God richly bless you. Love, Ione

Ione's second letter on January 9 was to her mother, wishing her a Happy New Year. Ione was without news for a while during her six weeks traveling with the Westcotts. The letters, forwarded to her, finally reached her at Bongondza. Ione had news of her mother via Hector but had a lot of her own questions:

.....It is hard to imagine Mother without a home, but I am glad you are able to be in full-time Christian service. I would like to know more about what you are doing, what hours you have, etc. In Hector's recent letter he said something about your being in love. I want to know more about that, too! Is it Mr Presnell? What are your plans for the future, or don't you know? Any chance of your coming out here?

Ione followed on with more about baby Katherine, whose Greek relatives were planning for her to attend a school run by missionaries in another region:

.....Little Katherine is being taught to speak English but she speaks Bangala most of the time. She calls me Mama Needy, and I guess I am, most of the time! The natives can't say R, so they substitute either L or N for it. And they can't end a word with a consonant, but always put Y or A or O at the end of a word. [Ione's last name being Reed.]

Despite this extra task, Ione still managed all her other activities:

.....I am carrying on my hospital and village meetings early in the morning, and when I take Katherine home at night to sleep with a responsible native woman, I generally make a few calls and sit about the fires and chat or sing. Last night I taught Machini, the head teacher, the bass part of 'Praise God from Whom All Blessings Flow'. I took Katherine to another house to talk to an evangelist and they asked her to sing. She sang the native words to 'Come Over on the Sunny Side,' which I had taught the boys this year. Then when they had ceased their

praise of it, she looked at them very soberly and said in their language, 'Let's pray', so they all bowed their heads and she prayed. It was awfully cute for she is so tiny, but very definitely loves Jesus.

.....I have averaged this year a native meeting every other day and there have been 22 souls saved. I tho't I was not able to do anything for my household duties and care for the sick, but the Lord is using my feeble efforts. When school starts, I am hoping to be able to conduct the boys' school entirely. But this depends wholly upon whether Mrs Westcott is able to carry on over there. They have much to do with giving the children their schoolwork, etc. Anne is doing some high school subjects now, and their studies are quite complicated. Mrs Westcott is not very strong yet, but does quite a bit.

.....I am feeling well, and am maintaining my added weight I think, altho' I've not weighed recently. My blood count was down and I took iron and I think it must have come back up. For whenever I prick my finger the blood is redder. I don't have the headaches I had then, too. Whenever headaches start for anyone out here it is a sign that the blood is anaemic. But iron helps. I am a bit nervous, but Doctor says everyone is their first term, getting adjusted to native life and needing help constantly. It would be much easier to do one's own [house] work often than try to teach them [staff]. They are straight from the forest in many cases and it is a strain to teach them. But I think I am getting adjusted and by the time I go home and come back I will find little trouble with nervousness. My greatest concern is that I'm doing too little for the Lord. He has done so much for me. May God richly bless you on your Birthday. I'll be thinking of you and praying for you.

Lovingly, Ione

The third letter Ione wrote on January 9, was to Hector. It was a long one and although it talked about information covered in previous letters that she wrote that day, it demonstrated the love, trust, and longing she was experiencing and what was uppermost in her mind at that time:

Dearest Hubby (2B),

Greetings in Jesus' Precious Name! This year I can say more truly than ever before, 'The Lord HATH done great things for us, whereof we are glad!' For me, in particular, because I have you. Soon we shall be engaged for a year, and even if the engagement plus separation, can't be such a comfort and satisfaction, what will it be to be married?? Don't ever think that I'm getting a 'pig in a sack'. I only want time and opportunity to show to you that I really do love you and want to be with you.

.....If [the] Westcotts find they can go home soon, I expect to come along, and THEN—can you think of anything that would prevent us from getting married? Even if you are still in the Airforce could you not be married? Or would it be prohibited?

The day before Christmas your Christmas cable arrived. How in the world did you time it so accurately? You surely are a peach to give me such a happy

Christmas. It was great to know of a soul's being saved, where Mother was, and that you had remembered the family. I would have loved to do something for them at Christmastime. But you are taking my place at home. It is such a comfort and joy to me to know this.

Your latest letter arrived on Dec. 30th. I don't know when or where it was written, for the first time it was cut off, perhaps for what was written on the back side, where you had been or something. At any rate, the silk hankie came in such nice shape, perfectly folded and with the beautiful wings of the RCAF in the corner. This is a lovely gift and I do thank you ever so much. I shall not use it until you are with me.

Your system is a good one for contacting people continually, and the Lord is giving you rich experiences in your service to your country (and mine!). I am encouraged to do more whenever I read your letters. I have been feeling discouraged because my time is so filled with sewing, feeding little mouths, combing hair, etc. But I added up the figures in my meeting book and found that I had averaged a native service every other day during 1943 and that 22 souls had been saved. Most of these, however, were saved during the two months I was in ½-time schedule and could get out more to the people. But the average is helpful to look back upon, when I tho't that perhaps I had been just marching time so far. Won't you pray that I will take advantage of EVERY opportunity? I was interested to read in 'Moody Monthly' a little account of the late Dr. Howard A. Kelly, world renowned scientist; 'A little question-mark pin always worn on Dr. Kelly's left coat lapel was the opening wedge to many a talk on Christian faith. He waited only for a query to respond that it stood for the greatest question ever put, 'What think ye of Christ?' He never allowed himself to be drawn into needless controversy over Jonah or the miracle of the virgin birth, but like a lodestar held the questioner to a clear decision; 'Define first what you think of Christ—whose Son is He—and all other questions will be settled naturally and easily.' The rose in his buttonhole was another valued approach to a testimony. Whenever one would exclaim on its beauty or freshness, he would always say, 'It is a Christian rose, because it has hidden sources of life and grace' as he turned over his lapel to reveal a small tube of water into which the stem was inserted.'

.....Your jokes are so welcome, and furnish me many a good chuckle, as well as others.

.....I heard last week that Mr Jenkinson was sort of hoping that you and I could stay here and carry on while he and his wife go home for furlough. He is counting a lot on your abilities to direct the practical things about the station. I don't suppose they would go, tho', until you shall have the language learned. But that doesn't take long. Miss Pengilly came in July I think, or August, and was giving messages in a few weeks. She has gone to Ekoko now, and will plunge right into girls' school work.

Naturally enough, everything I see and do, I am seeing it in the eyes of the future when you will be here. I wish I could more fully understand what you are doing now, but it is so hard to imagine. I am glad there is no restriction in your telling me what you are doing in the service of the Lord. Perhaps you could tell be more about the various offices in service. I know you are a Leading Aircraftsman, that is followed by Corporal, is it? And then what is next?

Well, I must close again. I am very happy in my work here, and have the pleasantest of relationships with the senior missionaries here. Just now I am the only junior on the station. I'm sure the seniors have more trouble with the junior than she is usually aware of! Pray for us all.

Loving you dearly, Ione

On January 14, Hector wrote a long letter to Ione in which he took the opportunity to show off his "French" language skills:

Ma Bien-aimee:

Anyway you are the dearest one in the world to me, well-beloved and all that goes with it.

I'm all alone this evening away over in a big city like St John. Jack McKellar who is here with me on <u>temporary duty</u> is out for the evening as he knew I would be writing to you and could not carry on a conversation when busy with such an important and pleasant task. We are living in a room in town and go out to the detachment each day to work. We eat mostly in restaurants and how we wish we both had our <u>wives</u> here to enjoy the grand feasts. I guess all this good food is serving a purpose because the other day I got on the scales to see it register 162 [pounds]. So as you said in one of your earlier letters I may be stout when I get out there.

Jack is married but his wife is in Toronto, doing his old job in the bank. She is a very beautiful girl by her pictures and of course according to what Jack says. He says he certainly isn't worthy of such a wife, so at least he and I have <u>that</u> in common. I am so glad for what he told me the other night, Ione dear. They have been very happy in their married life and I think I have profited much already, in preparation for the time when we two will set sail on the sea of marital happiness.

.....Well, dearest loved-one, I could scarcely find paper to put down all the things I think about you and plan for you. If you can be so sweet to me when you are so far away, just what will it be like to have my arms around you. I just become lost in the wonder of it. What an anchor you are for me as I mix among so many these days to whom marriage vows above all things seem so trivial! Surely the Lord has wonderful things for His own even here. And so I can go on from day to day, trusting Him and trusting my dear little Ione out in Africa.

*Praying to be with you soon,   **X** Your LOVER Hector*

It was to "Mother" (Mrs Reed) he revealed in a January 21st letter that his military service might possibly end:

.....You will be interested to know that there are some actions being taken in regard to my discharge. Rev. Linton from Toronto just wrote me this week and as a Chaplain in the RCAF he advised a certain line of procedure. First: Get the Council of the UFM to approve my discharge and ordination; and endorse my immediate departure for Africa. Secondly, have High Park Bapt. Church agree to my ordination. Having these two things arranged then I can see the Commanding Officer on the station here at Scoudouc. There is to be a UFM council meeting in Toronto on the 28th. However, Mr Linton did raise the question of waiting until the war is over, as the UFM would still be quite willing to take me on from where I left off. He is rather of the opinion that another year should see a big change. But I believe that the Lord would have me try. So now you may know how to pray. I want only the will of God in my life regardless of Ione or Africa. I have learned from bitter experience that there alone is the <u>happy</u> spot. But it would be just like the Lord to give us the desire of our hearts as Ione has often quoted. Well, mother dear I better close for now with a hug and a big long kiss. xxx Much Love, Hector

A week later, on January 27, Hector wrote to Ione about the ingenious way he had of carrying Ione's face with him wherever he goes:

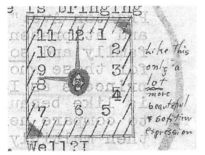

Hector's drawing of his new watch.

.....Do you remember me telling you about the little picture that Herbie and I cut out and put in the face of my watch? Well, I got a new watch since then but I took the picture and put in the new setting. For a long time it was up at the top and then later I put it down in the left hand corner. Last week I got a new idea for 'Ione'. I got some of this red cellulose tape and cut out little triangles and put two of them in opposite corners of the crystal. Then I cut out a circular one and put your picture in the centre and stuck it to the middle of the crystal. So now your beautiful countenance is surrounded by a little red frame and the hands peep out from behind to tell me that every minute is bringing me closer to you. This picture in type may be a miniature replica of that which is greatly coveted by all who see it. Here are some the expressions. 'Say, isn't that some idea.' . . . 'Well, you <u>must</u> be in love'. 'Where did you get such a small picture' . . . 'Is that just a picture of a girl or is it really her?' . . . 'When I first saw it I thought it was a new kind of watch' . . . 'Where is she?' 'What ! ! in Africa?' 'What is she, a nurse?'. So you see, dearie, you are preaching both in Africa and America.

In Hector's letters, if he was interrupted, he included this as news to Ione:

.....Pardon the interruption but two fellows just came by my bed and after noticing the typewriter they saw the Bible and asked if it was a dictionary. Of course they were not long in finding out that it is my most treasured possession. From there it was easy to tell them why, and since when and to where. Then your

life came into the picture and how the Lord took you all over the States and finally out to Africa. They were very interested and thrilled with it all. After that we talked about the need of the present generation and lack of formal churches. So another day has come and again the Lord has seen me safely through it and given me opportunity to tell of His power to save.

Hector ended the letter recounting the contents of a letter he had received from her mother and it was a testimony to the growing closeness of their relationship; perhaps this was to reassure Ione of his love for her and that her mother approved of him as a suitable prospective husband.

Leslie Goodman, Canadian Secretary of the UFM in Toronto, wrote to Hector on January 31, sending him papers that he would need to submit to register his ordination to mission work and thus secure his discharge from the Airforce. Should all go as planned, another couple, Chester and Dolena Burk, who had recently been accepted by the mission to go to the Belgian Congo, could well be traveling companions for Hector.

Hector received a letter from his father and sister dated January 31, 1944. His father thanked him for the shoes Hector gave him for Christmas. Hector's sister Jean added more detail to the letter, saying their father had visited family in Montreal and had not only acquired a cold but had brought a boy back to help with the farm. She described skating on the river with their brother Archie as being an enjoyable excursion. Although the family did not appear to resent Hector's choice of service, there was an underlying feeling that his input in the family and farm were missed by those left behind.

Maintaining family relationships was difficult for those who dedicated their lives to mission work, an aspect Ione referred to in a letter she wrote to her sister Doris on February 6, 1944:

.....I get a panicky feeling when I think of all that could happen to one's loved ones. It's that feeling that I just can't get there in a hurry because I'm too far away. But I have not forgotten the promise the Lord gave me for you when you went to California, 'With Me she shall be in safeguard.'

Ione reported that Mrs. Westcott was "happier than she used to be" and had taken over control of the children's education. There was still talk of the Westcotts traveling back to the United States, and Ione intimated that the doctor might be needed for military service, which would mean leaving the Belgian Congo quickly.

Hector wrote to Ione on February 13, telling about his most recent activity and his plans:

.....I have been out this afternoon preaching in a little country church. I met a man coming up the island on the train. He saw me with my Bible so later came over to talk to me. When he found out I was going to be near his home community for a few days, he arranged for me to preach this Sunday. He got word around & quite a number turned out. They were overjoyed to have a service since their pastor will not be back until June. I just love preaching, dearie. The Lord gave me a message in Acts—'Repentance toward God & faith toward our Lord Jesus

Christ.' They were keenly interested. And I know the Lord blessed His truth. Rather unusual was the fact that a Jewish lad (from Scoudouc) accompanied me. I believe he is becoming concerned about his soul. He was quite impressed and is a lad that thinks a great deal. They surprised me by giving me the offering— $2.

.....No doubt your plans will be settled in a few months or weeks. You almost shocked me when you said you might be coming home. Wouldn't it be grand if you could! ! How shall we act when we meet again! And the wedding—a church or home? Marcellyn will make such a lovely bridesmaid. And your mother with special music and—XX

I've written to both mission headquarters & your mother & I know they are rejoicing that things are turning out favourably. I haven't told my folks yet—a surprise! All the boys are so happy for me.

.....This letter has often been interrupted due to conversations. In fact it is after 11 p.m. & the little lights are all out except my own little light. So good-night dearie until I write or cable you.

Yours entirely, Hector X

On February 23, Hector wrote to Mrs. Reed. He was very excited at the prospect of Ione coming back to the States and hoped it coincided with his discharge:

.....Wouldn't it be just like the Lord to have her come back just as I was getting my discharge!!!! What a wonderful time we would have planning for the wedding. I know that my family would be so glad to meet her. I have still a few weeks to wait before getting to Toronto. My two weeks leave will be coming up the first of April and they advise that I get ordained then and on coming back to Scoudouc I will be able to apply for a discharge. I was talking to the padre this morning and he is very much in favour of it. I know that you will be praying much about it. Every so often I am reminded that the answers of your intercession are effective in my life and contacts. I could fill several pages telling you what marvellous times of witnessing I have had lately. It has been a very enriching experience.

.....Last Sunday I was able to take the service at the Air Force camp and the Lord laid a good message on my heart. Using Luke 15 as a basis I took the subject, 'Are you a prodigal son in the Air Force'. Quite a few of the boys spoke to me afterwards. There is a Jewish lad over there who took such a keen interest in spiritual things that I left my New T. with him, as he promised to read it right through. His name is Monro, 'Moe' Selby. One thing that really got him was the fact that I prayed for him. The next day he asked me if I had and I told him that I did. He said to me, 'Well, did you mention that it was Moe Selby?' He wanted to make sure that he wasn't being mistaken for some relative of his. He is a very comical fellow and a great favourite with the other boys.

.....Well, it is nearly time for my Bible reading and prayer. I'll let you know if anything extraordinary happens. In the meantime, we will resort to prayer.

Love and Kisses, Hector

On February 27, Hector wrote a long letter to Ione:

My crowning Queen: (Prov. 12:4)[29]

    So glad to be able to write again and tell you that I love you ! ! !

    I heard indirectly from you, through a letter that your mother sent. She also enclosed one from Marcellyn. What a lot of news to get in one letter! I had no idea that your mother was planning on going out to the field. What a miracle if the Lord should work that all out to His glory! With all that talent, we could take on the job of about half the Congo. You can be sure that the plans for this year are being moulded day by day, in prayer and practice. . . . I have just read through 9 of your letters, and it so refreshed me. I am all alone over in the room where we work in the daytime (when we are here); and it is so quiet. I have fixed up a stool with a back something like the ones the secretaries have. Letters, papers and two books (Bible and a book on Church history) are lying at my left; oh! Yes, and my little dictionary; a radio in front and a lovely light with a good strong bulb, and my thoughts about the loveliest, friendliest, funniest yet sincerest, youthfulest girl who will very shortly be my wife. Of course, then I won't have on a white sweat shirt, white running shoes and sand colored drill trousers; but I will have on my nice new rimless glasses and my decorated watch, Airforce ring, and a nice soft English suit, with you sitting on my lap.

    ..... I have turned on the radio and am listening to Fuller's broadcast. The chorus is singing, 'Let Jesus come into your heart.' I love listening to the bass and tenor parts. Now they are singing the old song, 'How beautiful to walk in the steps of the Saviour.' How I wish you were beside me! ! ! The next is a piece by the quartet for the children as well as older folks, 'Brighten the corner where you are.' I guess that is the greatest task we have in these days. The spiritual errands that can be done for the Lord are so frequent and interesting. Another Christian lad has come in to bring me a book, 'By Faith', written by Dr. & Mrs Howard Taylor.[30]

    .....I mustn't forget to tell you about my first plane ride. It was last Monday coming back from Prince Edward Island. There were two planes to come over to the mainland and we were in the second one to take off. I enjoyed seeing the ground drop out from under us and after a few minutes see the other plane flying right beside us and a little to the front. The pilots were very good, and so attentive to each other's movements. About half way over I took out my New T. and read a portion over in I Thess. 4., concerning the rapture ..... 'Caught up together with them in the clouds, to meet the Lord in the air; and so shall we ever be with the Lord.' Then we as believers will be going to our treasure and not away from it, as is the case with a man of the world going up in a plane. It was all very thrilling

---

[29] "A wife of noble character is her husband's crown, but a disgraceful wife is like decay in his bones."

[30] Howard and Geraldine Taylor, *By Faith: Henry W. Frost and the China Inland Mission* (Singapore: China Inland Mission, 1938).

and I am looking forward to more such exciting times. Maybe we'll take our honeymoon that way!!

This morning I came over to this quiet little room and began preparing my doctrinal statements for my ordination. It is grand to do something solid again. I am waiting for the day when you and I get to unite our efforts in the building up of souls in the faith, I was interested to read in the letter to your mother that every phase of the missionary program has a definite place. I'm afraid I'm getting rather slack on the medical angle but I do love preaching and teaching. I noticed too that you said you love to just travel around in evangelistic work. Well, I'm right with you in that. It is wonderful the way the Lord has been preparing both of us throughout all these years. I know you love a home and wouldn't I just love to fix one up for you, but it may be that we will be pilgrims for a number of years. Your health must be extraordinary. I was just thinking tonight what a hard time Pearl has had, but probably she was working too hard. Once again I realize that the hardest thing in the world is to keep balanced. I've only been sick a half a day since I got in the Airforce but conditions here have been much above normal. Lots of rest and good food.

Tomorrow is pay day again. I'll have over $200 saved up by the end of this month. When one is discharged, he is allowed a month's pay and an allowance of $65 for clothing. Since I have all that, I will be able to add it on our financial requirements for the field.

I've been working quite a lot with Butterfield this past week and we have become very good friends. We were doing mostly carpenter work on little things around the shop. I made quite a large filing card box and it caught the eye of quite a few. Someone remarked that I would make a good husband for some woman.

Well, dearie it is time to close again. I do hope it won't be long until I can hold you in my arms for the first time but not the last.

Love, Hector XXX

In a letter to Mrs. Reed on March 7, Hector revealed he had heard from Mr. Pudney that four Congo missionaries would be on furlough and the mission needed reinforcements. Hector also described buying a blue leather writing case for seven and a half dollars and the book, *By Faith* that he had been reading about the missionaries Mr. and Mrs. Henry Frost who worked with the China Inland Mission in the 1930s.

On March 14, he wrote to Ione:

.....The days have passed so quickly and it is time to write you again. But, my love, it is so easy to answer a letter such as I received last week, written Jan. 9. Without exceptions, that is the best letter I have ever had from you. I just love to read it through again and yet again. And the picture arrived, too. It must have been folded some time or other in transit but the crease was on the opposite side, and marred Joan [Pengilly] a little. I looked at it so longingly, and keep thinking, as I let my eyes have a real feast, is that lovely girl really going to become my

wife. Your face is as sweet as ever, if not more so, and you seem to be quite healthy. The background too came under close scrutiny. Is that spot near our little home, to be? I'm enclosing a little picture to remind you that I have not forgotten how to do carpenter work. Jack McKellar took it a few weeks ago.

Mr. Keen, Hector's pastor, helped him prepare the case for his ordination. Of Mr. Keen, Hector wrote:

.....He has been so good with it all and seems so much more like my <u>own</u> pastor all the time. It will be grand to be questioned by this group as regards my doctrinal beliefs. I have been enjoying quite a few hours making a study of an outline that Mr Pudney had used. I remember making a copy of it that summer that we were up at the Lake of Bays.

Ione wrote a magazine article in the spring of 1944 that hinted at some of the trials and frustrations she had endured but focused more on aspects that would interest her readers:

Serving the Lord with Gladness

I am well and happy and have much cause to praise the Lord that He sent me here. This strange combination of nurse-maid, dietician, nurse's aide, and doctor's assistant have not made me any less an evangelist. The number of souls does not compare with the number the Sunshine Trio from Moody Bible Institute used to see coming to the Lord when I was travelling with them, but the fact that souls are being saved is encouraging. And you need not think that in these silent months God is not doing some work in my own life. Before I came out at a farewell gathering in a church in Bristol, Va., the gentleman in charge enlarged upon the verse, 'What went ye out to see? A reed shaken in the wilderness?' He capitalized the word REED with the implication that he felt I would not be shaken in difficult situations. Well, that man's prophecy was not exactly true, for I confess I have been shaken many times but His promise has held—'the bruised reed will He not break' and no matter how far I've had to bend in one directions or the other in my varied tasks, the bending has only served to strengthen and toughen the calibre.

I am living in my four-room mud house, although I really only sleep there, eat a few meals and tell the cook what to do while I'm away. I don't get frightened but I don't exactly relish it. There was a snake in my orange tree for two weeks before doctor shot it with his rifle. There was a species of dog that haunts native villages and kills chickens that persisted in trying to get into my house and succeeded in killing two baby kittens in my living room. I put my hand on a huge mother rat, while reaching for oil to put in the typewriter just a few minutes ago. (I killed it, too!) The calls of the chimpanzees and the little hyrax in the trees break the stillness of the night, but they are all a part of this interesting life.

A Greek man came here recently and Doctor found he needed an appendectomy. He was very much afraid and his eyes looked wide and terrified at the thought of it. Then Dr. gave him a Greek New Testament which he began to read immediately. After a few days Dr. said he was ready to operate, but he expected the patient would be trembling when he went to the table. On the contrary his face was peaceful and happy. He said he had found something in the Bible. Then he told us that his uncle had died the seventh day after his appendix was removed and he feared the same would come to him, but now the Lord was with him. Later he said that he had accepted Christ as His Saviour at that time. Dr. does not tell about these things, but they happen quite frequently. He has Bibles in several languages and his point of contact in many conversations is often the Second Coming of Christ.

I am conducting classes for the native nurses and house helpers—seven or eight men—most of them Catholics. They have reading, writing, arithmetic, music, spelling, and Botiki, head assistant, has French. Our textbook is the New Testament and at present we are studying the Gospel of St. John, a good book to reveal to them the plan of salvation. These classes and the work with the women in morning meetings and the schoolboys give me a good balance of work among the natives.

On March 22, Ione wrote a letter to Hector. This was the first letter Ione had written to him since January 9, and she starts:

.....It sounded good to have you say you were lonesome for me, but it will sound better to hear it with my ears. When that happens you won't be lonesome anymore! I remember that handshake when you left Phila. I just <u>knew</u> you had squeezed my hand harder and with both of yours, but later I tried to convince Pearl that you felt the same toward everybody. But Pearl is not so dumb, either! I didn't know then what the future would hold for us, together.

She told Hector how he inspired her to try and reach one person a day:

.....Most of the time it is little boys who come evenings to my house singly or in groups, or in the early morning meetings. But twice this week I have dealt with a Mohammedan [a Muslim]. He is a Negro, but wears the garb of that sect and reads the Koran. He was operated on and was in the hospital, so I have the advantage of getting a testimony and a bit of scripture every now and then. He agrees with everything I say, but I know he does not trust in Christ as a living Saviour. Pray for him. He has promised to sell me one of his funny embroidered hats. The Lord is so good to me in giving opportunities to witness for him in the very line of duty each day. I have fretted so and tried so hard to get out to the neighbouring villages, but it makes me so cross and tired and I know it is hard on me physically when I try to get so far before breakfast then serve trays and attend to my own house before I go over to Doctor's. But in the women's meetings, the classes which I conduct with the nurses now at the hospital and the times with the boys I find countless times to witness to the unsaved.

Ione carefully chronicled all the letters she had received from Hector so he knew they were reaching her, and she also thanked him for photos and for remembering her family at Christmas. This kindness was touching, as Ione could not send gifts home herself. A flash of her humor came through in her letter:

.....That was good of you to say that one of my kisses would be worth the three that Marcellyn sent to you in her letter. I tho't that a bird in hand is worth two in the bush', but perhaps kisses in the African 'bush' are different.

I'll try to remember that it's Avonmore [Hector's hometown] *and not Avondale. Thanks for remembering the family with Christmas gifts.*

Later in the letter, Ione talked about the cause of her frustrations more precisely:

.....I was not able to take the boys' school even part time this semester, because Mrs Westcott said she did not feel she could do without me that long and with white patients continually to feed and care for, there were too many emergencies to permit me anything of a regular nature. So, in January I adjusted myself once more to the very irregular schedule that Doctor keeps. They gave me the nurses and house helpers to teach each afternoon at the hospital but if there is anything important on the Doctor's mind that is cancelled, like moving a triangular beam onto the frame of the new church, or an emergency operation, or any number of things. I have tried to get used to bending in this direction or that to fit the occasion, and find that rather than its upsetting me, it is making me stronger. 'A bruised Reed shall he not break'. Just now I have seven white children during the days: two little boys of the Lindquist family, from A.I.M., a little girl of a Norwegian missionary. This is the beginning of the rainy season, and when they've been outside and get all stuck up with red clay, it's no picnic. Today Charlotte fell headlong into a ditch of muddy water. I was shocked, but she said it felt 'awfully nice' down in that soft mud. Mrs Westcott spends most of her time in bed just now and I am trying to find something that will stimulate her appetite. Today I gave her added nourishment by putting three raw eggs in her cocoa. The Jenkinson's are ever sympathetic and helpful and kind. I was sick one day last week, but just couldn't stay the day in bed because I saw so much that needed to be done, and since then have been trying to cut down a little in schedule, and they have been good to help. I slept later and went to bed earlier and now am feeling fine again. And Doctor and Kinso are cooperating to get me a new leaf roof on the house to keep me from moving furniture thru the night when it rains! It rains every night now—and I mean RAINS. And the leaks play hide and seek with me.

Despite these challenges, she continued to stimulate her readers with details of the life she was engaged in:

I wish I had something exciting to write to you, something to make your eyes pop, as it were, but these days nothing worse happens than a fuss with the house helper of the theft of a kitchen knife. I received a new cord for my typewriter roller and it works fine again. You need not send me any now. I received a lovely big box from Montgomery Ward, as well as some pretty things from Mother and my sister Lucille. I am well fixed for some time now. The Lord is good to send in many special gifts, too. I am designating them all to my Work Fund except when designated Personal, so have an accumulated work fund and am only breaking even on household expenses. Since I do not have a boys' or girls' or women's work I do not have a place for Work Funds. But I am sure the Lord will find a place for it when the time comes. My trouble now is finding time to acknowledge gifts.

She wrote to Marjorie Baker, her friend who had come to her aid when her typewriter broke:

Dear Marjorie: Greetings and hallucinations—I mean salutations!

I was pleasantly surprised last week to receive from you the item [spring for her typewriter] *that I suggested in my Aug. letter last year. It was kind of you to send it. I trust you will write me soon and enclose a bill for the cost of it. As you can see, my typewriter is much improved. I can't hold it responsible for the spelling, but it is doing its best now to give me good service. Thanks very much.*

She told Marjorie about her trip to the mountains with the Westcotts a few months earlier and added:

.....Little Bobbie Westcott found a lizard and put it in my bed. He said in case any mosquitoes got thru the netting the lizard would eat them! I told him I really preferred the mosquitoes, tho'!

She also described her living accommodations, without mentioning the leaks in the roof:

.....I am living alone in my four-room mud house. Before the front door is an avenue of palm-trees going down the hill to the main road. There is a huge purple bougainvillea bush climbing over the front verandah and upon the roof; there are yellow bell-like flowers in several small bushes, red poinsettias, pink and white roses, and tall and short cacti all around the edge. My cook prepares my food in a little building back of this one and serves me in the end room, next room is the living room, next the bedroom and last the washroom. The house is fifty feet long, but very narrow and the roof looks like a narrow strip of paper folded lengthwise. The leaves fluff up in the wind and look like feathers.

I am having a good time and very happy I came. Please write me again when you find time.

Love in Christ, Ione

Hector started a letter to Ione on March 28 with:

Darling Ione:

'The righteous shall be glad in the Lord, and shall trust in Him; and all the upright in heart shall glory.' Psa. 64:10

And that is just what I am doing today. The Lord makes us so happy and then we are encouraged to trust with more daring. I was quite amazed this morning while having my devotions to come upon a verse . . . 'consider how great things He hath done for you.' The margin reads, 'what a great thing'. There is one important circumstance in my horizon and that is my 'sweetie pie' and a wedding in the offing.

It transpired in this letter that Mr. Pudney preferred Hector go to the Congo rather than wait for Ione to come back and marry him before he went. This had many implications for them, however. Hector wrote:

.....I'll be happy just to have things work out the way the Lord has planned. He never does anything wrong, so I can learn to be content in whatever state I am. As you stated in one of your letters some time ago, patience is the hardest lesson to learn. I've just taken time off for my devotions right here before it gets too late and I was praying for you again. I would just love to start for Africa tomorrow, but I have asked God to care for you until we are together and then to take us both on our way, soberly, sensibly, but most of all, happily. We have a big task before us, with plenty of responsibility, yet is not our work but His.

Hector wrote to Ione on April 16th, two days out from his routine as he had been preoccupied with his ordination into the ministry. After the details of the ordination were written out, he ended thus:

.....This is the first time that I have signed my name this way. I've been saving it for you.

Rev. J. Hector McMillan X

Hector referred to the Ludwig family coming back to the states and quipped that he'd have to check their baggage just in case Ione was hiding there. He goes on to say that although one hurdle had been cleared, he still had to obtain his discharge from the Air Force, a matter he picked up in his next letter to Ione on April 27:

My lovable sweetheart:

Out on temporary duty again, but I hope for only a few days or weeks, as I'm expecting news from Ottawa. Then I'll be counting the days as I move from city to city & finally to Africa XXX to see Ione. Your love is the acme of my coveted possessions. Heart affection vitalizes the whole being so I often have that kind of heart trouble. There is so much of you to think about & it's a grand pastime. So many things remind me of you; especially my watch. I imagine about 500 people have seen it in the last three weeks. Today I had some spare time & I was putting pictures in my album. After much hesitation I took those Phila. Pictures out of their folder & put them in with stickers. And this is what I want to tell you. In that picture of your room (I usually look at it the longest) I noticed for the first time that there is a little Baby Ben clock on the dresser. Is that the one that you mentioned several letters ago? The hands then were at ¼ to nine. So that reminded me of you. And then people frequently ask about 'Ione'—so many, I think, dearie, that when we get our wedding arranged, we'll just ask for an empire hook-up.[31] It would only take about 30 seconds to pay for it. We two will make some great scientific discovery or invention—like say—something to keep women from talking; that should bring in royalties from every nation. But I'd like to suggest this rule that it wouldn't be effective until after you sat on my lap & talked sweetly into my ear for three hours steady. You know dear I seem to hear your voice & merry laugh every so often. It will be glorious to be near you soon.

---

[31] Possible reference to a period radio term for broadcast news to the entire country.

Now for news. I visited Ottawa on the way back & the passport division are getting a few things lined up. In Montreal I went to see the Belgian Legation & they were very kind. One of the men gave me a huge envelope of literature on Belgium & especially the Congo. I've gone thru' most of it & have learned much about the colonial policy. He gave me three daily newspapers (French) from Elizabethville—printed last January. It has the amazing name of 'L'Essor du Congo.'

Last Friday evening I had the opportunity of preaching my first real sermon in my new capacity at the Soldiers & Airmen Christian Assoc. I enjoyed speaking on the works of the Spirit as outlined in John 16:8-11. I never really understood this section until I began preparing this message. Afterwards an airman accepted Christ as his Saviour. His name is Jimmie McLellan & he was on his last leave before going overseas. A fine young man.

Once back in Scoudouc, I wasn't long taking my ordination certificate down to the officials. The Flight Lieutenant was so interested he got his theological terms confused & asked me if I'd been confirmed alright. Evidently, they got everything fixed up that afternoon & were sending their recommendation for 'compassionate discharge' in to Ottawa. When he found out I was going out on temporary duty he said he hoped to have good news for me when I returned. So, keep praying & trusting, honey!

One more incident. While coming out to this station I got a ride from town with a local Anglican minister and [urged Hector to] *take the service next Sunday evening. What a golden opportunity!! I believe the Lord would have me speak on Gal 3:13, 'Christ hath redeemed us from the curse of the Law.' That should give ample material to tell of our state by nature & our available state by grace. I just love preaching!*

Closing for another time. Next year this time I'll be cutting some wood out of the forest to make a cradle & high-chair—Possible?

From your ardent lover, Hector XX

Hector marked Mother's Day that year by writing to Mrs. Reed on May 7:

To the dearest mother a fellow could have,

Special greetings for Mother's Day and a hearty hug & kiss X. My affection for you & yours is accumulating daily as the time draws near when I can really express it. Sometimes I feel you so close to me and I long for another motherly embrace.

When Hector's discharge finally came through, he cabled the news to Ione and dropped a brief letter to her mother on May 29, saying that he planned to stay a few weeks at the mission headquarters in Toronto.

On June 4, Ione started a letter to the Pudneys, which she finished on the 10th, noting she had not replied to the letters she received from them the previous year. She wrote:

.....The increase in salary was very welcome and we have been receiving our monthly allowances; however there is a three-month gap where Doctor finished

transferring our funds (June) and when Mr Kerrigan [stationed at Maganga] *began (Oct.). Doctor and Mr Kerrigan decided that Pearl and I would have to write the Pontiac church to make it up.*

.....Truly I have much to be thankful for. The Lord has kept me healthy and has given me choice opportunities to witness even when I thought I was too busy being a 'Martha' in the kitchen and nursery. Hector wrote me that he was endeavouring to speak to at least one soul each day about the Lord and when I saw what great results he was having, I determined that I would keep my eyes open for people right in my line of duty: *on my way past the hospital I walked thru the wards—prayed with a woman before she died; caught a Mohammedan reading his Koran and witnessed to the unsearchable Word of God; some school boys stopped at the house when I returned in the evening and we had several evenings of heart-to-heart talks and prayer and as a result one of them led his mother to the Lord; a group of boys came in on Sunday afternoon and 7 accepted Christ. And beside the opportunities going to and from the Doctor's house I have had two hospital meetings a week and a girls and boys joint meeting. I have the women just now three mornings a week while Vee* [Viola Walker] *is trekking; they have a devotional meeting and a reading class. I was to have taken over the boys' school this term with a half-time schedule at Doctor's but Mrs Westcott felt she could not carry on without me. There have been white patients almost continuously and feeding them as well as helping Doctor is too much for Ellen. But she is getting on admirably.*

Bongondza seems very strange without the Kinsos and right now Vee has gone. But the Faulkners are here as well as Joan Pengilly. The Faulkners are awaiting word of their possible furlough.

June 10 – Yesterday Doctor and Pearl and I (Pearl has been here a month packing up to go to Maganga) received an Airmail from Doctor Savage with the two motions made in the council meeting there, concerning Pearl's health and my engagement. I believe a cable is to be sent today with the response. You will have received [the information] *that I, too, am included in the furlough departures. I do not know what complications this will involve in America, but do not wish to upset Hector's plans. No doubt if he is released, he will be able to get passage very soon. It may be that we shall be crossing at the same time. Mr Kerrigan feels that Hector will get into the work quicker if he is not married for a while. This is agreeable to me, altho' I had hoped to either be married at home or to meet him when he had arrived in Congo. But by now I believe I know the value of rest when it is offered, and I could not refuse a furlough now when I should have to wait for Hector's furlough if I did not take it now. Jean Brown Faulkner's experience shows me that it will be better from the long view. The Lord will surely show me how to possess my soul in patience till I have rested and come back to Hector. By then he will have the language and we can relieve someone else who needs a furlough. I trust this sounds as reasonable to you as it does to us out here! Doctor is head over heels in packing and says he will get off in a month.*

Pearl and I have had a happy month together and we expect to have our little home very cozy for the next occupant. It has a new leaf roof, freshly plastered walls, new mud verandah, some beautiful clever grass in front, a place ready for planting of spider lilies on either side of the path; they will go in this week, and a new water drum for the cook house, and best of all running water at bath (Doctor built a bath in 2 hours!) from bricks and cement with a faucet thru the wall from a drum outside. The water falls first on the water stand and when the bowl is removed, it cascades down into the tub! A saving on faucets and pipes and it really works. Pearl loves the work here, and is willing to go to Maganga since that is the wish of the Council and it is tho't best for her just now.

Mr Kerrigan has been a real help and inspiration to us these three months he has been here. I expect Pearl will go with him when he goes to see his wife in July and attend to matters on his station.

.....No doubt the Doctor or Mr Kerrigan have informed you in detail of the recent decisions and happenings, but I do want you to know that whatever is tho't wisest in my case is acceptable to me. When Doctor and Mr Kerrigan asked me yesterday if I would be willing to wait another year to be married, I told them yes, if it would make me a better missionary and wife with the year of rest. The way I feel right now it seems I could easily go on for three or four years more, and especially with Hector. But if I do come home now with Doctor, I'll be able to keep up with Hector's pace. I am writing to Hector to tell him how I feel. In my heart I am holding a new hope that Hector may still be in the States when we arrive that I might see him anyway, but I don't suppose it would be wise for us to marry right then either if he is to go off so soon. And Mr Kerrigan thinks it is wise for him to come out single. Ah, me—it seems rather complicated, but 'our Heavenly Father knoweth . . .'

Please accept the greetings of the friends here, Pearl and Joan.

Yours in Christ, Ione Reed

Ione followed this letter with one to her sister Doris, giving her details of a recent bout of pneumonia and concurrent weight loss; no wonder she feels the need for a break and furlough, and despite being ill, she still maintains her work schedule which includes packing trunks for the Westcott family. Doris seemed to have had problems that elicited this response from Ione:

.....Your letter was like a melodrama and I wept and smiled over it. These experiences you have had and are having seem terrible to you right now but I believe you will turn out all right. 'All things work together for good to them who love the Lord, to them who are the called, according to His purpose.' If you can put a big period after each mistake and see that it doesn't happen again these times will be stepping stones rather than stumbling blocks. The main thing is to stay close to the good old Book—'sin will keep you from this Book; and this Book

will keep you from Sin'. Spend time in prayer and commit your life to <u>Him</u>. That's a big sister's advice!!

Doris also gets a description of the oven Ione is using:

.....The oven out in the cook house is made out of a kerosene drum and bakes acceptable bread. I bake my own bread every other day using no yeast, but a continuous leaven culture which you save out each time. If that should be forgotten a few days it will die, and then I would have to make a new culture from a fermented plantain or banana. It's a great life.

And again, on June 10, Ione wrote to Hector with news of her plans, which did not quite match up to his. Some of the letter was destroyed but it starts with:

Dearest Dear One,

Your cable reached me yesterday and I was so excited I just waved it in the air and shouted. At the same time that I learned that you had received your discharge I received a letter from Dr. Savage suggesting that I come down river to meet you when you arrive and that we be married and return to the work together. That all sounded great and I think I had the Doctor convinced that it was just the right thing. But Mr Kerrigan, in behalf of the Field Council shook his head. He advised that I take my furlough now when the Westcotts come home, else I should not get one at all. And he further stated that it was best for you to come here as a single man, get the language, and get adjusted to conditions before being married. I can see the wisdom, but I confess it had never occurred to me. And now very suddenly Doctor has decided that he must get off in a month's time and I am to go along, which is satisfactory with me, but I am wondering where you are, if you have left by now, and if, as I feared last November, we shall both be on the ocean but going in opposite directions. It may be possible, but the Lord will lead us both I am sure. But if I could just get to see you and talk to you, I would feel better about it. I want to go home and do need it before we are married, but I hadn't tho't it would be this way. If your sailing is delayed, we may yet see each other, and I am secretly wishing we could even be married there, but I would not wish you to be delayed when you are so needed out here. Six missionaries have already gone on furlough, and five more will be going in the next few months, maybe six. That only leaves eight.

Various plans were proposed: Hector could go to Boyulu to the learn the tribal language Kingwana (king-WAN-a); Hector and Ione could go to Maganga as a married couple if they married as soon as she got to the States or as outlined in the letter to the Pudneys. This meant Ione also had to learn Kingwana, since at present she spoke Bangala, the tribal dialect used at Bongondza and Ekoko. In earlier letters, the possibility of their going to Ekoko was suggested, but the mission did not have a "concession" from the Belgian government to work there, although it was being negotiated. The field leaders (Kinso and Kerrigan) would rather place an experienced couple there rather than the newlywed McMillans. As Ione said:

.....The future is rather indefinite but it is in His Almighty hands. If you get out here before we leave we can have some happy times together at any rate. But I

must pray for courage to go if you are here. Doctor said I might come back before the year is finished if I felt well. Perhaps a little sick spell I have just had made them fear that I would be too tired by the end of your term.

.....We have been praying all along for His guidance concerning our lives and now that there seems to be action at both ends of the line we cannot complain if He chooses to even move us both without seeing one another. We know that 'all things work together for good to them that love the Lord, to them who are the called according to His purpose.' If I should leave here in a month's time (a little more perhaps) I shall perhaps be allowed to travel on a medical boat with the Westcotts or to come with them by plane. They have no specific information as yet. At any rate I should be there in August or September. Doctor Savage said it would be several months before you could leave, but that letter was written before he knew you had been discharged. So peradventure you are on the high seas or about to leave. May I say, the Lord bless you abundantly and keep you safe from all harm. I want you kept safe for His Sake—and for mine. For I do love you dearly and want you for my very own husband.

Loving you always, Ione

June 10 was evidently a letter-writing day because Ione also found time to write to her friend Agnes Sturman. After thanking Agnes for her letters, she wrote:

.....Pearl was here to enjoy [your] *last one, as she came rather suddenly back, a little before time as Dr. Becker was leaving for the States and could give her a ride as far as Stanleyville. Then she took the courier bus and came to Kole where Doctor met her. She surprised us all by her rotundity and says she feels fine. Her blood count is high, much better than any of us, and she wants to get started. She has been designated for Maganga for a while until she is used to the work again. She has been packing and expects to go with Mr Kerrigan when he goes to his station again in July.*

We were surprised to receive Airmail from Dr Savage yesterday; and also, I received a cable telling of Hector's discharge from the Airforce. Since Pearl's health is good enough to work, that eliminates her from going home; she so much desires to put in some good months of real service before she goes home. I told Doctor I tho't it would be great to meet Hector at the sea and be married and I figured the change would give me a break before beginning the full-time missionary work. But the Field Council tho't differently. They want me to come home, too, and get a furlough before marrying so that I can serve a regular second term stretch without a breakdown. Mrs Faulkner was out here for a few years like myself and then instead of going home she married and now they are forced to go home because she just cannot carry on. Her blood count is only 45 and she has sinus trouble; and other things, I guess. So the Council used her as an example and want me to be rested and also they want Hector to spend some months on the field before he marries. It is commonly known that this climate is not the best; people get pneumonia so quickly and then—it is only a step to TB.

She told Agnes about her recent illness, which was treated with antibiotics and intravenous glucose, and added:

.....I presume Hector will get off on a boat soon. And it may be that we shall be travelling in opposite directions. I would like so well to at least see him on his way here and the Lord may work some coincidence. But otherwise . . . .I'll go home, be a single lady there and in the meantime he'll be learning Kingwana at Boyulu perhaps. Then I'll come back, we'll both be experienced and can take over any work that is offered, we hope! I suppose the States are full of returned missionaries who are deputating. I'll have a story to tell about the work here, Doctor will have some pictures, and when Doctor's modesty fails to speak of the miracle of his wife's recovery, I will take up the tale. She has had 16 operations you know, 11 this term. She could not lift her head when I came. Now she conducts the child health clinic, assists the Doctor with operations, and has a remarkable keen mental balance. She walks and even runs without a limp. You will marvel I think when you see her for she is still very beautiful and dresses the children very tastefully.

.....I am bringing your alligator-shaped ivory letter-opener instead of sending it. I have some other interesting things that I shall try to obtain permission to carry along. I expect I'll have my trunk sent to Charlevoix where Lucille is, since my home belongings are there and I shall have no other home. But if I can find a nail to hang on in Pontiac, I want to be there more than any other place. S'funny, isn't it, what a pull there is on the heart-strings for the folk at First Baptist. Pearl learned to love them as well as I.

I trust this letter finds you well.

Lovingly in Christ, Ione

On June 25, Ione sent Hector a birthday card and note:

Dearest Hector,

Soon four birthdays shall have passed since we first met. It does not seem possible. And you will be 29. I hope it will be a joyful day for you wherever you are. Surely another birthday will not pass before we are together. The Lord is leading I am sure and will not make us wait longer than is necessary for His Plan.

I sent you two letters a week apart and by now you have heard that the Westcotts and I shall be leaving shortly. The Faulkners hope to come soon, too. I am wondering whether you and I shall be sent at the same time so if we may be permitted to be together soon.

This week your April 27 letter came with your picture in ministerial garb. That's the first time I have seen you looking stern. Perhaps you'll look at me many times that way! I love you ever so much more now than ever before. I love your mischievous eyes and your strong hands.

Your cable indicated your imminent departure. If you are leaving America shortly may you be granted journeying mercies. If in His goodness you shall be detained a tiny bit to wait for me I shall be the happiest girl anywhere. Much love, Ione

[Birthday card] *PS: May every hour of* **Your Birthday** *and every day of the year to follow be filled with happiness. I mean the kind of happiness that comes when God opens the door to His chosen field of service; and when you open your arms and find them enfolding someone who loves you. —Ione*

While Ione was coming to terms with the possibility of traveling in the opposite direction from Hector, he was gaily preparing to see her, and on June 28, he wrote:

My dearest One and Only:

'Behold I send an Angel before thee, to keep thee in the way, and to bring thee into the place which I have prepared.' Ex. 23:20.

This is the promise that the Lord gave me on Oct. 22/43, when I first began to think about getting a discharge. Yesterday I received the official certificate. How wonderfully I have been kept in the way. In a few more months I should be at 'the Place' which the Lord has provided for me, by your side.

.....The other day I got a letter from Mr Pudney saying that they were negotiating with the Belgian Legation in New York in regard to a marriage document on arrival *on the field. Sounds allright doesn't it? But supposing there should be a time of waiting, I'll be able to see you most of the time. And you're not very hard to look at ! ! !*

Hector had been staying at the mission home with the Goodmans and provided childcare for their son, Harding:

.....You would love to hide around a corner and listen to what I've taught Harding to say. Last Sunday morning Mrs Goodman wanted to go up to Eglinton so asked me if I mind staying at home. So we told the lad all about the plans and he was willing to stay with 'Heh-heh'. He just loves stories; so baby Moses was of great interest to his little heart. As a diversion I took him around the room and he named out most of the people from their pictures. He goes wild over that one of you on the mantel piece. So I told him a little about our affair, and then asked him who Hector loved, and he came back with a close resemblance of 'Aye-yown'. When I reversed the question then he put my name in. So he has the right idea. Mrs Goodman didn't know what to say when she came home and I put him through his exercises. But the other evening at supper he went a step too far. I believe his mother asked him who Hector loved, and quick as he could be he said, 'Aye-yown, the bwack girl'. She has been telling him to pray for the little black boys and girls, and I guess he thinks you're one.

Then Hector added:

.....Maybe you would like to know what recommends the Airforce gave me. 'His conduct had character in the service . . . very good'. 'His qualifications during Air Force service in the trade shown . . . 'Superior'. But of course, you don't have to believe all they say. This parchment is invaluable to me and much coveted by others. 4XXXX This is Harding saying Hi. 'X this is for a little black girl. Love Harding'

145

It seemed that the plan was for Hector to sail in the fall with a group of other missionaries; in the meantime, he was enrolled in a language course, as he needed to learn French. Hector related to Ione that an acquaintance was going to the Sudan Inland Mission without having been to Bible college, whereas, the UFM took pride in preparing their prospective missionaries prior to leaving their home country.

In response to a gift of $10 from the First Baptist Church, Ione wrote to Mrs. Peterson (Lucille's mother-in-law) on July 7 to thank them. She included a story about a visit and provided a summary of her activities:

.....Recently we entertained Mr and Mrs Rogers from the French Congo. They told us of their experiences in the lion country, where daily they need the Lord's protection from bodily harm. Two days before leaving their station Mr Rogers had taken his gun to kill an antelope. He had just three cartridges, used two and then turned about to face a lion which rose in front of him.[32]

This has been an interesting year. A missionary's vocation involves many sub-vocations that of farmer, cook, administrator, carpenter, teacher, nurse. In the U.F.M. magazine, 'Light & Life' my name appears on the hospital staff. I am not a nurse, but this year more than last, I have found an ever-increasing demand upon my meagre knowledge in the care of the sick. Then there are the meals to supervise for both patients and attendants. For several months I was able to give instructions to the nurses as well. There were six or seven of them and a few staff members. We met each afternoon and studied reading (French and Bangala) writing, arithmetic as well as spelling and music. One nurse, Bangisa ('He makes people afraid') learned to read simple verses in the book of John in just one week. I do not know whether the continual study in that book made the impression, but soon after that he raised his hand in one of my hospital services and accepted Christ.

.....Our native orphan, Madoli, is growing rapidly, walks now and sings hymns. You would love to see him sitting at his little table in the back yard where he receives his meals when we eat. A little mulatto child, Katherine, sits at our table with us and sleeps with the Westcott kiddies. There are many for whom to pray— Botiki, Doctor's native head nurse who is a fine Christian. Samwele, the native pastor, Pelo, the head teacher of the boys' school.

Thank you for your kindness and generosity. I trust that you may continually 'abound to every good work'.

Yours in Christ, Ione Reed

Hector wrote a letter to Ione on his birthday, July 16. In it, he told Ione that the Goodmans had left him in charge of the mission headquarters. There was to be a council meeting and Mr. Pudney was arriving from the States; it appeared that Hector and Ione's marriage would form part of the agenda for discussion, and Hector hoped they would get permission to marry sooner rather than later. He wrote:

---

[32] We learn nothing of what happened next!

.....You said just what I want to say, 'I get so tired of myself it will be refreshing to have you around.' It will be sublime to have someone slip their arm around me and look coyly enticing. We will have many twilight treks, oblivious of even stray natives. Bwana Macky[33] will be the happiest man in the Congo.

Chester Burk and Hector McMillan in 1944 at UFM Headquarters dressed for Africa.

Another prospective missionary couple, Chester and Dolena Burk, were also resident at the mission headquarters. Like Hector, Chester was Canadian and grew up on a farm:

.....Chester Burk got the breakfast while Dolena and I were doing the washing. She is not very well acquainted with the machine. They are a fairly tall couple but both thin. He weighs about 130 and she might be about 115. They could both do with about 35 lbs more. Then they would be about the same as you and I. People are most amazed at my 'fat' cheeks as Mrs Roadhouse said. Chester and I were out there the other day picking cherries. At the dinner table in the kitchen Mr Roadhouse was recounting some incidents and his wife broke in with the comment that it takes Ione Reed to make things <u>really</u> interesting. So, I felt quite proud of you. That kind of pride is permissible I believe.

A letter Ione wrote from Matadi, at Congo's west coast, to Lucille and her husband started on August 8 and was finished on the 27th. It is clear she was already on her way home:

.....Doctor Westcott has left the work at Bongondza to go home at last. I am on the way with them, but cannot tell when we will arrive as we do not know. I am at the coast now after having completed the River journey. We are all in a hotel, Mrs Westcott too ill to go to the dining room, but able to eat a little. I hope we don't have too long to wait for her sake, as well as for Doctor's who is not well either. Most of the time I am both Mother and Father to the children. I am sure they could not travel without help. Pray for them.

The future looks bright—what could be nicer than to see my dear ones again—Mother, you-all, Marcellyn, Doris, the other relatives and real friends. And then—Hector! I would like to be married at Pontiac, but of course it depends on where you can all come and when. And it depends on Hector too.

Aug. 27: We are still waiting at the coast, unable to get passage. There are two or three remaining possibilities, via Lisbon, Portugal, via Liverpool, England, and by plane, which seems the most likely at present. If we come by plane we'll have a few more weeks' wait here and then come quickly. I'll either

---

[33] Bwana means husband or boss and Macky is a shortened "McMillan".

call or wire you when I arrive. We are living at the ABC Hotel, a Portuguese place, lots of sailors and drink, but the food is good & we have good rooms away from the noise & fights. I think I have gained back the pounds I lost with pneumonia this spring. Since coming here I've been having tri-weekly French lessons from the wife of the Customs agent. I have felt a little more confident in speaking French lately; it is a difficult language. If I can't make myself understood, I generally can find a native & talk Bangala to him and he interprets if he knows French. Some of the French people do know Bangala but it would be an insult to them to talk to them in the native language. The mission here is Swedish, but they speak English & French.

.....The weather here now is like September or June, lovely and cool—no rain. This is their nicest season. Tonight, we'll go up to the mission for tea & hymns and prayer—a 'sing-song' they call it. God bless you always,

Love, Ione XXX and more

The frustrations and difficulties of trying to get passage back to the States were evident in a letter Ione wrote on August 25 to her friend Pearl, now based at Maganga. Pearl was someone Ione was comfortable sharing a burden with:

Dear Pearl,

I miss your promises for beginnings of my letters. I'm thinking of that one about, 'He hath made and He will bear.' Kinso drew that one day at our house at Bongondza. I have been thinking about it for I've been so blue and kind of bitter. I was thinking that since the Lord made me, He has had a great deal to bear. I'm glad that 'grace works not with what it finds but with what it brings.'

This has been a strange time and as on the vacation trip it seems that if I want to write letters it must be either with interruptions or after everyone is asleep. Today it is with interruptions. I should not complain, for I have been having more rest than usual; I think I have gained back my lost pounds due to the good food all along the way; and people have been very good to us. Today we shall learn whether the Tarn, *a Norwegian boat will take us. The last one went a week ago and took the others who travelled down river with us, Dr. and Mrs Trout and Marian; Harold Paul and Paul Pontier; as well as Dr. from another mission and two single women missionaries. This boat is filled with those who have rights prior to ours, but there is a chance that several will not get here in time, for the boat will leave early; if that is so, we are on the spot and will be allowed to go. Otherwise, there is no other boat until the Portuguese one in Sept. or the Norwegian ones when they return on the next trip in Oct. or Nov. As yet there has been no opportunity of going by plane.*

The Stanleyville days were pleasant, always with responsibilities of course, but I did get a permanent and enjoyed the hotel. When I drew my money out of the bank there was not much to travel with; that was why I let Doctor go ahead and transfer the name on the bill for the milk and lard. I did not like to do it at all and I still feel badly about it. Then I realized soon afterward how much I owed you beside for other things. Would you please make a list of the things and let me know. I am transferring 500 francs today by the post office for the vegetable basket, but I believe there may have been other things, too. Don't hesitate to tell me.

I wore that brown blouse you gave me this week and it looked so nice. I know I shall have much wear from it. The green sweater has been a real help, too. I have needed it many times. This is a grand season at Matadi, real cool and pleasant all of the time. Sometimes it is even chilly. I presume we'll see the Faulkners when the [river] boat brings them this week if they come on here. We stayed a few days at Léopoldville, but the Consul advised us to come on here to talk to the Captains when these two boats arrived. I believe the rates are cheaper here, too. This hotel is cheaper than the Metropole and they make ice cream every day for us.

Ellen is awake now and I shall stop for now. She is sick most of the time, and at least one of the children most of the time. Doctor is not well either. It has been dysentery; now he's getting a cold. But things sometimes seem worse than they are I know. God is 'still on the throne' and Jesus Christ is 'the same, yesterday, today, and forever.' God bless you in all you are doing. Hope you had a happy birthday.

Love, Ione

On September 3, Ione found time to write four letters; the first to friends and supporters of her work, the Nordrums, in which she summarized the last three years:

Dear Friends,

I have thought of you many times and wished to express my appreciation for your generous gift to me. I have applied it toward the cement that was needed in building the native church which was completed this year. Doctor Westcott has built the church entirely with hospital proceeds, except for the gifts which came thru friends of mine. The old church fell down a few months ago and the new one was very much needed. It is 93 feet long, 36 feet wide, all done in burned brick. It has a slanting floor with a projection booth for stereopticon slides, two Sunday school rooms, a bell tower, a capacity for 600 people. Another society in Stanleyville built another, a similar church, and did not begin until they had $4,000 on hand, but Doctor Westcott's has cost much less.

As I summarize the past three years, I find much for which to rejoice. The Lord has been good to me and to those with whom I have been working. When Pearl Hiles and I said good bye to friends and loved ones in October '41, we scarcely dreamed of all that lay ahead: the wait at Philadelphia, the final departure a week after America had entered the War. The ocean journey during which time we travelled 'blackout', the safe delivery at Matadi, the fascinating Congo River, friends to welcome us at Bongondza on Feb. 7, '42, and then the beginning of my work, a strange combination of caring for the sick, and an ailing doctor's wife, their children, other patients' children of many nationalities, teaching in the native school, village work, trekking, etc.

During the second year I conducted three weeks of women's meetings, took charge of the two hospital meetings a week all year, had two or three periods daily in the evangelists' school for two months, taught about 40 school boys each Sunday afternoon, took tri-weekly village meetings for three months, and took a two-week trek with Miss Viola Walker. It was my joy to lead 22 to the Lord.

This last year I continued on with the early morning hospital meetings and in addition took charge of a class for hospital boys, the native nurses and house helpers. We met each afternoon and studied reading, writing, arithmetic, music, and French. One unlikely-looking nurse named Bangisa learned to read in a week's time simple sentences in the Gospel of John. Shortly after that he accepted Christ and entered the class for Baptism.

One of Doctor's native patients who had a TB spine has recovered, is a member of the evangelists' class, tells how he was saved while he lay in bed reading the scriptures. He has a fine testimony and if he remains true will be a great help to the work. His name is Tisembo, a tall thin fellow with a pleasant smile and earnest eyes.

Thank you for your kindly interest. I may see you soon, but until then, may God bless you both.

Yours in Christ, Ione Reed

And with more detail about her journey, Ione wrote a long letter on the 3rd of September to Hector ending with uncertainties of their days ahead:

.....Thanks for the flower you put on the letter you sent. Is it a forget-me-not? I have not forgotten you, tho; it has been a long time since I wrote. I am wearing your bracelet full-time now as the children give it better treatment than before when they broke it so often. I also wear a little ruby ring on the third finger of my left hand, a ring my Mother gave me when I was in high school. This is to give a silent testimony to any strangers on the journey.

This week I found some precious promises in Zechariah which have been a help to me. I sometimes feel quite handicapped with other people's needs, so bound down every minute of the day and night with things other than direct soul-winning that I get quite distressed. Then the Lord tells me that He will use these things in a way that He quite understands, even if I don't!

'Not by might, nor by power but by My Spirit, saith the Lord of hosts.' 4:6
'For who hath despised the day of small things?' 4:10
'And ye shall be a blessing: fear not, but let your hands be strong.' 8:13
Hos. 6:3 gave me a good message, too.

'Then shall we know if we follow on to know the Lord.' Verse 1 indicates that we're not ready now to know—we don't have a right to know even. Something has come between us and the Lord perhaps. 'Come and let us return unto the Lord: for He hath torn, and He will heal us; He hath smitten, and He will bind us up . . . . Then—shall we know.' Even after returning to Him that's not all: there's another condition—an if: 'if we follow on to know the Lord'. The only way we'll be able to know things is to first know the Lord. If we get hold of the

Key Man, He'll let us in on all the secrets. 'That I may know *Him and the power of His resurrection and the fellowship of His sufferings being made conformable unto His death.' Phil. 3:10. The sequence seems to be this: 1. Return to the Lord; 2. Follow on; and then 3. Know Him.*

I hope you can get a great deal of French before coming out, and if we are to come out together after the War is finished, I would like very much to come via Belgium to take the course in French. It has been much of a handicap to me and I don't want to miss an opportunity of getting it learned well as soon as possible. I believe the others who have gone out to the field have all been to Belgium first, and no doubt, since I did not have it the Mission will think it wise for me to go there on the way back again. Have the Pudneys spoken of that possibility, should hostilities cease before you leave? Things that looked so little before I came seem so big now. I didn't take much interest in my three lessons a week in Pontiac, but now I am studying with a woman who speaks no English at all and I must really dig to get along. We must speak French to everyone here except ourselves. The conjugations of the verbs have been the hardest and I have been carrying a paper around with me so that I can quickly look to see how to say it in the past, present or future tense. I made a bad mistake on the river boat. A French woman asked me if I was Doctor Westcott's wife, and I glibly said, 'Oui, Madame.' But luckily Mrs Westcott was near at hand and tho she is hard of hearing, heard that *and corrected me.*

I wish I knew what you were doing and what I will be doing a month from now. I hope we can see one another soon. I want to have some days or weeks to get my balance again, to become adjusted to civilization, to know you as a boyfriend for a little while, to be really sure you love me and that I love you, then I want to hear you say with your lips that you want to marry me. We have a right to a little courtship first, don't we, before we are married? I want it to be a time which we shall never forget. Our courtship has been far from normal thus far, but I want it to begin to be normal when I arrive, if you are still there. Do you think we could be satisfied to just hold hands even tho' a kiss would be preferable? I think it would be better for awhile and then we'll have no feelings later that we were being rushed too much. Goodbye, dear one, for now.

Lovingly, Ione

And finally, Ione wrote to Mr. Kerrigan:

.....A new month has begun and we are not yet on the way. We are beginning to get accustomed to seeing boats sail off without us, but perhaps someday soon we shall be the fortunate ones. At present, the only apparent possibility is the Portuguese line in October, unless the continued good news from Europe encourages some of these boats to carry less gunners and more missionaries! One can only 'look for the worst and hope for the best', as someone said. We have met some fine missionaries and have been seeing the family gain in strength, and the most hopeful thing recently was when Doctor obtained

penicillin to help counteract some of Ellen's ailments. It is rare and new, but has unusual possibilities (according to 'Reader's Digest'!).

I received a letter from Hector which I presume you have forwarded to me. Many thanks. Is there a chance that other first-class mail could be sent on, since we expect to be here another month? The magazines can stay, but I would appreciate the letters. And if you have salaries to send, would you kindly have them transferred to B.C.B., Matadi. I shall send a letter now to the office in the States in case they have not already stopped sending salaries here.

.....Hector's letter was an old one written in June, so I have no news as to his plans. He was beginning to study some French and was doing some work in the office of the Peoples Church, Toronto, staying at the Mission Home with the Goodmans. He spoke of a married couple with whom he expects to come in October. But I am not certain that our coming to America will not change his plans. I shall wait and see. Wouldn't it be funny if he came on the same boat that we go home on?

Give my greetings to the friends at Bongondza: Viola and Joan, the Faulkners, if they are yet there. If Ray has not yet gone, perhaps you could send my mail with him. Greet Mrs Kerrigan when you see her, and Pearl and Frances, too.

Very sincerely yours, Ione Reed

While Ione waited for transport at Matadi, Hector made preparations for meeting Ione, and on October 10, he wrote:

My own Darling:

No matter how close to me you are when you read this, you are still too far away. To think that I have only five more days before I can once more look into your eyes and tell you how much I love you over and over again in as many little ways as I can think of. For your sake I covet experiences causing a growth in heart qualities making me gentler, kindlier, less selfish, more thoughtful, more and more considerate of you, truer sympathy, numerous abilities and resources just to make you happier. I know that since last I saw you, I have learned much along some of these lines just from living with all kinds of people; but in all situations Christ was sufficient and who teacheth like Him?

As I travelled around Michigan for three weeks getting to know all your folks, I was told time and time again how fortunate I was to have you for my promised bride. Pontiac, Charlevoix, Belding, and Grand Rapids. Oh! so many people that knew you. But best of all was the week spent up with Lucille and Maurice and their three children. When I met Lucille, my heart was almost overjoyed. It was just like having you around. I used to watch her when she wasn't looking. Her kind, sweet face; soft voice; smile and laugh, poise, control of every situation. . . . I was seeing you living again before my eyes. And her children . . . well that will be one whole night's conversation.

You should see the way Mrs Pudney is fixing your room [at mission headquarters in Philadelphia]. *We've been working on it yesterday and today and it's all ready for you now; right next to mine. And we are to have the library and sometimes Mrs Pudney's private sitting room . . . to get better acquainted. WE ARE REALLY GOING TO SPOIL YOU.*

.....So, come away my love, my joy and crown; the touch of your hand will repay all the lonely hours. Ruth 1:16 for life.

Your lover now and always, Hector X

In October, the UFM published the following from Hector in its magazine, *Light & Life*:

..... 'The branch cannot bear fruit of itself, except it abide in the vine . . . '—John 15:4

The Lord uses various methods to teach His children lessens in faith and patience.

When I graduated from the Prairie Bible Institute in 1940, I verily thought within myself that in a few months I would be on the mission field. Four years have passed. In that interval I have learned that my help cometh from the Lord, for without Him I can do nothing.

These past two years in the Royal Canadian Air Force have been a great blessing in my life. I entered this branch of the Armed Forces on a promise given to Gideon, 'Go in this thy might . . . have I not sent thee.' This was a heaven-sent commission. When the Lord's time came for my release, He gave me another Old Testament promise one morning as I was having devotions in the barracks, 'Behold I send an angel before thee, to keep thee in the way, and to bring thee into the place which I have prepared.'

I am thankful for three specific blessings. The technical training was a great benefit and will prove invaluable on the Congo field. The close association with men who definitely needed Christ was a side of my life which needed to be developed. In the spiritual realm, the Lord gently cut away many unnecessary branches and revealed new truths of my union with Christ. I was then enabled to proclaim the wonders of His grace and provision for me throughout the past eight years since I trusted Him as my Saviour. I solicit an interest in your prayers as I now leave for Africa. — J. Hector McMillan.

On October 22, Viola, stationed at Bongondza, sent Ione a letter:

Dear Ione,

.....We are well, and happy. There is, actually, very little news, when one sits down to try to write! We are, needless to say, kept busy, very busy. There are the days when we praise the Lord for His handiwork in some life, in answer to prayer,—there are too the days when big disappointments come. You know all about that, both sides. On the whole we have been amazed and thrilled at the way the Lord is undertaking that a surprising large percentage of His work here is still being carried on (and by here I do not mean just Bongondza, but all our stations, you know) although with so few on the staff and that without any undue sense of strain. One can only conclude prayers of those at home are upholding the work the Lord has started. Personally, I am far stronger and less tired than

I was a year ago, with much less work. Joan is well and happy. This weekend she is out trekking. She will be in tomorrow morning early, Monday. I hope to go out in the other direction the end of the week. She is now studying Kibua [ki-BU-a], as I strive to set down the knowledge gleaned by the Kinsos or myself during the years, in lesson form. I have only 12 lessons done yet, and there will be, I should think, quoting someone, '1000 Uneasy lessons' so it is a moot question whether the book of lessons will ever be finished!

.....We miss your singing greatly in our little services. Only tonight I was wishing I would hear you sing, 'Out of the Ivory Palaces,' not that I ever did hear you sing that particular hymn, and maybe you do not like it, but somehow, I do! Glad to hear from Frances and Jean [Faulkner] that Ellen has been so well. Greetings to her. And goodnight—I didn't realize the page was full!

Sincerely, Viola

A letter to the Pudneys on October 28, found Ione now back at Léopoldville (the capital of Belgian Congo, miles inland from Matadi, Congo's port of entry) and no further forward in her plans to get back to the United States and Hector. She wrote:

.....There are at least 40 of us in Leo. Of our U.F.M. there are the Faulkner family of four, the Westcott family of five, Miss Longley, and myself. The Westcotts and I have waited two months at Matadi and nearly two months here. Living conditions are not too good, but we have been comfortably situated at the U.M.H. for the past three weeks.

.....We watched 4 boats leave Matadi, but could get passage on none. We packed hastily for air travel in Matadi but the plane was going in the wrong direction. Then we obtained a definite booking on Pan-Am to leave Oct 9th and came back here for that, but it was a new line and after a trial flight they felt they could not yet carry passengers. Another plane went and another, but still we wait, hesitating to notify anyone until we are in America. I have had no mail from the States, as it has been forwarded to Phila, so I don't know what has happened there since June.

Today Mrs W. and Bobbie are in bed. Doctor is not very well at any times, but he seldom stays in bed all day. They all eat better here than at the ABC Hotel in Matadi. I have gained back the lost pounds since my pneumonia this spring. The Faulkners look very tired and I'm sure will be glad to be in Canada. Frances appears very healthy and strong, but I know she is tired, too. This wait here is a rest of the right kind for all of us, of course, for myself, I have not been out three years yet, and don't need a rest, but will be happy to get home. I want to get some further training in teaching while I'm home. I want to return with adequate preparation to do a real job my next term. I am thankful for the 20 or 30 whom I have had the joy of leading to the Lord. Now I want to hurry back and teach them how to live for Christ. There is a little book called, 'They Were

Expendable,'[34] which tells of the soldiers sent to the Philippines. All men, good, were itemized and checked minutely until they were moved into line of battle; then all were crossed off the books as lost. The men & goods which returned were re-entered as gain. But they had to be willing to be counted as lost until they returned. I'd like to be expendable in that way.

Until we meet again, Ione Reed

On November 14, Ione, still in Léopoldville, wrote to Hector:

Dearest Hector, Greetings in Christ!

I'm really excited now, for we've had our call to leave by boat. Going from Matadi the 17th, or thereabouts, we should arrive in NY the early part or middle of Dec. It really looks as tho' you and I shall be together on Christmas. And I am very happy. I want so to see you to find out if you really still love me, after these long silent months. Not a word have I heard, but perhaps I'll find the letters in Phila. that you wrote before you knew we had left the station. At any rate, who cares about letters, when I'll see you in about 4 weeks, D.V.![35]

If you happen to be at Philadelphia, would you be able to find out about arrival time from the same line that we came out on. Mr Pudney knows, and he will be glad for you to inform him of our coming. And could you come to NY to meet us? I hold my breath when I ask, when I think it might be possible. But at any rate, I will get in touch with you somehow soon after arrival, if I don't see you.

.....I can't write much now, as we have only this day yet here. I packed last night after the news came, but I will be helping the Westcotts today. After I see that they are all with some of their relatives, I will be free—FREE from my long 3 years 'case'. There are a few places I want to stop while I am east, but I want mostly to talk to YOU. I hope I can see you soon. It's been a long wait, and getting away from here is not easily done. Most of the grey hairs that you will see have made their appearance during this wait. Waiting is always harder than working, isn't it? But now I don't care if they get seasick at once, for we'll be going somewhere!

I do love you Hector. I want to tell you that in a better way soon. Take good care of yourself until we meet. Leo is a real bottle-neck for tired & homesick missionaries.

See you soon. Lovingly in Him, Ione

Frustrating as it was for Ione, Hector was also suffering from lack of contact and information, and he filled Ione in as best he could in short, sharp sentences, in a letter written on November 23:

My only beloved and longed-for:

Thanksgiving Day! ! ! ! And haven't I plenty to be thankful for, especially YOU.

---

[34] W. L. White, *They Were Expendable: An American Torpedo Boat Squadron in the U.S. Retreat from the Philippines* (Washington, DC: Infantry Journal, 1942).
[35] Deo-volente – God willing.

Where will I start? What shall I say and what can I hope for? ? ? To think that I could have been writing to you all these months; I guess I should have done so anyway. My July letter came back to Phila. A cablegram waits you in Matadi, sent in October, and a copy of this letter lies dormant in Miami: and I wait here at 1150 with my heart all pulled out of shape.

.....My folks were all set to meet you and the letters of sympathy keep coming in, wondering how I can stand the suspense. They wanted me to come back up to Canada, but I am rather wary about crossing the border lest there be a delay.

.....Your letter to the Pudneys was full of good things. I never will cease to marvel at your ambition and abilities.

The days now are filled with plenty of activity. French, of course is the main project. I'll let you know every move, so just be patient—just wait a little longer and then ! ! !

Love . . . Hector

On November 28[th,] Hector wrote from Philadelphia to his sister Florence stating that Ione had written on the 14th saying she was leaving in a few days on a boat for New York; hoping to arrive the first part of December. He also told his sister that he was going to New York for the sole purpose of making reservations on that same boat when it returns to Africa (it usually docked for a week).

On December 19, apparently having at long last met Ione again, Hector wrote to his sister:

Dear Sister Florence & family:

Thanks for the lovely letter you sent Ione.

It was grand meeting her in New York; and every day has been getting <u>better</u>. You must have been much in prayer because everything worked out well.

The Westcott children, who have been Ione's charge for the past three years, are very lively. I enjoyed getting to know them for a few days.

We are together at Mission Headquarters now. Maybe Ione will be soon going down to visit her mother in Tenn., and coming back later. If I go on the first boat, I have only about two weeks left.

Glad to hear how the children are enjoying the snow.

Your Bro in Christ, Hector

After spending a few days with Hector, Ione did go to Tennessee to visit her mother. She wrote to Hector on December 22:

Dearest Hector,

Rather a funny time and place but I tho't I'd send a note anyway.

I arrived in Bristol at the scheduled time (12:25—Thurs.) and was met by my friends. They took me to their home and I had a nice dinner, after which we went shopping. She helped me choose a pretty taffeta dress and hat and a flower for my hair and then insisted on putting it on their account. That evening I went to a choir banquet and had a nice time. It brought back memories of evangelistic meetings and children in that church. We talked until after midnight and slept until 9 A.M. We sang and played the piano during the morning, had dinner and went shopping again. This time I bought some brown shoes, and a dress, but while I was trying the dress on, a dear Christian friend came in and when she shook hands, she left the price of the dress in my hand! The shop girl didn't know how much the check was for, but she was greatly impressed. When I talked to her a little bit about our work, she decided I should have a 20% reduction on the price. And strangely enough, the final cost was exactly what the check paid, so I just endorsed it and passed it over! The Lord seems to approve of ladies going shopping, doesn't He?

.....I surely miss my lover just now. In Christ, Ione

Sadly, little more is known of Hector and Ione's reunion in New York. While it must have been a climactic event after all the yearnings of their long-distance courtship, we can only assume that love letters were no longer needed when they had each other in their arms!

Chapter 7
RENEWING RELATIONSHIPS, RESPITE AND RELAXATION

Ione arrived back in the states at the end of December 1944 and she and Hector would have a mere three weeks together before his departure for the Congo. At the beginning of January, Ione was staying at Sudan Interior Mission Home (SIM) in New York so as to be near Hector up to his date of departure in mid-January. She wrote on January 8 to his sister Florence:

…..Your letter to Hector reached him today, and I remembered that in our busy whirl of events I had not really said Hello to you. I did appreciate so much your greeting when I arrived. I can't tell what a happy feeling it gives me to think that I have some new sisters-to-be.

I hope to go thru Montreal on my way to the farm at Avonmore and we can really get acquainted then. I will be stopping overnight, probably with Irene if she has a nail for me to hang upon. Maybe you two can find a good spot to park me for one night! But please don't give yourself trouble on my account. "I shall count it a privilege to be like one of the family."

I imagine I'll be coming around Feb. 1st, tho' there may be some alteration in plans.

Greet Eleanor when you see her and tell her I am anxious to meet her.

Hector's boat is postponed a few more days and we are taking advantage of the time. He is far nicer than I had remembered him to be. I wonder if his sisters have taught him how to be so nice. Whatever part you have had, I thank you for. I'm sure we are going to have some happy years together.

Hoping to see you soon.

With love in Christ, Ione

After being together in New York, Hector writes to Ione a few days later expressing his joy and love:

Beloved: - Equally disposed to love & be loved.

I thank God upon every remembrance of you! The Lord hath done great things for us whereof we are glad!

I love you!

When God made the worlds – He set the bounds of their habitation. He knew their orbits and circuits. When He made my little universe, it hath verily pleased Him to give me a lover to be a hub of an enlarging circumference. Your coming into my life has enlarged my desires, quickened my affections, broadened my outlook, clarified my up-look, deepened my responsibilities, strengthened my hopes for the future, satisfied my ambitions, rewarded me for past patience, comforted me after my mother's death, filled that place in my life divinely designed for you.

Well, "Honey". I shall hold you continually in the arms of prayer.

Just opened to this verse – In nothing I shall be ashamed, but that with all boldness, as always, so now also Christ shall be magnified in my body, whether it be by life or death. Phil. 1:20

Your lover, Hector

(45 minutes later...) Beloved:

Just listen to this: Song of Solomon 2:14...."in the secret places of the stairs, let me see thy countenance, let me hear thy voice; for sweet is thy voice and thy countenance is comely." You certainly kept me interested for those few weeks. Never mind honey you will be just as much according to the Lord's specifications at 45 as you are now – even after an investigation conducted confidentially. Your name is enough to make my heart happy helped on of course as I associate you & your department & various compartments – or maybe apartments.

Enjoyed you so much – the ear is not filled with hearing nor the eye with seeing nor the heart with loving. Just give me a chance dearie – the way of a man with a maid is as wonderful as the way of this ship in the midst of the sea.

The Lord has given me my heart's desire.

Yours. – Hector

On January 12, the Pudneys wrote to Hector and Ione:

.....I am glad that you have had such a blessed time together for a few days, both here and then in New York. It is such a big and important step when you give yourselves to each other for life. These days have helped you to know each other more intimately and given you a taste of the days to come.

The Lord will strengthen for the parting, Ione will be so busy visiting and thinking over the past, present and future! A trousseau [items collected by a bride for her marriage] *is a formidable undertaking and an interesting one, and to think that it is to be such a short furlough!*

Hector will live in a dreamland of memories on that voyage and have endless 'peeps' at THE RING! (this time it is the wedding ring) I had a game of anagrams to bring and forgot them, maybe you still have time to buy one. Ione's party found it such a help in getting acquainted with the folks. Others seemed to enjoy playing with them.

.....May the Lord bless and keep you both in His great love. With love in our blessed Lord Jesus,

Lilian G. Pudney - Ma Pudu

Hector sailed for Africa on January 14, 1945 and wrote to Ione from the ship. He mentioned a letter from Jean, written 16th of January, saying the McMillan clan were eager to meet and get to know her:

.....Jean says: "We are wondering if Hector is on the briny deep yet. I know that it will be a happy journey to his work but I just am sure that he will be awfully sea-sick. It was good to receive your letter saying that you will come to us to take your place in your "work". Let me tell you Ione, there is a spacious room for you and be assured that we are just waiting for you to come. The sooner you can

come too, Ione, the better for us and if you can make it in January, we'll be happy. We do want you, and need you, too. Dad and Archie too feel that if you were here all would be well. So do come as soon as you can."

On January 25, while staying with her friend Inez Slater in Pontiac, wrote to her mother, mindful that she had not given her much time while making the most of Hector's last few days in the States. She had also forgotten to take her quinine medication, which resulted in a short malaria attack:

.....And now I have a new set of plans. You remember I wanted to get some teacher's training and was thinking of going to Northwestern in the summer. Well, yesterday I talked to Mr French the Superintendent of Schools here and I can get the actual experience in teaching children to read and write if I will stay here and fill in a vacancy in the 1st or 2nd grade. I am really not qualified because I have no certificate, but they are pretty hard-pressed for teachers now. In this way I could get what I wanted now and when school is out in June, I'll go to Canada and visit around, and have a real rest.

.....Now, don't be concerned about me. I'm taking my quinine regularly now. I had forgotten to take it to N.Y. and that's why the fever. But it's all over now. I lost a few pounds, but Inez is feeding me up. She is very good to me. See you soon, I hope. Lovingly in Him, XXXX Ione

Ione also wrote to Marcellyn:

.....I surely miss Hector. We really got to know one another in N.Y. I stayed at the SIM Home and the folk there were just grand. I like Hector better than I ever tho't I could. I know we're going to have some grand times next fall. We bought the wedding rings and had them engraved; I have the one I shall give to him, and he took mine with him. They are identical and it will be fun getting together again. We had some pictures taken, too, which will sort of serve as wedding pictures. We visited the Canadian and Belgian Consulates to get necessary papers to be married as soon as I arrive. At Phila., they told me definitely I could go by plane in six months. Pray that nothing will hinder.

Please write and tell me what you want me to pray about.

Lovingly, Ione

On February 1, Hector wrote again to Ione from the ship which was the one that brought her back from Africa and the captain remembered her. Unlike Ione's letters, there are few details of the voyage apart from his seasickness but he did poignantly describe their parting in New York:

My Beloved:

"There is no fear in love; but perfect love casteth out fear."

This is just as true today as it was two weeks ago. The passing of time just gives a better understanding.

Where do you want me to start, dearie? Oh, yes, on the platform at the Penn Station after I last saw you through the window. Very fortunately, I knew my way back to the subway, because I would have been ashamed to ask anyone, with tears in my eyes. I had scarcely turned away from you when a surge of sorrow strained at my heart. Leaving the one who has meant more to me in three short weeks than anyone else.....on the escalator, in the subway, and later in the news reel I felt a loneliness that I had not anticipated. I tried to picture what you were doing; probably telling that girl about it all, explaining as best you could about our <u>*casual*</u> *parting. I think we rather surprised each other that we held to our contract. How brave you are; I think they call it stamina! Of course you can consider those you found in your housecoat pockets as having been given before.* [It is unclear what Hector is referring to here – maybe pictures or notes.] *The ones in the letters awaiting you and from now on, are the beginning of a new, and I hope short, regime.*

I almost forgot to tell you that I have been seasick all week. I had two full meals at the dining table; dinner or rather lunch today and lunch a week ago. Besides that, I have paid them four trial visits of about five minutes duration. The rest of my meals have been brought to my bedside. By now you have a distorted picture of a poor, languishing mortal. But no, I'm quite normal out on deck; sitting walking, talking, and reading. But the dining room up until today has been out of bounds to my anatomy. As I was telling one of the men yesterday, my sense of equilibrium isn't pivoted like an owl's head. But a balance or compromise seems to have been reached at last. One of the girls was accusing me of being more than seasick; but then I don't want to be cured of that until I see you again.

Two days later…

…..Here I am flat on my back again with the typewriter propped up in front of me. I have your big picture hung under the window; just your peaceful, patient self. The snaps [photos] *are right handy in my breast pocket.*

…..I'm going out for a walk now and when I return, I will tell you how I introduced myself to the captain.

He was not at the table the first meal, and I was not there for a long time after. But about the third night I went upstairs for coffee and happened to be sitting beside him. I quietly took out my snaps and handed him one and asked him if he knew who it was. He looked at it for a short moment and then with a smile looked up and said, "Miss Reed?" That opened up quite a conversation and I found out what he thought about you. He couldn't understand how you could be so <u>*patient*</u>*; and work such long hours. I told him what you told me about considering the situation if the children were your own. He has the greatest admiration for you.*

…..Do you know that I have had a lot of comfort out of the guitar. It seems to have a soothing effect. I've played most of the hymns in that little pocket hymnal. It's great to have those like, "How Firm a Foundation"; "Oh Safe to the Rock"; "Standing on the Promises". But then I come to part of the chorus where it says, …"Floods of joy o'er my soul like the sea billows roll", and I think that the one who wrote that must have been standing on the shore. At least he wasn't seasick!! Then too I have finished two of those books on masonry and that talked a lot

161

about stones, bricks, walls, footings and foundations. One would think that I soon should be established. But I'm happy. Plenty of time for Bible reading and prayer. How well I remember the precious sessions we had together. We seem to have gotten so much packed into those three weeks. It was all so wonderful and timely. Truly, Ione, these days have given me time to think and with all my thinking I cannot find anything wrong with you. Not to make you proud, because you are what you are. And most of all that you trust me. Things seem all different now. You're just a nice big armful of love ! ! !

    Goodbye for now, honey. Yours; past, present and future,   Hector

The January/February edition of UFM's *Light and Life* included the following:

    Rev. Hector McMillan has already sailed for the Belgian Congo. We take this opportunity to congratulate him and Miss Ione Reed on their official engagement. After a few months Miss Reed expects to return to the field where they will be united in marriage.

    …..Pray these young people arrive to the place of God's calling for them.

Hector arrived at Matadi on February 2nd and travelled on to Léopoldville on the 6th, where he arranged for a plane to take him up to Stanleyville on the 12th. He wrote to Ione:

    I was just reading a few verses before lunch and one in particular seems to apply. Acts 7:3…."Get thee out of thy country, and thy kindred, and come into the land which I shall show thee". The only difference is that Abraham had Sarah with him. But I have the promise which is almost as good.

    I'm wondering where you are just now. I have been trying to think of complications that might have arisen to change your schedule somewhat, but I know the Lord will continue to arrange all things as he has done for us in the past years.

    This is the 22nd letter I have written since we left Dakar [Senegal]. You will very likely read some of them as you travel around, but most importantly, I am sending regular mail, in fact all except the one home and to [page is torn here]. I suppose by now as you are reading along you are thinking, "Well, honey, when is he going to start telling me how much he loves me"? Well, honey, right now.

    The other evening just before I turned out the light above my little bed (number "12") I was gazing at your picture and said to myself, "Isn't she lovely. I suppose I would have been content with someone far inferior had not the Lord intervened. What a wonderful choice He has made for me!! ! !" Dearie, I want to continue always to love you for everything you are and have.

    …..That little set of tools have come in very handy. I have fixed two typewriters and two clocks already. I am able to schedule my time now that I am not bothered with seasickness. My trouble now is eating too much. I still read quite a lot and of course these letters have kept me gainfully employed. And I mustn't forget the washing and ironing.

    A little incident might interest you. At the table one day one of the girls regretted that she had no starch, so I loaned her my box. Several days later they were talking to the captain up on the second deck and I asked Miss Holland on the side if I could use the starch again. When she came back, I told the captain that you had sent it along with me. He suggested that I was becoming too dependent, and so I agreed and said I could hardly live without you. "Vell", he replied, "You have a wonderful girl; she had to look after the children and keep them happy, do all the washing and ironing and yet was always so pleasant and never tired. Tired, yes, but didn't show it." I assured him that I was going to treat you royally and spoil you for the first ten years. I didn't mention any thing about the six children.[36]

.....The guitar seems still to come in for a lot of use. I have developed a new system of fingering, which lends some variety. I hope it doesn't warp too much with the dampness.

There are a few verses that I want to put on before I close. Recently when I have been praying for you, I have looked them up and used them. "And this I pray, that your love may abound yet more and more in knowledge and in all judgement; and that ye may approve things that are excellent; that ye may be sincere and without offence till the day of Christ Jesus, unto the glory and praise of God." I'm sure that included everything and I know the Lord will answer abundantly.

Once again let me say that I love you with all my heart ! ! ! !
Yours only, X X Hector..

On the February 7, Ione wrote to the Westcotts at Ypsilanti from Pontiac:
Dear Doctor and Ellen and A B C[37]:

It has been several weeks since I talked to you over the telephone and I have been wondering what you are doing, what your plans are, etc. I believe you said that Ellen was in the hospital. Is she still there, or has she come home? Do the children like school? What subjects especially?

.....I spent a week with Lucille and Maurice at Charlevoix and we had a grand time. Esther, Lawrence and Ruthie are quite like your three and they ask so many questions about them. I visited Esther in school and spoke to the fifth and sixth grades in geography class. I spoke here at high school in three of four rooms. The teachers are all so interested in Africa. I have talked several times with the Sup't of Schools and he has put me on the substitute teacher's list, so I expect to be called at any time now beginning Monday. I will substitute in any grade. I think I have more nerve than good sense, but Inez thinks I'll get more out of this than some Normal School work. What do you think? There is an extension course starting here now from Ypsi in Child Psychology and I can get into that. And I also want to come down to Ypsi and visit the practice teaching classes. I talked to a recent graduate Monday and she said they allow anyone in. This teaching

---

[36] It seemed Hector and Ione had discussed how many children they would have. Indeed, they had 6 children!

[37] Ione's charming way of addressing Anne, Bobbie and Charlotte.

job pays $8 a day, and everyone who has taken this substitute work has been kept busy nearly all the time.

Started making arrangements for a Singer Sewing Machine Course. It costs $10 and takes 8 weeks of 2-hour lessons. They meet evenings and I can get into a 6-scholar class in March. But I haven't been able to make arrangements about French yet. Miss Avery is not teaching just now and I don't know who else to get in touch with. There is nothing in evening school here.

What do you think about my taking back a gun [to Africa]*? Someone wants to give me a rifle and a side-arm, I guess that's a pistol. Would it be a help, do you think, or a bother, and what permits do I have to have? I think it's a 30-30. What equipment should I take back in the line of general school supplies?*

How did you find your Mother and Father in Ypsi? And Florence? Have you seen the sister in Detroit yet? If I had her address I could see her sometime. With much love, Ione

In the margins of the letter are notes made by Ione of the Doctor's views on the guns and responses to her questions: OK; none; only have guns in cabin baggage readily accessible on entering at Boma; a 22 is good for small game, inexpensive of ammunition, light to carry & lots of fun; you'd seldom use a 30-30 but a 22 would be handy. A repeater is OK, better than an automatic; figure out when you take practice teaching.

Ione also wrote to Hector on February 7:

Dearest One,

.....What a surprise to have your letter written at sea. I just could hardly believe my eyes, for I tho't surely I would not hear again for at least a month! Thanks so much for getting this to me. Sorry you have been seasick. I have written two letters to you, sending one to the Swedish Mission in Matadi, and one to the U.M.H., at Leo. Maybe you can trace them if you haven't received them. This letter, to be on schedule, should not be written for a week yet, but I couldn't wait the two weeks this time. And if you get an extra one now and then you won't mind, will you?

I love you so much, Hector. No matter where I go, each new experience makes me love you more. When I see how marvellously the Lord has led us, I am ashamed that I doubted that I would be all right. I had so many doubts when I was coming across the ocean. I was afraid that after all you and I were not meant for one another. I was afraid that when I got back to Pontiac with the old crowd you would seem different from them and they would feel strange toward you. But here I am, and altho' you are not here, they are hearing plenty about you. And the more I talk, the keener I am for our anticipated marriage. And lonesome, -; I tho't I was lonesome out in the Ituri Forest [in northeastern Congo]*, but there was no comparison to here. In the midst of all the howdies and handshakes and good eats I am truly lonesome. And I know it's for you, because it is a relief to go to sleep when I can dream about you. Last night I dreamed you had come back, and I didn't know whether to feel terrible or good, for I want you there,* *but it's so lonely without you. If I could just talk over things with you and ask your advice it would be such a help. If I could just feel your arms around me and sigh and sigh it would be sooooo comfortable.*

The pictures came Monday and really are nice [see photo at left]. *I want you to tell me some folk you wish to have one. I have sent one of the small ones to the Pudneys and to you. Then I tho't we should send one to the sisters and the farm, my sisters and Mother. I believe I will need 20 more of that size. And I will send you some of the stamps* [stamp-sized ones] *too. I'll send for 200 more. Last night the class that supports me had a banquet reception, and I couldn't resist putting a stamp in each spoon at the tables. There were over 90 there. I handed the envelope to the head waitress and she never gave it back so I guess they were all taken. And the one I had at my place someone came and asked me for. They surely went crazy over them! I never saw such a silly bunch of women. You see it was near Valentine's Day and they were sentimental and finding the picture in a spoon makes one think of "spooning" or love-making and they had a lot of fun over it. They gave me $33 and two boxes of chocolates.*[38]

.....I came back to town on the 2nd and found your letter from the boat. And I also found that I was on the substitute teacher's list and will be called beginning the 12th so will need to stay around here. They are so in need of teachers that I expect to be busy, tho' not all of the time. I am glad it is not regular, for I can have free times to rest and study. I want to get French and an 8-week Singer Sewing Machine evening course and an extension course of Child Psychology from the Ypsi State Normal (correspondence). Then in June I'll take a real vacation. I have written Jean that it appears I will not be able to come [to the McMillan farm in Avonmore] *until then unless there is a long spring vacation.*

I hope I am making the right plans. I prayed definitely that the Lord would direct me about this teaching. I really didn't want to do it now, but it would be so much more expensive to go away to school and if it would give me the same training and same experience, I feel I just can't turn it down. I do want to be a better Congo teacher. I could have taken some nurse's training, but I have tried to watch operations and help Doctor and up to a certain point I'm all right and then I'm a flop. I get all woozy and have to get out. I hope you can do a better job of it. And the teaching goes along so closely with the evangelist work that I'm trained for and love so. I think you will be glad that I made this choice. I've gotten some good pointers already from the high school English teacher.

---

[38] Ione enjoyed chocolate her whole life.

Everyone is so good to answer my questions. And I learned how to string beads nicely in the jewelry store the other day.

I have been doing some speaking and renewing old acquaintances. Churches around here that have sent gifts and letters are wanting me to come for an evening or a Sunday service, and I have given a short word in various places. Tomorrow night I'll go to Clarkston and Friday to Brown City 1-1/2 hr's journey. Sunday morning I'll go to the Memorial Bapt. in town. Pray for these contacts that they may not be wasted. I want these people to learn how to be intercessory missionaries, and have deeper knowledge of what foreign missions mean.

.....I got in a good word for Pearl the other day. Poor girl, I don't want the friends here to feel that she is the insubordinate little rascal that Dr. Westcott pictures her to be! She is independent, but I admire her spunk and I believe it will help her to carry on in difficult times. I believe her class at the church still loves her and tho' I haven't talked to them yet, I think they are planning to send her some dispensary things. Give her my love and tell her I am trying to scatter the good seed in her behalf.

.....If you think of things that will be good equipment for the work write and tell me and I can apply some work funds in their behalf. Keep yourself well. I hope you can eat lots to make up for the lack of appetite you have had. Drink lots of water and don't forget your quinine. I still have to take mine! If I don't, I get achy and feverish.

Someone accused us of holding hands in our picture. It does sort of look like it, doesn't it? And they say your head is awfully close to mine. But why shouldn't it be, and has it not been closer? I didn't tell them that. But how I wish it were close right now? I MISS you, Hector. I just can't live much longer without you! You are so good to me. You did so much for me while we were together. I haven't forgotten the many little things as well as the big ones. Thank you so much. I love you.

Yours in Him, Ione

Ione wrote to the Pudneys about her recent activities and thanked them for the precious times in their sitting room when she and Hector visited and when Hector gave her the ring.

It is evident that the Westcotts were well known in her home church in Pontiac and a great deal of tact and diplomacy was required on Ione's part in dealing with the fragility of Ellen's mental state which was not disclosed. Ione divulged that almost no one in the church knew the truth about Mrs Westcott's condition. Ione hoped no one would ask.

She was trying to make arrangements to get Conversational French in the high school where she worked. She praised the Lord for making it possible for her to be in Congo these past years, and she trusted Him to direct in every plan for returning. Her greatest desire was that souls would come to know Christ as Saviour. And while she was home, she endeavored to be an intercessory missionary on behalf of those out in Congo.

On February 10, Hector wrote from Léopoldville to his family:

Dear Sister Florence and family:

How do you like getting a letter all the way from Africa? Well, I'm just as thrilled to write it.

I was just trying to compare it with some similar situation at home, when I suddenly realized that it was still February. I'm just sitting here comfortably warm. It is 5:20 in the afternoon, and the air is quite cool after a refreshing rain. It's something like a warm August day in Avonmore.

And what do you think of my sweetheart!!! I'm just waiting for letters from each member of the family and I know you all think just the same as I do. Well, the Lord has been good to us. The weeks spent together have left both of our hearts so happy and satisfied. She is everything that I expected in a girl; being neither forward nor backward.

The trip out was so enjoyable. We really hated to leave the boat. I was very fortunate to be able to make a plane reservation from here to Stanleyville, leaving next Monday Feb. 12. It means that I will have made the whole journey in less than a month at a cost of about $800.

Some prayer material might be summed up in these words. "How many of God's servants there are who, while giving their lives to His service, frankly confess that the feebleness of their spiritual life as a missionary, and the inadequate results of mission work as a whole, are due to the failure to make the leisure and, when secured, rightly to use it, for DAILY COMMUNION WITH GOD."

May the Lord enrich your life as a watered garden.

Yours, Hector

On February 19, George Kerrigan at Bongondza wrote to Ione describing Hector's arrival. The rambling letter shows Kerrigan's mischievous Scottish humour:

Dear Ione,

No doubt you will be hearing of the surprise which Bongondza had last Thursday. Mail had left in the morning and as the tabs,[39] were on holiday, I did not expect anything till Friday at the earliest. I had been busy typing the results of our meeting with the Doctor last July and then I had stencilled the copies and had got the machine out ready to duplicate them when a car drove on to the station and stopped outside the house. Went out to greet whoever it was, as I thought it was the Cotonco [cotton company] man who has come to reside at Kole and with whom I have had some talk. First a tall white man stepped out whose white suite seemed a little soiled; I went along and he said that he was McMillan. This (for some inexplicable reason) conveyed little to me as I was more interested in seeing Mr Bastin getting out of the driver's seat so greeted

---

[39] "Tab", is a shortened term form of "batarabai", sub-instructor below the head teacher.

him and the mines chap who seemed as though he had been pulled through a hedge backwards. Then the first white man who seemed rather old began to unload some things from the car so I thought that a visitor had come and very nearly said that the doctor had left on furlough when on looking at the things I saw H. and then it dawned on me that Hector had come. No word from the States, no word from Leo and here he was on the doorstep. Boy!!! (This is the word I have heard most from him since his arrival) weren't we glad to see him. Bastin and friends went off and then we immediately went along to Vee's. There we were invited to tea so back we went and your lordship had a wash and brush up (cost nothing) and then we went over to tea (largely water – you know how these boys act on a special occasion) and were invited to supper. My four sheets of stencils were lying there so I invited Hector to unpack as I was busy. He was soon back again and took over the job of the duplicating while I got the mail sack open and found his telegram from Leo. We worked well and the fifty sheets of each page were done with a few minutes left for me to shave and spruce myself up – in honour of our illustrious visitor. Over to supper where he passed on all the news of the various folks and your name seemed to come into the conversation rather more than it should but I suppose that is because he seems to be in LOVE.

Next day, so that there would be no mistakes made in his case and that he could not say he was misled by the lack of rules, regulations, suggestions, etc. I went through with him the bunch of papers mentioned above. We commenced before breakfast and we adjourned at 11:30 p.m. We covered a good deal of ground in that time. We did not move out of the house, nor did we have the usual midday siesta. I think that the day was profitably spent. We touched on most subjects under the sun but largely mission affairs.

Both cars were out of commission so he was going to commence [working] *on the Ekoko car; but as I had intended to try my hand on the spring of Kinso's car, one of the spring leaves broken, I got him commenced on that. He found three leaves broken so how I have been carrying on I do not know. Alas, we had only one replacement so I sent the lad off on Saturday afternoon to Mr Bastin to see if there were any springs to be had there. We had been over and got your gramophone (am getting rather tired of hearing your voice singing the few songs over and over again but he seems to like it – funny how tastes differ). So, we went again on Saturday last afternoon to get something else and he gave a gasp, as white ants had come up a pin-hole in the floor and had made tracks for the pile of boxes which contained things of yours and the Ludwig's. They seemed to have got into yours so as Hector had the keys, I got him commenced on the bottom of the box and quite a hole crumpled away in our fingers but they had not commenced on the contents. As I had been down the day or so before and had seen nothing, they had only had a day or so to work. We have scattered the boxes all over the place temporarily to see if the Paris Green works in the destruction of the pests. Hector was greatly interested in it all and as I say all I heard was "Boy" – I feel like telling him that I have now grown to man's estate.*

Sunday I spoke at the service and he visited a village in the afternoon with me while Vee and Joan went further afield. We again listened to a further repetition of your voice after the service on Sunday night.

This morning he had his first Bangala lesson after breakfast and then he set about the car again as the lad had returned with a couple of leaves. He worked on that the rest of the day, practically while I did what I do with the tabs – looked on and found tools for him to work with. As a matter of fact, he had started another job earlier on. I got up early, as the previous night I found the well had run dry, so I got up early and after I had pumped for a quarter of an hour, I found there was still no water as one of the taps had again gone haywire. So, I had no wash, nor he but he soon set it to rights, so were able to struggle so we filled the car and pumped up the tyres and we hope to leave for Buta tomorrow afternoon. I intend to stay if possible at two of the teachers along the main road probably Ngambo and Angada for a day each. This will get H. initiated into the work though it will throw back his Bangala lessons a bit – but not as much as in certain other people's cases I know. Well Hector has come at a most convenient time and from my conversations with him and his attitude to things in general, I think that he will make good. He is of the type who seem to make good out here. As no doubt he will grow thin under my expert cook's care there is only one thing to be done and that is to send an S.O.S. to the States for someone to come and look after him though I will extend to you what was extended to me by an old missionary, "Don't marry your cook, marry your queen". I accepted this advice and have been sorry ever since. Well, well, well, now I have blethered so much I will draw to a close hoping that you are having a good time wherever you are and gaining strength for a new term on the Field. Vee is sorry she has never heard from you. And you know my tears have fallen thick and fast for a like reason but do not believe all you hear or you will eat all you see. Cheerio and all the best. Remember me to anybody who asks after me but if they don't ask after me don't trouble. I take it H. is asleep in the guest room as it is now 10:45 so I will toddle also to the same place in the hopes of forgetting my troubles in the arms of Morpheus – do you know that gent?

Yours in Him, Keri

Another person pleased to hear of Hector's arrival was Jim Carter, the finance director of UFM in the field. He wrote to Hector from Boyulu on February 21, and although brief, it echoes Ione's thoughts that existing missionaries were very keen for new blood to help with the work:

Dear Mr McMillan,

Very many thanks for your cable and letter which I received by mail last Thursday. You know by now of course, that when I received them Thursday evening you were well on your way out to Bongondza. We have been looking forward to your arrival for a long time, and were so very pleased to hear of your arrival at Stanleyville. We await the Burks' arrival now and do so hope that they made contact with the steamer to leave Portugal this month. They are, as you probably know, coming out to us here at Boyulu.

Ione wrote to Hector's family, saying that after school closed on May 25, she planned to be on the train heading for Toronto, Dunnville, Montreal, and anywhere else she could find some McMillans!

She hoped to make a week-end trip to Chicago and buy a wedding dress:

.....Oh, I really don't have to buy it there, for I can get any number just like I want right here or anywhere. But there are some book firms I want to visit for Congo School supplies, and it will be fun getting the dress there, too. I want it to be cotton so the bugs won't chew it up and a design simple enough to cut off the skirt and use it for Sundays and parties (IF we have any parties!). Hector says he can wear white and my dress will be white. I will need to take cake decorations and all the things that make a nice wedding, for none can be purchased there. It was a bit of a disappointment not to be married here. I had bro't back things for light housekeeping should we be married here, and had planned the attendants, etc. But it will be nice for the natives to see a real Christian wedding.

Ione was sent two letters on February 24, the first was from Pearl:

Dear Ione,

What an age it does seem since you left us, but now Hector has come and is digging in to Bangala, and it makes us feel as if you are almost on the way back, although of course, we realize that it is a bit too soon for that. Vee and I are still meeting together for prayer each day, as we used to long ago in Ma Kinso's house, and you may be sure that you are constantly remembered at the Throne of Grace. Now we have heard you singing, and seen your snaps, so you seem somehow nearer.

Although Hector flew up from Leo, and so could not bring much baggage he found room for the frocks which you have so kindly sent us. You really are a dear, they are all so pretty. I tried mine on that very night, but the big lamp was up to its tricks, and in the light of the lantern it was not possible to see very well. It was easy to tell which one was mine as it was the longest. A big, big THANK YOU dear.

Pearl gave Ione up-to-date details of some of her students and a few of the house helpers on the station, then continues:

.....There was quite a lot of excitement on the station yesterday, for quite a big animal from the forest came right across, from the direction of the Doctor's. He went behind Vee's house, and broke the pipe bringing the water into her bathroom, came lumbering along, broke through the bushes between this house, and the empty one, and made off in the direction of the cooks' mafika [cook house]. Samwele and Sema went after him, but there has been such a long dry season that they lost his tracks. He was a dark colored animal, about as big as a very big pig. I happened to see him as I was returning to the house for some chalk.

The second letter was from Viola Walker:

Dear Ione,

You can very well imagine our amazement last week when a car drove onto the station and Hector emerged! It is true we had already here some of his boxes, but no further word of his, or of the Burk's departure had reached us, and I suppose we just felt "Nothing ever happens". Needless to say, we were as delighted as we were surprised, it seems as if the receding wave has started to return. Any day now we may also hear of the Burk's arrival at Leo. So, we praise the Lord and take courage. It should be now only four or five months till we hear of the Kinso's and of Eve and Isobel's (Whitehead) departure, and maybe our Verna and Miss Rutt. And then three more from England are not so very long after that.[40] I trust, dear Ione will be on the way back. 1945 should have to be a year of rejoicing.

It was sweet of you to send us a dress, and would you believe it, that young man of yours actually brought them in the plane to get them to us quickly! Mine is perfectly lovely (to my mind) than all the others. Because it just suits me. (I did not tell anyone that I thought so, however!) Thanks kutu-kutu [thousands] Ione. I will not be ashamed now if someday I go to Stan and stay in the hotel.

This hot season has been, and still is, the longest, hottest, driest season that even older people can remember. I have never been so hot for so long a period of time, I am sure of that! Yesterday some big animal of the forest, apparently crazed by the heat, ran across the station from one side and back into the forest on the other side. It broke the pipes of my bathroom tank in passing, so, in this sticky heat, I once more have to have water doled out by stingy pail-fulls. The natives (only children saw the animal, and Pearl) think it may have been an Okapi, from the conflicting descriptions.[41]

.....Do you remember the nice little teacher among the Basali, Anziambo? He has had quite a nasty accident, we hear. A gun exploded, and the powder entered his eyes. For a week or more he was not able to see at all, or open his eyes, but Ndunda says he can open one a bit now. I trust and pray he may not be blinded. Kibibi, whom he hopes to marry, or should I say, she hopes to marry him? is here with me now – her father is making a terrific trouble about it all and it seems that it may have to be abandoned. The old rascal. Kibibi just tells me her father came up today and Hector pulled one of his wicked old teeth. Wish I had known, and I could have told Hector to pull them all.

.....How is Ellen? Hector was saying how thrilled Charlotte was with New York! I can quite imagine! Are the children in school?

---

[40] Viola may well be alluding to the anticipated arrival of the Walby's; Alf and Eileen, parents of this book's co-author, Laureen. They sailed from Southhampton, UK, in the first ship to travel without naval convoy after the war as it was felt there was less threat from mines laid during the war.

[41] This is quite likely since the western edge of the Okapi Wildlife Reserve is only 70 miles east of Bongondza.

I must cease this ramble, Ione. Sorry there seems so pitifully little news. But as I say, I have just been here all holidays, and am nearly bored to death, so can't sound very interested even on paper! We pray for you all daily, and hope to see you back, Ione, but as soon as you are really, really rested and refreshed. Greetings to your mother and sisters, whose voices, - with yours, - on the records, gave us great pleasure Sunday evening. I could almost see you standing there by the piano singing. We often, often wish it were possible to hear your sweet voice, especially do I want to hear you sing our own favourite choruses, "I'll Sing it, & Tell it, Wherever I Go!".

Lovingly, Viola

On March 1, Pearl, now stationed at Maganga, wrote to Hector welcoming him:

Dear Hector,

Greetings, salutations and hallucinations too if you like them (as Ione would say). You certainly did surprise me. I didn't realize you would be here so soon, or would have had my greeting off to meet you on the way. I was expecting you and Ione to come as man and wife. So, you kissed her right on the pier. Well, being a nurse, I do know that part of her anatomy but I noticed that you were most cautious not to give the number – of course the number of the pier – wouldn't think of questioning the number of anything else – Ha! Ha! It's a real treat to be able to write a bit of humor in a letter. I do hope you fell in love with Bongondza like I did. It will forever and always be the place I call our African home (Ione's and mine), that house next to Kinso's house! Since you're not yet married, I can't congratulate you on that point, but I can say that if your time spent living with Ione is as happy and inspirationally spiritual as mine was, you will live happy ever after.

I noticed and appreciated the fact that you called me Pearl of great price. However, I am Pearl of no value now[42] so I'm singing, "Pennsylvania, here I come. Right back where I started from, etc." It's a great disappointment for me but perhaps it is "His appointment". There is the possibility that we may meet once before I leave. In the meantime, I'll say "Fight the good fight of faith and keep close, very close to the Master."

Yours in Him, Pearl

Ione wrote to Hector on the April 10, saying that her teaching experience provided many ideas and she hoped to go to Ypsilanti to investigate possibilities of further studies. She took French each Thursday evening for two hours and sewing on Tuesdays for two hours. Her life was meaningful but she looked forward more and more to the Canadian visit. There had been numerous gifts for the work as well as personal expenses. The Westcotts sent a check for $100 to pay for a food order for the Congo from a company in New York. She also looked for a set of dishes and

---

[42] A strange comment given the boundless work Pearl undertook before she contracted tuberculosis.

wondered if Hector was eating with Mr Jenkinson or chopping (preparing food) alone.

In a letter to the Westcotts on April 11, Ione thanked them for their gift. She also mentioned Russell Bemis, the man who was giving her a gun, wanted her to get a statement on paper that she could take a gun into the Congo. He was afraid there would be a limitation on the number of shells one could carry. Russell was going with her to the police station to get a license. Ione told Russell that she didn't need a revolver, but he insisted that she accept it and had paid at least $40 for it. They made plans to go out to the Gun Club for some instructions.

Three days later, Ione wrote to her friend, Pearl - mostly updating her on news since her boat trip across the Atlantic from Congo with the Westcotts. She gave details of her meeting with Hector in New York:

My dearest Pearl,

My neglect of you has not been intentional I assure you. I have thought of you so much and missed you, too, for, coming back to the Mission Home in Philadelphia did not seem the same without you. I intended to write but have been doing too much I guess for when I sit down, I go to sleep. For a few days I did nothing but sleep when I first came to Pontiac, and even now I feel that I never get enough. How tired you must be now. I wondered if you got the dress I had chosen for you when Hector passed out the dresses. I hope it was not too terribly large, and that I matched the hat Frances sent from Léopoldville.

The trip over was not hard, tho, during the hurricane I was busy both day and night.[43] It was grand having Hector meet the boat, and I was so surprised I dropped the things I had in my hand. And in spite of my appearance (I was all bundled up in a skirt and sweaters!) he took me off to a nice hotel to eat. We helped the Westcott's get off to her people in Pa., and then I let down. It seemed so strange having no one to take care of. I was in a daze, and I stayed in the daze until Hector had given me the love ring that I'm wearing! We had some grand days in Philadelphia, and then I went down to Tennessee where Mother and Marcellyn are attending Bob Jones College. I came back in time to stay at Philadelphia a few days more and then go to N.Y. to see Hector off on our same boat. [This confirms the previous reference in Hector's letter where the captain remembers Miss Reed]. *It was hard seeing him for just such a short time, but the future looks bright and it's so nice anticipating the wedding out there. I tho't you could be my attendant, but now I hear you are coming* [back to the United States] *the middle of May.*

So many people have asked about you. After Hector left, I was sick at Philadelphia for a few days with malaria, and Frances was there then and she showed me the letter you had sent about your needs there and the bad condition of the dispensary at first. Dr. was here ahead of me, and had a conference with

---

[43] This is perhaps why there are no letters describing her voyage home, unlike her voyage out to the Belgian Congo.

the Board of Missions. I don't know what was said, but several have asked me about why you are at Maganga. I just tell them as little as possible and stick to the truth. They do not blame you for anything. I have found that the less I refer to the difficulties, the better I get along. [This would suggest that there were issues between Pearl and the Doctor – which were probably professional - rather than just Ellen's illness.] *No one understands anyhow! It's hard for folk here to have a conception of how things are out there.*

Ione recounted her current program of activities: relief teaching, the sewing lessons, French classes etc.:

.....There's so much I want to do while I'm home that it's hard to rest. I intend visiting Hector's people in June. I had hoped to go there in Feb., but felt I should take advantage of this teaching experience. And the girls in Canada agree that June is a better month to spend there. I'm not really taking meetings like deputation, but there have been many places I have gone to greet them and give a short talk. I've averaged a meeting a day since I arrived. Funny how they count up.

Our life at Bongondza seems all a dream now. We had some grand times there together. I hope you get home before I go back and we can have a real talk about old times. I hope you can get to see our house once more before you leave. It seems so good that Hector's room faces out on it. But I don't suppose he'll be there very long, he'll probably be 'chopping' himself. I am wondering how long he will be at Bongondza. He seems to be getting along in Bangala. I get such a thrill out of the things he tells me and that he is experiencing some of the same things as we. I can see that it is a better for him to have had a head start and get used to things before we are married, but I surely wish I were there. I wish, too, that he could have waited for me, but he was so needed out there, I could not wish it otherwise really.

Folk here are wondering if you are coming home because of your health, or because your term is finished. Ellen has gained about 16 pounds and does look better. She has a hearing apparatus now and new glasses. She seems awfully tired, but I believe is stronger. They live with Dr's folks in Ypsilanti. His mother cannot walk and his father is blind in one eye. They have no one to help with the housework, so I guess it's not too easy for Ellen. The children are fine, Charlotte and Bob have had their tonsils out and Anne has glasses. They are in the 1st, 5th, 7th grades. They did a lot of school work on the way home.

I don't know whether you knew I am staying with Inez Slater. She teaches high school; I have gotten a lot of good pointers from her. My Mother surprised me by going to college this year. She is taking pipe organ, piano, English, Bible, Psychology, and not doing badly. She and Marcellyn have an apartment. Doris was divorced from her husband and now has a diamond from someone else. I have not seen her yet, but she has promised to come here May 4 or 5. Lucille and her husband have a new church just outside of Lansing. I spent a week with them.

.....Weren't you shocked to hear about our President? [Franklin D. Roosevelt] *I listened to the radio every spare minute today and heard all about the funeral. It surely seems strange to have him die so suddenly. Sometimes the Lord has to knock away our human props to make us trust Him more. He has been so precious to me. Life seems very strange and mysterious these days, and I wonder how everything will turn out. But God is still on the throne and "where His finger points, His hand will make a way." I have heard so many inspirational messages and such lovely music recently. It is good to be home once more.*

I have never forgiven myself for giving you back that bill as I did. I'm sure the Lord would have taken care of my needs somehow. I am so sorry about it. How did you come out with finances? I read your recent letter and the cable which answered it. I wondered what your reaction would be to the cable. Well, we'll talk about it when I see you. But write me now and maybe I'll get it before you come. I know you'll have a home if you come to Pontiac, so plan to stick around here a while. I think they will understand everything better if you stay a little while and fellowship with them. They really love you and want to see you.

Love to all the friends there. I haven't forgotten Vee and Joan. I still love them. Greet them when you see them. Greet the Kerrigan's, too. And tell the Carters to give the babies (Rosemary, Gordon, and Philip) a hug for me. Ask Betty if her dress fits.

Lovingly, Ione

Nothing is said in the letters about why Pearl left Bongondza. It seems odd that the mission leaders would move her from Bongondza as it was left without medical cover particularly when in the past Pearl deputised for the Doctor so ably. Perhaps it was an unspoken-of clash of personalities between Pearl and Dr Westcott. Also, people of all nationalities travelled from far and wide to the hospital to receive care. Perhaps the mission felt that by removing some personnel, word would spread that the hospital had limited facility and staff to care for so many. Regardless, Pearl took the message from the book of James (Ch. 1:19-25) as the right approach to dealing with the issues.

About this time of year, Hector wrote to his family. As there were no shops in the heart of Africa, mail order catalogues were the only way of purchasing gifts. Hector was obviously thinking ahead, probably to Christmas and realised there are things he didn't know about his family:

.....First of all, how are the children? I was looking through Montgomery-Ward's catalogue this afternoon and in the section for children's clothes there were different sized girls on each page and I was thinking about Joan and Audrey. Have they grown about 4" since I last saw them? I'm sure Dougie has anyway. Ione will soon be writing and telling me just how big they are. She was up visiting her sister Lucille in Northern Michigan and saying that the three children up there still prayed for Uncle Hector. She said she wanted to mean as much to my nieces and nephews. So, after her visit I will want to hear from you

just what has happened; how they went out walking with her and how she told them stories and sang for them ----- etc.

.....I'm expecting a letter from home soon. Ione was sorry that she had to change her plans about the visit to Canada. But it will still be alright in June. I do hope that she will have a time with Jean and probably will be able to help her spiritually. I do wish you could all come out to the wedding. I would like to have it in America but the Lord has seen fit to order things thus and it will receive His blessing just as well out here. I still can hardly believe that I am to be the bridegroom. I was reading in John 3 the other day and came upon this verse, "He that hath the bride is the bridegroom: but the friend of the bridegroom, which standeth and heareth him, rejoiceth greatly because of the bridegroom's voice..." I would count it quite a privilege to be the best man at Ione's wedding!!!

Well dearie, I better close for this time. Someday I am going to attempt writing a decent letter to each one of the family. I feel as though I have neglected each of you so much in these last few years. But I trust you will try to keep me informed regarding your affairs and especially how the Lord is blessing your family. I still remember the night that the girls and Bill accepted the Lord. May they continue to read their Bibles.

Good-bye for now and may the Lord's blessing be upon you until we are translated into His Heavenly Kingdom.

Yours, Hector

On May 2, Ione finally knew that Hector had arrived safely, and she wrote to him about having been in Pontiac nearly four months and averaging a meeting a day with 29 young people professing conversion and 5 offering their lives for the mission field. She also told of her reunion at long last with her sister Doris:

.....Last night I had the joy of meeting Doris at the bus depot. She came in at midnight from California and we will be together for a few weeks. We were so thrilled that we just clung to one another and couldn't say anything for a long time. It was a long journey and she did not take a sleeper, so I'm trying not to disturb her this morning (hence the pencil instead of the pen, which is in her room). I am not teaching today so we're going to have a real talk when she wakens. We'll have to make up for the past four years! She is planning to be married in August, and as far as I know he is not a Christian, but she says "he would make a good one"! She looks older, but not a great deal different. She seems more my age now and I feel we'll have more in common than before.

.....I am waiting for a letter telling me of your impressions and feelings now that you have gotten to know the work and the people there. How do you think Mr and Mrs Hector McMillan will fit into the picture? I am getting very anxious to be Mrs McMillan. It is a big responsibility but the Lord will make me equal to it. I remember so many things now about you that I did not think of when we were together. You are so full of pep and energy and keen to get started on everything. And you are so strong in physique and character. I know that you're going to be

the kind of husband that I've always dreamed I'd have. Please tell me more about everything out there.

I had a grand letter from both Vee and Joan, as well as Keri. So far as I know I am still planning to come out in August, tho' I've not heard from Mr Pudney on the matter. I expect to see your dear ones in just a few weeks now. I had a lovely letter from Alice yesterday. I am enclosing some things of interest to you:

"Singing is sweet, but be sure of this,
Lips only sing when they cannot kiss."

Very lovingly yours, Ione

In a letter to Dr Westcott and family, Ione filled them in on her teaching experience and some time at the rifle range with Russell Bemis practicing in anticipation of shooting snakes in Africa. She registered her pistol at the police station and received a nice holster for it with additional pockets on the right-hand side for the "harness-like thing" for extra shells and handcuffs. But instead of handcuffs, she'd put a drinking cup.

The May/June edition of *Light and Life* published the following article by Hector:

BELGIAN CONGO – Arrived – Unannounced   By Rev. Hector McMillan

The Lord has wonderfully answered prayer and I am sure that all things have worked out to His glory.

It would have been a rare sight for you [the reader] to have been standing behind a tree, watching Mr Kerrigan when the car drove into the yard here a week ago last Thursday. He had no idea that I had even left America. Just now I have been rehearsing the event with him as he sits at the other desk here in Mr Jenkinson's office. I take it that he is writing you a more graphic account than I can ever hope to give.

We quickly became the best of friends and these past few days have given me experiences and contacts that usually do not fall to missionaries until they have been on the field for some months. If I could have had fever this week the catalogue would have been complete. I arrived on Thursday, started language study on Monday and went out on trek on Tuesday, sleeping two nights in native villages, and enjoying the unique privilege of a close link between a prayer-meeting in America and the subjects of prayer on the field. I regret one thing, namely that each one of the prayer partners is not here to see what wonders the Lord hath wrought. I am left with this fact searching my heart. It is fairly easy to preach the truths of salvation and see results but then who is there to travail until Christ be formed in these converts.

The work here on the station is all very interesting, that is, outside of language study time. Last Sunday was especially impressive, when Miss Joan Pengilly's boys and Miss Walker's girls marched up in front of the church, in their various modes of dress. They cast curious glances at this new white man who had just arrived from a far-off land. To show their appreciation, the girls sang a little song that Ione taught them. The service was taken by Mr Kerrigan and even though I knew only a few words, his actions spoke louder than words! The God of the impossible was illustrated by Christ feeding the five thousand and Peter walking on the water.

This morning brought two interesting events. One was the hiring of my first staff member whose name means "this man is all right". The other was a man who came to have his sore tooth pulled out. It was a back molar, and fortunately quite loose. It was my first attempt so I was grateful for Mr Kerrigan's encouragement. The payment is to be a chicken ! !

Hector pulling teeth in the roadway at Bongondza.

Language study is a lot easier when one hears it spoken all the time. I'm always asking Mr Kerrigan what he says to the boys and their reply. We have our lesson usually after breakfast. Then the cars have come in for a bit of repair. It is very handy here since Mr Jenkinson had a platform built out beyond the end of the garage.

It will be a great day when this field is fully staffed. There is plenty of work for all, so we will continue to ask the Lord to lay the burden on many hearts.

Hector wrote to Ione on June 2 from Bongondza. Parts of the letter are missing, presumably chewed by mice. Hector wanted to write one letter to Ione at Avonmore, but the letter didn't reach her (while she was away visiting) and was forwarded on to Pontiac. Hector tried to imagine what it was like for Ione at Avonmore:

.....I have been thinking much about you and what you are doing just now. It will be such a thrill for my folks to meet you. The farm will seem strange to you at first but I hope that you will be able to walk all up and down the spacious fields and lanes where I spent so many years of my life. Dad will be showing you all the things that Hector made. But don't believe it all! Archie will try to keep him to the truth in all his story-telling. Jean will be glad that you were able to change your visit from Feb. to June. If I were there, we would have a JUNE wedding instead of Sept. (boyo te?) [isn't that so?].

And just to think that the mail came last week and there were no letters for me. Everybody seemed so sorry.[44] But I wrote in my diary that it isn't Ione's fault if the mail is slow. However, I did get something – rather eased the pain. I had sent a roll of film down with Pearl and prints came back. They turned out quite

---

[44] Hector's lack of mail seems to be of high interest amongst the missionaries as Jim Carter writes to Hector in a short pencil scribbled note thanking him for sharing a story about how he met Ione and ends with – "Trust the evening mail brings you reams".

well. I rather think that I'll make three of each, one for herself, one for you and one for me. I had planned on sending you one at least, but the weight would mean there would be just a short note on a tiny piece of paper, so I will do what I surmise is right. We are all wondering just what is going on over in America. Every time I expect to hear of the decisions reached in the council meetings. [part of letter is chewed away] *all come sooner or later. Kinsos will be the first of the station parties to leave. Sometime in July I think they said.*

.....This is about the length of my say-so.

All my love, Hector X

There are no records of letters written during Ione's first visit to Avonmore, however, in 1964 she wrote the following:

THEIR BROTHER HECTOR

Hector's sisters were always like my own sisters, from the time we first met. It was after Hector had gone out to Congo for the first time and I was waiting for my first furlough to end so that I could go out to be married to him.

In June, 1945, I took the train to Avonmore, Ontario, from my home in Pontiac, Michigan, to visit Jean, unmarried, and her brother Archie, also unmarried, and the old father, lovingly called, "D.L.", as his name was Daniel Lochiel (pronounced with a hard 'c').

The eighty-acre farm was situated one-half mile west of town. My train arrived at the station on the north side. It was necessary for Archie to meet me with the family car.

No one was on the platform when I stepped out of the train, but the fast-moving engine was scarcely out of sight when the brakes of a car were applied, rather abruptly, and I had my first glance of Archie of Avonmore.

During my brief stay in that small town I learned that there were many other Archie's but Hector's brother was to me the one special Archie of Avonmore.

The gleam of Archie's warm brown eyes and the white collar and tie which I was given to notice, was evidence that the girl his brother Hector had chosen was someone special to Archie.

From that time on, whenever I talked to Archie, the happy gleam was in his eyes, which made him look very handsome. So handsome, that I wrote Hector saying, "I think he is even better looking than you, Hector."

Archie is tall, like Hector, but not so thin, getting bald, also like Hector, and 10 years older, but just as strong and energetic.

Jean, who met us at the door of the white-frame house, had the same lovely brown eyes, and a lively personality which was necessary to keep a motherless home normal. The house was a pleasant place to visit. Its big comfortable kitchen became the reception room for many visitors during my stay in Avonmore. Hector's relatives and friends were gentle, with a sly Scottish wit that aroused in me the memory of a few good jokes which I knew and told. And there was genuine fun and laughter. When there were no visitors, I enjoyed watching the milking at the red barn, then following Archie to the milk house where the cans

179

of warm milk were plunged into the cool water to await their trip to the railroad station. I stood at the carriage shed and watched the horses being hitched, learning little by little what Hector was like.

Jean was a school teacher having left her previous work as deaconess with the United Church in New Brunswick because of her father's failing health. She took me the next day to the fourth grade and I saw how much her students loved her; and she drove me in the car to meet all the nearby relatives, brothers and sisters of the aging father and dead mother. Many cousins, many Archie's, many Alex's, many McMillan's, McElheran's, McDougall's, and McLean's, good Scotch Canadian folk descended from John McMillan who migrated from Caliche, Scotland in 1804.

The name McMillan, or more properly spelled MacMillan, came from the Gaelic name, MacGhilleMhaolain. The armorial bearings of the clan contain a rampant lion, and on the crest badge is a "dexter and a sinister hand brandishing a two-handed sword."

I learned that the McMillan motto under the sword of the crest was taken from Virgil, Book 1, line 630 and means, "I have learned to run to the aid of those in distress."

I noticed that although Hector and his father spelled their last name with a Mc, Jean and Archie used Mac.[45]

On August 17, Hector, writing again from Bongondza, started his letter to Ione with a series of xxxx's (kisses) and wrote:

.....Not the hurried kind like the last one at Pier 38, but rather like the one on New Year's Eve !!!"

He continued:

My Honey:

This isn't going to be very long but I will try and make it sweet. Where will you be when you get this, or will you be reading my carbon copy of it???? These and many other questions are pressing into my mind these days, Days and Daze. If only some of your letters could get through to me. The courier came in late last Wed, but the Kinsos opened it and sent my mail over with the runner, at 10:45. I struggled into wakefulness and answered his call at "our" front door. The flashlight was handy, so I was not long in getting the handful of letters and magazines. It looked encouraging, so I decided to light your little lantern. But these Congo Matches?? ! ! ! The heads of them wear off, they break, they sparkle, probably every tenth one; they do everything but light. Well, one did at last. And then a hasty look through the letters. One from IONE??? ....Not yet. But there was one from Jean, written last May and telling me about your plans. And that helped a little bit.

Did you get my two-word cable in time for your birthday party? I hope they didn't put all the candles on the cake. What a sized cake it would have to be ! ! !

---

[45] Why this occurred is unknown.

But never mind, Ione, I like them old and mellow, the latter word meaning <u>soft</u>. The other day I was going to fix Viola's watch strap, and so we traded watches. They seemed to be about the same size so we held them near each other to see for sure. And then as I felt her soft arm I realized that I hardly touched anyone since last January. Girls are such lovely creatures, at least the one I'm going to marry. I'm glad I had five sisters. And don't you think they are nice ! ! ! ! They have all been so good to me, and they all love <u>you</u>.

Well, honey, it is almost ten o'clock and I imagine I hear you calling from the bed room that it is time to have our devotions and get to sleep. And so I will ! ! !

Saturday, August 18 ... Almost supper time. Will be going over to Kinsos, Viola too, and after supper we will be having a station meeting, of which I am the sec'y [secretary]. *Kinso just gave me a haircut, rather short, said he is glad you are not able to see it! ! May write more if mail is delayed,*

LOVE X Hector

PS: (Just another note 9:20 p.m.) Good meeting – decided that Joan should have this house & I move over to Doc's house;[46] Kinso is going up to Ekoko for two weeks. I'm working on a machine to make roofing tiles.

Back in the States, Ione was still moving around, taking meetings and drumming up support for mission work. Detroit, Toledo, Cleveland, and Columbus were some of her stops. On September 14, 1945, she wrote to her mother from Columbus:

.....Mr Pudney has suggested that I come to Phila. after the meeting of the 30th, unless other meetings materialize. He wants me to present my passport to the Consulate before Oct. 10th. I am hoping to be able to send for you to come sometime around then. Do you think you will be free then?

.....Write me as soon as you can. I'll be anxious to know what you are doing. Mr Pudney said that Mr Jenkinson said that Hector is very blue because no mail is getting thru from the states now. I'm going to get out a cable to him today. I'm ashamed for writing so little.

On September 21, Hector wrote to Ione's sister Lucille and her husband, and it was evident he longed for Ione to join him:

Dear Lucille and family,

Wish you could come and visit me in my big house and drive away a little of the loneliness. But very, very soon your sweet little sister will do all that and we will be able to write to you in <u>one</u> envelope. I can hardly wait to hear that she has left America. It is 8 months since I kissed her goodbye. I still think back to the grand time we had running around New York. What a place to have a courtship. But if people thought we were a little too much in love, that's alright, they only saw us once. How much did Ione tell you about what went on in the

---

[46] Houses on mission stations acquired names like 'the Doc's house' depending on who had first residency, and they seemed to remain with the name even if the 'Doc' was no longer in the residence or even in the country; it never became 'Hector's House'.

SIM home? She had better not let out too much or I will have another candidate period in the mission!

Her letters were so long delayed for several months. The airmail was held up in West Africa so it was neither coming nor going. But that is all over now and it is so nice to be getting regular news. I got five of her delayed letters all in one mail. It was almost too much love to take at one time after so long a fast. She is such a sweet girl and I long to carry her across the threshold. We should be pretty happy, when she is both so pretty and so happy. All my folks were so much in love with her right from the start. I was so glad she was able to visit them all.

How is your new pastorate coming along? I will be so glad to hear about it the next time you write. Could you send along a picture of the family or is Ione bringing one? Give Ruthie a big hug for me, and if you have any strength left you could divide it between Esther and Lawrence.

I just love the work out here. So far, I have been very healthy. I have a good lad for a cook. He has been with me all the time. I just go out to work and hardly ever tell him what to get for the meals. He seems to know that I have a good appetite. He makes lovely bread. I keep telling him how much Ione will teach him when she comes. All the natives here love her and almost every day you hear someone praying for her soon return.

The next letter I write will likely be telling about the wedding, so I will save all my big words for that event. May the Lord continually bless you,

In Christ, Hector

Ione wrote to her mother on September 26 while in transit to Bluefield, West Virginia, and the tone of the letter suggests she had a lot occupying her mind, especially before going back to the Congo. She talked of a young people's meeting in Louisville where she chose a message about God's Surety and His provision for sin. She included dancing and drinking among other sins. During the invitation when the pastor was closing in prayer, Ione talked to two young girls and both accepted Christ praying the publican's prayer.

Ione spoke at three school groups and tried to get caught up on some office work. She was taken to Lexington and took a train overnight to Bluefield from Cincinnati. She had a "rushing time" of it going to Pittsburgh and back in three days saying they didn't give sleepers now for less than 400 miles, so she had several nights of sitting up.

On September 28, she wrote to Hector and summarised better her activities over the last few months. It was clear the Westcotts were not intending to return as they bequeathed most of their possessions in Congo to Hector and Ione. It was quite a boost to a young couple as the list included the piano, the redwood dining room set, a bed, desk, the sewing machine, washing machine, bicycle, shop tools and materials, and much more. It was a long list and both Dr Westcott and Ellen signed it. The Westcotts stipulated what they would like them to parcel up and send back to the States. Ione wrote to Hector:

My dearest One!

Your grand letter was just received and I do thank you so much. I trust you received my cable by now telling you that I am ready to come. After visiting my relatives for three weeks in Michigan and Wisconsin, I spent about one week in Pontiac trying to gather together the huge amount of things I had been accumulating to take back to the Congo. Mother helped me and by the time I had to leave for these deputation meetings things were pretty well under control, tho' a tremendous amount of work remained, which Mother has been doing while I am in meetings. She has been shellacking all my books, so that the bugs won't have such a good time as they had on my others out there!

I have been speaking in Erie, Michigan, Cleveland, Ohio, Columbus, Pittsburgh, Pennsylvania, Louisville, Kentucky, Frankfort, now in Bluefield, West Virginia, and lastly in Portsmouth, Virginia, after which I shall return to good old Philadelphia, where I hope to present my passport in N.Y., see if my visa is in good order and for how long. As yet, the boat possibilities are not too good. Mr. Pudney said they gave him as a possibility the last of Oct. or first of Nov. And if my visa runs out by Oct. 10th (as I fear), I will have to wait several months for another. If it does run out before I can get a boat, I believe I shall take courage and ask about a plane, if the church is willing to finance it. At any rate, you had better "stay put" until you do hear definitely. I had not tho't that you might be able to fly to the coast, but it was a thrill to read that you are thinking about it! I trust there will be sufficient funds to do it.

You did not say in your letters what house you have moved to, but the description sounds like the Doctor's. Does that mean that we will like it there? I think it is wonderful, tho' I don't think a couple of novices like ourselves deserve such a fine home!

.....I'm glad you are getting along so well. The manual training classes will help the children and the French will help you. I have some records of French lessons and an instruction book which will help, too. One can hear the pronunciation when the record is played. My cousin gave me the first 4 lessons & I will order the other 26. I'll try to pick out a nice tie, tho' I'm not a very good judge in men's ties! The ring is with me always and shall not leave until it is on your finger. I have already packed a case of batteries and they are in my trunk. I have a new flashlight, too. I bought some 116 films; someone told me that was the size of your camera. And I have some 620, hoping I remembered the size of mine. Have you looked at my camera to see if that broken lense is repairable? I am trying to get movie film but as yet none is available.

I know these next few weeks will be the hardest of all because they will be just waiting and enduring the endless space of time until we can be together. It has been nine months now. I love you so, Hector. I hope you will not be disappointed in me. The Lord is so good to give me your love.

In our Saviour's love, XXXX Ione PS: Greetings to Kinsos and Viola.

Hector had not received many letters and on September 29, he wrote to Ione from Bongondza:

Dearest BELOVED:

"We all with open face, beholding as in a glass the glory of the Lord, are changed into the same image."

No one has told me to stop writing yet so I will try to get another short letter off to you, me sweet WIFE. (soon!) I don't mean that you will be sweet soon, but you will combine your sweetness with being my wife. It sure sounds nice to hear that; just like you talk about me being your husband. I was praying this morning that I shall be a worthy one.

.....Do you know what we all did this afternoon. We went out for a picknick (pardon the K's). About 3 p.m. we got into the V8 and went out to Simo Mbamo's village out toward Bakapo, probably 40 km. We took Sema along with us (the teacher with six children). He may be stationed out near there, so is out trying the pulse of the people. [That missionaries were training and supporting local people to meet community needs was evidence of the forward-thinking philosophy held by the mission.] *We got there about 4:30 and Kinso and I went down to the stream, and found a lovely spot right by the bridge where we had the grass cut and all the good things carried down. And what a meal! Viola had prepared a chicken, then a vegetable salad (Joan forgot to put in the salad dressing, even tho it was right there on the table or maybe it was Ma Kinso). But it was good anyway, along with bread and biscuits. Then the dessert. It is a dreadful thing to sit where Ma Kinso can load up your plate. I think I had three helpings. And with it some nice condensed milk and muffins with filling that Viola had made. Don't ask me how many I had. I know I had the first one out of the box; and the last one and a lot in between. I took two pictures with Viola's camera. It was almost dark when we started home and it was my turn to drive. We had lots of fun as we came along. Joan is quite witty when she is sufficiently provoked. So, between the two of us we can keep Ma Kinso laughing most of the time.*

I got Kinso stirred up one day this week when I told him that I had seen an electric light plant [generator] *in Wards* [catalog]. *He came over and looked it up and was ever so pleased. $259 – allowing 250 watts to each of the four houses, which means quite a few bulbs, probably in the bedroom too, also small ones in other odd places. It doesn't have batteries, so the motor has to be going while we have the lights on. But it starts with a remote-control switch, one of which we hope to have in each house.*

Now to get away from the technicalities and talk about you. Inanimate objects don't have blue eyes.

I was reading in the August "Reader's Digest" that if one of the parents has blue eyes and there are blue eyes in the family of the other, chances are that the children will have blue eyes. So, there are yours and my sister Alice's. I enjoyed reading the whole article and am so glad that you are to be the mother of OUR children. Mrs Pudney used to frighten me when she told me what a refined lady you were. Sometimes I wondered if you could stand the kind of loving I preferred to give my wife. But that is all past tense now. I can see how you thrived on it. And Marcellyn told me how you wanted to be treated. You are surely made to order and I didn't get you out of the catalogue either. However, on the summer issue of Wards catalogue I did write your name on the lady's hat.

Well, it is getting late. The rain is gently pattering down on the tin roof and I am getting sleepy. I must tell you too about the nice shirt Ma Kinso cut out and made for me. I got the material in Stan when we were last there and she said she could do it, so this week I gave her the stuff and today she sent it over all finished. It will be so nice for the evening with white trousers, and shoes. I tried to do several little jobs for her in payment, like making a pot stand for her ferns and putting rubber strips on her rocking chair. We have started putting in the three arches in their front porch, and next week I hope to screen it in. There is surely plenty of work around here. Today I put little doors on the broom cupboard in the dining room of this house. No doubt you often looked at it. I have been using the shelves for a hat rack.

You have 31 days to get here for an October wedding. Don't put it off because I fail to see any advantage in not being married to a LOVELY GIRL LIKE YOU.

Yours more than ever,   Hector   XXXXXX

The furlough for Ione was fraught and frantic, her organisational skills were stretched and her planning was dependent on so many variables. She also had great concern for her mother's financial status. Leone Reed had experienced a major life upheaval over the last three years. When Ione sailed for Africa, her mother was forced to move out of the family home and live in rented accommodation. When Ione was back in the USA for a year, they could only meet in friends' houses – 'felt rather stranded' underplays the trauma of this experience. Presumably, on the death of her father, the family had to deal with un-paid debts, which perhaps explained the selling of the family home.

While Ione was happy to be doing 'the Lord's work', it did come at a cost, the ones who suffered most being family. It must have been difficult for Ione to balance 'dutiful daughter' with 'dutiful missionary'. As seen in her letters, she rarely voices her concerns out loud. She felt that she'd been disloyal to her mother and that she surely did not mean to. When she received money and did not send it to her mother and her sister, Marcellyn, it was because the donor wanted it to go to foreign missions. In a letter to her mother she talked of uncertainties, such as taking a plane to Africa but the cost was estimated to be between $1100 and $1200.

Ione also had no time to say goodbye to her sister Lucille in person and wrote to her family from New Jersey on October 12. She talked of her plans to sail on the SS *Gripsholm* going to Egypt, perhaps on Tuesday, October 16, but if the port strike continued, on the 18th. From Alexandria, she would have to take trains and boats up the Nile as far as she could go. Then Hector was to drive to Juba (JEW-ba), in Anglo-Egyptian Sudan (a week or so journey), where they might be married. The letter continued:

..... I'm so sorry not to see you and say goodbye; I tho't surely I would be able to get back once more and yet, it seems God is moving things rapidly.

Now don't be alarmed about me, even tho I will probably travel alone. It will be grand trip stopping at France, Spain, Italy, Greece, and I hope maybe the Holy Land. But there may be a long wait in Egypt and the trip on the Nile goes thru the hottest part of the desert in the hottest part of the year! But who knows, maybe I'll see those 7-foot Dinka men[47] or some crocodiles, or maybe King Tut himself! Well, do pray much for although I am feeling fine, I know there will be a strain.

.....Say goodbye to the church and friends there. Perhaps I'll see them 4 or 5 years from now. I have all my wedding things and they will be ready to slip into when I see Hector. I even have a part of the wedding cake and top that the Loyal's had at their farewell wedding party. I will try to find some little children just the right size for those dear little white dresses. Maybe we can get some pictures!

"May the Lord watch between me and thee while we are absent one from the other."

Very lovingly yours, Ione XXXXX

Ione set sail once again for Africa with her mother and Lucille seeing her off at the dock. While leaving loved ones behind, she was at last travelling to meet Hector and get married. On October 26 on board the *Gripsholm* moored in Naples, she wrote to her mother:

Dearest Mother,

Greetings from Naples!

We could not get off the boat, but mail can be sent so I tho't I'd tell you about the journey thus far. Everything has been lovely and I couldn't ask for better rest or nicer group of people. The woman with the small child left after the first night, and I had the cabin absolutely to myself until three Sudan Interior Mission girls joined me. Now we have grand times together and I have had some real inspirations spiritually, especially one girl, not with me, but who called on me the second day because she knows Hector and others in our mission. We have a prayer meeting every morning at 10 and I have heard some fine messages. I have sung one solo at that, and then the main church service last Sunday I sang a solo and a trio with an S.I.M. girl and a South Africa General Mission girl; quite a mixed group! We have sung several times already and due to sing at a singspiration tomorrow night. We have children's meetings every day and a number of boys and girls have accepted Christ. I led two so far and have dealt with several. Tony [the glove puppet] is a favourite and makes many contacts to deal with children in my cabin. I'm making him a life preserver.

---

[47] Ancient folklore stated that the Dinka in Southern Sudan were the first people on Earth and descended from Garang and Abuk – our equivalent Adam and Eve. They are tall, slim and adapted to living a nomadic life tending cattle. Nowadays, following famine and war, they are largely a displaced population.

The weather has been very calm and mild; we still wear sweaters on deck, but hardly need them except at night. Yesterday was a highlight as we passed thru the Straits of Gibraltar, and it was a wonderful sight, to see Africa on one side, French Morocco, I mean as that is the country in that part of Africa, and on the other side was Spain. We were nearest to the Africa side and I could not resist getting out my motion picture camera and a professional photographer helped me to get it ready and to take several views of the rocks on the Africa side, the waves beside the boat and the people looking at Gibraltar. The rock could be seen, but the haze made it impossible to photograph. We are in the Mediterranean Sea now and it is very calm and blue. We will not be allowed to get off at any of the ports except the one we disembark at, but I may get a picture of it.

I sit at the table with three South African General Mission folk, an elderly couple and a new girl, who is a very sweet lovely Christian girl. She teaches in the children's meetings, too, has the seven-year olds. I have the five-year old boys (10 of them) and they are quite a handful, but it is just for a few minutes a day. We have between 60 and 70 children here every day. I believe there are about 100 on board.

.....I'm so glad you could both come to the dock; it meant so much to me, especially since I had to go alone. I felt pretty lonely at first until that girl called on me and she introduced me to one after the other and some know Hector as he has three cousins in S.I.M., and some remembered the Sunshine Trio. Well, I do not know anything more about the future to tell you. I will find it all out as I go along. Perhaps I can write you from Alexandria or Cairo to tell you about how I am going up the Nile. I will try to get another message to Hector, too. It doesn't seem possible that I will soon be married!

Thank you again for all you did for me, Mother. I do so much appreciate your coming that long journey to see me off. I trust you got back safely. And I worried about that cable, for I'm afraid it cost more than I figured at the time. How did you manage?

Now I will be praying for your new work that the Lord will prosper it.

Oodles of love,   Ione

In a contemplative mood, Hector wrote to his father on October 27 from Bongondza:

Dear Dad:

This may be the last letter I shall ever write to you, before I get married.

Let me thank you from the bottom of my heart for all that you have done for me. Your life has been well spent. The Lord has been very faithful to you and I know He is all your desire. The other day I was reading in one of my books, commenting on this verse, "Now also when I am old and grey-headed, O God, forsake me not". When I read what followed it, I took my pencil and marked the page inside the back cover, with your name beside it. This is it.

"Have you green fruits still growing on you, as quickly and lively affections to God and Christ, and faith and love, as at the first and more abounding? Oh,

bless God you are so near the haven, and lift up your heart, your redemption draws near; and withal raise your confidence, that that God of grace, who hath called you into His eternal glory, will keep you for it, and possess you of it shortly."

You have had a long hard climb and much of the way has been lonely for you since mother died. I'm afraid we did not give you much help in your times of sorrow, but THANK the LORD you have stood true and I know you will have an abundant entrance into HEAVEN. I used to lie awake some times and hear you praying in the middle of the night. There must have been some battles to fight, but strong is the Captain of our Salvation.

I have had a rather care free existence so far. The reeds before me seemed to open up like the gates before Peter. Even before I was saved, I seemed to escape the many troubles that beset others. But since I have accepted the Saviour my life has been one of continued blessing. Now at this hour I am completely happy and satisfied. He has led and undertaken in ways that are marvellous beyond what I could ever have hoped.

In about two or three weeks I will be meeting my beloved IONE. She sailed on Oct 16 and will likely arrive at Alexandria on the 30th. From there she will travel up the Nile to a place called Juba in the Anglo Egyptian Sudan, just a little north of the boundary between Uganda, Sudan and the Congo. It will be a long trip, but Mr Jenkinson is lending me his car, and I may be taking Chester and Dolena Burk along to stand up with us. We will be well taken care of as there are some fine Christians there.

I am so glad that Ione has been able to visit you and she did enjoy herself. Someday we hope to be back with you and tell you something of our experiences in the Lord's work, but until then we will try to keep in touch with you by letter. May I prove the faithful husband that Ione deserves. I know we will be happy together.

Let me hear from you soon,   your son and heir,   Hector

On November 17, Ione wrote to her mother from somewhere on the Nile, furnishing her with more details of her travels after Naples; she recorded the temperature as 103° F:

Greetings from the Nile!

Well, the Lord has guided over many miles and now I am within a few days of Juba, where I hope to see a familiar face. I sent you a letter from Naples, but stopped at Cairo only a short while before coming this way; and this past week I have been feeling rather punk, due to a cold, imagine a cold in such a climate! I was prepared for hotter weather when I took the first steamer and the nights were quite chilly and the air was damp and the first thing I knew I was coughing with a deep chest cold. It kept on until I knew I must start taking the sulphapyredine I had bro't (I detected a bloody mucous which shows a danger of Pneumonia). Well, the medicine was very effective but as does nearly all sulpha drugs, it made me very nauseated and weak. And when I got on this boat a week ago, I was mighty glad to have a bed to pop into and stay for a few days. But now the cough is nearly gone, my appetite has returned, and I am gaining back the few pounds lost. I had gained a great deal on the ocean boat, so I guess I'll come out even! What an experience this coming down 2500 miles to Juba! And it's just as quaint as a story-book.

The Lord promised, "As thou goest step by step, I will open up the way before thee." And He surely has.

.....I missed the sights at Cairo, though and the pyramids, etc. I left the next day after landing. We got into Port Said instead of Alexandria, because we were trans-shipped at Naples. I didn't tell you in the other letter, but the motor broke on the Gripsholm *while we were out quite a ways in the Mediterranean and it managed to limp into Naples, but did not dare to go on.*

We went the other five days, with no stops on a troop transport, real army stuff – sleeping with 12 others in a cabin; one of the 12 was Madame Edis de Philippe Rabinoff, grand opera star, and her <u>26</u> pieces of baggage.[48] Altogether the ocean journey was 20 days, for we arrived Nov. 5. I was quite afraid of the Arabs for they looked so sneaky, and there were so many tales of their running their hand down the side of one and pulling off wrist watches, purses, etc. I wore my money in a money belt under my clothing, and when one brushed against me and ran his hand from my shoulder to my hips my purse was in my other hand! It was an awful experience, because I got into Cairo by train at midnight and at first there was no one of the missionaries, then some came out of the trains, and then there was no Cook's representative [travel agent], *and then he came , and HE WAS AN ARAB, and I was just as scared of him! When I got into my room I bounced into bed and covered my head.*

There had been a riot there two days before, and the Arabs had killed 31 people.[49] When I looked at the baggage the Arab porters had dumped into my room three handles were wrenched off and a tray I had bought on the boat was broken. I was glad to leave Cairo the next day, but none of the missionaries were ready to go, with papers, etc., so rather than wait two weeks in the hotel, I went alone. My compartment had a good lock in the train, so I slept well the first night. In all I have taken 4 trains and 2 steamers. Only one night I was unprotected when I had to sleep with an Egyptian woman and a baby and they kept the door open, and I had to get up frequently to vomit then, too. But that's over and I am with mostly British people on this boat.

---

[48] Edis De Philippe sang with both the Metropolitan and Paris Operas, as well as many others around the world, during the 1930s and 1940s. She founded the Israel National Opera Company in 1947, which she ran until her death in 1979.

[49] The Balfour Day riots November 2 and 3, 1945 in Cairo and Alexandria; these started out as anti-Jewish demonstrations on the 28th anniversary of the Balfour Declaration (1917 British statement of support for a national homeland in Palestine for the Jewish people).

Food is fair, sometimes queer, but I enjoy the English tea. And I am resting all the time. Have my veil finished; the bugs ate part of it but I have put lover's knots in lace over the mendings!

Lovingly, xx   Ione

A letter to Maurice and Lucille written by Ione on November 21 provided more insights about her journey to Egypt and down the Nile on her way to Hector:

Dearest Maurice and Lucille and family,

Greetings in Jesus' precious Name!

As you may guess, I am having a very thrilling time; of course, it is hotter than anything I've experienced, and when I passed thru the desert on the train I tho't I just could not stand it. But I lived thru it and the River is much more pleasant. The scenery is very interesting and just now I have just seen 8 hippos bobbing up and down beside the ship; yesterday I saw 19 in one group. And the funniest sight was when the boat made a turn, one hippo didn't get out of the way in time and he got spanked in the rear and he jumped up and ran, for it was very shallow, and his huge sides just waddled; actually his tail was between his legs, and he looked very frightened, while usually they are very ferocious looking.

Crocodiles are in equally great numbers. They are very cautious animals, and try to get under the water before we get to them, but occasionally one will be napping with his big mouth wide open. There are birds which pick their teeth while they sleep! This area is all swamp-land, with scarcely a piece of solid ground, grass and bull-rushes like Moses' mother used to hide her baby. I've been eating the leeks and onions of Egypt, too!

The ocean voyage was very restful and invigorating; I think I must have gained at least 5 pounds. There were nearly 200 missionaries on board (and 1,000 other people), and we had meetings every day for adults as well as for children, and there were a number of souls saved among the oil company's children and one young man, a deportee to Greece or Italy.

While on the blue Mediterranean the motors stopped on the boat, and we had difficulty in getting into Naples where we stayed five days and were trans-shipped to a troop transport where we lived like soldiers for another five days.[50] *Naples was quite in ruins from bombings. I had never actually seen what bombs do, and it is a horrible sight. There must have been many killed. Just giant wrecks of buildings left. We went in army trucks from one dock to the other. That's all we were allowed on shore, as there was little food there and the people were very poor and we were not allowed to go anywhere. One sailor went ashore and got drunk and when he came sober again, the civilians had stolen his clothes and money and he had to come back on ship naked!*

Then after the troop ship we landed, not in Alexandria, but Port Said, around the edge of the corner of Africa, down toward the Suez Canal. Customs was a

---

[50] The *Gripsholm* was sent back to Sweden for repairs.

mess and was very tiring as there were hundreds of people to go. But I had my Cook's representative to help me and was one of the first to get thru, having just six pieces and being alone. I was able to get a train out of P.S. by 6 P.M. and arrived at Cairo at 12 midnight, a bad time to arrive especially since there had been riots there two days before and white people's stores were rocked. 31 people had been killed. The Lord took care of me and eventually I found myself safe at the Victoria Hotel.

.....I have had to take four different trains and two river steamers already, and tomorrow, and I MAY see Hector then! (Someone just called me to see a herd of elephants, quite a sight!)

I have been making my wedding veil and now it is hanging up on a hanger in the middle of my cabin. I had it folded until I started to sew it, and then some bugs chewed big holes in it. I had to think what to do with the holes, so invented some bows and flowers out of lace and satin to cover them up! The decoration looks pretty I am told. I have fellowship with all English people on this boat. So far as I know, I am the only Christian.

.....It was so grand having Lucille there to see me off. I hope the money held out until you got back home, Lucille! I was afraid that that cable that I gave her and Mother to mail cost more than the $10 I had figured. I want to know about it. And I was wondering just when Mother and Lucille left the dock. I did not see them again after I waved at them. It was so good to have those last few hours together. I praise the Lord for such precious loved ones.

.....I bought a little brass bell at the last place we stopped, made by the natives and to be used on my table to call the staff [using a small brass bell was a traditional, perhaps colonial way to communicate with staff while dining].

My cabin boy here is a Muslim and wears a turban and long white robe, he has a nice moustache, too. He brings me tea the first thing in the morning and at 4 P.M. Well, I could ramble on and on, but I would like to send this Airmail if it's not too heavy. I hope to hear from you when I reach the station. The Lord be with you all.

Lovingly in Him,   Ione

Hector travelled a thousand miles from Bongondza to meet Ione. They finally married on November 27, 1945 in Juba, then travelled together back to Bongondza. Ione and Hector described the wedding, the journey and the welcome at the mission station in a long letter to Ione's mother on December 31:

.....We have thought so much about you and wondered what kind of Christmas you may have had.

.....How quickly we all were separated: it is good to look forward to a time when there will be no more separations.

After having been married one month we can say it was a splendid undertaking.

We are surely happy together, and there are so many things to laugh together about.

Hector & Ione McMillan in wedding-day dress for a reception at Bongondza.

It was wonderful the way we met: Hector arrived in Juba just the night before I did. And Hector was able to apply for the special license that made it possible to be married in just four days instead of waiting the usual three weeks. The hotel bills were very high and we were glad to have it finished quickly.

And to make matters nicer, the Burks from our station at Boyulu came by Congo Courier to stand up with us. They are old pals of Hector, and I met them in Phila. last January. The license arrived the same day that we had set for the wedding, and the Burks at about the same time. It was very exciting and while Dolena and I were picking bridal bouquets we were quite nervous. It was such a job to make a bride's bouquet just before the wedding, but it was the only way to have them fresh. I carried white frangipanis (odour like a gardenia and a lily-shaped blossom) and star of Bethlehem, a fine flower.

Dolena found the same flowers in pink. The men each wore an oleander in the button-hole.

Dolena looked very nice in the aqua-green gown that Doris had given to me. I had made my veil on the steamer and it had a lace edge and artificial flowers on the hat. Some cock-roaches had eaten some holes in it, but I put a lover's knot and two flowers of satin ribbon over the places: Mr Carey of the Church Mission Society of England gave me away. Miss Thrasher of the same society played a little organ.

The Chapel was beautifully decorated with flowers, mostly rose, bougainvillea and hibiscus. The preacher had a robe with all the trimmings on. The ceremony was long and we knelt three times. There were about 20 R.A.F. boys there and they had practiced, "Great is thy Faithfulness" and "O Perfect Love." They were singing the first when I came in.

There were a number of responses, etc., too, which made it an interesting service. At the close I received a nice Kiss and we went out under an arbour of bougainvillea while rice was thrown and one fellow took pictures on the Kodochrome movie camera. [Sadly, all of Hector's film footage has been lost.]

.....One of the first to congratulate us was Balimaga, the helper Hector had taken along on the trip from Bongondza to Juba. Balimaga was the bad one of the school but since he accepted Christ, he has proved very useful to Hector at the shop as well as on this journey.

We were put into a car which belonged to the District Commissioner and driven to Miss Thrasher's house where she had prepared a tea. An A.I.M.

missionary's cook had made a lovely white cake and frosted it and put on top the wedding decoration from Inez's party and everyone enjoyed it very much: there were small cakes and cookies, too, and ice cream and lemonade and tea. The R.A.F. boys served it with great gusto. It was lots of fun; there were about 35 people there, including one Egyptian barber and his wife and child. Then we went to the hospital to visit a man who had turned over four times in his car on the mountain, and to the hotel, where we changed clothes and went to dinner with the Burks.

There were no little white girls so we could not use the little white dresses. But will use them sometime here.

The next morning the Burks and we started on the long journey home, but we stopped in ever so many places. The Burks were only with us a week, and then we visited a number of A.I.M. stations and spent three nights at beautiful Mt. Ruwenzori, the highest peak in Congo.

We slept where we could see the snow-capped peak. The air was refreshing, the hike up the mountain invigorating, and then a plunge in the icy mountain pool. We stayed at a lovely hotel there and the manager picked strawberries just for us, and made ice cream. We waded in a river to the place where we could see and go under the water fall. And this is only part of the many delightful experiences on that wedding journey which took two weeks. We stopped at our two stations the other side of Stanleyville, Boyulu, and Maganga, and then arrived [at Bongondza] *Dec. 12th, two weeks and a day after the wedding. There was such a grand reception, folks running from everywhere. We had decorated the car with palms, and ribbons, etc.*

The Jenkinson's and Viola and Joan came running when they heard the horn blowing so vigorously. We had some tea and then went home to rest.

Hector carried me over the threshold, and set me down in the living room of Westcott's home, all re-plastered in grey instead of cream, and new curtains up, rug on the floor, pictures up, and every room furnished except two spare bedrooms.

It was nice coming into a clean house and vases of flowers everywhere. We had dinner at Kinsos and a nice fellowship after. The next morning, they had a formal reception in the church, and I gave the response. The church that Doctor built was beautiful with new platform, curtains, and flowers. And the station had been cleaned up so nicely.

Of course, I could go on telling about the return. It was so good of the Lord to give all this joy and it was doubly grand to come back to the place where I had been before and to come back with a husband whom they already know and loved.

Old Alfonse at the workshop who never went to church had started coming to church as soon as Hector took over the shop. And I could see a change in others. We do not know yet our work that is I don't, and will not until the General Conference which will be held next week at Boyulu. These weeks have been filled

193

with settling and holiday celebrating. A few days after I arrived back, I took on the care of a three weeks old native girlie whose Mother is here sick in the hospital, the baby's name is Lollypop, or Lolipopo in Bangala. She is going to live, tho she was quite starved at first. The Mother has syphilis and cannot walk. And there are two other children. The older, a girl of about 11 years does much of the care of the baby although she herself has leprosy. But the father stays here nights and is good about bathing the wife and children and feeding them.

I give the baby 20 ounces a day of Klim and sugar and glucose mixture. I beat it up myself and prepare the bottles. Then I check on the blankets and clothes. It is such a joy. You'll maybe hear more later about Lollypop. Then this week and last I have been teaching an hour a day singing lessons to the evangelists (13 of them) who are here on the station for the holidays. I am teaching them to direct singing and to sing well themselves – we hope. We have an organ now and I play it to lead them, but Viola plays every other day.

Hector is over at the evangelist's school right now giving a message, one of his series of doctrinal talks. They [the evangelists] will come here with their wives on Friday night for a social time; we'll give them popcorn, peanuts, cookies and coffee. They are a grand bunch and fine leaders.

I don't suppose my baggage will come for several months, and I am glad for some of the Westcotts' things to get along on for now.

The food problem is serious, as usual, but the Lord always gives enough. When the seeds come, I'll plant them and see if we can get more vegetables. Hector and I have both gained since coming to the station.

Please pass this letter along.

Lovingly in Christ, Hector and Ione.

Chapter 8
HECTOR AND IONE IN PARTNERSHIP

After their wedding in Anglo-Egyptian Sudan, Hector and Ione travelled back to Congo and began their life together at Bongondza. In a letter written in January, 1946 to the Westcotts, Ione shared their news:

.....We arrived back at the station on Dec. 12th, after stopping one night at Boyulu and one night at Stan. There are seven at Boyulu: Carters, Burks, Betty, Olive, and a John Arton from England, besides the three children (Rosemary, Gordon and Philip Carter). The kiddies are big now. And at Maganga are the Kerrigans, the Walbys (from England) and Isobel. Walbys are expecting a baby. And here [at Boyulu] *are the Kinsos and Joan and Vee. Joan is quite thin and not strong but is carrying on.*

.....Hector drove Kinso's car all the way [to the wedding and back]*– 4,700 miles - and with no spare!*

.....I know you would like to know about the station and they did have it looking very nice when we arrived; old Majuani and Bowito and Mobweki and a couple of others had been clearing the pineapple patch and all around and Ma Kinso had fixed up the flower house. I have counted five spruce trees higher than my head. There are some transplants of red roses and two beautiful gardenia bushes to my waist on either side of the back path. They have blossomed already. The avocado tree has many small pears on it. I am sleeping very well on your nice big double bed. And there are so many of the good things that you left to enjoy. I feel guilty every time I touch them and keep wondering if you did not forget to ask for certain things to be sent and if I could pack them in, too. I am getting together your list and trust that all will be packed allright. So, we will pack your things and send them to you. The mission does want to buy the microscope.

.....I trust that you will soon receive Botiki's letter sent last week. He was very pleased with the bicycle and phonograph and records. We hear them playing them nearly every day. I have been feeding a little new-born baby whose mother is here receiving shots; she has no milk and cannot walk. The baby's name is Lollypop. It is about a month old now. Maria will feed it while I am gone. I taught last two weeks a Singing Class for some special evangelist's meetings. I do not know yet what I will be doing here; we'll have a Station meeting about it when we get back from Boyulu. Well, my paper does not permit more, tho' there is much more. I am well, and Hector is gaining in weight. Please write soon. May the Lord be with you all.

With love, Ione
PS: Here's a bit of goat hair and snake scale.

In a letter to Marcellyn, Hector noted that Ione was so easy to love and tease and work with. They were pretty well acquainted now and had been in the best of health – mostly due to Ione's good cooking.

Hector and Ione in front of the Dr Westcott's House.

And in a letter to Hector's sister Alice, Ione noted that the house they were living in (Dr Westcott's house) was made of kiln bricks with a tin roof. It had three bedrooms, a sleeping porch, a screened in veranda and washing porch, a basement and attic, a nice stone fireplace and kitchen wood range, hot and cold running water and bathroom fixtures, and in a few months would have electricity. The house was spacious and roomy and sited at the top of a hill so it caught all the breezes which kept it cool in the tropical sun.

> .....And no rent to pay! The Lord is very good to make us so comfortably situated. But if we had nothing we'd be just as happy, "for I have learned that in whatsoever state I am, therewith to be content."

On January 27, 1946, Ione wrote her mother a long letter which detailed what life

The McMillan's Bongondza living room (L) and Hector (R) with one whole papaya on his breakfast plate – c1946.

was like for the newly married couple and what they were engaged in:

> .....To show you how the Lord always does the unexpected – I had longed so when I first came out to do just as much evangelistic work as I could when I came, and then because of my many duties with the sick and the white children, I was restrained. And during that time, I seemed to be always impressed that I would not be worth much without a knowledge of teaching. But now it appears that I will be free to do what my heart really longs to do, win souls. Of course, there will be times when I must teach them to read the Bible, but I am glad that there will be no restricting school hours to prevent me from getting right out into the villages. I hope to start a series of child evangelism classes and I think there will be a number of Christian women who will help. And I must learn how to trace down the villages of people who come to Botiki for medical aid, and go to

them and visit. I am quite certain that personal evangelism will reach them far quicker than classwork and meetings. Of course, I will be free to have as many meetings as I wish. Isn't it wonderful to take advantage of some of the unlimited opportunities to reach precious souls? We are waiting for a station meeting when Hector returns this week from Juba with Verna, but even tho I don't know what my official status will be, I am sure that the Lord has called me to a definite work of evangelism here. No doubt I will have a choir, too, and that will be a thrill. We have a little organ now and it helps a great deal.

But there I am spilling out all of my ambitions and I have not yet told you that I have not had one letter from you since arrival, nor from Marcellyn. Doris wrote me that she was leaving for Alaska in three weeks. And I had a letter from Lucille. Then Mr Pudney wrote telling of the great interest in Maurice's and Lucille's church in missions, and how they had agreed to provide a service fund of $300 a year. That is great, and it comes to me just at the time when Hector's service

A truck-load off to the Boyulu Conference – 1946.

fund has been stopped. You remember the church I visited in Portsmouth and its difficulties of which I told you? Well, they have had to drop Hector's because the people were all war-workers and have left town. But he still has his regular support. Mine comes, too. Our wedding was quite an expense and it will take several months to catch up, but it was worth it. Taking the extra trip around by Mt. Ruwenzori had to come out of our pockets, but the

Bongondza missionaries represented at UFM Gen. Conf. at Boyulu on Jan. 8, 1946. Back row (L-R): Herbert Jenkinson, Hector McMillan. Front row: Viola Walker, Alice Jenkinson, Ione McMillan, Joan Pengilly.

good food and refreshment repaid us. Hector needed it. He had gotten quite thin, and I persuaded him not to rush back to the station. He has put on more weight in just the last few weeks. And I am up to 127 pounds. The extra pounds are fat, not baby! We have been married two whole months and we don't have a baby yet!

The little back girl [Lollypop] is doing fine. We were away two weeks at Boyulu for the General Conference, and Botiki's wife took care of her then. She did very well, must have given rounding measurements of Klim, for the milk ran out one day before we arrived. Today I noticed that the baby has a skin disease, called panda [an autoimmune neurological disease that develops from a streptococcal infection]*; and it's funny, I think I have the same stuff on my legs! I must be more careful how I handle the little thing. The girl who takes care of Lollypop and bathes her has leprosy, all the more reason why I must be careful. The father does it when he is there, tho. But he has been working in the cotton gardens all day. Just yesterday he sold his season's crop of cotton to the government, six big baskets for 190 francs, about $4.00. His wife should have tended the garden, but she cannot walk because of paralysis since the baby came. It is a bad case of syphilis. She is getting shots for it but suffers a great deal. The father does not profess to be a Christian but prays beautiful prayers and seems very interested. Pray for them all, especially for the little leper girl of about 12 who cares for another younger child as well, and who is always smiling and seems very fond of coming to our house. I have had many women in for private talks on spiritual things. Some of them drag in mud, others carry palm oil over the rug, or their babies wet, but it is worth it to contact them. Yesterday I made a dress of some material a pagan woman brought and today she wore it smiling to church.*

.....There hasn't been a single snake here for two months! Nor a scorpion or a centipede. The driver ants surrounded the house on New Year's Day, but only a small contingent entered via the back door and a crack in the basement. We sprayed creolin around, and then they got side-tracked by a long snake that was in their path. We saw a brownish-black heap and my poking it a bit, discovered they (the driver ants) were feasting on the snake. They ate it right to the bone, and left the bones to bleach. Hector was bitten by a scorpion in one of Pearl's boxes, but he did not suffer seriously from it. I have to keep at him to attend to his jiggers, rather I take them out for him, for they get so big and leave such large holes; but none of his seem to infect. He has some very bad filaria swellings, tho, and sometimes his wrist watch won't fit on. He never complains but I know they must cause him discomfort. Incidentally he is the dearest, most thoughtful husband that I have ever had! The first and last I ever want.

I wish I could know whether you were able to replenish any of your needed winter clothes. Tell me what you need, and I can at least remember those items in prayer. What are Marcellyn's plans? Mr Pudney keeps speaking of her coming soon; he said he tho't Maurice's church would help her, too. Would it be useless for me to pray that you might come when she does?

.....Your black and orchid pompom curtains are now in Hector's study. And they do look lovely against the grey wall. I remember how nice they looked back home. I hope that you had a very happy Christmas Day and New Year's. And now I want you to know that you are the dearest mother any girl could have. I'm

sure I must have disappointed you many times. Please forgive me and be assured that I love you dearly. I am anxiously waiting to hear from you.

Love, Ione

In other news going out, Ione told a little of Hector's work. He blew a whistle in the mornings that started the drum going which called the men to work. Then he gave them a Biblical message and started them making bricks. He then went to his carpenter shop and started his carpenters, as well as Mr Jenkinson's. He was very busy at this time; they cut down a tree and were hauling the big planks to the shop to be transformed into furniture. She continued:

Hauling a big plank to the shop.

.....Hector is very thoughtful and lots of fun, too. He eats everything that is set before him, and sometimes that is pretty bad. Like last Sunday when the meat had spoiled and the rolls were like rocks, but with the cook to bear the blame, one can always set things aside that are too bland and find something else. When I am in meetings or occupied at the hospital, I spend very little time in the kitchen. The cook has learned to make good bread and can make cupcakes, upside down cake and biscuits.

Ione started one of a series of Child Evangelism Classes at Wameka, a village 8 kilometers away. Hector was hauling sand from nearby with the car, so she hopped in and while he was getting three loads of sand, she had the meeting and there were eight children to start with. Ione hoped eventually to have Christian mothers as the teachers for six or eight classes and she added in a letter:

.....Tomorrow I will make another attempt to get a choir together. They are very uncertain, these people, but they do love to sing. We are doing four-part harmonies in Bangala, "In the Sweet Bye and Bye", another, "Thou shalt call His Name Jesus," and "This is the house of the Lord." We have, "He Lives," now in Bangala, and I'm anxious to try them on it. Mother would be interested to know that I am trying to give the house helper, Abongakwai, piano lessons. But they memorize rather than read music!

In excerpts found in another letter written by Ione on February 25, we learn:

.....The native hunter has been busy since a gun arrived from the government for our use; it [the gun] was captured by the Belgians from the Italians. We have had wild pigs for two weeks and it is a great treat. Our cheapest tinned meat here is 25 cent sardines. Spam is about a dollar. We are glad to receive fresh

butter every other week. It comes from the Kivu mountains and costs about 50¢ a pound.

The cook who works for us usually makes quite good bread, but one day this week he delayed coming to put it into the oven and when he arrived it had risen and sank again. His heart sank when he saw it and he said, "It has died." He started to put it into the oven, but I showed him how he could knead it down and it would rise again; he was amazed for he didn't think it would ever live again.

.....Hector has a unique way of presenting Gospel truths to the natives which they find fascinating. He uses Bible illustrations with them in their work, and carpenter and farm illustrations with them in church. Pray for him in his ministry here.

Ione wrote to the family on March 15 and as a time-saving measure, it was sent to multiple recipients:

Dear Ones,

This afternoon I washed my hair with the grand shampoo that Mother gave me before I sailed. I had to wash it, for it was full of the funniest little bugs, no, not what you think at all, but let me tell you what happened. Early this morning I started out with the guitar, Tony the Monkey, a rubber ball, a bite to eat, and an object lesson. At the first village a former school girl decided to go along with me and carried the guitar. We passed a number of villages until we came to just the right one, for always at this time on Friday I have found a fair-sized child evangelism class. It was Alphonso's village, - he is a former hospital nurse, and he is very friendly, tho a Catholic. I opened the guitar case and began to play, "Come to Jesus", and Bipisa sang with me as the children gathered. At the roll call I discovered some new ones and gave points to the ones who invited them; when they've brought three, they receive a tiny bright metal automobile or airplane (they generally choose one like Bwana (Mr) Kinso drives for they see him go past frequently). Then we sang, "Jesus Love Me This I Know." And "For You, For Me, Jesus Died" and prayed the little prayer song, "We all rise up together". Then came time for my message, and I chose the tallest boy to be king and put a red pyjama top on him and a crown of thorns made out of paper. As the talk progressed, I drew objects out of each thorn, the third being a green paper cross. I asked them why it was green and they didn't know, so I tapped the pole above where I was sitting under the shelter of the house, and said, "This is dead, it is not green; Christ's cross is green because He gives life everlasting." Then I tapped it again to make sure they knew, and out from a hole in it came myriads of these tiny flies! They made my scalp creep and crawl, and I wiggled my head a lot during the rest of my talk.

Something else that you would have laughed at. At the last village, before I turned around to start back, I took out a pineapple jam sandwich and a cupcake to eat there. They gave me a chair and put it near their fire where the old grandfather was sitting picking jiggers out of his feet! Of course, I would not move the chair from where they had so graciously put it [honoring local custom], *so I munched my food pensively gazing into the clouds!*

An interesting characteristic about these people is their great ability to wail loudly at a death and at the same time to carry on quite a normal conversation. Their thoughts are almost continually on things to eat and things to wear. While relatives were digging a grave of a school boy who died at Maganga, their wailing was interspersed with a discussion on the price of a goat, 150 francs at Maganga, but 200 at Stanleyville.

Some days ago, a little girl died here. She had been treated at the hospital and I had been feeding her milk with glucose in it; she must have been about two years old and weighed only 12 pounds due to liver disorder. Naturally I felt the loss, for we had tried so hard to save her. When she was dying, I repeatedly put her into warm water to revive her. After spending some time with the hopelessly mourning parents, I turned to go. One of the station sawyers, named Baruti, or gunpowder, followed me and spoke in low, awed voice, "It is true, what you told them, not to make those loud noises or to hurt each other (the father had to be tied in a separate room from the mother, for he blamed the baby she was expecting to give birth to soon for the death of this child), and that the little child is in heaven and calling to the parents to turn their hearts and receive Christ and come there, too. I wanted to make loud noises, too, and did, too at first, for I said to myself, 'What is the use, anyway, of trying to be quiet, for my heart is sad, and these white people didn't save this child, and I brought my sewing machine a long time ago for Bwana McMillan to repair and he hasn't fixed it yet.' Then I told myself, 'No, I'll not wail, for it is good that the child is with the Lord, and I believe Bwana will repair my sewing machine soon!"

Imagine, choosing such a time for reminding us that the sewing machine is still in a state of disrepair! At any rate, he got his machine repaired.

Viola Walker (at right) and her women's class. Ma Kinso is 3rd from left.

We now have our full [mission] *staff once more on the station, seven members, Verna Schade arrived in January. Verna and Kinsos returned this week from a trip to Ekoko, and Viola Walker and Joan Pengilly returned from trek. Now Hector and I are making a trip to Stanleyville to get some bicycles for this station and Ekoko, as well as Maganga. Verna is going along and we probably will visit Maganga one day. We'll be gone about five days. Then when we return, we will probably go to Ekoko for two weeks to give them their bicycles. Ekoko is still without a white person and while we are there, I will have some women's classes and Hector will direct some building repairs.*

We had a letter from Mr Pudney, this week, just before he sailed on the Queen Elizabeth *for England and from thence to Congo for a visit. He said he had written Marcellyn to plan to rest for a while after graduation and then study some more French (conversational) for six months and then proceed to the Congo early in 1947. I think he must mean that she will go to that French YWCA in N.Y. where Pearl is getting some French. Two other candidates are there now. They have to speak it all the time and Marcellyn could get some experience before she comes. It is a disappointment, for I had hoped to see her this year, but Rom. 8:28 is still true. We received your letter, Marcellyn, and were ever so glad to have it. I will try to remember to enclose a list of things you could be getting together during the summer months. For you won't be able to get many cotton things when fall comes. Glad for your good marks and hope you haven't gotten too tired with such a heavy schedule.*

.....Our hunter is bringing in more meat now, Mother, so don't worry about our food supply, and we have had an unusually fine supply of eggs. I have planted some onions and celery, and have some squash seeds ready to put in. When my baggage comes, I will plant the seeds in my box. Oh, a big station garden has gone in, too, with corn and peanuts, and I gave Hector some popcorn to put in which we got on our honeymoon, so we'll not fare so badly unless the chickens get it all. Am so glad the work is going along well, Mother. We shall be waiting for more and more news. We'll be praying for the Bible study in the Loyal's monthly meetings. Give them my love. Any hope of a cottage to store your things in? I hope someday we will all be together again in a little cottage on a lake. Hector and I are very happy. He is so sweet and loving, sensitive to the least dissatisfaction on my part. And he works so hard, up at 5:30 every morning. He and his carpenters have just made some lovely choir loft benches for the choir I am directing. They will have robes by Easter, I hope. You would love to see the expressions on their faces when they file in to take their places.

Now please all write again soon. May the Lord richly bless you all. I am sending this letter to Mother, Marcellyn, and Lucille.

In His Service, Ione

On March 25, Ione had happy news for her mother:

Late Sat. night we returned from Stanleyville (as well as Boyulu and Maganga), and since yesterday was Sunday we're just getting settled in again. When we went to the P.O. we had a letter from Boyulu saying Betty Ingleson could come to us for a holiday if we liked (we had invited her before), so we drove on to their station and picked her up. She is a lovely English nurse and will be with us for about three weeks. She hasn't had a rest since she came out three years ago. She recently became engaged to John Arton, another of our missionaries at Boyulu.

I was glad to have Betty come for more than one reason, for I wanted her to verify the fact that I am expecting a baby, which she did! I missed my March period and last week started to get nauseated. As nearly as Hector and I can figure, the baby should arrive in November. Now don't you worry about that, for I am in excellent health and near to a Doctor. We can go either to the B.M.S. doctor a day and a half journey, or about two days to Oicha, the A.I.M., which I think I would prefer if we go a month ahead. While Betty is here, she will examine me, and a little later I can be measured by her palvimeter, to see if I can have a normal delivery, which I of course should. I am glad the class put a layette [baby clothes] *in the things, and that I have some maternity dresses on the way, too. As yet they haven't arrived, but should before long.*

The mail must go now, but you are the first one I am telling. You may tell the rest of the family and friends if you like. I wouldn't mind having the world know! I trust you are well. Please write again soon.

Lovingly in Him, Ione

The same day, Hector wrote to his father telling him that the letter would not be long but it was rather important. It stated that, if all went well, he and Ione would become parents sometime in November. Hector implored his father to tell the others in the family.

But the euphoria and happiness did not last long. Ione wrote in a letter to Marcellyn that she felt she'd walked a little too far for a children's meeting which seemed to have brought on a possible miscarriage.

She wrote to her mother on April 14 that she and Hector planned to go by motorboat a few hours down the Congo river to Yakusu (ya-KOO-soo) where she had an appointment with a Dr. Holmes with the British Baptist Mission Society, to assess the situation. In her letter, Ione starts by mentioning her long walk to her village meeting:

.....from now on we will use work funds for the gas it takes for such meetings, since gas is easier to get than babies! When I was on my way back my period came on, and do you know that just when I was wondering if I would get back home before I lost the baby, Hector drove up in the car. He has an uncanny sense of knowing just when I need him most! Bless his heart. He would have driven me in the first place but I did not let him. He was quite worried, but it is all over now [bleeding had stopped but she was still carrying the baby], *and the nausea all came back and after staying in bed for over a week I got up, but Betty says not to do much of anything or go walking until after I see the doctor.*

In a letter to her sister Lucille's church, Ione provided details of the trip to Yakusu:

.....We reached Stanleyville shortly after noon, very good time, for it sometimes takes eight or more hours. After much searching, we finally found a hotel which could squeeze us in. This was a day when both planes and a boat came into town and we were lucky to find a room. The name of the hotel was the Sabena and it was a few kilometres out at the airport. The room was cool and clean and the meals fine. Hector had business which took two days to finish and I did a little shopping and spent a good deal of time resting in the room and enjoying the luxuries that a hotel affords, - somebody else manages the native staff, somebody

else plans the meals, and each is a pleasant surprise, coffee comes to the room early in the morning, and delicious bakery bread and jam if one wishes.

I lay listening to the birds, hundreds of them outside, tiny black-hooded green birds with red faces, larger weaver-birds, a tame grey and red parrot, and a perky, long-beaked hummingbird [sunbird] which insistently pecked on the glass of the window nearest to me. Finally, the morning came when we were to take the launch to Yakusu on the Congo where we would find the Doctor expecting us. He had arranged to send his launch for us on Friday, the 19th, and we were waiting for it almost before daylight. It took 1-1/2 hours to go down-stream, and in the afternoon, when we returned against the current, it took 3 hours. In a canoe it would have taken about 5 hours I presume. The Doctor was cheerful and encouraging, and confirmed our hopes that there would [yet] be a baby by Thanksgiving. Two more journeys of this kind will be necessary, and you may be sure that we are thankful for your support.

Ione took time to contact her English nurse, Betty:

.....Thanks very much for your letter received this week. We are glad you did have a nice time with us, regretting only that you had so much work to do for the 'sick lady'. But is it with real thankfulness that we regard your being here just at the time when we needed you most. Thanks for coming, and do so again whenever you can spare the time.

.....Well, about Yakusu: We waited until about ten o'clock for the launch, or rather shortly after 9:30. We arrived at Yakusu a little after eleven, had some lemonade to drink, and Hector went off with Alfred (Walby) [missionary from the UK] *to see the station. We were surprised the Walby baby had not arrived* [as of] *this week. They promised to write us immediately upon its arrival.*[51]

I gave the Doctor the details of your note and he was very appreciative, took everything down on a sheet of his paper. Then he made a chest, abdominal, and vaginal examination, and announced my condition perfectly satisfactory.

That stiffness in the last vertebra the Doctor said was only a bit of rheumatism and would pass off; and it has. I am still just as nauseated, but am anticipating release from it by the middle of the month.

But on May 26, Hector wrote three letters from Bongondza, one to Pastor Clarence Keen in Toronto, one to his dear friends Chester and Dolena Burk and the third to Ione's mother. They are all slightly different but the central theme in all three focus on the sorrowful details of the miscarriage that indeed happened.

Dearest MOTHER:

---

[51] Although not documented in the letters, the Walby baby's arrival was traumatic. After a long labor, the baby's head was stuck and facilities were not available for a cesarean section. The only option was to rupture the baby's skull membranes. which would result in a stillbirth. While trying to determine the best route to take, the baby's skull membranes ruptured spontaneously. Alfred was relieved to at least have his wife, as he was in danger of losing them both.

Well, I think I will be safe in saying that this letter will be all my own work. Ione is in bed.

Saturday she was working around the house and was able to get our accounts all lined up. In the afternoon I rearranged the office furniture, putting in a little camp bed so that we could have an extra place just to lie down for a few minutes. Saturday evening, I was doing some work at the new desk and she was sitting on the bed. She had a few cramps so finally curled up to rest. About 8:30 we went to get ready for bed. She had scarcely gone in the bathroom when she called to me. I asked her if I could come in, then she told me she was afraid to move, lest something would come. However, I took some of her things and she was able to get to the bed. I took off her shoes and socks and gave her the bedpan. Once she was lying down, she was more relaxed. I got ready for bed and knelt down and read a chapter from Exodus and we had prayer together, and put out the light. I have been sleeping in another room, but I thought I better stay near her in case of trouble. She took out the pan and tried to settle down for the night, but the pains were getting worse again. About 10:30 she got the pan again and as I was about half asleep, I just heard a faint noise but Ione said, "Oh, Hector, something has come". I gave her the flashlight and went to get dressed to go over and call the Jenkinson's. When I came back to get the flashlight and to give her a candle for the time I would be gone, she showed me our little baby. The poor girl just broke down and said, "I didn't want to lose it". I tried to comfort her by remembering what we had asked the Lord to do for us just a few hours before. She realized afresh that He makes no mistakes. I made sure she would be all right and dashed off to get the Jenkinson's.

.....As soon as I came back, I lit the big gas lamp and then Mrs Jenkinson took control of the situation in a wonderful way. Mr Jenkinson helped me get a fire going, and then we sat in the living room, waiting. Ma Kinso worked over Ione for about an hour and then she asked us to come in and raise the foot of the bed. The placenta had come away, but now Ma Kinso was afraid of haemorrhage. She asked me to go down and get Verna Schade. Together they decided to give an injection of Ergotine. Kinso went down to the hospital and I went to call Botiki, as he knew where the equipment is kept.

After the injection, everything settled down nicely. Kinso and I got the ladies some tea as they were just finishing up around the bedroom. They had another look at the foetus to make sure that everything was there and went in to tell Ione that it was a little girl. Then Kinso and I went out to bury it under an orange tree in the back garden. Ma Kinso stayed here all night as it was now 2:00 a.m. Kinso led in prayer before we separated and I went in to see that Ione went to sleep all right.

So now everything is back to normal. She had a bit of temperature yesterday morning, but that passed away and she has been eating well. Everyone has been so good to us and Ma Kinso spent most of the morning over there today. She will get the very best care.....

Your devoted Son - X Hector

To Chester and Dolena Burk, Hector added:

.....pretty soon Ma Kinso took control. A thousand blessings on her. She worked over her from 10:45 until 2 a.m. After the placenta had come then the bleeding started [a description Hector did not share with his mother in law].

Botiki was ever so kind and patient last night. Kinso was around too, helping where he could. Both he and Ma Kinso had left their dental bridges at their house. They just would hardly take any thanks for the trouble, here. Everybody has been so good. Ma Kinso slept in the office and today Verna is on duty. Ione will have to stay in bed for at least 10 days.

Since starting the last paragraph, we have had dinner and a rest. Ione is coming along nicely.

Be glad to hear from you again.

As ever,   Hector & Ione

There is little doubt that Ione's passion for evangelizing in the local villages was her greatest heart's desire. At many times during the care-giving years with the Westcotts she pleaded with God to allow her to get out and share her joy with the natives – what she really came to Africa for. The simple dirt road through the dense forest from Bongondza to Kole (the nearest town), is 25 kilometers and the only vehicular traffic would be the few missionaries going to and from Bongondza station once or twice a day at most. The 10-mile walk Ione had taken must have been a blissful time of soaking in the natural wonders around her - the singing of birds, the churring of insects – and heart-to-heart talks to those walking with her. So, it is not surprising that she was so enraptured with the experience, she lost track of her limitations, especially those brought on by her pregnancy.

As Ione recuperated, Hector carried on at the station and in June 1946, he wrote for a magazine, demonstrating that while Bangala would be easier to learn than Kingwana, he had not yet grasped all the nuances of the language as explained in the following story:

My class in manual training is just across the pineapple patch, in the carpenter shop. They are making deck chairs from a pattern of one I have. Some of the lads are quite good with tools.

After the morning meetings I have to find work for the carpenters and explain in my best Bangala what is required. When words fail, I lay hands on some pieces of wood and give them an illustrated lecture. Two weeks ago, a man came in to buy some boards to make a casket for a relative who had died during the night. Mr Jenkinson thought of having one made to sell when needed, and with this thought in mind I instructed two men to make this box. The following day I entered the shop and there it stood...about a foot-and-a-half square and four feet long. I looked at the men and demonstrated how impossible it was for a man to get in the box. Then the truth came out; they did not know that I wanted a casket for a dead man. They thought it was a box to pack goods in.

With the right idea they commenced another – the former could be used for a clothes cupboard. The next day they brought to me what looked like a square cone. The length was alright, but now there was no room for the feet and too much room for the head. After expostulating, the natives had a good laugh and I suppose we must use this one for a gate post!

Ione wrote to her friend Evie on June 7, and although she mentioned her loss, she focused more on other matters, describing some of Hector's work schedule:

.....In spite of our disappointment about the baby I have been very happy here. Hector is so good to me and never seems to be cross or lose his temper. He seems to have a grand disposition, and such a sense of humour. His appetite is good, too. And I do enjoy preparing meals when they are appreciated. He works very hard and I wonder how he maintains his weight and even is gaining a little, but he drinks about two quarts of milk a day. Recently he has had charge of the station again when Mr Jenkinson went to Juba to get two new missionaries and there were 75 workmen for Hector to oversee, besides the carpenters at the shop, the Manual Training Class for boys, the hospital workmen and nurses, besides our own staff members. He had the job of demolition of a sundried mud house which the wind had somewhat wrecked, the making of bricks in the kiln for a new house, the addition of new rooms on Miss Walker's house, roofing some school buildings with leaves, and as a side-line just for fun he erected a 40-foot flagpole to fly the Belgian flag when Kinso arrived with the new girls. We are nine now on the station, but some will go to Ekoko eventually. The latest two are Mary Baker from Va., and Mary Rutt from Pa., very nice girls, just my age. Mary B is living with me temporarily while Hector is on a trip to Stan and Wamba. They will have rooms soon in the back of the church, prophets' chambers, so to speak.

Believe it or not, my baggage has not yet arrived. Recently I received the keys and the final papers so they must be coming up the Congo River now. You asked me if I needed anything. My needs will be pretty well met when the things come, but if movie films come back into circulation and you can get hold of one, I would appreciate it. Mine is an Eastman 16 millimetre. But don't feel you must get more than one, for they are quite expensive. We took wedding pictures but sad to say, not one turned out well. Now that Hector can check on the camera we would like to try again. For our still camera the number is 616 if you should want to stick in a few of them.

How is everyone at your house? Mother well? Did the strikes affect you much? Write me again real soon. Your last letter was so interesting and newsy. Don't ever feel that I have forgotten you for I never shall.

Love, Ione

On June 9, Ione felt strong enough to write to the family, the first letter was to her Mother:

.....I just found the carbon copy of the letter Hector sent to you two weeks ago, and I shed tears all over it! But I'm glad he wrote you such explicit details for you no doubt would want to know all about it. However, it has not been a really

difficult time as there has been no pain or discomfort since that night. I had excellent care and both Ma Kinso and Verna kept things very sterile and tidy in the room. I had a bath every day. Then the day that Hector had to go to Stanleyville, on the third day (Tuesday), Mary Baker came over and stayed right with me all of the while. From then on, she waited on me and we had the cook set the table in the bedroom and she ate with me there. Mary has only just arrived and knows very little Bangala, but we have had lots of fun while she has tried to tell the staff members what to do. One time when she was pouring kerosene oil into a lamp and the helpers were tipping up the oil drum, she shouted excitedly, "Oh, Ione, tell me quickly how to say 'slowly' – " She is a delightful southern girl and made hot biscuits for breakfast three mornings. She has gained about four pounds helping me gain one! She weighs about 143. Hector was delayed longer than we expected on his trip and didn't get back until just yesterday. And such a wonderful reunion we have been having. We have tried heretofore not to show our affection in front of others, but it is hard, for the separation, just at this time, has made us more in love than ever. Honestly, I never realized I could care so much for him.

My weight went down to 108 pounds, but recently (according to these uncertain scales) I have gained about three pounds. I really think I must weigh more than that for my clothes do not look baggy on me. True, they were getting a little tight but now I seem just about the size I was when I left home. Only my arms and legs are a bit thinner. But a good egg-nog every day is a help, and Mary B. has given me a supply of liver and iron tablets. I also have Inez' vitamins, but I will wait until I finish with the liver tablets before I take the vitamins again in case they might not mix. Since the nausea is gone, I have been eating like a horse. When I am a bit stronger Hector and I plan a visit to Ekoko. Then will be the grand time when the Pudneys come.

We expect them in August, after they attend a big conference in Léopoldville. They will spend about a month on each station. And they want us to have a general conference of all Congo U.F.M. missionaries, so that will mean a lot of travel for some and a lot of entertaining for others. I have a feeling we'll do the entertaining, since our station has the facilities. I hope I can help plan the meals, for I love that, and cooking in large quantities is nothing new to me.

Just then I was feeling the most useless with spending so much time in bed, two hospital women accepted Christ when Verna spoke to them, as well as Lollypop's sister the leper girl. Praise God with us for this. I can hardly wait to get out in the children's meetings again. But I must wait until I see the Doctor again next week. I must make another trip by car and boat and unless I need what they call a 'curettage' [cleaning of the uterus], I can come right back. I'm quite certain everything will be alright.

I was praying nearly all day during Marcellyn's graduation, and felt assured that it was a blessed time. I shall be anxiously waiting to hear all about it. Don't worry about me. We won't hang up the extra stocking this Christmas, but hope for the next Christmas!

Loads of love, XXXXX Ione

On the 13th of June, when Leone Reed responded to Ione and Hector's news, she had obviously heard about quinine and its possible negative impact on pregnancies:

Dearest Precious Ione and Hector:

Your letter written May 27 was received last Monday June 10th. My heart surely went out to you in your sorrow, illness and great disappointment. We do know our God doeth all things well and some time we will know why God does certain things. I lost my first baby, too, and I, too, was so disappointed. I answered an ad in the paper and took a little 3 month-old baby and took care of it until I expected Lucille. I had to take gallons of medicine (a certain kind) the summer before Lucille was born to keep from losing her. One day at the 6-mo. stage, I was kept under a hypo all day to keep the pains from increasing. They finally wore away. Ione darling perhaps the quinine is your difficulty. Women who want to get rid of babies often take quinine. Isn't there anything else you could take to ward off malaria? I heard that the soldiers in the last war took a certain drug in place of quinine. Please Ione take extra care of yourself now and rest and build up all the health you can. Then no doubt you can become pregnant again. ....Perhaps this baby would not have been normal given the trouble you had since the day you walked so far. The Lord surely knows best. It is too bad though that you had to be so nauseated so long. I could sure feel for you. Remember when I was in bed for three months before Doris came? It's a great life if you don't weaken. Keep looking up.

By June 21st, Ione had travelled to Yakusu with Joan, to see the doctor for a final check after losing the baby. Hector had to stay behind and manage the mission. They returned to Stanleyville and had to stay over a few days until they could be picked up by Kinso. They were staying at a home belonging to the Baptist Missionary Society, which seemed well equipped; Ione wrote to her mother:

.....We have a house helper to care for our needs and an electric refrigerator. We found a store that sells ice cream powder & have already made ICE CREAM! Tomorrow we are going to a butcher to see if we can find a roast beef! Such luxuries as these folks have in Stanleyville.

.....I got some new ideas when I walked around the BMS mission station at Yakusu. Their children in the girls' school are making rope doormats of banana fibre, something we could try. And they were doing some lovely fagotting on hand-made slips. And they have a kindergarten school, which I would love to have at Bongondza.

.....I have had such precious fellowship with the Lord during these quiet days, and now I feel quite ready to go to my work again. We are going to be busy painting, getting ready for the Pudneys, whom we expect in August. And I am hoping to do more visitation among the sick folk who come once a week for shots.

Hector is very busy just now, putting shingles on the house Viola lives in. They have built on an extra room & a verandah and raised the roof. He is 'batching it' this week. There are three single girls on the station but without his wife there he dare not eat with them, else the natives would think he was wanting more wives! I don't know what he'd do if he had two! He is so attentive to the one! Honestly, Mother, I didn't know a husband could be so dear and so thoughtful. Pray that I may never lose him. May the Lord bless and guide you continually.

Very lovingly, Ione   XXXX Kisses to all.

Hector wrote to his Father on the 22nd of June and started with Viola's roof:

.....It has been ever so busy these past few days as we have been putting some shingles on Miss Viola Walker's house. It was really too small a house for comfort so we added two more rooms in brick and then took down the old leaf roof while she went out on trek. We wanted to get the new one on before the walls and inside got too much rain. This is our first venture with shingles. The natives cut down the trees and saw them into 18" wide blocks and then cut off half inch slabs. At any rate anything is better than these leaves. I kept remembering the time Archie and I did the hog pen. It would be a treat to get some nice cedar shingles out here. Tin [roofing] is about 4 dollars a sheet and then it is very hard to get since so many big companies have priority.

I was thinking the other day about some of the things I would like to hear again around the old farm; such as a robin singing down in the cherry trees, or a whip-poor-will north of the railroad track, or the old fanning mill on a wet spring day. How I longed to hitch an engine unto it ! ! ! !

Needless to say, Ione and I have been a bit disappointed in losing our baby. Ione has gained in health a lot since then and it has made quite a change to be able to eat normally once more. Our love for each other has grown deeper and we seem to be really husband and wife now in a new way. I never thought I could care for anyone quite so much. She is my ideal in everything. It is hard to be separated. For the past week she has been down to Stanleyville to see the doctor for a check-up.

I'm still in good health and drinking lots of milk. Klim is rather expensive but it keeps me in top notch. But I would like to pay a visit to the milk house on the farm. Just wait until I get back there! ! ! Our allowances and gifts are coming through regularly.

On June 24 Hector wrote to friends and explained how the Africans communicated using a drum. The sounds produced were phonetic but the untrained ear might not appreciate the language used:

.....This morning when I was going over for the early meeting with the workmen, it was rather foggy and I didn't see anyone around when I whistled for them to beat the drum [to call the others]. So, I made my way over to it and decided to try my hand at this ancient art. The drum is a log cut out of a tree trunk, three

feet across and about six feet long. With native tools they cut out the center of it, working through a narrow slit, and leaving the ends intact.

The hammers are just two short pieces of hardwood limb. And so, I picked up these two formidable weapons and gingerly began to send out my RADIO message that it was time for everyone to be at the meeting! I tried to imitate the rhythm that I have heard three or four times each day. I think I might have done better on a three-console pipe organ! Using only one hammer I started on one side for about five beats. Then came the business of using two hammers on two sides. About every ten beats I would get off the rhythm. It must have sounded dreadful to the trained ears of the natives. The finale of it consists in forcibly bringing both hammers down almost simultaneously on one side. I just got nicely finished and settled at the desk in the class room, when the head-man came out of a house, picked up the hammers, and – you should have heard the difference! Anyway, when the men all gathered, we had a good study in Acts 9 about Paul's conversion and his call to missionary service. Verse 16 reads thus, "But I will show him how many sorrows he will eat because of My name."

Something quite interesting came to light the other day. While we were finishing the ridge of a new shingle roof, the sound of the hammer was <u>echoing</u> *on another building nearby. I asked the natives what they called it. They told me some word in their language and then went on to explain that this other sound was the SALUTE to the one I was making.*

Then came the news of yet another death, in a postscript from Ione:

.....Just a word and a thank you to all for your many kindnesses. We are happy to know you are interested in us. Perhaps you remember my telling about little Lollypop, the native baby I was feeding. I am sorry to tell you that she died. We tho't she was safely weaned and eating soft foods and dismissed her to a nearby village and learned just yesterday that they had given her too much plantain and she got diarrhoea and died. Pray for the Lord's wisdom in caring for a new little native boy who was bro't to us yesterday. I am now teaching handwork and singing each day in the boys' school; the boys are learning "Great is Thy Faithfulness," and "Lamb of God" in French.

Much love to everyone in Jesus's Name, Ione

On July 13, Hector wrote to his sister, Eleanor. Hector described the environmental changes when rain clouds gather and their need for a downpour:

.....A cloud in the western sky is making it real dark now, although it is only five o'clock and there is still 1-1/2 hours of daylight yet. But we do hope it will rain. Normally there is enough water from the tin roof of our house to keep us with a good supply in the big tank. From there a helper pumps it up into two big 50-gallon gasoline drums, and from there it is piped into the kitchen and bathroom. Now he has to take two pails and go away down the hill to a little forest stream where he fills them, puts them on each end of a stick and puts the stick on his shoulder. We ran out of water three times this morning, so he was pretty busy.

He continued with a couple more things:

211

.....If I can keep Ione from reading this, I would like to make a suggestion. Her Bible is getting rather worn and I'm just wondering if you could pick out a nice one and send it out, I could give it to my BELOVED for Christmas. Now would you like to do that for me? I would really appreciate it. Maybe if it gets here in time, I could give it to her on Nov. 27 --- our first wedding anniversary. Sometimes you can get those fairly thin ones with nice print, but just suit yourself. There is a good store on the side street along by Peoples Church, on the opposite side of the street. I got the one we gave Dad a few years ago in that store. It just thrills me to think I may be able to have one for her soon.

Kindest regards to your Mother and Dad.[52] We will try to write more often to tell you some of the interesting things people do.   Hector

Hector and Ione go to Ekoko, 210 miles from Bongondza, on the 20th of July for a one-week visit. Ione responded to the letter from Evie which she received before she left Bongondza:

.....I am feeling very good again and have gained back all the lost pounds. I don't seem to be very fortunate with babies for two weeks ago Lollypop died. We had fed her for six months and tho't she would be all right now, but babies go very suddenly. Now I have taken on the feeding of a little boy two weeks old. He is very tiny and his eyes are somewhat protruding, like a little frog's eyes. We have no name for him as yet.

.....That is very thoughtful of you to get together some cosmetic items for me. They will be very welcome. The things I bro't in my hand baggage must come to an end soon and my boxes haven't arrived yet. Imagine waiting all this time! But I have not really lacked for any necessity as yet. We can get tooth paste and tooth brushes out here and a few other items.

.....I am writing to you from Ekoko where Hector and I have been visiting. It is sad that no white person is here just now. And the natives beg us to stay on permanently, but Jenkinson's feel we are more needed at Bongondza for all the building and remodelling Hector must finish soon. The Faulkner's will soon return from Canada and take over here and there will be one or more single ladies, too. But the buildings have gone into bad condition. The school is fine with over 100 boys under Deny's [native evangelist] able care, with evangelists' school and women's classes, too. Hector is settling a palaver [argument] today about the rice rations received for the school from the three nearby capitas [chiefs] of villages.

I had a grand women's meeting yesterday and we had the evangelists in last night. We will return next week. It is our first experience together of camping and we love it. We live in Ludwig's house, but use trek equipment. They have bro't us all the chickens we can eat and dozens of eggs, corn, pineapple, and bananas.   Ione

---

[52] Eleanor has been living with the Wells, who adopted her at an early age when the Avonmore McMillans were unable to care for her after the death of their mother.

Hector, a day later, explained to his Canadian friends:

.....After about a year and a half in the Congo, I feel like an old missionary. At present Ione and I are up at the station called Ekoko between Buta and the Congo river. We are just here for a week.

.....We are expecting Mr and Mrs Pudney after the Léopoldville conference. They will stay until the October boat leaves Matadi. After they visit each of the stations, we all hope to gather at Boyulu. There will be 28 of us all together.

.....This afternoon Ione and I went for a walk out to some of the villages, stopping and looking at their gardens and houses. One old man started grumbling right away about the white ants. And I don't blame him. We went in to see the house he was building. He had the roof leafed and was starting to mud the walls. But the ants beat him to it. They had eaten out one pole and had a good start on some of the others. I'm afraid they're going to beat him out ! ! !

There is enough work at Bongondza to keep the whole carpenter gang of

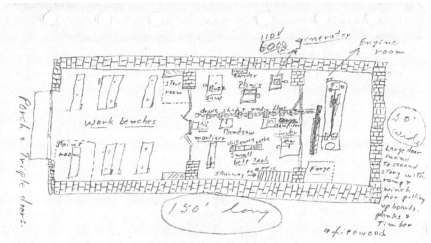

Hector's sketch of the workshop at Bongondza. - c1946

Prairie Bible Institute busy for at least a year. There are a few power machines such as a small buzz saw, grinder, and lathe, but I would just love to have a planer and a saw mill [see workshop plan above]. *Some of the native lads are doing well, and that is a bit of encouragement. Ione is helping in the boys' school, teaching singing and hand-craft classes.*

Letters were scarce for a while as Hector and Ione brought the Pudneys to Bongondza. They drove the 160 miles to Stanleyville in Mr. Jenkinson's little V8-37 and were able to get a little shopping done before the stores closed that night. The next day they greeted the Pudneys at the airport.

In a short letter to his pastor in Toronto, on the 28th of July, Hector wrote:

.....They seemed quite fresh from the long day's trip, but they do need a good rest. The reception here on the station was quite touching. They had not seen Mr and Mrs Jenkinson for nearly 14 years. It has been a wonderful week here. Our evangelists were in for the occasion and before they went away again, Mr and

Mrs Pudney wanted to have a session with them, so I joined in. We were trying to encourage them to work harder in their villages and build up their congregations. We gave them High Park Baptist as an example!

The Jenkinson's and Pudneys are now at Ekoko, about 200 miles north and west of here. So once more I have to look after the station, but there is plenty of help from my wife and five single ladies. This morning I enjoyed taking the church service; speaking on the two natures from II Peter 1.

The McMillans must have been kept busy at Bongondza, but now they had a great deal to rejoice about – Ione's luggage finally arrived nine months after she arrived. On the 17th of August, she wrote to her family:

Dear Friends in Christ: "Who giveth us richly all things to enjoy!

Last week the baggage came! What a thrill after waiting nine months. We received notice from Kole, that the boxes and trunks and kegs were there waiting for us to pick up. It didn't take us long to gather up the 18 pieces [one was missing; it arrived in Africa empty] and to deposit them safely in the basement of the Doctors house. It was there that we discovered the value of Mother's careful packing, for there was very little damage; mirror glass, dishes, pottery, all were in good condition. And the books that Mother had shellacked lay shiny and new in their respective boxes. We take off our hats to Mother and Mr Burton Hempstead, Mr Ball, Miss Slater, and Mr Fulcher for their efficient work.

The mimeograph [an early version of a copier] arrived perfect with all of its accessories, thanks to the Newberry Church at Clarkston. The school supplies were opened and a number of items are already in use in the boys' school. The handcraft models and supplies will soon be put to use in the afternoon class. And Hector's trumpet has been all week penetrating the station quietness with its blats and poofs. The linens, as well as the pale blue glass dishes arrived in time to set a nice table for the Pudneys when they arrived here a week ago. The bedspread from the Loyal's was just the right colour to match the green furniture in the bedroom and the quilts (Mrs Stewart's group) fit the bed and one is on it right now. I was ever so glad to have some clothes for I had been trying to make do with the things I came in.

The compass that my brother-in-law gave me has now become part of the equipment at the native school at Ekoko. And the grand lot of dresses and sun suits given by the White Cross and woman's groups at Five Points and Salvation Harbour as well as the First Baptist Church were just in time to dress up the school children for Pudneys and for the Administrator who came the following Monday. Some of the children's clothing went to the children of evangelists who came in to Bongondza for the annual Motondo Harvest Thanksgiving Service. The layette was examined thoroughly; also, the little flannel quilts from the Joy Philathea Class, and put into a box with a sigh, hoping that they will be used next year.

And the cast-off things that you sent with me instead of the Good Will Clothing Drive, Ines Slater! You would be surprised to see some of them walking around on worthy black bodies. And I think Hector has his eye on the green jacket for some cool nights. The curtains that you tho't were of no use, Hazel Slater, are now gracing our cushions in the living room: and the feltograph and filing material will soon go into active service in children's meetings, etc. Lucille, your old gas waffle iron will provide many more suppers: we've had one. And Doris' grape juice was a special treat; all the canned goods arrived in perfect condition. I can't begin to thank you all for your loving forethought to give all of these things. Be assured that we count ourselves your missionaries and that we are made comfortable by your kindness to us. May the Lord abundantly bless you.

Lovingly, Ione Reed McMillan

P.S. Hello Everybody. I didn't mention how pleased Hector was to see that collapsible frying pan – it's just the thing. We are feasting on the delicious canned things. They are so satisfying.

On the 27th, Hector wrote to yet another church group at the Houston Street Baptist Church in Tennessee. He spoke of the difficulty of getting anything across to the people unless it was illustrated:

.....I had looked up the word 'to hide' in the concordance and came across this verse (Colossians 2:3). In a wonderful way the Lord brought to my mind a way to show its truth to the natives. I got two identical boxes and half-filled them with sawdust. I put a franc piece (worth 2-1/2¢) in one box and none in the other. When I started the message, I put a box on each side of the pulpit and asked a school boy to come up on the platform. Pointing to the box which was to represent the world, I said, "there is a franc in there, see if you can find it". Of course, he looked in vain. The promises of the world are vain. There is no peace, or joy, or life. Then the other box was investigated representing the things of the Lord. This yielded the true treasure.

And of the ongoing projects including the growing number of boys in the school:

.....The work here is so varied from day to day. There are so many tasks that natives cannot do alone; special carpenter jobs, plumbing, mechanics, etc. When the Doctor was here, he had a stationary engine driving his big electric generator for charging 20 batteries. He also ran a circular saw from it. The bearings on the saw were quite worn, so last week I had a great time redesigning the whole thing and putting a shingle roof on one of the school buildings, and the saw is ever so handy for ripping lumber for strips over the rafters. Three of the lads in the carpenter shop are Christians and I enjoy being with them. Some of the older school boys have classes in manual training and they do very nice work. Ione teaches them all for an hour and a half each afternoon in handcraft. Two other ladies take them for their morning classes. There are 89 on the roll now. We have recently drawn up a plan for a new boys' school in brick, according to gov't specifications. So, there will be plenty of work ahead.

On the 30th, Hector and Ione wrote to another church. First, from Hector:

Dear Friends:

"I will send thee far hence unto the Gentiles".

It means taking part in a warfare, sometimes on a lonely outpost, even inside enemy territory with a few resident members of a resistance force. And so, the story could go on.

In some ways this could apply to us but certainly not in regards to the 'lonely outpost'. We are a large happy family here. I didn't realize that missionaries could work together so harmoniously. It is true that we are more or less cut off from the tangled skein of the political and financial world, but nevertheless there are plenty of perplexing problems within the bounds of our few cleared acres in the jungle. These difficulties tend to remind us that we are at the battle front. If the ever-present enemy of our souls could once get us out of tune with our Lord and our fellow workers, it would then become a case of "toiling all night and taking nothing". It is impossible to have civil war and at the same time do battle with a common enemy. So, as a preventive measure we have a daily prayer meeting from 5-5:30 p.m.

To mention something about a local resistance force, we are encouraged indeed by the fine stand that some of these natives have taken. I suppose we shall never know what it has cost some of them to break with age-bound customs. An evangelist, Tasembo, is such a one. From an uncouth life lived selfishly he has changed into an amiable, polite young man: he treats his wife like a partner instead of a burden-bearer. Moreover, he encourages us to study the native language, rather than trying to hinder us as so many do by their lack of cooperation. He sees it as a keen weapon to present God's truth.

This morning when I was pulling nails out of a woolly head of hair (not my own) to spike some rafters to a ridge pole, several of the carpenters and masons were trying to help pronounce various words. It must be my Canadian accent that makes me seem hopeless. So, in return I tried them out on the English word for the same thing. As distinctly as possible I said "Rafter". Then came a chorus of voices, "Laughter". They see no difference between R and L.

.....May this letter find each one of you walking in the Lord's will, with all joy and peace in believing.

Sincerely, Hector McMillan

And Ione wrote:

.....Moses complained that he was slow of speech and of a slow tongue. And that seems to be our complaint of late, for we are trying to learn and speak a new language, Libua. Our Bangala is good enough in business and in general meetings, but to really converse with the people, especially the old people, the Libua language is the only medium. So, we have taken upon ourselves the task of daily lessons taught by Viola Walker, who has made a very special study and has gathered a grammar and vocabulary from her contacts with the Babua tribe, and has translated some parts of the New Testament. I trust it will not take us as long as it did Moses before he could give those splendid farewell talks to his

people forty years after he first tried. Won't you pray that our tongues may be loosened that we may pour forth the wondrous riches of His love for us.

.....Four little new boys came into the boy's school today, bringing the total up to almost one hundred. How thrilled they were with the sun suits sent by three missionary groups. For some it was their first bit of clothing other than a loin-cloth. Verna Schade has charge of the school, Mary Baker helps her in the mornings and in their outdoor activities, and I come in for music in the morning and handcraft in the afternoon. You should see them making string for animal nets out of fibrous grass: they do not need to be taught how to do that! We hope they will have their own net ready for the next hunting expedition. The net must be at least four rods long [16-1/2 ft]. A number of boys have accepted Christ and four were baptized recently. Pray for them in their morning devotional time.

Thanks for the good letters and the gifts which were very acceptable. Greetings to all from Botiki, the nurse at the hospital; Limandigumi, the school teacher; Moses, the littlest boy in the school, who makes up in wiggles where his speech fails; from Pudu, the wee African baby boy; Flicker, the tame antelope; and from Hector, whose letter is on the other side of this!

Lovingly in Him, Ione Reed McMillan

Finally, on the 30th, Ione wrote to her Mother 'and all' in the knowledge that her news would be passed around the family. Some excerpts:

.....A few weeks before the baggage came, I took on some added duties in the boys' school. Joan has not been well and has given up the work to Verna Schade, who had it before when she was here. Joan hopes to leave for England next week. She has been out for over three years and has had amoebic dysentery the entire time.

.....Hector and I are feeling fine now, having both gained a little. He gets very tired, but in this rainy season when the work has to stop, he has some extra times for a long afternoon nap. Yesterday it rained from noon until four o'clock and the rain seemed to come down in pail-fulls. Our water fellow never has to gather water during this, for the eaves-troughing directs the rain into a large cistern which supplies the house thru pipes; and because of the water tank and coils in the kitchen, we have hot water as well. What a job that must have been for Doctor Westcott to do! Every little while Hector shakes his head over some lovely piece of work left by Doctor, and says, "What a man he was to do all of this!" He is realizing more and more what it means to build up a mission station and then keep it in repairs.

Plans are being made now for a new boys' school. The boys have outnumbered their dormitories and classrooms and something must be done for accommodation for them. There are nearly 100 of them. When I have my handcraft, I divide them into thirds, and put them in three separate classrooms. The native teacher has one group and two older schoolboys the other two, and I pass from one to the other, giving instructions and checking on their work. Sometimes I wish I were triplets!

.....The school supplies them with nice two-piece khaki suits for Sundays and during the week they are supposed to wear the suits that were last year's Sunday suits, but there are so many boys that were not here last year and they have nothing. What has been sent fills a real need and they love them. You should have seen the proud look on a little boy who received a bright purple one! The clothing that I brought from home that was old and cast off has served for some bigger boys who have worked every noon for us in our garden for one month. Dorothy Keylon's bathing suit went to a chubby boy named Avakuma. He is proud of the name embroidered on the front.

By the way, we have peas and parsnips and turnips, radishes and peppers and tomatoes growing. I don't know whether they will live to bear fruit, but there are hopes. The roots of the peas look a little rotten already from the rain. We have had a splendid crop of popcorn and is it ever a treat.

This morning I took out of my trunk a little painted frame for pots and pan holders. It is a colored mammy holding up two hooks which hold the two red holders. I took it to the kitchen and asked the staff what it was. One said it was an animal (the scarf around mammy's head sticks out in two places at the top!); Tabia said it was a bird; and Lendo, who was doing the ironing said it was an animal with horns. They laughed when I told them it was a woman. Then they began to see the features of it. I told them I was going to nail it in the kitchen by the stove. I called it Tabia's wife, and that bro't a chuckle out of him, and when I nailed it up, I said, "And she can't run away from you," (his other one ran away from him!). Then I put two more holders inside the top of the stove, one had a top like a chicken. I said, "This is the house of the chicken; perhaps it will lay eggs here." He laughed and said, "Will a cloth give birth to a child?" They have such funny ways of saying things.

We have had the Pudneys in our area for nearly a month now. But they have spent one week of that at Ekoko and are now trekking among the pygmies and the Basali folk. Today Mrs Pudney and Viola come back from the pygmies. Their journey was an interesting one and we'll be glad to hear all about it. Part of the trip was to have been made by canoe. Monday Mr Jenkinson and Mr Pudney will be back from their journey. Then they will be with us one week more, and leave for Maganga and Boyulu. Two weeks later we will all go to Boyulu for a large General Conference.

Two weeks ago, there were about 16 baptized here. Among them were two school boys who have really come right out for the Lord. They are giving messages and praying very frequently. One of them is Botiki's cousin who came back here with him when Botiki returned last year. Now my paper is finishing too quickly.

I am so anxious to hear from you, Mother. I missed telling you on Mother's Day that I love you very much and I long for the day when we can be together again. Thanks for all the hard work of packing my things. I keep finding little tokens of your tender touch.

Lovingly, Ione

Joan Pengilly left for England (for an unknown reason) and Hector and Ione drove her to Stanleyville so she could catch her plane. It was an opportunity to get the car repaired but more importantly, the trip meant Ione could meet up with the Doctor at Yakusu for a maternity check-up.

As a guest at the Sabena Hotel in Stanleyville, Ione had more time for letter writing and provided useful description and insight into her aplomb when faced with surprises. One incident (described in a letter dated September 9th) occurred when Viola took Mrs Pudney on a route which fringed pygmy territory. The ladies had the excitement of stopping a war between the forest pygmies and the village ones:

.....A man had absconded with a girl, a sufficient cause for the blowing of the war horn. The forest folk came up the road but at sight of the white woman they retreated as quickly as they had come. "What's the use of fighting and wounding people?" asked Viola of one of the little men. "Wound?" said he, "We kill, we do not wound." True, their poisoned arrows never miss the mark. Farther on they had the joy of seeing a whole village indicate their desire to follow the Lord. Who would teach them? There was no one. They pooled their resources and bought a village Bible. One of the lads who can read a bit will read the precious Book to them. Who will be their teacher? The Holy Spirit.

Also, Ione found time to write to a church in Michigan on October 5th. She thanked them for their gifts of money and explained how it was put to service and described life as a missionary and what the recent days entailed:

.....As I look down the list of expenditures from this service support, I am more than grateful that your gifts have made possible shop supplies, gasoline for a trip to the doctor's a microscope for the hospital, and many other smaller items. I do not know how we could have managed without your help for living expenses are higher here than before I went home on furlough. Someone said, "two can live cheaper than one, but not so long." I am glad we have the assurance that friends at home are interested in us out here, and are helping in such a material way.

Today another baby came to be fed and healed, the wee son of our Big Chief Toya; his wife is a sweet woman whom we hope to reach for the Lord. Each one of these African infants that we help costs about $37.50 for the first six months; it is a real project and I am thankful that the Lord enables me to do it. We lost Lollypop, the little girl, but another little boy, Pudu, is doing very well.

.....It was a thrill to come home this week after nearly two weeks at a General Conference at another UFM station, Boyulu, and to find that altho' there was no white person here at Bongondza for that time, there were three souls saved. How often one finds that the Lord can work thru other channels than ourselves. We praise the Lord for Christian Africans who can be trusted to carry on the Lord's work. The boys' school of 112 was left in charge of Limandigumi, and the numbers increased to 120.

In August, my trunks came, then the Pudneys from America to see our station, and I was glad to have a nice white tablecloth on the table! It was just about then that I took on the handcraft and music classes in the boys' school, as well as child evangelism, and then a number of boys accepted the Lord. I was glad that we had taught them to pray at the beginning and end of each class, for when we came back from the Conference, we found them doing it. They are memorizing Isa. 55, Psalm 100, and a verse from each book in the N.T. "The entrance of Thy Word giveth light." For a number of months, we had daily lessons in the tribal tongue, Libua, and found it fascinating. Now we have found it necessary to spend an hour a day in French study to get ready for an examination in January. My husband and I have just completed our second examination in Bangala; would you like to know our marks? Hector 88-1/2 and I, 92-1/2.

DIARY OCT 3rd: 5 A.M. Mother of native baby, Pudu, calling that she might receive some milk for the baby; got up and prepared it and went back to sleep until 7, when carpenters came for Hector, a fellow applied to me for work, went to the hospital to see the patients, stopped at garden & picked fresh peas, turnips, radishes, put medicine in antelope's sore eye, put oil on scabby head of the native baby, visited boys' school music class and was thrilled to find that teacher was able to beat time correctly and teach in 3 parts. Breakfast at 8:45 – devotions in Bangala with the staff. Spent some time with the Lord. At 9:45 unpacked our things and gave soiled things to helper to wash and iron. Many things were wet and had to be put into trays in the sun – stationary zipper case, many stamps, envelopes, paper. Set our food for the cook to prepare for dinner, rice, sweet potatoes, spinach, some tinned meat, fresh rhubarb sauce from some rhubarb we bro't with us from Boyulu (their vegetable basket from the Kivu mountains has some in it); dinner at 12; rest until 2; hot bath, went to visit the native women on the station; Atosa gave me 4 eggs. Station prayer meeting at Jenkinson's at 5. Hector mentioned how good a rhubarb pie would taste so the cook and I made one for supper and sent two pieces to Jenkinson's. Made a shell for a cream filling tomorrow. Supper at seven, read a while and went to bed.

Next week will be a bit different, with the regular station activities again, with hospital meetings Mon. Wed. Fri. at 6:30 A.M.; Music Classes each day at 8:30; Child Evangelism Mon. & Wed. 2- 3:30; Handicraft Tues. & Thurs.; Choir Mon. & Thurs. French for whites each day at 4.

On the 12th, in a letter to her sister Lucille, Ione wrote:

.....I have translated Mother's DVBS [Daily Vacation Bible School] *program into Bangala, even the creed and "Thank God for the Bible" song. I have stand up and sit-down chords and one boy, Ngbayo, plays them (I stuck red papers on the organ keys for one chord, and blue papers on the notes of the other chord! He can't miss it!). There are several boys working on trios. This morning I took two out with me to some villages for meetings for a little practical work. The boys are memorizing Isa. 55, Psa. 100 and a favourite verse for each book in the N.T.*

You should see the smallest boy, the child of the head teacher. Little Moses can salute, march, and has even tried to speak French (he is about 3 years old and very chubby with a look of constant wonder on his round brown satin face; his lashes curl like silk and his body is like lumps of chocolate!) They say when he prayed the other day he said, (in French) "I am, Thou art, He is, Amen." He is one of the first of second-generation Christians, providing he accepts Christ, for he is from parents who are both Christians, a rare thing. We just heard the other day that Anziambo and Kibibi are expecting a baby. Anziambo is a very promising evangelist on the Basili Trail. This baby we hope will be another trophy. It means so much to have Christian parents; I hope you children realize that.

This week I have fed three African babies, the diet ranging from weak Klim to strong, Cod-liver Oil, glucose, sugar, castor oil, crushed bananas, tangerine juice, flour gruel, antelope soup, and raw eggs.

.....Now I must close. Won't you pray for us, too, for we are so busy with this big house and so many African girls and boys. We are very happy and could not ask anything except that we hear oftener from you dear ones at home.

Lovingly in Christ, Hector & Ione

On the 17th, Ione wrote to their hosts, the Burks, regarding the conference held at Boyulu:

.....We missed last week's mail with a letter to you as we had intended, so will get an early start this week. We want you to know how we enjoyed staying at your house during the Conference. You made us feel so welcome and right "at home". Thank you so much for all you did for us. It must have been a tremendous job to satisfy so many people with so many things for so long a time, beside all of your schoolboys! You must have been very tired.

.....Enclosed is a check for 600 francs for our share of the food; Hector had so many 'seconds' that we really should be paying more! And this hardly pays for half of the jam you bought, and we ate ever so much of it, it was so good! It was a real treat for us.

.....Hector surprised me tonight by bringing in a lovely revolving table stand for condiments, jam, etc. It is of one lovely large piece of reddish wood. It runs with ball-bearings, and has a nice metal stand under it [a lazy Susan?]. He just varnished it and it is hanging just now from the ceiling over our heads. A few days ago, he fixed a 'noiseless' door fastener in the bathroom. I expect next he will be padding the tub!

Please be assured that we love you and long to have your fellowship again real soon.

Work for Hector was never ending at Bongondza. He spent quite a while on Ione's watch and got it to go for a few days but it started acting up again. However, Marcellyn's little Ben was repaired and it sat on the table ticking softly and faithfully.

Hector's latest accomplishments included: benches for the school boys, a re-model of "Benton Hall" (another classroom) with seating forty at brick and wood desks; venetian blinds, an office desk, a shoe rack, a clothes closet, a ceiling, and other odds and ends for some of the single ladies. For some of Bongondza's dwellings, Hector built venetian windows inspired by a design he saw on a new building in Stanleyville. These windows kept out the wind and rain but allowed circulation and were easy to install and clean. Hector felt the occupants would not have to rush home to close up the house when a storm came up. So, he, once again, demonstrated his capacity to turn his hand to anything.

Hector's aluminum Venetian shutters (interior photo).

Hector gave his pastor in Toronto a short report on November 22nd, describing the various departments of the work at Bongondza, and he included some humour:

.....The evangelistic work is being taken care of now by Miss Viola Walker together with Miss Francis Longley (Toronto) who is now on Bongondza personnel, learning the language which she will use when she and Miss Baker go to Ekoko next January. They are on a three-week trek now and after a few

days rest next week, will again go into another district among the pygmies. Mrs Pudney will be able to tell you something about those people since she trekked with Miss Walker about two months ago.

Machini leads a march at Bongondza – c1946. Doctor's House is behind the large tree in center, the hospital is at left and the shop is on the right.

.....Boys' School – under the direction of Miss Verna Schade. There are about 120 on the roll, having each one 206 bones with muscles attached, making a grand total of a LOT OF WIGGLES. Of late we have been giving them about a half hour of physical training each morning, which uses up some excess energy. Miss Baker helps in the teaching, and Ione takes the classes for singing, handcraft and child evangelism. Quite a number have accepted the Lord, and those who are Christians are dealing with others. Pray for the new school building which we are planning to put up soon. It will take a lot of men and bricks and hard work.

Also, for a young man to come out from America or Canada with qualifications to teach.

Here is the end of the page and there are three more depts.! But with this I will close. The other day I began to think of where we could place three young men if they were available. Then I asked Ione where she would put them. She said, two in the boys' school and one out doing child evangelism. The three jobs I had picked out were, Doctor, teacher for the evangelist, and trekking the outstations. Hence Pray!! Hector

Hector's sister Eleanor got a 'thank you' for doing his Christmas shopping for him:

Dear Sister Eleanor:

.....It would be so much easier to sit down and talk to you; but after the nice Bible you picked out and had sent out here !!! well, I'll just have to do the next best thing, and write you a letter.

When the weekly mail came on October 23, there were a few letters and two parcels. I was working in the carpenter shop, when Mr Jenkinson sent a native lad around with the mail to the various houses, about 4 p.m. When I came to the house Ione had read some of the letters and had opened one parcel, (not yours). Everything was on the dining room table, so I picked up the other package and came in the office. I must say that the Bible was well wrapped. When I finally got the last paper off and saw it, I could hardly believe my eyes. It was so thin and yet such good print. Could I contain myself until Christmas ???? It didn't take very long to make up my mind. I picked it up and went into our bedroom, asking Ione if she would like to come in for a minute. We sat down together and I told her that I wanted to give her a Christmas present. When she saw it, I can tell you that I got a nice big thank-you kiss. She does appreciate it very, very much and wants to send along her thanks.

A week later, Hector wrote to his father and Archie:

Dear Dad and Archie:

Thanks for the nice letters you have been sending and I did appreciate the clippings from the paper. I read all I could see, on both sides. It was nice to see Mr. McDonnell's picture too.

And we do want to thank you and Aunt Marjorie for the $25. It will find plenty of uses. Living is quite expensive here compared to what it used to be. It is amazing how much meat comes to our door. A small hind leg of a little antelope costs about 30¢. It lasts about two days. If we try to keep it longer that that it begins to spoil. Milk is the most expensive thing, about $1.75 a week. This Klim is wonderful stuff. It is whole milk atomized. The water is evaporated and the rest falls to the bottom of the container as powder. That is sealed and sent out. We put two tablespoons of this powder for each glass, mixing it with boiled filtered water.

Did you know that Aunt Marjorie gave Ione some seed corn when she visited Avonmore? Just the other day I put three kernels in a glass of water with a blotter in it. I have the glass on the desk in front of me and two of the kernels have sprouted. One is up about three inches. It must feel funny growing in November !!!! But it is nice and warm here.

Bongondza worker "churning" a barrel cement mixer built by Hector.

Ione is going to dictate now for a few minutes. She is lying down, as she is not too well these days. We are hoping for a baby next June but she seems to have a difficult time the first three months.[53] [Ione wrote:]

We are hoping to plant all the corn when the rains come on in Feb. The baggage and the corn did not come in time to plant it in the last rainy season. I put the peas in but they didn't do well. We wish that we could be with you at Christmas time; I can't think of a nicer place to spend Christmas than on the farm. Our Christmas tree here will be a paper one. We do have some spruce trees in the yard, which we brought from the mountains. We do enjoy very much receiving your letters and hope you will keep up the good work. You must miss Jean a great deal. We were glad to have a letter from her recently. My pet hobby these days is the school boys. That is all Hector hears me talk about. Just now we are making new clothes for them to wear next year. One hundred skirts and pairs of short trousers is quite an undertaking; but all the ladies on the station have joined forces and 77 have been finished now. We are planning a Christmas program. The boys are going to act out the little story, "Why the Chimes"; and Hector is going to fix the church bells (brake drums) so they will ring with no one pulling the cord. I don't think he knows himself yet how he will do it. The native girls and women also have a part in the program, but Hector's workmen will just sit and listen.

Hector's work load increased as noted in a letter written by Ione on December 5th:

.....Hector will have to get busy and build some more houses! Pearl Hiles has chosen the spot where she wants her house when she arrives, next door to Doctor's on the hill. Verna Schade's will be between Mary Baker's and Viola's. The ground has been broken for a new boys school on the slope across from the work shop. A young people's club room is nearly finished near the site of the old church. Then Machini, the head teacher, will need a house back of the boy's school. The old brick kiln will have to do a lot of firing in the near future. No more leaf roofs now, for we are replacing them with wooden shingles made in the Bongondza "shingle factory".

---

[53] The hoped-for pregnancy is quietly announced here midst details of activities on the station.

It had been at times, a difficult year for Hector and Ione, veering from the excitement of their wedding to the disappointment of losing their baby daughter. They had set up a home and opened it up to visitors and fostered children. Lollipop died but Katherine, one of the first children Ione cared for seemed to be surviving at school in Katwa.

They seemed to barely have time to record in detail all their activities, especially the time they had with the Pudneys. It must have been a joy for the Pudneys to see the two young people they had brought together and encouraged to be missionaries, now teamed up and working hard at Bongondza.

Chapter 9
RAISING A FAMILY ON THE MISSION FIELD

The year started with a pensive Ione at Bongondza as shown in an extract from her diary dated January 9, 1947:

8 AM Dear Diary, What a long time it has taken me to realize that I have been slipping back in my relationship with the Lord! As one grows older there is that inclination to rest on the blessings of the past, to recall how the Lord has used us before, to be satisfied having a prayer-list folded between one's hands, thinking you are remembering everyone faithfully. Then comes the sudden realization that the wonderful pressure of His Spirit's urge is gone, and working, witnessing, reading and praying has become too mechanical.

I am not sure just what did it this morning, or whether it was last night when I found that I had done poorly on my French exam. When Hector left in the car, I was on the wrong side of him and missed the last tender glance and the press of his hand. And it left me empty and realizing that without Christ I am nothing. And altho' I have known all along that I am not without Him, yet I have not partaken of His best things for me. I've been satisfied to accept Hector's comforts and compliments and to believe that everything was all right between me and the Lord. But I know there has been a gap, ever-widening, until today when I was forced to admit everything.
Confession:

I made my mistake by not getting away where I could talk aloud in prayer, for constant whispering soon becomes merely thoughts, and how thoughts do wander and sometimes one falls asleep entirely.

My prayer-list was not formed prayer-fully enough, had no suggested Scriptures or means of inspiration and checking from time to time on one's spiritual warmth.

I did not write down the precious verses as they came to me.

I did not keep an account of those dealt with and those who accepted the Lord that I might pray intelligently for them.

I have not visited the natives enough.

I have not spent time enough in prayer over messages.

I have not learned to control the desires of the flesh.

I have not found that victory in ALL things is thru Christ.

I have neglected some of the fundamental things necessary to a practical Christian living.
AND I HAVE BEEN EXPECTING GOD TO BLESS ME!!

When I returned from seeing Hector off, I turned to II Thess. 2:13-17 and found real help. It is wonderful to know that even tho' I have failed so miserably in this first year of our married life, still I was chosen by Him (vs.13) to salvation thru sanctification of the Spirit. I was called, too (vs.14) but it was not for my own gratification or satisfaction but for HIS GLORY. But I have not STOOD FAST (vs.15) nor have I held to that which I have been taught. But I slipped gradually into a rut and my mind as well as my spirit became dulled. Hence the poorly done French and the lack of passion for or ability to win souls. "Standing fast....by word" means you have to say something. And I haven't said half enough to Him and to others about the wonderful Saviour I have. I was taught "by word...and by epistle". I can't expect to see results in the lives of others except I do the same. And then to think that the Lord Jesus Christ Himself, our God, our Father, is the One who loves ME, even now in my useless condition, and has given ME EVERLASTING CONSOLATION, (and He has!) and good hope thru grace. Yes, my heart IS comforted, but it could never be if I did not know that He will also STABLISH me. That's what I have longed for many years. I KNOW that He will do it. "Faithful is He that calleth you, who also will DO it."

9 A.M. I listed the different things that I thought would be put right when He stablishes me and I believe He will make possible the doing of them. He will need to give me physical strength to put first things first and make the effort to reach these people. For when I think of my body in its present condition, I am inclined to take the easy way. And that is not good for me mentally or spiritually. I must learn to do and be His best in this my present circumstance with relation to every phase of my missionary life, as an Ambassador first, as a wife, as a girl-friend, as a 'mother' (to these people and to the school children) as a mother to the child I hope to have, as a teacher, as a leader, evangelist, student, as a housekeeper, as a church-visitor, counsellor, accountant, secretary, not forgetting that I am also a daughter, a daughter-in-law, a sister, a sister-in-law and an auntie!! "And God is able to make all grace abound toward you that ye ALWAYS having ALL sufficiency in ALL things may abound unto EVERY good work."

WHAT AM I DOING AS:

A correspondent. Don't forget Mother, Doris, and frequent form letters.

A member of the Games Committee. Finish the report and mimeograph copies.

A student of French. Daily reading from Bible and some other book.

[A] Libua [student], Lessons from Vee while she is here.

A music teacher. Make a Modulator, help Mary. Easter music for Choir, Corrections in hymnbooks. Complete hymnal organ copy. Visit villages each day at 4 when there is no French, or before then.

A Child Evangelism Director. Letter to French Dept., other stations. Children's classes nearby. In school. Flannel graphs. Check on new idea for board.

A helper to other missionaries. Vee Sewing? Mary & Frances breakfast set, umbrella. Ma Kinso, garden, Kindergarten (?)

A wife. Hector's mending, keep the house more orderly. Insist on the best from the staff. Be easy to talk things over with.

A mother. Baby dresses, bed, etc., maternity dress.

A housewife. Keep storeroom better. Flower house arrangement. Basement. Sewing cupboard.

An accountant. Get the Work Fund up-to-date and audited.

A secretary. Keep record of diary, meetings, souls dealt with, won.

A "Mother" to natives. Talk more to them about their lives & how to improve them.

9:30 Already I can see the Lord working in my behalf, showing me what I CAN do, in spite of my having to be careful physically just now. Verna has come telling me that she will study Libua with me and that we can have a daily lesson while Viola is here. Praise the Lord.

Ione was not afraid to set herself a tough agenda.

On January 25, 1947, Ione wrote to her mother and shared events during Christmas:

Dearest Mother,

This is a birthday letter, tho' it will arrive a little late. I want you to know that I shall be thinking of you and praying for you on your birthday. I am praying that the Lord will guide you with the A 'skilfulness of His hands' in all your plans for this coming year. He has not failed in the past, as you so nicely put in your Dec. letter. The little mat which I shall try to enclose is a wee birthday present. It is native-done with that pretty soft raffia which grows out here.

There is so much to say I hardly know where to begin. I am so glad that Lucille could go to Stockbridge for the baby. As yet I have not heard a word about the baby but perhaps it will come this week. I do hope that everything has gone all right this time. I am just about half-way now and am feeling fine for the first time in months. It is thrilling to keep out-growing my dresses, and it is good to have larger ones to put on. I think it would be a pity to be both misshapen and poorly dressed. I am, gaining in weight (120 now) but all in ONE SPOT! Hector calls me fatty. He is ever so thrilled that I have gotten along this far. Next week I should be able to feel the baby's movements. We have talked a great deal about plans to see a doctor, as I have not seen one as yet. I wanted very much to see a certain doctor in the A.I.M. but the distance is quite formidable, but now it seems that the Lord is making possible a journey to that district. Hector and I have been asked to attend as delegates a convention held at Rethy and if we go (next week) we could find him and have an examination and maybe make some arrangements for the delivery in June.

I am so glad Marcellyn has been having such a good time in meetings and preparations for coming to Congo. I suppose she is in Philadelphia right now. We have not received the Christmas box as yet, but I suppose it will be coming along soon. I am glad you have sent the pillow cases and the canned turkey will be a real treat!

We had a nice time here at Christmas. We decided to celebrate with the natives on Christmas Day itself and postpone the white people's get-together until New Year's Day, for it is difficult to do it all in one day. But unknown to each other, everyone had prepared little presents, thinking to send them over some time during the day and the night before Christmas we were all to gather for a station meeting. Well, Hector and I got the inspiration to bring our presents (we had prepared and filled little red-checked gingham stockings for all) at that time and Hector dressed up like Santa and came barging in with Martha Johnson's riding breeches on and opened his sack in the centre of the floor. Then quickly the others slipped out and got their presents and we had a lovely evening laughing and nibbling on fudge, cookies, popcorn and nuts that were in the socks. Then on Christmas Day the native boys and girls went around early carolling at our windows and at 7 everyone gathered for a prayer meeting. Then at 10 we had the program; I had charge of the boys' play, "Why the Chimes Rang" and Hector had fixed up the automatic bell in the belfry which would ring without anyone touching it and it rang when two little boys accepted Christ.

In the afternoon the natives feasted and there was a ball game and in the evening Mr Jenkinson and Hector showed slides on the life of Joseph and Daniel. We were happy to have the Kerrigans with us at that time. Mrs Kerrigan was recuperating from an illness which all but took her life while she was trekking in the forest. The Lord performed a real miracle in sparing her, for usually Black Water Fever is fatal, and she had begun to pass blackened urine, which is a sign of that. They have a wonderful story to tell of how she came those 24 kilometres out of the forest; her husband was with her and he was so exhausted that he could scarcely walk further. Mr Carter and Mr Burk had cycled in to help to get her and finally Mr Walby, who took some butter and soup-concentrate which was a real help to Mrs Kerrigan. They carried her on a stretcher and finally came to the main road, but it was almost impassable and they had to go over a bridge that was covered with water. Mr Jenkinson went to get Mr & Mrs Kerrigan at their station with his car and he bro't them here. Now they have heard that they can go to England for their much-needed furlough and they are packing for the boat.

It was strange that just at the time that we received the message that Mrs Kerrigan was so ill and Kinso had left to get her, we also heard that Viola Walker was very ill where she was trekking. She, too, needs a furlough. You remember she came out with us in '41. She has severe chills and was in a critical condition and needed to be come for in the car. I tell you we prayed that Kinso would come back soon with the car so that we could get Viola! She now is better, too, but hopes to go home soon. Then came the message that our best evangelist had had a relapse of an old illness which had kept him in bed for weeks and weeks while Doctor was here. Doctor had operated on him for TB of the spine. Now he is back on the station but is not at all well. The incision has opened and is draining pus which causes much pain. Pray for Tasembo, as well as for Viola and Mrs Kerrigan. How we praise the Lord that they are all three alive.

We had expected two couples to spend New Year's season with us, but only one came and that only last week. The Walbys are a lovely English couple and will take over the Maganga station when Kerrigans go home. They have not been out two years yet. The wife's name is Eileen but is called Topsy because her maiden name was Turvey [as in topsy-turvy]. She is lots of fun and a real help and inspiration. And Alfred, big, slow, good-natured is a nice companion for Hector. They were very tired and we hope they have rested some here. We have had lots of good things to eat, roast pork, antelope, chicken and tins of meat, and today I made doughnuts which Mr Walby liked very much. We serve them tea the first thing in the morning, Mrs Walby has milk at 10 and tea at noon, tea at 4 as well as in the evening. We are pretty well tea-ed by now![54] But I enjoy it. Topsy cut out a maternity dress for me this morning. They will leave next week and we will drive them back on our way to Rethy.

Hector continues to be well and weighs about 164 pounds. He has filled out a little but never gets too fat. He is rather tired and I think the little trip to Rethy will be a rest to him. He may have full charge of the station if Mr Jenkinson is called to the Sudan to spend some time getting his ordination. Now the staff at Bongondza is nine, but soon Mary Baker and Frances Longley will go to Ekoko. Frances is an experienced missionary from Canada and very capable and a good manager. Mary is a southern girl with a warm heart and abounding energy. She has been out nearly a year. She is in her early thirties, a graduate of Moody, after Marcellyn, I think. I learned to love Mary very much while working with her in the boys' school. She is a skilled accountant and will have charge of the books at Ekoko.

.....We saw an interesting thing a short while ago. A praying mantis attacked and killed a small bird. You know what the mantis is, a chunky insect with a disjointed head which can turn all around and looks at you with beady eyes. And it holds its front feet up as tho' it were praying. Those front feet are very powerful and that is how it captured the little green and red bird. When I saw it, the mantis was hanging on a bush up-side-down suspended by its hind legs and holding the bird by the shoulders with its front legs, chewing around the bird's neck; then as I looked closer it appeared to be sucking the blood from the bird. The natives say that it is very strange for an insect like that to attack a bird.

Now I must close. I do love you ever so much, Mother, both of us do. We'd like to give you a big hug right now! Please write real soon. I trust this will be your happiest Birthday yet.

---

[54] One American missionary told Topsy it was possible to drink water without first boiling it and pouring it over tea leaves! To which she retorted that she had good manners and drank it without ditching it into the sea—a snide reference to the historical Boston Tea Party.

Love, Ione and Hector XX

About three weeks later, a letter to supporters and friends on February 19, 1947, was filled with the usual mix of thank yous and description of life.

Dear Friends and Loved Ones,

Two more gifts of $50 have arrived, one Dec. 11th and one this week, for which I thank you very much. I believe this brings your total up to $300 for 1946, or an average of $25 per month. That is splendid and I congratulate you. It is these gifts that keep going the car, the shop and the hospital.

The Chief's baby that I spoke of in my Oct. letter died in my arms. It had a venereal disease. That is the third baby that I have lost this year, besides my own. But we are not discouraged, for two have lived of the Africans and we expect one of our own in June! One sees much of death and sickness, but you just keep trying and then by and by you have some real trophies to present to the Lord. Milk has been so expensive and difficult to get that I have welcomed a new recipe for making peanut milk. Now as soon as the peanuts come in season again, we shall be able to feed orphans and sickly babies with a minimum of cost.

.....Hector has equipped a radio left here by Mr Kerrigan when he went on furlough, so now we have news every day. It makes us feel as tho' we're more connected with the outside world. However, we are glad that we are so sheltered from the strikes and shortages in other parts. The Lord is very good to give us everything we need.

Hector and I were able to represent our mission at the big A.I.M. Conference at Rethy in the mountains last two weeks. It was a journey of nearly a week, but it was worth it. We were really cold and our appetites were whipped up and we ate ever so much of the good things there, roast beef, pork, fresh milk, fresh vegetables, watermelon one day, and peaches. We were able to bring back a load of vegetables, smoked meat and honey, so we are feasting here, now, too.

The Conference was attended by over 100 and we were thrilled to be a part of it. On the way we saw many pygmies and some chimpanzees and baboons dashed into the forest ahead of the car. We met a hunter who is searching for Okapis, a peculiar animal somewhat similar to a giraffe.[55]

Yesterday in the middle of a children's meeting at Wameka's village, I heard the headman shout and every child in the service disappeared into the forest. It seems that a chimpanzee needed chasing. It reminded me of the time when our old Sunshine Trio was holding a revival in the fire hall in Asheville, N.C. and the alarm went off and all of our audience slid down the pole to the first floor and went off in the fire engines!

About two years more and we hope to see you all. Until then keep praying and we will try do our part out here. Praise the Lord with us that our wood and water fellow accepted Christ a few weeks ago. Today he attended the Baptism

---

[55] Now an endangered species, the okapi is an herbivore of Central Africa It has a reddish-brown coat and striped legs like a zebra.

Class for the first time. Pray for the fellow who does our washings; his name is Gregory.

Lovingly in His Name, Ione Reed McMillan (Mrs Hector McMillan)[56]

Hector practices the guitar.

The next letter to her sister, mother "and all," Ione wrote:

.....In this week's mail we received the guitar strings Maurice sent. We were both able to sing with the guitar last Sunday night in our white people's church. Hector and I sang, "God Leads His Dear Children Along" and a visitor, Bill Dawn, former classmate of Hector's put in a third part.

We are happy that Lucille and Maurice have another boy. It makes an ideal family. I was glad to have all of the details. Sorry Lucille had a difficult time, but I'm sure she feels he is worth it. Just think he'll be two years old when we see him. Maybe he'll be a pal to our little girl or boy! I can hardly wait now for ours. Everything is coming along all right this time. And I have decided to go to the American doctor [Dr. Becker] at Oicha. I can fly from Stanleyville to Irumu and hope to make connections with the doctor when he passes thru there on his monthly rounds. I will probably go the first of June. The baby should come June 24th, tho' our mission nurse thinks I am a month ahead of that, or perhaps it is twins! I have felt movements for a couple weeks. I am feeling fine now and hope to do much more between now and that time.

Now I must close. This is brief, but to let you know we are well and very happy. Hector is working on the moving picture camera tonight, as yesterday we received 100 feet of movie film from Evelyn Ankarberg and want to use it before it deteriorates. She also sent some toilet articles and hankies, bless her heart.

May the Lord richly bless and use you all.

Lovingly, Ione XXXXXXX

On February 26, 1948, Ione wrote to her sister Marcellyn with news and advice for her forthcoming trip:

Dearest little Sister,

We have surely neglected you of late and I am truly sorry. This morning Mr Jenkinson is driving to Stanleyville and I will get a letter off with him, hoping that it will reach you in time.

Did you get your French-English Phonetic Dictionary that you were telling me about? You should have some sort of dictionary and also a little pocket book for one to have handy when you are shopping, etc. Your prayer cards are lovely, and I am sure you have been ever so glad you had them done that way. The

---

[56] Ione is now establishing links to Hector's supporters as well as writing to her own.

picture is very good of you. We have the big one up in the office, waiting for the real thing! We showed the card to everyone here and they agreed that it was very nice.

I am glad you have met Olive Bjerkseth.[57] She is to arrive today when Kinso returns (or tomorrow). We'll be glad to see her, and I will feel almost as tho' I had seen you when she so recently has been with you.

I'm sorry we have been of such little assistance in your getting ready. Yes, you will need a camp cot, and if possible, a small roll-away bed as well, altho' if you have the mattress, a bed could be made. Innerspring mattresses are not so good here for they rust inside and you can't paint them. While you are here, you might live with Miss Bjerkseth, and when you go to Ekoko you will probably have a rammed earth house until some can be made of cement blocks. Miss Bjerkseth will live in the same house that Pearl and I lived in last term. There is some furniture already there, a bookcase, dresser, etc. If you should have the funds to bring a small wood-burning cook stove you would be glad of it. The one in Miss B's house is not good anymore, and I'm sure you would need it at Ekoko. Your portable oven will be good for trek. Try to get a charcoal iron, as gasoline is so dangerous and you could not trust the cooks to use it. You may be able to get one after you arrive in the Congo. Rain boots or rubbers are fine if you have them, but don't buy anything special. Make sure you have rubber to fit your walking shoes. You'll be glad you have the treadle sewing machine, and so will the other girls at Ekoko for they have none. Yes, you need a good-sized bed sack and ground sheet; also, camp chair and table and dishes. About the garment bag that you are sending—we are not sure yet how plastic does here. Surely plastic dishes and accessories which need washing in boiling water do not do at all, for the water spoils them, but things that don't need hot water probably will keep. We'll be very glad to have a garment bag, and I don't think the bugs will penetrate it; we shall see!

.....You may be sure that we want to do everything we can to help you and we'll go as far as we can to meet you, tho' we don't have a car of our own (yet) and Kinso's is very old and cannot go much. But we'll be there with bells on whenever you arrive!

Loving you very dearly, Ione

On March 1, 1947, Hector wrote to Houston Street Baptist Church, one of his supporting churches and shared his story of the trip to the AIM conference:

.....My wife and I were privileged to represent our mission at a conference of the A.I.M. It was a long trip over rough roads, and I really felt sorry for the car. It took us about four days to get there but the week of fellowship was worth it all. We took a native lad along with us and he enjoyed seeing all the different scenery. When we finally got out of this huge Ituri forest on the third day, it was grand to be able to see far off hills in the grasslands. Peter, the native lad, had

---

[57] Olive was a new missionary coming to Bongondza from western Canada.

never seen or heard a turkey before so at one stopping place he came and asked us, "What is that chicken that talks big?" These people have such a unique way of saying things.

Last week I had my first attack of malaria fever. It wasn't very severe but it leaves one weak for a few days. But I must say that I do thank the Lord for the better-than-usual health I have enjoyed since coming to Congo.

I would be glad if you would remember us the next few months. We are expecting a little one in June and it will mean a trip to a Doctor who is about 650 miles away, partly by car and the rest by plane.

On March 20, 1947, Dr. Becker,[58] in a brief note, replied to Ione's letter regarding her impending birth with good news for the baby's delivery:

.....We would make room for you if necessary. For a servant of our Lord would have first demand on any of our time and efforts.

Hector monitors the boys' physical training class at Bongondza, c1947.

Ione found less and less time for her correspondence, so she resorted to writing one letter to several people, and using carbon copies so each received the same news. On March 29, 1947, she wrote to family:

I have never known Hector as busy as he is just now. He is well, and has entirely recovered his appetite after the week of malaria. Two friends from Boyulu, John Arton and Chester Burk, have been here for two weeks with the big mission truck and they have been hauling rocks to make a foundation for the new boys' school; they have gotten much sand and lumber as well, and it is a real help to our work here. Next week after the men go, there will be 50 extra native workmen bro't onto the station by the territorial agent and they will give a real lift in our work. We need bricks for the new school and shingles for roofs of a number of buildings. Today the white men are trying to finish putting a new box on the back of the truck. It is quite a job and it is very hot. This afternoon they consumed quantities of orangeade and tea. Beside all of the special jobs with the truck, Hector has charge of all station work, buying the food for the 130 school boys and 22 school girls, our own workmen and carpenters, the boys' physical training classes daily, and the many little jobs that he ALWAYS finds time to do for his wife! He will be glad when Mr Jenkinson returns Monday or Tuesday and can take over responsibilities.

---

[58] Dr Becker saw many missionary children safely into the world, he being the doctor who steered Laureen Hemming's own safe arrival, her mother – Topsy – having lost her first baby in childbirth.

You would laugh at the substitutions we serve at the table. One day synthetic hamburgers made from bread and onions, today mashed potatoes made from manioc root boiled and beaten with milk; we had a pumpkin and one meal it was served as squash and the next in a pumpkin pie! Our applesauce is stewed maracouja (tropical passion fruit), our chilli sauce is pai-pai (papaya), tomato and onions, our jam is carambola (star-shaped sweet and sour fruit) and pai-pai, our butter is peanut butter when we cannot get it from the Kivu Mountains. We fare very well, and very cheaply I think, compared to eating at home.

.....Hector and I are still hoping to fly to Irumu in June and go by car the rest of the way to the hospital at Oicha. I have the nice flannel layette that the Loyal Philatheas made for me with blankets, quilts, etc. And the little woollen jackets that I bought when I was in Canada. And two native girls are making little petticoats, dresses, sheets and pillow cases by hand. This baby will not lack. And best of all, Hector has brought 4 springs and a strip of rubber tubing to make a baby carriage! You should have seen his face when he showed us these things recently when he returned from a trip to Buta! There is a nice wooden baby bed and mattress, and a dear little native-made basket which will soon be a bassinet for the baby's journey. I have netting in pink and blue and white, so the baby can take his choice!

.....Enough about that. We want you to know that you are not forgotten tho' you are far away. Thank you so much for your prayers and letters and interest. We shall be looking for more letters.

Lovingly yours in Christ, Hector and Ione

In a letter on April 9, 1947, to Mrs. McLaughlin in Virginia, a supporter, Ione mentioned a letter she received from Anne (Westcott):

.....This week I had such a sweet letter from Anne and I did appreciate it. I am sure I shall never forget those three years that we spent together. I do thank the Lord for leading me to Congo just when He did. We had some precious times together, tho' often difficult. It seemed very strange at first coming to their house and finding it empty of children. I have missed them. Now we are hoping to have a baby of our own and the coming of a little one will fill the gap somewhat. I expect to use the little bed where Charlotte slept when I first came. I am thankful that Westcotts left it.

.....We have finished our hottest season and it did seem hotter this year than ever before. I have never known Westcott's clover grass to turn quite so brown. I thought that it would die entirely, but now it is putting out new little sprouts. We are busy separating the lovely white lily plants Ellen put in. The 'mother' lilies have so many 'babies' around them and we are transplanting all the babies in other places. It is fun. I think there will be enough for a lovely border all the way to Doctor's shop [situated away from the main house].

The shop is a noisy place, like when Doctor was there. Hector has two saws cutting at once, and the men are shaping shingles that will make a pretty diamond pattern on the roofs of several new buildings. This evening while I am

The shop at Bongondza framed by the arched entrance of the church – c1947.

typing, Hector is preparing a diagram of a new desk for me, with a swivel chair and a place for the typewriter which pulls out of the desk. I should get many letters written when that is finished! I am teaching music and handwork in the boys' school and have the choir and child evangelism work and boys' devotions twice a week. We have an advanced school here now, called Ecole Moyenne, tho' it is only an effort to bring the boys up to gov't standard. It has bro't boys from two of our other stations and a station of the Brethren Mission.

In a long letter to her mother on April 25, Ione indicated that she was thrilled with the arrival of the long-looked-for Christmas package which included a little tool kit and suspenders for Hector, some combs for Ione's hair, and much-appreciated food: tins of chicken and turkey, cranberries and mushrooms, and nut brittle, pecans, and peppermints. Ione also wrote about her plans for the baby's arrival:

.....You asked me what I am doing for dresses. Well, not too badly. I have the two maternity dresses which I bro't out, plus a couple of dresses made over, a new dress made after the pattern of a house coat, and a pretty one lent to me by Mrs Walby. She also gave me a smock. But the smock I bro't out is far too small now. I have another new dress cut out of the red and white French gingham which one of the Pontiac ladies gave me; it is cut like Mrs Walby's with snaps at the back of the shoulders and it laps over in back. I hope to finish it before we go. I'll use it for the journey and then put it away for the next baby! I wish you could see the dear little bassinet made from a wooden box. I have a nice wooden bed that the Westcotts left, but I wanted something for the time we're at Oicha, and the box can be used to mail the babies belongings in. I have a skirt with a ribbon-drawstring made of pink cotton covered with pink net (what I had bought for the wedding!); pink ribbon covers the arches made of wire which are detachable and will hold the mosquito net which drapes like a little princess' bed. I have two (sometimes four!) teacher's wives making dear little dainty dresses and slips, sheets, bands, etc. all by hand. They will be trophies to show you when I come home. The girls have done them quite nicely. And they are so interested in the baby's coming. I guess I told you Hector is making a baby carriage. He bought the springs and rubber tubing for tires, and that's apparently all he needs for a start. He is making beautifully turned redwood discs for wheels. I am making little cotton knit long-sleeved shirts and cross over in front; I can get three out of two pairs of Hector's shorts! Rubber pants I am

making out of the rubberized pillow-cover that Hector bro't out. It is fun trying to decide what to use as I go thru the 'necessary' list in the baby book.

Although I have been very careful, especially one week a month, I have not found it necessary to give up the school work. I cannot go to the villages for the

One of the buildings at Bongondza under Hector's supervision.

child evangelism classes, but I go to choir practice Saturday nights, and it is good to keep going. I feel I need the excercise, I am so large. And when the first of the year Verna made out the school schedule, she made it 3 hours lighter than last term. I have the three departments of the boys' school as well as the evangelists' school for music, but they divide themselves into two class-periods a day and meet three times a week.

.....Another mother and father came with their baby for milk, but I did not feel we could spare any milk just now, and asked them to try to bring goat's milk for me to fix. Ma Kinso talked to them too, and as a result they did come for some time. It was lovely milk and I only wish we could get the natives to bring it to us. But that stopped recently as the mother goat was expecting another baby. And these people don't seem to be able to get another one. But it is not as tho' the baby will starve for the mother does have some milk, and this time on goat's milk has given it a boost. Natives here just DON'T use goat's milk; and they laugh at people who do. Yet their babies are dying without it when the mothers don't have enough. It is a tragedy. Ma Kinso and I are experimenting with peanut milk, and think soon we'll have a proper consistency for tiny babies. I have dismissed the little boy, Pudu, who now is entirely on solids and have just tiny little Priscilla on the bottle. We must shift her to peanut milk as soon as possible, as it costs about $40 to take care of a baby for six months.

Now I must close. I hope this finds you well, Mother. I have not heard yet from Marcellyn, but perhaps you have. You are ever in my thoughts and I love you dearly. You are the loveliest Mother any girl could ever hope to have. If you ever feel you could come out here, we would love to have you with us.

Lovingly, Ione

On April 26, 1947, Hector responded to a letter from his friend Doug Brock, and shared details of his work:

.....As regarding tools, we can get quite a few things in Stanleyville. Just a few weeks ago, I got a little parcel from Vern Ryerse [a Canadian friend] *with about 40 hacksaw blades and 25 small assorted drills. The hack saws I had been getting in Stan were good for about three jobs. I think I have had one of these in*

the saw for about a month now, and it's still going strong. So, you can see that we just take what we are given out here, while at home there is a selection. So now if you want to send some little thing along, I would suggest a combination circular saw, 7" diameter, ½" hole. I am using it to trim shingles that the natives cut from softwood trees. It helps us solve our tremendous roofing problem, since we can't get sheet metal. Some time I must draw you a sketch of the buildings on this station, and a map of the area. Maybe I can entice you and Jean out here for a two-month vacation!

I'm sorry I must close so soon, as I should talk with you about the spiritual side of this work, but that will come next time. Yours in the Lord's Service,
Hector

The Christmas parcel from Ione's mother was not the only package to arrive out of sync with the seasons, as seen from excerpts of a letter written by Ione to her friend Mildred on May 2nd:

Dear Mildred:

The box of Christmas cards came and I do appreciate them very much. It was very thoughtful of you to collect that large boxful and send it. Thank you. Bright, cheery pictures are always welcome and there are many uses in scrap books and just now I am interested in using some of the pictures for the backs of schoolboys' raffia picture frames. We are using raffia that the children have gotten from a nearby place and it is dyed several colours with Rit I bro't out. I have three classes doing this in the primary school, and in the advanced two classes they have been sewing pen wipers and Bible covers.

.....Well, Mildred, I guess you knew that the first of our 'six hoped-for' babies is just about due. It is a real joy to make the preparations for a little one. I have had to be rather careful the entire time, but it will be worth it if we can have a baby!

We have a wonderful Lord and Saviour. 'He daily loadeth us with benefits.'
Love, Ione

The UFM missionaries in the Congo were spread across a large region, were supportive of each other and took time to correspond as witnessed in the letter to Mary Carter written on May 10, 1947:

Dear Mary,

It had been a long time since I have written you and it seems there are so many things to say. First I want to thank you for your letter which I received this week.

I am sorry that the tricycles were a disappointment.[59] It is hard to compare children to other things when they're miles apart! I thought surely they were bigger than that.

---

[59] In all probability these are toys left from when the Westcotts were at Bongondza. By now, Mary and Jim Carter, the UFM field secretary, had three children: the twins, Gordon and Rosemary, born in 1943; Philip, and Michael who was born in September of 1947 at Mambasa, Congo.

We did enjoy having Chester and John Arton here. Hector surely missed them after they left. They were so easy to care for and so appreciative of every little attention. I do hope they were not too tired when they returned. They worked hard all the while they were here. I think John was somewhat lonesome for Betty, especially the last week, when they wanted so badly to get away and couldn't. He sat in our rocking chair and rocked himself to the tune of, 'Far from My Home'.

My sister (Marcellyn) is in Belgium now and I expect will come on to Congo in July, although I have not heard from her directly as yet. We are glad Pearl is really taking that course, after the false report that she was skipping it and coming on to Congo. We must pray much that she will pass and be able to come to Congo in July, too. I wonder where Marcellyn will be stationed. She first was called of the Lord to Ekoko, she believes, but of course she must be willing to go where the Field Committee feels the Lord would have her to be. She is six years younger than I.

I am looking forward to next month with great anticipation. I have been quite well, but have been very careful, for as you say, babies are very precious! I hope mine can be as sweet and nice as yours.   Love, Ione

Near the end of May, Hector and Ione left on their way to Dr. Becker in preparation for the birth of their child. The journey was not an easy one as was apparent in this brief letter Hector wrote on May 31 to Leone Reed during their plane flight from Stanleyville to Irumu:

.....On the way to the big event. Everything is just fine. The road was rough by car from Bongondza to Stan but we went slow & had Ione lying down on the roll-away bed mattress & she had a good trip. We did some shopping with the Jenkinson's yesterday & Ione was ever so pleased to be able to get a permanent. Now we will soon be at the Doctor's. A lady missionary from the Brethren Mission is meeting the plane with her new Plymouth station wagon. I just looked out the window with the field glasses Russell Bemis sent us & saw the rough old road far below. The plane is ever so much better.

Ione has been quite well although she has to be careful. Last night she said the baby was quite far down, so it won't be long now?!!! We will wire Mr Pudney & ask him to let our folks know.

Yours as Ever in Christ – Hector & Ione

A few days later, on June 5, 1947, Ione provided a more detailed account of the journey from Bongondza to Oicha in a letter to her mother:

Well, now it is just a question of waiting for the big event. And it is fun and interesting, especially so since Hector is here, too. The journey from Bongondza was made easier by the mattress of the roll-away bed. I slept a good deal of the way and the bumps were not bad. It took us 10 hours because Kinso and Hector drove slowly, and we had to cross three rivers by pontoon. Mrs Jenkinson [Ma Kinso] had a nice lunch prepared and was very helpful. They [Botiki and she] had complete equipment ready in case the baby came on the way. We had made reservations at the Airport Hotel so I went right to the room and rested while Hector got the airplane tickets and had the baggage weighed. We had a lovely dinner at the hotel and I especially enjoyed the salad and steak.

Next morning, we went hunting for some trousers for Hector. I found a nice brown felt hat, too, and then I found that the beauty shop was giving permanents again by a Portuguese man, and the price was cheaper. Then Hector and I had dinner in another hotel and I went to the B.M.S. (British Baptist Mission Society) and rested on Ma Kinso's bed until Hector came to tell me they were going to get some ice cream. That was a real treat. Then we invited the Jenkinsons [and their BMS hosts] *as well as two visiting missionaries to have dinner with us at our hotel, se we had a nice little dinner party.*

Hector at a pygmy hut near Oicha.

.....Our quarters here are very comfortable.[60] We share a tile-roofed brick house with Peter and Mrs Stam and little Sharon. Peter is John Stam's nephew; they are Wheatonites and lots of fun.[61] Peter hasn't arrived yet for he is teaching at the Rethy Academy for two weeks more.

I understand the baby will be born right in this room, unless there are complications. I have a lovely Simon's hospital bed. Hector was gone two nights when he went over to Butembo to see the Ludwig's (just 2 hours away). He had strawberries four times there and brought some back & some vegetables, too. Ludwig's are in a garden spot and seem very happy. She gave me two little shirts which I needed very much.

We bought a native-made basket and I have it all prettied up with a pink netting skirt (you remember the netting I bought for the wedding?) and hoops to hold the filmy white mosquito netting up like a miniature covered wagon. I have everything laid out ready but nothing has happened yet. They do give a sedative here and will make it as painless as possible. The two Christian nurses are lovely girls. And there is a dear little mulatto helper who is lots of fun. The mines doctor has two chimpanzees which are kept in the store house back of us, so we have strange noises sometimes. They feed them bananas & pai-pai and milk in a baby bottle. The first thing I saw this morning when I went outside was a monkey face peeking at me from a window!

This is a time of precious Christian fellowships with these missionaries and also a time to be apart with the Lord. You will hear from us about the baby by cable via Mr Pudney.

---

[60] Having flown from Stanleyville to Irumu, they were picked up by Oicha missionaries and driven the rest of the journey to the hospital at Oicha.

[61] It was John Stam's story of missionary work in China that first motivated lone to enquire about missionary work. Peter and Mrs Stam attended Wheaten College.

Love to everyone in Jesus' name. Ione

Dr Becker was not only adept at looking after his patients, but also in keeping expectant fathers busy, which enabled their wives to rest before labour commenced. In a letter dated June 15, 1947 to Kinso, Hector recounted his activities:

Thanks for the nice lot of mail. Everything arrived in good shape. We enjoyed the letters from you especially. Thanks for taking time to write. I trust by now you received the letter we sent last week. In case you think this is the letter telling about the baby, I better tell you that that will have to wait a few more days. Of the five ladies waiting here, three have already had theirs, two boys and a girl. So there is just Mrs Stam and Ione left.

The other day Doctor handed me some cameras and a light meter and told me to enjoy myself taking pictures around the station. One, a nice new 35 mm, another was the film pack type, Graflex (a real good one) and then I had a movie camera, and lots of film....I fixed up a small blackboard and started out at the highway, just as if I were getting ready to visit the station. While I was taking the picture of the Irumu-Beni sign, a pygmy and his little wife and family walked into the scene. The film pack doctor developed here in the X-Ray tank were quite good.

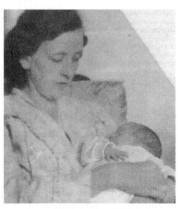

Ione with little Kenneth Reed.

We are listening to the news these days and wondering how long it will be before America and Britain calls Russia's bluff.[62]

We will close for now. Look for a telegram next mail.

Yours in His Love, Hector

Kenneth Reed McMillan was finally born on June 19, 1947, at 1 p.m. and weighed a respectable 8 pounds. There were five sets of parents at Oicha at the time, Kenneth being one of the last to appear and the fourth boy! So much for the pink netting around the crib!

Letter-writing started almost immediately.

To Mrs. Wideman, one of Ione's supporters, Hector wrote:

I guess this is my introduction to you and the other members of the class that supports Ione. I have heard much about you and we both wish to thank you for your interest in us. We received your letter of May 18. The news of the church happenings is always welcome. We appreciate the close contact with those in the homeland. We are glad you asked about the big event. The next paragraph will give you the details. I will take an extract of what Ione wrote in the diary:

June 19...All morning this continued. It was terrific at times. About noon I was taken to the operating room and the last big effort was made. The doctor

---

[62] Referring to the start of the Cold War—America and its Western allies feared the spread of Communism and Russian influence in Eastern Europe and the Middle East.

was very encouraging and when I was about to give up, the baby came, at 1 o'clock. He cried loud right away and Lois said, "It's a boy"!! Then they laid him on the table and his head was turned toward me, and he opened his big eyes and looked. I thought that I had never seen such a lovely face, broad forehead, eyes wide apart, fat cheeks and chin and a rose bud mouth. His hair was dark and closely cropped. His chest was broad, and his legs well-formed and fat. Hector was called in and was happy that it was a boy.

And to his niece, Joan in Montreal, Hector wrote:

.....Ione and I have been made very happy by the arrival of our little boy. He came last Thurs. the 19th. Of course, I was very proud to carry him from the hospital back to our little cottage. He seems so new, I felt as though I were driving a new car out of the factory. Ione had a fair time with no complications. The Dr and nurses have been very good.

Here is a little of what Ione wrote in the diary:

.....Hector was called in and was happy that it was a boy. He held my head while I screamed with the pain of the stitches. About 1:30 all was finished and I dropped to sleep for a while. I was not very comfortable until the next day. Hector was awake nearly all night, watching and caring for the baby. It cried quite a bit at first and choked several times on the liquid in its throat; but Hector got along all right and didn't have to call anyone. The next day he said he changed its diaper even tho it didn't need to be changed. "What's a little waste of flannel", he said, "When you can stop the baby from crying"! He had him in every conceivable position when he was choking. In the morning Kenneth showed only a slightly swollen eye. When put to the breast that first night he knew exactly what to do. While I had him with me, I found that his head is shaped just like Hector's, his hair is the same colour, and his eyes look like they will be blue. He is the biggest of the five babies born here this month.

The lights have gone out so I better close for now.

Yours as a proud father.   Hector

And to fellow missionary friend, Viola Walker, who was on furlough in American, Hector wrote:

Dear Viola,

.....I guess you know that Ione and I intended coming here [Oicha] *for the big event. Well here we are and here IT is. Just you wait until you get back to Bongondza and see the little laddie who is going to take charge of the carpenter shop for his daddy!!!*

I used to wonder how anyone could write a whole letter about a baby, but when it's your own you think everyone else is interested. But I'll calm down after a while!

.....Hector

On June 26, 1947, Hector wrote to Ione's mother:

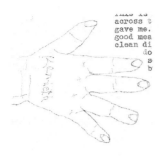

Dearest Grandma: This is my little hand that wants to reach right across to you. Thank you for the nice mummie you gave me. She is so sweet to me and gives me 7 or 8 good meals every day; and changes me into nice clean diapers when I need it. Sometimes daddy does that job too, but mummie doesn't stick so many pins into me! ! ! I cry a little bit but only when it's near meal time or when I haven't anything else to think about. Last night I was real good. Mummie and daddy were so happy about it this morning that they sang to me while I was having my six o'clock breakfast, and it was especially nice with the guitar. "Pass me not oh gentle Saviour"; "I am a stranger here"; "What a friend we have in Jesus". I'm glad they named me Kenneth Reed, and now I would like to say good-bye. Be sure to keep praying for me.

It was a touching and sensitive gesture to send an actual hand size, something tangible for Leone Reed. The letter goes on to give more exact detail about the labour, the lumbar epidural anaesthesia and the delivery.

The next day, Hector penned a letter to his father (speaking as baby Kenneth):

Dearest Grandpa:

I know you have lots of other grandchildren, but I think you're pretty glad that my name is McMillan [the first grandchild born to a male McMillan]. *I will try to carry on the family name as well as I can; but I must say mummie and daddy have me a pretty long one when they called me Kenneth Reed. I'll just have my evening meal but between times I'm telling daddy what to write. They treat me very, very good. Mummie feeds me six times a day, and daddy changes me sometimes. I sure keep the staff busy getting clean things ready for me to put on. I weigh 8 lbs and am quite fat. I hear Mummie and daddy talking about me sometimes and they say that I have some characteristics like a fellow called Archie* [Hector's older brother]. *I'm not too sure who he is, but if I'm like him, he must have a broad forehead, a round face and a good thick chest. I haven't really heard daddy say this, but I know he thinks now that Archie is a pretty good looking fellow, since I'm a little bit like him.*

I'm getting sleepy now, so daddy will tell you the rest of the news. The next time I write I will be back at Bongondza, after my plane journey. Pray for me that I may be kept safely out here in Africa.

A few weeks elapsed before the journey back to Bongondza, and on July 20 Hector wrote a letter that was sent to several friends, supporters and family:

.....We have arrived back on the station after being away for six weeks at Oicha. I know you will want a picture of what we brought back from there. We will try to have some ready for the next mail. Life is a little more varied now that we have little Kenneth; but we will soon get acquainted with him. We plan to dedicate him to the Lord in a week or two along with some native couples who have recently had babies.

Just one more short paragraph about the little lad – a few days ago one of the native carpenters came to see the new baby and of course Ione soon showed him into the bedroom where Kenneth was lying in his bed. Ione asked Balemaga who Kenneth looked like and he answered - Bwana McMillan. Then she waited for a further comment, such as 'he is beautiful' or such like; but Balemaga just said "Huh" and walked out----.

This week we had the pleasure of being introduced to the Prince Regent of Belgium.[63] Our school boys, all dressed in their new uniforms, were lined up along the road and when the official cars drove up, they sang the Belgium National Anthem. The Prince talked with us for a few minutes, thanking us for coming the 17 miles out to the main highway. He said the school boys looked very healthy. He spoke to us in both English and French.

.....The work on the station is as plentiful as ever. We hope to get aluminium roofing for our church; but for some of the other buildings we are using wooden shingles, which we wire together in the shop and then put them up in big sheets. We need something substantial: last night we had 5" of rain in about ten hours.

Praise the Lord with us for those who have recently accepted the Saviour; pray for His continued blessing.

In a letter written on August 2, 1947 to Eleanor, a missionary living between Oicha and Stanleyville, Ione shared more details of the Prince Regent's visit. She wrote:

.....We arrived in Kole Tuesday after the Sunday we left you, and we were just ahead of the Prince Regent! My, how the people bowed and waved as we passed! I guess they tho't we were the advance party. It was fun seeing all the arches, flowers, groups assembled, etc. When we reached Kole, I took Kenneth to the Administrator's house to cool him off and to wait until the excitement was over when we could go on to Bongondza with Mr. Jenkinson. All of our school children, nearly 150 were brought the 30 kilometres for the occasion and they sang, "La Brabanconne" and cheered, "hip-hip-hooray!" The Prince shook hands with everyone and came back a second time to talk to our Mr. Jenkinson and expressed appreciation for bringing the school out to the main road.

We found our house all ready for us, with flowers, etc. And our cook was on hand, for which I was thankful, for so often when one returns from a long journey they aren't to be found! We had a few weeks respite before school started, but the fun begins next Monday. The baby is growing ever so much and weighs over 9 pounds now; he smiles and seems much stronger than before. Dr. Brown of A.I.M. stopped here on his way to Stanleyville for his 'stage' of one month and he said the baby was O.K. He will look at him again on his return to Banda. We are thankful to the Lord for bringing him here for each of these months in a baby's life are most important; and then in September we are expecting to welcome Pearl Hiles, our nurse, for she has passed that difficult medical exam in Brussels and can come as soon as she has transportation.

---

[63] Charles was on the second Royal tour of the Belgian Congo.

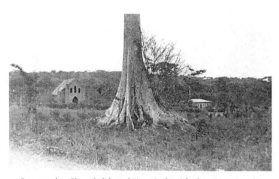

Bongondza Church (L) and Hospital, with the giant tree in foreground. Photo is taken from the Doctor's House - c1947.

Back at Bongondza, the natives had been bringing gifts of eggs and peanuts for the past two weeks and tip-toeing in to see the baby in his bed. He was the only little white child for many miles around just now and was quite a curiosity. The women told Ione that she should feed him every time he cries, saying, "Go and take care of your baby now!" They never put their babies down, saying that one mother did one time while she worked in her garden and a monkey came and picked it up and ran up a tree with it. But when they made a fuss and came after him, the monkey threw down the baby and leaped away. Needless to say, the baby was killed.

While the car was being repaired in Stanleyville, Hector cycled all the way to the station from Kole and back and was pretty tired. He was trying to get a bicycle motor to work to make the trip easier. Ione shared a little more about the changes in her routine in a letter to a supporter, Ms. Hess in Michigan:

.....I find it very interesting to work out a schedule which includes him [Kenneth] and gets the Lord's work done, too. I have classes in the boys' school which I fit around his bath and feeding times, and I can oversee the work at the hospital and get out to the villages as well. My husband has made a baby carriage which we think will be quite adequate for these Bumpy roads; it has rubber tires, ball bearings and knee action! Little Kenneth seems quite content to go anywhere in it, and the mosquito net protects him from insects and black hands which would love to touch him but carry disease.

The first village I took him to is the one adjoining our station, named Bongondza. An old man of the village clapped his hands and said, "We shall call this child 'Bongondza', for is he not our child?" They all laugh at him because Kenneth has a lack of hair in the same spot as his daddy! The women are keen to see how I care for him, as there is not any other white child anywhere around, and some have imitated us by providing a net for their baby, giving it drinking water, and even putting on a diaper, which is never done usually among native mothers. Perhaps we can show them also how to teach their little ones to love and serve the Lord.

And to Mr. Gowdy, a supporter at Three Hills, Alberta, Ione wrote from Bongondza:

.....We are enjoying the Lord's blessings. Souls are being saved. We had a filled church and somewhat overflowing on the last Sunday (the church seats 600) when we celebrated the Harvest Festival or Thanksgiving. The natives brought gifts to the front while we sang. The space in front of the altar rail was filled with peanuts, sweet potatoes, sugar cane, native squash, eggs, etc. Some even brought

spears, and several of Hector's carpenters bro't little stools. When they don't have many francs, these gifts take their place. There are money gifts as well, amounting to 900 francs, about $20.

Hector has been very busy with the several building projects in progress just now. A native meeting house was just finished, and a dwelling is going up, to be used for a while for a new missionary coming out, and then it will go the natives head teacher.

I am working in the boys' school teaching music, handwork and have the Sunday school. I have the church choir, too, and they have white robes which add to the 'dignity' of the service. Then there are the Child Evangelism classes, but I have not resumed those yet. I have gotten to the third village with the baby carriage and as soon as I can get to the fourth, I can gather the children there. One's strength comes back gradually but surely with constantly 'getting out' and doing things.

Ione wrote to Dad and Archie at Avonmore on August 16, 1947:

Hector's double desk.

.....Today Hector finished ten double desks in hard wood for the evangelists' school and the advanced boys' school. He enjoys working with his four carpenters, all Christians. They have been out in meetings together and I think will go hunting together too. The desks are very sturdy and the teachers are glad to have them. These fellows are preparing to teach and preach in the native villages all around. They spend a couple of years here and then they are stationed somewhere. Recently a woman has gone into the classes, the wife of a fellow in the advanced boys' school. And when an examination was given, she excelled them all.

.....This week I cleaned the two guns getting them ready for the shells that should be coming in the next mail. We haven't had meat (except from tins and an occasional chicken) for a long time and it will be fun for Hector to go hunting. One is a Winchester 30-30 and the other a revolver Smith and Wesson 38. The natives are getting quite anxious to get going. They hunt with nets and traps. I don't suppose Hector will try for anything bigger than antelopes or wild pigs, but there are elephants and leopards around. I think I would rather go with him than to sit home wondering if he got the animal or the animal got him!

We are so thankful to the Lord for His continued blessing. He has bro't us to a pleasant place and given us a work which we love to do, and now has given us a dear little baby. We have a wonderful Lord. May He continue to be with you and keep you well and happy.

Lovingly, Ione

In a letter to Lucille and family written on August 22nd, Ione wrote of the dedication service for the baby:

.....We dedicated little Kenneth Reed at that time [during the harvest festival], *along with a native baby, Etienne Lomea, wee son born the same week as ours. He was good but the little black baby cried real hard, and everyone around was whispering to the mother to hurry up and feed him. She had a new dress on and the neck was small, so it was quite a job for her to bend over to get her dress screwed around so that she could satisfy the baby. By that time the ceremony was nearly finished. It has been fun comparing that baby with ours. He weighed the same at birth but was one inch shorter. Now he weighs less and is still shorter, but can hold his head up without support and ours cannot. I guess I should start carrying Kenneth on my back! It might give him a stiff backbone. They both cry equally loud!*

And in a letter to her mother, Ione talked about day-to-day life for her since the baby's arrival:

.....I am sleepy very early these days, but now I am not missing so much sleep for the baby sleeps from 10 to 5 now and we have skipped his middle of the night feeding. My schedule is not too heavy, tho, and I can rest in the daytime. I have a hospital meeting each morning at 6:30, give the baby orange juice at 7:30, eat with Hector at 8, give the staff their orders and then bathe the baby and feed him. By that time it is 9:30 and I get ready for the music classes. I have three groups together at 10:30 in elementary music and three more groups at 11 for advanced. (I started the advanced group on chromatic scale today; I am teaching this in French). Since the classes are at the church and just at the foot of the hill on which we live, I leave the baby on the verandah, where I can hear if he cries. I feed him again just before we eat at 12 but try to give him water after that as well as sometime during the morning. I have handwork classes at 2 on Tues. and Thursday and leave him in his bedroom during that, but I am not very far away, and Hector is just next door at the shop and runs in to see him occasionally. Now that I have charge of the boys' Sunday school, I will be meeting with the 8 fellows who are teaching each Thurs at 3, but they will come to the verandah. At 4 each day we meet at Jenkinson's for an hour of French and our white prayer meeting. I take the baby along for this and he sleeps or plays with his rattle out in the yard.

On August 23rd, Hector wrote an excited letter to Mr Bemis in Pontiac:

Good News ! ! ! ! THE SHELLS ARRIVED

.....Ione was finishing bathing Kenneth and was just putting him back in bed when I asked her if she wanted to shoot off the first revolver shell. She came outside and took the gun, looked at it a few times. I asked her if she wanted me to shoot the first one but she was still confident. She held it up again and faltered; then handed it to me. Later she said that she began to think that she could look after the baby better than I could in case anything happened!!! But I must give her credit for shooting the second one. I went over and got Mr Jenkinson (he

was a corporal in the 1914-18 war). He said he couldn't do anything with the revolver, but when we got a target up, he came right close to the bull's eye with the rifle; whereas I was lucky to even hit the paper. However, practice will help. We have sent for a hunting license this mail and should have it next week.

Thanks ever so much ! ! ! !

Ione's sister Marcellyn, left the USA in April of 1947 and travelled to Africa via Belgium where she had to stay a short while to learn French. Being a missionary in the Belgium Congo required language skills, a variety of tribal dialects were spoken in this part of the country, however, as a Belgian colony, the recognised language was French and without it, foreigners had difficulty in communicating. Ione had been longing for family members to join her and finally, Marcellyn is on her way.

Even though Ione lacked family around her, she had an extended family of missionaries and supporters. Mr. and Mrs Jenkinson never had a family, so they thought the world of Kenneth. They and the Kerrigans became honorary grandparents to all the missionary children whose parents served with the UFM. The adult missionaries were called Aunty and Uncle by the children. Ione's supporters at the church in Pontiac had also adopted Kenneth as their little missionary and sent $10 a month.

On September 5, 1947, Hector wrote his family in Canada thanking them for the many gifts they had sent and sharing his life in the Congo, especially about the need for a new car:

Dear Dad, Archie and Jean (if she is home):

If I had written to you every time I thought of you, the mail would be quite plentiful. But there are so many other things to attend to. This is Friday evening, and the mail is gathered in tomorrow night, so we naturally try to have some letters answered. Just when Ione and I got settled at our desks in the office. I opened the right-hand drawer to get some stationery, I saw a mouse's tail disappearing over the back of the drawer. By the time I got up to move the couch away from the wall, he was on the floor and down his hole to the basement. Ione grabbed the Coleman lamp and we hit out for the basement. The nearest stick along the way was the handle of the flyswatter, I had made some time ago. But when we got down there, he had gotten to some snug corner and we couldn't find him. (A few weeks ago, we saw another one in the office, and we got down in time to see him running along a wire on the basement ceiling. Ione was the one with the stick that time and she smote him nose and tail). But there was something else that was interesting. A great big spider was over in the corner. It is only the second one of that kind that I have ever seen. He has eight long legs, can walk backwards, sideways or front wards; has a pair of three-inch feelers; and most amazing of all, two jointed grasping arms with claws on the ends. I wanted to see him in action; so I saw an old hard-shelled bug lying on his back and pushed him over to the spider. It was better than a circus to see the spider take slaps at the bug then jump back. Of course, I was cheering for the bug, and pushing him into the fight. Finally, the spider got right back against the wall and the bug walked right over him. Ione had come back up to the office, and after killing the spider, I did the same and now I will try to get on with the letter.

.....We want to thank Jean for the parcel we received last mail day. It was the first thing we opened. The Duck was ready for a swim, the cute little brush and comb just match Ione's set. The plastic sheet will find its place in the carriage. Thanks ever so much for my car and trailer. (By the way, if Archie wants to sell a hog or two, we would be glad for the proceeds to be put into a car fund for Bongondza station.) Miss Rutt has given $250; another gift from England of $125. Miss Viola Walker who is now on furlough, has just sent in $50 to the Toronto Office. So, with a little bit more we should be able to get something soon. We have asked Mr Pudney to see both the Chev and International about a suburban carryall. The Chev costs about $1200 in America; but it takes about $600 to get it out to Africa. Mr Jenkinson's car is just about worn out.

.....Ione's sister Marcellyn will be leaving Belgium this month for here. We will

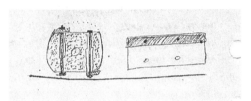

be very glad to welcome her along with Pearl Hiles, our nurse. We haven't a house finished for Marcellyn and Pearl yet, but it is about half way along. It is so difficult to get these people here to work.[64] . . .All the buildings must be in brick and cement to be

Hector's drawings of the lead-molded planer blade spindle showing the blades made from car springs.

permanent. It's a long process from the clay to bricks; the drying; burning; hauling and building.[65]

.....But I must say that the carpenter shop is getting well equipped. The band saw I rigged up is most useful and a great time saver. I'm working now on a 16" planer. I have poured molten lead around the crankshaft of an old model T, and put that back into the engine, turned it upside down, and the planer head just comes up enough to make the cut. I have to make the blades yet. A fellow wanted to sell me the head and blades for $200; but this is cheaper and more interesting.

.....Since most of my time is spent with the carpenters, I naturally try to get things as convenient as possible....the crankshaft is built up with a babbit, to make the planer head. I have yet to make the blades from car springs. They say it is a heart-breaking job, but I guess the secret is to leave them in the fire for about two hours; take them out for straightening and drilling and then put temper back in. If it is a failure, I will probably send to America for some. And just tonight I

---

[64] The concept of work is somewhat alien to the tribal forest people of the Belgian Congo; the people Hector would like to work usually only work to satisfy a given need, that is to make a shelter and hunt for food; once their basic human needs are met – they stop working.

[65] When they run out of bricks, building is delayed while they build another kiln and fire the bricks.

*thought of an idea for running six long saws (like our crosscut only for ripping)
off a six-cylinder crankshaft. But this is for some future day.[66]*

    Goodbye for now.

Love & prayers, Hector, Ione & Kenneth

Ione wrote to fellow missionaries Frances and Mary at Ekoko. As with other letters,
she mentioned Kenneth's progress:

> *.....He is becoming more and more dear to us, for he recognizes us and smiles
> and twinkles ever so nicely. He is sitting straighter and straighter and can hold
> up his head when he is on his tummy. Next week we'll start him on solid foods.
> We are thankful to the Lord that altho' we are far from a doctor or nurse, he is
> doing so well.*

Ione thanked supporters for the gift of a quilt and, as always, included some
description of the mission work as in her letter of September 19 to Agnes Sturman:

> *Dear Agnes:*
>
> *.....I do not know which group is responsible, but hope that you know and can
> convey my appreciation. Tell the ladies the quilt is reposing right now on the bed
> which [the] Westcotts left us and its colour scheme goes nicely with the spread
> which the Loyals gave me. It is just the thing for these damp rainy days. I know
> that a quilt means a lot of labour by many hands and I want to express my thanks
> to whomever is responsible for such a fine gift.*
>
> *.....This Wednesday I met with the women at 2 P.M. and instead of a lesson on
> bathing a baby as I had planned, I went with the entire group to a village where
> a woman had died in the forest. She had gone with a group to get fish in the
> forest and a storm came up, one of those quick heavy windy rains, and the others
> ran and left her. She lost her way and when she stopped to put down her pot she
> somehow fell, and that's the way they found her dead, with no wound or even an
> indication of a snake bite. She was not a Christian, nor were many of the people
> in that village. I enjoyed that half-hour walk with the 26 women. They chattered
> in Libua which I am still trying to understand. When we arrived, we sang and
> Botiki's wife gave a splendid message which was directed toward the unsaved.
> They were very quiet until they were well out of hearing of the village and then
> they started to be jolly again and they laughed all the way home. It was good to
> see these hard-working women who carry such heavy loads of wood and water
> and food, without burdens for a little while. And the fellowship seemed so
> refreshing to them. Some of them are really beautiful and so neat and clean. They
> have come a long way from the dirty pagan women which Mrs Jenkinson found
> here 14 years ago.*

Photos of the hand-built pram Hector (the inventor) constructed were included in a
letter he sent to his sister Florence on the 21st of September:

> *You always write such good letters; and it is a shame that we don't take more
> time to answer. As usual it is just time to wrap up the mail. The native is waiting*

---

[66] Hector states in another letter that about 90% of his missionary work is manual labour.

on the porch to carry the sack 17 miles into Kole where the transport truck picks it up tomorrow morning.

I am laid up for a few days. That same knee that went out on me when I was in the Air Force played me up yesterday. I had just fixed up standards for volley ball and was teaching some of the natives how to play when I landed with my leg off balance and it crumpled under me. I have it bandaged up and am using crutches; but it should be all right in a few days.

Hector's baby carriage with rubberized knee-action wheels.

I am enclosing a picture of the baby carriage, with knee action [independent suspension] *on all four wheels and rubber tires. It was lots of fun to make it, rather than paying $150 for one we saw in Stanleyville. All I had to buy for this was four coil springs and the hose for the wooden wheels.*

In a brief October 10 note to his friend Art Forester, an RCAF pall, Hector shares his daily devotional schedule:

We get up when the first bird sings, which is about twenty to 6. She feeds Kenneth while I shave and get dressed and then we read in First Thessalonians (just now), looking up the references, and then we each pray. She takes a meeting for the hospital patients from 6:30 – 7; while I usually take the service for the native workmen. At breakfast we have family worship with the three house helpers in their language. At noon we pray for a different country each day of the week. At 5 p.m. we have prayer meeting with the five other missionaries. After supper we have our own family worship in English, and once more before we go to bed, we read and pray together usually remembering folks in America. That sounds like a lot of wasted time but it is amazing how much more one is able to do.

And of more practical matters, he wrote on October 24, 1947 to his Aunt Mable McElheran:

.....I could fill three pages telling what happens [here]. *There are hundreds of jobs to be attended to. The wearing part of it is that you have to think for about twenty or thirty other people. I seem to have charge of the practical work around the station. That is where all the good PBI training comes in handy.*[67] *The*

---

[67] Hector wrote in another letter, "I really enjoy it. I get a chance at carpentry work, plumbing, masonry, electrical work, painting, and all sorts of repairs; guns, clocks and watches, locks, cars, etc."

carpenter shop is the busiest place. We have the sawyers out in the forest with long two-man saws, slowly ripping out boards and planks. They build a scaffold of small trees tied together with forest vines and when everything is ready, then they tell me in the morning at roll-call and all the workmen go out to put up the log. If you could hear the headman go through his little song to get them all to pull together. He says something and they all reply, then after about the second or third time they take a lift. I'll have to try to get a picture of it sometime. After the log is in place it takes two men about 10-14 days to rip out 15 boards. These are brought in to the station and piled to dry. But as a matter of fact, they are usually used right away, unless it is for furniture.

I have rigged up a good bandsaw running off a 5-horse engine. When Chester Burk was up here last spring with the 3-ton truck from their station, we decided to put a new platform and rack on it. We used the bandsaw to cut out 6" timber, and it did it quite well. The natives think it is wonderful to be able to saw so fast. I've been working on a planer too, but it it's not quite finished yet. Just now I'm doing a plumbing job for one of the single ladies. She bought a stove and I'm trying to fix it up so it will heat water. It makes a lot of work when material is a bit scarce but we have had quite a good supply from Stanleyville. There is another new house going up and we will soon be starting the carpenter work on that. For a good many years the missionaries were putting up temporary buildings but the gov't wants us to build in brick. And I must say that it is a lot more satisfying to be working with things that are a little more permanent.

While Hector seemed well equipped to undertake this work, it did come with frustrations. He and Ione had to deal with a clash of several cultures which would seem not to have formed part of his missionary preparation. His frustration came out in an October 31st letter he wrote to a Mrs. Warren:

.....I seem to be looking after the practical work on the station and that takes about everything you've got. But in the rush of looking after sawyers, carpenters, masons and brick-makers; physical training for the boys at 7:30 a.m. and girls at 9:30: one soon gets his fill of dealing with natives. Patience is so necessary lest someone be offended and yet discipline alone can gird up their minds and bodies. And then on the side there are locks to repair for natives who insist on bringing in eggs (which of course we need), but then I have to take time off from some other parents of the school children, especially the girls. Just last week the father of one of the oldest girls came to talk over the matter of her marriage with one of the Christian boys on the station. This was Mr Jenkinson's interview, as head of this station [Hector was standing in for the Jenkinsons, who were on a trek to outlying villages] but the father brought along a gun that needed to be repaired. So, you see that it all adds up to making one a walking repair shop.

Ione also found life frustrating at times, and she described the natives' behavior as "funny," as she outlined in a letter to the Roberts (missionaries) on October 31, 1947:

.....The natives are really funny. They send a letter in for the mail and usually send less money than is required. Or if they come before hand, they ask for a stamp, and after leaving what you were doing getting it for them, taking the money and settling down to your work again, then they say that they want one for their relative. And so, you go through the whole thing again. Likely as not they will want a sheet of paper and later on, an envelope. But knowing that they are not far removed from paganism[68], we try to be patient with them.

Ione also wrote to the family on the same day, acknowledging letters and packages she had received, but also voiced concerns over Marcellyn, as she has had no news of her. Even though Marcellyn had left the States in April, she still had not arrived. It appeared that Marcellyn and Pearl were no longer traveling together as anticipated.

In a letter to the Roadhouses of the UFM on November 5, 1947, Hector provided an update on his work as well as on Kenneth:

.....Kenneth is a real boy. He is just now in his carriage beside the desk. He is usually a pleasant little chap but I guess we all cried when we were getting our first teeth. The two on the bottom are through but there is just a <u>sore bump</u> where the top ones are. He has been so healthy and Ione is still able to feed him. We are thankful for such a nice little <u>new</u> missionary.

The Kinsos are out on trek now. We miss Viola for that job. When they come back after three weeks, Kinso and I are going up to Ekoko to put up a house. The workmen are getting all the things assembled, so two weeks should see the task about finished.

On November 6, 1947, Ione wrote to the eldest of the Westcott children, Anne, who she cared for when she first arrived at Bongondza:

Dear Anne and All,

I am ashamed that it has been so long since I received your very welcome letter. It was so nice of you to write; I wept big tears when I read it for I wanted to see you. It was so good to hear all about everything you have been doing. I suppose the list of pets is much different by now. What about a horse? I remember how much you wanted a 'Flicka'.

.....We are very happy with Kenneth, our baby and he is growing very well, is now five months old. He has two teeth coming in and a swelling for a third. One day we found Kinso's cat curled up at the foot of Kennie's bed. He had crawled right over the baby to get where we found him. Hector didn't like that very much. I am still nursing the baby, but he takes anything else that I give him, cereal, fruits, spinach, etc. He more than doubled his weight in four months. We thank the Lord that he is well, for we have no doctor or nurse to take care of him.

.....I have so many reminders here of you all. The baby sleeps in Charlotte's little bed, wears some of the little garments I found on the clinic shelf at the hospital;

---

[68] The term 'paganism' was not used pejoratively here but was common parlance at the time of writing.

others will serve and have served as patterns to sew more. And just this week I was sorting out a bag of small pieces of cloth and found a part of a little romper which gave me a good idea for making some for Kenneth. And the apron that Charlotte cut holes in one time when she was real small and a little naughty, I found and used what the bugs had left to make a pretty beribboned bunting for the baby. Hector and I speak so often of how fortunate we are to be able to have so many useful things here. The house is so well built and is such a comfort and protection.

I guess you knew that two of my sisters have babied this year, too. Lucille in Lansing - a boy in Jan., and Doris in Alaska a little girl. By the way, Hector saw Katrina when he visited the Ludwig's at Katwa. She was a lovely big girl and seemed very happy at the mulatto school.

.....Write again soon, Love, Ione

In a letter to his father dated November 8, 1947, Hector was still trying to come to terms with "man management" realizing his father probably had similar issues and might provide some advice:

Dearest Dad:

.....Now that I have others to oversee, I realize what you were up against. Not that Kenneth is any problem; but on the mission field there are always workmen and that is my trouble just this week.

For some time, I have been looking after the shop and a few other jobs such as plumbing, electrical work, car repair and sometimes the masons, as well as all the carpenter work. Sort of like Old Del Wiggins, Shirmie Alquire, Chas. Nesbit, Angus McLean, and Jimmie Tinkess [probably old Avonmore characters] all put into one man. Usually Mr Jenkinson takes care of the rest of the workmen. He is out on a three weeks trek now and the station was left in my care. As usual I left the outside workmen to the native headman, as he is supposed to check on their work. It just seemed as though there was nothing being done. On Monday evening of this week I had a talk with some of the leading Christian natives and they said the same thing was heavy on their hearts. After some suggestions, I asked the head school teacher, if he would come up in the morning and give the men a talk in their own language He really did too. He knows his own people so well and has their respect too.

First thing to do was to demote the headman. He got sore and quit work altogether; so, since then I have closed the shop and have been acting as "capita" [ca-PEE-tah] – or foreman. The men have to be on roll-call at 6:30 a.m. and 2 p.m.; unless they are on a special job. If they come in the morning and not in the afternoon, they get zero, which means no pay for that day. Those who say they are sick are taken down to the hospital and checked over by the native lad in charge, and he tells me whether or not they are fit for work. (Even old Sid Gunn would have a job fooling us out here). If food is brought to them, they can take time to eat but they must not go to their villages – suppose our road from Avonmore was twisted and turned, and had heavy forest and underbrush right out to the road. Avonmore could be the Chief's village, and each farmer's gate along the road would be a cluster of huts called a village. When you got to Sutherland's corner it would be Bongondza, with more villages beyond. The place called Kole would be down about Apple Hill.[69] So now you know a few more things about this land.

The Jenkinson's will be back next week we hope. A few days after that he and I will be going up to another of our stations for two weeks to oversee the putting up of a temporary building. That means a building not made of bricks but logs, sticks and using mud as a plaster. It will have rooms, doors and windows and a leaf roof. A good job might make it last four or five years. The men have been getting all the things ready, so we will be able to push the work, when we both go. The two single ladies who have been there for 7 months now have done remarkably well for the challenges they have had. While we are gone from here, we expect to put two shifts on the brick machine, each shift making 1500 bricks.[70] For the new school it will take about 150,000. So, you can see that the Bongondza workmen will not be idle.

Will be waiting for a letter from you soon. Kenneth and Ione send their love. God bless you all, Hector

In a letter on November 10, 1947, to his Aunt Marjorie and Uncle Alex, Hector provided an update on Marcellyn as well as the car situation:

.....In reading your letter of March 17th over again I see you were asking about Ione's sister Marcellyn. She is still in Belgium, but we heard recently that both she and Miss Hiles are expecting to get a boat the first part of Dec. We will be ever so glad to welcome them here. I will probably have to make the 160-mile trip into Stanleyville to meet them there. Mr Jenkinson's car is getting pretty old, been going over these rough gravel roads since 1938. It usually has to have something done to it after every trip it makes.

.....We have been getting together some money for a new car fund, and it already amounts to quite a sum. It is wonderful the way the Lord supplies our needs. He is so FAITHFUL.

.....I must close now. Kenneth sends his love to you. Maybe you will see him in a little more than a year from now.

Yours in the Bonds of the Gospel, Hector

Many of Hector and Ione's letters referred to Ione's sister Marcellyn joining them in their missionary work and it was evident that lack of news had them both worried. Ione, in a November 22nd letter, wrote that her younger sister was undergoing difficult times, though the exact nature of them was not revealed. Being a missionary in the middle of Africa is not for the fainthearted as revealed in all the letters Hector

---

[69] All the trucks and cars travelling between Stanleyville and Buta pass by Kole.

[70] Not bad for a press that only produces 2 bricks at a time! This means they have 7 minutes to put in the right quantity of mud and grass into each slot, bring the hammer down to compress the mixture, remove the bricks and start again – fairly relentless!

and Ione write and it is not surprising that Marcellyn's commitment has been placed under scrutiny. Ione wrote:

Thanks so much for your letter received this week. It was such a relief to hear from you yourself. We were wondering what was wrong. We are still wondering; I wish you would tell us. We want so badly to help you and cannot unless we know. But at any rate, you must have a good reason for wishing to wait to tell us. I am so sorry that you have been misunderstood; it must be very very hard for you. I have such confidence in you that I cannot imagine anyone doubting your word or intentions. It must be Satan's way of blocking your coming to Congo. The Jenkinsons have not said anything to us about you; they would try to shelter and protect you all they could I am sure. I do hope everything will be all right and that there will be no stigma to mar the wonderfulness of your arrival to Congo. It will be such a grand event for us and we want it to be a happy time for you, too. Remember that 'underneath are the Everlasting Arms' and that you 'need not fear what man shall do to you'. We have a wonderful Lord who is able to solve every problem.

.....I am typing under difficulties for my tummy wants to turn inside out. If this keeps up we may have a little sister for Kenneth on his first birthday! More information later!

Hector is away for two weeks with Kinso. They are at Ekoko starting a new house for single ladies! That might interest you [as this is a house for Marcellyn]. *.....I miss Hector so much when he is away. He is so cheerful and full of pep. But Kenneth is good company daytimes and Ma Kinso sleeps nights here. Kenneth is cutting his fourth tooth. He drinks milk from a little glass, too, which he feels is quite an accomplishment. I still give him my milk when he is very sleepy, but am gradually weaning him.*

Tell Pearl we discovered some hospital 'treasures' in the basement here. Stacks of 6-yard pieces of peli, a couple bundles of Americani,[71] some flannel, some figured blue stuff that might do for hospital curtains, and quite a number of nice blankets, some all-white and some brown. That will be a good start for her, as that stuff is so expensive.

.....In Him, Ione

By the 23rd of November, Hector found himself at Ekoko, 260 miles northwest of Bongondza from where he wrote to Mr. and Mrs. McDonald, two supporters. It is evident that, Hector, like Ione before him, had to reconcile his preconceptions about his role as a missionary with the reality of what the job entailed. With people back home supporting him financially in this role, the hope was that they understood the exact nature of what the role entailed.

.....There are two single ladies here, Miss Frances Longley (second term) from Toronto, and a new missionary, Miss Baker, from Virginia. Mr Jenkinson and I

---

[71] Americani is an unbleached cotton sheeting originally woven in Massachusetts and carried in the mid-19th century to Zanzibar by American traders.

have come here for two weeks in his '38 Ford, to oversee the building of a temporary house. We sometimes think that we are bad off at Bongondza, but here there is not a single permanent building. By that I mean nothing in brick or cement.

.....There are so many possible departments on a mission station. But strange as it seems each new worker adds to the work of others. We are expecting a nurse at Bongondza in Feb. so that means that now we are rushed trying to get a brick house built for her. We have to make the bricks, build the drying sheds, build the kiln, have the firewood cut, oversee the burning and then have the bricks hauled on wheel-barrows about 400 yards to the site of the new house, AND ITS ALL UP HILL. The masons are quite good workman and we are quite proud of some of the jobs they have done. As for the roof, it is very likely that we will use leaves, since we are in a hurry. Otherwise we would try to make shingles from soft native wood nearby. This is really the most important part of the house. A few weeks ago, we had 5" of rain in 10 hours [loosely termed the "rainy season"].

And so, the work goes on. One's idea of missionary work is rapidly changed once you get into the harness. The picture of a man under a shade tree with a Bible in his hand is only half the story. True he still has the Bible in one hand but in the other he has a hammer, saw, square, level, shovel, trowel, pipe wrench, blowtorch, electrician's pliers, school books, medical books, and a typewriter. I wish I could get a cartoonist to draw a picture of such a present-day missionary.

While Ione missed Hector, Hector missed her as well and he wrote on the 29th:

My own Beloved,

Thanks for your note. It made you more precious than ever to me. You were worth waiting for as these past two years have proved. Sorry we couldn't be together for our second anniversary but I've been thinking about you.

And how's our laddie? Don't let him forget that he has a daddy who loves him.

I hope you've been feeling better since your cold is gone. Take care of yourself and for the sake of Linda Lou [a reference to the new baby].

News Items:

The house is coming along nicely.

We've taken a bagful of rattles out of the Ford in our spare time. It was almost falling apart.

Mary [Carter] *is in the Aketi hospital after being a week in bed here with a temperature that wouldn't come down to normal. Kinso took her in last Tues & the Doctor thought it was kidney infection.*

Kinso is going in to Aketi this morning to spend the week at the church there. He'll see how Mary is getting on & that will decide our plans for returning to Bongondza (i.e. leave here Thur. Dec 4 at 4 a.m., shop at Aketi. Leave Kinso at the road going in to last village, shop at Buta & be home about 3 or 4 p.m.)

Folks enjoyed films very much. (I've sent the other one to Pudneys.)

Kinso has been praising up our Bongondza workers. It would encourage your hearts to know what he thinks of each one.

Well, honey, so long for now. Love is a wonderful thing when you're the other half.

    Hector

On December 2, 1947, Hector responded to a letter from his father and brother Archie who had shared news of home. He wrote of his views on farming in Congo:

.....*I guess the rain rather ruined the crops* [in Avonmore]. *It's a long time since we only threshed 40 bags.*[72] *But you should be thankful for the rich land that we have on that farm. Out here the ground is very poor. If it wasn't for the abundant rainfall everything would wither up. One of these big jungle trees uses 80 gallons of water every day. When the forest is cut down for big gardens it never grows up with these big trees again, but just soft trees and <u>thick</u> undergrowth. The big cause of poverty of the land is that there is no time when everything dries up and dies, as during the winter at home. If these people want to use the same land for a second time, they would have to wait 10-12 years. So, they just don't bother. They just move over into a new patch of fresh forest and cut that down. They plant peanuts first and in four months harvest them, then they plant cotton and gather it in 6 months. Some people then plant (cooking) bananas, but the land is all worn out by then. If they want good bananas, they cut a special garden and plant them right away. All the work is done by hand and all the carrying is done by the women, having huge baskets on their heads or back. If they have a baby he must be fastened on somewhere too. They have no donkeys or horses, carts or wheel-barrows. A man and his wife with hard work may make $25-$30 a year. Out of that they pay $2 tax, buy their clothes (which costs plenty since the war), and usually their relatives get a share of it, to pay for some fine that is imposed on them. Naturally their food cost very little, but they don't live very well. Just yesterday I was telling a fellow about my father's farm. He thought you must be VERY rich. However, I told him how hard we have to work to get anything.*

Of temporary building in Africa, Hector gave a description of the effort that went into constructing a house that would only last a few years. All the materials for the house, even the one being built at Ekoko that was 65 ft x 32-1/2 ft, came from the forest or the earth nearby. Poles set into the ground made up the main structure to support the roof which were poles of varying diameters and length. Room partitions were also poles set into the ground. The pole rafters were tied together with dried strips of bark or forest vine that was split. Roof materials were the long broad leaves of a plant of the forest floor brought to the building site in large bundles. Barbs were formed with a knife in the stems of the leaves which were hung in layers on a lattice work of reeds. The resulting roof was a thickness of 20 to 30 leaves.

Then came the walls which started out as tightly spaced reeds or small poles. Earth was dug and mixed with water and plastered on the wall from both sides. After drying, it cracked so a mixture of sand and water was applied. When that had dried,

---

[72] Hector is remembering a bad year on the Avonmore farm.

the walls were brushed with a clay whitewash mixture. The doors and windows were then fitted in to complete the house.

The whole process was repeated every four years or so as termites ate away the poles, the leaves shrivelled up and blew off little by little, and before long the house sagged and fell.

He continued:

.....SUCH IS TEMPORARY BUILDING IN AFRICA. Missionaries have done it for years until now when there are 6-8 white people on a station someone has the disheartening job of continually pushing the workmen to rebuild these miserable MUD houses. Is it any wonder that we want to use bricks and metal roofs? Almost everyone will tell you that they are much cheaper in the long run. But it is having the capital to start with. A brick machine costs $275. Labour to build the drying sheds, and kiln and make the bricks might cost $100. Transporting the bricks and building house (masons) $200. Cement - $75. Roofing – Aluminium or corrugated iron $400. Furnishings - $150. So, the total is around $1000. Say this house lasts 20 years. In that time, you would have had probably 5 mud houses at an average cost of $450. So that is the story.

The missionaries decided Ekoko required a male presence if the house they were building for the three ladies was to be completed in time for Marcellyn's arrival. As it would be improper for Hector to be with two single ladies for such a length of time, it was decided at short notice that Ione should accompany him. So, the McMillans moved to Ekoko for six weeks over the Christmas period. They left Bongondza at 10pm, arriving at Ekoko the next afternoon. Ione wrote on December 16th that the facilities at Ekoko were far more basic than at Bongondza:

.....We are not so secure from the wiles of the jungle here at Ekoko; lack of screening exposed us to more and itchier bugs: we do not have the variety of vegetables as at Bongondza, nor the meat: we do not have the security of brick walls and sheet metal roof. But it is a real joy to be 'needed'. We are many miles from a doctor or a nurse, but little Kenneth enjoys the best of health and weighs now more than a child many months older should weigh. Ekoko's school year is about to begin with more boys enrolled than ever before. We counted 168 on parade this morning. The outstation reports are encouraging, as many as 90 souls won to the Lord by one teacher alone; the offerings 20,000 francs for the year at the outstations. Ekoko deserves to have help, and we are glad to be here for a while.

We are thankful to be starting this year with a small refrigerator, with a nurse on our station. The Lord does 'prosper' and we want you to know that He is using you to supply our every need. Truly, 'The Lord hath done great things for us, whereof we are glad!' If you could see the little boy who comes daily for medicine for his burned leg, the babies who have received milk and medicine, the villages that are calling for teachers, the girls saved from polygamy, the boys who will be good husbands for them, the women whose family life is gradually becoming 'different', you would be glad that you have encouraged and prayed and given. May the Lord richly bless each one of you.

Lovingly yours in Christ, Hector & Ione McMillan

Hector then wrote on the 23rd to Kinso about a little of his progress:

.....The house is coming along well. They have finished the roof on the front and about 2/3rds up the far side. I imagine the "ndelis"[73] will be [pleased] *but it might be a tight race.*

We have fixed up a shop out behind the other one; repaired the two benches and fixed up a nice saw table. I have already tried out the power plant with the car, but I have it all ready. I'll try to take a picture of it. I have another table inside the garage on the cement floor and use the little engine in there for work during the odd evenings. I'm making a sign for the new road entrance, in my spare time. Those router bits are the real thing for cutting letters into a board. It works well off the little motor. The other day the motor stopped and after some investigation we found the Bakelite part on the points that ride on the eccentric [cam] *shaft had cracked off. I was able to fix it with small copper rivets.*

Hector's car-powered table saw.

Meanwhile, in a letter Ione wrote to Ma Kinso on the same day, she shared her work with the local school girls who had their dresses washed and ironed, and who were helping with the new house:

.....[For three days] *they are working awhile during the mornings getting earth for 'mudding' the house. They seem happy to have a part in the new house, too. Frances told them their mud was for their Mademoiselle's room! They are also making paper decorations for the church and the Christmas tree. We have chosen a pretty lemon tree down near the church and hope they will enjoy seeing Mary's pretty decorations on it, plus the ones they are making. Denys[74] had his boys practicing at the church until after 9:30 last night. They seem to enjoy it, tho. They are working hard days now that their exams are over* all doing something toward the building of the new house. And the catechists are working full time too. They practiced their play at 5 last evening. They are so tired and hot, but they did very well. Their play is worked out together with the women.

I have not been able to do as much as I would like, but I am taking charge of the meals, and the girls' program and helping with the church decorations. I am trying to get the staff members to do 'Gloria' well enough for Christmas Day. Hector will be speaking that day, and I will give a message to families in the

---

[73] Ndeli is a shortend, "mondeli", or white person, in Bangala.

[74] Denys Likanga, a Congolese evangelist.

afternoon. I have a class, too in the conference on the teaching of hymns. The conference will really be only Friday and Sunday, but we are trying to pack in all we can and yet keep as many hours as possible free for everyone to work on the house.

Christmas at Ekoko was described thus by Ione on the 29th of December:

We left Bongondza just before Christmas, at the close of a precious year in His service. The last season I had with the teachers of the boys' Sunday School was interesting. They were concerned for their scholar's spiritual welfare. . . . I do not know the exact number who have been saved but they have come to us every week or so, in twos and threes and sometimes fives, to accept Christ. The number of boys attending school this year is 142.

.....Christmas at Ekoko has been a very busy, interesting affair. All of the outstation teachers and evangelists are in, and the fellowship and fun are great. The first thing we heard Christmas morning was carols in the villages around about then it came nearer and nearer and by day light the school boys were before our house singing and waving flowers. They shouted 'Joyeux Noel' and we shouted back. The church was packed and a large overflow crowd stood around for the 3-hour morning service. No one was in a hurry to leave. That service was only the beginning and for four days there were festivities of all kinds, plays, outdoor races. On Christmas night Miss Longley called them all around the Christmas tree (a lemon tree) for gifts. Candy and nuts would not have pleased the children nearly so much as the two lovely squares of red disinfectant soap. The meat from their roast didn't arrive until Saturday, but when they finally had it prepared and in dishes on tables set with flowers it looked almost like a white people's feast.

The climax of festivities came when at the last service on Sunday, the station teacher, Denys, announced that for two days everyone would work before leaving for the holidays. The new white lady was on her way and if everyone worked together, they could get the house all 'mudded' before they left, then when they returned, they would have only the joy of welcoming her, with no sorrow that she had no place to sleep. The results were amazing for on Monday morning men, women and children were present to take their part in gathering ant-hill mud, crushing it, mixing it with water and putting it on the walls. This is the second day and I believe it will be finished. Women with little babies on their backs made mud and plastered it on the walls; skilled labourer worked side by side with unpaid volunteer, and all were singing and making the work a real joy. We have been hearing a variety of songs from the different ones as they worked, and whenever we go over, there is a cheerful atmosphere of cooperation. The white shirts have come off, all are working together, teachers, monitors, catechists, the shoe-repair man, the tailor, as well as the paid workmen. They don't know it yet, but Miss Longley is planning to give each one who has helped a cupful of salt as a gift. That will bring some smiles.

So, even though Marcellyn's house was unfinished, a letter written by Hector on the 6th of January, 1948 was the first (and only) indication that she had arrived and she and Ione were able to share time together. But as it was Hector writing, the focus was more on the work he had been doing for his 'boss' Kinso:

.....You would all appreciate sitting where I am and listening to Marcellyn and Ione singing as they are sitting at the organ. Ione had started a letter to Verna on this typewriter but I just silently slipped out the letter and started this one as I'm sure the organ will occupy them for an hour or two.

The plane was in a little late at Lisala [lee-SA-la]. because it got stuck in the mud on the stop before that. I guess the pilot went too close to the end of the runway. They had to get a tractor to pull it out. There were only five passengers when they left Leo and they picked up a few more on the way. We left Lisala about 1:30 p.m. Sunday. It was just about dark when we got to Bumba [BOOM-ba, on the Congo River].

Hector and Kenneth

.....We got in about 10:30. Ione and Marcellyn had a real meeting and soon a crowd of natives were in the yard. We had a light lunch, took Kenneth out to see his AUNTIE, and then went to rest.

.....Tomorrow should finish the floors, and then we can sand and pembi [whitewash] the walls. They are drying out quite well.

We saw a Jeep station wagon in Bumba on the way to Lisala last Friday. It has gone about 4000 km. We just talked to the chauffeur, but he said it drives just like a car. There is only back-wheel drive. The springs are ever so soft. He caught the front end and bounced it up and down so easily. The engine is remodelled and the seating arrangement is ample for seven. We were ever so pleased with it.

On the 13th of January, Hector provided the team at Bongondza an update on his activities at Ekoko:

.....The house and furniture are coming along well. Frances is looking after the tabs while I'm trying to stay at carpenter work. We were planning the kitchen stove this afternoon. I think we have hit upon something quite good. It will have one ash pit, a grate made of pipes out of old bicycle frames, a large top using a flattened out drum, and oven to the side made of a half 200 litre drum, with the closed end having a square door cut in it; the other end being bricked up; a damper to let the fire get started up the chimney and then closed off so that the heat will have to go over top of the drum, down the other side, underneath, and along the bottom to the back of the stove and up the chimney. It is the nearest thing to a stove from home that I know of. In fact, the front of it will be in about the same proportions.

Kenneth is getting so big and strong, even standing up in his carriage. We'll have to put an eaves trough [fall protection] *around it or else tie him down! !! Ione is giving us good meals. We haven't had our French exam yet. Frances is always threatening, but I tell her that I'll have to stop making furniture to study, so she recants!!!*

We are remembering the work there each day and pray that the Lord will bless. Hector

Ione found out that some churches (in Michigan) had dropped their support for the McMillans. It must have been a blow to her but she kept her faith that the Lord would provide in another way. She reflected in a letter to her sister Lucille and her family on March 13, 1948 that missionary work was not exactly how it had been perceived but she seemed to be more at ease with the situation:

.....On the missionary field there are the tasks done by the 'specialists', the doctors, nurses and teachers, and then there are those who find it their lot to 'fit in' and occupy various positions, sometimes several at one time. My husband and I are these 'fitters-in', and we can say it has been a blessing to have the Lord with us, and to let Him make the work to prosper.

We might go down on record as having had charge of the workshop and hospital. Surely most of Hector's time has been at the shop, for there were buildings to be erected and furniture to be made. I have spent very little time at the hospital except to conduct their morning meetings and give a few words of advice now and again, for Botiki knows more than I do about what should be done for the sick. Most of my time has been spent in the boys' school, where I taught music and handwork and helped in their devotional services. I had music, too, for the evangelist's class and the school teachers, as well as a Sunday choir. Then there were the times, choice and precious to me, when the Jenkinson's were away and I had the women's classes and the evangelists. Hector alternated with Mr Jenkinson in taking the station church services and has been out for several short trips to the villages for meetings.

And in a letter written on March 27th, Ione can't help mention her encounters with forest critters:

.....The animal life is still active here. This week we killed another snake in the dining room, right behind the chair where I was feeding the baby; I couldn't kill it until I had deposited both the dishes and the baby, and then I got the shovel and smashed his head; then there was a scorpion in the kitchen which jumped out of the wood box when I reached in for shavings. I was thankful I had a good light so that I could see it immediately, for it travelled pretty fast. I killed it with an axe head! Such fun!,

Pearl Hiles must have arrived at Bongondza by March 28th, for Ione told of her usefulness soon after she gets settled in, as well as other recent events:

.....I enjoy the women's work very much, but lately have not been able to do calling on the sick, etc. Partly because I am not very strong, and tire easily, and partly because of so many cases now of Small Pox. Pearl has several isolated (if

you can _ever_ isolate an African!!) near the station, and some temperatures have been quite high. She reported the epidemic at once to the Banalia [ba-NA-lia] *doctor. He has made one trip and has sent vaccine for everyone from here to about 15 kilometres away, so Pearl has been swamped, vaccinating hundreds daily. Today she has a native nurse helping her, whom the doctor sent. She vaccinated Kenneth several days ago and he has been having a good reaction. He is not feeling too well, but eats some of his food, and drinks lots of water. A few days ago, the mother of our cook fell ill, and it turned out to be Small Pox, so Gaston* [the McMillan's house helper] *was ordered to leave his village and stay right on the station at night. He did one night, but the next day both the doctor and nurse caught him in his mother's village. They said he could not work for the duration of the epidemic, so he left last night. It is hard to protect ourselves from such a catching thing. Will you pray that there may be no serious results in the schools or among ourselves. There is just one case in the girls' school as yet.*

Kenneth keeps pulling my left arm; that accounts for the mistakes. I have his carriage a little too close, I guess. These last few days he has been a "mother's baby", for he doesn't want me out of his sight and he perspires so much I have to change his clothing often. He knocked the scab off the vaccination today, but I guess it will still work.

Ione and Hector must have been very busy at this point, preparing so that they could go to Yakusu at the end of May for the birth of their second child. Yakusu was a station of the Baptist Missionary Society of England. Kpodo, one of their helpers from Bongondza, went along and it is apparent that they arrived safely at Yakusu. Kinso and Hector worked closely on projects and each kept the other up to date on unfinished business as seen in Kinso's letter to them both on the 12th of June:

.....Verna's house goes up slowly. The bricks will all finish today but I don't anticipate too long a delay. The State [the Belgian government officials stationed at Kole) *is giving us some men to cut wood for the kiln and 28 turned up this morning (+ 30 more at midday) to start in Monday and we expect many more. Thus, I hope to put the fire in the kiln Tuesday and then get enough wood cut for perhaps three other kilns.*

It is almost noon and the Carters have not yet put in an appearance but we are all ready for them. We have a fire put in your kitchen so that they will have hot water to bath the kids etc. We managed to get the shingles on to your mafika [shed] *yesterday but the ridge is not on yet.*

The generator has arrived from Boyulu. I found it at the C.V.C. Stan and forwarded it.

Ma Kinso fell off the Corgi[75] last week and made a bit of a mess of herself – grazed forearm, cut knee and bruised all over the place. However, she has been

---

[75] A Corgi was a small motorbike developed during the war for couriers that was fairly cheap to buy and maintain.

on it again and says she will either master the little beggar or else leave me a widower!

As when Ione was awaiting the birth of Kenneth at Oicha, Hector kept busy at Yakusu, where he was fixing things. He also had time for a good gossip - on the 19th of June, he wrote to Kinso and folks at Bongondza (note: all caps in first section of text is due to broken typewriter):

.....RECEIVED YOUR WELCOME LETTER LAST EVENING, AND APPRECIATE YOUR TAKING THE TIME OUT TO WRITE TO US. IT'S GOOD TO KNOW THAT ALL THOSE MEN HAVE COME IN FROM THE VILLAGES TO HELP THE WORK FOR A FEW WEEKS.

WE WILL BE GLAD TO KNOW HOW THE CARTERS GOT ALONG ON THEIR TRIP. I WAS GLAD HE WAS ABLE TO GET THE TRUCK REPAIRED.

THAT IS GOOD NEWS ABOUT YOUR NEW PLANS FOR A LIGHT TRUCK. VERNA IS A GREAT SCOUT ! ! ! SHE SEEMS TO FALL IN WITH GOOD IDEAS. HOWEVER I FEEL SORRY FOR POOR MR PUDNEY. HE JUST DOESN'T SEEM TO HIT THE RIGHT NAIL ON THE HEAD WHEN IT COMES TO DEALING IN CARS ETC. BUT AS YOU SAY, IT MAY WORK OUT TO OUR ADVANTAGE.

I have just taken half an hour out to repair this typewriter so that it would write without capitals all the time. I don't know what I did but it seems better now.

Ione is still holding out. Just like the new cars; delivery uncertain. However, the folks here on the station are happy, due to several repair jobs being done.

One repair project was the big diesel motor used to run the 5KW generator that had been out of commission for two years. After Hector dismantled and reassembled it, he managed to get it to started – without the muffler on.

.....It was a very exciting time...the noise of the exhaust was almost deafening. People began to gather from all over. The girls up at Miss Wilkerson's compound were in great glee. "Are we going to have electric lights tonight?" After it was running for a few minutes I saw Ione and Kenneth coming into the shop. She said she had to push her way through the crowd.

.....I have been talking with Yakusu folks who say the specialist from Stan gave them very little hope. Any machine that has done seven or eight years' service is counted as junk, unless it has a complete overhaul job.

.....Did you get the Corgi fixed up again? And the Ford brakes?

In case Joan (Pengilly) did not give you the details of the thieving at Sabena[76] I'll try to give a report on it. When the plane came in from [illegible] on Friday evening, one of the passengers was put in the Sabena with Mr Simpson. In the dead of the night these fellows came in, took the suitcases, and other valuables and slipped away down toward the river. They forced open the cases, took what they wanted and left the rest by the side of the path. When they awoke in the

---

[76] The hotel at the Stanleyville airport.

morning the chaps who had come in on the plane saw what had taken place. He had lost his PANTS, so sat on the side of the bed and cried. Mr Simpson was fair mad. All his money, some shoes, shirts, glasses (he was almost blind without them), and wrist watch that his wife had given him on their anniversary. The other fellow lost about 7000 francs in cash. And so, it was reported to the police. But Mr Chesterton of Yakusu station, helped out with a loan of money and the plane left next day. Several days later Mr Chesterton was called over to the police station. They had caught a whole gang, among them two former Yakusu staff members, and one of the Sabena staff. They were about 13 or 14 yrs. of age. One chap had the watch and wallet (they say that natives are afraid of these bifocal glasses so threw them out in the forest). As regards the clothing ---the chief of police told three policemen to bring in the clothes that had been found. It amounted to a pile a meter high and a couple of meters across. Something like 40 shirts, yard goods, shoes etc. This is the third recent thievery from Sabena.

On the 21st of June, 1948, Ione wrote a letter to her mother describing her time at Yakusu:

Dearest Mother,

.....We have been here nearly three weeks now and the baby has not come yet, tho' I keep thinking every day it surely will arrive. I have not felt so good as last year, and so have been lying down most of the time, tho' I do manage some kind of a walk each day usually. I suppose I use a lot of strength on Kenneth, but it seems that Hector has most of his care. The varicose condition does not seem any worse and this doctor does not seem at all disturbed about it, so I guess there is no danger of a haemorrhage as the state doctor tho't might happen when labour began. I weigh around 140 pounds which is 20 extra for me and I feel rather heavy. My appetite is fine, and we do have better food here than at home, because it is so near to Stanleyville. We order a vegetable basket every week here instead of every other week as at home, and we have fresher and larger quantity of things. Then we get fresh butter, beef or pork, and even bread from the bakery! Hector's cheeks are filling out and I am glad to see him looking better. He is having a good rest here. The baby is really due on the 24th, but as Kenneth came ahead of time, we looked for this one early, but now Kenneth's birthday has come and gone and we are still waiting.

We had the nicest birthday party for him, and there were two little missionary's boys age 1 and 2 who shared it, the children of Dr. Browne[77] [the delivery doctor]. We had a four-layer cake of alternating chocolate and white, with a big single candle which reads Happy Birthday on it. They sat at a cute little blue table and chairs and first had sandwiches, then custard with canned peaches on, and cookies then the cake, and Grenadine-ade to drink. It made me

---

[77] Dr. Stanley George Browne was a renowned medical missionary and leprologist in Africa. He worked for the BMS in the Congo, covering an area of 10,000 square miles. He pioneered a community care program that became a model in Africa for controlling endemic diseases.

so happy to have such a nice time at the first birthday party I ever had for my own little child! I've gotten so many parties for other little ones, and this was the nicest of all!

Baptist Hospital at Yakusu – c1920

.....They [the folks here] *are very kind to us, and have sent us many things to make our stay pleasant. There have been gifts of chickens, vegetables, flowers, etc. besides the regular rations of eggs and fish twice a week.*

.....We have nicer things for this baby than for Kenneth, for we have some of his things left and just recently a box came from some ladies in Hector's church. There are some lovely little wool sweaters, blankets, etc. And I have saved many things that came in the big box from the Loyal's. Inez says there is another box on the way. That is a real surprise. And I have heard the 3rd Phil Class is getting another ready. We shall be very well cared for. There was nothing broken in that big box and everything was so welcome. We have tried to stretch the eatables out as far as we can. I have one more bottle of baby food yet. I know things like that cost a lot, but different things to eat are so welcome here, especially sweet and sour things. We get pickles very seldom. But whenever we have tomatoes, I can make ketchup or chili sauce. If you see some children's tooth brushes a few would be nice for Kenneth. He has 16 teeth now and must start to brush them! He needs more little sox and shoes already. He's wearing size 5 sox now but they will soon be too small. I believe his shoes are 5 too. He has no decent little boy's hat, only one I have made out of a brown felt of Hector's. He has the straw braid for me to make him a straw hat when I can, but a felt is quite important, too. I am afraid I shall not be able to wear my nice dresses that I bro't out with me, because my hips are larger now. So, if there should be opportunity to choose a cotton afternoon dress, it would be welcome, probably size 16 or 18 now. As far as clothes, Hector needs about everything, but we are thinking that we might have an allowance saved out soon and ask Maurice to buy Hector a good lightweight suit and some shirts and under things. But we will try first to see if we can get him anything when we pass thru Stanleyville again. I have never seen any nice suits there tho'.

I just asked Hector if there was anything else to mention, since you had asked us to 'unburden ourselves'. He had Kenneth in his arms to take him out for a little airing, and his eyes twinkled as he said, "Tell her to come and get Kenneth!" And Kenneth's little eyes twinkled just like his Daddy's! He imitates everything Hector does; just now they were crowing like roosters. He follows

Hector everywhere and tries to take big steps. He can say 'ball', 'bye-bye', 'mommie', 'daddy', and the rest is in his own language. All 3 of us love you very much, and want you to write real soon. Lovingly, Ione

.....I decided that I had not written enough, so in spite of the extra postage it will require I am adding some. I was thinking you did not know when Kenneth walked or anything of our recent activities. Then, too, I wanted to tell you a little story which might be useful in your meetings.

Kenneth took his first steps at ten months but it wasn't until he was eleven months that he began walking in earnest. Now at one year he is very nimble on his feet and even tries to run. He is not quite so large as the other baby here who is two months older, but he is solid all over, weighs about 25 pounds, and his legs are very strong. He had eight teeth at 4 months and now at 1 year has 16, all of his molars and his canine teeth, which make it possible for him to have solid foods he otherwise would not have. He claps his hands when I sing, "Joy, Joy, Joy with joy my heart is ringing" and tries to point his chubby fingers up to heaven. We are real happy with our little boy, Mother. Hector has his heart on a girl now, Linda Lu (Lucille), but I will be just as happy if we have another boy.

.....While we are here Hector is getting together a history of protestant missions in the Congo in order to speak on it when he returns to the station. It will be for the celebration of the 70th Anniversary of the Belgian Congo Missions. It has been interesting reading in books which we are able to get here. This mission, Baptist Missionary Society of England, is the oldest mission in Congo and they have many interesting stories of early days. During the Arab slave raiding days, a little girl was rescued from the Arabs by a Dutch trader and he and his wife protected her until they met some BMS missionaries who took her. When they were to make a journey up the Congo to this new and unexplored territory, they took her with them. The natives were very hostile and shot arrows at them, some of them poison arrows, and tried on many occasions to kill them. One day when their boat was up in this territory where we now are, their boat had to pass near the shore for it was narrow and the little girl noticed that the natives had markings on their faces just like she did. She was thrilled, but did not know then they were of her tribe, for she had been very small when the Arabs stole her. Very soon the missionaries tried to land but the natives began to say in their tongue that they would kill them. And wonders of wonders, the little girl understood what they said! Her old language came back to her. And she immediately spoke to them and said not to kill these people for they were very kind. And because of the little girl's words they waited. A little bit later a man appeared and it turned out that he was the little girl's own father. He was so thrilled to find her that he did not leave her again. And when the missionaries came on a little ways farther to Yakusu (where we are) the father came right along. That little girl was their interpreter and she was used of the Lord to draw many to Christ. Yet today some of her relatives are still on this station. It is a good example of what a little child can do for the Lord.

The 'extended family' back at Bongondza were all missing Hector, Ione and Kenneth. The following are short notes written in June, and sent to the family demonstrating the affection they had for each other:

Dear little Kenneth, First of all, a very happy birthday to you. When you come home, we have got a little piggy bank for you. We hope you have a lovely birthday – and a lovely little "ndeko" (sibling) from Mummy and Daddy too. With love from Auntie & Uncle Kinso.

Dearest Ione & Hector, All jogging along here – just waiting for your return. Carters came. They did enjoy your house. Mary said once or twice – "This is such a lovely house." I was so glad! They were quite comfy I'm sure. They left for Ekoko on Wed. to sleep en route – expect to return on next Wed. All else well except Anziambo very seriously ill. My class slow this week as two are helping in the school, 2 out going after their wives. I hope we shall perk up next week.

We're continually praying for you & thank God upon every remembrance of you. Hoping to get good news this week. Love from both. Kinsos (Ma Kinso).

Yes, we'll be mightily glad to have you back with us again. Things are somewhat slow. All bricks finished – fire now in kiln but very disappointed. It has been going already 2 days & 2 nights and the fires have not been kept good but it is not by any means cooked. We now have enough wood cut for at least two more kilns & I rather think it will do three so I hope that will help us along.

My! I have been thankful for the Corgi - a great energy saver both day and night. Getting up in the night isn't such a burden when one hasn't to walk down & up the hill. On my last trip in the dark the lamp bulb burned out. Maybe you can get us one or two in Stanleyville– 6 V. 6 W. bayonet cap, centre contact. Tonight is moon-light. Kinso

PS: Hope to get permit for 2 tons cement from Buta – less transport there than Stan & I heard that Sedec had 40 tons waiting for purchases.

Dear Ione & Hector, - Quelle nouvelle? Linda Lou or Hector Jr.? Hope all is over and has gone well. I trust your time there has provided a good rest for you both and that your new addition will bring you much joy & happiness. We are not rushing in maternity work last two weeks – only one case (B.O.A.) born on arrival (plastered with mud from the road en-route to the hospital). Best wishes and lots of love. May God bless. Pearl

Dear Ione and Hector and Kenny and Linda Lou [obviously a pet name for the yet unborn baby should it be a girl!].

Greetings! How are all of you! We are getting lonesome to see you! How about coming back soon! And here is some work for you Hector. Do you suppose you will be able to carry back the cash for the enclosed check! Thank you so much. It is for the round house. It is coming along great. You will be surprised I am sure. And one more thing, if you have any shopping sprees would you bring me about three yards of some rather nice white material for making shirts – not Americani – something at about 30 francs a yard, or less if you can find something nice at that rate. Sorry to always be a nuisance, but I must leave room for the rest of the family. My love to you – or shall I say, appropriate greetings to Hector and love to the rest. Even singing class goes quickly for me now, Ione. Nothing like practice. But how glad we will be when you are back! Much love. Verna

Dear Ione & Hector & wee Kenneth, We are anxiously waiting for the good news. Our native brethren are praying for you too. We enjoyed having the Carters with us and will be happy to see them again when they return from Ekoko. We gathered at your house last Sunday night for our service. I had an attack of malaria & have been a bit upset since. Our teacher Erneste went with the Carters as far as Aketi [a-KEH-tee] to get his bride. Asani has been teaching in his room. Ngbayo is teaching in Anziembo's room. We almost thought we would lose A. this week but God has touched his body. There has been a sudden influx of children in A.'s room. Ione you might be interested to know that our little Mulatto boy loves to sing. Maybe he will be a real credit to our school someday. With prayer & training he might prove a real blessing in this land someday. Love, Olive

Now dear ones. Looking forward to your return & best love. Even Minuet (Her black cat) is here pushing her nose in to say greetings. Ma K.

PS: STOP PRESS Corgi's gone on the blink. Spent a long time on it today without any result. I am ever so sorry. Maybe Jim will try his hand on it. God bless you. Kinso

It would seem Kinso was jinxed with all things mechanical when Hector was away.

The waiting continued and Dr Browne thought they may have another three weeks to wait. Hector wrote to the Bongondza team that they just lived from one day to the next, buying Klim by the tin and petrol by the bottle. Mrs Parris (of the Yakusu station) said that they would just add them to their staff and that made Hector feel a little better to be of some help. Both Hector and Ione had evidently established personal policies to use their skills in the service of others around them (something that has been passed on to all the McMillan boys).

Hector consented to overhaul the diesel motor on the big motor launch. The station had a whole stock of spare parts. As the boat left to go up to Stan, the rudder played up and Hector made a temporary repair. Parts were ordered earlier from England by a plantation chief engineer who overhauled it and the station had been waiting for an opportunity to have the job done. The station committee thanked Hector for all he had done and hoped yet to do. Hector and Ione felt that they were not imposing on them so much when they were able to be of help.

Kinso wrote and added a list of some needs at Bongondza:

SOLDER
2 CYCLE TYRES FOR KASE 26 X 1-1/4
4 POINTING TROWELS from Sidis
PUMP PACKING –can't think of real name, you know, the stuff for sealing joints
CARRIAGE BOLTS (Assorted)
SMALL NAILS FOR SHOE REPAIRS

SPARK PLUGS FOR CORGI
TILLY GLOBES (glass casings for the gas lamps)
NEW AUTOMOBILE
MCMILLANS RETURN
A whole heap of other things too, but I can't think of them at the moment. Further lists will follow.

On the 13th of July, Ione updated those at Bongondza:

Dear Friends,

The baby [Kenneth] *has just awakened from his morning nap and is playing around on the mats here on the veranda. Hector has had another siege in bed, this time from a torn muscle which he injured while lifting Mr Parris' bicycle box; he helped the natives a little with it when they were moving it ready for him to open and assemble; it didn't bother him all day much and he unpacked and assembled bicycles for Dr. and Mrs Grey as well, and then repaired a typewriter for Mr Parris. But Sunday morning he could not move from bed and has been in bed for two days. This morning he took Kpodo with him and walked over to the shop and has bro't back a few boards to make a better barricade for the entrance to the house; we have been putting chairs down to keep Kenneth in. Kpodo is doing the work for Hector can't bend or use his arm.* [Appatently, one of Hector's back muscles on the right side had torn away slightly from the rib.] *It is raining today and here it is very desolate, damp and cheerless. But we can always "encourage ourselves in the Lord."*

.....Last Friday the Parris' went back to Stanleyville and on that day this station was honoured by the visit of the President of the Belgian Senate and his daughter, along with the Governor of Stanleyville. Naturally we stayed out of sight, but we caught glimpses of the celebrities. And we 'tidied up' just in case they should see us. Just about 3:30 a native came and asked for Hector, and a Belgian man walked up and introduced himself as the mechanicien [mechanic] *of their boat. He was wanting a little assistance with the blow torch to fix up a lamp for the return journey. When he went with Hector to the shop, he told him that he was the man who had come here and spent one day in trying to get the diesel engine to work. He had learned somehow that Hector got it to go!*

And then came the news everyone was waiting for (in a letter from Hector):

Wednesday JULY 14, 1948 - PAUL DANIEL WAS BORN THIS MORNING AT 4:30. The announcement will give the main items of interest. Things did not get really started until midnight, I called the nurse at 2, and after she had done a few jobs, said to call her again when things looked serious. It was nearly 4 when Ione woke me again and said I had better call the nurse. She sent me to call our helpers to get a fire and hot water ready; when I came back she sent me for the Dr. He put his rubber boots and white dressing gown on, grabbed a white coat and got here shortly after I did. I went out to see how the hot water was coming and Dr. met me and said to call Miss Varley as well. She took a minute or two to get ready so I went out for hot water, on the way back in she met me

271

and I said, "You better hurry or you'll miss it ! ! ! Only too true. The astonished doctor and <u>bustling</u> nurse were standing on each side of the bed, in the light of our Coleman lamp, holding a baby up by its feet, while it cried its lungs full of air, mother hardly knowing when it was born because it slipped out nestled right in its little sac. The first words I heard doctor say, "That's the first time I ever delivered a baby in a caul [placenta]." When he broke it, little Paul got a sudden introduction into a new world.

.....We have come to the conclusion that if this baby was to have a Chinese name it would be, "Six-long-wails".

Ione and little Paul

And so, we have what we came to get. The first chance I got to see him properly, I said right away that he looks like Ione's sister Marcellyn. His face is so round, mouth quite large, eyes not too widely opened, double chin and fat cheeks. The shape of his head is quite different to Kenneth's. His legs are more slender but his body well formed. I guess that is where he has the extra weight packed away. I went into the next room (Kenneth's now) where the scales are kept and watched Miss McGregor weigh him [at 9 lbs, 4-1/4 oz.] The basket is just about the right size, when he's stretched out his head and feet almost touch the ends.

Don't think for a minute that I'm disappointed in not getting a girl. Two little boys can make a life just as interesting! ! !

We asked the Doctor if he could give us an approximate date for departure and he said it would be about 14 days, since he wanted to have Ione strong enough to stand the trip. That will give us time to get up to Stanleyville, do the shopping and get ready for CVC on Saturday.[78] We will have money enough to get home on but scarcely enough to buy things for others, unless it be on account. However, there is some time yet and these matters can be arranged.

I better draw this to a close and get it ready for the mail.

July 21st saw Ione writing to Ma Kinso, a letter that demonstrates not only the motherliness of Ma Kinso but also the esteem in which she was held:

Dear Ma Kinso,

I am writing in bed and have not a good place to make a good job of it, but will try. This is the eighth day and I have the promise of setting out in a chair tomorrow and on the verandah on Saturday. It is hard to stay in bed when I feel all right but Nurse McGregor is firm. She shook her finger at me last night when she caught me "dangling" my feet over the edge of the bed! As Hector has

---

[78] CVC stands for 'Courier Vici Congo', a rural bus service.

written you in last week's letter, we expect to leave here as soon after the 28th as
possible.

.....Hector has been working on the Mokili every moment he can be away from
here. And he is repairing Miss McGregor's gramophone while he is at home. He
does find time, too, to cheer up his wife! And that is not too easy sometimes. I
am ashamed to be so discouraged at times, for we have so much for which to
thank the Lord. We have a healthy baby (he is back up to 9 lbs again and will
regain his birth weight in a few days we think), and are getting very good care.
But when Nurse scolds me I get so upset. Hector just laughs if off and jollies her
along but I can't seem to. Oh, well, she is only doing it for our good and I should
be thankful that she errs "on the right side"!! I miss very much the lovely, even
soothing temperament of our own Mama Kinso.

Thank you so much for looking after our house after the Carters left. Mary
has written me telling of their nice time at Bongondza. I appreciate your having
the linens washed. We will be glad to be back in our convenient home again.

Lovingly, Ione

It was not until the 27th July that Ione started a letter to her mother while still at
Yakusu:

If you could see me now, you would say that I was really happy. How good of
the Lord to give me, not only the joy of serving Him in Africa, but a good husband
and now two nice boys. I am sitting on a verandah, so close to little Paul that my
elbow rubs the blue net of his basket, and Kenneth is playing with his toys at my
feet. And Hector is not far away. He is making himself useful here by overhauling
the motor of the smaller hospital launch. He did their bigger "Mokili" already,
and for that work the Baptist Missionary Society gave us a gift of ten pounds or
about $40.

There is a break in the letter and Ione continued on the 3rd of August from
Bongondza:

.....We are home again now and how good it seems. Am writing with Kenneth on
my lap. He has a cold & is "mama's boy" today. The baby stood the trip all right
but has a bad heat rash. At last I have found a fountain pen! I hope you received
our cable via Mission Headquarters about the arrival of Paul. I am feeling fine
again. [Ione's positivity is returning.] *Had a tooth pulled while at Yakusu & have*
a bruise on my jaw but am rid of the hurting tooth. Kenneth had a middle ear
infection while at Yakusu but Penicillin injections cured it.

The night we arrived here Hector surprised me with a birthday gift, a new
wrist watch, sent Airmail from Canada. Will write more soon. Love, Ione

The journey from Yakusu back to Bongondza is aptly described in an August 12th
letter from Hector to Mr and Mrs Ennals, missionaries they helped while waiting
for Paul's birth:

.....Our trip by the CVC (an old Plymouth car) was real speedy. We were
traveling with one other couple. They sat in the front and Mr Crabbe gave us the
whole back seat to ourselves. There was room to put Paul on the floor in his

basket, as well as quite a lot of our baggage. The various pontoons [ferries needed to cross the various tributaries flowing into the Congo River on their journey] *gave us a little change; but best of all was the fact that the other couple who were state people knew the Administrators at Bengamisa* [at] *Kilometre 10, so we all went in there for about an hour and had refreshments.*

We arrived at Kole about 1:20 and found that Mr Jenkinson had just got his car turned around when we came in sight. Mrs Jenkinson had sent along some hot coffee and hot chocolate with cakes, so after our little lunch we made our way in to Bongondza. It was a royal welcome we received. After we got established in our own home again Mr Jenkinson went back in to Kole to get our two staff members and the baggage.

During the first week we were able to set up the generator and now we have lights in most of the houses and even three street lights. It was necessary to attach

an old radiator (off a car) to the old five horse engine, and later a water pump like we use for pumping water by hand (I think Dr Holmes has one on his side porch). By fastening an extension into the handle, it was possible to have the engine make the pump operate. I hope to soon have it fixed so that I can shut if off at 9:30 from our house, or maybe by means of an old alarm clock.

Hector working on the electric generator at Bongondza.

The new house for Miss Schade has come along well while we were away. We have just been pre-casting some cement lintels for over the doors and windows, re-enforcing the cement with barb wire or rods. I'm thankful for the helpful hints that Dr. Browne gave me. We will be able to go ahead with more brick work today. Yesterday the school boys helped us and we moved about 12,000 bricks. The breakage was practically nil since the bricks were only handled two or three times. Everyone was very co-operative. There is plenty of work ahead but the Lord gives strength and wisdom.   – Hector

On the 18th of August, Ione used an opportunity to write to supporters (perhaps a beginner's Sunday School Class) back home citing Kenneth as the correspondent:

Dear Beginners,

I guess you know that I have a little brother now and his name is Paul. The money you sent came just in time for him to have when he arrived. And the $5 for my birthday came about a month later. Thanks very much for my money and for Paul's, too. I was able to get a pair of everyday shoes with mine. Paul's $5 helped to pay for his trip from the hospital. We put him in a basket and took him to the river side, like little Moses. Then we put him in a motor boat which took us to Stanleyville. We stayed overnight there and then his basket was put in the *back seat of a car which took us to Kole and there another car met us and we were soon at Bongondza. He was only 2 weeks old then.*

Paul and Kenneth sitting with 'friends'.

Have you had 100 in attendance yet on Sunday? I would love to hear you sing the Marching Song. What other songs do you know?

Don't forget to pray for us out here. With love, Kenneth McMillan

The next letter Ione wrote to her mother on the 2nd of September once again describes the harshness of raising babies in the Congo and what she had to deal with:

.....The packages came this week, the one with the screwdrivers from the company and then the one from you with toys and bibs for the children. 'Frisky' arrived in very good condition and Kenneth just loves him. Only a few months ago he was holding him and squeaking him, then Kenneth would make a noise just like it. He likes the little car, too, and I am trying to keep it put away for Christmas, since there is nothing about that will spoil; (rubber things sort of melt after they're here awhile, especially if not in use, and metal things rust, but this little car has neither so I will try to keep it as a special treat a little later) The bib is grand, just the thing to protect his good suits when he eats out. Thank you so much. Paul's rattle is ready to use in probably a few more weeks. His eyes are following objects already and he waves his hands around. He is so big that he can already wear a little romper suit that Kenneth wore in 6 months!

You will probably be shocked when I tell you what happened to him a couple of days ago. But it really isn't as bad as it sounds. He had had a little 'cradle cap' on his head which I had been giving especial attention to when I bathe him, and one morning I noticed that instead of the whitish scabs the spot had gone red, so I gathered him up in my arms and ran down to Pearl. She said it looked like a little bruise and said it was nothing serious. I tho't he had rubbed his head when he kicked himself to the end of his carriage or bed, so didn't think much about it until night before last when at 8 o'clock, above the noise of a heavy rainstorm I heard him crying. It was an unusual time for him to waken and I examined him very carefully before I picked him up and discovered a line of tiny red ants leading up to his head. Then I found his head covered with ants which were eating there, and they were drawing blood to the surface. I immediately washed them off with water and bathed his head with disinfectant solution and plastered it with a castor oil ointment. Then came the job of tearing his bed apart, the bedding I mean, shaking it all and washing the bed and renewing the cans of water under each leg. The water I had had in the cans had gotten a coating of dust over which the ants travelled. I felt terrible to think that I had not changed the water often enough. Right now, the ants are very numerous and if I lay down a blanket on which he had drewled or vomited, in just a few moments it is covered with them. But this is Congo, Mother, and I am glad we have come. I don't think Paul was uncomfortable very long, for I was not far away when he started to cry. But I hate the tho't of ants eating on our baby's head! I have heard of rats chewing on the toes of natives while they slept.

That was thoughtful of you, Mother to write to me on my birthday. I had a lovely birthday party; it was joined with Pearl's and Ma Kinso's birthday. But celebrated on my day. Joan baked the cake and we had a buffet supper at Mary's house. I received a pair of Nylon hose from Ma Kinso, some glass individual salt dishes from Pearl, soap from Kinso, 8 little fruit drinking glasses from Verna Schade, Coty's toilet water and a hanky from Olive, a hoover apron from Joan, some pot holders from Mary, and book ends from Paul and Kenneth. Of course, my nice watch from Hector, which I do appreciate so much. The one Evelyn gave me got caught on the baby's high chair when I was taking him out (Kenneth, I mean) and dropped on the cement floor and broke inside. I had been carrying an alarm clock to classes with me. We had nice things to eat at the party and especially nice was some Bavarian cream which Verna made, and some cracker jack which had come from America. Hector's carpenter stayed at the house to watch Kenneth, and we took Paul in the carriage.

I am teaching again, but on a rather reduced scale. I have the same Music Class Mondays, Wednesdays, and Friday from 10:15 to 11:15 and Hector stays with the children (does work in the office here). On Wednesday afternoons I have the women from 2 to 4 for sewing, hygiene, and a message, but I am taking Paul so that I can feed him at 3 o'clock. The women are quite thrilled to have me feed him in the meeting! They marvel that they are so close together, Kenneth and Paul. I am seeing if I can keep up my health with this work and if so, can take more. I want to learn to ride the motorbike (Corgi) and take some children's meetings in a rather distant village. We have French class every day at 4 and prayer meeting at 5, besides our regular native gatherings. The children keep me pretty busy from 7 to 9:30 and from 2:30 to 4 but with the help that I have with washing and ironing and cooking I am able to do some missionary work.

.....We are praying daily for you that you may have His guidance for your fall work and that you may be established in a home again by furlough time. We love you very much and long to see you. In His service, Ione XXXX

Ione got back into the swing of life as a missionary. No longer an expectant mother, she resumed writing to her supporters on the 18th of September:

Hurrah! The big package came last night. And how hard it was to finish feeding Kenneth and Paul and then to eat my own supper with Hector before we could open it. We brought it in here to the office and tried to do it systematically and look at each thing together, but then a native came to see Hector and I got ahead of him. I couldn't wait! It was so exciting and when we came to the candy, we just sat down and ate. I must tell you that everything, even the candy came *thru in perfect condition. And that it tasted just like it had come fresh from the store. That is very unusual here, for I cannot ever remember receiving anything like that without it being somewhat melted and sticky. The caramels did not even stick to their papers when removed. How good they taste. I guess we have eaten about half already, but the rest I have put into quart fruit jars so that the ants and dampness cannot spoil them. We want them to last a little while at least. Hector has the cooling unit 'cooking' over a little gasoline pressure stove, so that we'll have COLD <u>Jello</u> today from our Icyball Refrigerator.*

I don't know what to say first about the clothing, I am so thrilled. EVERYTHING is so useful and I must say needed at this stage, for every week now I have to put away things that Kenneth is too large for now. He can step right into some of the little suits and will look lots nicer than he would if I had spent hours and hours sewing for him. His socks were getting to the stage where I tho't he would have to go without, and these size six are just right for him to put right on.

.....He looks so cute that I have sent him over in his monocycle to show his

Daddy. A native fellow with a green apron and big dreamy eyes is pushing him proudly. His conveyance is a single bicycle wheel with a seat on the front and handle bars for pushing; also, two little wheels for when the 'passenger' gets in and out and in case the 'pusher' is unsteady. The little suit with the navy-blue trousers is quite like [what] the schoolboys wear on Sunday, so I will let him wear it then to please the boys. About 140 of them will be watching Kenny when he comes into church. There are so many nice things for him to wear and I appreciate each one. And those lovely blankets – I just love to sit and pat them. Thank you so much. The

Hector's 'monocycle' stroller for little Kenneth.

bunting is fine for Paul if he has to make a journey on a chilly day in the damp season; or for when we are on our way to America. I don't know yet when that will be, but before long, I guess. Our station leader has notified Mr Pudney that our time (my husband's) to go is due in Feb. I will try to save the blue sweater till then, too, but Kenneth could wear it any time if I get in a pinch. You have sent everything I suggested and much more. I think one of the most thoughtful things is the little bathroom fixture for the boys. It is exactly right for the little chair my husband had made.

Saturday is always a day of interruptions, buying 'poso', or food from the natives who come to the door, helping various women with sewing hints and showing schoolboys which parts of our big yard and garden need cleaning, trying to keep the cook from spoiling the baking, etc.

.....Kenneth has gone to Kole with Hector and he has worn his new blue corduroy suit, with navy blue socks, and of course, his new white beret! I don't know how to thank you for all of these things. I just put away the clean clothes and was so thankful to discard to the 'native' cupboard some old shirts that Westcott's had left for native babies at the hospital. I had confiscated four of them when I had nothing to put on Kenneth. By the way, the Jello was delicious for dinner. It stiffened beautifully and was a real treat. I have put the remaining boxes in a jar for if I leave them out the dampness will spoil the stiffening process.

Tomorrow will be a special Sunday service celebrating the arrival of Viola Walker who came on Wednesday. There will be special songs by the women, the schoolgirls, and the schoolboys, and a presentation of flowers. Viola has a car following her and that will be a help to our station. There is also a car coming for Verna Schade, a Commer pick-up truck. This brings us all sorts of possibilities of trekking and short and long trips. I think there will be some sort of trip made at New Years' time and Marcellyn will return to spend a couple of weeks with us. Ekoko, her station is about 250 miles away. I am fortunate to have my own sister so near. Our Bongondza personnel is now nine, eleven counting our two babies.

Hector is trying to get Verna Schade's house finished by Christmas time. Then Pearl Hiles will move into Verna's present house, which is the guest house that Doctor Westcott built.

Now mail day has come, and before this goes out, I will add a little more. We send and receive our mail once a week. This has been an interesting week. In the music classes we are beginning to work in earnest on the national anthems for an inspector will be here in a few weeks. We want also to sing for him the French words to a lovely song, "The Lamb of God." They have been learning to sight read "The Son of God Goes Forth to War," in Lingala [lin-GA-la], (the language Marcellyn speaks). Lingala is more difficult than Bangala, my language. I am teaching them the tonic sol-fa system as well as the notes and staff, for the former is used here a good deal. I had music classes on Monday. Tuesday, I went out with Mama Kinso to Nzei's village where a new church was erected recently. She had a reading class with the women while I took the children's meeting. Then while she had a regular church service, I took the children outside for some games. There were about 20 children. A number there have professed to accept Christ. Tuesday night we all ate together at Kinsos because it was Mr J's birthday. I gave them all a treat of JELLO. With a bit of marshmallow on top! And we ate the rest of the candy. Wednesday Music again and the women in the afternoon. They sewed for an hour on some appliquéd tablecloths and then we had the meeting. I spoke on soul winning and family worship. Last evening, I cut some more appliqué pieces and cut out a shirt to be given to the schoolboy who best weeds our lawn and paths then I spent some time writing the four parts of 'La Brabanconne' for the music class. And now it is Thursday, Mail Day.

One feels the presence of Satan so strongly here, much more than at home I believe. Sometimes I must almost run to the bedroom where I can pray, and when I am feeding the baby or doing something else, I just quietly quote as many scriptures as I can. And another thing that has helped to combat his power I found in that verse, Rev. 12:11 "And they overcame him by the blood of the Lamb, and by the work of their testimony." The word of testimony helps greatly and I try to WITNESS as hard as ever I can!!

Now I must close. Kenneth is pulling on my left hand and punching the Shift Key and he needs attention.

Verna Schade's new round house.

Thank you so much, everyone. Lovingly in Christ, Ione

In another letter to supporters, this time unspecified and written on the 29th of September, Ione's enthusiasm for her work and life is very evident:

.....It is wonderful that these black folk here who believe shall wear white robes of cleansing from sin, and they shall have 'palms in their hands' as well. Then they shall unite in the glorious song, 'Salvation unto our God who sitteth upon the throne, and unto the Lamb.' What a wonderful privilege is ours to be a part of this great work of evangelizing the nations! The vanguard has passed out of sight, but as Zinzendorf's friends said to him when they arrived on a certain island and learned that their predecessors were imprisoned, 'So be it; we are here.'[79] The work must go on. Wherever men sit in darkness the light must be taken. God must have men. 'Whom shall I send, and who will go 'asked the Lord of Hosts. 'I am here,' said Isaiah, and we are here.

.....When we returned to our own station [from being at Yakusu], Hector found the building of Verna Schade's house progressing fine, and he started to make cement lintels for the windows and doors so that the white ants would find no woodwork to eat. It is an attractive five-room bungalow, perfectly round made of brick. It faces over the brink of a hill into deep forest. Verna hopes to occupy it by Christmas time. We are waiting now for the roofing for it. I was glad to teach again my singing classes and it has not been too difficult to take along one or both children. I found it exciting this week to push the baby carriage over driver ants which were threatening to raid our house; I can tell you I went fast!

---

[79] A reference to Count Nikolaus Ludwig von Zinzendorf, a major figure in eighteenth-century Protestantism and a Christian mission pioneer.

In class I found it necessary one day to remind the 96 boys about being quiet. In fact, I said that the next one who spoke without permission would go to Bwana McMillan [for reprimanding]. *To my surprise, a child spoke right up and said, "If you please, Madame, there is a bad animal right behind you! I turned, and sure enough, a long squirmy centipede was gaining speed toward me. That boy got a stick, but it was to kill the centipede! We haven't had many 'bad animals' around recently, but there was a snake which attempted to enter at the roof of the washing room, and the house helper saw him and called over to Hector's carpenters, and together they frightened it out on top of the water drums. Then, to my amazement, I saw it leap deliberately from that high position, some 10 or 12 feet, to the ground. They tell me this type of snake does leap; that is why it is dangerous sometimes to walk under trees.*

I have a new Child Evangelism class at Nzei's village, where Mrs Jenkinson has organized a fine work and they have built a church. I have been going with her, as she has a reading class for the women while I have the children's meeting. After that, I take the children outside for games and she calls all adults into the church for a Gospel service. The church is so tiny that there is hardly room for children as well as adults. There have been some saved there nearly every week. It is precious to see a little child turn his heart to Jesus. Paul has been going out with me and Kenneth stays with his Daddy.

Today in the women's meeting here on the station we discussed foods in a hygiene lesson; two women bro't a plate of food like they serve their husbands and we talked about each. I showed them how they can improve the balance of their diet and demonstrated the value of tomato sauce. Then we had our Gospel service and made plans to all go out next week for a village meeting. Sonatu will speak, and her grown-up Christian daughter will sing with three other women, "Amazing Grace." One woman, Kibibi, holds her baby while she sings, but nobody minds, and I must hold mine, too!

Yesterday Hector cut his finger quite badly on a rotary planer he runs electrically. As Nurse Hiles went off today on a medical trip, I must be his nurse for a few days. He will have the use of the finger again but it is doubtful whether the nail will ever come back. But he says, "a carpenter loses a finger every seven years."

This week I am leaving the sewing machine open all of the time for use at every "odd moment." It seems that I am singing "a song of the shirt," for there are shirts of every kind in progress: I am cutting off the sleeves of some for Hector; making a new one for Kenneth; making four for native lads who are receiving them as prizes for cleaning the weeds from the large front and back yards; and with the help of the washing helper I am trying to finish nine schoolboys' shirts for next year, to mend schoolboys' old shirts, and to make two shirts and a pair of trousers for the 8-year-old mulatto boy who eats with us.[80] But "I ain't got weary yet!"

It seems I cannot finish this letter without a reminder that we are in Africa, for Hector has just come in with driver ants on his legs. We have taken a light and discovered that a raid is upon us and the black columns have already spread into the house. They have filled the kitchen, have entered the dining room, and even while I write they are coming into the hall leading to the children's room. My husband is endeavouring to head them off with his blow torch, but he thinks that we may have to evacuate, for they have spread so far already. It is interesting to see them even going into our refrigerator which sits in basins of water. The refrigerator is not very cold just now, but it is amazing how they got across the water. Excuse me while I look again to see how near they are to Kenneth and Paul.....They haven't gone any farther into the bedrooms, but have concentrated more in the kitchen. Outside they have covered the backyard area. I am watching to see if they will climb into the windows. Now Hector is going to try to stop them with D.D.T.[81] We don't mind if they kill some cockroaches and other insects and rats, but we don't want them to get in where the children are....You would laugh to see us hopping first on one foot and then the other with the spray guns and lights in our hands. That helps to keep them back but it is hopeless to try to kill them all. We found a table in the washroom had none on it, so we sat there with our legs dangling, looking down on them. The shadow of the light upon them makes them appear to have a hump and they seemed to us to be galloping along like an endless caravan of camels.

Back in the office now I find they are here; I will have to leave for they are covering my desk! They are very speedy for even while I look they seem to close in on me and I have already felt several nips...I have moved to the front porch now, and I have sprayed my shoes with D.D.T. but they get across somehow. I have made another round of spraying. They have spread to the side of the house and have gone into the basement. Hector is fascinated by them and watches everything they eat, but it makes me sick to see them devouring alive other insects. Hector has sprayed his legs up to his knees so that he can stay close to them. Unless they cross over to the other side of the house, the children are still safe. This raid has lasted now - nearly two hours. It is 10:15 P.M. They usually take about three hours to raid one house, so I guess we'll continue our fight and try to keep them from disturbing our little ones. We can sleep at Mrs Jenkinson's if necessary. The place where I was sitting in the office is now quite black with driver ants. They are now on the front steps, which means they have encircled half of the house. The right half of the front yard is creepy with them. I wish I could describe how quickly they move and how viciously they attack and how

---

[80] It appears that once again, Ione was acting as a foster mother.

[81] Dichloro-diphenyl-trichloroethane was developed as the first of the modern synthetic insecticides in the 1940s and is now banned in many countries.

expertly their little guards engineer their activities. The largest of them is about half an inch long. They seem to stand on their hind legs but all six legs are still on the ground when they reach up with their powerful mandibles. 11:15 – they are dispersing now we think, without entering the children's room. A dazed cockroach escaped there and I killed him. Just now when I was attending to Paul, Hector called to me to come and see the drivers attacking and capturing a stinging centipede on the front steps. I'm glad they got him. They have done a good house-cleaning job for us. I think it will be safe to go to bed now, for if they continue to raid, they will probably reach our bedroom before the children's.

Next morning – still one or two drivers but the raid is finished. The little mulatto boy says that one night in the house of a friend of his, driver ants came and captured a snake and were dragging it out when the man awakened and was bitten by the snake.

Enough of that, but I will say in closing that in spite of a few inconveniences that living in the tropics brings, we are very happy here, and glad that we answered the Lord's call to 'go'. Thank you so much for making it possible for us to be here. Your gifts have been a great help and blessing. And be assured that prayer is being answered and souls are being saved. We love you and hope we shall never be a disappointment to you. Do continue to pray that the Lord will keep us humble and useable in His Service. Please pray with us concerning our coming home for furlough early in the spring.

Yours in Christ, Hector & Ione McMillan

On October 7, 1948, Hector wrote to the Kerrigans who had been on furlough from Maganga since 1947, and had now returned to the Congo:

It was so good to hear that you arrived back and that you found everything in good order. I suppose you were glad to have the long trip finished, and to get settled once more in your Congo home.

And too we hear that you have enough money for your Commer truck. That will be a great day when all these years of prayer and savings have been answered. We are eagerly looking forward to having one here on this station.

.....What do you think of Chester's saw mill? I guess you will want him to come along to Maganga some time and give you a helping hand.

.....Yours in Christ, Hector

Ione sent a secret letter to her mother on October 13, 1948, while Hector was in Stanleyville:

Dearest Mother and whoever else is there, too!

.....First, I will take care of the business of this letter, for if I have an interruption I can quickly close and slip it into an envelope and get it over to Kinso's to put in the mail bag before Hector returns from Stanleyville. I don't want him to see this or know I've sent it for I want to ask if you could get him a Christmas present at home from me and send it out Airmail. He lost his fountain pen on the journey taking Joan Pengilly to Ekoko recently and he misses it so much. He is using mine in Stanleyville now, and I miss mine! Do you think you could get him

another? He needs a pencil, too, but Airmail postage is very high and he could wait for that. I will pay you whatever it costs.

Hector thinks he can wait for clothes until he comes home [to the US], but really, he has nothing to come in, for everything is worn out except a wool suit. His underthings we can replace in Stanleyville, and shoes and sox and shirt, and I think, even a hat. But they have no nice lightweight suits like for travelling in. And he needs a couple pairs of work pants for every day. I have tried to make them, but they just don't fit him nicely. And he is so active he needs something plenty large and strong. If something were sent straight mail right away it would get here before we leave, I am sure. His trousers measure 33 inches at the waist now and his shirt 15 and ½. About paying for it, as soon as you wish you can ask Phila. [mission headquarters] for one allowance $40 (not more if you can help it!). Our gifts over and above allowances from now on will have to be saved toward our furlough unless that need is all met.

.....I am very well now, and outside of a badly cut finger Hector is O.K. Paul weighs 16 lbs. My milk comes well for him but I have to drink it at every meal. We spend one whole allowance on Klim alone!! But the Lord is good to us and we do not lack other things.

Thanks so much for all you have done already. If this is too much expense and trouble, please feel free to tell me. Nothing is urgent.

Love, Ione

Her mother managed to get the special little package sent and Ione responded in a November 25th letter to her, also mentioning upcoming travel arrangements:

Dearest Mother,

At last we had news of Doris's visit and it was so good to hear. Sorry your other letter didn't reach us about the preparations. Yes, the baby is a big boy, and gaining right along. Kenneth is big, too, but still doesn't talk much. He tried to say Bonjour, and a Libua word, too, but most of the time it is just Mama and Daddy, a jumble which means drink of water, etc.

The 'special' little package came this week and I have it hidden but I'm afraid I can't wait until Christmas and he does need it, so I might give it to him on our 3rd Anniversary, next Saturday. Hector's shoe size is 9 width medium, and brown is especially nice on him. His hat size is 7-1/8, but both those items he really can get out here. 11-1/2 is OK for sox; not any smaller.

I will need to buy some kind of travelling shoes before I can come home, but I think I can get them here; I am not sure yet. If you are able to send some, probably brown would be best, and a low heel. I think my width is bigger now, probably 8 triple A would do. I may be able to remodel the dresses that are too small and too short for travel. If I had one dress suitable for either summer or winter, I could use it on the way and when I first arrive in cooler climate. I have sweaters to wear and my same coat. I think the children will be cared for in the boxes that are coming.

.....It was good to hear all of the details about Doris' visit. I was so thrilled I wept. Wish I could have been there with Marcellyn, too. I wish Marcellyn and I could be together oftener. But she writes very frequently and I do feel near to her. I hope nothing interferes with her coming here during the holidays. Transportation is very difficult right now, as the old Ford is on its last legs and she may have to come on the Congo service which is expensive and takes several days. We are waiting now for the Bongondza new truck to arrive. It should be here at any time. She is expecting a new car at Ekoko, too, that Frances Longley bought. Did you know that Frances' mother died and she went home. I guess Marcellyn told you.

Hector's cut finger which I wrote about in our form letter is healed but it doesn't look very nice. It will always be disfigured. Hector is working so hard to get Verna Schade's house finished and furnished before we go home. It is a nice little house and she seems pleased with every new thing he does in it. But Hector doesn't get enough rest, for now he is running an extra shift of school boys during the noon hours as well as a group from 3 pm to 5 pm beside the regular workmen and carpenters and masons, etc. Then he teaches Science once a week in the boys' school. And when I am away, he manages to keep the children. We never leave them with natives.

Week ago Sunday, Hector and I got out to a couple of villages with the children. He let me off at one with Paul, and took the car on to another with Kenneth. We had forgotten the boiled water for Kenneth's milk and since we would be gone for a number of hours (about 60 miles each way) I had a native woman boil some water and I strained it thru a diaper and had it cooled by the time Hector returned to my village. The following Tuesday I went to Nzei's village with Mrs J. but left the children with Hector; and then on Wednesday went with the women to a village about 2 miles away. We walked and I took Paul.

I am feeling fine now, and do love to keep going. Am planning some parts of the Christmas program and do love that. I have charge of the women's part as well as the boys'. No room to tell about them in detail.

Thanks so much for the wee package for me to give to Hector. I will pay you whenever you let me know the price.

Lovingly in Him, Ione

In December, Hector was again in Stanleyville, and wrote to Ione while staying at the BMS guesthouse:

Dearest Belovedest Ionesphere:

I hope you're busy writing me about all that has happened since I saw you last. I meant to send you the flashlight but missed out. Hope you can borrow Pearl's!

.....Fri morning 6:15 a.m. I went to bed early last night & so I'll try to get more off to you this morning. I was remembering you in my devotions this morning along with Kenneth & Paul. I know the Lord will care for you all (& for me too) while we are separated. It is so nice to have a family as the centre of one's

interest & I've got such a commendable one! ! ! There is no one who can ever be as wonderful as my Ione & the two boys. XXXX

You'll be glad to know that I've been able to get a nice pair of American slacks at Aladoff's for 298 francs. They even have a zipper. There was a stray thread in the cloth on the left leg but I've carefully cut it out & it's hardly noticeable (there was a tag on the trousers saying they were "seconds"). They are light brown & I'm very pleased with them. I also was able to get 3 undershorts & two undershirts. I was looking at the suits in Aladoff's & I imagine we can afford 2,200 francs after Christmas. There is one nice one there, all wool but medium weight. However, I'd like you to be with me when we pick it out. You have such good taste.

The man who is putting the body on the truck is doing a good job. It will probably be finished at noon today. We have taken 2 sheets of flat aluminium down to him for the roof. The garage man expects the bulbs by plane today so we'll be all set to leave tomorrow. It will make a good load with 3 drums & all the other things that Parry & Keri have purchased. Keri is busy reading thru' the instruction book. When we get to Maganga I'll probably spend a day with him going over the broken electrical system & gas lines; as they are the most likely causes of trouble. He has purchased a fair supply of tools.

.....Yesterday when we were in the "Commer" place there was a passenger car sitting in the yard. The mechanic was adjusting the brakes. Later he told us it belonged to the manager of Banque Belge D'Afrique. It is a Humber. The manager brought it up from Matadi to Léopoldville when this mechanic was down there. After he had gone over it, he took it out for a road test – 130 km an hour - & if he'd pressed it a little more, he'd have gone 150. It must be some car. Cost – 180,000 francs.

.....It's almost time for breakfast so I'll leave the letter & try to add more later. X

11:30 a.m. Now I have something interesting for you to read. I visited the Agency of the Maritime International (right beyond the Post Office) & he was ever such a nice man. From his suggestions & schedules I've been able to work out the following:

River: Leave Stanleyville March. 3 (Gen. Olsen), Arrive Léopoldville March 11, Arrive Matadi March 12 = 2 fares = $165. Children free.

Ocean: Leave Matadi March 14, Arrive New York March 28, (Belgian line direct) = 2 fares = $1050. Kenneth = $263 = Total $1478.

When we are sure of going this agent can book our passages & issue our tickets.

Yours since Nov/45. Hector

The McMillan's preparations for a visit back to the States is starting to take shape. The last letter of the year was to Ione's mother written on the 18th of December:

Dearest Mother,

What a grand box you sent and it came in time for Christmas! It was so thrilling to receive it. It came with the mail the night Hector and Jenkinsons brought the new car to Bongondza a few days ago. While I was getting a bit of supper for them, I was all the while peeking into the box. The only thing broken was the glass container around Kenneth's toothbrush, and the candy was somewhat sticky and had dampened a few garments but I can wear it for Christmas. Thank you <u>so</u> much. It fits just right. The boys' suits are grand and fit too, and will fit them for quite a while as the buttons can be moved along the straps. They look darling on them together. The socks are so welcome and the little silk cap darling. And Kenneth's cap & jacket will surely be fine for going home on furlough.

As I write this, I can say nothing as yet about when we will leave. Hector is in Stanleyville again, this time helping Mr Kerrigan become acquainted with the new car for Maganga station. I am hoping he will have some travel information to tell when he returns in a few days.

Speaking about my new dress reminds me to tell you that several native women have seen it and have had me cut tops for their Christmas dresses just like it! I have so much enjoyed working with the women this year. I have only led one woman to the Lord but Mrs Jenkinson has led several. And a number have been baptized. Women are real trophies here. They have such a hard lot.

I have sent over to J's just now to see if there is any mail for me. I tho't tonight I'd hear from Marcellyn. I'm holding my breath for fear that she can't come. The new Ekoko car was to have arrived there about now & might be available, but if not, she may have to come by Courier & it may be too expensive. I do so much want to see Marcellyn. This will probably be our last visit before our furlough. She is such a dear sister and I'm thankful to have her near. Wish she were on this station; there are so many more conveniences. But she is <u>so</u> needed at Ekoko.

Next morning.

Well, the Courier came and I received a letter from Marcellyn saying she has reserved a place for herself on a bus that comes from Aketi to Kole. That means <u>next</u> <u>week</u> we'll be together!! We'll meet her at Kole. Sorry we couldn't have gone all the way for her. Marcellyn also said you <u>received</u> the job at South Baptist Church! Hurrah! I'm so glad.

I also had a letter from Hector and he will be here Tuesday or Wednesday. That means we'll have a few days together to paint the bathroom & get new curtains up before Christmas. Hector has gotten information on our furlough trip and says he could even buy the tickets in Stanleyville if the money comes. There is a connection which leaves Stanleyville March 3rd and arrives in New York March 28, all the way by boat. Will let you know if we can take this.

Now before I close & get the children ready for church, I'll tell you what happened after I wrote you last night. While I was writing Ma Kinso came and we talked until the lights went out at almost 10 (we have electricity now). Then I *lit a candle and got ready for a bath. As I lifted the bath mat from the edge of the tub to put it on the floor, something dropped from it. The wee light of my candle revealed a snake, quite small. I almost put out the candle in my haste to kill it with a broom handle. I carried it outside & returned to the tub and found two more snakes <u>in the tub</u>! I got sort of excited then and was a bit panicky by the time I killed them so I got a better light and searched around and Verna Schade slept here in case any more turned up while I was nursing the baby. Must close for now. Lovingly in Christ, Ione*

PS: Dec. 23, Hector back now & says don't bother to get him a suit. He has seen one in Stanleyville. Reservations booked – see you soon. X Hector

And, so ends 1948. It had been an eventful year for Ione, one that had been testing, yet brought joy with the birth of her second son. She managed to combine motherhood with missionary work and survive all the challenges of living in the Congo.

Chapter 10
GOING HOME ON FURLOUGH

Arranging furlough was always going to be difficult. Aside from tying in all the different travel sections, there were also the two little boys to consider. Ione wrote to Lucille and family on the 23rd of February, 1949 stating that they hoped to take the March 3rd river boat, then the ocean boat on the 14th, arriving in New York the 28th.

Ken & Paul advertising for Klim powdered milk.

Naturally both sides of the family wanted to see them and spend quality time with them. However, furlough for missionaries was not a vacation. While they are home from the Congo, the McMillans needed to reconnect with all their supporters and engage with new ones who would contribute to the mission finances and thus enable them to continue with the work. There were also conferences in Pontiac and Toronto to attend as soon as they landed in North America. Hector had promised his father that he would spend two months on the farm so that would take up May and June. The boys also needed some stability in all of this. It was impossible for Ione to make some kind of definite timetable from such a distance and when so many other people and factors needed to be taken into consideration. Ione tried to explain the situation to her family and suggested that they could maybe all meet up in Pontiac. Both she and Hector were tired from the work and ready for the break.

Kenneth strolling towards Kinsos' house.

.....But we are hungry, so hungry for American foods:

white potatoes, beef and pork, and most of all ice cream!

.....Our babies have been awfully sick as a result of their yellow fever shots [immunizations]. Kenneth had one convulsion. But they are better now. There is yellow fever around here now. Three children had died with it. We are thankful they are inoculated. The Lord is good to bring them thru this illness.

Hector is awfully tired now, and yet is working day and night to get all he can done on Verna's house. He is now making venetian windows (shutters) in

288

aluminum sheeting. His round house has turned out quite nice, and should last many years. Tho' Hector is very tired, he never utters a cross word. He is so patient when I get upset, and so good with the children. I am still teaching music, but I think today is the last day! I have our trunks mostly packed, and have stuck in some bits of candied pineapple and peel and Congo sugar lumps! Wish I could bring some avocado pears! We have a large head of bananas hanging in our wash room. We can't possibly finish them all.

Love to all, Hector and Ione.

The family eventually set off as planned and their arrival home was recorded in the local paper. On April 6th, the *Pontiac Daily News* carried the following story under a dramatic, albeit wordy headline, written by Florence Seldon:

Aboard the *Rein Astrid* on the Congo River, heading from Stanleyville to Leopoldville on their way to furlough in Canada, March, 1949

Belgian Congo Missionary's Wife and Sons Visiting in Pontiac Tell of Wild Pygmies.

Travelling the long distance from the heart of the Belgian Congo to Pontiac with two babies is a task which would daunt a less courageous person than Mrs J. Hector McMillan. As Ione Reed, Mrs McMillan was known to many residents of Pontiac when she lived here and graduated from Pontiac High School. She entered the mission field and with her husband went to a post at Bongondza, Kole, Belgian Congo. Mrs McMillan came to Pontiac to speak at the Missionary Institute and the First Baptist Church.

The airplane journey (from N.Y.) brought a quick transition from a temperature of 130 degrees at their home two degrees north of the equator to our Michigan early spring. It also brought new experiences for the two little boys, 22 months and 8 months of age. Last week they tasted fresh milk and white potatoes for the first time. As for the older McMillans, one of the first things they bought upon arrival in the States was a big piece of apple pie a la mode for the Rev McMillan and a 'hot dog' in a bun for Mrs McMillan. Those two indulgences satisfied longings they had cherished from the time they knew they were coming 'back home'.

Ione with Ken and Paul

At Bongondza the great lack is fats of all kinds. Meat, too, is unavailable unless you are a good hunter. Mrs McMillan learned to use both a pistol and a rifle before she went to the Congo and sometimes she has joined her husband in his hunting quests for meat for the family.

A wild pig, a dwarf antelope or a buffalo is considered good eating. Rice is a great staple, the brown unpolished kind, and the manioc plant is also a staple, both for its green leaves and its roots which can be eaten as a vegetable or ground into flour. The white persons of the post, eight in all, make their own bread from cultured hops and the yeast is passed about among them and kept alive. One of Mrs McMillan's projects has been the translation of American recipes into the native tongue and teaching native women cooking, sewing and homemaking. She also teaches handicraft, music, and religion in a boys' school.

Under the present Belgian rule, natives are encouraged to be industrious and thrifty. Each man is obligated to raise his own garden and also a crop of rice, cotton and peanuts. This the government buys at a good price. Failure to raise a crop means imprisonment. The land is free to anyone who will till it. A man takes acreage to cultivate according to the number of wives as they do a great deal of the manual labour. The government also encourages monogamy by offering exemption from taxes to any man who has one wife and four or more children. 'Infant mortality and sterility are very prevalent because of the high rate of social disease. In a village of 1,000 you will often find only one infant,' says Mrs McMillan. 'There is a great effort at health education and gratifying results come about at once when a native becomes Christian.'

One of the finest native preachers is a man whose father was a cannibal. The mission post is located only 40 miles from the famous pygmy village. Next door neighbor to the McMillans is Viola Walker, the first white person to gain entry to the pygmy village. In her daily trips to the village, through a huge swamp infested with hook-worm, Miss Walker has formed a small nucleus of Christian converts. Braving the poison arrows, learning a language they could partially understand, this dauntless woman brings back many interesting accounts of the strange little people. Rev McMillan also has visited the pygmies. He found them living in burrowed out tunnels and wearing scanty leaf clothing. Among themselves they wage warfare and always have been considered inaccessible to white influences.

Mrs McMillan underwent harrowing journeys for the birth of her children. Accompanied by her husband, she started out a month before the expected events. Two hundred miles by car, 400 miles by plane and another 100 miles overland brought her to the hospital. The last time she made the trip, she arrived only to find that the doctor was no longer there and she added a 400-mile boat

journey to her already lengthy trip. In two weeks the first time and twelve days on the second, she was on her way back to the jungle with her new baby.

When it is time to send Kenneth and Paul to school, they will go to a 'nearby' school 900 miles away. The school is run in three month shifts when the children go home for a month. Some of the parents in the district accompany them on each trip and they all take turns.

Mrs McMillan considers the Belgian Congo a healthful place in spite of the fact that she

Archie MacMillan with little Paul.

takes five grains of quinine every day and has had malaria several times in the seven years she has lived there. Her little boys are rosy and sturdy, seldom ill.

The McMillan family will be on furlough in the United States for one year.

DL McMillan enjoying his grandchildren. On the pump is Barbara Pierce, Ken (to her left) and Donald Pierce - 1949

As is often the case some literary license was used by this member of the press. Though perhaps not exactly Ione's very words, it gave an idea to the readers of the extraordinarily different lifestyle lived on a mission station.

With interviews, deputation work and conferences, it is two months later when Ione finally finds herself and the family at the farm in Ontario, Canada. She still had not spent much time with her mother and castigated herself for not having made more effort to see her or even get a card sent for Mother's Day. Her first furlough (in 1944) was spent preparing for her wedding, now on her second furlough she had a husband and two small children. With all the things she had to do she knew that her mother was the one person who would understand that she was simply running out of time. So, she wrote her a long letter in May 1949 to unburden herself of the guilt. In it she apologized for the long delay, reiterated many times how much she loved her and laid out plans for the two of them to have some time together travelling to Michigan for meetings, at which time Hector would look after the children.

Ione poses with Archie MacMillan and Ken on the Avonmore Farm, 1949

.....I am sure there must be no loneliness like that which comes when your dearest ones neglect you. I'll probably experience it someday and then I'll know how you have often felt. Don't blame Hector, Mother for it is not his fault. I could have written if I had just pushed myself a little. Now Mother, please know that nothing has changed my heart toward you. I love you very much and since I am a mother, I appreciate more and more what you mean to me. It is just that I have not yet completely made the adjustment of loving a husband and two children, as well as my mother and sisters. Be patient with me until I get used to it and another time, I'll prove that I do not love you any less for having more dear ones to love. You are such a good sweet Mother and anyone who hurts you ought to be punished.

Hector's sisters (L-R): Jean, Alice, Irene, Florence and Eleanor in front, 1949

In December, Ione explained to her mother that their time in Canada and the States might be shortened. There was a possibility that Hector would take over as station leader, and as such, would be required to undertake a course in French in Belgium. He would spend a few months there and then return to America in order to travel immediately out with the family to Bongondza. It was a matter of discussion and prayer as it would require a great deal of money which they could barely afford along with the complications of the children. Ione was thinking she would not make the trip to see her mother. She wrote:

.....If we were to go in April, say after the conference here, I would have to decide where I want to be. I could go to Hector's farm, but the house here would be much easier to care for and living expenses are not high.[82] People are just wonderful to missionaries; we have had two sacks of potatoes given, a sack of

---

[82] Ione and Hector are based with Hector's mother's family, the McElherans in Three Hills, Alberta.

carrots (big sacks like two bushels), nearly 100 jars of fruit, vegetables, pickles and this week we will probably receive a quarter of a beef, about 100 lbs which we'll put in a locker for now.[83] *Our rent is cut down $5 because Hector works on the house. We could live on the remainder of what Hector does not need for Belgium. And if I were to stay here, I would like you to come here when the baby comes* [Ione is pregnant again] *and from then on for several months until Hector returns. But that is all 'What I would like'!! You probably will be head over heels in a new project there by that time. It sounded from your letter as though you will not want to leave there for some time. And you must do just what the Lord leads you to do. Don't let anything interfere with His Will.......I am sure that the Lord led in bringing us here. He is really dealing with my heart. And the Lord is blessing in Hector's deputation meetings. He attends some classes too. It's a wonderful atmosphere to live in, with everyone Christians, the milkmen, the farmers, the many people we contact in business, etc. It would be a rest and a blessing for you.*

By the New Year, still no decision had been taken regarding the Belgium trip but the family enjoyed a wonderful American-style Christmas, praising God with family and friends and opening gifts from so many kind and generous people. On the 2nd of January 1950, Ione wrote to her mother:

.....You gave us so many wonderful things I hardly know where to start. Hector was so pleased with his candy. You know just the kind he likes! You should have seen the children when they opened their packages. It was so much fun.

Kenneth's eyes opened wide when he found a truck all full of candy. And they are both very fond of their knife & fork sets. I guess you knew they had never had any just for them. Those blocks are lovely and so interesting to play with. Paul enjoys piling them up. Oh, the ducks, too, are very popular. Paul takes his in the bath tub and Kenneth is learning to wind his up by its tail. They are taking a real interest now in books & I'm glad to have a Christian nursery rhymes book. And five presents for me. I think I should scold you. I'm afraid you are going without necessities to buy things for us. That jacket & slippers are darling and will be grand to use when I go to the hospital. The hose & holder are lovely and I surely do thank you. I had been using a slip cover from an old white purse to

Hector & Ione in winter coats.

---

[83] Rationing was introduced to Canada in 1942 and USA in 1943 and stopped in 1946, Canada continuing another year. During this time, Canadians and Americans resorted to growing their own food and preserving it, thus they catered for at least 40% of their needs; a habit that was still very much in evidence.

hold my stockings. Thank you very, very much for everything. But you must promise not to do so much next time. We know you are in His service too, and need things yourself. We would love you just as much if you sent us just a card.

Ione reported that though the temperature was horrendously cold (minus 38 degrees), she was able to walk the half mile to town, especially on a fine day. The car they had bought to facilitate all the travelling did not have anti-freeze but Hector usually managed to coax some life from it if necessary. This car continued to function, thanks to a generous neighbor who fixed it up with about $100 worth of new parts. Once they return to the Congo, Hector hoped to give his brother the car.

Ione had limited childcare help from two of the neighbor's daughters. As of January 17th, Ione was active but cautious as she was quite large (with David). The previous week she started having cramps at intervals and it kept up for several days.

There are no letters or photos available describing the arrival of David Lynn, who was born on the 17th of March 1950 at Three Hills, Alberta. The lack of letters might perhaps be due to Ione and Hector being on 'home territory'. Telephones were by now standard items in homes, thus eliminating the need for announcements to all interested parties by letter.

With the family based in Three Hills, it's not just Ione's mother that missed out on family time. DL (Hector's father) was also missing them, and although in this letter written to the family on 1ST May, he indicated he is struggling, he did not ask for them to come and help but recognized the sacrifice all made for the Lord's work:

Dear Hector Ione Ken & Paul,

It's about time I would drop you a line. We have stormy weather for about ten days – high wind every day. Archie was laid up with a sore leg, varicose vein, he had to have Dr Pollick strap his leg up for about ten days. We hired John Blair to do the chores at the barn until Archie got well enough to do the work. I am not able to do very much. I have to take it easy. I get tired out. We heard you will be up in Peace River holding meetings. I hope that you will have success that God may be with you at all times to bless & strengthen you. Ask God to guide you in all that you undertake in His name.

With love from Dad & Archie to all the family

In another letter written on May 19, DL said:

.....the sow had 13 little pigs and Ken & Paul will have lots of fun when they get on Grampa's farm, young D.L. (David Lynn) will have to wait until next year before he can chase the pigs.

The family made it through the winter with only minor colds and sore throats but the finances were tight. Ione took advantage of being 'home' to have dental checks and booster injections against yellow fever. As they did not obtain certificates for the yellow fever injections the boys had in the Congo, the whole family was revaccinated.

On the 19th of June, Ione wrote to her mother, listing some of the money friends had sent to the family for their work. The boys had a joint birthday party with exciting presents each.

.....The box for Kenneth and Paul arrived Saturday and we kept it until today noon when we had two little cakes with candles lighted on them; two for Paul

Hector and Ione with Kenneth, Paul & David

and three for Kenny. They had fun blowing them out then we opened up your package and they were so thrilled with those big rubber tractors. Kenneth slyly tried to exchange his green one for Paul's red, but after we explained that the red one was the one Gamma meant for Paul, he was satisfied and I saw him later hand Paul the red one. We bought them red American Beauty wagons that are big enough to sit in. We couldn't get two colours so Hector painted their names on the back. Already Kenneth knows which one is which. These wagons can be dismantled and packed in our tin box [footlocker] *with their other toys. ......Both children speak often of Gamma and I don't think Kenneth will ever forget that long train ride. Thank you so much for their presents.......The baby talks real 'conversations' now. He is as fat as ever and is outgrowing so many clothes. He's getting a good color from the sunshine as I put him on the porch every day........We'll be here until July 3rd.*

Lovingly in Him, Ione

More packing was added to the footlocker. There were a few things the family bought in New York before sailing, such as clothes and shoes to last for the next five years. Ione and Hector had concerns about their return to the Congo, this was transparent in the tone set by their contribution to the UFM's *Light Life* magazine which started with:

And the arms of his hands were made strong by the hands of the mighty God." Gen. 49:24.

The time for returning to the Belgian Congo has come and we are finding it a bigger responsibility than the last time. As we thought of getting ready three small children under three years of age, with clothing for five years, and then the actual journey, which is rather complicated, we felt we almost had a load. Then we received a letter from the field which told us of a native woman who had been working in her garden. At the close of the day she prepared her bundles of firewood and tried to lift them to her back, but could not, for they were far too heavy. So, she sat down in her garden and spent some time in prayer. When she rose to go and took hold of her bundles they went to her back quite easily and the journey to her home was made without strain. She said it was as though there were hands under the load. "Hands under the load" was the phrase that stayed with us, for that was what we were needing.

The year away from the Congo seemed to fly by and it would seem that friends and supporters had expressed concern about Ione returning once more to the Congo. On the 30th of June, Ione wrote to Mr Hempstead (at UFM HQ):

.....About my health. You will see that the enclosed statement explains that I am alright. These extra weeks on the farm with good milk, eggs, strawberries and quiet rest have put on some extra pounds for all of us. I weigh 125 lbs now which is more than I have weighed for quite a few years. It is such a joy and satisfaction to have my own folk in my church so concerned about my welfare and I appreciate all you have done and wish to do in my behalf. I really want to get off on this boat and trust that it will be possible to sail at the scheduled time. The Lord has been so good in the past and because he has not failed in the past, I trust Him for all that lies in the days to come.

Finally, they had all the baggage ready including an organ for Marcellyn. Aside from the toys and clothes for everyone, there were medications, flanelgraphs and other teaching aids, and canned foodstuffs (two supporters had canned two cows as hamburgers, steaks, etc). Some supporters donated clothing for the Congolese. Extra provisions for the ocean crossing also had to be taken into account. There were almost 30 boxes in all and only an excess of $21 to pay.

Once again, Ione's mother was unable to see them off and so Ione was obliged to send her farewells in a final letter from the ship.

.....We have two cabins next to each other, two beds in each. Tonight, Kenneth is sleeping in the room with his daddy. I think that will be the way we continue. David's little bed is fastened to mine and I can feel of him anytime!......Our meals are wonderful, but only condensed milk...

However, the journey proved to be more arduous than ever before. The family reached Matadi on the 27th of July. In letters written on the 30th to her mother and sister Lucille, Ione described their voyage. The crossing was peaceful enough although Hector, as on his last voyage, suffered from debilitating sea-sickness a good deal of the time. For twenty-one days all Ione needed to do was look after her three boys and her ailing husband but this did not leave time for letter writing. She never took all three children out at once and used reins to restrict Ken and Paul when on the top deck. From the deck they watched whales 'spouting and splashing around in the water'. The ship docked twice: Savannah, Georgia, and St Vincent in the Cape Verde Islands, where Ione traded some soap for three colored shell necklaces and watched the island boys diving into the crystal-clear water after coins, which they always found. The rest of the non-crew members on the Belgian cargo ship were all missionaries with like-minded spirituality. Ione was able to share communion and prayer time with them. She then wrote:

.....We arrived at Matadi on the 27th at about 2 o'clock. I stayed on the boat with the children until Hector was sure of a hotel room. He got me installed in a lovely big room and then, upon returning for our hand baggage, found that he could not get it through customs that night. So, we were without some rather important things for a while. I had just the baby's diaper bag but I had a few books and

toys tucked into it and a chocolate bar and [an] *orange.* [Ione was without training panties for Paul, however, another missionary, Mrs Carper came to her rescue and she fashioned a diaper/nappy for Paul.]

.....I had the children's supper and breakfast served in the room.[84] We came from Matadi to Léopoldville yesterday (29th), eleven hours by train. That was a long time for the children but they had two naps and it was cool. Hector opened the seats out into beds and I covered them with a sheet.....We were met at the train by the Union Mission car and were in time for dinner here, a delicious meal of creamed tuna fish, mashed potatoes, peas, salad and peaches (canned), oh, yes, and soup.

The next stage of the journey would be a river boat (the *Reine Astrid*) up to Stanleyville which was due to leave on the 4th of August and would have the family back in Bongondza around the 18th, about the time the Kinsos were about to leave. However, they had to wait for their main baggage, including Marcellyn's organ, to come from Matadi. Ione started a letter home on the 18th August but it did not get completed until much later. In it, she recorded that her first night on the ship was a good one. While Hector took Ken and Paul round the deck, Ione spent time on Bible reading and reflection, she read:

Isaiah 45 and a few verses from 42: "...and I will give thee the treasures of darkness, and hidden riches of secret places... I will go before thee, and make the crooked places straight... I will lead them in paths that they have not known; I will make darkness light before them."

And she reflected how her first term as a missionary was spent looking after the Westcotts, which meant she was not instrumental in bringing 'souls' to the Lord, nor was she able to evangelize in the villages. Her second term of office was predominantly focused on marriage and having children and she recognized that there was "a coldness in my heart toward the Lord." And she noted that once she was back home "over 700 came to Christ". She wrote to the family on the 18th of August stating:

.....While at Three Hills, Alberta, a change took place, and the Lord renewed His covenant with me, in fact, He said it was now to be an 'everlasting covenant' and so I go forth once more with a burning desire to see His will performed in this place. The fire within my heart burns hotter than any fire without that might oppose. I am claiming, yes, I am demanding from the Lord these "treasures of darkness", these "hidden riches of secret places".

Yet, once again in Léopoldville, Ione was brought face to face with the possibility of losing a child in Africa. A family who were on their way home for furlough had just lost their two-year-old daughter who had died of cerebral malaria. Kenneth suddenly spikes a temperature of 105° Fahrenheit. Fortunately, he returned to normal within 48 hours. But there was more illness on the horizon.

---

[84] They establish a routine where Hector eats with Ken, and Ione with Paul; apparently David is the easiest, most placid and undemanding of them all.

Every bend in the river brought familiar sights, sounds and smells, but Ione wondered what the 'crooked places and paths' that she had read in Isaiah meant for her. The second day on the boat, all became clear.

Ione developed bacillary dysentery (diarrhea), where abdominal pains are severe. A doctor is summoned aboard at Coquiatville, a short way downstream, who prescribed 'sulfaguanadine', a drug these days used primarily in the treatment of animals which had the desired effect. By the time they reached Stanleyville a few days later, Hector, too, was very ill having spent two nights with a high temperature and malaria and then dysentery. Ione was staying up all night trying to keep up with the laundering of diapers and soiled clothing and in the end as time runs out, was obliged to tip the last load of washing into the river. The whole family were transported by ambulance to the hospital. Hector deteriorated and started to experience paralysis in his whole body.

With all these challenges, Ione was determined not to let her new found commitment to her Lord waver. On the 6th of September, she committed a prayer to paper in a letter:

Dear Lord: Thank Thee for revealing to me that there is NOTHING important except THY WILL, thy, LOVING KINDNESS. "Because thy loving kindness is better than life, my lips shall praise thee."

Thou hast shown me that I have no control over my children, my home, the work, except THOU givest me strength, wisdom, love, to do it. So much has seemed important for me to do. So much for my hands to do; I have not hands enough to care for my three children at once, and the women, and the staff, and the schoolboys who come under my influence. Just the tho't of so much to do makes my hands limp and hang down.

But now I can lift up my heart WITH MY HANDS unto God in the heavens. Lamentations chapter 3:41 "I stretch forth my hands unto Thee." Oh, bless them, strengthen them, make them to do first things first. "This ONE THING I do." "I will lift up my hands in Thy Name."

Ione had to go on to Bongondza with the boys and leave Hector in the hospital, still seriously ill with the dysentery and paralysis complicated by arthritis. On the 7th of September, she wrote to the family of her very difficult situation:

.....How I dreaded the night last night! Electric lights not working, flashlight batteries exhausted, not much kerosene. And Hector still sick in the hospital. I was so depressed as I looked in many places until late before I found some candles. I hate the night in Africa with its creeping things! I saw a huge spider and imagined many other things; chased a big mouse out of the sleeping rooms. I finally found the candles, and left one burning but it would have been so inadequate if a snake should come or a strong wind. I was up many times with the children carefully putting on my slippers each time lest I step on something. I longed for the day when I could protect my children better. Then this morning I read, 'My soul waiteth for the Lord more than they that watch for the morning.'

How emphatic it is! How necessary for me to place all that extreme longing in His very direction.

.....It is hard unpacking without Hector and the children are not yet adjusted to Congo. What hope I have for the future, what desire toward Him.

Paul, David and Kenneth at Bongondza - 1951

Eventually, Ione made up her mind to carry on with the work and leave the worries about Hector and the children to the Lord. She had to get the children up and breakfasted first thing in order to make a special time for her devotions when they were napping during the day. She was determined to have daily worship not only with the family but also with the staff.

She wrote to Hector a couple of weeks later telling him of the improvement in their own boys' health though they still were not sleeping well at night. She had to miss many of the services but did manage to stay through one whole morning service and was able to respond to the official welcome that she had been given.

.....It was a fine service and my heart ached to think you were not there. Everything is so empty without you. Nothing seems right. I don't see how I could ever get along without you. I love you so much.

.....I found only 4,000 francs in the bank so deposited Marcellyn's 2,000 and drew out 2,000, enough to buy store for a month. That leaves only 4,000 for your immediate needs and nothing for Léopoldville bills.

.....We have no light, and I didn't have enough money to buy a lamp, so Kinso brought one over and so did Vee. I have no equipment to light Kinso's and last night he was busy and didn't get it lit and I tried to light Vee's and broke the chimney. Could you buy another for her if it is available? You know what she has...I think it's an Aladdin. Can you bring some kind of light too and some more batteries for the flashlight.....I surely miss electric lights! I dread for evening to come on that account.

.....I hope you are feeling better and will soon be coming home.

.....The house was beautifully cleaned and whitewashed. You'll be pleasantly surprised at a good many things. The Lord is good to us and how I do praise Him for everything. Not much mail really here. Will save it for you. The baby is crying for a bath and the boys are getting restless. May the Lord be with you and make you a blessing.

Letter writing home was placed on hold. Ione later wrote in mid-October that while Hector lay in the hospital, helpless with arms and legs stiffened with the arthritis and a raging fever for ten days, that he prayed constantly and felt that he was wrestling with the Lord as Jacob had wrestled with the angel. He clung on to his faith despite feeling physically wretched and after several weeks was allowed to leave the doctor's care. He was a shadow of his former self though the paralysis had completely gone. However, his faith was even stronger and his sermons and dealings with people when he returned to the mission had a real power to touch their lives. He came back to Bongondza at the beginning of October 1950 and immediately set about fixing things for Ione.

For Ione and Hector, their return to the Congo after their furlough was very traumatic, yet they not only survived but emerged triumphant and revitalized. And so, the next term swung into action.

Chapter 11
BEING AT THE HELM

Ione and Hector and their three little boys are soon back at Bongondza having finally recovered from their illnesses. Ione wrote in a newsletter dated October 5, 1950:

Bongondza Church (photo taken in 1968 shortly after the first service since held 1964).

And so, He has made darkness light for us. Hector is home and the paralyzing condition of arthritis is completely gone. We are all well again Hector has the lights shining once more, several motors humming, and new aluminium sheets are going up on top of the Bongondza church. School boys are singing, and there is a contented murmur in the women's reading class.

"These things will I do unto them, and not forsake them."

.....Yesterday I went out with Hector and the children to the place where over 700 have been saved recently. We took our dinner and stayed all day. It was a wonderful day and the enthusiasm of the people was great. There were over 300 at both morning and afternoon services and when they went down the road to baptize 24, they were all singing together. There are several who want Christian marriages, but there was not time for that yesterday. The little 'rest house' was right next door to the church, so I could divide my time in the two places and manage the children so that Hector was free for each service. He conducted their very first communion service.

At Ma Kinso's suggestion, Ione starts holding her women's meetings in her backyard. That way David got to nap in his room and Ken and Paul played nearby. In a letter to her mother, Ione described how she managed children and work, although she found walking to a village with the children in a baby carriage too much. Bongondza is perched on a hill, so this was no mean feat. Going down was relatively easy but going up must have been a struggle. So, Ione waited until she could use the car. For these outings, she made sure the children were well covered with long sleeved shirts and long trousers protecting them from the sun and insects. Baby David continued to thrive, he took readily to the powdered Klim milk and Ione described him as 'a real little butterball'.

Hector's activities are detailed in several letters that he wrote to the Kinsos. He reported:

301

One brick shed is full and the masons have started the footings for the kiln.
The church roof is finished now except for the eave troughs and cistern. The roof
for the church took 321 sheets [of corrugated aluminum].[85]

When I get some more nails, I will try to put a new roof on the hospital.

Bongondza Hospital (photo taken in 1968).

In another letter by Hector written on the 3rd of December, he was not just dealing with building works, but also managing the men:

.....By the way, we have bad news about Botiki.[86] He has two young women in difficulty, one of them came down from Rethy with Dr. Trout. He has evidently had to go before Government officials. Mrs Ludwig writes of it in detail, but we are not saying much until we hear it from several more people. In our own circle, Bazapanai has had to be put off because of two affairs with young women when his own wife was helping her relatives plant cotton.[87] Samuele (one of the evangelists) checked on it, and yesterday Viola, Sam and Machini went out to settle up on books etc. and write him off [dismiss him].

As Christmas approached, plans were made for mini breaks away from the station and Hector and Ione planned to visit Marcellyn directly after the festivities at Ekoko. It was a good time for breaks as most of the workmen and school children returned to their villages from mid-December until the end of January. Olive Berkseth and Verna Schade were looking for a break in January and Pearl Hiles hoped to visit the Ludwigs in February. With so many colleagues away on furlough (it's not just the Kinsos, the Walbys stationed at Maganga were on furlough in the UK), a great deal of planning had to be done to cover the work. However, before holidays in the New Year, there was Christmas.

Ione wrote that on Christmas Day there would be 'hundreds' of people coming into the station, including the African evangelists from the outstations and their congregations. In preparation, Hector went out to hunt for meat for the anticipated gathering. He was gone for a few days with African hunters and slept in an open lean-to made of leaves. Ione described how they kept a fire going all night to ward off predatory animals. It was Hector who described the festivities in a letter to Mr Pudney on the 2nd of January:

.....All the evangelists were in for Christmas and seem to have had a profitable time. I had them for the early morning meetings and then a class from 11:15 – noon; during the week before Christmas. I took up the subject of Identification,

---

[85] Corrosion-resistant roofing material must have become available.

[86] Botiki is a medical aid worker who assisted Dr Westcott in the early 1940's.

[87] The Congolese were not monogamists but missionaries expected monogamy for Christians.

(1) with Adam, (2) with Christ. During three of the evenings we had moving pictures.[88] The largest crowd must have numbered close to 500. We have an outdoor "auditorium" in that triangle in front of our house and the slope of the ground makes it ideal. The screen is framed in Bamboo, for a tropical setting, and the projector table is up on seven-foot legs, so that it doesn't hinder visibility. I have two wires run up from Pearl's hospital electric plant. Baptista surely did me a good turn when he sold me this little projector and gave me those seven Christian films. The natives love the one on the prodigal son.

On the 8th January, Ione wrote to her mother:

.....A section of the hospital wall fell over during a heavy rain last week. Two rooms were put out of commission. And the workmen are away on holiday just now! There was a patient inside when it happened and I guess he was quite scared, but the wall fell out instead of in. Pearl is soon going to have the hospital reroofed, and have the metal extend out farther so that the walls will not crumble. Last week's rain took the ridge off our chicken and duck coop, and Hector and I put up a big piece of tin and last night the wind took that off.

Kenny has his first jigger taken out of his little toe, but he didn't cry. It was a big one and when I snipped the top of the dead skin off with the scissors, the eggs and 'mama' jigger just popped right out. Paul's world is made up of "lellow futterbies, yizzards, naughty 'nakes, 'piders, and bottle bugs, yitto wee ones, like David, and big Kenny ones".

Kenneth is only just now talking Bangala, after all these months, but he surprises us with whole sentences, using words we never dreamed he knew. And he translates them into English when he says them in Bangala. Learning is like a game to him. For months he has had me repeat to him everything I say to the natives. It has been disturbing at times, and embarrassing to have to stop and translate for him, but he surely stored up all I told him.

.....Our dysentery has never returned, and I am so thankful. We are all quite well and fat now. I don't know how much I weigh, but my dresses are getting tight! We have only been without butter two of three days since our arrival, and we still have cans of beef to draw from, as well as the canned potatoes. And we regularly get fresh vegetables every other week, enough potatoes for two meals, enough carrots for one, parsnips, turnips, and sometimes red cabbage. From the seeds I planted we got quite a few cucumbers, but I have had to make pickles out of all of them because there were worms in them. There were a few tiny ears of corn, beans, radishes, and squash, but the latter, too, was wormy. We are getting little tomatoes from some starts in our flower house, and a few tiny potatoes from some I had planted from the vegetable basket.

---

[88] Hector has acquired four films; one featuring animal haunts; another, a contractor building a house – with French subtitles; the third is underwater pearl hunting/diving and the fourth being an English sport's film with men hurdling, pole vaulting etc. in slow motion.

.....I must close and get to bed. It is going on 11 o'clock. Hector and I just had a piece of 'synthetic' pumpkin pie, made from papaya. I made another pie today using the recipe given by Mayme Baker, called 'Canadian Tarts'; it is nuts, brown sugar, egg, vanilla, etc. I used peanuts and pineapple combined. Kenneth and Paul helped me cut out some tiny tarts, little enough and tender enough for even David to bite on with his six teeth. He is so cute, now, big hands and big feet, fat yet all over, and so good natured. He has a huge appetite, eats as much as the other boys. He is trying to walk from chair to chair. They were so happy on Christmas morning when they found their stockings. In the afternoon when the 'Aunties' came to dinner, Auntie Pearl brought them some big net stockings crammed full of all sorts of things, rubber balls, gum, lifesavers, charms, packets of Christmas candy, tiny rolls of adhesive tape (which I needed) bandaids, baby powder, etc. So along with their nutcup favours they felt like they had a second Christmas. And when we get to Ekoko we'll celebrate again even if it is on Jan 11th or 12th.

Write soon. We love to hear from you.   Lovingly in Him, Ione

One morning in January, Ione was up before dawn writing to a supporter in the States:

.....This is just a little note written in the early morning by lantern light. There were baboons near-by and the head-teacher came and got a gun very early. I have been listening to hear the 'bang' of the gun, or the shrieking of the monkeys. Kenneth is still asleep in the same room with Paul. Altho' it is 5 o'clock here, you may be just going to bed in America, do pray for Kenneth that he will soon give his heart to Jesus, for he will soon be big enough. There are many other boys and girls here, black ones, much bigger than Kenneth, who have not even heard about Jesus, so they don't know how to accept Him. We are trying to reach them, but the missionaries are not many enough to reach them all.

Ione's zeal was as strong as ever, fueled by an article written in *Youth for Christ* magazine:

.....I have been reading in the Youth for Christ *magazine of the wonderful Revivals in Pasadena Rosebowl, Minneapolis, Kansas City and other large centres, and an article by Merv Rosell convinces me that Revival can just as well come to us here at Bongondza. Last night as our missionary staff met for prayer, we discussed this, and everyone is in accord that we must definitely set our hearts toward that very thing. Will you join us in prayer for a real awakening here. We are already seeing 'mercy drops' round us, especially in the Balolo region. A letter has just come in telling us of at least 60 more converts ready for baptism, 6 more men offering for Christian service, and 21 couples wanting a Christian marriage.*

.....On the other side of us, in the Basali region, Viola Walker has just come out of the forest, and tells us of real spiritual awakening there, with many saved. But right on our station things are cold; pray, pray much that by the time of our midsummer native conference the Lord will do a new thing for us. At that time

natives as well as some white people, are coming here from all four U.F.M station. If Revival comes then, it will affect the future of our entire Congo U.F.M. We must have it, or there is no use of our being here.

The January lull gave Hector a chance to write home:

Dear Dad, Archie and Jean:

It isn't quite daylight yet but I want to get a letter off to you. Two of the ladies are making a trip to Banalia today, about 70 miles away, and they can mail it there.

Thank you for your letter, Dad. I also got one from Uncle Alex in this last mail. I hope you have all had a good Christmas and New Year's. It must be nice to have Jean home again.

We have just come home from a week's visit up with Ione's sister at Ekoko. The children enjoyed it very much. Kenneth and Paul are great playmates now and run all over. They can talk at a great rate. David is very sweet. Their Auntie Marcellyn surely loves them all.

This is holiday month so there are no school children around, or workmen. It is nice to have it quiet for a while. It gives us a chance to catch up on a few odd jobs.

It is a real privilege to be a servant of the Lord in these days. We have a wonderful message for these last days especially when men's hearts are failing them for fear.

May the Lord bless each of you. Yours as ever, Hector & family

Ione wrote to Hector's sister Alice on the 5th of February, essentially to thank her for the Christmas parcel which had only just arrived, however, the letter gave insight into the McMillan lifestyle at the time and Ione's chief concerns:

.....Your package arrived just two days ago, and we had Christmas all over again. It was so much fun opening presents in February! The children could hardly believe their eyes when they saw the trains, two sets of them, and have been no trouble ever since, for they have plenty to amuse themselves. They are learning to hook the cars together. They do love them ever so much, and so does David love his ball; he finds it nice to chew on. The books are nice, too, and let me say that the suckers did not last out the day; they were very popular, for they haven't had any since we left New York! I have saved the sticks and will try to mold some more 'sucker' candy around the stick. Hector stuck the pen in his pocket and it has been there ever since;

it was just what he wanted. He helped us open the cans too, and the honey appeals to his sweet tooth. We had it on pancakes the same day it came!! Thanks, too, for the lemon juice. There are so many uses for it. And the salmon is something we find almost impossible to buy here, for the prohibitive cost. Perhaps it was expensive for you, too!! At any rate, we do appreciate that it is a real treat, and will keep it for special occasions. The birthday candles are in time for David's celebration in March. There will still be plenty of candles in the packages for the June, July and August celebrations, tho I guess there won't be enough for the cakes for Hector and me!

We are thankful to be in the best of health now. Hector is thankful to be getting rounder than he has ever been, except for when he was in the Air Force. But he is worried because his clothes are much too tight now. Even his best Sunday suit looks like a wiener with a string tied around it! He weighs 166 pounds now, and is very energetic and happy. The burden of being leader of this station doesn't seem to affect him (like it does me!!) for he just doesn't let anything worry him, and things do come out all right. Every department of the work seems dependent on him for something or other, and things go wrong and need repairs, but he does keep the single girls happy, with a bit of cement here, and a paint job there, a roof on the hospital for the nurse, etc. And he is always available for taking the cars where they want them, if they are too busy to drive themselves. And he keeps the cars in grease and repairs. I think the secret of his good health is drinking lots of milk and not worrying. Of course, he does spend much time in prayer and the Lord honours that sort of thing.

Our boys are yet too small to let them play outside without supervision, but they are doing better. I think they would know a snake now when they see it. One fell out of a tree at their feet, and Paul came to see me and said, "I saw a big grasshopper, but I couldn't catch it!!" They are learning to touch worms with sticks only, as I fear they might pick up a centipede or a tarantula or a scorpion! The best place for them to play is on the wide verandah which is screened-in. David likes to be with them, but I have to guard him lest they ride his back like a 'horsey'. He does not walk yet, but makes pretty good speed on hands and knees. His hair is dark like Kenneth's and Hector's but his eyes are light blue like Paul's. Paul's hair continues to be whiter and whiter; I guess the sun must bleach it; he is truly a blonde.

We were sorry to learn of Aunt Marjorie's departure to be with the Lord, tho' for her it is far better. We have had one good letter from Jean since her arrival at Avonmore.

Do write us soon. Lovingly, Hector & Ione & boys

The delays in parcel post prompted Ione to write to her mother on the 17th February; Leone Reed had asked about sending the boys larger toys such as bikes:

.....if you can get some they would do for birthday presents in June and July. Packages take so long to come, but if they are in separate packages, they might travel faster. I'm afraid the freight will be as much as the bikes, however, so you'd better inquire into that before you buy anything. Whatever you pay for each just count on as much more for freight. It may be the $20 will not do it at all. Please don't go over that amount, for they still enjoy their wagons and there is a wooden kiddie car here. David can use the kiddie car, when his legs get a little longer, if the other boys do have tricycles. If you find you have enough money for small toys, just remember that plastic things are not worth sending so far, as they break so soon. Metal things are good, if they do not have cardboard wheels. Rubber does pretty well, but is not so long-lived as metal (not tin, tho).

Ione had other practical concerns for her young family:

.....I always hope none of the children will be sick when there is no car on the station. All are well, but just now I am noticing that Paul's appetite is not so good. This noon he fell asleep before he had eaten anything, and when I offered him his dinner when he wakened, he just looked at it. The only thing that appealed to him was a glass of pineapple juice. He is just getting over being constipated from too much native food, so I guess it will be good to rest his tummy and give him lots of fruit juices. He has a fat tummy, but he is frailer than Kenny, who is very stocky and solid, and he is so fair that he looks a little too pale to suit me.

Besides her own three boys, Ione was still acting as a foster mother as she did in her early days on the mission station:

.....The little mulatto boy is back with us again, and he is nice to our children; they converse freely now in Bangala. And Paul and Kenny are also adding many new English words to their vocabulary. Paul's latest is "carefully". He carried an egg carefully from the chicken coop to the house, and another time he informed me that he had killed a bug "carefully".

Ione shared with her mother news of her sister Marcellyn:

.....I found Marcellyn quite well stocked with lovely eatables from home like ready mix, tins of special things, etc. And she looked so well - better than I have seen her before. She weighs as much or more than I. She keeps herself looking nice in spite of being so isolated. Her home is beautiful, and so roomy and comfortable. She has it very well planned and organized. She had gotten into the habit of scolding her house staff a lot and I talked to her about that. She had helpers that were especially trying and sort of new, as her regular one was gone. Hector laughingly said she talked nicer to her cats than to her staff, and she realized it too, and tried to do better. Mother you can't imagine how hard it is to see the work done poorly and nice things spoiled, when we have been so used to a nice clean home. Pray that Marcellyn may have the utmost patience. But on the whole Marcellyn's house looks cleaner than any of the others. Scolding helps, but I'm sure it is a poor testimony to do it all of the time. I'm sure you would find this part of life out here very trying.

Hector's letters are more work than family focused; he wrote to his brother Archie on the 5th of March:

> .....This is the hot dry season here now and it is hard to keep going with all the many jobs that need to be done. We have just finished taking a brick kiln down. We got about 18,000 bricks out of it, which is quite good. The masons are working on the huge new school building having six big class rooms and two offices.[89] I would like to have quite a bit of it done by the time Mr Jenkinson comes back. We have put a new roof on the hospital; but it was so hot that we worked sometimes at night with electric lights. In the day time you can only stand the heat on the roof until about 10:00 a.m. then we have to find other work in the shop or someplace. However, the rains will soon be coming and working conditions will be better. That big cistern that we dug before Christmas is a great help now. It is almost up to the top yet. It must hold 250-300 big drums of water.
>
> I was out a few weekends ago to a village where we have a native evangelist. The Lord has done wonderful things in many hearts there. That one Sunday I was there, I baptized 55 people[90] and performed a marriage ceremony for 19 couples, the latter being people who have been married according to state laws but who now wanted to have a Christian wedding. It does your heart good to be among such a changed group of people.
>
> It must be nice for you to have Jean with you again. Thanks for the letter, Jean.   Hector

On the 10th of March, Ione had more 'special' news for the family at home:

> .....I wanted to tell you first that I think we're going to have another baby, the latest sign being the nausea. But do not be surprised if you hear in my next letter that I have lost it, for even tho' I am being especially careful right now I have cramps every day and other signs. The second month is a critical month for me. If I am able to keep it, we may expect the baby's arrival in October. It surely looks as tho' I am running competition with Doris.
>
> We did not feel we should have a baby while Kinsos were away, as responsibilities were heavier on us just now, so we do hope they will be back by that time. They left last September. If it were not that I have some very good house helpers who do all the work except the care of the children, I couldn't get along. One helper is quite clean and I am having him whenever possible to carry David from bed to baby carriage, etc. and to the high chair for his meals. But I always feed them, bathe them, dress and put to bed, etc. as well as stay right with them for their playtime. Kenneth is beginning to dress himself, and both he and Paul can go to the bathroom by themselves. The only trouble David makes is that he needs to be changed, fed, etc. He is the best boy I have. I was thinking this morning how easy he is to care for. After his morning nap, I dress him, and put

---

[89] In another letter to supporters, Hector believes he will need 150,000 bricks for the project. Every room is to have ventilators near the floor and near the ceiling and metal windows which will not be eaten by termites.

[90] This meant standing in a river for two hours.

him into his carriage and he watches the work in the kitchen all morning.......He's a darling right now, will be one year next week. His hair goes into little curls in his neck and his teeth are so lovely when he smiles. He has such a broad forehead and square jaw that the girls here call him Winston Churchill.

.....We did have such a nice time at Marcellyn's house and were so glad to find her well. It is so nice to be with your own relatives 'way out here. I'll surely be lonesome when she goes on furlough. When the boys get bigger I can let them visit her and stay awhile by themselves, at times when she is not too busy. Mrs Carter tells me that the English and Australian school systems do not coincide with the courses given at Rethy and they are not sending their children there, but are teaching them themselves; several others in our mission are non-Americans and I may find the same difficulty when we come to the time when our children go to school. I had hoped that others would be sending theirs to Rethy and we could share the trips financially as it is so far. But we'll have another furlough before that time, and if we can bring back a car of our own, we shall be able to take them to Rethy on our own. Rethy is a splendid school and the children come out really ahead of those in America, when they finish.

The family had been out to one of the villages to help and support a local evangelist. Ione continued:

.....You maybe are wondering how we could spend a week in a native village and care for the children properly. One thing was in our favour: there were no mosquitoes at the time. We slept under nets at night, for there were big bugs that flew around at night. A big spider landed on David's net, and shortly after, a flying bug jumped on the spider! The first night there were more noises at night, then the little creatures realized that white people were there, or maybe we just slept thru it all!! Mice found our bits of newspaper very tempting and night after night could be heard dragging large sheets which they carefully folded and pulled down their holes.

Hector went hunting once and they bro't back a baboon; some other hunters who came along shot two birds and an antelope. While there we heard our chief hunter back at the station had killed an elephant. A second elephant was shot right near here after we returned.

People all around us are asking us to please come with the gun to shoot elephants as they are spoiling the plantain gardens. We are only allowed by the gov't 4 per year, but if they are molesting station property any number can be killed. Hector is going to Stanleyville this week and ask special permission to kill as many as 10, for we have already had our quota. I hope Hector never tries to shoot one, for we have heard some sad stories about other white people (as well as blacks). A beloved missionary up near Ludwig's was very recently attacked by an elephant whom he had wounded, and the elephant ran his tusk right thru him.

Hector took time out to update Kinso on his activities: he made a shopping trip to Stanleyville and had been buying provisions wholesale as this was cheaper.

.....We got some good bargains at Ollivants, Savas, and Sedec Gros. Everyone was well pleased with the shopping tour. It surely pays to buy wholesale.

While in Stanleyville, Hector saw the 'Monsieur' at the 'Service de l'Agriculture' and gained permission to kill more than the allotted four elephants a year in their locality.

Most of the letters written through March 1951 were from Hector, Ione seemingly preoccupied with three small children and the nausea of early pregnancy. In these letters, Hector always thanked the supporters for their contributions and reiterated the story of making bricks two by two amongst other tasks that occupied his time. There are several mentions about being the only male missionary. In one letter he ended with:

.....Once in a while we are able to get out to the villages in the district. There is always something to encourage our hearts, as we see numbers turning to the Lord and leaving off their heathen practices. The Lord is answering the prayers of the folks at home. I know you will remember us from time to time before the throne.

Ione also wrote to Mrs Hess, a church supporter:

.....Two of our house staff members have married recently and their wives have accepted the Lord. One who has now been a Christian for several months bro't a friend of hers to my door and when we prayed together I noticed Malani used the very verse in her prayer which I had used to lead her to the Lord – Romans 10:9,10. Another woman was bro't to me this morning by a young evangelist's wife, and she was helpful in leading her to the Lord.

I am able to carry on with my regular teaching altho' my schedule is not so full as the single girls as I do not like to leave our children for anyone else to care for. Hector and I manage to take turns in their care. We appreciate the help of the staff in the home for house work, but do not leave the children with them. Our Kenneth and Paul love these helpers and remember them when they pray. The other night Paul was going over their names and Kenneth reminded him, "Remember to pray for Balimaga." Paul said, "I did pray for him alweddy." But Kenneth wasn't satisfied and said, "Well, he carried a tire over to the shop for Daddy; bless him for that."

.....We have had a wonderful answer to prayer recently. For two years we have had a Bible famine. We were absolutely unable to get them in Bangala, and so many new Christians who could read were needing them, as well as aspiring young student evangelists. We made it a very definite matter of prayer, and then sent one more letter to a printer, and almost before the letter was well on its way, we suddenly found ten large sacks at the gov't post and each box contained 50!!

Unsurprisingly, Christmas parcels were still coming and Ione wrote to supporters on the 10th of April:

.....Now about the package – it has just come in yesterday's mail! It was a time of real excitement when we opened it. We appreciate the Christmas cards, and the bathroom tissue, so lovely and soft, it can be used as Kleenex. And the odour

that struck our noses from the soap was so refreshing. We were badly needing hand soap. And I had no shampoo and was just ready for a good head wash! I presume the dress is the one you told me about. I am glad to have her address and will thank her right away. Is the silk slip your gift? If so, I do thank you very much. Also, for all of the clothes for the children. Most of the things fit Paul. However, the pretty new blue socks are big enough for Kenneth and also the training panties. One sun suit we will use for David. Every piece is so useful. The blue sweater I could use for David, but I think I will start saving up for the next one, due in October!! Oh, the toothpaste, too is very welcome. You seem to know how long it lasts our family! I had just taken out the last tube which you sent at Christmastime! Thank you so much for everything. If you could only know what a box means to us here! Paul doesn't miss going to stores but Kenny remembers and shows me pictures of ice cream and suckers. Pearl Hiles has a refrigerator which makes good ice cream and yesterday she bro't up a tearful, and I had baked some "ice cream cones" out of piecrust, and you should have seen Kenny's face when we fitted the ice cream into the "cone" (made over a funnel! Then I took the funnel out when it was stiff). We made suckers, too, one day, in a muffin tin and colored the boiled sugar yellow and green, and stuck sticks in while it was hot.

I cannot write more now, but want you to know we are thinking about you. Two more women saved this week.   Ione

Mrs Pudney also was sent a letter. Ione told her of the pregnancy, the work they were doing and Pearl's new clinic at Kole:

Dear Mrs. Pudney:

Greetings in His Precious Name!

No doubt you will appreciate being informed at this seemingly early date that the McMillans are expecting another baby in October. I have not found it necessary to give up any of my meetings; in fact, I have an added 'Hymnsing' in Kingwana each Friday night in preparation for singing Kingwana songs during the Conference in July. The little songbook prepared has ten songs in Bangala, ten in Kingwana, contributed by each of the 4 stations.

Hector and I had a good week out at Makpolo's with the children, living in a two-room mud house. We spread mats on the mud floor where the children played, and put David in the baggage carrier for a playpen!! It was not on top of the car, however! The hunters killed two birds, a monkey and an antelope, and we enjoyed the latter. There have been three elephants killed since Christmas, but Hector got permission in Stan to kill 10 since they were a real nuisance around here, spoiling many gardens.

.....Hector is replacing some of the woodwork at the hospital and extending the metal roof over the ward walls where the rain caused the brick walls to collapse. He has arranged a new water system for Pearl with eavestroughing and a battery of drums. He flies between hospital and the new boys' school on Ma Kinso's motorized Corgi. He has it rigged out with a baggage carrier labeled, "Keba!!"

C.V.C. – U.F.M. And the speed he travels everyone needs to Keba! (Look out!)
He has it equipped now with a spotlight, or he did until last night when I heard
him bump a gasoline drum ! ! Fortunately the drum was rolling in the same
direction. Today he was making cement lintels for the doors in the boys' school.
That building is coming right up. He has a moveable shed to keep the sun off his
masons! ! He's doing the office end of the school first, trying to complete Olive's
and Verna's classrooms, he says because they might bother each other!

Pearl expects to have the opportunity in the near future of conducting a clinic
[at] Cotonco at Kole. This may be a fine opening for a Gospel ministry. Pray
about it. The State doctor is making all arrangements, and says that Cotonco
will in turn provide Pearl with cloth for her babies and small children sewing
projects. Hector is building 3 leper dwellings this week so that she can have an
isolated spot nearby to treat these needy folk.

My women have been sewing handkerchiefs (for themselves) baby bonnets for
those who have babies, and piecing a quilt for a poor old lady. Tomorrow I will
give out some pieces of pretty native cloth to the best sewers (seamstresses!) to
make a new table cloth for the church and curtains for the altar rail. We hope to
have the church dressed up by the time Kinsos get back. But they will also get a
message on the Servant Girl who witnessed to Naaman the Leper. We've had
some wonderful messages by the women themselves of late. One woman said the
Gospel found her boiling 10 pots of wine, and she poured them out to follow
Jesus. Two women were led to the Lord by Kinso's faithful Mayani. Several
others came because of the testimony of another native. This is encouraging
when we realize that we may not have much more time with these people. We
want them to carry the Good News themselves. One woman who could hardly
read and had no Bible, found her verse in "Njela na Kubikisa" Acts 4:12. She
gave a much more stirring Gospel message than I could have given, with
illustration after illustration, and she stuck to her text, too! I praise the Lord for
this.
.....Give our kindest greetings to all at the home.
Lovingly in Him, Ione

Ione's letters at this time remained upbeat. The family's diet was varied - they had
their canned meat from Canada and fresh produce provided locally:

.....Of course, we can nearly always depend on peanuts, papaya, pineapple,
lemons, eggs, and just now lovely big avocado pears. We do thank the Lord for
His provision of our every need. Our little boys are all big and strong and real
fat. David has just started to walk now, at 13 months!
.....Hector gained back his lost pounds and has been feeling quite well. The Lord
is so good to give us all good health again after that time of illness [on the river
boat]. The Lord met Hector in a time of severe pain, and blessed him in an
unusual way. Hector's life has been changed thru it. He needed so much a
special work of the Lord, to prepare him for his many responsibilities this term.
He has had some difficult cases to settle, and just this morning, two tribes in our

Central School turned on each other, and he had a very hard time settling it. He worked until late last night with both sides and from morning until noon. I believe it was the worst time we've had. When you realize that probably their grand-fathers or great-grandfathers dared not trespass each other's territory without bloodshed, it makes one not too surprised to find such enmity between school boys. We have several tribes coming here, but never had a real fight like this one. Do pray that we may be able to show them that Christ can help them to put aside old anger and jealousy.

I am enjoying working with the women, and we've had some blessed times. The hardest to deal with are white people who are out here for other purposes than missionary [work].

Towards the end of May, 1951, Ione wrote a long letter to her mother. It would seem that family and supporters were concerned that she was again pregnant and Ione was taking much effort to reassure all that she was fine:

.....It is two o'clock and the birds are doing their best to bring us a shower. I hear the shrill, clamorous chirping of the weaver bird; the tuneful song of the canary; the low, plaintive, liquid cheeping of the swallow; the "quick, doctor, quick" of the [yellow-vented] *bulbul; the pleasant continuous squeak of the wagtail; and many others, churring, cheery, lively and attractive. Congo is a wonderful place for those who love birds.[91]*

My little birds are having their nap. Kenneth was the last to settle down, and he begged me to lie close to him and tell him again about the time I went on the train when I was a little girl as big as he; about the song we used to sing at the table instead of praying when I was a little girl; then, did I think Grandma might be with the box of bikes when it came to Kole; and did Jimmy try both bikes to see if they would fit Paul and Kenny; and would that package of suckers come this week. I left him before he was asleep, but he seemed satisfied, and after singing a marching song in Bangala, he became quiet.

Paul gets thru the morning now without a nap, but he hardly finished his dessert before he slips into his room and tumbles to bed. He was quite thrilled today because I had the cook make them some "songo" a native root, very starchy, but which they like because their beloved house helpers like it. We had a vegetable dinner of rice, creamed celery, carrots and beets, the three latter from our vegetable basket which comes every other week. Dessert was a sweet ripe pineapple. Paul is getting broader in face and tummy and is almost as tall as Kenny. He has such a keen sense of humor and a twinkle in his eye, and whatever he does he does it quicker than a wink. You'd laugh to hear them telling the words that represent the letters of the alphabet – A –automobile, B-blowing bubbles, C-coasting, etc. The little book we have has V-Velocopide, and of all

---

[91] Until reading this letter, John, who has been watching birds for over 40 years, did not know his mother was a bird watcher!

the words he remembered that best. I heard him practicing it by calling Kenneth that name. He said, "Here, Velocopide, take this to the store for me."

.....I received your letter this week and want to thank you for it. I got one from Inez in the same mail. She was of the same opinion as you regarding the fourth baby in five years. I am trying to figure out whether I am just hard-headed and

Ken & Paul

cannot be told, or whether what I feel is true, that the call to have children is just as clear to me as my call to the work of the Lord. I do not feel the robust health during that nine months that I feel at other times, but the work gets done, and I don't feel that my general health has suffered from it. Other people who are run down get malaria often. I never have it, or colds, etc. Now that the nausea is past, I am able to carry on quite well. I don't expect to take trips with Hector, but I am able to care for the children while he is away. We have good native help, even a man to light the lamp

when Hector is away. I couldn't manage if I were home, but things certainly do go smoothly out here, and we have such a good home in which to keep them.

I am thankful for all your advice, for it does remind me of many things I should be doing, and I will try to put them into practice. Don't stop giving it, and don't stop praying. I trust your health will be better soon.

We are thinking about you on Mother's Day, and hoping it was not a lonely day for you. I hope you had a white flower to wear. Next year Marcellyn will fix you up fine, as she will probably be home for that occasion. You are still my beautiful little Mother and always will be. Mothers never get old, do they? At least not to their children. I'm so glad that you are keeping so active in the Lord's service.

.....Our heavy rains were late in coming this year, but now we have rain every day. It is refreshing and cool, but sometimes the clothes get a sour smell before they are dry for it takes two days to dry them. I'll never forget how hard it was to get diapers dry the week Paul was born. It rained almost steady for five days, and we had no fire in the house, so tried to dry them by the heat of a pressure lamp! October is a little better time than July for a new baby.

.....David's hands are into everything, but he loves to try, too. You should see how cute he looks in the little red shirt and blue overalls with red apples. That outfit is just right on him now, and when it is a bit chilly because of rain he wears them. Today we are having sweet potatoes, gravy with corned beef in, baked beans and chocolate pudding.

Hooray!! A sack of packages which had been delayed from last week's mail has arrived, and the SUCKERS! You should have seen the children's faces; they were all awake from their naps, and as I read each name on the little plastic Easter basket, each child took his suckers proudly. Kenneth found a way to open his right away and had the paper off one and was sucking it, while I took the paper off Paul's. I found David clutching his sack tight against his fat tummy with his two little hands, and when I took it to open it up and get the sucker for him, he cried, but he was soon all smiles when he had the sucker in his mouth. I have 'bottled' the suckers now, after they had several and they will have a few every day until they are gone. Thank you so much for sending them. It makes some very happy times for them.

.....Now I must close. My cook has invited all the single ladies here for supper tonight, as he is making waffles on that big iron griddle. He has had pretty good success lately, so is taking courage to invite guests. We have some maple flavoured syrup which he has made. First, we'll have vegetable soup and pineapple and cottage cheese salad (providing the milk we 'soured' turns into cottage cheese!). Hector is in Buta today getting a large load of prepared rafters to make the roof of the new boy's school. A Mr Bryers in Canada has sent $1500 to pay for the roofing. And he is going to send more money in smaller amounts for the evangelists' school.

.....Kenneth had a piece of paper in his hand and came showing it to Hector. "It says on it, Dear Kenneth," he explained. Paul was not far behind, also with a piece of paper. He said, "Mine says, Dear Me!"

The Lord bless and keep you day by day in His service.

Lovingly, Hector and Ione, Kenneth, Paul & David

Hector referred to the upcoming conference in July, however, in his letter to the family we note that other 'notables' are in Stanleyville. He wrote on June 10, 1951:

Dear Dad and All:

It is a bright Sunday morning. We haven't had breakfast yet, but I want to get a letter off to you this week.

We do want to thank you for the latest gift of $50. We do appreciate the way you are remembering us. The cost of living is rising out here as well as at home.

It is fortunate that the price of powdered milk stays about the same or is even a little lower. I wish we had the old "Quin" cow out here. Her pail-full of milk twice a day would be a bountiful supply!!!

I made a trip to Stanleyville about three weeks ago and there was a party of 43 people from England and America preparing to make a film about 100 miles from Stan. They were spending a week in preparation. Needless to say, all the hotels were full. I was able to stay with another

Kenny & Paul on the merry-go-round.

missionary in a mission home; while Miss

Bjerkseth stayed with some Scotch people who run a big wholesale store. When we first arrived in town, we called around at all the hotels without knowing why they were all filled up. At one place two ladies were walking leisurely speaking English if you please. I passed within about five feet of them. Later we found out that one of them was KATHARINE HEPBURN from Hollywood.[92]

.....The children are all well and busy. Kenneth is getting to be quite a help now. He loves books. Both he and Paul can go through a little alphabet book now. .....David tries to do the same things the others do now. He is real roly-poly with a good big appetite. I made a little merry-go-round for them; which they spend hours on.

The school building is going ahead quite well. We have about 40 workmen now, so I don't have much time to sit around. I will be glad when Mr Jenkinson returns from furlough in November. We may have another man on the station by that time or it may be a little girl this time. We are expecting the baby sometime in October.

Ione wants me to ask Jean for Aunt Marjorie's recipe for oatmeal cookies. Ione copied it out when she was in Avonmore but left it on a calendar somewhere in the kitchen.

We have written Irene but haven't heard from her yet. We will be glad to know what she plans to do. Write when you can..... Love to all....Hector

On June 10th, 1951, Ione had other preoccupations and wrote to Dr Paul Brown, who, with his wife, had been at Moody Bible Institute with Ione and worked for the African Inland Mission (AIM) at Banda:

.....We are expecting another baby around October 4th and are speculating on just where to go. In your December letter we read of your latest developments in operating room, etc., and we wonder if you are set up to take care of our case. If you feel it is just too much for you when you are so busy already, we shall not mind if you say so. But to us it would be such a relief to know that you 'had charge'. We do not expect any complications and since this baby is just 19 months later than the last, one would expect to meet about the same circumstances. We hope that we have calculated our time so that it will mean only 2 or 3 weeks off our station.

Perhaps the biggest item to mention is the fact that we would like to come as a family, since leaving the children would be difficult, and little David would have to be with his mama anyway, so we might as well do for three what we would do for him as they are all so small. We would suggest coming with 2 or 3

---

[92] Katharine Hepburn, Humphrey Bogart, John Houston and others, were filming *The African Queen*, a story set during the First World War. This was quite a novelty, as few films were shot on location at this time. Most of the cast and crew were ill except for Mr. Bogart and Mr. Houston who boasted that they were saved from being ill by only drinking whiskey! The other lady was quite likely Lauren Bacall who, at the time, was married to Humphrey Bogart and was good friends with Miss Hepburn. The film was released in America in December 1951 and has become a classic.

staff members to care for our cooking and washing, providing you feel you can make room for us all to 'park' there that long. We can bring our own provisions and set ourselves up as we would on trek.

Around this time, Ione wrote to supporters at home about the death of an elderly Christian lady who had walked miles to Bongondza for medical help. When she died, no one would help Pearl with 'last rights' until two Christian ladies offered to help. Ione wrote:

.....I took my women's class to the funeral and spoke to them on I Thess. 4:13, 14. The procession was interesting, as she was wrapped in a white blanket, lying on a stretcher (which was not buried with her, however), and we had to go single file along the little path into the forest where the hole was prepared. There were a number of hymns about heaven, and I gave a brief message, and during the

Ken, Paul and David in the brown, green, and red felt hats that Ione bought in NY – 1951.

singing of more hymns, forest vines were slipped under her in two places and she was gently lifted into the hole. The ones bearing her sprinkled a little of the earth on top of her, and that was all while the crowd was there. It is so good to be at a funeral where there is not a lot of screaming and crying. One young man in the evangelists' class said that was the first real Christian funeral he had attended and he was so glad to know there was a nice way of burying the Lord's people. He was impressed when I said that we might see the woman even next week, for the Lord may come very soon.

Ione continued to reassure her mother that all was well; on the 9th of July, she wrote:

Just a few lines while I am watching the children as they play in front of the fireplace. It is raining today and chilly and a fire feels good. [Hard to imagine that central Africa gets cold!] *Wish we had some marshmallows to roast! Pearl gave me two packages gelatine and we will try to make some. We don't miss many pleasures out here. We had hamburgers last week, on buns, but the meat was made from a wild animal, I don't know what it was, for it wasn't a pig and it wasn't a deer, tho' it had a skin like a pig; the meat was all dark; it was very good and made up well into hamburgers with some onion and egg and a little bread. We served them in the living room with a little vegetable salad and chili sauce, with doughnuts and coffee for dessert. We had a Scotch lady visiting us for a week from Stanleyville. We found out she is a real Christian woman and she was craving for some spiritual talks. Her husband manages a wholesale store in Stanleyville. They bro't us some delicious chocolate candy and caramels, as well as little tins of various things, sweetened milk, chocolate sauce, lobsters, and margarine.*

317

I am looking at the plan you sent me of your apartment, and wondering what you are doing, how the rent payments are coming, etc. It has been upon my heart in prayer especially lately. I wish there was more we could do, for it would be too bad to give up such a nice place. Do tell us how things are coming. How are you feeling now?

We are surely looking forward to the bikes' arrival, have had a notice that they are in the Congo, but that is all. The other day Kenny was making believe opening mail as we do, and he spread out a sheet of folded paper, and looked up with animated face and said, "The bikes are in Stanleyville!!" I wish it were true. Already Kenny's birthday has passed and Paul's is due next Saturday, but we are trying to teach the children to be patient, and not to be disappointed when they don't come.

Congo is so indefinite sometimes about things we are looking for. K had a nice party, with ice cream, cake and "chocolate" tea, and there were some nice presents, a lovely little blue plastic flute to play, and ABC book, some Tootsie rolls, gum and a package of Jello and a tin of cherries. He opened the first present, and the second one he turned to Paul and said, "I think this is for you," so we let it be so, and Paul opened it. Paul was so sweet about it and didn't expect anything for himself.

I am very well now, and I don't even fall asleep in the early evenings as I used to, I seem to be able to do more. I think it is because we continue to have good food, varieties of fresh vegetables, fruit, and milk. The Lord is so good to provide enough money to pay for these things. David is very large now and heavy, weighs 28 lbs; Paul weighs 34 and Kenny 41. It will be soon hard to tell them apart. You can see by the pictures how close together K and P are in height. David is just as big around, but his legs are shorter yet. He is so good-natured and happy and loveable.

.....Just this week a big black monkey caused a lot of excitement for 3 or 4 hours until he was caught. He was all over the place, even ran right in front of our house, much to the boys' pleasure. I kept them on the porch most of the time and they could see the monkey swinging high in a big tree.

We killed a snake in the bedroom a few days ago, I had seen it just as it was crawling from the floor up into the springs. When the house helpers came to kill it, they couldn't see it at all so I just picked up the corner of the mattress and swung it back double and there was the snake! They said it would kill a person, but we never do know for sure.

Love, Hector & Ione

On the 16th of July, Ione wrote to Hector's family:

.....We're celebrating birthdays just now. Yesterday Paul was three, and tomorrow Hector will be --? We are forgetting, I guess. We had a nice little

birthday tea at 4 o'clock and the "aunties"[93] came. It is so difficult out here to have presents, especially for children that we have requested for all three of their birthdays that they bring no presents. The birthday, to them, is the cake, and we

Paul's 3rd birthday.

try to decorate it as brilliantly as possible. Paul said when wakened from his nap, "Is the happy birthday ready?" So I let him peek into the refrigerator and see it, three-tiers high, of pink, white, yellow and chocolate with white frosting on the bottom two layers and prune custard on the top one with a green turtle candle in the middle and two white ones beside it. There were flattened prune halves on the sides and these were studded by vari-colored fruit drops from a little package Hector had bro't from a trip to Buta. One auntie found a Mother Goose book somewhere to give him, and two other aunties had wrapped beautifully a big can of pears and a big can of plums. These were exclaimed about as tho' they were very precious. Three weeks ago, Kenneth got a plastic whistle and a book and some jello and a can of cherries. I am thankful that we are in a place where little things are appreciated. It makes so much more wonderful the priceless treasure of our wonderful Lord. We want Him to be the most important.

.....Hector keeps very busy these days, since he is the only man on the station. In this past week he has been in three different directions and some journeys have taken him away several days at a time. Sometimes Kenneth or Paul go with him and that makes it less complicated here for me. He has been baptizing, marrying, having communion with various groups, getting supplies for us whites as well as for the native conference which begins next week. I have meetings three times a week.

Besides birthdays, the McMillans were chief hosts for the July Conference, which did not go quite the way Ione and Hector hoped it would; Ione wrote to her closest supporters, the Loyals on the 19th of August:

.....Remember I had asked you to pray for revival at the time of our conference. Well, we are not satisfied with the results. There was great conviction, and a real break-down on the part of some but there is great distress among others who refuse to go all the way. Some claim there is nothing wrong, really are not Christians, and are criticizing and all kinds of stories are going around. It is true when the Lord wishes to send revival and the way is blocked, there is only confusion. Do pray much that this condition will be resolved into a real heaven-sent revival. We cannot carry on without it. God must bless us or we shall utterly fail. There is strong feeling against white people and Communism is creeping in

---

[93] Lady missionaries working with the McMillans – Verna Schade, Viola Walker and Olive Bjerkseth.

so fast, we are amazed. The other missionaries and we agree that the trouble is entirely spiritual, and can be solved with real conversation on the part of the trouble-makers. So please pray much for us at this time. Then there is an organization started that claims to be Protestant, but is not good we are sure, that may even be Communistic, and we are taking our stand against it. Oh, our time may not be long here, but we must be true and strike out against sin, and hold Christ up before these people. Pray much for us at this time.

And to Ma Kinso, she confided:

.....Yes, the Conference was somewhat of a disappointment to us. I am sure there has been ever so much conviction and hence much criticism between various groups and tribes. It seemed for a time that all of the criticism was in our direction (white people), but we have since learned it is not so, but of various natives as well, and we believe it is a spiritual thing and when people get right with the Lord, He takes away criticism. Since the Conference we have more than ever made an effort to make the Word plain, and keep to the fundamentals of the Cross, blood etc., and I believe the Holy Spirit is working.

The conference was eventful in other ways; Gordon Carter, the eldest of the Carter boys was ill in the hospital, nursed by his mother. Viola Walker was also ill. This meant Ione had Jim Carter and the other three Carter children, Rosemary, Philip and Michael to care for. Ione explained that at this time she was catering for 10-12 people for a three-week period. This letter was predominantly a 'thank you' as the Loyals had sent her a package. She wrote:

.....I opened the packages with all six children looking on, and it was difficult to keep the cards right with the gifts, so I have not been able to identify each thing with the giver. Please forgive me for this, for every gift is so much appreciated. The children so much enjoyed watching, and you should have heard the whoops of joy when we came to the suckers and lemon drops. I'm afraid we delved right into the other 'eatables' as well, some of the ready-mix cakes were very welcome, puddings, jello, etc. Folk were arriving at midnight and others leaving at dawn, so the instant cocoa came into use, as well as Ada Wideman's instant coffee which she sent a short time ago. I never saw a time when more was required of me, at all hours of day and night, but in spite of my heaviness of body just now, I kept feeling quite well. The good food was a real help.

And it wasn't just food that Ione was grateful for and she hints of expecting another baby:

*.....All of my garments will be just right to put on when I come from the hospital. It will be so nice to have fresh things then. I am especially grateful for the nightie, for I needed that right away. Was that from you, Inie? Your card seemed the nearest to it of any. If so, thank you very much. The crème shampoo went into use very soon after it was discovered, and I'm afraid it won't last long, Mrs McNair, for it seems so many heads need washing so often. Thank you for it.
.....I still have lots of pretty dresses, and I am wearing only maternity dresses right now. Those very welcome cotton panties are large enough for me to use*

now, as well as later. The half-slip, cotton blouse and silk hose are ever so useful. Thanks for them. With Peggy Reh's pair of hose, that makes 3 pair, and that is all I need for now. I have bottled them to keep them from insects. Had I told you, Peggy, how we needed training panties for the boys? Anyway, you have sent just what they needed and I thank you, and the darling little blue knit suit is just right for David now.

Whoever sent that talcum powder gets a thanks in my heart at every bath time, for I like to use powder every day, but it goes so fast we must ration that like the suckers! These two tins will do for quite a while as they are large. I will keep one for the new baby. Thanks too for the tooth powder, hand cream and soaps, and the soft pieces of tissue paper and the odd ribbons as well as the ribbons on the packages. Oh, yes, the pot-holders were another splendid tho't, for our cook uses them up very fast. That's a very practical kind. And the transfer patterns are grand, Mrs Wideman. I have looked them all over and find some I can use right away for little baby things.

.....I was speaking to her about diapers and found that she could give me enough to 'get me by'. Then Marcellyn received a box of new baby things and because she tho't Pearl needed them more than she, sent them to her, and Pearl called me when she opened it, and do you know that is was made up entirely of baby gowns and receiving blankets! Isn't the Lord good? Pearl gave me all I need for now, so I am ready to take the long journey to the hospital. Unless we feel we must leave before, we'll not leave here until two weeks before the baby is due, and that will be the last of September. We'll go 550 kilometres, about 350 miles to an American doctor, Dr. Paul Brown, I have such peace about going there, even tho' it is so far. We will live in a two-room rest house and eat our meals under a big tree.

.....A leopard was reported on the station, but have not seen it. No more snakes in the bedrooms lately; just a few cockroaches and bats banging around at night. I dyed my living and dining room curtains ecru as they were discolouring from dampness. Did I ever tell you that the dishes you gave me came without a breakage, and they had even put in two extra cups, so I really have a set! The beautiful blue teapot is lovely whenever I serve tea. I have so many reminders of the Loyals. Thank you so much for everything.

Lovingly, Ione McMillan

In September, the family moved to Banda in preparation for the baby's arrival. Hector wrote to Kinso:

.....At last we have some time to write to you without having to rush. It is wonderful to be relieved of responsibility for a few weeks, although we realize it makes it more difficult for the others at Bongondza. We left about midnight last Sunday, spent Monday and Tuesday night with the Millikins at Titule (they have a new 6 wks old baby), and came on here the next day. We have taken Viola's car, which brought us along without any trouble. Our house helpers, Tele &

Nichola & his wife came with us. Ione stood the trip quite well except that she was a bit tired on arrival.

Mr and Mrs Dix are in charge of this station. They came here a little before you folks opened Bongondza. They have built it on a flat-topped hill with a view of at least 70 kms on every side. Our helpers were amazed that such a place existed, where there is no jungle.

Dr and Mrs Brown are finding plenty to do. There are about 300 patients on the waiting list for operations besides all the regular patients. Then there is a camp for lepers, probably another 300. I was down with the Doctor for a service this morning, when I spoke in Bangala. The missionaries here all use Bazandi, but the natives hear Bangala. The Doctor says they do not encourage white people to come, in fact Millikins were the first ones to have a baby here. Ione and Mrs Brown hadn't met since '35 so they have been having some good visits.

Some of Hector's carpenters. (Photo taken in 1968)

I have left the workmen doing several big jobs which should keep them busy until we get back. We just finished a kiln of bricks before we left, so that has to be taken down and moved. Another job was the getting out of more stones for the school foundation. The masons are finishing off the store-room, office and class-room, so that there will be a class in it by the time the inspector comes this month. Verna wanted to move Likali's 2nd year down to the new room and let Ngbayo take his group up to the girls' school. Then the original boys' school can be used for a sort of shop for manual training.

.....The new bridge at Buta is real nice. It has been open for almost two months now. The area around Bambili is undergoing some wonderful changes. They have machinery there which will make 5 kms of road every day. They are getting the natives on little farms and gradually introducing cattle.

I'll leave a few lines for Ione now. – Dear Kinsos: I will just greet you and then this letter must go. Hector has been showing his pictures nearly every night. These people are very kind.   Love, Ione

Ione wrote to supporters and family who had provided a steady supply of packages and parcels. These seemed to arrive with very good timing and all with treats for the children. They consisted of clothing, food packets, flavorings they could add to fresh local produce and cake mixes. In her letters, Ione told how she had used the supplies, most of which survived the transit time intact and in good condition. This time most of the baby things were colored pink, so friends and family back home seemed to be hoping a girl would arrive.

However, in a letter to her mother on the 1st of October, she wrote:

.....Everything seems to be all right after examination. The first examination (and by the way the first I have had for this baby!) the doctor said the heartbeat was that of a boy; the next two weeks later, he was doubtful and said it sounded like twins! But he could only locate one baby. You know how big I get, and I guess he tho't I was big enough for two.

.....The Loyal's layette arrived just before we left and it was such a big one. Mrs Flemington put in a darling little bonnet. There is a darling nylon pink hairbrush and comb set, tiny white kid shoes with pink rosettes, everything PINK practically, so they at least are showing their desire for a girl.

But the baby was indeed a boy. John Howard put in an appearance on the 18th of October, 1951, weighing 8 pounds and thirteen ounces. Leone got a short note telling her:

Ken, Paul, David & little John.

.....I am O.K. and didn't have a very bad time. Baby came quickly. Love, Ione

Then her mother got a lengthier letter on the 21st of November:

.....The new baby is one month old and is gaining steadily. He is looking more and more like David. I love to take care of him, and it seems that every time Hector comes into the house, he finds me holding John. It is so restful just to sit and enjoy him; I am so glad that I can nurse him. It is nice to be feeling good again myself, so ambitious and light. Hector continues to gain weight and his clothes have become quite a problem, all too small or ripped or buttons off. But he is very patient. (Pause while I laugh at Kenneth: he is chasing a big blue hornet around with his little rubber hammer. He got him cornered up in the window and put his hands on his hips and said, "Boy, he doesn't have much clothes on, nothing in the middle!" It is one of those 'wasp-waist' hornets!) Paul is the heart-breaker these days, with his big wistful (mischievous!) eyes. And David is a round little ball with dreamy blue eyes and still those wispy curls over his forehead. He is an 'ammal' most of the time, and one can expect at any time to see him put on his fierce look and come at you with all fours. He has been trying to climb out of his crib and I'm afraid he'll have a bad fall, so we have given him a single bed like the older boys. It is quite low and if he falls out he'll land on a folded quilt.

Six weeks later, the family were back at Bongondza and although happy to be back 'home', they were looking forward to Kinso and Ma Kinso's return. Unfortunately, Kinso required surgery for a hernia and their return was delayed until February 1952.

As the year drew to a close there were changes on the horizon for the mission, Verna Schade would be going home to be replaced by a returning Mary Baker, two new nurses were expected which meant Pearl Hiles would get a break. Yet more parcels arrived, including the long-awaited tricycles – and Marcellyn arrived just in time to support Ione with the new baby. The family experienced another bout of bacillary dysentery, but this time Ione was prepared and knew what medication to take to get well.

Ken & Paul on their new bikes. David takes a spin but his feet don't quite reach the pedals.

Chapter 12
FOCUSED AND FIGHTING

In January 1952, Ione picked up on a phrase her fellow missionary used - 'prayer must be focused and fighting'. Indeed, the year presented Ione with more challenges of life in the Congo - her growing family, missionary work, illness, invading wildlife and the news of deaths at other mission stations.

Ione's first letter of the year was to Peggy Reh, a supporter, thanking her for clothes, toys, candy, and packages of canned meats and fruits that were sent to the family:

.....I am so thankful you do pray for us. We cannot get along without it. We are beginning a new year now and I will be gathering together my women as soon as I can get them out of the forest. They go back in the cooler parts of the forest just now and fish, etc. It will be well into March before they all are back. But I am having a little meeting next week to see how many will come; I think I will serve them a cup of tea and some cookies. Then we will have a prayer meeting with them, and announce the coming events. There should be around 50. Pray that these women will grow in grace. Most of them are Christians. I am happy to be working with them but am thankful for every opportunity which allows me to go out to the villages, for they are needier. When my children are a little larger, I can get out more, and will eventually organize a native Gospel team to sing and give testimonies as I used to in America. Will you pray for this? I have the singers in training in music class, but they cannot go out by themselves, as they are not advanced enough yet in the things of the Lord.

I must close now. Another snake appeared yesterday – just a small green one, near the bed where Hector was resting on the sleeping porch. He killed it with his bedroom slipper, and we went on with our rest. I forgot to ask him if he threw it outside, and when I did think of it, he just joked about it, because I always make such a fuss about snakes. Now I finally learn that he did NOT throw it out, and dead or not, it has disappeared! I looked everywhere, so I guess it revived and is hiding somewhere. To me that is more serious than it seems, for it just might not be a baby one, as we tho't yesterday, but one of those miniature vipers. Well, such is Africa. All for now.

With much love to all, Ione

On the 3rd of February she wrote to a supporter about a wildcat:

.....I hope you all realize how missionaries appreciate being prayed for. Several times this year we have felt at certain times that someone must have been remembering us in the homeland. I don't suppose a wildcat would hurt a person if he could get out of it. But once in the white man's house it was a problem how to get out. He had smelled ripe bananas and had squeezed thru a square opening

near the sheet metal roof. He ate all of the bananas that he wanted and began to get a bit worried toward morning, and in his restlessness, he tipped over some basins. I didn't reach for the flashlight as I got up, for we have become more or less accustomed to the luxury of electric lights. But in order to illuminate the wildcat I had to step to the centre of the room where it was and pull the cord! It was more than I had courage to do, so I went for my husband, and when he came, he flashed the light into the beast's eyes and this blinded him for a few moments while I ran for the gun. I didn't want to waken the children or my sister Marcellyn who was visiting us. Hector took the gun, and as I held the light on the staring cat's eyes, Hector prepared to shoot. Having some difficulty because of shaking and holding the light steady, I anxiously whispered to Hector, "Hurry and shoot!" At this point, we both heard sounds of my sister getting up. Hector said out of the side of his mouth, "I can't shoot!" "Why," I said, breathlessly. "Marcellyn's coming and I don't have my bathrobe on!" So, I carefully turned the light over to Hector, ran for his robe, put it around his shoulders and as Marcellyn appeared he shot and the creature was dead with the first shot. Perhaps you were the ones who were praying for us just then.

May the Lord bless you in your service for Him. Lovingly, Ione

On February 11th, Ione anticipated saying goodbye to Marcellyn who was due to go back to the States and added more tales of wild animals:

Dearest Mother,

Marcellyn will soon be leaving us, and it will surely be lonely. It looks as tho she will get off on a river boat that leaves Stan Feb 28th, and sail early in March from Matadi. You will no doubt have the facts right from her. I expect she will sail with Verna Schade and Olive Bjerkseth. I do hope so, as it will be good company for her.

I cannot write very much as I am trying to nurse John at the same time and must finish in time to straighten the house before everyone comes for the daily prayer meeting. Every time I press the left-hand keys John scowls, but he won't let go, and doesn't miss a beat in his sucking! He's not going to miss much by being the fourth! He takes the activities of the others in stride, and enjoys watching them.

.....Hector had shot another wildcat on New Year's Day which was asleep in a tree just behind our house. Then just a few nights ago, a liboli, another type of wildcat which is not striped but black, got one of our roosters and its cries pierced the calm night air, waking Paul who sat bolt upright with hair sticking up and eyes wide. He was breathless while I told him what had happened. Then he sought Kenny and said, "Kenny, a wildcat's got Nikola's chicken, it's run off with him and he's not even hanging out of the wildcat's mouf! Now, (with anguish in his voice) what will Nikola say to his chicken?!" John has had his first jigger, and Paul his first filaria worm in his eye, so, on we go, living in Africa.

The Lord bless you and meet every need of yours which I so long to meet.

Lovingly, Ione

In March, Ione got disturbing news from her friend Pearl about the Brown family with whom she stayed when giving birth to John and wrote to them on the 7th of March:

Dear Doctor and Raunie,

I'm afraid to write for fear that I might be wrong, but I feel definitely constrained, for it must be true, the news that I have heard about your little Timmie. Our nurse Pearl Hiles was in the mountains for a holiday and the news came by radio that Timmie had died. Oh, dear friends, how I long to tell you of my own sorrow for you. Your precious little lamb, so ready to go, but so hard to part with! He was on my lap such a little while ago. I was putting his shoes and stockings on, he listened so quietly to the story, and now he has slipped away to gladden Jesus' heart! I just now looked at Paul; the hair is the same, the eyes are blue, only one month apart, their height was nearly the same, both a good healthy colour, and I marvel that I have mine, and yours is gone. I could have spared mine more easily for I have two others tinier, yet the Lord has <u>chosen</u> Timmie, and taken him from your arms to the Father's bosom. How close that must bring you to Heaven, how real must be the Saviour, how keen must be His Presence! What an experience! To meet the Lord in this manner, to know the depths of such sorrow. To find that underneath ARE "the everlasting Arms".

No doubt you will soon be going home for furlough, as I hear that Dr Becker is back. If I don't see or hear from you before then you will know that I cherish dearly the weeks spent with you, and little Timmie, and will be praying for you.

Lovingly in Christ, Ione

And to Mrs Wideman, Ione wrote on March 9th with thanks for a shaving kit for Hector, aprons and packaged treats for the family. She told of foods that are available locally such as corn, rice, tomato sauce, wild meat and jam. She continued with stories about her boys:

.....I wish you could see how much the children enjoy drinking with their straw sets. It says on the package these will help the children to drink more milk, and Hector laughingly said he wondered if there was a way to get them to drink less for ours do go heavy on the milk!! David still "blows" instead of sucks, but will soon learn, I think. He insists on having his Elfunt every time the others use theirs. They have been having fun stringing the wooden beads. They stack up nicely like blocks, too. And the magic slates are a marvel to Kenneth and Paul. But most popular of all have been the toy trucks. They are grand. John's darling afghan is over him right now. It is cool and light and just fine for this climate. It has such luscious colours and makes his little grey bed look pretty. It is just the right size, by the way! I have found that aluminum foil very useful for wrapping things. And the Kleenex I am using these days by the handful as I have a bad cold. Thanks for the gift papers, too.

In a letter Ione wrote on the 31st of March we learn that the Kinsos have returned. Hector drove to Stanleyville taking David with him. As with most letters, this one starts with thanks for packages and gifts. Ione detailed how each item was used and how she passed on what she could not use. This time Rosemary Carter at Ekoko got a 'darling' yellow dress. Ione usually included some aspect of her work:

.....*Before I close, I must tell you about our African women's "reception" which we held in honour of the arrival of Mrs Jenkinson from England. The women planned it themselves, something brand new for them, and I helped provide the refreshments. It was held at the home of one of the oldest members, or rather in her front yard under an orange tree. There were about 40 women and 20 children. There were speeches, gifts of eggs, chickens, rice, peanuts, for her, a message from her, and in the middle of it all we heard a scream down on the main road and almost every woman jumped to her feet and ran. A baby which had just come from the hospital after treatment had gone into convulsions and they tho't it was dead. The mother of the baby rushed back to our group (she was well-known, tho' not a Christian) and threw herself on the ground. It was difficult to calm everyone down, and get the child on its way back to Pearl Hiles, who treated it immediately and it recovered. Then the sugar which I had put at the disposal for the occasion was used indiscreetly and about half were served, the rest were informed that they would get no sugar, so the rest politely (but firmly!) stated that they would have none at all! So, I hastily sent to my house for more sugar and put a Gospel Recordings on the Victrola lest we have a fight in the meeting over it. In times past these little forest women have flown at each other in a rage over such a little matter. Then the sugar came, and there was enough to put a tiny spoonful in the hand of each child as well, so everyone went away happy.*

Do pray much for the women this year. It looks like I will continue to have them, even tho Mrs J. is back. She will be having the Bible School. Pray, too, for much stealing which is going on.[94] We never know from day to day what will be missing next. The Lord can take this terrible thing away by changing their hearts.

Lovingly in Him, Ione

Although the Kinsos were back, it had not resulted in a change of responsibilities for Hector and Ione; they continued doing what they were doing and Kinso and Ma Kinso took on new roles. Kinso was nominated Field Director and took on Treasurer duties, probably because Stan Nichols and family had gone on furlough.

On the matter of Hector and Ione having only boys, there is an informative excerpt from a letter they wrote on April 17, which follows:

.....*Hector has the boys repeat the Bible reading after him, phrase by phrase, and now that David can talk, he tries too, though his comes after the other two have said theirs, and what he says is generally just the last word or so of the phrase. Hector waited patiently this morning as this was going on, verse by verse, first Kenny and Paul, then David, until the very last phrase, and Kenny*

---

[94] The Congolese did not view stealing as 'theft'; they did not 'steal' from the jungle, they merely used what was at their disposal. As the missionaries seemed to have so much, the temptation would have become sizeable and therefore problematic.

and Paul said it, - then a pause for David's, but nothing came: Hector waited a long time and finally David opened his mouth ------ and hiccuped!

John has four teeth and big blue eyes. The natives have a special name for him as he is our fourth boy. It is Jean Boabazu – [which] means of course, John for the first name, and for the last – "God makes boys as well as girls".

Technology started to make an impact, more people had radios so despite being in remote areas, the missionaries knew some of what was happening further afield. In a letter to her mother on April 21st, Ione wrote:

.....Mary Baker has a tape recorder and we are busy making recordings to send home. I may be able to send you one if you know someone who has a recorder [player]. We have done about ten minutes of schoolboys' songs, some greetings from natives with interpretation, and I expect to coach a woman today with her "speech" which I will interpret. Hector got the drum being beaten yesterday for church, and expects to get native sounds while the workmen push a log. It takes about an hour to use a whole tape. I'm going to send one of Mary's to First Baptist in Pontiac and ask them if they wish to send another to be filled. I'll have to ask Mary again the name of the recorder so that you will know it. Only that kind of tape can be used.

So, at last Leone Reed got to hear what her grandsons' sound like.

In May, Ione wrote to her sister Lucille describing a recent fatality:

.....Hector was driving Verna Schade's pick-up truck with plantain and sand on it and four native men. Hector got the sand as a favour to his head mason who was wanting it to finish his house. Kasi asked two of his brothers and a relative to go along to help dig and the younger brother was Kpodo (Pwodo), our house helper who has worked for us for four years, a Christian (baptized). Kpodo decided to ride on the back half of the running board and Hector did not see him. Kpodo's brother told him twice to get into the truck, but the young man apparently tho't he'd have a thrill, so stayed right there. Hector made a turn, was going about 18 miles an hour as the load was heavy, and he thinks a small branch must have hit him or he tho't it was going to and ducked, for he fell off backwards, struck his head, turned on his side and died instantly with multiple fracture.

My, how shocked we all were. Going thru this experience and seeing how kind the Christians have been to us, knowing how badly we feel, has given me a new love for them I did not know I that I had. Several young men have believed as a result of it. Hector is going to board up that part of the running board that is out of his vision so that it will never happen again. Hector and the carpenters made a coffin the next morning and I draped it with white cloth and put a new blanket in the bottom. The flowers Kpodo had cut for me the day before were still fresh and I put them into it when our children went into the church for the funeral, they each placed a white gardenia on his coffin. They were very fond of Kpodo. He was the one who saved them from the snake that fell out of the big tree.

Another boy had a luckier escape; Ione wrote:

.....Aurora Gabriel was a schoolboy at Bongondza. He often watched Mama Kinso or Mademoiselle Rutt or Bwana McMillan riding on a small motor scooter and it became an obsession with him to get hold of the vehicle and ride it for himself. During one sports day at school several of the bigger boys were allowed to try it on a small spot in a level field. He only knew enough about it to start it and steer it.

Young Gabriel looked for his chance to take it when no one was around, and then started down the steep hill which led from my old mud house to the main road and the stream. Hector with Kenneth and Paul were at the bottom of the hill where the old Ford called 'Molimo' was being used to carry water from the stream ('Molimo', meaning spirit, as it no longer had a body!). The little boys and their Daddy looked on amazed as they saw the black boy, now quite pale-faced, come tearing down the hill full speed. He had forgotten how to shut off the motor!

By now, not feeling very angel-like, Gabriel narrowly missed Hector, but hit the 'Molimo', left the bike and flew right over the old car, landing in a patch of jungle forest not far from the river. The boy was terribly frightened, but had only a scratch on his leg. The bike and car had some damage, however.

Hector was pretty pale himself, but he marched the boy up the hill to tell the lady owners of the bike what he had done, and then sent him to his parents to collect the money for repairs.

Ione encountered other staffing issues as she related to her sister Lucille on the 10th of August:

.....We had a dinner already except that; I say "we" for the little house helper and I did it, for the young fellow who does the cooking is sick today. Our older and most capable cook is gone now, and we are all feeling sick about it. He has had two cases of adultery since we came back from furlough and this week, he staged a "walkout" of all of our staff members for higher pay, which right now we cannot give. Since he was the leader, he had to be let go. He is a Christian, and that makes it very bad. Now we have one less staff member and it is better really, as the others can do the work if they try. If you were here, you would know how big is the business of our "help", dealing with them spiritually first of all, and then keeping them working happily together. All are Christians, and we have nice times of worship each morning together.

Ione recounted that all the family had malaria. She had been trying to triple the quinine doses but had not accounted for how much the children had grown. To make matters worse, Hector ran out of his supply and was taking children's doses, so for a short time was unprotected from this preventative medication.

It is at this point that Ione broke the news of her forthcoming pregnancy:

.....I could go to this same doctor when our baby comes in January but as yet we are not sure. The road is not good and it is farther than we have yet driven for a

baby. But the doctor we had for John is now on furlough. My, how I wish we had a doctor in our mission. Do pray for one.

In October, Ione focused on her sons' education and writes to the Calvert Course organization. She asked if they had courses of study by correspondence which would be suitable for beginning children.

To Hector's sister Alice, Ione wrote on October 26, describing what was going on around her at the time:

.....We are all well, and thankful that our family has not been affected by an epidemic that has passed around among the natives. A number of local people have been found with hookworm lately; that means we must be very careful; it is a horrible disease and hard to cure. If we wear stockings or long trousers when we walk thru long grass that lessens the danger. The little worms cling to damp grass. Hector is getting quite stout. His waist-line has expanded from 32 to 36 since we have been married! .....This week he is labouring under difficulties. He broke his upper plate [dentures] *and cannot wear the old one he had. He cannot make the trip to Stan for repairs for another week I'm afraid, so he is going around with his mouth shut!*

Our boys are just like steps and it is interesting to watch them develop. Their weights range from 35 to 50 pounds. The youngest is more like Paul, quite fair. David is a handsome, square-jawed fellow, who at this particular age (2-1/2) is feeling his importance to the extent of contradicting everything we say. If we say it's a "little one" he immediately corrects us. It is a "big one". The other night I found out that "Sing a song of six-pence" had been green birds instead of black ones! Paul is quite blond and Kenneth quite dark. We are starting a "Reading Readiness" course with Kenneth and Paul. I have sent for the Calvert Course, which should follow this; it will be first grade I think. But for now I am trying to develop colour sense, seeing likenesses and differences, left to right eye movements, developing number sense, size discrimination, matching letters and words, pictures, etc. Kenneth was five in June. Do you know that before Kenneth is six we'll have, the Lord willing, our fifth child! The big date is Jan. 14.

Here Ione disclosed the amount of correspondence that needed to go out – 400 form letters with 60 personal notes in time for Christmas. Letter writing was more difficult when contending with babies and toddlers demanding attention. On the 16th of November, Ione grabbed an opportunity while Hector was entertaining the children to write to her mother:

.....Hector has the children out for a little walk and I will type fast. Your letter came last week and was very welcome.

.....Mary Rutt has arrived from furlough and is helping me with the women until the baby comes. She is planning and taking charge of their Christmas program. This is a big relief to me, as I am getting a bit heavy. I have written out the schoolboys' Christmas program, but the 5th and 6th year are translating it into Lingala and will chose their own parts and under Mary Baker's supervision will not need me. I am only drilling them in the six songs that go with the program. I

am teaching the women a song, too. That's about all I am doing right now, and am glad for a little break. You see Christmas Day is a little too near the baby's arrival to count on my doing too much then. And I am hoping I can attend the General Conference which meets January 1-8 at Ekoko, then take a boat from Bumba to Yakusu for the baby. That's the latest plan.

.....Kenny is learning to read and spell by leaps and bounds. I find he is able to take all I can give him. And he follows me around getting words of songs and the alto part! His mind is so eager to learn. I will need to give him more and more time.

We were all sitting in the living room one evening, all the missionaries, the children were in bed, when a large praying mantis flew across the room and lit on the door opening into the office. Immediately a tarantula leaped out of the darkness, from the ceiling of the office, I guess, and grabbed the praying mantis. We were so surprised! Then of course, there was a grand scramble to kill the tarantula.

.....Now to close. Kenny has come and the rest are on the way. Our Sun nite supper is French toast and syrup. It smells good.

Love, Ione

Christmas celebrations went with a swing. In a letter penned on December 28, 1952 to her sister Marcellyn, now back in the States, Ione wrote:

.....Yesterday we had our Christmas dinner at Kinsos, eleven adults and 4 children. We had three ducks, and all that we could wish to go with it. Nothing really typical, tho in the eats line for Christmas, for not one of us got a Christmas package yet! There are many on the way, so we'll look for some cranberry sauce or nuts later. I was afraid the children would lack for toys, for we had not been able to get any when folk went to Stan, but the Snyders[95] had forethought to bring 4 little presents from Belgium, two tops, an airplane, and a miniature farm. And Pearl had bought more tops, some ninepins, etc. Viola Walker gave them some cute little leatherette suitcases which she had bought in a native shop. They had lots of chocolate bars, gum, life savers, peanuts, etc. Pearl had big gauze socks more than filled with things; they were hanging on Kinso's mantle when we arrived for dinner yesterday. The Friday between the native Christmas and ours Hector had to go to Buta, and brought back cute little cars for all four, that nice sturdy tiny size. We had both dinner and supper at Kinsos. Supper was so much fun. It had rained and was chilly so they built a fire and we roasted wieners and had them on buns and bread with piccalilli and potato salad. There was pumpkin and lemon pie and cherry ice cream, and lots of Putu salted nuts that Pearl had saved from last year.[96] Then as a surprise Bill Snyder brought in some marshmallows and we roasted them. Kinso read us several funny poems and some more serious things, and we sang carols. John went to sleep nicely in his

---

[95] Bill and Coral Snyder were new missionaries from the US.

[96] These nuts were from the States; Putu means white man's land.

carriage, David on Kinso's bed, and finally Paul on the couch. Kenny stayed
awake until we left about 9:30. The children had just as much fun as we did.

No sooner was Christmas over when preparations started for the New Year
Conference at Ekoko; people gathered at Bongondza with the intent of all travelling
together. Seats were put in the back of the truck. Ione wrote:

.....The Burks and McAllister's will sleep and eat here.[97] All will rest as much as
possible tomorrow evening and night and Tuesday, and then we'll leave about 8
o'clock Tuesday night, hoping to get to Ekoko in the morning. We'll make
breakfast on the road, however, as they expect us at Ekoko for dinner. I guess
the cars will try to keep together. We'll put the choir benches in the truck and
you can imagine the fun (and discomfort!) of those who ride there! ! The
Conference starts on New Year's Day and lasts until the 8th. My baby is due the
14th, but I think it will come before then. You will soon know. If it is a girl it will
be Ruth Leone.

But things do not go to plan as Ione told her mother on the 3rd of January, 1953:

.....This is the first letter since the arrival of the baby, and I want it to be to you.
By now you should have received the telegram Hector sent. Stephen Arthur was
born at about 7:30 P.M. Dec. 31st, 1952. He didn't quite make it to the New Year!
His birth was a little abnormal for he came face first. He weighed 8 lbs 2 oz. but
looks easily as fat as David did, with the chubby cheeks, pug nose and broad
forehead. I have a very clever and kind doctor, to whom all the Belgian women
go from all around. He did everything possible to make it quick and easy and
painless, and best of all, he let Pearl Hiles stay with me and even administer
anaesthetic!

.....I slept right thru the night, and again the next night, but last night I didn't
sleep so well. The doctor thinks it is a touch of malaria – but I have no fever. I
think it was the pains that come when the milk comes in. The baby started nursing
today. He is darling, so much like David. And such a good disposition!

Hector and Mrs Jenkinson bro't them all (our children) to see their brother
yesterday and all were impressed except John, who wouldn't even come to me,
after just three days 'absence'! He is fond of Mrs J. and it is just as well. I will
win him back when I leave the hospital. The children are having a good time
with 11 other children, and good meals and supervision. Dolena Burk is giving
them baths and keeping their clothes straight. They sleep with Hector.

.....Lovingly, Ione

---

[97] McAllisters are a new UFM missionary family from Ireland, first stationed at Boyulu with the Burks.

Chapter 13
SHOCKS AND SURPRISES

In March of 1953, Hector was in Stanleyville having some dentistry work carried out. Kinso travelled with him and took the opportunity during the five day stop over to investigate the non-Catholic Belgian School (Athénée Royale). Besides the growing McMillan family, other missionaries on the other stations had children; the Carters at Ekoko had four, the Artons at Boyulu had one, the Walbys at Maganga had two with a third on the way, the Boyes family at Banjwadi (ban-JWA-dee) had three. This meant that a lot of missionary time would be spent home schooling. The alternative was to send all the children to Rethy, which was not only much further for everyone to travel, being 800 miles away but was also expensive. The mission needed a better solution and Ione favored a third option for the children's education. She wrote to her mother on 1st March:

> .....if they live in the U.F.M Home we hope to build soon in Stan, they can be cared for by our own missionaries and therefore not miss a real Christian environment.

The education of the missionary children was resolved several years later.

In her mother's late-arriving Christmas package came shoes for all the boys and new overalls, which they wore to church for Stephen's dedication service. Stephen wore a 40-year old dress that had been used when Ione was a baby!

Ione hid away some of the things for upcoming birthday presents. In her 'thank you' letter to her mother, she revealed that she now had 6 children under her wing:

> .....You are thinking we have five boys now, but it is six. We have taken a mulatto boy to live with us now. He is 13 years old and his name is Joseph. He is a darling little fellow and a real Christian. He was raised by one of our best missionary ladies, Mabel Wenger, from Pennsylvania. She found him down country when she was with another mission and has kept him until now, along with two others and several little black orphans. She has done wonderfully in training them all. But now Joseph needs schooling and our native school has the classes he needs for 5th and 6th year. We have agreed to keep him two years and let him go to the day school here. He sleeps in our first basement room which opens out at the side of the house, but when it is cold or rainy or when Hector is away I have him sleep in John's room and I take David with me. He is really an answer to prayer for someone to help me with the children. He is loveable and comical too, with so many cute little jokes. He speaks English very well. He is a good eater, can put away about four times as much rice as Hector!

At the beginning of the year, Ione had many 'thank you' letters, one being to a church in Michigan who had decided to send a monthly allowance for Stephen's upkeep. Ione's letters included some description of life in Africa, such as when the family was, once again, driven out by driver ants:

> .....*The people are forest farmers; they keep cutting down trees to make their gardens, but the forest seems never to end. Because the trees are so near to us, we sometimes have visits from animals, snakes and bugs of different kinds. Last week driver ants all but drove us out of our large brick house. They decided to raid our house and with one account swarmed in a million strong into Paul's bed, David's bed, Hector's bed, Kenneth's bed – and one by one came trouping into the big double bed, which after all does have limitations! There was only one room left and there were stragglers even there. The only way to keep them back is with lots of fire or water, and in the wee hours of the night we decided to just try to keep our little family sleeping and just remove them to another house if the ants came to the last room. The ants didn't come any farther that night but toward evening the next night began to make another attack and we got started earlier and swished at them with water and burned papers around the entrance until they went away.*

In a letter to Alice on the 19th of March, Ione informed the family that she now dedicated time to home schooling Kenny and Paul:

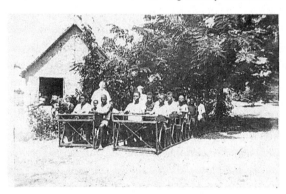

Desks for the native school.

> .....*The books and crayons are going into our new school cupboard in our "classroom". Thank you so much for everything. We do not mind at all that they did not arrive at Christmas, for the things mean a great deal to us just now.*
>
> .....*I am trying to give Kenneth and Paul 2-1/2 hours school a day. We have sent for the first-year work of the Calvert Course, which costs us $80 for materials, for teacher (me!), and two pupils for one year. Kenneth is beginning to read a little; Paul is still in "reading readiness". Our recently bricked-in sleeping porch makes a nice bright classroom and Hector has installed a blackboard which covers one wall. We have the little desks the Westcott children left here.*
>
> .....*Hector announced tonight that he has just finished making 24 desks for the native school. He's got some wonderful tools now and high-powered machinery and can turn them out like an assembly line. He's just completed another unit of the 7-unit boys' school and wants to furnish the room now.*

Packages from family and supporters often arrived just when the family needed new supplies as noted in a letter to her mother on March 28:

.....Toothpaste, too, was just at an end with us. Am glad for a good big tube. The talcum is almost gone already, as I have had to use it for the baby's bath every day, and sometimes oftener as he gets prickly heat easily among his layers of fat! Yesterday Pearl found a big tin of baby talc which she gave me among other things which she is getting rid of while she's packing. So I can save the rest of the Cashmere Bouquet for myself. I am popping the corn by the cupful, and have had two lots of it already. It is so good. The nuts we bro't out on David's birthday and the children used some dental forceps and had fun cracking them. But I saved enough for some fudge, and I think there are 5 more in the can for something else. I hid the hankies away before Hector saw them and will give them on his birthday; I might share them with Joseph, am not sure. Joseph's birthday is in September. The plastic panties are nice for Stephen, and the bread wrapper has a good many uses. The puzzle is just fine for the children. Thank you so much for everything.

Now for the other package, which came at another time, I can't remember the date, the one with the big Noah's ark game. That is just grand for the children, and they do enjoy it a lot. The two older boys and Joseph play it and they let David put the animals into the boat. He loves to take charge of the boat. The best John can do is chew the tails off the animals! We are trying to preserve them, tho'! The animals, I mean, not the tails. And all of those books are a real help to our supply. It is so good to have the Bible story books with such attractive pictures. And the four just alike of the Three Bears, etc., they carry around everywhere with them, as they have such pretty scalloped edges. They like best to go straight thru all four, and now I find Kenneth 'reading' them to Paul. I am taking the stories in the Bible story book and enlarging upon it from the Bible, then putting it on our big blackboard in stick-man, with a Bible verse appropriate. After Jonah, I let them draw little whales with chalk on the bottom of the blackboard. Thank you so much for all of the things you sent. I don't see how you got together all the money it meant to buy and send so much.

Coral and Bill Snyder were at Bongondza at this time and were having meals with the McMillans. While this may have been extra work, it was also extra support as Coral took charge of the children which allowed Ione freedom to go out to the neighboring villages with Viola Walker – something which pleased her immensely. Stephen was Ione's first bottle fed baby, which was another factor that enabled her this freedom. Coral wrote much later that Ione and Hector were good role models for them and that Ione was the only person on the station who seemed interested in the fact that she was pregnant.

Ione continues with an update on bugs and life with her boys:

.....We had a scorpion in our women's class last week, a big sprawl grey one, on a box that one woman was sitting on while sewing, in our basement. I killed it with my shoe, as the other women didn't have shoes on.

It is now 3 P.M., and everyone is awake but Kenny. John is back (with wet panties) David needs shoes put on, John is asking for meeilk. He talks much plainer than David did his age; Milk was always wunk with David. Not much chance of letter-writing now, but I'll keep trying. Stephen's needs are few. It's the David and John age that keep me jumping. But they're so cute, Mother, just like soft little dolls. Oh, Oh – I guess I'm finished for a while. John spilled his milk on the floor, and while I was getting the cloth Paul occupied my chair, and is now sitting on the window sill facing me, trying to cut a Christmas card with some little plastic scissors. "Dey don't cut," he's saying, and he's about right. They're no good. Now David's intimidating John with the knock-out bench hammer. John's not easily scared, but screams anyway. Now David's using the hammer to open the windows in the living room (they are not glass, thankfully.)

Well, I will close, as John is in my lap. As I was attending to the little needs of the children, it seemed that the Lord said to me, "Lovest thou me more than these children?" And I quickly answered in my heart, "Ye Lord, thou knowest that I love Thee." Then it seemed as tho He said, "Feed my lambs." I am trying to give the children spiritual food, and these native women with whom I work, as well as the staff members. Pray for me. Lovingly, Ione

In April, Ione got another charge. Janet Cowger (a nurse who had replaced Pearl Hiles), asked Ione to foster a month-old baby weighing only 3 pounds.

The gifts kept coming. In a letter Ione wrote in May, she thanked Mrs Smith for a monthly donation for John's upkeep and for contributing to the correspondence course Ione used to teach the boys. As with all gifts, Ione's letters aimed to convey a little about the people they were supporting and of John she wrote:

.....He is still so little and needs lots of care. He feeds himself, but milk is still his favourite. He tried to get me to go to the kitchen and give him some a few days ago, and kept pulling on my skirts until I finally turned around and then he gave me a push from behind, and as if that weren't enuf, he gave the marching orders he hears at the school boys' drill, "Gauche, droit, un, deux," (left, right, one, two!) He's such a funny little fellow! You hear him calling out Mbote (hello) to the natives, then on occasion he will politely shake hands with a Bonjour, but for me it's just, Hello, Mommie! He's not smart, I want you to know, it's just that he keeps hearing these words in Bangala, French and English.

.....I would say this has been our best year yet on our field, for we have seen more saved recently than ever before. Every few days someone comes to us as inquirers. There were 90 in the class this week for those who have accepted Christ. There have been a great many schoolboys, and this is something for which we have been praying for years. Some women, too. I am having fine times with the women. I have been getting out more frequently to the villages since February.

This is all for now. Love, Ione

Ione's upbeat mood of the mission work spilled over into a letter to another supporter:

.....There has been a remarkable turning in the large boys' school, for which we are very thankful. There were 90 in the baptism class last week. Some of my

women have been coming, too. One day when I tho't I had had the hardest time in history (imagine trying to satisfy 50 little backwoods mothers and wives with bits of cloth and the proper instruction to achieve under garments for themselves and their babies!), with my last ounce of strength, after a message that I tho't was as weak as water, threw out a general invitation to accept Christ and three promptly said out loud, "That's for me."

And while most letters are full of love for her 'boys' there is evidence that Ione and Hector were disciplinarians:

.....Well the children are in bed, but still making noises, and there is no meeting tonight. The missionaries usually meet Mon. nite to study French. Paul tip-toed in the office and handed me the strap, "You left this in the bedroom," he said. "Do you think I'll need it?" I said, rather sternly, and he caught the hint and went back. It's Hector that really uses it with success [even just as a warning].

Ironically, just as Ione was feeling so positive, illness strikes. On the 11th of July, Hector wrote to the family back home:

.....This is a note that we want to get off with the telegram. It must be short as it goes the first thing in the morning. Ione wants to dictate it [as follows:]

I'm sorry if the telegram has upset you. We made it urgent because I want Marcellyn to come so badly and I felt that she will somehow be able to arrange it. I'm not seriously ill but this morning I had a little spell that convinced me that there is something wrong with my heart although it may not be serious. It was over in a few moments and it wasn't a bad pain but because of that and the fact that the doctor at Banalia wanted me to come in for a cardiograph to Stanleyville, I know now there is something wrong with my heart.

We were out on trek with the family because this is holiday time. And when I left, I felt grand and was thrilled with the first three days because there were nearly a hundred souls saved on the Panga road, where there are nice new rest houses. Then each of the children one by one had vomiting spells and then got over it immediately. We thought we had gotten a little germ of some kind. Then one morning Hector took sick with the same thing and recovered quickly too. But then my turn came I couldn't stop vomiting and I vomited so hard that by night time I was feeling a tightening in my throat every time I vomited. I had no pain in my heart but I got a bit short of breath and asked Hector for an extra pillow. Then he decided he'd better send for the doctor at Banalia which was fortunately much closer than if I had been home (that is, 45 Kms). The doctor came right out and stayed with me an hour, and then came back the next day. The Lord must have put us near <u>him</u> *because he is a heart specialist.*

.....Now don't worry. The children are all well and are well cared for, for the time being. After the spell I felt good again and ate a good dinner and feel quite alright for the doctor to come to see me tomorrow. No stone will be unturned to see that I get the best of care, but I want Marcellyn. John 14:1, Heb. 13:5b

With all my love, Ione

Kinso recalled on July 13th and 14th, 1953:

.....The doctor had said that if Ione continued to make progress he thought she could get up after one week in bed. She tried at the end of one week but didn't feel fit enough so she wisely stayed in bed. She had tried once or twice after that. The last time she was sitting up for quite a time. However, it proved to be too much of a strain and last Saturday, July 11th, she was very ill and we all felt it was wise to send you the above wire. [Wire: Ione very ill. Heart condition. Marcellyn come. Please pray. Notify church and relatives. McMillan.]

At the same time, we sent word to the doctor to ask him to come to see Ione as soon as possible. Yesterday, Sunday, afternoon and evening she was very ill indeed and during the night we certainly had good reasons to fear the worst. All night long prayer was offered – we whites were in the sick room and our African brethren gathered in the next room and kept up an all-night vigil. Relief came early this morning but she has been very low again since then and right at this moment she is a very very sick woman and still very much on the danger list. Miss Cowger is now giving her glucose injection.

Banalia Ferry , c1950

That brings us right up to the moment – 11:30 P.M. Monday, July 13th. The doctor has not yet come. We will keep you informed of developments.

Yesterday afternoon Ione was very low and there was no sign of the doctor coming. Miss Cowger and the rest of us had done all we could so I decided to go Banalia to see why the doctor had not come.

.....It was close to midnight when we got back to Bongondza and I was happy to learn that Ione is now out of danger. He has left instructions and medicines for her treatment and has promised to write at once to the heart specialist in Stanleyville to arrange for Ione to go there and he expects that we will have an answer by next Friday's mail.

Our African brethren have been a source of strength to us at this time. I wish you could have seen them on their knees and on their faces pleading with God for Ione. I am sure it is in answer to their prayers and the prayers of you friends at home that Ione is now declared to be out of danger. There is still much need for prayer but we believe we have the victory.

Cable Received July 24th from Bongondza: Marcellyn arrived. Ione better. Stanleyville hospital heart specialist.

Hector recorded the events in a July 17th letter thus:

Dear Friends,

339

Many of you will have heard about Ione's serious illness of which we informed our headquarters by cablegram.

The heart attack came about 11 A.M. Saturday July 11. Our nurse, Janet Cowger, was soon at her bedside. The pain went down her left arm and soon made her whole body tingle. By late afternoon we got her to rest quietly and she dictated a letter for me to send to her Mother and sisters. At four in the morning she had me call the nurse again and just after daylight a letter to call the doctor got on its way.

Unfortunately for us the doctor was being recalled to Stanleyville from his place in Banalia, our gov't post. His replacement didn't realize the seriousness of her case amidst all the confusion of his first day in a new territory. During that day he had performed 5 different operations; 4 of them were unsuccessful. All this was unknown to us as we waited for him to come to our aid. Mr Jenkinson finally made the long trip to Banalia on Monday afternoon. The doctor arrived about midnight.

Sunday evening was a <u>very</u> critical time when a real battle for her life began. When we gathered around her bed about 7:00 P.M. we little imagined we would be there until 4 A.M. The 6 missionaries became involved in getting hot coffee, fanning, patting, praying, singing, reading promises from the Word. In our living room the native leaders gathered, weeping and crying as they besought the Lord to spare her life. Fortunately, the children slept through it all. We kept the light plant going all night.

As we neared exhaustion from singing, Miss Baker slipped away and got her electric record-player that changes records automatically. She picked out some appropriate hymns and brought the machine to the room. What a blessing this was for Ione! Little by little her nerves quieted down, she finally laid back on the pillow and seemed to relax. Now she went to the other extreme and all activity ceased except about 8 respirations a minute. She whispered, "Just let me hear one more hymn then I'll go. That finished, we asked Mr Jenkinson to pray, expecting him to commit her to the Lord. (Unknown to some of us, he had said earlier in the evening that God had given him the confidence that Ione would be raised up again.) Even in that darkest hour, when even Ione had given up her heroic struggle, our dear Mr Jenkinson once more asked the Lord to raise her up. One slow breath followed another until she made a slight improvement and soon after fell into a sleep of exhaustion. The rest of us did likewise for two hours until daylight.

One of the first things Ione remembered in the morning was the promise, "Weeping may endure for a night, but joy cometh in the morning." I looked it up and read all the verses before and after it in Psalm 30. She said her life hung by such a slender thread and really the air on the "other side" was fresher than down here. The singing of the lovely tropical birds was refreshing to her. One inquisitive little fellow came quite close to the window looking in as much as to say, "It's all right, the Lord takes care of us, too."

Soon a heavy rain came on with thunder and lightning. During the day two more spells came on accompanied by pain which caused us much anxiety. However, we knew that the cablegram was on its way asking God's people to pray and also requesting Ione's sister to come out to us from the States.

The nurse's skillfulness and wisdom are to be highly commended. Other dear missionaries gave unstintingly of their time and ability. The children are receiving competent care and have quickly made the necessary adjustment. Ione so much appreciates the ice and jello from the refrigerator.

The doctor said she must be flown to New York. We hope to have all the arrangements made within a week or ten days. Plans for my return with the children can be made when Ione's sister arrives.

.....If you want any further information you may receive it at 1150 N.63rd Phila 31 Pa.

Yours in Christ, Hector

Ione got to Stanleyville and in a letter to Hector and the boys, she reassures them and delivers surprising news:

Dearest Hector and Boys,

I will write a little note to send along. Janet and Marcellyn are here just now writing letters too. I'm glad they're staying tonight yet for I was afraid they'd go back right after dinner and they had only been in & out quickly a couple of times. You must pray much for me for I see now how difficult it is going to be to bring about the relief I need. The doctor is kind but it's I who has to face the nurses and I seem to be a bit off to a wrong start, and as yet I don't feel he has much of a reputation here. Maybe I just imagine it. But I told him this morning I would rather go to America than to stay here as things are. Just pray that I may keep from getting anxious.

There will be more to say after the doctor comes again. He wants to consult with two other doctors.

Now Kenny, my bed looks out of a window where I can see the Congo River all day and the big boats passing. I like to hear them whistle. Paul, you must not tease the others but be a good boy and run fast to Auntie Marcellyn when she calls. David, keep on sharing with John and play nicely with him. John, you tell Daddy or Auntie Marcellyn when you need the pottie. Stephen, you mustn't make noises anymore at night.

Now, Hector, you do your best to keep them prayed-up and happy, and do stand by Marcellyn and help her a lot. If you think it wise, come in on the courier. If you don't come, send a letter.

The doctor bro't another doctor and they are now sure a baby is coming, but my heart is so good now that they are not justified in doing anything about it. So the doctor is recommending to our Legal Rep. (Kinso) that I go home for the duration of the pregnancy and a couchment [rest]. So, from now on let Kinso do what he feels wisest. No more cables until I'm on the way. Then, I don't know what. Marcellyn says she's willing to go back with you if there's no one else, but

341

is afraid the mission might balk at the cost. However, the church might rally.
Don't urge where you will go just now when you arrive. Let me talk to Mother
first. And don't try to follow me too soon. Let me arrange about a plane first.
    Love, Ione

Again, from her hospital bed in Stanleyville, Ione wrote to Marion at the mission headquarters thanking her for finding the funds to get Marcellyn out to Africa so quickly:

.....I don't know how you did it financially but I am much concerned now because
the doctors here said yesterday, I must fly home right away. They gave me a
vaccination today. Tomorrow they do an electro-cardiograph. You're supposed
to wait 15 days after vaccinations so there may be a little time to get the money.
Don't worry <u>yet</u> about the family coming. There's no hurry as Marcellyn will
stay with them. But get the church straight as to how much money might be
accredited to our name unless you have had to use that for Marcellyn!! You
probably have done all this & <u>more!!!</u>

She finished the letter with a request that Dr Westcott attend to her and wrote with her typical wry humor:

.....I have been pretty sick, but <u>don't forget, I'm not dead yet</u>.

Ione also wrote to her mother trying to reassure her that she was well enough to travel but that she was two months into what will be her 7th pregnancy.

She also thanked the church members – Asalake, Ana, Denys, Masini, Samuele, Mayani, Anziambo etc. for their prayers and intercession on her behalf, that she was flying home to the States and testifying to the Lord's goodness.

The first leg of Ione's journey home was by plane to Léopoldville as she explained in a letter dated July 30th:

Dearest Daddy and Boys, and Marcellyn,

    This will be the only letter before I leave for N.Y. as I am booked for 5:45,
today.

    When I left you at Stan, I couldn't see my way into the plane very well because
of tears. I blinked my eyes when I got inside and looked for a seat. I saw one, but
as I sat down, I stumbled over a book on the floor. Then I heard a little English
voice say, "Daddy, this lady has our seat!" So, I quickly got up and found one
just behind, across the aisle. Then I looked to see what I stumbled over and it
was a Bible! So, I took notice of the family of five, and pretty soon the lady spied
my Bible in the basket and conversation began. They were the Greenhow's from
Nyankunde! And what precious fellowship we had!

    .....I am a bit tired with all this rush, but perhaps I can rest when we get there.
My appetite is good and these little missionary children have helped me to not
cry for my own little boys.

    I hope the family will be able to come as quickly and as nicely as I have. But
I will try to be patient and wait. I will try to write every week.

    Give my love to Kinsos, Mary R., Mary B., Janet and Snyder's.

Tell the boys when Auntie Marcellyn gets enough Sunday clothes made, they can come, too, and I'll get a place ready. For now, goodbye, and remember "His yoke is easy, His burden is light."

Lovingly, Mommie

Ione provided Hector with another update on the 4th of August from Ypsilanti, Michigan, where Dr Westcott practiced medicine:

.....Well, now I have something more definite to tell you. First, let me say I am feeling much, much better, and I am praising the Lord for His guidance all the way.

I took a plane Saturday night from Philadelphia and in less than 2 hours was at Willow Run, Detroit. Maurice, Lucille and Mother were there to meet me and it was a happy reunion. It was quite a way to Fenton and they did not go thru Pontiac. We arrived at about 11 P.M. and found Mr and Mrs Kenneth Hempstead there. They had come over to see when I was arriving and the Peterson children told them to wait and they would see me. So, we talked awhile and they said they would tell the folk at the church I had arrived. The news must have gotten around, for the next afternoon Dr. and Mrs Westcott came, and after a little discussion decided to take me to the Ypsilanti hospital that same day and I was given a room with a dear Christian lady who had a paralytic stoke. Monday morning, I was started on a very busy day of tests, etc. and finished up with a blood transfusion. It has been the same today, with a second pint of blood. I guess it's the new blood that makes me feel so good!

Dr. Westcott had a long talk with me this morning and told his diagnosis of my case:

The heart attacks were a result of the epidemic infection that touched our family. He said it should have been treated immediately with penicillin or sulpha. It was a temporary thing and passed with the infection with no damage to the heart. We should be able to have next baby all right, but I must have two minor operations afterward and then we can never have any more babies. I guess that sums it all up. He gave the blood because I am anemic, and I should bring my normal weight up to 130. I'm 117 now.

I think I'll be released from the hospital tomorrow and will stay at Westcott's until Mother is ready to have me at the apartment. It is just a small place, but just right for us. My first job is going to be to get ready little packages of clothes for the boys and I'll send them Air Mail as I can. Just the bare necessities for travel. And we shall hope that there will soon be sufficient money for our family to be reunited.

.....All for now. Am looking for your first letter.

Lovingly, Ione

And back in Africa, Hector and the boys sent Ione messages on the 4th of August:

Thank you for the Mechano[98] set. I love you Mommie; Paul, David, John, & Stephen do too. - Kenny

Dearest Ione,

I'll send this to Headquarters hoping they will forward it.

.....We are anxiously awaiting news of your trip.

You surely looked lovely with your hair so nicely fixed up. I'm sure it made your trip more enjoyable. Even tho' so far away from you I'm still thankful that I have the privilege of being your husband. As Mary Baker says, "I've got the cream of the crop."

The children have surely enjoyed that Mechano Set. Kenneth has made all sorts of little things & the others play with them. Marcellyn has the house in good shape & I've done some work in the office. David is singing "Tom, Tom the Pipers Son". Marcellyn has been teaching them some new songs. In fact, they had one all memorized when we got back from Stan. Their little shelves in the bedroom are a great help for their daily dressing. Even John can hang up his 'jamas.

.....Marcellyn moved down to Viola's house & likes it quite well. She goes there for Siesta and sometimes stays until 4 p.m.

Janet has kind of gone to pieces again. We expect some of these times. She will say [when] she wants to take the next plane home. Coral is getting more into the work. Ma Kinso says Margaret Ogilvie will stay here for several months to help out.

Well, mummie, I'll say bye bye for now. I'd be willing to stay here until you come back. But Pudneys will know what is best.

All my love, Hector   X

A few days later and Ione was out of hospital:

Dearest Daddy, Auntie Marcellyn and Boys,

Now you know my new house number, and I surely hope to hear from you soon. No letter as yet from my dearest ones. We have a beautiful apartment on the second floor, "where every prospect pleases," except the rent each month! But it is good to be with Mother, and to be next door to Lucille. We can see their house from kitchen, dining room, and Mother's bedroom window. My bedroom is on the other corner. I am feeling pretty good and am up a good part of the day. We listened to tape recordings this morning of the Joy Trio, etc. How I wish we could get them out there soon to you! They are such a blessing.

.....Since I have been here, I have been just resting. I am wondering what I can do about helping you get the many things together for the journey home. I think I have a few ideas! Marcellyn, don't feel you must do a lot of sewing for now. I can see a way to get clothes for the children to you in a hurry. I already have

---

[98] Meccano (here spelled correctly) is a model construction system created in 1898 by Frank Hornby in Liverpool, United Kingdom. The system consists of reusable metal strips, plates, angle girders, wheels, axles and gears, and plastic parts that are connected using nuts and bolts. It enables the building of working models and mechanical devices.

nearly enough new things for their journey and will get Kenny's packet off first Airmail if it doesn't break me. Just a coat & hat (from Jimmie - nephew) 2 pairs trousers, shirts, under wear & pajamas. Maybe a little toy to be saved for the journey, a balloon to blow now and a sucker to suck now! I will try to find a light-weight suitcase to send it in, and the same will follow for Paul, David and John. Steven has quite a few clothes, so I'll just send a duffle bag full of disposable diapers! Stephen has a pink girl's coat that should fit him & there is a grey coat & hat for John, a tan one for David. I'll have to buy only one, for Paul, and flannel pajamas for K.P.& D. Anything else you must let me know quickly.

Now, boys, Mommie is real lonesome for you and grandma, too. We are praying you can come soon.

Love, Mommie X X X X

PS: I am sending balloons & toy for Joseph, too.

For Ione's birthday, Hector wrote on 11th August:

HAPPY BIRTHDAY!!! <u>Mummie</u>

Dear Ione: X

I'll take a few minutes now to write while David & John are having a sleep before dinner & Marcellyn is teaching the other two. It is just starting to rain a little, having been cloudy all morning.

We've finished the book of Acts in family worship & we all enjoyed it. Paul keeps praying for you that the airplane won't fall down. He can't understand that you arrived <u>Kalakala</u> [a long time ago]. Stephen has 6 teeth & 2 more just about thru! He's sleeping much better now. Everybody loves him to pieces. I try to tell him how tight mummy is going to squeeze him when she sees him again. I guess by his chuckle, he understands!!

.....We are getting along as well as could be expected from an amputated family.

Love,   Hector

Hector, again wrote to Ione on the 18th of August:

Beloved Ione:

Were we ever glad to get those two letters last Friday. I think I have read them so often I could repeat all you said. You have had good attention. Those blood transfusions must have been a big help to you. We will be looking forward to your letter telling about your birthday.

We got the package from Mrs. Smith, Imlay City. She had gotten together four little outfits all the same and right to size. They will be nice for arriving in. She also put in 5 T shirts. Three nice books have kept the children amused; a wooden train for John and a racer car for David. She had made a beautiful quilt of colored corduroy patches. I used it on David yesterday when he had fever. I've written to thank her. The other package was from United Press Church of Drayton Plains. Ever so many little shorts and shirts, a dress for you, some slips; a few diapers, a nice little coat and cap for John. So, don't spend too much money sending things out airmail.

I figure it will cost $2170 for our trip to N.Y. It seems a terrible amount of money and we can only trust the Lord to send it in when He knows we should go.

I hope you can make out the children's letters (see below).

Well, the time has slipped away. Joe is just about finished getting the children dressed after their bath. He's a good little soldier.

Sometimes I don't know what's wrong with me; but there is a sweetheart far away who could supply the answers. Kenny has put in a good quota of kisses, so I'll have mine before and after his.

At the modified merry-go-round are (clockwise) Ken (in front), John, Joe Dhansis, Steve (in crib), Paul and David.

So long for now and write us often. All our love all the time. Hector X

The boys all added their greetings and news:

This is David: Dear Mommie: X

I'm sitting here on Daddy's lap and want to tell you how much I love you. I was sick with a little bit of fever yesterday but am alright today. I pray for my Mommie every day and hope the Lord will take care of her. I like to sing, "His Yoke is Easy..." I'm waiting to give you a big hug when we get to where you are. Bye Bye for now, David Lynn

This is John: Dear darling Mommy: X

I'm getting bigger every day. Yesterday I prayed for the first time, remembering especially my mommie. All my love, John

This is Paul: Dear Mommie: X

First, I want to tell you that I love you with all my heart. We received some nice things in two packages this week. I'm so shy that when Daddy asks me what I want to say next, I just lick my lower lip. David is sharing with John. Auntie Marcellyn taught us a song in school the other day. That first letter you sent from Leo I put it under my pillow the first night. Love, Paul

This is Kenneth: Dearest Mommie: X

Thank you for the nice letters. We are glad you are feeling better. About those donkeys running away and then the other part about Saul and about the heart. Samuel told Saul about his heart after the servant went on ahead. Did you have a good time in the airplane? What did you have for your birthday? I love you very much. When I come where you are I'm going to give you 12 kisses. (after Daddy gets finished!!!) Auntie Marcellyn is teaching us nice French school. And feeding us French fried potatoes & French toast, etc. Much Love, Kenneth

Despite convalescing from her ordeal, Ione cannot really relax until she has her family with her. On the 20th of August she wrote:

Dearest Daddy, Auntie Marcellyn and Boys,

Now I can write more as I am using Auntie Marcellyn's typewriter. You must take my big typewriter down to your house to use. I do hope you are not getting too tired, Marcellyn. I hope it will be very soon when the family can come home and you will be relieved of your big job.

Hector, I think unless you hear from Pudneys by the time you get this letter, it is for you to write to them and tell them when you want to leave. A letter written August 15 from Ma Pudu says, "We shall be awaiting news from Hector concerning the coming of the rest of the family." If you have not written to High Park and others, perhaps they will, in order to gather in as much as possible for the journey. I should think you will need about $2400. Has there been anything said about Marcellyn's helping you to get them home or is there a furlough of somebody else near? From all I can tell there is no one here who expects anything else but that you come home immediately (be <u>sure</u> *you have someone* <u>all</u> *the way.). So, if that is the plan, I will send these three small duffle bags of air clothes (they can wear everyday clothes to Stan & leave them to be taken back to Bong.) by Airmail so that you will get them. I will try to find a pair of brown trousers for Daddy, in case the waistband of his good suit is too tight. No doubt it is by now, with all of the good cooking Auntie Marcellyn is doing!*

And now for the plan: the Lord has shown me that I must not try to pry too far into His future plans for us. But what seems best for the immediate future is that you go straight to Montreal, put yourself in the hands of your capable sisters for a few days to get adjusted, then with one or two accompanying you, proceed to Dunnville, it would be best by car if possible. Stay there long enough to get the children rested up and checked for colds, etc., then try to drive them all here. The apartment is big enough for us all to be here if Kenny and Paul sleep next door at Auntie Lucille's, eat breakfast there and come here for the other meals. This arrangement will be all right for a few weeks; then if no better arrangement can be found, Daddy would take the three smallest back to Alice's at Dunnville [a city between Toronto and Hamilton] *for a few more weeks. Neither Mother nor Lucille can physically cope with the task of all the children for any long period of time. Let us not talk of future plans beyond that. I am thinking much and praying much, but a lot can be decided when we have a few weeks together. Just remember, Hector, in your many thoughts about it, that I love the States very much and I do want Mother to be near us.*

.....Lovingly, Mommie

Hector wrote to Ione from the Baptist Mission Society's guest house in Stanleyville on the 26th of August with an update on travel plans:

My own Beloved Ione:

.....I visited A.M.I. & Sabena today; we can leave here on a Tuesday at 1 p.m. & be in Montreal Thursday at 1:15 p.m. for the sum of 82,620 francs or $1650. This is much cheaper than I figured since it's possible to take John <u>as well as</u> *Stephen on the 1/10 fares. Normally they only allow one if there are two under 2 yrs of age. But with another adult along, they (the adult) merely have to sign a*

paper saying they will care for the second child. Kinso is writing to ask about Mable Wenger. She could take a train from Montreal to Lancaster, Pa.

After a day or two on the farm or in Montreal we could take a bedroom suite for the overnight trip to Toronto (6 hours) & Alice could meet us there.

The only catch now is that we will have to go before John's birthday. Am enclosing some negatives & snaps. Aren't our boys cute ! ! !

The doctor here says we should be able to get vaccination & yellow fever at Banalia. That saves a long trip here to Stan.

.....If I were easily moved to tears, I surely would have used ½ dozen hankies on Tuesday when I got here to Stanleyville. I went to the Post Office in great anticipation & found a letter from you to the Kinsos (sent Aug 19) but nothing for Ione's husband. Maybe tomorrow. If not, I'll just wait here in Stan until I do get <u>one</u> ! ! !

.....Our boys still love that Mechano Set. Family worship in I Samuel has been good. Continue to spend much time in prayer. It helps so much at this end.

Your lover   Hector   X

Would the McMillans have to retire from the mission field because of Ione's health? If so, this would echo what happened to the Pudneys and the Westcotts before her. Discussions of this issue became more apparent in the next letter to Hector and the boys (to whom she wrote individually) written on the 28th of August:

Dear Kenny,   Your letter came today. When you send letters on Thursday night, they arrive here Friday the following week - just ten days. I am beginning to watch for letters on Fridays. One came last week, too. Yes, I had a good time on the plane, and I think you will, too. But you must help Daddy take care of John. There is a little plastic harness [and leash] in the duffle bag for when he gets in and out of the plane. For my birthday we had hamburgers, fried over a fire outside and ice cream and a cherry cake. I received a nice bed jacket, some underwear. Also, money from several ladies in Pontiac. I'm glad you remembered the story about Saul and the donkeys. You must remember as many as you can and tell me more in your next letter. I shall look forward to the kisses. Lovingly, Mommie

Dear Paul, Thank you for your nice letter. I'm glad you kept my first one under your pillow. I would like to see the clothes you received in the packages. You must save them to wear when you come to Mommie. I want to hear your French song, too. Tell Auntie Marcellyn to keep teaching you lots of things in French. Mommie is going to collect lots of kisses when she sees her little boys again. I am getting so fat that you may not know me! I don't think it will be very many more weeks before we are together. Lovingly, Mommie

Dear David, I got your letter and your kiss. I'm sorry you were sick, but glad you soon were all right. You must remember the nice new songs you are learning. But don't forget "His Yoke is Easy," and "Hark Tis the Shepherd's Voice I Hear." Keep sharing with John, and be a good boy. Lovingly, Mommie

Dear John, I'm glad to know you prayed in family worship. Please don't forget about Mommie. I wonder if you will remember her when you see her again. I am wondering if you will be sick after your yellow fever injection. Mommie is praying much for you, and I have a lovely soft little bed for you to sleep in when you come here, right beside Mommie. I don't believe I'll ever let you go again. Be a good boy like David is. Lovingly, Mommie

Dear Stephen, I am wondering if your six teeth are all the way thru now. I know all of your brothers love you a lot and try to help Auntie Marcellyn take care of you. You are a precious little fellow. Mommie has lots of kisses saved up for all of her boys. Lovingly, Mommie

Dear Hector, I'm not sure I acknowledged your birthday letter, for I think I wrote you a few days before your letter came. I was glad to know that you were planning to take John & Stephen to Stan for yellow fever shots. Your Aug. 18 letter didn't mention that you had gone so I guess Miss Ogilvie hadn't arrived yet by then. I know you will remember to watch them carefully after the shots for signs of convulsions. Remember both other times?

.....I received a letter from Mrs. Pudney today. She spoke about the advisability of our having no more children after this one and then said,

Mr P. asked me to write to you in his absence but definite decisions have not yet been made. We feel however that Hector should come home with the children and that you should be established by yourselves as a family unit. Just what provision you have in mind, we do not know. It would be too much to expect to live with relatives, but of course that decision must be your own and no doubt will depend upon your circumstances.

We must have some indication of funds and you will be praying with us I know. You have not been out long enough to accumulate furlough funds sufficient for these expenses but we are looking for special gifts for you and we know that the Lord is able.

.....The Lord has wonderfully supplied every need thus far, and I have not taken even my salary from Philadelphia, as I want it to go to you. I believe the Lord will give us a home where children can play; with a garden; some livestock and pets; shade trees & fruit trees; airy, cheerful rooms; warm in winter; modern conveniences; near stores, church, school; ample bedroom space, rooms for Mother, etc. And someone to come in & help with the work. I believe He will do it, Hector.

And another thing, unless I have any more trouble with my heart, I don't see why we cannot go on planning to return to the field, and then it will be up to the Lord to close the door if He desires. We must come to some decision in our own hearts even before the mission tell us. I have recently renewed my covenant with Him, and believe in my own heart that the only safe and contented life we can live in these uncertain days is to stay very close to what we <u>know</u> <u>now</u> is His will.

If we can be counted as missionaries on furlough, I will be content to stay with the children and let you do all the deputizing that you can. If I have someone to help me, and Mother in and out, I'm sure I can manage. You must be free to go as much as you wish.

I heard Mr Maxwell last Tuesday & talked to him (Flint). He was surprised to know about us. It was his message on "Ye did run well, what did hinder you?" that spoke to me, and made me sure that if I had a proper home I could give you up for meetings! All for now.

Lovingly, Ione X

PS: *I helped Grandma can 1 bushel of peaches today! We're going to do pears and pickles, too!*

Ione's next letter to Hector on September 3rd, illustrated the turmoil that was her life – she thought she had a problem resolved only to find it wasn't, yet she tried to remain upbeat:

Dearest Hector and Children,

.....I believe the Lord will make it possible for you to come before John's birthday and thus pay the smaller fare. We may be paying back the General Fund for a while, but that is all right. You should come as soon as possible.

This week's mail bro't the letter from Alice I had been waiting for and altho' it hurt me a little, I could see the Lord's hand in it all. I wanted to give your sisters opportunity to help if they felt they could, and that we have done. But Alice had just come from visiting the others, and they came to the conclusion that we should choose one of two things: either separating the younger children in various directions, or you staying on the field until after our next baby comes. Alice says it is absolutely out of the question for her to help you with the children except as you pass thru! She wrote in love but was very definite, which makes me to know that the Lord has a better way.

Having much time to spend with Him, things are coming to me more clearly now. "And the angel of the Lord went further, and stood in a narrow place, there was no way to turn either to the right hand or to the left." Num. 22:26. The Lord led Israel out of the usual way till He got them to the Red Sea. Then there was room for His power to be manifested.

..... "So the Lord alone did lead him, and there was no strange god with him." Deut.32:12

The fellowship with Him has been priceless. I will give you my "impressions" after seeking Him about returning to Africa:

I cannot go far in my reasoning without being convinced that the Lord will give me health to go back.

The children are safer in Africa in the will of God, than at home and outside of His will.

For Hector, the "best" he can do is all out there.

Therefore, why not proceed with the plan of returning unless He leads definitely otherwise?

The only safe and contented life we can live in these uncertain days is to stay very close to what we know now is His will.

I felt I could make no plans for us until Mother was settled. Then the need became apparent in my mind for a place for us during what seemed to be evident - a furlough of about two years. Mrs. Pudney's August 26 letter said, "We feel that Hector should come home...and that you should be established by yourselves as a family unit."

Well, I wrote about this in my last letter to you, but since Alice's letter it is quite evident to me that He would have us go to our own place immediately when you come. And I will be strong enough I know. You will see, Hector. The Lord has already done wonderful things for me physically. I only feel that in order to free you for meetings right away. I should be as near as possible to Mother and Lucille. They are whole-heartedly in agreement with me, and will help even more than I tho't they could. If you think it's all right, I can start accepting engagements for you around here. I will not take any meetings for me, tho'. I must be present at a welcome service at 1st Baptist Church on September 23. I will be able to take care of the children if I have a convenient house. The thing I am asking Him about right now is whether to rent or to buy. I asked Him for a token of a gift of money the day we looked at a house near here, and that evening $10 was handed me from an unexpected source and we had a visit from the pastor of Lake Orion Baptist Church and they have already started sending $25 per month instead of the $10. This is not much but a definite "token" that He will supply our many needs. Do not be alarmed at the prospects of a big debt, for I will not take a step without your consent, and I do not feel we should borrow. But I will find a place where we can live, so that you'll come here as directly as possible.

All for now.   Love, Ione

Two days later, and Ione was mothering from a distance when writing to Hector:

.....It's hardly light yet, but I wanted to write a note. I wakened suddenly hearing John crying and found it was only a rooster crowing! I tho't I would remind you of a few things. Marcellyn says the children have colds, and I'm afraid they're not getting the proper care. They didn't have colds when I became sick and I think it was because I was careful to see that they never had baths after 5 o'clock. And they should have sweaters on these cold rainy days the first thing in the morning and in the early evening. But be <u>sure</u> to remember to <u>take them off</u> at breakfast time or as soon as it starts to get hot. Another thing, were those thin pajamas all put away? I think I asked Marcellyn to do that. There should be <u>no pajamas</u> on their shelves except <u>flannel</u> ones, and even <u>they</u> are not enough. The children <u>must</u> be kept <u>covered at night</u>. Oh, please, Hector, if I could be sure you were doing this. Penicillin doesn't do much good if they aren't cared for enough at night. I trust you to check all you are doing and see where you can improve your routine. And don't let their little bare feet go trolling around early in the morning on the cold cement. Please, please, Hector, give me some small assurance about this! I find it increasingly hard to keep on in this separated way. Do try to get them over their colds before they start on that long journey.

351

Don't be surprised, if you find me at the coast when you arrive!

Much, Much love, Ione

Fortunately, Hector understood Ione enough and loved her well enough to know the criticism was out of frustration. He responded on the 6th of September:

Dearest Mommie:

I feel just like writing three sentences.

How about a love letter.

To me.

Every week.

There surely was an awful hole in my heart when I opened the mail sack last Friday and found no letter from you. And the one to me last week didn't even have a kiss!!! Don't I feel sorry for myself??? But I hope it will help you to know that I love you with all of my heart. I know you are concerned about the family and find the time long without them. But it shouldn't be for long now. You just keep on having a good rest and getting closer to the Lord so that I will know the same sweet Ione that left us five weeks ago. There is no one else like you in all the world, so please don't change except for the better, if that's possible. I may be a bit different but it will mainly be a deeper appreciation for you.

.....Kinsos and Carters discussed our going home and suggested Marcellyn stop off in Belgium (in case Mabel Wenger can't go). We could book thru to London by Sabena and then Marcellyn could see us off for Montreal by Trans Canada Airline. However, I'm still hoping that Mabel can come. We will have up until Oct 13th. I have half a mind to ask Kinso to book us for that date. We have to have our injections and yellow fever yet and we wouldn't want to travel until we were sure the children wouldn't be sick from the shots. It would give us more time to get the money together as well.

.....Well Mommie dear I'll close for now. Keep praying and writing and loving and waiting.

Your OWN   Hector XXXXXX One for every day until next letter.

Ione's spirits were soon revived and on the 9th of September, she accompanied her mother to the First Baptist Church in Pontiac, home of the Loyals, her wonderful supporters. Ione was given the opportunity to speak to the Sunday school and she shared her need for a home. The Westcotts were present and took her back to their home for dinner and Ione got to meet Anne again who was studying music.

Ione wrote on the 10th to Hector with acknowledgement of his good news and added more good news:

I just received your two Stan. Letters August 31 & September 1, and in the same mail as Jean's letter telling about your inheritance from Uncle Alex. I have written to Jean, and told her you may need to use it to come home. I also informed Mr Pudney.

Then last evening the pastor and deacon of Lake Orion 1st Baptist called and presented me with a check for $1,000!! To be used for a house for us, or for *anything else we wish. I expect to deposit it in the bank here, unless you will need it to come home.*

Knowing that it is here, you will not need to delay your coming because of money. However, don't attempt to do any of the journey without help, not even the few hours from Montreal to Toronto. And don't leave until you let me know, for I will do everything in my power to meet you in Montreal.

Much, much love,   Ione

Hector was heartened by Ione's letter; he wrote on the 13th of September:

My dear DARLING IONE. xXxXxXxXxXxXxX etc.

"Many daughters have done virtuously, but thou excellest them all." xxx
"The heart of her husband doth safely trust in her." XXXX.

Now does that make you happy you old sweetheart ! ! ! ! I could hug and kiss you for an hour.

......As I have been thinking things over, I wonder if we could arrange to live there if the house [in Avonmore] *hasn't been sold already. It is off the main street, has a garden (some livestock if you like, maybe a pony in the little barn), shade trees and fruit trees, three bedrooms upstairs, and the living room could be made into one for you and the baby, indoor bath room and water pressure, electricity, Bruce Wert's store the Presbyterian Church and the school quite near (+ being rent-free). Think it over and pray about it, beloved. I told Jean I was writing you about it.*

.....Well, my lover bye-bye for now.

All my love, Hector   X

PS: 9:00 p.m. The service was very good and we had communion this evening. While talking to Mr Harris afterwards I mentioned what a privilege it was to work with the Kinsos. He said, "That's allright brother, they think quite a lot of you too, so it's mutual." It's nice to be appreciated isn't it?   More love,   XXX Hector

Now that Hector had the money and travelling companion to help with the children, on the 14th of September he wasted no time organizing his trip and wrote to the travel agent in Stanleyville:

.....I would now like to make tentative bookings for the SABENA plane Stanleyville -London leaving Oct 13th. Then the best connections TCA, London – Montreal.

The following is the list of passengers:
Miss Mabel Wenger
Mr Hector McMillan
Kenneth (6)
Paul (5)
David (3)
John (1)
Stephen (9 mos)

I believe you suggested that the second youngest could also go for 1/10th fare.
We would very much appreciate this if it could be arranged.

Ione was very thankful that the Lord had guided her and supplied her needs, she explained all that had happened in her thank you letter to Lake Orion First Baptist Church on the 15th:

Dear Friends in Christ,

It has been a pleasure for many years to know your church was interested in us. But from the time I arrived in this country on August 1st, it seemed the Lord had given you a special burden for our needs for there, waiting in Philadelphia, was a large check to meet my immediate expenses. Then, after resting several weeks, I began to feel that I would be well enough to take care of my children again, if I only had a place to go with them. It was then that I was led to read this verse:

Psalm 84:3 – "Yea the sparrow hath found an house, and the swallow a nest for herself where she may lay her young...." Also Psalm 84:11 – "No good thing will He withhold from them that walk uprightly."

So, Mother and I began to pray for a house, and being assured also by Psalm 81:16 – "He should have fed them also with the finest of the wheat," we were led to pray for a good house and one large enough for five little boys. I even listed fifteen points that seemed to be necessary for such a house!

But we had nothing to start with, and asked him for just a little token that it was His good pleasure to provide a place by the time our little ones and their father arrived from Africa. The same day a ten-dollar bill was put into my hands very unexpectedly, and that evening your pastor and head deacon called. Of course, it was fresh in our hearts and on our lips that the Lord would provide a home. And then they left, and it seemed as though we were not alone in our desires about this.

Days passed, and we had little more to assure us than Deuteronomy 28:12, "The Lord shall open unto thee His good treasure."

When last Friday your pastor and deacon called again, it was to present the check for $1,000.00. So, you see "His good treasure" has been opened, and you dear friends have been the blessed instruments of His divine provision for us. Thank you very, very much for your exceeding kindness and for your confidence to put in our stewardship such a large amount. I trust we shall not disappoint you in the way in which we shall account for it. It is safe at present in the savings bank until we shall see the house which the Lord would have us take.

.....May the Lord bless you all is my prayer.

Very Lovingly in Christ,   Ione McMillan

Ione maintained her long-distance mothering and the letter dated 23rd of September is full of instructions for Hector:

.....I realize that you will receive only two more mails before you leave, so want to give some last-minute instructions. Don't forget there's a harness for John if needed (I hope the 3 duffle bags arrived!) and it may be quite cold before the

journey is finished, especially in Belgium. The children will each need a sweater as well as a coat at all times, that is, handy to put on if both are needed. I have been wearing a winter coat. There are sweaters in a laundry bag in the green cupboard in our room; also, in the plastic bag in the baby's room. The coat for Stephen is a pink little girl's coat [!] and I think it was either in a suitcase or a trunk. Don't forget your black overcoat, Hector, and try to get a decent hat in Stan. But it will need to be brown if you have brown shoes and suit. You have a brown sweater that you could wear under your suit coat if you're cold. Take as many warm things as you can with you, and any other clothes can come freight with the household things. Don't be afraid to change the children's clothes on the way, for I will have fresh things for them to put on when I meet you.

And don't stint on taking things for them to eat, as you know how there will be little on the plane for children to eat. They should have on hand all the way, some fruit, sandwiches or cookies, and something to drink. There will be nothing but carbonated water all the way, so you will need boiled water. Could you fix that round metal water bottle so it doesn't leak, and replenish it whenever you can? I don't think you should take any smaller amount of Klim than a 5 lb. tin. The bigger boys will probably enjoy the fresh milk right away, but Stephen & John may object. How is Stephen fixed for baby bottles? I hope you've been able to get some, so he won't have to use syrup bottles!! Be sure the nipple holes are O.K. and keep them clean!!

Now if the boys are well fed, and not too hot or cold, and their clothes are not too tight, they should be able to sleep in their seats. If they're restless it's probably because the rubber is too tight around the waists and if you are sick, Hector, be sure their seat belts are fastened before you lie down. Get some Dramamine. I found it such a help, just a half tablet at a time or else you'll get too drowsy, about a half hour before you expect to be sick.

I believe you'll do your best, and I have confidence in you. I love you so much and am just living for the day we'll be together again. I want you close and don't want to be parted from you again. One more letter to you, and then I'll see you.

Lovingly, Ione   X

In her final letter to Hector before his return, she reiterated some of her travel and housing concerns:

.....There was no drinking water on the plane except carbonated. I think they changed planes another time before Brussels, so you'll have to find out where so that you can get the hand baggage assembled in time. If you don't change you just get off with the children for a little while and leave the baggage on. I'd like to know ahead of time if you have the reservation for sure, as I don't want to get Herb Boyes to drive to Montreal a week ahead of time. And I'd like a cable sent to Irene's or Florence's when you leave. Florence has asked me to stay there. I think we'll stay one night at Montreal, and then a night at Avonmore. That should not hold her up too much.

Hector, I can see that Uncle Alex's house would surely suit us, I tho't of it even before you wrote. But it's not just a <u>house</u> we need. We will need to be near the doctor and hospital at Ypsilanti, as well as Mother and Lucille, for some time yet. You see, there's two operations after the baby comes. We will talk about it, and pray together about it when you come. I am trying to arrange with the sisters at Montreal some sleeping arrangements that first night so that we can be together with the children. Then we can talk and pray before we go on to Avonmore.

I am getting so anxious to see you. It just doesn't seem possible that I can wait a few more weeks. It will be so nice to be a normal family again. I'm glad to have all this rest, but now I'll be restless until you come. I know I'll have to be careful when there will be so much to do, but maybe you will remind me about lifting heavy things, reaching too high, and staying on my feet too long, just the usual precautions before a baby comes, plus special tho't when there's a little pain in the heart. Dr. says I may have these pains for about a year, but they may never lead to an attack if I am careful.

This morning I visited the school where Kenny and Paul will probably go. The principal thinks Kenny will go in the first grade and Paul in Kindergarden. If you tell them this explain that they will just go for a little while each day and will eat and sleep at home. I think Kenny has a little fear he may be sent away to school like Rethy. Tell him Mommie will go with him. They are using Sally, Dick & Jane stories in the 1ˢᵗ grade and Kenny already knows some of these.

Love, Ione XXXXX

Once again, Ione had faced her challenges and come through bolstered and supported by her faith and continued belief in the Lord's goodness for her. If Hector was tested through illness a few years earlier, this was now Ione's turn.

Chapter 14
FORCED FURLOUGH / SETTING UP THE CHILDREN'S HOME

Due to a severe heart condition and pregnancy, Ione returned to America in July, 1953. She lived with her mother in an apartment in Fenton, Michigan. This meant she was close to her sister Lucille, thus having two very good support networks. She was also near to her supporting church based in Pontiac and equidistant to Dr Westcott and family.

Ione, with family while recovering from her heart illness - Fall 1953

Once Hector joined her in October, the family set up in their own house, so as not to overcrowd Grandma Reed.

Timothy George McMillan was born on 6th February, 1954. There are few letters giving details of the birth, much as it was when David Lynn was born.

.....Hector wrote to Mr Pudney on the 8th of February:

.....*The pastorate here in Fenton have been giving me $50.00 per week. This should take care of our rent and heat. From now on the office should be able to keep back all the gifts which come in, sending Ione's and the children's support, and mine from Peoples Church. The cost of living is still quite high, but we have a fair supply of goods*

Ione with a happy Timothy George

ahead now. I imagine I will be able to take some outside meetings when Ione is a little stronger. Just this week I have filled out the form for clearing that $500 that my uncle left. I am enjoying having this opportunity of being a pastor. The Sunday congregation is growing and folks seem eager for Bible teaching.

I trust you received the telegram about our new boy. Ione had a fairly easy time but had a little setback when they allowed her to get up the next day. They are so crowded that they like to have them go home in two or three days, so they encourage them to get around. The little lad is real cute, something like David. He weighed 8.8 lbs.
.....*Yours in Christ, Hector*

Also, in February, the Pudneys sent out a newsletter which included an account of UFM's growth and the need to move the headquarters from 1150 N 63rd St in Philadelphia to a more suitable property located in Bala Cynwyd, a township just outside of Philadelphia:

.....The advance of the U.F.M. during the past 10 years has been most gratifying. New fields have been occupied in Haiti, Dominican Republic, British Guiana, and Dutch New Guinea, in addition to extending our activities in Papua, Belgian Congo, and Brazil. We now total 240 missionaries with many others soon to join them. Records show 360 churches, 100-day schools, 5 Bible schools, 5 boarding schools, 4 hospitals, printing press and an estimated 40,000 converts. To God be the glory, very literally our cords have been lengthened; but, what of strengthening the stakes! Future possibilities are unlimited. To be scriptural this must also be considered.

Hector wrote to the Pudneys once again on June 11:

Dear Mr Pudney:

Thank you for your letter and the allowance.

.....I'm sorry not to have written sooner, but the questions of the pastorate was a bit uncertain right up until the first of June.[99] Wednesday evening, they had a nice farewell service for me. They were most appreciative of the Lord's blessing through our ministry and I too want to thank the Lord for the very profitable time spent with them. The missionary conference was very worthwhile and may mean something in the future for John Stevenson. He plans to spend some time visiting various pastors in the area.

On the allowance slip Ione's service support seems to have been mentioned twice. In regards to finances, I believe we will need a little more for this month if any has come in. One extra item is the parts I have had sent out for the Bongondza lighting plant, amounting to $40. I understand that Alf Walby[100] has received the parcel, but when I ordered them for him, I told the Company in Wisconsin that I would settle the bill.

The doctor has given Ione quite an encouraging report. She had her medical examination [for her insurance] this past week and it was satisfactory. She has to go back in two weeks and maybe one month after that again to check on any adhesions, due to the recent operation.

We trust you will have a blessed time on Saturday at the dedication.

Yours in Christ, Hector & Ione

---

[99] It would appear that a church in Fenton was without a Pastor when the McMillans turned up, so they paid him $50 dollars a month to undertake pastoral duties while the church debated their next move. Hector, seeing the money as a useful stopgap, does not seem too disappointed that another minister is found and he is relieved of his pastoral duties – he can now focus more on missionary deputation work.

[100] The Walbys moved from Maganga to Bongondza to assume the responsibilities left by Hector and Ione.

The McMillans moved from Fenton to Newington, Ontario, located near Hector's family and on the 12th of September, Ione wrote to her mother:

.....Jean bro't in roast veal and gravy and potatoes, fresh vegetables and baked goods almost every day. She bro't salmon loaf yesterday. The children have been having fun exploring in the barn and all around the place. The big electric train was the biggest attraction the day the truck came. I wish Mrs. Dickenson could know how much I appreciated having it for them just now. It gave them a central interest while we made their surroundings normal.

Kenny & Paul like their school. It is a 3-room brick, quite modern, with the 1st & 2nd grades in one room, and the teacher said K & P could sit together for

a while. She starts & finishes the day with prayer & reads the Bible to them.

I had some nice talks with Barbara about the things of the Lord.

I am feeling fine and getting over the tiredness of our busy time.

Lovingly, Ione

Two weeks later, Ione wrote again to her Mother and Lucille as she had not heard from them:

.....I haven't heard a word from you since our arrival twenty-six days ago, and I am wondering if you have written to the wrong town! Did you get my letter? I am wondering how you are and what everyone's doing.

.....I have been amazed at the pep I have had here, and just at the time I need it to get things systematically going. I certainly appreciate all the help I had all last year, to get me back on my feet. It was so good to know that I had my

Ione with her six sons, Fenton, Michigan - 1954

Mother and sister right there to step in. And by doing a little bit more all along, I gained strength. I think I must weigh about 145 now, and I feel so good. Our food is simple here but good and plentiful. We have enuf potatoes for nearly all winter, a big box of carrots sanded down, a bushel of apples, tomatoes, cabbages, turnips, eggs, etc. You can get a chicken for 50¢ and eggs are 22¢ but I had 3 doz. given to us last week. We are not out in the country anymore really than in Fenton, but it seems more open as there are not the bushes, there are shade trees and fruit trees, too, and we get a strong wind which makes the diapers fluffy and the cheeks pink.

.....Hector has been helping Archie and some of the other farmers do their threshing this week, and has had many opportunities to witness. Did I tell you Hector drives to Avonmore school mornings for 1-1/2 hours and again in the

afternoon? We are so thankful to have a car to use. The few days we were without
it were hard, but Archie let Hector have his car when he could.

I have been finding it a real joy to sing at my work, and I can sing <u>*loud*</u> *as we*
have no near neighbours as in Fenton! I remember years ago asking the Lord to
bless my voice, and he did so that I could sing with the Trio. But now I am asking
him to give me a song. There is quite a difference. "He took me out of the pit ---
set my feet on a rock...He put a song <u>*in my heart*</u>*." The latest song- "I Stand*
Amazed in the Presence of Jesus the Nazarene." Kenny sings the tenor.

All for now. Please write. The children have adjusted themselves quickly, but
they are not forgetting you.

With loads of love, Ione   XXXXXXX

During October, Hector and Ione wrote a newsletter summarising their recent
activities, explaining why the sudden rush back to the States but also reassuring
everyone that Ione had made a good recovery. Dr Westcott suggested that the family
count the first few weeks as 'sick leave' thus giving the family an extended furlough
in which to fully recover. However, it is evident that the family would like to return
to Congo but this time they had a wish list that included a car.

Planning to return to Congo meant Ione was accommodating meetings to spread
the word, and she told her mother that she had a date at the United Reform Church
to speak at their morning service. Being in Canada meant Hector's niece Florence,
could help Ione with childcare and the other bonus was the supply of food. When a
pig was killed, they got steaks and a soup bone. Ione wrote to her mother in
November:

.....I have learned to milk the cow. She had a nice little girl calf. Which we sold
for $20. Bread is delivered 3 times a week, also cookies, etc. Don't worry. Come
and see for yourself! I weigh 133 lbs. Lovingly, Ione

This letter although short, indicates that there were family matters worrying Ione;
her Aunt Kate had died, so one reason for writing was to send her mother money to
cover flowers that were bought. Money remained a major preoccupation. Ione was
mindful that in getting Marcellyn out to Africa and all the family back, there was
still money owed to the Mission.

As ever, Ione's letters to her mother sought to reassure that the family were well:

.....They all have warm clothes, as well as leggings and boots. We received two
parcels from ladies at Toronto of overalls and flannel-lined jeans, etc. We're
destitute for sox right now but by washing them when we do the baby diapers
they manage with about two pairs apiece. Stephen's snowsuit fits Timmie now
and Stephen can wear the dark blue heavy coat that John wore for good last
winter. I hate to have him wear it for every day, but it's all he has and it is easy
for me to put on. He doesn't go many places and I hope it'll not be too dirty when
I want to take him to church in it.

Ione's management skills were made evident in the next sentence:

.....I have the summer things packed away in tea towels marked with their
initials, so there won't be so much sorting in the spring, I hope!

.....and ended with a touch of humor:

.....The children's school teacher is Miss Dickey and you would have laughed the first few days. They came home calling her Miss 'Stickey' and the boy that impressed them the most was someone whose name sounded like 'Magooey'. Rather a gummy bunch! Now they've got it straightened out; the boy's name is 'MacQuay'. Our telephone is just as unprivate [a shared line] *as the one at Fenton was private. There are no private lines right here, and we have all the rings and combinations from 1 to 6. I was talking to our neighbour one day and a rooster crowed over the wire. I asked if she had a rooster and she replied No, but did I? Then we both laughed and she said, "I'll bet that one'll get his head chopped off for dinner!" We nearly always hear someone lift up the receiver when we start to talk! But when Hector and I talk we speak in Bangala!*

All for now. I am feeling grand.

Love, Ione

Christmas at Newington, Ontario – 1954.

In a letter written on December 18, Ione wrote:

.....I am going to miss you all this Christmas, but will be thinking of you all together there with Lucille. I think we will go to Montreal to Irene's unless they decide to come to the farm with Jean. I have let them decide. Jean has the house decorated beautifully. Our house is going to be pretty, too, with the tree on the end of the train table.

Loads of love, Ione

As one year ends and another starts, Ione's letters began with 'thank yous' but it is clear her eyes were fixed on future horizons:

Dearest Mother,

The packages of books for us all came and I want to thank you ever so much. That large number of books must have cost a lot, but it surely does add considerably to our small library. The children's books are so well chosen for their ages. I am helping Kenny a little with the one to be filled in, but he does well to find a lot of the Bible references. He can read quite well now. Hector & I enjoy ours a lot, too. The one by Mrs. Aldrich I have wanted for some time as I follow her "Mixing Bowl" in Moody Monthly. The "Thoughts for the Quiet Hour" are excellent.

.....I hope Marcellyn had a real Happy Birthday. I want to hear all about it. Stephen was honoured at a birthday dinner at Aunt Jean's. It was fun watching him blow out the candles. We spent Christmas Day there and she served a lovely turkey dinner. Alice called long distance and she and Claude talked to us

"conference style" as they have an upstairs phone. Irene was there with her two and we went for a sleigh ride sitting on bales of hay.

.....Pray especially for us as we speak at a local church here next Sun. Jan. 9th. I spoke once in the Sunday school Rally Day and now they have asked us to take the evening service.

Timmie can sit himself up, flop over, get on his knees, and stand with a little help. No colds, and I don't know how to account for it as I keep forgetting to give them their Vitamin C capsules!

We are thinking that when we leave here, we will store a minimum of household things so that we'll have something to have immediately upon arrival next furlough – the heavy furniture and some of the dishes. If we don't have a "Happy Furlough House" we'll at least have "Happy Furlough Furnishings"!!

Love, Ione

She mused as to when she may get to see her youngest sister Doris. While in Africa, Ione had no opportunity to see her family, yet once in America/Canada, it seemed incredibly difficult to touch base with each other.

Another concern for her was the state of some churches and the differences and changes in them; in an earlier letter to her mother, she wrote:

.....There is a really fundamental preacher in the Presbyterian Church at Finch, near here, and we were all there this morning. There is nothing in Avonmore and the Wesleyan Methodist here seems fundamental, but a bit shallow & noisy. I have agreed to give a 15-minute message in their Rally Day Sunday School next Sunday. We'll all go there then. This area is a real mission field. I have had some talks with my nearest neighbour, Mrs. Duval, who has two children who go to school here. They are United Church, but no family worship, no Gospel message, children unaccustomed to anything but rituals of church.

Ione returned to this theme in a letter to her mother on January 8:

.....Tomorrow we have charge of the service in the Wesleyan Methodist Church here, the only fundamental group, and they don't dig very deep for real spiritual food. Cornwall has a spiritual Baptist Church, tiny and in need of our encouragement, but not much deep teaching there either. Ottawa is the nearest, I guess. This week Hector got into a Bible study group in a home which was excellent, taught by a lawyer, who came out of the United Church. He asked his pastor several times to conduct a study of this kind but he did not even care to have a mid-week prayer service. Hector hopes to be able to bring him or another teacher like him, to a nucleus of believers in the community. I have spoken in some pretty dead churches, but I praise the Lord for opportunity to present a Gospel message.

All for now. Love, Ione

Ione's next letter to Leone on the 14th of March concentrated on the next big move back to Congo. She kept her heart in the attitude of expectancy - ready, and looking to Him for each step:

.....*"My soul, wait thou only upon God, for my expectation is from Him."* [Having] *learned a few little signs and tokens to go by, from the Word, and circumstances, etc., I think He will show me ways to simplify the ordeal.*

One thing I know, it will not be useful to [pack up] *a tremendous amount of equipment here, of course, any offers of help will be welcome, but it would be easier for me to have funds of money allotted to household furnishings, clothes, etc., and buy them in Stanleyville. One reason for this would be because we'd like to fly, and baggage <u>may</u> or may <u>not</u> arrive in time to get the house in working order by the time school starts. I'd like to get all heavy luggage off before we ever leave Newington.*

.....*I'd like to buy an electric stove in Stanleyville, also some other appliances that work on the current there. It will be quite necessary for caring for so many children, with fresh milk, etc to keep.* [Ione is not just referring to her six children, the plan is for her and Hector to look after all the Mission's children, so they can attend school.]

.....*Last Friday night about 8:30 we had a telephone call from Jean for Hector to "come right over". He went, and we both tho't Dad was worse. But when Hector got there, he found he was to help Archie give a <u>bath</u> to their Dad! He has been getting steadily more and more feeble in his mind and he came to the decision that he would not take a bath. Archie couldn't hold him & it <u>took</u> the <u>two</u> to do it. Everybody felt better afterward tho!!*

All for now. Love, Ione

By May 4th, the family's plans were taking shape, Ione wrote to her mother:

Thanks for your letter received this morning. I was glad to hear you have a house at last. It sounds like a nice place.

.....*We'll be doing some packing soon. And I don't look forward to it. But it's nice to be able now to get the winter things put away first. We are going to store snowsuits, etc., right here at the farm at Avonmore. I think we'll have to store the electric train as the current in Stanleyville will be different, and it isn't good for it to be run without electricity. But it will be a nice thing to play with next furlough. They have surely enjoyed it this winter. We have just moved it from playroom to garage, as it is warm now and there is a nice cement floor out there, a few chairs, etc., a double garage.*

.....*We have had confirmation of space for our family on the plane which leaves Montreal August 25th. It would be nice to work toward that date, tho' we must be sure of our fare before we leave as we cannot have another overdrawn for a long period of time. I think Hector's church is going to pay what is left of ours, but I am (and Hector is too) still concerned for Marcellyn's and maybe we can help her finish hers off. How did she manage to pay her way home from the field? Or is that yet to care for? The plane provides a Sky cot for the baby.*

.....*Stephen just came to me informing me that he has killed a fly, and it went on the f'oor, and he 'sepped on it wif his soos. That's a long sentence for the little baby Marcellyn took care of! He's still as round-eyed and plump but is quite a boy now.*

I'll be speaking at a Mother and Daughter Banquet at Moulenette, near here, the 25th. Stephen now tells me he sees a bird that is big and long and he's measuring with his hand, spreading his fingers apart. Timmie is taking his first steps and climbs up the stairs and slides down backwards on his tummy. Good thing it is carpeted. I must go take the clothes down now, and fold them up. There'll be precious little to get ironed, I think! Hector has three nylon shirts, now, so I don't even have to do the white shirts. There's no laundry around here, like in Fenton, to have it done now and then. But Hector has had a bunch of shirts done up at a Chinaman's in Toronto and keeping for the future. All for now. Write when you get settled, if you live thru it!

Ione XXXXXXX

In May, Ione and Hector wrote another newsletter to their supporters:

"I sent him therefore the more carefully..." Phil. 2:28

This verse seems to be on our hearts just now as we are making plans to return to the Belgian Congo. Epaphroditus, Paul's companion, had been sick, but was now returning to Philippi as a messenger and minister, and Paul was sending him 'the more carefully'. So, do we walk softly before the Lord these days making preparations, gently, slowly, but surely. There are six little boys now who must be sure of the way, the feet "shod with the preparation of the gospel of peace". And day by day we shall be nearer to the time of the final quick journey, made necessarily short because of the youthfulness of some of the travellers.

Kenneth is 7 now and Paul is 6, David is 5, John is 3-1/2, Stephen is 2 and Timothy is 1. We approach them on the subject of certain pleasures and foods not available in Africa wondering if they really wanted to go. Kenneth spoke up rather reproachfully, saying, "But didn't the Lord call us to go there?" So, you see it is with one accord that we return. And Mother's health has been fully recovered. We have had a happy and healthy winter on the farm in Canada and expect to spend a few weeks in the States as soon as school is finished the last of June. There is space on a plane for Congo, leaving August 25, and we hope to be able to make reservations.

There is a job on the mission field which no real missionary wants because of its limitations so far as extensive itineration's and village to village contacts. But because of our own need of schooling for our children, we believe the Lord would have us take this job of caring for the school children of the Unevangelized Fields Mission. This step necessitates the purchasing of land and the building of a large home in Stanleyville, one day's journey from our former station, Bongondza. Until this building project can be completed, we must rent a house.

And so we shall go carefully, and yet 'careful for nothing', knowing that 'at the last your care of us hath flourished again; wherein ye were also careful but ye lacked opportunity…Not that I desire a gift, but I desire fruit that may abound to your account" Phil.4.

It will be possible for us to take a few meetings while we are in Michigan during July and August and we can be reached at First Baptist Church, Pontiac.

Lovingly yours in Him, Hector and Ione

En-route to Africa – Aug 1955

The McMillans flew to Congo in August but had some delays when John broke his arm after someone pushed him off a deck during a game. On the 9th of September, Ione wrote from the 1st Children's Home in Stanleyville:

Dear Ones at Home,

A broken arm!! Just as we were about to leave for Congo! But we had promised the Lord we would go "carefully" in this venture of returning to the field. And it wasn't just the arm, there was money involved, too. We didn't have all we needed for the plane, and the Airway Corporation was wanting to know in three days if we wished a cancellation. Well, the hospital was first, six days of it, and finally John was dismissed. We decided to pack when the doctor said the little arm would be all right if we travelled by train to the coast, instead of by car. We bought a ticket for Montreal, but knew that we would not get any farther unless the Lord undertook in a special way. We could go to the farm and wait, if need be. As we put the things into the cases the following conversation ensued:

Ione: This is like Abraham, "going out not knowing whither he went."

Hector: Yes, and because of the uncertainty of things, he took along Lot.

Ione: (sighing as she looked at the packing yet to be done) Well, we've got a lot, too!

So, we left Michigan by train on Wednesday afternoon, the 24th of August. Late that night the train stopped at Toronto, and during the 20-minute stop-over it happened – the remaining $550 was made up, thru Frances Longley and Mr. Small. When Hector came back to the place in the train where I was resting, but not sleeping, he whispered, "We can go!" And so we did. The journey was a fast one, and the following Sunday found us here.

We found a furnished house to rent in Stanleyville until Jan. 1st at $150, but then rent would increase to $200, so we are looking for a more permanent resting spot, whatever the Lord may have. School started Sept. 9th and the school-age begins at 3. There are many young children in our mission and we expect to have a full house. Kenny Boyes and Barbara Nicholls are with us already, and Billy Boyes will soon be here and two little Walby girls [Laureen and Veronica]. *We like this house and it is right in town* [Sergeant Ketele Street, next door to a patisserie shop] *and the school bus calls for the children at the corner (at the door on rainy days!). We have electricity and running water, two very large bedrooms and two smaller, several beds, dining room furniture, living room furniture, a five-burner kerosene stove with oven. Four of our children are in school, and they are rapidly learning French.*

.....The roads are typical, tho' somewhat improved over the past two years. The children looked for animals, but the wildest things they met up with were some lizards, some very uncomfortable driver ants, and a praying mantis (John called it a praying mattress).

"For whosoever will save his life shall lose it; but whosoever shall lose his life for my sake and the gospel's the same shall save it." Mark 8:35

Lovingly, Ione

By accepting the task of caring for the Mission children in Stanleyville, a new chapter opened up in Ione's missionary life.

Since the family's arrival back in Congo in August of 1955, Ione seemed to have little time for letter writing. The McMillans rented a house on Sergeant Ketele Street in Stanleyville. They took on parental responsibilities for another five children and got them all settled into a school where most could not speak the language.

Ione explained:

.....we're starting school here[101], with...a total of 12 school children and Timmie and Stephen. Marcellyn will be interested to know that Jim Carter arrived a week ago yesterday with his 3 boys (Gordon, Philip and Michael). They are such nice boys and a real inspiration to ours. I peeked in their room the other night and found them all reading their Bibles.[102]

.....Only 3 little girls [girls were destined to always be in the minority]. *I washed heads today and braided hair. I do enjoy them all so much and the help question is getting less acute. I have a couple of city fellows and one wife who knows the city ways and lives nearby - Christians. The wife works right along, too, and is a whiz. We're turning out the laundry by the basketful! The Lord is so good. Everyone is in good health here. Dolena Burk had to go home suddenly last week for an operation. They thought at first it was cancer, but it is a growth. They left a week ago today and 4 stations turned out to see them off. We had the crowd to dinner and supper – about 40 in all. We have the school children in 3 booths against the wall, 4 to a table. They like that – restaurant style. We have two other long tables and a small one for the adults and visitors. Our stuff from Bongondza came with the Walbys when they brought Janet Cowger in for medical care. Conversation between the 3 ladies – Janet, Mrs. Walby and Mrs. Burk:*

---

[101] The Belgian school, Athénée Royal, in Stanleyville.

[102] Ione fails to mention that during Gordon's first few weeks at school he returned with a box of six large black beetles. Not having a cage, they were placed in a bowl with greenery. Surprisingly, next morning, all had escaped and were never seen again. That did not deter Gordon! He returned with two white mice in a box. Fortunately, a cage was procured from somewhere and the mice resided with him in his room and procreated at will!

Dolena Burk – "I've got cancer – what are you here for?"

Topsy Walby – "I've got T.B." [The tropics did not suit Laureen's mother, she lost weight but carried on resolutely.]

Dolena Burk (turning to Janet) "I suppose you've got leprosy!"

But it has not turned out that bad. The report for Mrs. Burk was better before she left and Topsy may get over hers with more rest. I have just had some teeth fixed!

I am feeling fine. I mix up the cookies and the cook bakes them (a double batch every day!) [and we buy] *3 loaves of bread a day from the bakery next door.*

Love, Ione

Ione was not only managing the children, but the home became a base for missionaries travelling in and out of Stanleyville. This was an extra challenge Ione faced throughout her work as host at the three Children's Homes set up in/near Stanleyville. She recounted to her mother on the 22nd of October:

.....Today the children were entertained at "tea" at the B.M.S. (British Bapt. Missionaries) Mr. & Mrs. Seoul. Had a nice time and all behaved – all 14! I had a date, too, with the Protestant Chaplain & his wife, the Salvation Army man & wife to sing some mixed quartets for the radio here. They are recordings and will be used a week from Sunday – 3 songs from Chants de Victoire [Victory Songs] *in French. I guess this is going to be a steady job. I didn't know they had started a radio station here. I am singing the alto in these numbers. I love it.*

We are without guests tonight as the Carpers [Del, Lois and daughter Marilyn, recently arrived from America] *and Valerie Buckingham* [a British Nurse] *left this morning. Yesterday Viola Walker and Olive Bjerkseth were here on their way back from taking Verna Schade to Boyulu to take Mrs. Burk's place, who flew home for an operation. Mary Rutt had been waiting here for a ride to her station and left then. About 15 guests in all thru this week. We have some better help now in the kitchen and washroom – in all, 4 natives. I am trying a man and his wife, the latter to serve the children's tables where we seat 4 at a table, restaurant booths.*

The Lord is good. Marcellyn was right about there being few dishes and linens and our drums haven't arrived yet. But we had a gift of 8 tea cups and saucers and 12 glasses and with a bolt of Americani, have made pillows, cases, sheets, table clothes, etc. Our "guests" have helped a lot in this work and have given extra gifts of money. From day to day we see His hand moving in our behalf. Our promise yesterday "not a feeble one among them", and a "happy mother of children".

Tomorrow a group of former native Bongondza-ites who live here now are coming to give an "official" welcome. We'll have them at 9 A.M. and a visit from Mr. Coumidy at 5. He wants to rent us "very cheaply" a larger house and furnish it. But we are careful, for altho' he is a professing Christian, he has a very critical spirit. A Greek man – Marcellyn knows him.

And now how about some news from you. Our biggest news yesterday – a letter from Jean [Hector's sister] telling of going forward in a Billy Graham[103] meeting in Ottawa, also John D. Dunbar. The letter glows with a real experience*! Praise the Lord.*

And now a head wash and bath and to bed. One package we mailed to ourselves has already arrived. Hope the drums come soon. No jiggers here and fresh Capitani fish [Nile Perch from the Congo River] *every week. Hamburgers two days ago. We had a gift of money to go to the ice cream parlour next door (the bakery).*

All for now. Love, Ione

There are few letters from Hector at this time, however, on November 2nd, he wrote to his sister Irene and her two children, Barbara and Donald:

.....I have some time so I thought I better just sit right down and answer. John's arm is as normal as the other one. After the doctor took the bandage off Sept 10th he told me to gently straighten it a little every day. I made a little tray for the arm to be measured in as it straightened out and we noticed the mark at the wrist was moving about ½". I took him back to the doctor two weeks later and the arm was almost straight. He felt around the back of the elbow and said it would not straighten any more. He showed us his own left arm which he said was hurt when he was small but the parents didn't know about it. He has the use of it but cannot rotate the lower arm. Then he asked John to try – quick as a wink John gave it a flip both ways and the doctor threw up his hands in laughter and said, "I guess he will live with it." But better than that, the arm did continue to straighten out and he can put it out flat as a board. I know a lot of folks were praying about it.

You better send Donald out here to be a model for our children. Their writing could stand a lot of improving but if these first two months are any indication, their teachers will give them no peace until their books are real neat. They have a real good educational system here and everyone so far seems highly in favour of the new set-up for the UFM. The 8 extra children come from four families representing Australia, England and USA.... There are 12 of them to get off to school twice a day on the bus which comes to the corner. Two are in 6th grade, 3 in second, 2 in first, 4 in kindergarden, and John in "ecole maternelle". They take little lunches to eat in the middle of the morning, so Stephen likes to imitate them and pack a little sandwich which he carries as far as the bus when he goes with me to see the others off. Then when we come home, he eats his on the front step! French is coming along nicely. I, too, am finding it much easier, since I have to use it every day.

.....It is nice to hear of your visit up home and to hear so much about Dad. Jean wrote us about her experience in the Billy Graham meeting in Ottawa. Glad to

---

[103] Billy Graham was an American evangelist whose passion and zeal for the teachings of the Bible led to him organize large rallies/crusades all over the World.

hear about Florence's holiday too. Give Eleanor our love when you see her next. I must get a letter off to Alice soon.

.....We have lovely times in family worship. Some of the new children are quite good singers so we enjoy our sing time too. We just started in Genesis this week in the morning readings after we had finished Daniel and Jonah. There were some splendid lessons in those two books. In the evening we are reading in Matthew. It was nice to have enough children to take the name of each one of the disciples. They had lots of fun remembering who was who.

We have been looking at some other property and some seems to suit our need. One nice acre of land in a residential district has a price of $3,500. The man who owns it has not put up any building, but as he is retiring and returning to Belgium, he is giving us first choice for the same price as he paid for it. Please remember to pray for this choice of a permanent home. We do want to get the place the Lord has for us.

Well, the children will soon be home for dinner and I want to get this down to the Post Office. . . . . Bye for now,

LOVE AND PRAYER, Hector and family

A few days later, Ione penned her own reply to Irene telling about the new Belgian school and the children learning French:

.....French comes hard as yet, but our children have had none, whereas the others have had lessons in French from their parents. Kenny asked yesterday what is meant by, "qu'est ce que c'est ce la?" [What is that?] And they all know sit down and stand up, etc. Our boys need improving in writing, too. The children here do beautiful work, and the school is very strict about blots, etc. They write with pens in Grade 2. Last week we had to make two gymnastic costumes and now comes a note for the four kindergarteners asking for Noel costumes, 2 shirts and two "jupes" (skirts) in horizontal green stripes. Whatever can these represent? Their copybooks must be signed weekly as well as their report books. You should see Hector pouring over the dozens of lessons. The number for Excellent is 10, and each week they get a report for 4 items, I can't just remember, Ordre, Application, Conduit-savoir vite, and the 4th I can't think of. Last week Kenny got 10 in three of them. The kindergartners have a card with four squares and if all goes well a red line is in all four, for 'tres bien' (very good). Alas, John got one blue mark last week, for Propre (that's the 4th I couldn't think of!), so I guess he must be messy and not tidy. Maybe I can slick him up a little!

Enough of the school affairs. I have a "date" today with an English lady married to a Greek hotel-keeper, for a walk and a bit of fellowship. There are many white people here who are lonely we have found. Perhaps we can "first give our own selves" and then point them to the Saviour. And last but not least of our opportunities is among the native population, a daily chat and Bible study on the front porch, with this one and that, house staff principally, and others who come in. There is time for this just after the children go off to school.

369

You would enjoy the balmy weather we're having. It was 85 last evening until well into the night. In the heat of the day we find our excess pounds melting away. My dresses are already too loose. And Hector is a little flatter in profile! But all keep healthy. "Not a feeble one among them." We have enjoyed so much reading from Hudson Taylor's life. He says, "Let us see that in theory we hold that God is faithful; that in daily life we count upon it; and at all times and under all circumstances we are fully persuaded of this blessed truth." "And they overcame by the blood of the Lamb, and by the word of their testimony."

All for now, Love, Ione

There were many advantages to living in the middle of Stanleyville, but as Hector mentioned in his letter to his sister, the house they were renting was not fit for their needs and was exceeding the budget allocated. Within a month, the Children's Home was moved out of town.

Chapter 15
KILOMETER 9: NASSER'S PLACE

As Christmas approached, Ione and Hector moved the Children's Home along with the 14 children, some of whom were ill with measles! They also had 10 house guests but rather than being a burden, they all helped with the move. The house was far from ready and there were no quarters for the staff. Ione wrote to her mother and sisters on the 12th of December, 1955:

.....About a week and a half ago we moved from the place next to the bakery to a place nine kilometers [about 6 miles] out of town on the old Buta Road. There are about 3 hectares of land, that is about 7-1/2 acres of forest, garden and cleared space. It sits on a hill, well off the road, rather above it with a hedge across. Lots of palm trees, papaya, berries, pineapple, and native greens, etc. We are renting the two houses and the land all for $100, a month. The larger is a good dormitory and the smaller a guest house. It is fitted with electricity and run by a gasoline motor and there is a well of water.

Our stove, an almost new one brought to Stanleyville by Viola when she could not get it to work. She bought herself another. And we have found that it just needed a very large chimney and have been getting very good results with it. A wood stove, a little larger than Marcellyn's at Ekoko. We have a two-burner kerosene stove as well. Also, an outside fire for heating bath water, much like on all stations. In fact, this reminds us very much of setting up a new station, and it is quite a challenge. Were it not that we have had our hands full with an epidemic of measles we might be quite thrilled! 8 of the 14 have had measles and the last two just wouldn't break out for ever so long and kept vomiting night and day. But I guess it is all over now, and we are so thankful for no serious complications. We had the advice from the school doctor as well as the B.M.S. doctor, and a visit from Betty Arton who helped with care and advice, so we have not been without medical care.

We have had some splendid verses especially in the Psalms, 31:8-"Thou has set my feet in a large room." (I wish you could see it!) And the verses about being delivered from the "straightness of our way" being removed from the horrible pit and miry clay (you should have seen the mucky ditch water in front of the other place!)

And we have had some real blessings in reading from Hudson Taylor's life. This project is a step of faith, and must go on, without subsidy or special support for the time being, and we BELIEVE GOD will not fail us in it. You maybe remember the verse in Revelation chapter 3 verse 8 about an open door and a little strength. Well, this is surely it. On one of the very first visits to this new

*house some natives pled with Hector and Kinso to set up a church on this road,
and because we are this far out I believe we can do it without infringing on BMS
or Salvation Army territory.[104] There is no protestant work right here at all. Last
Sunday we held a service and the first audience was ten from right on the spot,
but by afternoon others came inquiring and said they will attend, too.*

*.....As Hudson Taylor said, "Our needs are great but they do not exceed the
resources of our Heavenly Father".*

*What we would like to do is buy the property, and then we can improve it as
we would like. The total cost would be $14,000. Will you pray for this, and also
for transportation? The bus comes here four times a day for the children but we
would like a large station wagon or Volkswagen and are trusting Him for this.*

*The children are learning French fast.[105] It is a very high-class school, and
everything must be just right, even to covers for copybooks of a certain colour,
etc. And detailed notes came one after the other concerning the costumes
required for the Christmas program. The final results were ten different
costumes, some with four parts. There were soldiers, Dutchmen, hunters, white
rats, and little John was to be dressed all in white, and they put a big red bow at
the neck and their song was darling. It was last Monday. Everything in French.
Two had the measles. I am keeping well, and Hector too. Our baggage came just
after we had moved (the Lord's good timing!) and we have Christmas
decorations, etc., plus the good strawberry jam and rhubarb. Not one broken.
Only two dishes. All for now.*

Lovingly, Ione

Over the Christmas vacation, the porch was cemented, walls were whitewashed and
windows installed. The staff marked out and set up the floor plans for their huts and
inserted wooden poles which would form the outline of their homes. New Year's
Day 1956, Ione wrote:

Dearest Mother, Marcellyn, and Lucille,

.....The pictures came this week! And they are beautiful!

*.....We had a nice Christmas. Filled stockings but no tree. 33 natives came and
we gave them a little "feast"! Not much in the mail, but a letter from Doris with
a check for five dollars, five dollars from Mother, and a dollar for Stephen's
birthday, which was yesterday. We couldn't get into town to change these so
will get something when we do go. Stephen needs to pass his rubber boots on to
Timmy and have some new ones. Timmy is talking so much now, and he rolls his
eyes so expressively. He had his first taste of 'pai-pai potopoto'.[106] Can't you
just see his eyes registering the flavour, and then he made the statement, "It's*

---

[104] The various Christian organizations had an agreement not to compete directly with
each other, given the vastness of the area.

[105] The Belgians had indeed set high standards for the school since the majority of the
students at this time were from the Belgian expatriate community. Any non-Belgian
children had to be able to keep up with lessons in French.

[106] A mixture of Klim powdered milk and soft papaya creating potopoto or 'mud'.

goob!" In family worship one can often hear his voice as he says to the other boys, "Voove over!" He prayed his first little prayer the other day. John has been wearing the little baseball-figured two-piece cotton suit that Lucille gave to Paul for his birthday. And today he announced that it was too tight in the middle, so Stephen has it now. You can see how fast they are growing. I suppose Jim is almost as tall as his mother by now. Kenny is rejoicing because his fat tummy is thinning out and he is taller. The Protestant Chaplain and his wife and daughter presented our missionary children with some gifts for Christmas. Shirts, trousers, tennis shoes, whistles, mouth organs, all sorts of things. Three huge packets, and she helped me divide them into packets for each child.

Thank you so much, Mother for the gift of money. You should not have done that, as I know you need it yourself. And Lucille, for a magazine [idea], My Chum would be fine. The children seem to have sufficient clothing. Shoes are our next need. We can get them out here however. I am thankful I have those shoes provided by the Sunnyvale Chapel ladies and the Loyal's. They are so comfortable, I never think of my feet and whether on cement floors or stones or mud they are the same. I must send the bill to Geraldine Lonie to prove to her I did spend that money on shoes! I wish I had someone to give me a Toni [hair permanent]. I am tempted to try it myself, but my hair would need cutting and that takes a little skill. Maybe I can get some of our visitor's help.

"And the house of Jacob shall possess their possessions." Obadiah 17

This has been going thru my mind. We've entered into this project as a single definite act. But the possessing is step by step. "As thou goest step by step..." It is one thing to enter in by faith; another to possess it. This jungle must be conquered, pushed back, more buildings put up, the people reached. By the time we had made shelves a tarantula had crept into one suitcase of things, and when I lifted out the pile of clothes, it jumped back into the suitcase. I called the house helper to kill it. And Hector killed another in the washroom off our bedroom. We are reminded daily that we are in the forest. A storm last week whipped around a way that it usually does not come and four rooms were wet. And Christmas decorations were spoiled (some from Marcellyn's trunk!); bulbs that had survived six months of travel in a metal drum now met their doom, and the force of the rain sent a spray of red crepe paper raindrops thru the wire screening on the white tablecloth and the open dish cupboard. We were two days drying piles of children's clothing. But that is nothing to the damage that might have come. We have a strong roof.

I am thinking of the stanza Mother put in my precious promise New Testament when I spent my first Christmas on the mission field;

"O Strengthen me, that while I stand

Firm on the Rock, and strong in Thee,

I stretch out a loving hand to wrestle with the troubled sea"

Please excuse this messy letter. Loads of love, Ione

January continued to be a very busy month; Ione described it to her mother on the 27th:

.....Mr. Nasser, the Indian, who owns this property said if Hector dug the well, he'd furnish the tiling to finish it. So that's where we are right now. Already Hector has the water piped to the house and a pump at the well pumps it. You asked about electricity; there is a motor which Mr. Nasser gave us, but it is old and we hope to have a new one soon. There is a possibility of a large Diesel engine being designated for us. It is on its way out from Ireland, and Mr. Kerrigan is the receiver, but he has said that it is too big for his needs. Well, it wouldn't be too big for us, and a vote was taken on all the stations, and as nearly as we can tell so far, most think we should have it! Do pray about this. We have lights going at night and also in the morning as we must be up before daylight, and the lamps that we bro't do look pretty with their nice shades. When we moved to this unfurnished house it looked pretty bare and the missionaries from Banjwadi brought in a whole truckload of things, so that we have most everything now. Hector has made a number of things, tables, cupboards, a long living room seat with nylon cord woven for the seat, desk, bamboo rings for curtain rods, etc. The rugs look nice in the living room and bedrooms. The whole house has a dark red cement floor and mottled creamy-white walls. The woodwork in the bedrooms is light pink.

After many interruptions, on the 30th of January, Ione continued:

.....Well, now it's the mumps! In the last few days one after the other has come down with a swelling on one side or the other or both, until today we have one child from each of the four families sick. I am following the advice given in the Child Care book, and it says to be especially careful with boys and watch for swellings elsewhere, so I am as we have such a number of boys here. And one of the Carter boys, Philip, is 11, rather a serious age. He became ill first. John is the latest and has the basin beside him this morning. One side is swollen, of his jaw I mean.

After the lights were out last night we were lying in bed talking about Grandma and John spoke up brightly and said, "Grandma likes me!" And then little Timmie echoed, "Gamma wike me!" It was sweet. I am sure they have not forgotten you. But you must send a picture where they can see your face. The one you sent with Timmie just shows big fat Timmie! And he is still just as fat and soft. You should hear him singing "Are you sleeping, brother John," in both French and English. He is talking much sooner than most of ours. The Carter boys are so nice to him and love to dress him and help him in many ways. I hope he will not be spoiled.

Well, I've had a round with the kitchen staff and I think the dishwashing is improved now, for a while. I'll keep out awhile and see what they can do, then I'll go out and tell them what to prepare for dinner. We are expecting Kinso and Marge Boyes and maybe Marshall Southard from Banjwadi. [Ione has 27 house guests through January].

11:15 A.M. Things are pretty well ready for dinner now: browned potatoes, slices of hot Smack (like Spam), Harvard beets, creamed carrots, lots and lots of diced bananas prettied up with a tin of strawberries. Whether our company comes or not, we'll enjoy it. And then there is a big three-layer frosted cake ready for supper.

5:30 P.M. Well, I guess it's hopeless to try to write more. There are a number of places for me just now. Bowl-baths for all the sick ones (now a fifth), the two babies in the tub, and now the rest have finished and I've sent for the cook to get supper. I need a wash and take a few more temperatures.

Some precious verses today from Daily Light *about running. Yes, the road is uphill all the way, but what a lovely ending! To see His face will be enough. Crowns, well, we'll cast them at His feet. "Take this child and nurse it for ME, and I will give thee thy wages."*

Loads of love, Hector and Ione

It is mainly the older children that had mumps and they proved to be more difficult to nurse than the younger ones. Ione got a chance to write to Hector's sister Irene on the 5th of February while Hector took some of the children out for a walk. Hector's walks were usually one kilometer. At Kilometer 8 there was a house he liked the look of (more on that later).

.....The going here is uphill all the way, but the exercise of our faith is a blessing to our souls. Perhaps you can picture Hector and the bigger boys digging a well in 100 degrees temperature, so that we won't have to carry the water from the next property; Hector trying to bring to life a long-dead electric motor for lights; me standing over a small wood stove cooking for 20 or more. It's a humble beginning, but we have the first qualification for a children's home --- the children! And if the parents have confidence enough to send us their little ones, we can carry on until things are better. We are in a healthier place now than in town, and I think we feel the inconveniences more than do the children. The Lord is good to trust us with the job. And the natives keep coming for meetings, too. And the guests, at least three a week. We have a family of four with us now, missionaries from a station about 200 miles away. When they leave their children with me and go to town shopping, to doctor, etc., that adds to the job, but the Lord gives grace. It will be better if some day we can have another couple in charge of the guest house.

Last night we were sitting in the living room talking with the missionary couple, and Mrs. McAllister heard a slight rustle behind her. The lantern light revealed a snake, which Mr. McAllister bravely trampled with his shoe. I thought it a bit risky to kill it that way as he couldn't see the head too well, and it kept trying to wind around his leg. Usually it's better to cut off the head with a machete. But I was thankful to have it killed that way as there was no blood left on the rug.[107] We have killed two tarantulas since coming here.

---

[107] Bob McAllister was a stocky Irishman, more than capable of stamping on a snake!

Hector back now and a meal to think of. Loads of love, Ione

Ione encouraged the children to write letters, Sundays were usually dedicated to writing to parents. As the McMillan boys had their parents on hand, they were encouraged to write to Grandma. On the 1st of April, Paul wrote:

Dear Grandma, Thank you for your nice letter and for the stamps. I do not have a good stamp album. I am using a note book. We are having a nice April fool time. We fool Daddy in giving him candy paper with stones in. David is collecting pictures of cow boys. I would like a Bible game to play and a book called Lassie and Joe. We have read Lassie Come Home. I would like an ice-cream cone when I come. What would you like from Africa?

Here is a verse. "What time I am afraid I will trust in the Lord." With love from Paul (those are kisses) XXXXXXX

On Easter, Ione wrote to her mother:

.....Our biggest news you maybe know already, as it is that the Loyal's Philatheas have voted to buy us a refrigerator. They asked if we might be able to buy it out here, and I sent back a letter return mail with a picture of one we can get right here, a lovely big deluxe Servel kerosene one with a big freezing compartment beside places for ice cubes or ice cream! My, will we be glad to have it! We continue to have guests sometimes two and three parties at once, and with a special gift received at Christmas we hope to get good beds and mattresses for the children. We use the big double bed that Westcott's left at Bongondza which was brought down to us here. We have the piano now, too, and a rocking chair that was given to Dr. Westcott when he was down country with the other mission. I do enjoy it, and have rocked all of the children in it. When Walbys asked if there was anything else we wanted from there, I mentioned that and the piano and they brought them on the 1st March.

.....Money keeps coming in for the children's home, but as yet we are not sure whether we should stay here or look for another piece of land. Our mission has applied for a free government grant, but these things take years to get. And what do you do in the meantime we are not sure. We might find a place which the government might consider and rent it for the time, but it would mean building, and I don't see how Hector can be doing building in another place, and be any help here, and I feel I cannot carry on without his help. So, pray about this. It would be easier to stay here, but the cost is quite high. As Mrs. Taylor once said, "The Lord gave us a single eye to do His will, and then guide us just where He would have us..."

.....And so, we carry on, putting up walls which can be moved, for an additional bathroom, removable pipes for our water supply, temporary partitions between rooms, etc. Two nice teeter-totters, a big slide, a swing and a "cable car" which travels on a couple wheels over a cable down a slope. Everyone says the playground place here is ideal.

.....Now I must close. The secret of happiness I have found this week is to LET NOT your heart be troubled...It is a definite act and must be guarded carefully.

If we believe in God, believe also in the Lord Jesus, then we can systematically be instant in prayer, casting ALL our care upon Him. It saves worrying.

Thanks so much for your good letters and for your faithful ministry in our behalf. The Lord bless you and keep your heart singing.

Lovingly, Ione

On the 10th of April, in a letter enquiring about Esther's upcoming wedding, Ione writes to both her sister Lucille and niece Esther. In it, she described a little of her day which started just after 5.30 am. Family worship started at 6.15 am so that everyone was ready for the school bus which arrived at 6.45 am. As they did not have a car, Hector set out on foot, the six miles into Stanleyville. Ione wrote:

.....Hector bought some small chickens and sent them back with a native lad so that I could cook them for dinner while he did other shopping. But alas, the chickens arrived after the guests! But the Lord always undertakes for us, and the guests, that is the first ones, presented me with a package of cold meat from the butcher shop. Quite often people have thoughtfully stopped to get us meat as that is a problem. So, we are having fried chicken for supper, the second time since coming back.

.....We are so happy here, especially so because we feel we are needed. Missionary mothers have expressed their gratefulness that we are caring for their children while they are able to get out into the village work more extensively.

.....Since I started the letter, we have had 27 different guests. Part of them were because school was starting again after the holiday, and the children were brought back by their parents. But we are noticing a definite increase of guests, from other missions as well as our own. Until Christmas the average was three a week and now it is ten a week! Do pray much for this, as our first job is the care of the children, and we do not want to be too tired to be a father and mother to them. The two little girls[108] have gone on furlough, so now it is 11 boys. "And I was strengthened as the hand of the Lord my God was upon me, and I gathered together out of Israel chief men of God to go up with me." Pray that the Lord will lay it upon someone's heart to come out and help us. There is no one free of all our present group of missionaries on the field.

.....We have figured up that within four years there will be 30 children in our present field group that will be of school age.

Another heartache – during the holiday time I did something which has been heavy upon my heart since we came. There are little children all around us who cannot go to school because they are too far from Stanleyville so since I was already giving some reading and writing lessons and sewing to the wives of our house staff, I let their children come, too, and got as many as I cared to handle! Then the bombshell! Our field secretary made a visit and told me I must not try to have any classes, as it was too much for me. But I can continue with the sewing

---

[108] Laureen and Veronica Walby left on the 3rd of April.

classes as it gets our mending done! Well, it is a thing to pray about. Pray that we may be able to find a native teacher who knows the Lord who can take this group regularly. Hector has been making beds out of inch pipes threaded together and a webbing of nylon cord stretched across.

Three times today little Stephen got into the driver ants, and each time had to be lifted out of them as he was frozen to the spot with fright. The hurt only lasts until you pick them off. They are right near the house where a stump has been removed, and he keeps forgetting. Timmy rolled his big eyes and said, "I didn't get into them!" John was supposed to be in the bath tub today but I found him climbing up on the shower fixture, grinning guiltily, and he couldn't get down by himself.

By May, the hot season was getting to Ione, she wrote to Hector's sister Florence:

.....It's so hot that the paper wants to stick on everything, and the little biting flies want to stick on me, but it's a case of now or never, as the children are outside for a while, and Hector is supervising them.

We got a package from Canada (Newington) the other day, and inside was a fruit cake and a 4-lb. tin of honey. My, did that taste good! I wish we could exchange some of our bananas for such things; where we are living now there are many bananas and they are a special kind called lady fingers, as they are small, only about 3 inches. We just finished one head and another is ripe.[109]

.....The oldest boy (Gordon Carter) was home with mumps and was sitting on his bed with his feet dangling and happened to kick a small basket and out from the basket came a tarantula, large, black and hairy. It touched his foot, but did not bite, and we are thankful. We can tell them from ordinary spiders because they are so hairy and the body is fuzzy with fur. This is the third tarantula we have killed since we came. And two snakes, one in the living room and one in the bathroom. The toads we let stay as they kill ever so many small insects, and there are several in each room. Their little shadows hopping in the dark places are common sights. One night I got up without my slippers and put my foot on one; it was soft and cold!

On May 12th, Ione wrote:

Dearest Mother,

I wanted to tell you of three wonderful answers to prayer in the last three weeks. Three weeks ago yesterday, April 20th, we received a letter from Kenneth Hempstead, authorizing us to go ahead and buy a refrigerator out here, and we did, and were able to get the very one I had been wanting, a deluxe model Servel run by kerosene, 8 ft. size. It is lovely and has a light blue colour inside, and a large freezing compartment for ice cubes, ice cream and meat, etc. It was delivered the next day and we have had ice cream almost every day since! The cold things and even the cold water seem to improve everyone's appetites. It cost

---

[109] Lady finger bananas were almost a 'staple' part of the diet. One day, money had run out and all that was left to eat were the bananas!

$440. I was afraid that even if we had it there wouldn't be enough money to buy the fresh meats and vegetables to make it worthwhile but again the Lord has undertaken and we have not lacked.

.....The second answer to prayer came May first, after I had been reading from Daily Light, *"And my people shall dwell in a peaceable habitation, and in sure dwellings, and in quiet resting places." Isa. 32:18. I especially claimed the 'sure dwellings', for in so many ways our dwelling is yet unsure, and we have not been able to secure land even yet. We felt if we were to stay in this place, there would have to be some very large gifts of money toward buying it. That same day a notification came to our Field Treasurer of a gift of $2,000 for the Children's Home, from Mr. Bryers, the same man who gave us $100 when we stopped to see him when Mrs. Wideman drove us to Toronto while we were in Fenton. Our guest house is filled now for a month, and a letter came asking us to keep some Rethy children on their way to their school, that is for one night.*

Hector & Ione with some children in front of the donated Jeep.

.....And now for number three! Not least, to be sure! I don't think I told you about two visitors we had some time in March, about 6 P.M., two smart looking American men in raincoats drove in a Jeep station wagon. They asked for Hector and I took them thru our puddle road to the guest house where he was working. There were no chairs there to offer them, so I gave them boxes and they sat around sort of friendly like and I left to go stay with the children. It seemed they were tourists who had travelled around Africa and were wanting to go home now to California and leave the two Jeeps that the two couples had used. They wanted to do something for some American missionaries and had been told about us by the British Baptist Mission in town. They were willing to sell their Jeeps for 80,000 francs (about half price.) We saw no way of obtaining that much money but told them there were others in the mission who were hoping soon to get cars. He asked Hector ever so many questions and I guess was convinced that we needed a car.

He took Mr. Pudney's address and telephone no. They said they would write us in about ten days. The next day Hector met them again in the bank and one man, Mr. Bruener, came right over to Hector and said rather secretively, "My friend and I do not see alike in this thing: I want to give you my Jeep, if you will make it possible for me to put it thru the income tax for exemptions." Well, we looked and looked in the mail and heard nothing more, but Hector knew that when the men left, they put the two Jeeps in storage at the same place where we bought the refrigerator. So as long as they were yet in town, there was hope. The children took it for granted that we would receive it and began to thank the Lord for it. But I was afraid to write anyone about it. Well, last Tuesday when Hector went into town the letter came, and a beautiful one at that, from the man in charge of a chain of furniture stores all across Cal., presenting us with a Jeep station wagon ('56)!! And Hector came home with [the 'Jeep from Heaven'] that noon. I was so overcome that I cried instead of laughing. Such a nice new green one, and with seats enough for everyone. Isn't the Lord good?

.....The enclosed picture [shown at left] *was taken in front of our house.*

.....In the snap the two larger boys nearest to me are the sixth graders, Gordon and Philip Carter (12 and 11). The third Carter boy is next to Kenny, and they are both in grade 2. Billy Boyes is next to Michael Carter, and Kenny Boyes has the bandaged finger (following his accident on the cable car)[110]; and the two girls (Laureen and Veronica Walby) are in Grade 2 and Kindergarten. They've gone on furlough now, so we just have 11 boys. (Barbara Nicholls also left for furlough with her family).

The children had done well at the Belgian school. In her letters Ione does not expand on school life, however, each academic year, the headmaster of the school produced an end-of-year report called *Palmares* written in both French and Flemish. From the 1955-1956 edition, it is noted that John received a special prize for drawing, Ken, David and Kenny Boyes for application and Paul, Mike and Philip Carter for 'Conduite' (behaviour). Paul came 11th in his class with Bill Boyes in 18th place; Ken McMillan was 13th with Mike close at 15th. It is evident that Philip and Gordon struggled with the lack of French language as they are noted to have an overall score of less than 50% for their school work. Obviously, Ione and Hector had done a great job in supporting the children through their school work if 7 came away with special prizes for excellence in their endeavors.

As it turned out, Nasser's Place was not to be the 'sure dwellings' which were foretold in Isaiah that day in May. It would have cost $14,000 to buy and the well was insufficient for their needs. The pump failed, despite renovation, causing no small degree of discouragement. For lack of clean well water some of the clothes

---

[110] Unfortunately, Kenny Boyes reached up and put his finger on the cable and almost lost the tip as the wheels ran over it. He ended up with a very bad cut swathed in bandages and the cable car ended up 'out of bounds' to the little ones.

had to be washed in a nearby stream which would not leave them looking good. The dishes were difficult to clean properly using the local soap as there was no detergent available. Everyone at the home needed a bath every day and the school children's heads needed to be shampooed. They were covered in dust by travelling back and forth every day on the school bus with its open windows. Just keeping clean and sanitary was becoming a real problem. The facilities were just too basic and the lack of running water, a burden too great. The McMillans and their entourage moved one kilometer down the road.

Chapter 16
KILOMETER 8

The move to KM 8, as this property was to become known, took place in October 1956 and was to be the last location for the Children's Home. Ione told her mother:

KM 8 and kids - 1956

.....We are moving, for the fourth time, and to a place more suitable to these dozen children who are now with us, plus the guests who come from time to time from surrounding mission stations. We are renting a house on a plot of land [2-1/2 acres] which we would like to buy. It is five miles (8 kilometres) out of Stanleyville.

The plot of land had a large shed/hanger partly brick built which was up for sale. The McMillans had a fund to pay for it, should they get permission to buy it.

.....This place is a real improvement in our living conditions. There is plenty of water and a nice new electric pump to bring it up from the well. And because we are on the town side of the intersection, the bus comes 15 minutes later so the

The school bus dropping off the children for lunch.

children have a little more time at home. And it stops right in front of the house. There is a large 'football field', a croquet [area], flowers, fruit trees (we have transplanted about 100 mulberry bushes since coming) all in a little over an acre.

The adjoining property has the shed and we could surely use that too. But for now, we have made a long staff members' *house into a dormitory room for the six older boys, three rooms and a bathroom with shower as well as tub. Kenneth sleeps with Michael Carter and Paul with Billy Boyes and they enjoy being on their own, tho it is only a few steps from our back porch. (Gordon and Philip Carter share the other room). We have three large porches and a big storeroom.*

In an additional note to Lucille she wrote:

George Kerrigan with the Commer truck and curious kids.

It is good to be in a nice house again, and it is partly furnished. A lovely living room outfit, some curtains, dining table and chairs, kitchen equipment. The well is deep and can produce 8 barrels at one time. That means we can wash clothes at the house instead of carrying to the stream. A new diesel Lister motor gives us lights all over and a new small diesel Lister pumps the water from the well. Hector and some of the missionary men have made over the building just behind the house which was meant for our staff and now it is a nice dormitory for the six larger boys. It has a bathroom of its own. The owner is very considerate and it may be that this will be the place that we will buy.

Turning this place into a home for her family and also for the other children, was a joy for Ione and included cleaning and repainting the piano that Dr Wescott had given her. Hector replaced all of the little springs which make the keys go back in place after playing - showing that there was really nothing that he could not turn his hand to, especially for Ione. The refurbished piano was then tuned by a Catholic priest, a friend of the protestant chaplain's wife which, in those less ecumenical times, was a very enlightened step. Ione was very uneasy about this since she and Hector had preached that –

.....anyone who exalts Mary above our Lord, is really an enemy of the Lord.[111]

KM8 dining areas – 1956-1957

Once the piano was tuned, Ione then secured someone to come to the Home and give the older children lessons. Some did better than others. Laureen had great difficulty balancing a coin on the back of her hand while playing scales; which effectively ended any notions of a career as a pianist. Philip Carter and Kenny McMillan were the stars and progressed the furthest.

In November, Ione wrote to her mother:

.....We had a nice dinner: soup made of browned onions, carrots with rice, creamed potatoes, sliced cold meat from the butchers, fried ripe plantain, cucumbers and butterscotch pie with mock whipped cream on. They liked the pie and it was so easily made with brown sugar. The cook made the crust and it was

---

[111] Ione would soften her feelings about Catholics later on during the times when Protestants and Catholics were subjected to the same brutal killings at the hands of the rebels.

tender. It is only his second try. We have the children at two tables, Hector at
one and I at the other. We change around from time to time, but today I had
Gordon (the 13-year-old) at the other end of my table and he was helpful in
serving the little ones and reaching things. Timmie and Stevie were on either
side of me, and John, David, and Kenny Boyes on one side or the other. Their
little conversation is so different from the bigger boys. I hope eventually to have
them in three divisions, as the teen-agers like to be on their own.

We can do this when our nurse comes next year. She is from England and has
a slight impediment of speech they say. She knows she is to come here and is
quite happy about it.[112]

As always, Ione's letters home included inquiries about the family back home;
both hers and Hectors. It is evident that she is mindful of missing events such as
graduations, weddings and the births of great nieces and nephews. From the letters,
she learns that Marcellyn and her new family are not returning to the mission field
in the Congo but starting out a fresh in the Dominican Republic. Besides letter
writing, Ione experiments with tape recordings and sends her mother one of Kenny
singing 'God Leads His Dear Children Along'.

As the year ends, Ione wrote to her sister Lucille and her husband Maurice:

.....We have had the nicest Christmas we have ever had in Congo. The children
had the most toys, as six parcels arrived just a week before (Packages reach us
quicker here than at Bongondza), and they were lovely things.[113] The boxes from
the Loyals arrived and there were things in them from Mother, which included a
dress.

We had our own Christmas early so that we could get ready for a large group
of natives who were coming here for Christmas night and day. There were about
75 who slept all around the place, some in the open and about 100 who were at
the main service. It was like a little Conference. And it was such a blessing to
our hearts. There were three tribes and they divided into three groups and kept
singing, testifying, praying and reading the Word one after the other until 3 A.M.
When they were surprised that I could stay up that night, I laughed and said, "I
have sat up many nights with a sick child, and can I not spend one-night singing
praises to the Lord with you all!" When they finally did settle down, they just sat
around their fires, and only the little children and mothers went into the
dormitory rooms I had left available. And they were singing carols before
daylight! Such a contrast with the many who were at liquor places. There were
three women who accepted the Lord.

---

[112] Ione is referring to the imminent arrival of Margaret Hayes, affectionately known to all
as Maggie.
[113] The package included a huge road grader, 3 kinds of dump trucks, one of them
hydraulic, a moving van with exchangeable trailers, an auto haul-away with little autos, six
complete sets of toys.

Next week the decision will be made about this property and we will soon be letting you know. Keep praying.[114] *All for now,*

Lovingly in Him, Hector & Ione

In a 'thank you' letter to her mother on the 29th of January, it appears that there were enough bits and pieces sent for Christmas that Ione was able to make up Christmas sacks for the Carter and Boyes families to take home with them. Everything was lovingly shared between the missionaries.

Ione also told her mother that the Pudneys had sent their permission for Hector and Ione to go ahead and buy the land on behalf of the mission; she wrote of:

.....the marvellous answer to prayer in the form of a telegram from Mr. Pudney saying to go ahead and purchase this property. So, we will be staying here, the Lord willing, and we can begin getting ready for more children.

However, it was not all plain sailing for Ione, the euphoria of Christmas gave way to problems with the children:

Phillip C, Gordon C, Ken M, Michael C, Billy B, Paul M
Kenny B, David M, Emile B, Steve M, John M, Timmy M

.....At the beginning of school this month Paul had the measles, which he apparently had missed during the epidemic last year. Shortly after Michael Carter had the same rash and fever, or it seemed the same, and we had the diagnosis of a different doctor and he called it red fever and said it would be finished in 48 hours. And it was, but hardly had he gotten into his clothes again when Timmie had malaria, and then Stephen started in the night with a violent fever and diarrhoea. In just a few hours he was in convulsions and went from one convulsion to another until we could get him into the hospital. They had quite a struggle there, and he finally was relaxed. They gave him an adult injection of terramycin, a new and very expensive drug, and that, with injections for malaria and to quiet, did the work. The doctor said it was malaria and dysentery.

He was two days in the hospital and a good many more in bed at home until he was strong again. The dysentery did not leave for a week or more. He is certainly eating well now. I didn't see how we could stay with him in the hospital (there are no special nurses, and not even real nurse's care like at home, tho the

---

[114] During December, Ione and Hector had 60 visitors and used this opportunity to write to the three main Mission Headquarters (America, Canada and the UK). They needed $15,000 over 6 years to buy the land; they had already accrued a deposit. There was enough land to build a church and they had the hangar as basis for a guest house/dormitory.

doctors are very good and the nurses kind tho not all skilled) and manage transportation back and forth and care for the children remaining at home. But as always, the Lord undertakes. Hector got Sonia Grant (a qualified nurse) to come out from Banjwadi and she slept right in the same room with him, and then he was not frightened when the nurses talked to him in French. Sonia is so lovely with the children, and Stephen called her mama and responded so nicely to her sweet care. It was a bit of a rest for Sonia too and the meals were good and they didn't charge anything for medicines or doctor, only about four dollars for food. We are given medical care free here, which is such a help.

There were some hard moments while Hector was gone for Sonia and we had [Stephen] here yet and wondering if he would ever regain consciousness, but the children were praying and ever so quiet, and the Lord made it a blessing.

It seems there is never any progress in His work without heartaches and illnesses, but the progress comes, if we are able to bear the cost. So, this week comes the word to go forward, and right today negotiations are being made at the bank between our mission and the owner of the house. I trust all the difficulties can be ironed out, and the papers set in order. Do remember this.

Our new Dr. and Mrs. Sharpe have arrived from England with their five-month-old girl; also Mr. and Mrs. Urech and Audrey Edwards. We have the first two and Audrey here for about five weeks to do their 'stage' at the hospital. The Urechs are at Banjwadi and will probably go to Ekoko or Aketi. They have been in China for about 22 years and are veteran missionaries, a real addition to our work. Their only barrier just now, the language, but they are fluent in French. He is Swiss and she Scotch. She is about your age, Mother and looks quite like you.

Next week we keep overnight the Director of the Missions Department of Moody, Dr. Harold Cook, and the following week Bishop Culbertson. I am sorry I have no real nice place to keep them as this is first a children's home, but pray for His blessing.

Love, Ione   X

Having told her mother all about Stephen's illness, in the next letter on the 1st of February, Ione wrote to Lucille:

Writing to you from here while sitting beside a little [sedated] boy is rather unusual. This is the second little boy we've bro't to this hospital within two weeks!

.....Last night David broke his arm by falling out of a tree in our yard. Both the big bones above the wrist of his left arm. They didn't set it last night as we expected but put it in a sling and padded it all over and he was given something to take. He had a pretty good night (at home) and this morning they took an X-ray and then set it. They let me watch. He took the ether very well. Now we are waiting at "Radiographie" for another picture of it, and then we will go home and come back at 3. They must not have given him much ether as he was soon out [of the hospital].

He is pale but able to walk about. He was determined not to cry and did not. I told him Paul had not when this same doctor sewed up Paul's hand recently (he too, had ether). Paul had been for a walk in the edge of the forest and had stumbled and fallen on a big broken bottle which had been thrown in a hidden place. Well, that's enuf of catastrophies.

With all these difficulties there is PROGRESS for the Lord! We had a cable from Mr. Pudney to arrange for purchase of property, so negotiations are being made to buy the house where we live, plus furniture, land, etc. We can stop paying rent and start putting up more dormitories.

Praise the Lord with us. We're going to have a foothold here!

Lovingly in Him, Ione

On April 29th, Ione again wrote to her Mother:

A little boy with big brownish eyes was fishing thru my letter basket this afternoon for a letter that his big brother had written for him to his Grandma. When the other boys were doing letters this morning, he said he wanted to write to Grandma and ask her to send some cookies, so Paul volunteered to do it for Timmie. Kenny wrote to a boy who wants to be his pen pal, and David to the Focklers who support him, and John to Aunt Jean.

You maybe are wondering why they are not in school. We are quarantined for two weeks because of polio, that is, the children (ours) can't go to school. There were several cases of polio at Banjwadi, and little Cynthia Boyes has had it, and it has left her with a slight limp. Since she came here during the holidays and played with our children, they must stay out of school, as well as Cyndy's brothers (Billy, Kenny and Ernie). The Carter children can go, as they were not here when Cindy was sick. We are hoping that no one else gets the disease and would appreciate being remembered in prayer about this. Our children have had shots (last week), but they may not have been given in time.

The same day that our polio ban was placed on us, Hector had an accident with the Jeep. A car came out from a side street without stopping and Hector could not help hitting him. No one was injured but both cars suffered damage. While the Jeep is in the garage, the insurance company has provided us with another car which is rented by the day. The day these things took place, I received the promise, "The Lord is able to deliver thee from all evil." And so, He has.

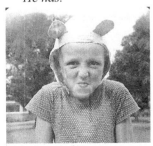

John in part of his rat costume.

I wish you could have heard John tonight in family worship, singing the tenor part to the song, "All your anxiety, all your care, bring to the mercy-seat, leave it there." It was so refreshing, and he sang it so sweetly. He's been whistling nice tunes lately, too, and when I asked him about it, he said he couldn't whistle out yet, but was still whistling in! The other day he was sitting on his bed, and remarked, "I know a whole bunch of French words, and I know some

387

English, too!" He does speak French fluently now and has started speaking in the native language as well. David's arm looked crooked for a while after the cast was off, but it seems to be getting straighter all the time, and there is hardly any difference now with his other one. He uses it all the time.

.....Much love, Ione

Ione can finally report that she had help:

.....A nurse from England has been designated to stay here until after her medical "stage", and in all it will be about four months. She is a dear girl who has a quiet way of making herself very useful and knows just the jobs that tire me most and then does them first. And she is such a good organizer, that she has started some methods of tidiness which are a real help. She has a chart and starts out the week with 20 points, and the ones who have the fewest points taken off at the end of that week, get chocolate bars. Their rooms do look real tidy now. Her name is Margaret Hayes. She is really good in French, too, and is able to help the bigger children with their studying.

Ione loved recounting tales of the unexpected happenings that were part of life in the Congo, and wrote:

.....Last week a queer thing happened on the main street here. We saw a [vehicle] stopped and a crowd of Africans around it with knives and sticks ready for a fight. One person was gingerly raising the hood. I said to Hector, "I'll bet there's a snake in there," and then I heard an African saying "It's a big one!" We had to leave, but later passed the same place, and there in the road was a seven-foot snake, and we heard that it had stopped the motor of the car, and when the man opened the hood and this head raised up, he just threw up his hands and fled. It must have crawled in there while the car was stopped somewhere in the forest.

It's not long before that school year is over, and on 11th of July the family was at

Hector (3rd missionary from top) and others at a baptism service at Banjwadi – c1957

Banjwadi for a Mission conference. Ione wrote to her mother:

.....We have come over to this station for ten days to attend our General Conference.[115] I haven't had very much to do and it is nice to be away from our responsibilities. We are living in the Boyes' new house. There are 24 people there just now, nine big boys in their garage, our four youngest in a room with us. Carters in another room, also Logan's and the Boyes' family. In all there are about 70 missionaries and 30 children.

[115] The conference is a great success with many people converting to Christianity. Many people were Baptised in the Lindi River, so many that a whole team of people were in the river baptising people simultaneously, totally disregarding the possibility of crocodiles lurking!

There are meetings for the children each day and mothers appointed to watch them during their play times. Hector has some films to show them when they all have to be inside. We have brought over most of our equipment from Stanleyville and shall have to take it back in time to care for a good many who will be stopping over afterward.

.....Love, Ione

In the letters home, there is no reference to just how well the children were doing at the Belgian school. But by reading the school journal, *Palmares*, for 1956-57, it is evident they were continuing to do well; Paul, Mike, Philip and Gordon Carter were awarded prizes in religious studies, John yet again won a prize for drawing; Ernie Boyes for being a model student; David got a prize for best effort through the year and Philip, a prize for effort in general and another for politeness. In their year grades, David was 14th in the class and Kenny Boyes - 21st; Billy Boyes is 8th and Paul was 11th; Ken - 12th and Mike 15th. These results were a testament to the effort and success Ione and Hector expended on building a home that nurtured and cared for all.

DL McMillan 1868 – 1957

Hector received news that his father had died on July 18, 1957. Daniel Lochiel (DL) McMillan, was a hard-working Scotch Canadian farmer who married Jane McElheran in 1903 when DL was 34 and she was 28. In a terrible flu epidemic in 1917, the entire family was ill, except for Jane, who nursed the rest of the family. While Jane survived this epidemic, she later developed tuberculosis and died when Hector was only five. Ione tells her sister about DL's passing:

.....He had no suffering but stopped eating one day and just slept away the next. He was breathing heavily, and then they found him gone. It is quite a change for Jean, as she was caring for him like a baby for so long.

Back in Africa, it would seem that the conference at Banjwadi was a great success. On the 7th of August, Ione wrote to her mother:

.....The biggest thing was that our three youngest children accepted the Lord. There were ten missionary children who took their stand for the first time during the meetings held for the children. We are so glad about this.

The Conference was the best one yet, with 100 people there, 30 of these were children. It was July 4th to 12th. We got a lot of visitors before and after, because of so many furloughs due just then, and other reasons. The week before we had 10 of 11 besides our children and the Carters who were waiting here for their parents to come to the Conference. Then the day Conference broke up we had to hurry away with beds to get them set up here for the ones who would be here by noon for dinner.

We have had 60 different guests since the conference, and departures each week, so it hasn't been as quiet as we tho't it would be when school let out. My, how we need guest accommodations. But the Lord is undertaking, and it looks like day after tomorrow the papers will be signed so that Hector can start putting a cement floor in this big building next to this. As soon as we can get up the walls

KM8 - 'Family Worship' – 1957. Isabel is sitting at far right.

partitioning off one end, we'll move over there, with the 9 little boys who are 7 years and under (they come back in three weeks' time) and leave the six big boys in the small building behind this which they have occupied this past year. Then the little girls can stay in the lovely big house where we have been sleeping. And Isabel Whitehead will be living with us to help care for them. She is a girl Marcellyn knows, who came out before I did, a real sweet English girl.

We are taking out a wall in this house to make an enlarged dining room, have put three sinks in the kitchen, and are ready to establish a utility room. When Pudneys were here just now, they promised us the money for a big washing machine. So, you see we have much to praise the Lord for. A year ago, we were in that awful barn where the wind and rain came in as it wished, and where baths were available only outside in half a drum! But any struggle is worthwhile if it can bring about a satisfactory way of caring for missionaries' children while they are seeking to win these Congolese to Christ. We were thrilled to find out that two other children besides our own, had testified to having accepted Christ while they were living in our home. These are the future missionaries. Do pray for them.

Our African staff is growing, in numbers as well as in Grace, and it is a joy to minister to them daily from the Word, and on Sundays our porch is filled with neighbours and those who walk some distance as well. I wish you could see these bright-eyed young men and their beautiful wives setting our tables, washing dishes, mending clothes. We have three couples now who do quite well. But just today I had to tell one young man to stay away tomorrow because he has dysentery. When we have as many as 30 or more eating and sleeping, I am mighty thankful of their help! Mother can you believe that a report has gone around that the food is "excellent" here! If my poor planning and efforts rate that high, what would yours be!! Do pray much that I may set my heart on winning souls rather than the fun of just cooking for so many!

The whole family is well, and Hector is quite heavy now, that is, he is no thinner! I eat well, and feel fine, but the scales don't show much increase. We had a family picture taken this week, and you will be getting one in some form, we are trying to have it printed on a form letter.

We picked up the packages for the children from the Post Office on the 12th and they were in perfect condition, the cookies just as fresh as you could wish, and the chocolate coating was not even turned white! It was such a treat, and we are so thankful for them. Timmie sends his special thanks. He has marvelled ever since he wrote a letter and Grandma got it and sent him just what he asked for. I showed him your picture holding him in your arms and you are quite a real person to him. He is just at that darling stage where everything sounds cute. The four-people living with us for their medical 'stage' just can't get over his interesting conversation. And he can whistle any tune that you can sing. Stephen is so different but has depths that Timmie never reaches. Timmie plays up to his public, but Stephen, never. He sits quietly and lets Timmie get the praise, and only smiles and twinkles sort of shy-like when someone talks to him. He clings to me more than Timmie, and it almost seems like he remembers when I went away from him in '53 and he is afraid I might do it again. John's cuteness could occupy a whole paragraph but I must save it. David's as handsome as ever, and Paul the best disposition of the lot. Kenny - always dependable.

Joyfully, Ione

P.S. the pajamas are grand. Just right. Thanks so much.

Letters home were not just about news of Congo. Occasionally Ione had to send a special thank you letter, deal with financial matters with her supporters or the mission staff, or offer condolences for someone that had recently died. Many such events are omitted here in the interest of brevity, but it should not diminish Ione's concern and love for others, or her concern for the day-to-day finances.

On the 16th of August, Ione wrote to Lucille about her work at the Children's Home:

.....We have just passed thru the busiest time since coming back, the affair of the property was cleared up & now the $14,000 property is in our hands! And not only has there been a physical advance, a Bible study has been started in Stanleyville for whites and is meeting every week. A real answer to prayer. And Africans continue to inquire the way of salvation. Our hands and hearts are full. We have had well over a hundred different guests in the last four weeks. Yesterday we served four tables of missionaries at noon & night plus two tables of Africans. So many come in to Stanleyville to see the Jenkinson's leave for furlough. They are going to America.

.....In spite of our busy time we managed a little family holiday of one week-end at one of our bush stations, Wanie-Rukula. The children enjoyed watching monkeys and blue pheasants [Great Blue Turacos] in the trees in back of the

house where we stayed. The missionaries there had two sick children. The mother, a new worker, said it was diarrhoea, but I was shocked to discover blood in the stool, the symptom of bacillary dysentery, the same awful thing that hit us on the way out in 1950. They have no nurse or doctor there, but I had her call a native nurse from a nearby dispensary and he gave sulfaguanadine. By the time we left the children were responding. The Lord sent us there just in time.

I see His precious hand in everything we do. He has anointed my own soul with "the oil of gladness," and I've never found before so many reasons to praise Him!

Lovingly, Ione

On 25th of August, Ione updated her supporters in the USA:

.....Work has begun on the new building which will be big enough to house 28 children. And as soon as the first unit of four rooms and bath is finished, we will move ourselves and the smaller boys. Then the present house can be used for kitchen and dining room and guests and the little building just behind which has (inadequately) housed 6 big boys, can be the utility building. And we have been promised a washing machine!!

Although our efforts all seem bent toward the care of missionary children, we cannot be blind to the need of the Africans all around us. This morning as we saw our large veranda quickly filling up with eager listeners while Hector gave a Gospel message, I prayed that the Lord would make possible a meeting place for these who have no other Gospel witness. And African women are begging for reading and sewing classes. Little children as well. "IF thou draw out thy soul

The older KM8 boys playing marbles. (L-R): Bill Boyes, Paul McMillan, Michael Carter, Philip Carter, Gordon Carter, David McMillan, Ken McMillan

to the hungry – IF thou satisfy the afflicted soul; THEN....thou shalt be like a watered garden".

Hastily, but joyfully, Hector and Ione

September 29th saw Ione yet again writing a thank you letter to Lucille and Maurice who had sent out a package:

We received the package yesterday, in good condition, tho the box was a bit squeezed. I tho't the cookies would be broken, but most of them were just fine, and still fresh!

.....The suckers by the yard were a pleasant surprise, and we have told the children there will be four apiece, but they can only take them one by one. So we have a secretary check them out, and they must take the colour that comes next. All the sticks are saved to make popsicles. The peppermints are Hector's favourite. Thank you so much for this Christmas box in September. Oh yes, and the plastic bags, I'm glad you sent

them as we have no way of getting any here, and they wear out after a while, so I was glad to have some fresh ones.

.....It is a trying job this entertaining, along with the children, but a real blessing, to be a servant to the servants of the Lord. And the children have gotten a real inspiration for their own future work from the testimonies we have heard.

We have 13 children right now, one little girl, [probably Hazel Parry] *but two more little girls have arrived from furlough and will be coming along in a short while. By January we'll probably have 16. The Stanleyville pool has already been closed.* [It would seem that there were worries of Asiatic flu.] *Kenneth and David, the two Carter boys, and tonight John, have all had fever and colds this week. John scared us when he found he couldn't walk, and I thought right away of polio. But watched him carefully, and in a little while he went to the bathroom and didn't seem to have any trouble. Sometimes malaria makes joints ache. He said his knees hurt. Well, do pray for this epidemic of Asiatic flu that seems to be sweeping the world. I am thankful it has not been serious around here.*

Our Jeep station wagon is crowded so much now that we have to go in shifts. Isobel Whitehead is with us temporarily to help with the children so that makes our regular crowd 16. And most of the time there are others as well. When we

KM8 Kids playing in the sandy driveway which provided a giant space for a host of games.

are all in, we feel like opening up the hatch at the top to let out steam! Will you pray for a small bus or Volkswagen of a size that would be suitable?

This business of pets has gone a little too far. Gordon Carter just loves all kinds of animals, and I have not objected to his monkey, (although the animal bites), the scores of white mice, and the turtles and pigeons, but three days ago he bought a horned viper from a native when I was busy about the supper. It stayed overnight in a pail with a lid and a stone on top. But I was afraid it would get out. Then the next day I came just in time to catch him bargaining for a boa-constrictor! I stopped that sale, but he arranged for the native to bring it back the next morning, which he did. So, I urged Hector to take Gordon and me, and the two snakes to the zoo, where he sold them for 1 dollar. He made a little profit. I have forbidden him buying anything more without permission.

Michael Carter remembers sitting on Phillip's bed reading comics when Ione came in and inquired as to the contents of a bucket in the room. Michael sensing trouble, feigned ignorance and carried on reading. When Ione lifted the lid and discovered the contents, she was not pleased! However, they all relished seeing Gordon's snakes every time they visited the zoo. For the younger kids he had 'hero' status.

Despite house guests, managing the Children's Home with 16 children, Ione still found time to keep up her flow of letters to her mother. The one written on the 1st of October tells that the boys had received letters from America:

.....They were so thrilled to have an airmail letter each. When I went out to check on the 8 14-year-olds I found Paul lying in his bed reading his over again,

squeezing the juicy bits of interest out of it right to the last! They may not write to you right away as they have so much homework these days, but I hope they will get letters off soon. They are finding French easier writing than English now. But we are trying to keep them from forgetting their English. It appears in their spelling

The older boys each with their "trucks" that they rolled around the compound.

sometimes, as "ch" is pronounced like "sh", and fish becomes fich. I saw in one of the older boys' letters the word "line" spelled "ligne", like in French. Perhaps letters to you will help them not to forget.

I am trying to demonstrate more love to the children, and it is not hard, as they are so loveable, and it is not impossible to extend that love to the other children whose mothers are far away.

.....How many times I have been blessed with the verse, "There hath no temptation overtaken you but such as is common to man, but God is faithful and will with the temptation, make a way of escape." Temptations to discouragement, irritableness, criticism, jealousy, and a good many others, but the 'way to escape' thru confession and His precious blood – always a sure cure! God lead His dear children along!!

Well, this is all of the paper but not the news. Keep your heart happy in Him, Mother. And be assured that someone loves you away out here in Congo!

Much love in Him, Hector & Ione

In November, Ione's sister celebrated her birthday and Ione wrote:

.....You, and I, are not getting any younger, but each year is another milestone for Him. It is another year for Him to work with us to make something of us. "He will perfect that which pertaineth to us..." to present you holy and unblameable and unreproveable in His sight." What a happy life it is tho painful sometimes. I trust that tomorrow will be the happiest birthday yet, and that He will spare you for many more before He comes.

As usual there is an update on her work:

.....We just had a letter from Fergus Kirk [Hector's uncle, who is president of Prairie Bible Institute] *who is sending $800 for our Children's Home. This will go toward the purchase of the property. And a few days before that came a letter from Mrs. Pudney, who is sending $100 toward a new washing machine. We need $100 more for the big one that we can get in Belgium, plus $100 for transportation. Will you remember this need? We are not suffering thru the lack of it, as the Africans are used to washing by hand, but we will get a much more efficient and speedy job done with a machine.*

The two little girls [Laureen and Veronica] *came whom we were expecting and they have been with us about a month, a real addition to the Home. That makes 15. The flu epidemic is finished, and Isobel and I are thankful that all thru the time of the children's sickness we had no guests. The Lord always knows our needs and capacities!*

The 'hangar' dormitory at KM 8 being remodeled.

.....Hector is working very steadily on the new dormitory, and day by day we see new evidence of the Lord's goodness there. At first there was only a pile of bricks to work with, then donations of bathroom fixtures from three downtown business people. A drugstore was tearing down its walls, and Hector arrived just in time to relieve them of the windows and doors which they wanted carted off that very day. They made the price very cheap. He has already put up a number and is building rammed earth walls between the pillars of brick. There was no cement for floors and one missionary shouted, "Now, get to work, Hector!" So he did, and when that was gone, another car drove up and another missionary asked Hector to go downtown and take delivery on a ton of cement. So the Lord cares for His own.

Hector had the unpleasant task of killing four snakes in one day in the shed, making seven in all in as many days. One was a horned viper.[116]

.....Joyfully in Him, Ione

Incidents were never far away and, on the 10th of December, Ione wrote to her mother:

.....I will try to finish this while waiting to see the doctor. Gordon Carter has been running a little temperature in the evening and has a cold which has given him some pain in his ear. Then to make matters worse, a boy at school took a pea-shooter (or the likeness of such) and shot a grain of rice in that ear. Isobel put some warm oil in and the rice floated out, but we tho't he should see a doctor.

---

[116] Hector sometimes allowed the older boys (and Laureen) to dissect the snake and skin it. He viewed this as educational! The kids were hoping to establish what it last ate!

A few days ago, our Stephen put a little round black seed in his ear, but a nurse was visiting us and took it out!

.....Love, Ione

The Christmas vacation meant all the children went back to their respective mission stations to be with their families, thus giving the McMillans a little respite and an opportunity to be a 'family' in the true sense of the word rather than the large extended family they had become. Ione and Hector took the chance to get some well-earned quality time with the boys at the end of 1957 with a holiday up country. They had worked relentlessly since taking on their first children's home, and the last one consumed an inordinate amount of time and energy. But Ione seemed to thrive on this, it was work she loved doing despite the setbacks and worries. She lovingly trusted the Lord to provide for her needs and give her the wherewithal to continue.

Chapter 17
A YEAR OF GROWTH

At the end of 1957, the McMillans' holiday to the Slaters at Katwa (KA-twa), in the Kivu region of the Congo, was to be a 'working' holiday in part. Stan Nicholls, the mission treasurer, was returning to Australia with his family for furlough; he agreed the McMillans could have the use of their car while they were away for the year. This meant driving them all up to Kampala, Uganda from whence the Nicholls would get a train to Nairobi and a plane home. This arrangement was convenient for all concerned because the Nicholls paid the expenses on the outward journey, so the McMillans only had to fund the return trip. It wasn't as simple as it sounds, since

The McMillans at Katwa on vacation.

Hector and Ione had very little money at this time. But, as always, the Lord provided; Ione wrote to her mother:

.....Just as we were trying to figure how we could afford it, a letter came telling of the Christmas gift from First Baptist. It was $100, more than it has ever been, and was earmarked 'for the whole family'. Well, it was exactly enough, even to buying hostess gifts and Christmas gifts for the Ludwig and Slater children. The Lord always does the "exceeding abundantly above.."

As with everything Ione engaged with, this required meticulous planning. Besides the Nicholls family, the Kerrigans and Jenkinsons accompanied them as well. As the journey would take them near Katwa, it gave the family an opportunity to catch up with fellow American missionaries who were working at Katwa, the Ludwigs (Ione's associates from their church in Pontiac, Michigan). They all set out from Stanleyville on 21st December as soon as school ended and arrived at Katwa for Christmas Eve. The Kivu region, being mountainous was much colder than Stanleyville so cardigans and coats were needed. The family kept to Ione's target except for one little hiccup; Ione wrote:

.....We kept right to schedule, except for one night which we had to spend in the car at the barrier between Congo and Uganda.[117]

---

[117] This was when the family travelled through the Albert National Park (now Virunga Park) and Queen Elizabeth National Park in Uganda (now Rwindi Park).

We found the hotel filled up and couldn't persuade the native guard to call the white man. He said it was after hours, and it was, but in the morning, when the white man saw that a family of eight had slept in the car in the wind-swept mountains (we used all the coats and sweaters that we had with us!) where wild animals roam, he dismissed the guard as he said he had not used common sense.

Mrs. Kerrigan, Hector and Ione at Albert National Park - December 1957.

Having slept in the car, the family was able to make an early start; Ione wrote:

.....we got a very early start and had only gone a few miles when we started seeing lots of animals, a big elephant lumbered across in front of us, and looked at us and then walked on leisurely; buffaloes in large herds stopped eating long enough to frown at us, gentle waterbucks wiggled their ears and tails. We also saw a wonderful herd of long horned cattle, so common in Uganda.

On their way home, the McMillans managed another short stay with their friends at Katwa; Ione wrote:

.....Verna Ludwig gave us fresh strawberries and many other treats, and so many plants and flowers that the car looked like a greenhouse. We bought little stools and other bits of basketry. The children enjoyed every bit of it.

They arrived back at Kilometer 8 on New Year's Day ready to start again:

.....And now we are starting a year of enlargement. One corner of the new building has cement floors and we have moved into that part with six of the children. It means 'roughing it' like we did at the Nasser place, for a little while, but we have the Home to come to for meals and a pleasant sitting room, and bathroom, so we don't mind, and it does make more sleeping space. We have had $150 given, thru Mrs. Pudney, toward the washing machine, and some large gifts from Prairie Bible Institute have been a real help especially at the end of the year when we were feeling discouraged because "ends" were not "meeting"! Do praise the Lord with us. Mrs. Deconynk has sent us several gifts and a package of soap samples.

Ione was very grateful that Isabel Whitehead had stayed and maintained the home in her absence since the day they got back from their holiday, four car loads of visitors also landed.

The New Year brought fresh concerns about the family's health; Kenny fainted at school and was taken to a doctor who observed he was mildly obese but reassured Ione that nothing else was remiss. Unfortunately, Hector suffered a bout of malaria and had to spend a few days in bed. Then Stephen had malaria and two other children got chicken pox. Ione attributed the malaria to having slept without mosquito nets for a couple of nights while they were away.

On the 4th of February, Ione wrote to her mother:

.....Timmy has his fourth birthday on Thursday. He is getting excited. Isobel has redressed his teddy bear and some other folks visiting us left a ball and truck to be given to him. His cake will be a ready mix that we received in a Christmas box. Timmy is quite manly and holds the car door open for me, and talks quite grown-up. Stevie is more babyish, tho he tries to sit and stand like a man. He still has his sly-crooked grin which makes him a favourite. John is much like a greyhound in sleekness, size and speed. But his eyes are big and loving. David is perhaps the most affectionate of all and is getting bigger than Paul. Paul is still like a little boy tho he runs about with Kenneth's crowd. I have been reading "Lassie Come Home" to them on afternoons when they don't have to go to school and those big boys have loved it. I rest out in their dormitory those afternoons to get to be with them. The six smallest ones get a story after they are tucked under their mosquito nets each night. Last night they said the two wolves and the troll made them dream bad dreams!! The stories were Little Red Riding Hood, Three Pigs, and Billy Goat's Gruff.

The McMillan boys, c1958

Ione finally heard from her mother mid-February; it would seem that Leone had experienced testing times for Ione wrote:

.....I am asking the Lord to supply your physical needs, and also to meet the loneliness, in whatever way He sees best. I'm sorry you have lost your job. But the fact that you had nothing to do with it, makes me think that it is the Lord who closed this door, as he sometimes does, in order to open another, which will be better. I wish I were there to comfort you and to help in some way.

Some of the Children's Home kids in the KM 8 driveway dressed for a special event at school in Stanleyville. Photo was taken near the main road.

It's in this letter that Ione shared that there were ups and downs in her life too:

.....We are at a turning point in our big experiment here. It could mean failure or success depending on how far we want to go with the Lord. But having "launched out into the deep", we will not turn back. But each new move is disarming and sometimes

frightening, as we see the extent of influence it will make. We have had hard financial testing's and have decided that for us it is wrong to incur any kind of a debt. The Lord bro't us thru a severe testing at the end of the year, and a wonderful gift from PBI paid it all off. But, with our mistakes behind us, they are ever before us, too, and we shall not be tempted again. It has been after this issue was faced that the Lord moved in a special way in sending the first designated gift for the new building, and an architect to draw up a plan superior to the old one. Praise the Lord with us, that He lets us stay on in such a responsible position, with so much money to handle; I have four books to keep and I don't know how many Hector has, and the treasurer looks at them every few weeks. We live like in a glass house, yet have wonderful times with the Lord, and with our children, and wouldn't trade places with anyone!

In a letter to friends and supporters on the 9th April, Ione reported on the progress made so far with their work:

.....If you have been wondering if the big shed has been turned into a missionary children's dormitory, you wouldn't be sure right now, if you could see it. It is taking shape, thru the work of many consecrated hands! Our nearby station of Banjwadi, sent to us about twenty workmen and Bible Institute students, on holiday, and they are all over the place. Some are working on a new well, some on a septic tank, digging ditches, laying pipes, cement block walls, plastering, or cutting long grass around the place. It is good to hear them singing hymns or responding cheerfully to Hector's suggestions. Five women are preparing their food, and some little children are running about.

The missionary children are on holiday and we are working hard, inside and out, to have a better place ready for them when they come back next week. The

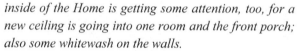

inside of the Home is getting some attention, too, for a new ceiling is going into one room and the front porch; also some whitewash on the walls.

We expect sixteen children this term, ages 4 to 14. From the big children's "student council", down to the little one's cute sayings, it is an interesting work and in the last few moments of the day, when all is quiet, we like to talk over these things. And in the middle of the morning, after they are in school, Isobel and I stop for special prayer for the problems. Isobel Whitehead is the other missionary who is helping here full time.

David with the cat.

You would laugh to see David "staring" the cat out of the chair where it is not allowed. Instead of lifting the cat away, he just glares at it until the cat removes itself! Or you would be surprised, as I was, when Timmie stands before you singing, "Happy birthday to you", with his hands behind him, and then presents you with – of all things – the butcher knife! You need eyes all around, but above all, you need eyes that look up.

Recently we had a letter from Hector's Aunt Mabel, who always sends some helpful portions of Scripture, and this one was Romans 4:18 to 21 – "Abraham (vs.20) staggered not at the promise of God, through unbelief; but was strong in faith, giving glory to God".

So many things are staggering and I find myself with greater responsibilities than ever before, especially with older children to guide. But we are determined that no child of ours, or the others under our care, are going to be raised for the devil. There'll be no black sheep. And the only way we can see them going on for God is to keep out of sight ourselves and not let any selfish affection for them interfere. We have given them to God, and now we are going to hold onto God for them, one by one. It is not easy. And He has not promised that there will be no trial of faith, but He has said, "Everything that may abide the fire, ye shall make it go thru the fire". We get to know God intelligently thru the Word, but experimentally by means of trial.

Thanks so much for all you are doing in our behalf! May the Lord richly bless you!

Joyfully in Him, Ione, Hector & Boys

KM 8 group photo at the Stanleyville Airport – July 1958
Back Row (L-R): Margaret Hayes, Laurel McCullum, Ione McMillan, Jean Radden, Lois Carper, Del Carper, Hector McMillan
Ken McMillan, Paul McMillan, David McMillan, Laureen Walby, Eileen Walby (w/Adrian), Isobel Whitehead
John McMillan, Tim McMillan, Wilfred Walby, Steve McMillan, Marilyn Carper, Veronica Walby

To reduce Ione's work load, the Mission Field Council made a decision; Ione wrote to her mother on the 28th of April:

.....Did I tell you, Mother, that the Field Council made a rule that no visitors were to come to the Children's Home while the school term was is session, except

the parents of the children. A hotel in town has made a special rate to missionaries. We still have quite a few people in and out, but they most always come in between meals and when the children are in school. It was hard for me to write to missionaries of other missions and tell them of this ruling, but I felt it was of the Lord as I had the verse, "This also is from the Lord, who is wise in counsel and wonderful in working". Isaiah. We are able to get ahead better with the building program. I'm sure you must have been praying about this.

.....Love, Ione

This letter was written from a doctor's office and Ione omitted to tell her mother why she was at the Doctor's. Leone had to wait for a letter written on the 9th of July 1958 for an explanation:

.....I'm sorry I did not tell you why I was there. Hector and I had taken five of the missionary children to see the doctor. Four of them were diagnosed as flu and the other received medicine for a bad cold. So many were getting fever that we began to think it was more than ordinary malaria, and it was, although no one was really very ill or with complications. I had several bouts with it, and I began to think there was something wrong with me, as I was so nauseated and ran a little temperature every day. But that has passed away, and I am fine again. It just took a while to get over the flu. I really feel better and more able to cope with the job than last year at this time. We did not have any guests except parents until school was out, and since then it has not been very hard. Just now we have our newest mission doctor and his wife and small child. The wife is not well.

.....We met Joseph Dansis, the mulatto boy (now a man!) who used to live with us before I was sick at Bongondza. He stayed last night and went on to Mabel Wenger's today. He is one of the three mulatto children Mabel has raised. He has his teacher's certificate now and is a sweet Christian young man. We will have Mabel and the other mulatto girls, plus Joe, next week. They are going to do some gardening and landscaping for us. We have ordered a lot of fruit trees (free from the gov't) and grass, and want someone who knows how to put them in. We have 15 beds made up already for a number of people stopping here after a field council now in session at Banjwadi. We have done a lot of meeting of boats and planes, and are finding this a real expense, when trips are made and the people don't arrive. But the Lord knows about this and will give wisdom concerning our financial affairs.

We received the Sunday school material and are so thankful to have more copies. We are continuing Sunday school during the vacation; we still have some from the last set to finish up. Then we'll start on what you sent when all of the children are here as there are enough copies. The books you sent were so welcome. I think all of the children who can read have read all of them. They are just ravenous to read interesting stories and it's good to have something that will help them to love the Lord more.

The mail is going, now, and I will only take time to enclose a picture of each child. Hope you like them! Love, Ione

The 1957-58 edition of *Palmares*, written by the Headmaster of the Belgian School made interesting reading. The children gained an array of prizes and awards:

.....*Stevie McMillan gets a prize for singing; Religious knowledge prizes go to Laureen and Veronica Walby, Hazel Parry, Ken Boyes, Mike Carter, Paul and David McMillan. John gets yet another prize for drawing as does Stephen Parry. The* Sedec *prize for application goes to Mike Carter who also gets a prize for maths. Paul McMillan and Mike Carter get prizes for being model students and Laureen for making the most progress in one year. Language prizes go to Billy Boyes, Paul and Ken McMillan.*

In their individual classes, Veronica is ranked 3rd, Hazel 5th and Ken Boyes 24th; David is 16th in his year; Laureen 12th; Billy 4th and Paul 7th; Ken 5th and Mike 7th in their respective years, so good attainment by all especially when considering all classes are undertaken in a foreign language.

Ironically Laureen's mother was extremely proud when her daughter (Veronica) received 100 lines to write as a punishment. She had to write, "Je suis une bavarde" – that is: I am a chatterbox! Quite an achievement for an English girl in a Belgian school.

The end of the scholastic year in June gave Ione an opportunity to catch up with things that had slipped with the frenzy of caring for children, ensuring they get homework done, entertaining guests and parents collecting children and supporting Hector while he engaged in building work. On the 22nd of July, she got time to respond to Hector's family and thank them for their faithful support and letters. She wrote:

.....*School finished the 21st of June, and Hector celebrated by shooting off a little sky rocket.[118] The children were thrilled and called it a satellite. When the children, other than our own left, the guests began, and at present we have ten.*

It was just a short time ago that a splendid letter came from Irene with local news and interesting bits about all of the family. And just today a birthday letter for Hector from Jean. Kenneth and Paul enjoyed the poems (original!) on their birthdays.

.....*Paul is sitting beside me writing Donald Pierce, to thank him for the pictures he sent. The beautiful wedding pictures of Muriel and Jim are posted on our big board in the dining room. I wonder if I ever thanked you, Alice, for them. Also, for the good letter written in March. Florence's letter and new address were both interesting. In answer to Irene's letter, we expect to take our furlough in July or August of '60.*

So far as news from my family, Mother has a job she likes in a large 5,000 patient hospital for elderly and crippled people. She is secretary to the Chaplain. She has access to a pipe organ and plays for a wheelchair choir as well as her

---

[118] Laureen remembers being given the choice of either grapes or a sky rocket as a prize for achievement at school. She chose a rocket and proudly took it back to Bongondza and her father set it off as night time fell. It caused a real commotion as no one in that part of the Ituri forest had experienced anything like it.

office work. She does a lot of visitation, too, in the wards. She has a new car and drives thru all sorts of Chicago traffic. I am amazed that she has learned to drive at her age! My sister Lucille and her husband have a new pastorate in Pawpaw, Michigan. Lucille is probably in the hospital just now in Ypsilanti, having an operation. Her oldest daughter expects to come to Africa this year as a missionary. Marcellyn expects another baby next month; this will be six children in three years, which of course beats my record! But her husband had three already when they were married. They are doing a good work in Dominican Republic.

We continue to enjoy the Lord's rich blessings. "For the Lord God is a sun and shield: the Lord will give grace and glory; no good thing will He withhold from them that walk uprightly". Psa. 84:11

Joyfully in Him, (Hector and) Ione

If Ione was expecting a break during the school holidays, it wasn't to be a reality. On the 10th of September, she wrote to friends and supporters at Westwood Baptist church:

.....While the children are in school, I have more time for letters. All summer it was difficult as we had not only our 6 children, but altogether 114 house guests.[119] We had DVBS [Daily Vacation Bible School] part of the time and finished some Sunday school workbooks which were sent to us. If you ever have any unused workbooks or things to cut out or colour will you send them up for us? If you can't send them, we can get them when we come home in 1960.

Now school has begun and we are more or less on schedule. There are 16 children here, and as fast as we can increase our sleeping space and staff there will be more. Other missions are wishing to send their children and we want to be able to have them. Pray for Hector as he lays cement blocks for rooms and puts down cement and bathroom fixtures.[120] Also pray that another missionary couple will be free to come and help.

In a letter to her mother five days later, it appeared Ione, Hector and family managed to get a break to return to Bongondza where they had left behind certain belongings. While some had perished it appeared that some treasured items remained intact. Ione got special pleasure from listening to records:

.....My how thrilled I was when I played (after five years) the records which we just now received again from Bongondza: "In My Heart There Rings a Melody," "He Came to Me One Day", "The Stranger of Galilee".

Ione shared news about her health and the bouts of 'flu she had experienced over the last few months. She was perplexed by the cyclical nature of her illness, until someone pointed out that she may well be experiencing the onset of menopause.

---

[119] The embargo on house guests seems to have been lifted for the school holidays and everyone has capitalized on this.

[120] It transpires that the work Hector started earlier in the year was without formal approval from the Field Mission, however, it was all made official in July.

Hector and the children made her birthday celebrations special and gave her a toy okapi:[121]

.....Hector and the children bought me a little velvet stuffed okapi. It is a rare animal which is only found in the Congo. You will see it when we come home, something between a giraffe and a zebra.

The request made to her supporters for Sunday school material was reiterated to the family and it's no surprise that Ione's letter contained news of materials received:

.....We have started using the Scripture Press S.S. material with the children and certainly do enjoy them. I only hope the next set will reach us in time to continue right on when these finish in December. And thanks so much, Mother, for the Christian Readers Club membership. We have been receiving some very fine books and tracts. We are looking forward to that box.

In the next letter, Ione commiserates with her mother about her need to buy things on an installment plan. Her own experience has led her to believe that if at all possible, being in debt is not the right way to go. She wrote:

.....How I do pray, Mother that all of your obligations may be met and that you will never again have to pay for anything on the instalment plan. I'm sure that is a greater burden than anything else in your life. I was reading some of the old letters we bro't back from Bongondza and it reminded me of the debts I used to have. I don't believe the Lord ever meant for us to have that sort of burden.

McMillans at KM 8 – c1958

With a new term, Hector resumed work on the 'hanger', turning it into a dormitory. Ione wrote to the family in Canada in October:

.....All are keeping quite well. Hector is not getting any thinner, though he is doing work which takes a lot of strength and energy.

The center of the big building looks pretty much like a workshop yet, but the right-hand side one would recognize as a dormitory, though perhaps only from the fact that beds are there! Hector and I have a room between the two finished (??) dormitory rooms and by having walls on either side that fold back we can give necessary supervision at times of getting up, studying, and going to bed. The folding walls are also convenient for cleaning and for more air when it is excessively hot.

---

[121] See photo above of the actual item Ione saved. It was eventually given to John McMillan and is one of his cherished possessions.

Hector was an inventive builder. The round house he built at Bongondza for Verna Schade was talked about by the travelling British Home Mission Secretary and the McMillans got a letter from a mission in Haiti asking Hector to share his knowledge.

Ione continued in this letter describing an outing they undertook with all the children:

.....Yesterday we took the children after Sunday school in the afternoon to a chicken farm near here. In order to take them all we had to let some walk part way, but since it was too far to walk, Hector shuttled with the Jeep and picked them up before they were too tired. After leaving the farm, we went on some distance and had a "paper sack" supper. The children carried the drinking water bottles which they usually take when going to school or on any trip. The last stage of the journey was made with all in or on the Jeep (20!), very slowly of course, with the back down and four big boys sitting with their feet hanging out the back. Perhaps you can form a picture in your mind. Isobel and I were a bit squashed, and when we arrived, I said to Isobel, "Was this any easier than getting them to wash the dishes?!" They get the meal and wash the dishes Sunday night as the cook has that time off.

Always having an ear for a good laugh, Ione wrote that everyone usually goes to the B.M.S. (Baptist Mission Society) church and they spoke of it by those initials. She overheard one of the bigger boys at the Sunday breakfast table comment on another boy looking too untidy for church, "Are you going to be a mess (BMS) like that?"

Birthday parcels (like Christmas) never arrive in time for the event but seemed to arrive in a timely manner; Ione wrote to her mother on the 14th of October:

.....Just after I sent your last letter the first package came. That was Sept. 18th, with the cotton kimonos, dresses, books and 3 boxes of candy. Then on the 20th the other one came with the other box of Sky-Peps, more dresses, slips, ties, and the luscious Yardleys. Thank you so much for remembering my birthday! The candy arrived in very good condition, as did everything else. We have given the children a roll each for two weeks and then single ones and I'm afraid I have had more than my share for I know where I keep them. And just now there is only one package left. I guess we'll offer that as a prize! We have never had anything more delicious, and we have certainly enjoyed this treat. Thank you so much.

Ione saved parts of the packages so she has a stock of things she could use on the boys' birthdays so they'd have something 'on the day':

.....The box of nuts I am saving for John's birthday which is coming Saturday. We have a confetti angel cake mix to make, and some rolls of life savers to decorate.

On the mission station, everything was shared:

.....Will you also thank Mr. and Mrs. Wm. Thornberg for the dresses, and tell them if you see them, that four of them fitted me exactly! Two were the right size for Isobel, and also a slip and a nightgown. They were very welcome, as I have no more new dresses to pull out of the trunk. I was wishing for a white dress to wear for formal occasions at the school, programs, etc., as all of the children

are in white (with badges on their pockets) and while we were at Bongondza, the new doctor's wife gave me just the thing which she could not wear. I had not a hat as I had given the one I travelled in to Mrs. Walby for her furlough trip, and a German lady in town passed on to me a pretty wide-brimmed straw. I have had three dresses given to me by Marge Boyes, two of them cut out and made up especially for me. People are so good and observe when we need things! Reinforcing the timeliness of the packages!

It's not just clothes that Ione was grateful for:

.....I want specially to mention our appreciation for the doctrine book for children. It is just what we were wanting for the children's family worship, and Hector has read a chapter every day. I think there is only one chapter left. The children are so interested and love the question time. I see you sent an extra copy, which we would like to give to someone else. Do they sell books without covers cheaper, and do you think we could get an order of more Christian stories for the children to read themselves, like the Winky Series and Patty Lou? They just can't get enough, and there are so many children now who can read. If we don't fill their cravings for reading matter with this sort of thing, they will seek it in the comic books which are available here now. I remember curling up with books – I was an avid reader. You are doing so much for us already I don't like to mention anything, except as I know how much you have been used of the Lord in meeting our needs and others.

As the year ended, there are few mentions in Ione's letters about Christmas, what the family did or what parcels were received. The family got one trip out, albeit with one more incident. Ione wrote:

.....We took an overnight trip during the Christmas holidays to a place called Yangambi, an agricultural center [downriver from Stanleyville]*, where we could get replacements for fruit trees that had died, some flower plants, and grass.* [122] *Everything went well until we rounded the last bend between Stanleyville and our Home. Hector slowed down for a bad bridge and then a turn. Just on the turn the door opened and John fell out. He sat down on the gravel road and then fell forward so that he had gravel marks on his forehead, nose, chin, elbows and knees, but they weren't deep. After cleaning him up at the house and putting on seven bandages, he felt better* [that or he simply did not want another hospital visit]. *He went to sleep, and when he wakened, he felt like playing again. We are so thankful that Hector was not driving fast. And we will be more careful now about that door; we still don't know whether it wasn't shut tight or whether he bumped the handle.* [He bumped the handle!]

It was a busy year, and a physically taxing one.

---

[122] 150 trees and shrubs had been planted earlier in the year.

Chapter 18
DILEMMAS AND TENSIONS

It's not surprising that Ione's letters in January of 1959 do not focus on Christmas and 'thank yous' as in other years. Ione had catered for 20 missionary visitors and the number of children she cared for had risen to 18. In the letters to family and supporters, she wrote of making ends meet and meeting the needs – physical, spiritual and emotional, of all those in her care. To her mother she stated:

.....We have had to go without some things, but I am thankful the food has been enough to satisfy all and the children have round, rosy faces. Our financial account has been sent to all of the stations, and they are marveling that we are spending each month 2000 francs ($40) more than we are receiving from the parents, and still have no debts! All missionaries have been urged to donate any work funds, which are not already committed, to this need. The Lord continues to do the impossible, and we thank the Lord for gifts from time to time which make up this needed amount.

.....There is still a debt of $7,000 on this property, though the amount is owed in our mission rather than to the former owner. And just yesterday we learned that a gift of $2,000 was on the way from Mr. and Mrs. Bryers in Hamilton Ontario. Prairie Bible Institute friends and relatives have contributed heavily all this term and it is because of their interest and prayers that we plan to go out there again this furlough.

While thinking about the children, Ione knew what to ask for:

.....If anyone has used games that you think we could use, they will be welcome. Outdoor as well as indoor games. And we never have enough of colour books, crayons, paper dolls, etc., which are nice for rainy days. Stub pencils cast off from offices or schools at home can be used here for amusement at home.

I want you to know how much we appreciate your interest in us. You have a tremendous job if you are going to try to help all of the missionaries, and we will understand if we are left out.

She went on to explain:

.....I do hope you will not fail to keep us supplied with some sort of S.S. material, as it has helped the children so much, not only spiritually, but it helps their spelling and reading in English. This has been neglected while they study in French.

Also, at the forefront of Ione's mind was their anticipated break/furlough coming in July of 1960. She was mindful of the support she had received, like the donation mentioned above. She told her mother that she would like to visit supporters but more than anything, she would like to include her mother in her July/August travel plans. On the 15th of January she spoke of flying from Congo to Europe and picking up a second-hand Volkswagen from a German friend, drive it around Europe, then putting the car on the ocean liner, *United States,* and sailing to America. Ione tried to entice her mother to join them for this venture including the voyage back on the liner.

Finally, in letters to various members of family and friends, Ione addressed the disturbing reports of current affairs in Congo:

.....I know you will be anxious to know what is happening in the Congo. According to the radio and papers there was a riot in Léopoldville three weeks ago. The report was that 42 Africans were killed, 250 injured, and 10 whites injured. It started with a political-religious group called ABAKO. The Salvation Army property was in their path of destruction so they lost 5 buildings. The Salvation Army missionaries left their homes and put their valuables with friends. Last week there was tension felt here between blacks and whites; it was announced that there would be a general strike if the proclamation from Belgium was not satisfactory. Evidently it was satisfactory as there was no strike. Belgian Congo has severed relationship politically with Belgium.

According to Fabian (1996) in his book, *Remembering the Present: Painting and Popular History in Zaire*, Kasavubu, a political activist, had gone to Léopoldville to demand independence for the provinces of the lower Congo. These provinces were the wealthiest mining areas of Congo. He was imprisoned after the riots and extradited to Belgium. The ABAKO was the largest political group and it was not long before other leaders began to emerge from other parts of the country.

.....Our children attend school which has a large proportion of Africans. Police were stationed around the school for a few days, and the children were not happy together. When the teacher wasn't there, one black girl hit one of our girls with a jumping rope and said something mean. Laureen cried when she came home but declared she had said nothing to the girl. We had a good talk to all of the children about remembering what their mothers and fathers came out here for, and to keep loving the African children as they had before. We have heard rumours of another riot in Léopoldville. Two dispensaries were attacked. The Belgians are somewhat bitter and it reflects in their children. Do pray that we will keep our hearts at rest in Jesus and our minds stayed on Him.

The Belgians were getting nervous and equipping themselves with guns while the Africans were emboldened to voice their dissatisfaction with Belgian colonial rule. There was no indication at this time of the physical difficulties and threats that everyone would face in the future. Neither were the feelings of unrest and the frustrated, localized acts of rebellion against the oppression of colonial rule unique to the Belgian Congo. This was a period when so many emerging nations across the world could not find the patience to wait for the independence they had been promised by their European masters. Where the Congo differed from most countries was in its brutal history. While the advancements in improved infrastructure, health and education were undeniably enjoyed by the people, it was the attitudes of many

Belgians and the deep-rooted resentment of the indigenous population towards them that set this nation on a downward spiral from which it has never fully recovered.

The first introduction for Congolese people to the Europeans occurred in the 18th century when Portuguese ships sailed into view and weighed anchor in the vast mouth of the Congo river in direct confrontation to the then Kingdom of Congo. Purporting to be traders who might bring advancement and wealth to the region, the intentions of the Portuguese sailors were entirely predatory. Contrary to their initial expectations they found themselves face to face with a complex society, living in an organized city structure which was governed by a supreme king. Nevertheless, they began their 'trade' offering guns in return for slaves. They set African against fellow African in their pernicious ventures and thus destroyed the balance of that society. The population of the kingdom, which was a relatively small area compared with the size of the country that it was to become in later years, was completely decimated. Four million slaves were dispatched to the West Indies alone. The lucrative trade in slaves brought many more Europeans, including the British, who attempted to forge their way into the hinterland by sailing up the river. None were able to progress any further than 100 miles. The 220 miles of rapids and cataracts had kept invaders out of central Africa for decades. It is estimated that these same rapids could provide hydraulic electricity for the whole of Africa. However, late in the 19th century the explorer Henry Morten Stanley, was finally able to navigate the mighty Congo River by starting from the other end. Travelling across the continent from Zanzibar in Eastern Africa, he located the source of the river and traced its route northwards and eventually westwards to the Atlantic Ocean. He arrived in Boma, the capital, in 1887 having taken 999 days to cross Africa from East to West. Initially he had wanted to annex the whole area enclosed by the course of the river for the British and he was expecting their financial input. But at that time, the eyes of the British were firmly fixed on India and the east. So, Stanley approached King Leopold of Belgium who was more than happy to fund his expeditions. Stanley swiftly laid claim to this vast area making Boma the capital of the new 'Congo Free State', a personal fiefdom for King Leopold which was eighty times larger than the country for which he was monarch. As the trade in slaves eventually declined owing to international social pressure, the Congo basin came up with the next commodity that the modern world required most – rubber.

At the turn of the century rubber was needed not only for the insulation of electric cables but also for the manufacturing of tires, first for bicycles and later for the burgeoning motor car industry. Half of the tires in the world were made from Congolese rubber. Wild rubber in its unrefined state would make a personal fortune for King Leopold. Having established that the river and its tributaries could transport this precious commodity, he set about arranging for the labor to harvest it. It is no secret that the military were engaged in forcing the population into the forests to do the work. Their regime was brutal. If the allocated quotas were not achieved, a number of those responsible for the harvest would have their hands summarily cut off as a warning to others. It is not known precisely how many people died from the maltreatment used to fuel the world's need for rubber but it is generally considered to be a half of the entire population. It was probably one of the worst atrocities of the 20th century and yet it is now all but forgotten by the rest of the world apart from the Congolese people. At least, at the time, pressure was put on the King to bring to an end this 'businesses 'of his and in 1908 the whole area was handed over to the Belgian state to take over as a colony.

Turning away from the rubber trade, the next vital raw product to be found in the Congo was a vast supply of copper in the southern Katanga province. It was the largest deposit of copper in the world and came to light just in time to be used in the manufacture of shell casings for bombs and bullets required for the first World War. A few years later, and from the same area, the Congo yielded another precious metallic element at the appropriate moment in the form of the finest high-grade uranium. This was used in the construction of the atomic bombs used to bring an end to the second World War. It is a little-known fact that the Congolese army fought in both wars on behalf of the Belgians. They, in turn, invested the wealth from the mining and other projects into building roads, railways, schools and hospitals. The living conditions for the African people were indisputably raised but the extremely large expatriate community living in the country exercised a rigid apartheid society. It was this, compounded with a history of brutality that fueled the resentment of the people in the months before the Congo's declaration of independence.

It was in this atmosphere of unrest (with still a year and a half to go until Independence Day) that the incident Ione earlier referred to occurred at the school. A general strike had been announced which prompted many of the Belgians to arm themselves as a precaution and this in turn caused the police to be out in force near the school creating tension in the air.

Ione's letters in February of 1959 included one to her friend Pearl Hiles, the missionary nurse who travelled out to Congo with Ione in 1942. Pearl was still at home in the States and Ione wrote to her on the 5th of February:

.....It just seems like old times to be in touch with you again, and it looks like we can be together again. I surely am happy about this and hope it won't be a disappointment to you to be doing this work for a while. I wish it would be permanently, but I know that there will probably be a shift of personnel at Conference time in June or July, so can't set my heart on anything except to be happy that we can have you until then.

.....Will you be coming by plane? We want to know when to meet you. Be ready for some HOT weather in Stanleyville! It stays hot nights here, too. It is so thrilling to know that you really are coming.

The Walbys are here right now, meeting the Siggs[123], and they want me to send you their greetings. Wilfred (their third child) will be coming to the Home after Easter.

Lovingly, Ione

As usual, some packages did not arrive in time for Christmas: Ione wrote to Irene Pierce on February 20th:

.....Your wonderful package arrived the middle of January and I can tell you there was a lively bunch of hands ready to open it. Thank you all so much for giving us this lovely Christmas in January! We don't mind at all having them later as they did have a parcel for Christmas Day as well as a number of things Hector bought with a $20 bill someone sent. I think they take better care of their things when they don't get too many all at once! Kenneth and Paul have been using their dictionaries and it was good for them to have English as well as French, for when they write English letters, they find difficulty in spelling. The French is useful for their schoolwork. The socks were just right for K and P as well, and they do send you their grateful thanks. The little boys' toys were darling and they were so pleased. Three of them were sick in bed when they arrived, so they had lots of time to play with them. (We have had two epidemics of flu since September 1958, the last ending in whooping cough.)

And to Marguerite and Hazel - thanks for another package:

.....What a happy surprise we received when, on January 23rd your package arrived! It was beautifully packed and everything came in excellent condition.

.....Hector was pleased with his tie and socks, and the pretty things to go with them! He has a shirt which requires cuff-links but he had none and was always borrowing some that the Loyals sent to the children last year! Now he has his own, and such smart ones. The slipperettes and half-slip fit me just fine and I am so glad to have them; these items are very handy, especially when we travel. Thank you so much. Kenneth has always wanted a brush and comb set, and this is his first. I hope he takes good care of it, and the nice hankies as well. Paul is real pleased with his harmonica and finds nice tunes on it. The hankies are especially welcome as the only ones they have had until now are the kind made out of flour sacks! Miss Whitehead, who helps us with the sewing, has stitched their numbers on so that they can tell them apart. David and John felt especially honored to be trusted with jack knives. They are old enough to know how to use them safely and are keeping them wisely on their shelves. Stevie's importance went up 100% when he became the possessor of a wallet, and with money in it. He will save the money for when we come on furlough, unless he is tempted to trade it for francs when someone goes on furlough ahead of us. It is always handy to have some American coins in your pocket when you arrive, for tips, etc. Timmy's baseball came at an opportune time, as the bigger boys had just

---

[123] Dick and Mimi Sigg were new, young American missionaries from Florida and Indiana and they had a 1-1/2-yr old son, Sammy. They were designated to take the place of Hector and Ione during their furlough.

received from Focklers who support David, a real baseball, and Timmy is very anxious to learn how to play the game with his own first. His duck [apparently Timmie had a duck!] *is very sturdy and his squawk has not faltered once, though it has been going for almost a month!! Yesterday a little African lad 'fed' it with small stones and Timmy was quite upset and spared no energies to cause a regurgitation and relieve the creature! Thanks so much for just everything.*

.....Joyfully in Him, Hector & Ione

On the 24th of February, Ione wrote to supporters at Westwood Baptist Church. The letter gives a good overview of life in the Children's Home:

Dear Friends of the Primary Department,

We have recently received $12 from you and want to thank you for it in behalf of our son Stephen.

Stephen behind Tim in the wagon at KM 8.

Stephen recently had his 6th birthday. I am sending you a picture of him sitting in the wagon behind his younger brother Timothy. John is in the back coming down the steps. There are 20 missionary children here now; the youngest is 5 and the oldest 16.

Did I ever tell you what these children do here? They always get up before daylight, except on Sunday. And in order to help them waken and be able to find their clothes, Uncle Hector starts the big diesel engine and the lights come on for a few minutes. But by the time the children have dressed, washed and made their beds and met for family worship, the lights can go out again, and they eat breakfast by daylight. They have papaya, a nice fruit like muskmelon, with a few drops of lemon on, oatmeal and rice porridge, bread and peanut butter and jam,

Children's Home kids are shown here awaiting the school bus.

413

and of course milk, but the milk is made from powdered milk bought in cans. While they are at the table they make a sandwich and fill a drinking water bottle to carry with them. Sometimes they have some francs and can buy some cold pop or a big bun at school. They play around the yard until 7, when the bus comes and then they get in line. In the morning the tiny children go in first, but at noon, whoever gets there first. The Belgian children have taught our children to be very polite. Everyone shakes hands and says bonjour whenever they meet an adult that they know.

From the time our children leave home until they come back at noon they must talk in French. It does not take very long to learn when you are little. We try to have their dinner ready for them to eat as soon as they come home because they do not have much time. They ate their sandwich during recess at 10, and it is now 12:30. The bus comes again at 1:30 and this time they take just water to drink, as there is none that can be used at school. In the afternoons they do not have hard lessons, but handwork and the girls sewing, etc., as it is very hot. They arrive home again at 5 and have family worship again and then supper. Right after supper there is homework, and everybody does it except those in kindergarten. First graders are already writing with ink and have time to play ball before it gets dark. When the big diesel starts up again that means that there will be hot water for baths, as the water that cools the motor gives us hot water for all the children. The diesel [motor] also pumps it from the well at the same time.

Kindergarten and first grade are in bed by 7, the rest in primary school by 7:30, and those in high school have more homework which sometimes keeps them up until 8:30 or 9. It is a busy life, but they are happier when they have lots to do. We have time for birthday parties, picnics and swimming and trips to the zoo, but now because we are so many, we have taken turns going. Our hearts are happy in Jesus, and we hope each one of you know Him as your very own Saviour. Write to us sometime.

Lovingly, Ione

The Stanleyville swimming pool was close to the Congo River. It wasn't tiled but simply a concrete construction filled with filtered water from the river. There was a small children's pool with a slide – a slide so rough it ruined many swimsuits. There was a spring board and a diving board at the deep end of the pool and a row of showers at the shallow end. As for the zoo, that too was adjacent to the river but by Tshopo falls, nearer to the children's home at Kilometer 8. The chimpanzees who roamed freely liked visitors' picnics and often came begging or scrounging for anything that was dropped.

Ione wrote to Canadian family friends and at the forefront of her mind were plans for returning to America with her large family:

.....we would like very much to put the children in the school in Three Hills for the time that we are in the homeland (fall of '60 and spring of '61). If we can get a house to rent like we did in '50 it would be nice. Hector and I will have to be

away a number of times for conferences in the States and eastern Canada, but we will try to alternate so that one can be with the children all the time. I don't know what the children will eat, when it's Hector's turn to stay!! In that case, I hope our house is not too far away from yours!!

Aunt Mabel had been advised that the children needed to be registered early for school on their return, presumably because choice was restricted if not done in advance. Ione continued:

.....This past term P.B.I. has done so much for us, and we want our children to get all they can from there. The school here is a public school and all their Christian training must come from our home. It will encourage their hearts to be in a Christian school for a while. I am wondering if any of ours will be near to the ages of your girls. Kenneth is 11 now; Paul is 10; David almost 9; John is 7; Stephen is 6; and Timothy is 5. They will all be in school when we come home, and I suppose Kenneth, and maybe Paul, will be ready for high school. The grades are so different here, it is hard to tell until we see the work they do there in high school. Kenneth, if he passes, will be ready for what they call the secondary school here, by the time we come home. But we have noticed the work is about a year ahead of school at home. It is in French and Flemish.

In a letter written later in the year, Ione described an incident where Hector felt the need to talk to the teacher at Athénée Royal de Stanleyville which probably affirmed for them the need for a Christian education program; Ione wrote:

.....We have a problem right now that Hector has gone to town about this morning. The first-grade teacher requested in the 'journal de classe' which each child carries and we have to sign every night, a pack of playing cards for them to do their 'calcul' (math). Hector went to see the teacher and asked if there were any other cards that we could provide so that we would not have to put into their hands the gambler's tool. She had no other alternative, and had prepared the term's work around this theme, and it distressed her to think of changing. Hector left, but decided today, he could ask the school principal about it, and as there were four classes of 1st grade, it might be that we may be a bright and shining light here in this town, and not allow anything that would hinder us from witnessing for Christ. It will be nice when we are on furlough to be able to send our children to a Christian school.

Indeed, Ione was looking ahead to school arrangements and wrote to her mother on 24th:

.....The letter from Jean and Archie invited us to the farm. Jean is expecting to be married and may be leaving. Her boyfriend, Bob Jones, is a Christian banker in Calgary or Winnipeg, out in western Canada. Archie would like us to live with him as long as we can. We would like to spend some time there during the summer but feel that our children deserve to be in a Christian school at least while we are on furlough and would not like to put them into the school at Avonmore.

Her rationale for this was explained as follows:

During this furlough impressions will be made which will help them to know the Lord's will for their lives. If we can show them what other Christian young people are planning to do, they won't be limited to the inspiration of being a truck driver or shop-keeper in Stanleyville! That was our reason for thinking of the grade school at P.B.I. But I know there are other Christian schools as well, but I don't know of any in Canada, and it's there we can get the children's allowance of $30 a month.

Hector was away for Easter Sunday at Waine Rukula station to preach and Ione and Kenneth stayed home with Stephen who was sick:

.....Kenneth is laboring away over an old typewriter, having his first try at it, and Stevie is lying down, copying his letter to you. I am making believe for a few days that I [am a young mother with] *just two well-spaced children, and that my husband is away on business! We were all going to spend Easter at Waine-Rukula, but when Stevie had symptoms of jaundice the plans had to be changed. It is very quiet here (being the Easter break). We are hoping to hear soon about Pearl's departure for Congo.*

All for now. It is wonderful just to trust Him day by day. His joy is sufficient for every need.   Lovingly, Ione

Besides the package from her Mother, Ione received one from the Reh's and she wrote on the 28th of March:

Dear Peggy and Walter,

On March 26th the looked-for package arrived and was it ever big! Bigger than any package they have ever received. Such delight and excitement there was as Daddy unwrapped it. Somebody was busy reading the ticket. Someone shouted, "Oh, good, now we can take some presents to Waine-Rukula!"

They appointed Auntie Isobel to decide what toys each should receive. She enjoys a job like that, and all would be satisfied. The two helicopters went to John and David; the Honkalong to Timmy; one bus to Stevie, the hydrogen fire engine to Kenny and baggage carrier bump'n go to Paul. There were still four large toys, and because they were planning to spend a long Easter week-end at a station where there were four missionary children, they decided it would not be right for us to have two each and those children have non, so the other bus was designated for a Logan boy, and the beautiful organ-like top for the tiny Cunningham girl. Everyone agreed that Daddy should have the lantern and he has taken it with him to Waine. But we all couldn't go, for Stephen became ill with jaundice, and will have to be in bed for a while. Kenneth stayed at home with me and Stevie.

.....Thank you so much for all of these things. It is a lot of money to spend on just us, and we appreciate it so much. May the Lord bless you and supply your every need.

Lovingly, Ione

It's not long before whatever caused Stevie's jaundice eventually infected his younger brother, Timmie, however, they were mild cases. Work continued on the new building with more cement floors and getting the rest of the curtains up. Hector made six nice desks for the middle-sized boys. He remarked that only three screws hold up four desks, but Ione wondered what would happen if those 3 screws came out and four boys went down!

One dilemma facing missionaries abroad centered on the family they had left behind. Frequently in Ione's letters, particularly to her mother, Ione asked for information, checking that her mother had enough to live on, worrying where she was living and what she was doing. Besides her mother, there were her sisters. Letters between Marcellyn, Lucille and herself were frequent, but Ione's youngest sister, Doris did not write often which was something that worried Ione considerably over the years. Doris seemed to make questionable life choices and avoided writing to Ione - leaving her with no news except what was received from her mother and her sisters. Ione learned that Doris' husband, Bill Biederman had sued for divorce and won custody of all their five children. Ione, loving and caring for her family as she did, wrote directly to both Bill and Doris. Despite her attempts to get them to reconcile their differences and obligations as parents, Bill wrote back that the story was a bit more complicated than what Ione may have thought or heard and that, after 12 years of marriage, Doris had gotten tired of living with the same man. Bill thanked Ione for her concerns and asked for prayers for the children left in his care.

Many of Ione's letters are to supporters, in part explaining what her and Hector's missionary work entailed. She told of caring for 21 missionary children while they attend public school. Hector had them for morning and evening devotions and the children were taken to two services on Sunday held in town, one in French and one in English. In the afternoon, Ione arranged the Sunday School. In addition, Hector had a weekly Bible study for white people in town.

The children's parents provided their clothing and paid for their food. The Home was the style of most Belgian tropical homes, large and airy, well-ventilated. It was not like any of the missionary houses, which were smaller and more like the natives have. The rooms were large but not nearly enough for so many people, so doors and windows (purchased second-hand) were put up into a big open shed which adjoined the main house. This kept Hector busy while the children were in school. During the vacation months missionaries stayed here in order to do their shopping and get their cars fixed. There were over 100 visitors in the previous summer.

Fortunately for Ione and all those under her care, packages kept coming from America. Vanilla, shirts and pajamas for the boys, dresses for Ione, balloons, books, and socks. Ione started thinking about travel clothes as they neared their time of furlough. Almost every item is mentioned in Ione's letters along with what they are used for and she does not forget to thank each donor.

Pearl had now settled in at Kilometer 8 to care for the infirmed (with flu-like symptoms) and Ione enjoyed her breezy way in such a hot place. The teachers asked the sick ones not to come back too soon, as there were many cases of relapse and re-infection. Eighty percent of Stanleyville had the flu. In the junior boys' room, three out of four were in bed. Ione was thankful Pearl had come just when she did.

Missionary Kids at Banjwadi Conf. – July 1959.
Back Row (L-R): Bill Boyes, Philip Carter, Rosemary Carter (holding Cindy Boyes), Ken McMillan, Gordon Carter. **Second Back Row:** David McMillan, Michael Carter, Ken Boyes, Ernie Boyes. **Third Back Row:** Barbara Nichols, Hazel Parry, Stephen Parry, Allan Nichols, Paul McMillan, John McMillan. **Front Row:** Matthew Logan, Grace Parry, Marilyn Carper, Catherine Streight, Steve McMillan, Tim McMillan

In her role as house mother, Ione kept her charges' parents informed of events at the Children's Home. She kept a file of each of her 8 parents, explaining school regulations, expenses, comings and goings of children, etc. It got more and more complicated as the numbers of families increased. She wrote that this school term would likely end with sickness as it began. All the children were in school for only one day of the whole term. Timmy now had chicken pox, but most of the children had the flu two and three times. David had been in bed for about three weeks. The doctor finally took an X-ray of his lungs but found nothing to explain for the temperature but it just seemed to take a long time to get over it.

Ione enjoyed the Conference at Banjwadi as she stated in a July 8th letter to her sister Marcellyn:

.....*We just finished the best Conference yet, and I think my greatest pleasure was singing duets with Alma McAllister and trios with Sarah Schmidt and Coral Snyder. Kenneth sang in a quartet with the 3 Carter boys in four parts. Hector is on the Field Council now so has to help solve the many problems that arise.*

Pearl Hiles has been designated for Banjwadi. When we go on furlough the Siggs and Isobel will carry on. There will be 23 to 25 children this year when they all get there, but when we go the Boyes go, too, and also the Parry's, which reduces the number of Home children considerably!   Ione

In a letter written on August 4th, Ione told of progress on the new building. She found Hector there using the Jeep and a pulley to lift a heavy double door frame into place. He was also looking at some dirt levelling and covering bare brick walls. It was hard to imagine any kind of living quarters yet as most of it was still a work shed. But the rest of the rooms had been made comfortable with the same sort of imagination, faith and energy.

As the school year came to an end, there was no respite for Ione with the Mission Conference coming so soon after the end of term. In *Palmares*, Tim got a prize for good behavior, Stephen, a prize for drawing. Bill McAllister got the 'Prix de Sagesse' (knowledge), prizes for excellence in Religious studies went to Hazel Parry, Veronica and Laureen Walby, John and Stephen McMillan and Ken Boyes. Prize for Effort went to Heather Arton, and Good Behavior to Paul. Ernie Boyes got a prize for being a model student as did Ken McMillan. John McMillan got a prize for overall outstanding performance and Stephen Parry came second to him for the first-year students. Ken Boyes earned the same prize for the second-year students. Allan and Barbara Nicholls got prizes for demonstrating the best effort in their studies.

In terms of position in class: John came first in his year with Stephen Parry 3rd, Ernie Boyes 9th, David McMillan, 18th, Ken Boyes, 19th and Barbara Nicholls 25th. For some reason – perhaps school absence due to illness, Veronica Walby, Hazel Parry Allan Nicholls and Heather Arton were not placed. Laureen Walby and Bill Boyes were both placed 5th (girls and boys were segregated at this stage) and Paul was 13th. Close rivalry between Ken and Mike Carter was maintained with Ken coming 5th and Mike 7th. Philip came third in his year group. So once again, the missionary children did well. This was due to the supervised homework sessions that Hector, Ione, Isabel and the Siggs provided.

Shedding some light on the children's schedule and school work, Ione stated:

.....When the bus comes at 5 [PM], they sit down for family worship, then go immediately to eat. After that we listen to their reading and check on their lessons and sign a book that they have done their assignment. All have homework except kindergarten and it sometimes lasts an hour. They do not print but start writing in ink right away in the 1st grade. You can imagine how much ink is spilled as they must use dip pens! But they eventually learn to write nicely, the Belgian style. One little kindergartner came home this week proud to report that when asked in French to go to the bathroom, the teacher had said it was 'tres bien francais'. The children who come to us young enough to start in kindergarten have learned French the easy way. The ones who came at 9 and 10 have had to repeat grades. Our John started in before he was 4 and had three years of kindergarten. Now he keeps around the first in his class. He is 7 and in the 2nd grade.

Ione wrote of receiving groups of missionaries on their way back from a short time in the mountains. The general report from AIM territory (on the borders of Congo and Rwanda) was 'unrest'. It would seem that the missions were preparing for

Independence and a time when Congolese were to take over administration of their country. There had been riots in Brazzaville (across the river from Léopoldville), violence in Uganda, whispers of 'independence' here and there, and unrest everywhere.

The Children's Home had 24 children at this time. The week-ends were the busiest when they were home all the time, and Ione had to keep pretty much to a schedule to have things work out all right. They had Wednesday and Saturday afternoons at home. The Siggs had a big Chevrolet carryall which they changed into a bus and there was just room for all inside. They went swimming Wednesdays, played games Saturday night and attended church Sunday morning. After Sunday night supper the children cleaned up afterwards. In a land where missionary children were used to being waited on by natives, this was necessary, even though their weekday schedule did not permit much housework. They made their own beds and seemed quite happy, not minding the strict discipline that must have been maintained. The missionaries wanted them to learn to obey while young, so they would hear and obey His voice when He calls to service.

Games on Saturday for older children often included 'just a minute', where one had to speak for a minute on any given topic without hesitation, repetition and long pauses! Occasionally, Hector would get out the projector and all would watch a film – silent of course, such as the one telling the David Livingstone story. The other films were mainly from National Geographic.

Ione was incredibly busy despite the additional pairs of hands (the Sigg family). She hopped from one topic to the next in her letters. In this one, written to her mother on September 11th, food is one topic followed by plans for furlough.

.....Can you imagine counting out 90 potatoes for a meal? I have checked to see if the spaghetti and meatballs are done. There are fresh green beans and banana and peanut salad, with a half cupcake and a cookie for dessert. I have just counted to see if we have 30 eggs for supper, as the man who cooks them will be coming about 12:30. Hector has come from town with tomatoes and lettuce, and they will have rice cakes for dessert for supper. It is fun planning meals, but sometimes I must be content to let the Lord plan them, and when we have to have things that do not seem well-balanced, the Lord continues to give them healthy bodies all the same! Praise the Lord, he knows what is best for us.

.....It is good that we can get cane sugar quite cheap here. (We use a 100 lb sack of sugar in less than a month!)

.....Hector has made some tentative reservations for a plane for June 18. That is the last day of school. We had a letter from Marcellyn and she was hoping we could have our reunion in late July or August. If she cannot come home before then, we can plan our visit to Avonmore first and then come to Michigan for the latter part of the summer. We had thought we could come to Michigan first via N.Y., and then go to Avonmore the last of July or first of Aug. If we go to Canada first, we will get our ticket to Montreal.

.....These boys love their Grandma and are really looking forward to seeing you

again. David is thinking about the ice cream cone and fully expects to be eating it a few minutes after getting off the plane! You will be sorry to hear that John has broken his arm again, in the same place as before, but this time the ball of his elbow was not moved so far and only one bone was broken. He has it in a cast and a sling and is going to school but finds it a bit hard to dress and use a ruler, etc. The picture of him sitting in the milk drum horse was taken a short time before he broke his arm. The hat is a mouse's hat he wore in the school program. One little boy who visited us recently was talking to him. Timmy asked, "Can you whistle?" The boy answered, "Yes", Says Timmy, "So can I.......in AND out!"

John in the milk-drum horse that his father built.

Hector and Ione

Whistling was something Tim was desperate to master. He practiced morning noon and night. Sometimes his eyes bulged with the effort. Older boys tried to teach him or torment him by doing it effortlessly but he persisted until he mastered it – as Ione says – both in and out!

Apparently, Pearl's forte was not caring for missionary kids but rather in full time nursing for the African people. She was now at Banjwadi but still a real pal to Ione.

It could not have been easy managing such a large household but the McMillans, Siggs and Aunty Isabel were a well-suited group, each bringing something to the children's care. Hector and Ione epitomized 'tough' love, they were strict, the main disciplinarians, the ones you wouldn't want to offend; in contrast, Isabel was like a warm soft duvet to cuddle into when things went wrong or if you were sad and unhappy. Isabel also had a steely determination about her and certainly picked up a child who disobeyed and did not conform or behave as he or she should. The Siggs represented young love, they were an absolute joy to have around and their method of achieving respect was using fun and laughter- whatever each brought to the table – it worked.

When Ione wrote to supporters, especially if she was needing something specific including specific prayer points, the detail in the letters is descriptive of life in the Congo and the letter written on the 18th of September to People's Church is very poetic:

Dear Friends,

The musical 'ding-ding' of water running from the roof into buckets and drums comes to us above the roar of the rain. It is a good sound as rain is clear and clean, and so much better than the stream water which we have been using since our well started to run dry. The beginning of school is a hard time for a shortage of water, but since our "times are in His hands," we can be thankful that this condition is to His glory. If water is low, kitchen staff do not wash their hands as frequently, and there is a greater chance of disease common to the Congo. Will you remember this need, please, for enough water for our Children's Home.

In another letter Ione writes:

.....When Hector had dug a well, he attached the diesel motor to a pump and until recently there has been enough water. But as we have gone thru a very serious dry spell, we have many times been carrying pails and sending to the distant spring or river. Hector must deepen the well now, and in order to do this he has to figure out a system to get air down so far while he digs. And as he broadens the bottom, there is danger of the many tiles falling down on him. Will you pray about this?

.....Another need, which was as great a surprise as the lack of water, is concerning the tuition which we pay at the Belgian school for our children. At first, we paid no tuition, then last year we were asked to pay one-third, but this year when Hector went into the office, he was informed that our missionaries must pay the same as the others. The Director was very kind and wished that it were not so, and even suggested that we present a special request to the Governor-General.[124] Our UFM legal representative is going to do this. Will you pray that it may not be necessary for any of our missionaries to take their children out of this very good school, just because of lack of money.

Ione got to catch up with correspondence on the 21st of September, with updates of the future of the Children's Home:

.....When the Field Conference met in June they made some plans for the future which greatly affect our Children's Home. We had suggested ways of enlarging the eating area, but they moved to build a new large dining hall (maximum 100) and kitchen and storeroom. It is to be after the pattern of the Bible Institute refectory at Banjwadi and will be just behind the present 'Home'. We praise the Lord for this and are finding it easier to endure the cramped conditions this year, knowing that something better is coming. Another important decision was to obtain the land right next to this for an Administrative Centre for UFM. They applied to buy it, and then learned that there was a possibility of a free government grant, so have made out different application papers, and are waiting to know whether it will come this way. Already materials are beginning to come for buildings on this land, as soon as the papers are signed. The first building will be a large guest house, and this will accommodate our parents when they bring their children to school, as well as any other visitors. Then there will be an office building and dwellings for the two couples who do the

---

[124] The school must have been experiencing a drop in revenue as many Belgians had already started to leave the country ahead of Independence.

administrative work. An application has also been made for 6 or 7 hectares of land just back of this, for ball fields and gardens. How thankful we are that we came so far out of town. Now there is room for expansion, and the power plant and well can be shared.

In this very busy period for Ione and Hector, it hardly seemed like the calm before the storm. Letters at the start of the year hinted at trouble in Congo but in this vast country it seemed far removed from where they were. However, the news did not go away. On the 20th of October, Ione wrote to the Fellowship Bible class back in the States:

.....We spend some time before our radio these days, getting what we can of news about trouble in Matadi, trouble in Luluaberg, and the Otraco shipping strike. No passenger boats are going now, and the only way out is by plane. The unrest seems to be coming closer and we wonder how long Stanleyville will be so quiet. There is lots of talk of 'depinda' (independence), but I am not sure just what it means to them. [Many thought independence was what you carried around in a briefcase!] *I spoke of this unrest and trouble to our African helpers and their wives (about 15 in all), and read 2 Peter chapter 3:14 – "Wherefore, beloved, seeing that ye look for such things, be diligent that ye may be found of Him in peace, without spot, and blameless." I thought it had left an impression on them, until I heard later some of them remarking as some soldiers passed by, "They are coming to kill us like they are doing in Congo-bas* [southern Congo]*!" Pray for our relationship with them.*

Lovingly in Him, Ione

On October 31, Ione chronicled the situation in Stanleyville thus:

.....The trouble in Mangobo [one of the five African townships at the edge of Stanleyville] *started Sunday with an unfortunate car accident, but when the children came home ahead of time yesterday, we knew that the political meetings had come to a bad end. The note said, "School closed by the medical authorities." Some of the teachers told them there was small pox around, but this may have been their way of getting the children out without trouble between white and black children.*

.....This incident at the time when a strong movement had just started in Stanleyville, has made an unusual tension, though we hardly realized it fully until yesterday. Our missionary children arrived home from school before noon, and they said their teachers had hurried them away, some without their report cards which they were supposed to bring with their first period reports.

.....They were supposed to have gone to school thru the afternoon, and then there would be a holiday of three days over All-Saints Day. The Siggs had planned to meet the children after school and take the Maganga and Boyulu ones to their stations that night. Shortly afterwards, we discovered that the city was under military law. The soldiers were doing the work that had formerly been done by police and were guarding all exits of Stanleyville. Since this morning I have seen two Jeeps with soldiers passing. I marvel, when the issues seem to be between

black and white, that the African soldiers can stand the criticism they must receive from the others.

They finally got off, as did the Banjwadi children and Isobel, which left only the McMillans at the Home. We thanked the Lord that this had all been pre-arranged and that the children got to their parents so quickly. Some natives passing by, probably drunk, called out, "White people made us to suffer, now they will feel fear!"

Same day, 3 P.M. This morning we heard a series of 10 or 12 explosions in the direction of Stanleyville. We are about 6 miles out of town. We have heard sounds like this in past months when they were dynamiting rocks on the big new Kivu Highway. But today, though to us only Halloween, is All-Saints Day to them, a very special and sacred day and there is no work and special services in the Catholic Church (providing anyone got thru the 'barricades'). Our house helper told us the noise was shooting, when a white man shot two Africans, but the Belgian man who brings us eggs, said there were big guns used in the part of Stanleyville that is the other side of the Congo River. At any rate, we shudder to think of the results, for one could almost hear the earth shake with each explosion.

3:30 - Malenza and his wife [Congolese helpers] *have come to get us some supper. I asked (as I had seen him go away on his bike after his morning work) if he had been in Stanleyville. He looked disgusted and said, "Do you think any of us can go there?" Then his wife spoke up and said, "No one can come out of Stanleyville and no one can go in, since the market was closed at 10 this morning." Then they told us that they heard many shots during the night and could not sleep (their ears are better than ours for we slept well all night!). When they could not sleep, they arose, lit a light, read their Bible (they have the WHOLE Bible now in Bangala!) and sang and prayed.*

...Our usual staff of eight has dwindled to two, plus Malenza's wife. But this is partly due to the fact that it is a holiday. I had told the washing men to come and iron until noon or until it was finished, as we like to give them as much of a holiday as we can. And we thought we could not wash on Monday and let them have that whole day off, that is the washing men. And the cooks I had told to come by ones instead of twos as we had only eight people to cook for. And the two old outside men were not to have come anyway. We know of two of these who were held by soldiers when they went in to town yesterday, but hope they were able to hunt up their needed papers. At any rate if they are in town, they'll not get out until the trouble is over.

The next day 8 A.M. We heard from the Stanleyville radio station around 5, but no names were given and an announcement was made that soldiers were arriving from Gombari with tanks and other equipment. We were thinking that this group would have passed our station Boyulu and some of our children, now with their parents, would be excited when they saw them pass. Malenza and his wife listened with us to get as much news as we could get from our local station.

Then we listened to the news from Brazzaville and Léopoldville. Seven were reported killed. But later that night Hector heard on the BBC World News that 24 had been killed.

While we were having family worship with the children, just after dark a group of people, perhaps drunk, went past noisily and at first it looked like they were coming here, and just then there was a loud bang, like a gun, but as we listened for another or for them to come closer, we realized that it was some sort of a make-believe gun, or a bang of something against our big stump. Anyway, they went on, and it was absolutely quiet from then on. Hector went across the road to visit our nearest neighbours, Belgians, but their lights were off and they must have gone into their bedroom, so he came back.

As it seems now from what we have heard on the radio and the many verbal reports, the rioting only actually started at the time the children were rushed off home to their parents, from an unofficial political meeting which got out of hand. The man, Patrice (Lumumba), we have been hearing about for some weeks, had been gathering a following, and some wanted him to become like a king. He must have a pretty good opinion of himself, as we have heard that when he went into a supermarket here in Stanleyville, he felt it beneath his dignity to push his own food cart, so engaged a little African lad to do it, and when he came to the butter department he would not have the local product, but it had to be imported from Holland! Our impression of Patrice is none too good, and right now the soldiers and police are looking for him, but he is hiding somewhere. It seems the incident of last Sunday of the child being run over must have been an unhappy coincidence which preceded these other very serious events.

So now, we are in the third day of real trouble. Hector heard shots at night, but unless they are really big guns, we could not hear much from Stanleyville. How glad we are that we moved this far out. For as it is now, our six are happily playing on the front porch, with no soldiers in sight, while in Stanleyville there is a solid line of soldiers around the section where the white people live. But even if we were right in town as we were four years ago, we should still know His protecting presence. "For He shall give His angels charge over thee, to keep thee in all thy ways."

The children asked, "Shall we run into the forest?" But their Daddy, laughing, said, "There is only one safe place, and that is where He has put us, and we could not be safer than in His care." John's face showed more concern than the others, and when after he was put to bed, he appeared again saying, "My bed is nearest the door and window, and it's a long ways from everybody else," I could not resist taking him into our big bed, where he could have some flesh and blood arms as well as those of the Lord Jesus.

.....I heard a shot from the direction away from Stanleyville. I am not sure what it means, perhaps nothing. I am sitting where I can see the road, and as I write I see a native woman with a basket going in that direction. Now, a second shot, and the woman turns around, throws her basket in the bushes and disappears. It

is not very loud and has not awakened Hector and the children who are sleeping or resting in the dormitory next to this building, at least so far as I can see. Like as not, if he does hear it, he'll keep them calm, like he did last night in family worship. Only their eyes showed the apprehension that was inside, but John had little lines of worry over his eyes.

3 P.M. The Stanleyville radio station just announced that they have arrested Patrice Lumumba, the leader of the Mouvement Nationale Congolese (MNC), at the home of his parents.[125] Others have been arrested, including one European woman.

Lumumba had attended a protestant primary school and then a Catholic secondary school. The Finishing School was the Government's Post Office Training School and he passed the course with distinction. He then worked for the post office in both Léopoldville and Stanleyville and was reported to have continued his education reading works of Rousseau, Voltaire, Moliere and Victor Hugo. He was perceived as well educated and held in high regard by others in Africa, such as Nkrumah, President of Ghana.

However, he was labelled a militant nationalist by Belgian colonial authorities. As leader of the MNC, Lumumba had planned a congress for the 23-28th of October but the Mayor of Stanleyville stopped it from taking place and called in the military to maintain public order. Lumumba's arrest and flogging resulted in him being seen as a political prisoner and raised his status locally and across the country. He gained popularity because his vision was for an independent Congo not just a Province of the Congo. Ione continued:

Nov. 2 [next day] 6:30 A.M. We spent a very quiet evening, interspersing "Papa was a Preacher," with news flashes from the radio until family worship and bath time. We enjoyed this week-end with our children, the first in a very long time. We listened together to the Governor's message and were of the impression that all should be quite tranquil now. But by midnight there were again the sounds of heavy guns and by this morning the radio announced 70 dead.[126] I was awakened by crying in a village not far away, and there have been shouts from the road. I hardly know what to say to Malenza, who is in the kitchen now getting our breakfast. Last night when we told his wife that buildings had been burned in Mangobo, shops, a school, a church (we don't know yet whether Baptist Missionary Society buildings were involved) she immediately said, "It was probably the white men's guns that did it." Foramina [Malenza's wife] is a Christian, but she is under a strain, and she told me she has many relatives in town, a soldier, a policeman, a ndombi (sec't) and others. Hector says we had best not tell them every radio report, but it seems better that they get it straight

---

[125] Patrice Lumumba who founded the MNC, the first nation-wide Congolese National Party, advocated unification of all Congolese regardless of ethnicity.

[126] Cars travelling in and out of Stanleyville must wait for several hours and then be accompanied by soldiers in convoy.

than thru rumors. And most of the time the news is given (except for World News) in Lingala and Kingwana as well as French, so they are bound to hear it.

9:15 A.M. As I write, the strains of "Lead Kindly Light" come over the public-address system Hector maintains in our two main buildings. As I think of our circumstances and the possibilities ahead, the words are a message to my heart, "Lead kindly Light, amid the encircling gloom, Lead Thou me on; The night is dark, and I am far from home, Lead Thou me on; Keep Thou my feet; I do not ask to see the distant scene, - one step enough for me."

A nice time of family worship with the children, then a good breakfast, and Hector called for staff members' service as I helped the children to gather a big basketful of ripe oranges. This is our fourth basket (about twice the size of a bushel) taken from one tree, and there are many more yet.

.....1:50 P.M. I just came back from across the road where I paid a visit to Mr. and Mrs. Bonte. He is president of the city's Chamber of Commerce. I asked about the latest news [and was told] *that cars only travel on Buta and Ituri Roads in convoy and with soldiers' escort.* [I mentioned that] *stones had been thrown just outside of town and especially so on the road to Yakusu, but they had nothing to say about this, only that our road was OK and that his wife was going in at 3 and would take any letters we have (hence this) including letters to our Field Leader and Mr. Pudney in Philadelphia.* [Later], *2 army Jeeps drove in at the Bonte* [residence] *and we think maybe* [they] *have asked for protection out here tonight.*

.....They also said that school was to be resumed tomorrow!! If the bus comes, I suppose we should send the children, but I doubt very much whether the ones Boyulu way will be coming, if they have so much trouble getting thru; likewise, the children at Banjwadi and Bopepe [bo-PE-pe]. *School isn't all that important that we should risk their being stoned! The attitude seems to be to try to get going as usual and it is not exactly possible with repeated uprisings! We shall pray about our decision for sending the children to school.*

Really, we are safer near so many soldiers than those in isolated places where natives are angry and there are no soldiers near. Even on our mission stations it is not safe from the standpoint of the attitude of the people. But we are sure that the Lord sent us here, and we love the people just as much. If you feel concern for us, just read II Chron. 20:12-17, and be sure that we shall be singing and praising (vs. 22) and that the Lord will do that which will bring to Him glory. Now to get this off. We will let you know more later.

Joyfully in Him, Hector and Ione

Ione's theory that the children would not return from their breaks with their parents was misjudged. From 6pm onwards, cars rolled in with their cargo of children ready to start school. On the 5th of November wrote to Mr Pudney, head of the mission in the USA:

Dear Pudu,

As you may be wondering what has happened since my lengthy letter a few days ago, this is the sequel.

Much to our surprise, the parents sent their children back Monday evening and early Tuesday morning. We took them to the school which did meet, but only a few were there and not a full staff. And they told them not to come back in the afternoon. Wednesday the bus appeared with two soldiers as escort, so we sent them to school, and have done the same today.

We had not expected to have the responsibility of our mission children during such a troubled time and in such a dangerous place. And had we a chance to notify the parents we should surely have advised them to keep the children at least a few days more. But our letters went only once a week to some, and they arrived here even before the courier went! And there was nothing to do but what we did. And although we kept the tiny ones here on Tuesday, we felt it was best to let them go yesterday and today as they were really safer under armed guard than out here with no guard, and then there was the problem of keeping them occupied, plus keeping the work going here with a staff none too steady! Kinso has been all week at Bopepe and we have not seen him since the trouble started.

But what a wonderful certainty we have in the Lord who said, "Certainly I will be with thee." Again, and again, and again, we must run to Him, and say, "Oh Lord, this, too!" Isa. 28:29 – "This also cometh forth from the Lord of hosts, which is wonderful in counsel, and excellent in working."

Praise the Lord for bringing us here, and for keeping us here, "for such a time as this." Though the guard of the soldiers has not been diminished, we trust it soon with be and that there will be a better spirit soon.

Joyfully in Him,   Ione

Ione told that:

.....the soldiers rode our bus for a week, and then departed. So, we are without guard now. Of course, we have our invisible host, and have no need for alarm even if trouble starts again suddenly. Our parents are wondering if school will start on time in January or if they will wait to see if there is trouble over the date set of 'Independence'. It seems so reasonable to accept the responsibility for independence more slowly, but there are many Africans who are unreasonable or who are pushed to a frenzy by leaders of Communistic background.

It was generally rumored that Patrice Lumumba was a communist but this was debatable; he viewed colonialism and communism as equally malignant. He was an idealist who believed in a Pan African state. He approached various countries for support against the Belgian rule, the UK and USA both stalled but the Soviet Union was prepared to support his push for Independence and hence the assumption that he was a communist. Most leaders kept tribal or feudal relationships and disputes would eventually lead to genocide in later years.

The situation was uppermost in Ione's mind in her letters. As of the 24th of November, most folk expect stormy times in December and January. UFM mission was planning a Field Council during this time, but now they were wondering if it was wise for the station leaders to be gone at all just now. And Ione was not keen for Hector to be gone. A letter came from the UFM American Council giving advice if there should be danger. It meant possible evacuation in a hurry and they were to notify authorities if protection was needed. They were to carry on otherwise.

In a letter to sister Lucille on the 25th of November, Ione wrote:

.....*We hope to have a little celebration here day after tomorrow, partly for Thanksgiving and partly for our wedding anniversary. Last year Hector bought a desk file drawer for where I write letters, and it has been a useful remembrance of our years together. In it I have building project papers, children's records, staff books, household purchases, letters to answer, letters answered, visitor's book, valuable papers, stamps, envelopes, and a file for furlough addresses, etc. Also notes, diary, etc. for the book which will be written by someone someday, probably not me. I wonder if Mother will be too busy to take my 'collection' and do something with it? I have not said anything to her about it, but have carbons, from when we first came to the field, and especially since the Children's Home project started.*

It is amazing that Ione had the time and energy to run the affairs of the Children's Home, keep parents informed of each child's progress and ensure they stayed healthy, write letters to supporters, AND keep a diary. (Sadly, no diary has been found but Ione stated that she kept it in preparation for a book to be written!) No wonder she needed a desk and she would have been well served to have an executive assistant.

On the 16th of December, Ione and Hector, while listening to their radio, discovered that King Baudouin of Belgium was making a visit and instead of going to Léopoldville, the capital, he was flying directly into Stanleyville. There was no time to prepare for this auspicious event. However, the staff at Athénée Royal de Stanleyville thought they could use the school children to form a welcoming party so they were sent home with instruction to wear white 'school' uniform and that the buses would arrive early to transport everyone including the teachers to the airport. Evidently, it was deemed unsuitable for some of the children such as the Kindergarten children and high school students to go so they stayed home.

The McMillans and their staff decided that they too would make their way into Stanleyville to see the King. However, this journey was more eventful than that experienced by the school children. Dick Sigg drove them all to the outskirts and they picked a suitable spot between the Airport and the Governor's Palace to watch the cavalcade pass. They were near other white people and the mood of the crowed was not hostile, although one or two Africans began to make their feelings known. Soldiers lined up in front of the sightseers and order was temporarily restored. Ione wrote of the incident:

.....*When a native dignitary arrived, there were cheers, "Long Live Independence!" There were not any cheers for the King when he appeared, just a long continuation of, "Long Live Independence!" The car in which he rode was closed, and he was surrounded by soldiers with bayonets. The car went too fast for the soldiers on foot, so they kicked up their heels and chased behind. It was over in a moment, the seeing of the King, as he was quickly whisked into the Palace which was surrounded by soldiers.*

King Baudouin had visited the country in 1955 and had a rapturous welcome, but not so this time. He was in favor of Congo gaining independence. In January of this year, he had made a speech about pushing for independence for the Colony without 'irresponsible rashness', advocating that there be a push for education of the people, and training of suitable persons to assume power. The Belgian government in Brussels had not previously interfered with the administration of the Colony and those living in Congo did not appreciate the changes the central government were advocating.

The King's poor reception, not only in Stanleyville but in all the other towns that he visited led the Belgium government to rethink their ideas of a gradual transfer of power. Ione continued:

.....But our troubles were only begun, as we had to make our way through the now excited crowd to get to the car. I had Timmy by one hand and John by the other, and took every opportunity to politely get through, but as we continued, the others following me, we seemed to be pressed on every side, and there were many bicycles. Isobel Whitehead, our English worker, was separated from the rest of us when Dick and the big boys stopped to pick up and carry the little girls. When Isobel was handled roughly, she objected, and one said, "Knock her down!" She turned and said, "I have given 20 years of service in the Congo and you want to knock me down!" Someone said, "She's a missionary, leave her alone." Another said, "She's a liar!" Isobel managed to climb up on a high grassy place beside a laboratory sign. The African who had been following her, angrily pulled up the sign and waved it about. Oh, they were a rough crowd! We promised the Lord we would not ever again take such a risk, not even for a King!

About this time, our little Timmy was tripped, perhaps accidentally. As he fell, someone said, "Why do they come here with such delicate eggs (meaning the children)!" I clung to Timmy, but John was having trouble at the other hand, and the pull in two directions was making me dizzy. I thought I would fall, but just then two of our staff members appeared; I did not know that they were anywhere around. One, Pierre, picked up Timmy, and the other, Marcel, took John, and carried the two children high above the heads of the pushing crowd. We thus reached the car, but there was no hope of moving it for some time. Mimi Sigg opened the door and sat in the front seat, but when someone pulled her hair, she felt she could not stay there. We all sat in back then, and Isobel finally joined us. For the first time I was thankful that Sigg's car had no windows at the sides. By this time, they were banging their hands on the outside and it made a terrific noise.

A white man nearby was having troubles, too. His car was dented, and we saw his hat knocked off. The American lady found two natives in her car and had great difficulty in persuading them to leave; and it was one of those tiny [cars].

The lady's son was struck. All this time we saw not a police[man], nor a soldier, and we heard later that they were all concentrated around the King. Now we began to see some police coming, and the violence became less, but not before Gordon had a cuff on his head and was knocked against the car.

More of our staff appeared, and there was a heated argument as to whether they would get into our car. Two out of four were brave enough to identify themselves with us when the chances were rather poor for us. These two sat in the back of the car, and whenever a taunt was flung by a passer-by, they poked their heads out, as though to protect us. When it was finally possible to move the car, Dick asked one boy to sit in the front with him, and we moved along very carefully lest even a touch might fan the flame of anger. A great sea of people was moving in the direction of downtown. A little later we passed by the prison, and saw their destination was the place where Lumumba was interned. Their hero and leader had been imprisoned at the time of the riots.

The children came home on their bus escorted by two soldiers. They had exciting stories to tell, of angry shouts, and fighting near the prison. Where they stood at the Palace entrance, they had a good view of the Belgian King.

I remember seeing five or six men near the car, each with a garden tool. There were two pitchforks, a rake, a hoe, and I believe a shovel. The men's eyes were wild with hate, but their arms were down and they were standing quietly. I thought of Daniel's lions when the Lord had shut their mouths! When we were safely home, Mimi read Psalm 27, and we thrilled at the reality of the word, "Though a host should encamp against me, my heart shall not fear...For in the time of trouble He shall hide me in His pavilion."

"Who knows but that thou art come to the Kingdom for such a time as this!"

In Him, Hector and Ione McMillan

After all this tension school closed for the Christmas break and life resumed a calmer pace for but a brief interval.

Chapter 19
THE DOOR IS CLOSING

Despite the political unrest, trauma and turmoil that Ione and her family experienced leading up to Christmas of 1959, Ione started her letters in January 1960 on a fairly positive note covering three main topics: the fast-approaching independence for Congo, the trip home and her work of the expanding scope at the Children's Home. However, there was still much tension.

The Belgian Congo had evidently been making the headlines; Patrice Lumumba was released from prison so that he could attend meetings in Brussels with Kasavubu to discuss transition of power, elections to be held in May and Independence which was scheduled for the 30th of June. The riots and poor reception of the King meant the government in Brussels did not relish a protracted period of unrest and civil war, so they acquiesced to most of the demands made by the Congolese delegation who put up a united front. Kasavubu would be President and Lumumba would be the Premier and hopefully the population of Congo would sanction the division of power. The country would remain unified and work collaboratively, putting aside previous divisions.[127]

On February 2, Ione wrote:

.....Well, our helpers are still with us, tending the wood fires, ironing with charcoal irons, and hanging up the huge washings. It might be better to put it, <u>we</u> are still here, as there is more chance of <u>our</u> going than their going! We were impressed when we read that Congo would have its Independence June 30 with a statement in the newspaper (in French) "After the Independence the European population is assured of good living conditions." So, it does not sound like they want us to go. Well, we know that what is His Will, will continue to be His Will, no matter what may be the conditions. In fact, it is He who alters the conditions to suit His good pleasure. And if He wants us to make it possible for our missionaries to penetrate into the deeper parts of the jungle, places where their children would not be able to pursue their schooling, then He will keep us here. We feel our Children's Missionary Home is as definitely a work of God as is any of our stations. We have just recently been voted a "station".

Ione found challenges coming from quarters she did not expect, like the cook. She outlined the following incident on the 12th of February:

.....This morning the cook who knows how to make cakes and pies was making life difficult for all of us by his loud shouts and declarations about what would happen to the white people when Independence came. He has been getting more

---

[127] In reality, the Belgians were leaving the country without an official head to formally govern the country.

and more objectionable, and his Christian testimony is not worth much when he gets angry. I told him he'd better talk more softly and say only things which would help us all to work happily together. This brought louder talk, so I said, "Did we not say in our morning prayers that we would behave ourselves today as Christians?" This was met with the reply, "It isn't a question of Christians or non-Christians, it is a question of blacks and whites." "In that case, I said, "Since I have asked you three times to hush and you have not, I will say that we would rather not have your help if we must take the bad talk with it." He walked out, hopped on his bike and left. This left 8 pies, 30 tarts and 8 dozen cookies to be finished before noon, but Mrs. Sigg helped and all was finished by 11 o'clock except the oven watching which could be done (sometimes burned!) by the little lad who helps. While we have no cook, we will have simpler things, which is better for us anyway. What is that verse about, "a dinner of herbs where love is"?

Each day I ask the Lord to help me in every relationship with the Africans, and He always does. I do not ask that things always run smoothly, but that it may be to His glory. Perhaps this incident will help the other 8 or 9 members of our African staff to see the emphasis is not so much on their usefulness to us as their usefulness to the Lord.

Joyfully in Him, Ione

More incidents of unrest were shared with another supporter:

.....The British Baptist have a station called Lingungu and it was recently put under military occupation when it was found out that their missionary nurse had removed a bullet from the wound of a fugitive whom a white officer had shot. The nurse did not know he was a fugitive, and as many times hunters get bullet wounds, she felt she should help him. It made trouble and when the soldiers occupied, they had to close their school for a while. All houses had to be re-white-washed and grass cut back for so many meters. The station next to this, with a large medical work, Yakusu, had a call to rescue a white man who was being attacked by his road workmen. The station leader rescued him, treated him and sent him away as quickly as possible, so that there would not be trouble. Do keep praying for our right attitude during these trying times.

The increased number of children in resident at the Children's Home required UFM to reduce visitors. Parents and any other guests, could no longer stay at Kilometer 8 but must find accommodation elsewhere. The plan was to eventually build a guest house and an office for central administration of the mission at Kilometer 8. In the meantime, property had been rented in Stanleyville for this purpose. In response to a letter about the development of the Children's Home site, Ione wrote:

.....Just this week the state man and local African chief got together here and made a settlement about our having the land that we asked for. Things take a long time here to materialize. We have yet to pay for a certain number of palm trees planted by a certain woman, and the chief will come in for his share. But the land is a free grant. And we should soon be able to start the building. I think

433

the building will be of cement blocks and tile roofing, and will be financed by money the parents send in. As yet funds have not been available for beginning the building of the dining-room and kitchen for the Children's Home. But if we can manage the rest of the school year, next Sept. there will be fewer children and not such a strain on present kitchen facilities. Three large families go on furlough at the same time. All of the children are from missionaries serving under the UFM. We have had three requests from three different missions asking us to take their children, but our Committee has not as yet consented, as we have not the accommodation until the dormitory is finished.

The dormitory or 'hanger' as it was affectionately named, was a building site. Although it had windows and doorways, these were just openings. The building was not secure. The end nearest the main house did have dividing walls and designated sleeping areas but the other half of the building was a store for building materials. It was a shell with a roof on it.

In a letter to her mother on the 15th of February, Ione revealed the amount of forward planning needed to get her family back to Canada/America *and* suitably dressed for the occasion. She may have been living in Africa for years but the smart young lady who sang in a trio and undertook many public engagements before her missionary experience was still very much in evidence.

Many in the Congo were anxious for freedom of Belgian rule and varying opinions were voiced around the country. Some Congolese would continue as before, but with increased power in government and commerce. Others wanted to be entirely rid of the white people. Just a few years had passed since a more savage way of living, and Ione was not sure whether the majority of feeling would come from the wilder element. And then there was a common fear that if all white people were expelled, a cruel dictatorship would take control. The missionaries hoped that wise and well-educated Congolese would not let things get out of hand. Churches were rapidly being put into the hands of trustworthy Christian Africans who would bear the responsibilities of the work and the missionaries would only share part of it. It was hoped that some of these church leaders would be greatly used of the Lord.

.....Whether our time be long or short, we are committed to Him, to serve Him in just the way that pleases Him most. These troubles are bringing more opportunities to witness, and to show how the Bible has a promise for every need. Some are turning to Christ who have tried the world and found that it does not satisfy. Pray for our Sunday meetings in the native quarters and the daily services with staff and neighbors. And for the children as they pass out tracts at the school.

To the family, Ione's letters remained reassuring as was her letter to another of Hector's sisters, Florence:

.....The children have felt a little antagonism going to school with so many African children, but there are many who are kind as well. And the teachers are always watchful to stop any race troubles (17 different nationalities!). We have talked to our children and feel that they understand that we came to help them

to know the Lord, and if they are unkind, we should still continue to love them as Jesus did. They even spit in Jesus' face, didn't they?

We are happy in our work here, and glad to have help which can carry on while we are at home. Our household numbers 31 now, with the arrival of 2 more new children. This is our maximum so far, but will exceed this when we return in '61. The Lord is good to lead us thus far. We can safely trust in Him. Audrey's verse was a blessing – Joshua 23:14 "...not one thing hath failed of all the good things which the Lord spoke."

Lovingly, Hector and Ione

Ione still retained her sense of fun during these changing times as seen in her letter to Alice and Claude (Hector's sister and brother-in-law):

.....Although assured by many that white people will be permitted to carry on as usual, no one is too sure, and even our mission work is planned so that in the event of our leaving the work will go on. For years we have dreamed of the indigenous church, and have seen a number come into being. And now, in the speed of Africans taking over all important jobs, the churches are finishing quickly a job which we thought would take many more years. It is really wonderful, and yet some work is turned over with many misgivings! There is so much prejudice and hatred between tribes that there is not much hope of justice in any line except thru a white intermediator, whom they have made use of for years.

Just this week, our gardener and his wife had a quarrel. As the little old man and the little old lady continued to hold forth, the shouts came to blows and then the old lady made a run for the workshop where Hector was. As Hector stood between them in a narrow passage and preceded to give his words of wisdom, the little old lady pursed her lips, squinted one eye and then reached past Hector and smacked the little old man right in the face. I guess you can see it in a mental picture!! I came just in time to see it all, and then had to duck behind something so that they could not see me laughing. I don't know how many times in a day one or the other comes for advice and to settle some dispute.

Well, the Lord knows what the future holds. And our present is yielded to Him. May the Lord use us yet to the salvation of many souls to Christ.

Ione kept up with her letter writing on April 15th:

.....There has been a change in the way we get our allowance now, and we have to plan ahead a bit. We are not sure what will happen to the economic conditions here. They say the Congo franc has already devaluated since the Belgians have taken away the gold on deposit at the banks. No more checks are accepted. And the banks are cautious about giving out money even when you give in a check. One of our missionaries was refused when he asked to take out money a second time in one week. Another person who was standing ahead of Hector in line was told to come back later in the afternoon. Our exchange will probably not be less, but we cannot be sure that when we put money into the bank it can be taken out again. And we dare not keep cash in the house because of thieving.

The music teacher had the equivalent of 40,000 fs. stolen in the night a few weeks ago. They took not only the money in his pants, but the pants as well! Much of the thieving is done by children who have older folk hidden nearby. Some take the loot across the river and get it on the train and right out of town quick. We have heard that half of the white people have left Stan. It is probably the Belgians who are seeking employment elsewhere. There are still a lot of Greeks and Indians and Portuguese people. We have not heard that there will be no school in Sept., but folk are saying the school will be the last establishment to be disbanded. The Lord knows what all this will mean to us. But if we are here thru the crisis, we can best advise our young helpers. Pray for our safety.

The white people who have made African enemies have left because of danger of revenge. But we feel we have many African friends here, in the Lord. The priest of the Catholic Mission near Banjwadi accidentally ran over a black man, and had he not dashed hastily to the administrator he would have been killed on the spot. Another man did stop when he ran over somebody, but the only thing to do is hurry to the police or soldier camp. Sometimes Africans make their bikes go deliberately near a car, so they will have to pay damage. It surely makes you careful in driving.

Do you remember the time when we were at Bongondza and an African who was riding on the pick-up truck fell off while Hector was driving, and was killed? Well, there were some pagan relatives who were all for killing one of our children as a means of revenge. If this accident had happened today, we would have had to leave the country. The priest who had the accident at Banjwadi had to go away completely either to Belgium or a remote place in Congo. And ever since then they have been stopping priests to see if it is the one. Well, these are unusual days, and I do believe that we "have come to the kingdom for such a time as this." If it can bring glory to Him, we shall not mind the difficulties. Our Christians are watching us now as never before. And a number are accepting Christ. Just last week another staff member, as well as the parents of our house helpers' wife. And we do see some fruits of the Spirit, though at times they get so wrought up over 'Independence', and suspicious that they are going to be tricked.

Although there was political unrest in the country, there were still new missionaries committed to coming out and serving in the Belgian Congo. Families like the Muchmores would have been in Europe learning French in preparation for their first term in the Congo. In a letter from Ione to Mrs Muchmore on the 17th of April, there was much talk of goings on at the Children's Home including a synopsis of the daily food that was available:

.....We have dry skim milk, but for drinking and for cereal, etc., we use whole dry milk which we get wholesale here. Breakfast; oatmeal cereal, papaya or banana, bread, butter (Planta margarine), peanut-butter and jam. When we can get wheat, we use half and half for porridge. They like to put ground roasted peanuts on their porridge but we do not require them to do this, but we do ask

that the children take a little bit of everything that is offered for the usual items. Dinner we try to have quite like at home, with meat and potatoes, vegetable, salad and dessert, but frequently substitute rice or manioc for potatoes, and a native green called sombi, or cooking banana (plantain). The children have rose apples.[128] Real apples are not impossible as occasionally we see them on the bargain counter price and we don't want the children to forget what they taste like. Supper is salad, leftovers, bread or toast. We eat at 6:30 in the morning during school; dinner 12:30; supper 5:15. They take a sandwich and their own drinking water bottles to school in the morning. The bus comes at 7, brings them home at 12:30; goes again at 1:30 and comes at 5.

After the Easter Vacation, Ione wrote to Tom Downey at UFM Headquarters on the 20th of April:

.....Today marks the beginning of another trimester here at Athenée Royal. Most of the children arrived last night and the Banjwadi ones went straight to school from their station this morning, as it is only an hour's ride. We have noticed a slight relief from the usual feeling of being crowded, as the Larson's were able to take a few of the parents for eating or sleeping.[129] I guess you may know that they have engaged a house to rent nearby in order to get going on the Administration Centre project. But others went to the hotel, and some just planned to come into Stanleyville and right out because of no accommodations. Even with just the children and staff we are bursting at the seams, wishing for that new dining room and kitchen. The refrigerator contents are groaning for the next size box. The washing machine stops now and then, just for a rest.

But what a happy, jolly group of children. So, thrilled to be back with one another, after two weeks with their loved ones, some have been in large native conferences, some trekking, all feeling a part of the wonderful work the Lord is doing here in the Congo. The little boys don't notice that we still haven't installed washbasins in their quarters. Brushing teeth outside with a tin cup is always fun when you can see who can spit the farthest!

At this time there were about 40 mission societies working in the Congo. The ones nearest to Ione and Hector were the British Baptist Mission Society, the World Evangelization Crusade (or Heart of Africa Mission), the Africa Inland Mission, the Norwegian Baptists, the Swedish Covenant Church, (MEU) and the Brethren (Immanuel Mission).

Ione wrote that the types of professions needed for work in Congo were: Bible teachers (which training can only come from a Bible Institute or College); teachers of all types and background; doctors, nurses, children's workers, Christian

---

[128] A fruit with red skin, white flesh and a hard seed that is related to guavas rather than apples.

[129] Al Larson and his wife, Jean had recently arrived in Stanleyville as new missionaries from the US. Later on, Al was to take on the duties of Field Director for UFM in Congo and would play a major role in the rescue of the McMillan family and others in 1964.

education specialists, dieticians (wishing she had this training!), business training, engineering of all kinds for building projects, etc.

As far as they knew, they would be able to continue on in the Congo, even though the Belgians would probably leave (2,000 had abruptly left already). Ione stated that living conditions would probably deteriorate, as the Belgians had a high standard of living. Ione trusted the Lord for grace to bear the changes yet to come.

At the beginning of May there was a rapid disruption to life in Stanleyville. Lumumba had just flown into town from Belgium to organize the forthcoming elections. There were several different political parties vying for control of the country, most were based on tribal relationships. As the Congolese had never voted before, the concept of democratic rule was new. The indication the McMillans had of impending trouble was when the children got sent home from school early on buses with soldiers riding as guards. Mabel Wenger, a fellow missionary happened to be in town and her car window got smashed. Ione wrote:

> .....This week a car window was broken when one of our missionaries drove near to the crowd around the African leader, Lumumba. It was Lumumba himself who rescued her, for the car door was opened and those in the car were spat upon.[130] When the missionary (Mabel Wenger) sought refuge with us, Hector cleaned up her car a bit, and put the name of our mission on it in white paint, and she had no more trouble. That same day our children had soldier escort on their school bus, as windows had been broken. Yesterday the school authorities asked that we keep the children home in the afternoon until crowds had subsided.

> .....While we are having trouble with race feelings, the people themselves are getting more and more animated about their various political parties. Some have guns, and are using them. I am thankful that we are six miles out of town, as we can protect the children better from scenes of violence.

Ione provided her sister Marcellyn more detail in a letter written the 10th of May:

> .....The Belgians are leaving and losing their plantations, and everything planted, and are only allowed to take $200 with them......We are beginning to mark our mission cars so that they will not be damaged. It is a queer feeling to be without a Governor, and we are wondering if this will be a stormy time. All sorts of stories are going around, but we do know that Banalia is under military law as of yesterday from fighting and that all of the single girls at Bongondza are sleeping at Walbys. One of the new missionaries was wakened suddenly in the night when an African man was pulling her bed covers off. She is not easily scared, and set up a great noise, and he ran away. The Bongondza folk are concerned about the big girls we take care of here. Laureen is 12 now. So, we are being very careful to get them inside the house at dark, and they are always with us. I have not told Mother any of this, and I hope you don't, as she would worry. We will be thankful when these 26 children are with their parents and the

---

[130] The missionaries have been given the assurance from Lumumba that the Protestant Missions will enjoy favor after Congo's Independence.

responsibility will be for only our own. Final exams are being rushed a bit and it looks like school will not last until June 18 as planned. June 30th is the big Independence Day with 4 days of celebration, when they say even the police will be celebrating. Our missionaries have felt all along that they should stay on their stations and encourage fetes of the right kind. We shall see if this will be possible. We are not having our Annual Conference as usual, and leaving the Field Council till the end of summer when we "know how the matter will fall".

And to her mother:

.....We are listening a lot to the World News, and the seriousness of affairs between Russia and the States sort of puts our troubles here in the shade. [The cold war between United States and Russia was heating up.] *Our local papers tell only of battles with bows and arrows, spears, etc. There are incidents all over, and right here in Stanleyville. Yesterday the African leader Lumumba published that the voting was fraud and the votes don't count. And because Belgium is sending in white paratroops, there is to be a demonstration against whites in Stanleyville. In fact, United Nations became involved and troops arrived from Ghana, Britain, Eire and America provided troop carrier planes. Do pray for our children, as we feel we should keep them in school as long as we can. They will tell the children not to come if military occupation prevents.*

Trouble escalated as Ione chronicled in a letter on the 25th of May:

.....As I write, there are soldiers circulating about town, and a helicopter flying low, looking for trouble. As the Congo is going to have its Independence in just a few weeks, a lot of changes are being made. And these changes are not pleasing to everybody. Political parties made up of people so recently out of savagery, cannot settle disputes without violence. Volunteer white soldiers and paratroops which arrived last week are not very welcome, and because of strong protests in the newspapers, two newspapers were seized. The Congolese leader here says that he can keep things quiet without white soldiers, but the Belgians are not going to chance anything.

A good many white people have left, especially the wives and children. Our field Secretary had a talk with the Congolese leader, Lumumba, and he says the Protestant missionaries are welcome to stay. But we are not basing our hopes on his word, as we have a higher Authority, who called us some time ago, and when He closes the door, we'll know our work here is finished.

Perhaps you remember what Mordecai said to Esther, "Who knows but that thou art come to the Kingdom for such a time as this." We feel that the Lord has a special purpose in keeping us here at this very critical time. Over the days of Independence Celebrations many white people are lodging in hotels with food and guns. The wives and children of the British Missionary Society at Yakusu are coming to stay in the home of the British Vice Council, in Stanleyville. We expect to stay right here, unless told by our mission to do otherwise. There will be soldier protection in town. But we have our invisible host.

Lovingly, Ione

Ione seemed to be experiencing a mixture of emotions, excited to be going home, her day-to-day work and worry about the state of affairs; to Marion Hutchinson on the 13th of June, she wrote:

.....We are getting excited about coming home, and the children have just a few more days of school. We expect to stock up on food and gas. We're cutting down our staff (Congolese) as soon as the children leave on Saturday, and the only ones will be those who live on the place. This morning Isobel heard one of them say that they're going to bring rotten eggs to the door to sell and if they don't buy them, they'll throw them at us! Well, there may be some April fool tricks. Hector is going to give a gift to the local chief and hope that this will prevent everybody coming to the door for a present.

On June 14th, she wrote to Hector's sister Irene:

.....I am feeling fine now, but we hope to have a thorough check-up on the whole family after our arrival for worms, amoebic cyst, chest [exam] for John, and anaemia for all. Everyone except Stevie and I have had fever this past two weeks, and David is in bed right now. The illness may be a type of flu as it seems to be epidemic, but treatment for malaria brings the fever down.

.....The children are putting little things for the journey in the Sabena bags we bought for them. Their Grandma sent them each a notebook and ballpoint pen to keep a diary of the journey, pictorially for those who cannot write much yet. The suits she sent them are nice and have been already shortened where needed. My suit is beige and has a nice straw beret to match. I wore the skirt and hat and gloves to a reception last Saturday held at the Embassy to honour the Queen's birthday. That is the second British reception I have attended, the other being in honour of Sir George somebody or other who is the Ambassador from Britain to Belgium.

Now I must close. We are having another little birthday party [for Kenneth]. There is ice cream and a special cake, with a big chocolate butterfly on it. I made it by cutting a small round cake in two and turning the round sides together with a chunk of cake for a body between. It has silver ball eyes and is studded with silver balls, a bright aqua green with spots made of raisins, and a shiny green sugar dusted over it. The seven candles are around the butterfly, resting on the rectangular bottom layer. [Ione made animal-shaped birthday cakes for all her boys.] This is the last birthday of the term, as Kenneth's is the day after the children separate. Parents will be arriving beginning today and lasting all week, but most will be staying at another house down the road which our mission has rented for now until our guest house is up.

It is amazing and typical of Ione to maintain, as much as possible, a semblance of normality in the midst of political unrest and imminent upheaval. Her love for the children enabled her to ensure normal life continued and to put aside whatever feelings she harbored. She saved realism for her letters and on the 29th of June wrote to her mother:

.....The last trip to town will be made now, and I want to get a note off before the Independence festivities. There are not many white people left, and those staying for these uncertain days are sort of going into hibernation. We do not expect to go where crowds are until things quiet down.

Yesterday as Hector passed the market place there were three truckloads of soldiers trying to disperse a big sea of people. There is more fear than joy just now, as the people really do not know what it is all about. Our staff say they will stay in their houses during the fete, as they are afraid that a big crowd will bring trouble, which it usually does.

We are letting our staff go tonight after work, for the four days of celebration. The King is to arrive in Léopoldville today, and tomorrow he will officially give the Congo its Independence. There will be parades, fireworks, special services in Catholic and Protestant churches, bells ringing, etc.

There have been many incidents of violence, and even just yesterday a white man tried to shoot his chauffeur, and when he missed him an African woman was hit. There are more troubles in Léopoldville than here, as that is where the gov't is being formed. People in town have soldiers around them; and we have a jeep patrolling twice a day past our house. We are getting damageable's out of the way, and the children will stay pretty close to home.

We are getting anxious to go home. All the children have gone to their homes.

Events in Congo took a turn for the worse right after Congo's Independence on June 30th. The Congolese army, at the point of Independence, were still being managed by Belgians and they mutinied because they felt they were underpaid. The Congo, being made up of large provinces, each with differing tribes, languages and ideas was not a unified country. While Lumumba strove to unify all these areas, leaders in these parts strove to establish their own areas of power. The province of Katanga under the leadership of Tshombe broke away with support from Western Countries, in effect, stirring civil unrest. The Belgians sought support from the United Nations. Lumumba approached both the United Nations and his Russian allies for support. His involvement with Communist sympathizers alienated him from the Americans and ultimately, the United Nations. Few Belgian civilians remained. The British Vice Consul realized that there was no protection from a mutinous army or guarantee that British subjects would be safe should they remain in the country, despite assurances from Lumumba. They advised Kinso and key missionary figures in all missions that they should evacuate at least all their women and children. Kinso drove from station to station throughout the night with news that everyone should pack the essentials and prepare for evacuation within four hours as there was no time to lose. This was particularly hard for those living in more remote areas who had not experienced the unrest and racial tensions that were exhibited in the townships such as Léopoldville and Stanleyville.

Ione described these events in a newsletter to supporters that was eventually sent in February of 1961. She titled it, *Flight from Congo*:

We were planning to go on furlough in five days [on July 18th]. *Each of the six children had his clothes laid out ready to wear on the journey. Suddenly conditions in the Congo became very difficult. Soldiers, freed from Belgian command because of Congo's Independence, now were out of control and terrorizing white people as well as the Congolese. In Léopoldville, the missionaries and many other white people, fled across the Congo River into French territory. But when the soldiers began searching cars and houses in Stanleyville, there was nowhere to go, except by plane. Sunday, July 10, Hector went into the city to see if it was safe for us to travel the six miles with the children to church, and later retuned saying it was not safe. He had been roughly treated by soldiers and the car and his briefcase and his clothes were searched to find a gun or shells or a knife. We stayed quietly at home that day but heard Monday that the soldiers were starting to search houses, and where a gun was found, the owner was beaten and taken to jail. We had two hunting guns in the closet of our bedroom, and felt concerned lest we be found with them. Hector went to town to find out where to take them, but decided that it would not be safe to be caught with them in the car even. The guns remained in the closet. On Tuesday things were getting worse, and the order came from the British Vice-Consul to advise our Field Secretary to get our missionary women and children to Stanleyville in readiness for evacuation.*

Hector had to carry the message of evacuation to Banjwadi, 50 miles away. It was quite peaceable there, and Hector said his announcement was like dropping a bombshell in their midst. He had received the order to go to Banjwadi just twenty minutes before the city curfew fell. He was unable to get back until the curfew lifted the next morning. This meant that Isobel Whitehead and I would be alone with the children (and the guns!) through the night. Our co-workers, the Siggs, living in the next house, suggested that we rig up a dinner bell in our quarters, to ring in case the soldiers came. I agreed to this. After supper I gathered the children around the Word and found some precious promises like, "Be not afraid, neither be thou dismayed, for the Lord thy God is with thee, withersoever thou goest." A great calm came over us, and we forgot about the dinner bell arrangement, and went to sleep peacefully, with no alarm set up.

That night the house next to us, a half kilometre nearer to town, was searched and when a gun was found, the man was beaten and taken to jail. In the morning when I took the children to the Siggs house for breakfast, the staff told us about our neighbour and we realized that our house would be next to be visited. I lost my appetite and was in deep thought about those guns when Hector drove in. Along with him came the Field Secretary and also the Treasurer, prepared to set up evacuation if necessary. All available men were sent to pick up women and children from distant stations. Hector was told to take his wife and children to the airport immediately. When Hector turned to me and said, "Can you go, now:" I replied, "Yes, but you must get rid of those guns first".

Hector took the guns from the closet, and while the children put on the clothes they had laid out, he made a hurried journey to the police station. He was not stopped on the way, and was able to leave the guns and all papers there. There was only twenty minutes in all for us to get ready, but I paused for a moment at the bedside to shed a few tears as I realized that although I was not afraid, I found it hard to not be 'dismayed'. But the Lord's command was, "neither be thou dismayed", so I dried the tears and preceded to pack.

Hector took us and Miss Whitehead to the airport and said a hasty goodbye. He returned to the home to find Mrs Sigg and her little boy alone. Very soon after this, the soldiers came to search the house. Some of our Congolese neighbours went out to meet them, and held out their hands as though to prevent them, saying, "Everybody behind us is good, everybody in front of us (indicating our Belgian neighbours) is bad". When Hector saw that the soldiers might become difficult, he went out also to meet them and told them that he had turned in our guns to the police. The soldiers believed him and went their way.

In the meantime, I was waiting at the airport for our turn to leave. The children had had very little breakfast and when the crowds prevented our leaving before mid-afternoon, they were getting quite hungry. But they did not complain, and seemed to understand that this was a very unusual time. They asked what it meant to be a refugee. I looked in the concordance of my Bible and read all the verses I could find on the word refugee. This prepared them for the stops that they would make in the refugee centres, and they knew that they would not have any attentions like we had expected on our journey. As we went off in the big plane that took us eventually to Belgium we could say, "Yea, in the shadow of Thy wings will I make my refuge, until these calamites be overpass." Psalm. 57:1. We were given some supper on the plane and the children slept quite well through the night, though we made a stop at Malta. Here we were offered a very greasy fried egg and a slice of bread. I couldn't eat as I was feeling ill, and had I realized that this would be the last meal the children would have for the next eight hours, I would have urged them to eat more of it. They were quite hungry when the plane finally arrived in Belgium, and here we were herded into an enclosure with thousands of anxious faces staring at us, across the ropes. Several of the Belgians broke through the ropes to ask me if I knew anything about some loved one, missing since the trouble started. I was glad to give news to two of these. The children were given buns and Coca-Cola at the Salvation Army canteen and toys at the Red Cross. I had to leave them for several hours in the roped-off sections of the Salvation Army for I was told my papers were not in order. The route I wished to travel must be changed. I was also told that the hotel and meals formerly offered on my furlough tickets were not available. And I had just four dollars. Furthermore, to arrange my papers might take 8 to 10 days.

Well, the verse came again to me – "be not afraid, neither be thou dismayed". And the belief and trust came into my heart that the Lord would show us what to do. Through the American Consul in Brussels I was able to get in touch with the secretary of all protestant missions in Congo, and this man [Mr. Stenstrom], *knew me as I had entertained him one day in Stanleyville.* [He] *came to the airport to help us, and had papers which were needed and $40 so that we would not lack money. Our ticket was then changed quite quickly and we went to England in order to get a plane to Montreal.*

Laureen recalls that the conditions in Stanleyville's small concrete air terminal were indeed chaotic as her family prepared to evacuate. It was crowded with women and children of all nationalities hoping for a flight. Anxious menfolk who were not being permitted to travel and who did not know when or if they would ever see their families again, harassed officials trying to organize their evacuation. Army personnel tried to maintain some semblance of law and order. The Walby family were part of that humane crisis. Being 12 years of age and the eldest of her siblings, Laureen was keenly aware of the situation. Her mother lost her wedding ring on an American troop carrier on the first leg of their flight to England. She felt utterly bereft, especially as her husband and Laureen's father had been left behind to catch a later flight. Laureen had a French book with her, one of her school prizes from the last term at school which had been given to her for academic achievement. She loaned it to an Indian girl, who was bored on the journey and never met again, and she never saw her prize again. Like Ione and the McMillan boys, the Walbys made several stops and had to wait for available flights, ending up in Brussels where they spent four days waiting for a flight to London.

On the 18th of July, Ione, who had not lost her sense of humor, wrote:

.....I looked around at the other passengers – in various stages of disorder, some hardly dressed at all. I was the only passenger who wore a hat. I said to myself, "Well, I am glad to be properly dressed." Then I looked down at my feet and to my surprise I discovered I was wearing one red shoe and one tan! So, I took off my hat.

Ione also wrote to Hector from Montreal:

Dearest Hector,

Our first letter to you since our parting! We sent a cable to tell you we came here instead of New York. The American Consul in Brussels suggested it as the papers weren't in order for going directly to America. Now I am able to go to U.S. as a Canadian resident. I want to carry on with our planned schedule whether you are here or not. I miss you terribly, but the children have been good, and keep well. And with God ALL things are possible. .....Newsmen have been here the past 3 days with television cameras, etc. from Ottawa, Toronto, Cornwall. They think I'm the first Canadian (?) woman to be evacuated from Congo! We'll see ourselves tonight reading the Bible, praying, even telephoning to see what's happened to you!

.....Love much, XXXXXXX Ione

A week later, the Ottawa Citizen News reported:

Rev. J. Hector McMillan, the Congo missionary who saw his wife and six sons off to safety last Wednesday from Stanleyville, has joined his family at his brother's Avonmore home. Avonmore is 60 miles southeast of Ottawa.

His wife and sons, who arrived last weekend at the Avonmore farm of Archie and Jean McMillan, brother and sister of the minister, had entertained fears for his safety because he could not leave with them.

Mrs. McMillan and the children, hearing yesterday that the missionary was due to arrive in Montreal last night, went there to meet him. He had arrived at Dorval from Nairobi via Khartoum, Athens, Zurich, Frankfurt, Copenhagen and London.

There is a lull in letter writing as the family settled back to living at Three Hills, Alberta. On the 21st of September, Ione found time to update her mother:

.....There is plenty to do here, but I am not killing myself. Have had some visitors from around here (UFM missionaries mostly).

The children are happy and we are getting acquainted with their friends & teachers. Today I inquired about the 4 oldest taking piano. We have a piano here & a teacher next door! $26 for the year's lessons for each child. – Ione

By the 17th of October, Hector was taking 14 hours of study and enjoyed being in school again. Ione took a high school girls Sunday School class. She had a correspondence course from PBI and ordered another from Moody.

Stan Nicholls, the UFM Field Treasurer, decided to stay in Stanleyville when his two children and his wife evacuated. She went back to Stanleyville later but only after leaving the children in the care of Hector and Ione in Canada due to all the uncertainties in Congo. Allan was 9 and Barbara, 10 years old. The children knew Ione and family well as they were part of the Children's Home family. Ione offered to care for them along with her six sons until they were able to return to their parents. The Nicholls children seemed happy, and were obedient. There were three little girls in the immediate neighborhood with whom Barbara played.

Ione missed her African staff members' help in the washings and cleaning, but Hector did a lot between classes, and occasionally took over for an hour. Each child had at least two jobs a day, like sweeping, dusting, emptying garbage, burning papers, washing dishes, wiping, clearing table, etc. All this besides making their own beds and sweeping their rooms.

Timmie had malaria and was responding to treatment but stayed in bed. After the second round of vomiting, he settled back on his pillow saying he felt, 'just yards better'. The children had only started using yard as a means of measure. It was a change from kilometres to miles, centimetres to inches, etc. They got their report cards and all did pretty well, but one or more of the McMillan boys were required to redo the previous year's studies as they did not know how to read in English!

The last letter of the year that Ione wrote was to her mother:

.....My last letter to you was just a carbon-copy kind, and I have been wanting to write a personal one. I am wondering if you will be in Otsego when Doris comes and what your future plans will be. It looks like we'll be entertaining her

around New Year's Day. Hector's sister, Jean, may be with us at Christmas. We'll have one of the Nicholls' children then.

.....It is zero here today but no wind. The children have rosy cheeks when they go outside. All are well just now. Stephen has a scar on his chin from the cut he received when he fell from the top bunk and hit the rail of the bottom. The doctor said he would have to grow a beard to cover the scar! It healed quickly but one little hole stayed open longer and when the bandage was off, we were surprised to find him whistling thru it. We put the bandages back and it soon closed. Hector has a rail on the top bunk now.

We're going after a Christmas tree next Saturday. It's a long way to the foothills of the Rockies & we'll have to take a lunch but it will be fun & we have a good heater in the car. Loads of love, Ione

The year was like a roller coaster ride with many twists and turns, and full of surprises. Whether in Congo or Canada, the family was still exposed and needed the watchful eye of Ione. She herself was feeling the strain as she was experiencing health problems. But as ever, she relied on her faith to support her and see her through.

Chapter 20
A CANADIAN INTERLUDE

Despite the hurried exodus from Congo, the McMillans, now back in Canada, were able to enjoy time with family over the 1960 Christmas period. Ione's sister Doris came to visit them at Three Hills, Alberta and later wrote:

.....Am so thankful to see you all & won't forget the wonderful visit for a long time to come. Thank you much for the courses from Prairie Bible Institute. We will enjoy them very much I know. Hope you are still considering coming up here [to Alaska] in the Spring. We will be thrilled if you find you can make it. Any arrangements you might wish concerning meetings, etc. let me know & it can be arranged.

Doris told of some heart-breaking times with the children being separated from her except for certain visitations. Her ex-husband, Bill had remarried and any visits were tense. But Doris was confident that the Lord would help them through it.

In January, while living in Canada, Ione wrote to her mother, who was now living in Washington DC, sending her birthday wishes. She also told that Hector, while helping a neighbor on his free day from school, got his right hand in the works of a grain auger, breaking the 3rd and 4th finger. 15 stitches and casts were necessary, but it was healing. He could use the hand but he had to give up typing class.

She added:

.....We feel quite ready for this cold spell that is beginning just now, 10 degrees below this morning. We have plenty to eat, moose, lamb, rabbit, turkey and some smoked salmon Doris brought. There are 30 fish in the freezer all cleaned and brought to us last night by the Bill Grants. We're getting our eggs & milk free right now as Hector is doing all chores at Cullums for a few days while they are away. When we buy them from the small chicken & turkey farm behind us they are 25¢ or 35¢ a dozen. The turkeys we bought were 35¢ a pd. We get the children's allowance from the government for the Nicholls children as well as our own.

We have been home 6 months now & it looks less likely now that we'll get back to Congo in July. Today's news is bad for our province & in Katwa they have worse troubles.

The Nicholls children have been getting letters [from their parents in Congo] every week until 3 weeks ago. Now nothing comes. Pray that we'll know how to counsel them if this continues. The children write every week but only about 3 of their letters have reached their parents since November.

The children do not seem to be worrying, but we wonder if their folks will be forced to leave. I've asked Hector's sister, Jean to come here for 2 weeks while

I attend Conference at Pontiac & other meetings, but haven't had her answer yet. It would be April 19-23 in Pontiac.

Love, Ione

As the next letter shows, Ione and Hector talked of future plans and are kept very busy looking after 8 children. Ione wrote to her mother on April 1st:

.....The children are settled down for the night and Hector is repairing a broken table.

Yes, I do owe you a letter and that's no fooling, even on April Fool's Day! I was too busy to play a single prank on anybody though I had spent a good deal of time at the doctor's office today & two days ago, filling out medical papers required by the mission. We have had a letter from UFM saying that only strategic missionaries would be permitted to go back to Congo. I guess that lets us out, for it seems to me we are not strategic. They are considering opening new work in North Africa, Europe or Pakistan. Our doctor here was a missionary in Pakistan and he says there is a splendid school there for missionary children. That is a big consideration for us as we plan to take all the children if we go to the field within the next two years.

Of more concern was Ione's health. She asked Hector's sister, Jean to come and stay a few weeks with Hector and the children while she was away at meetings on the east coast plus getting some medical attention later at Three Hills. The doctor said the problem with her pelvis bone might clear up at menopause. But at the moment, Ione did not have much discomfort even though the floor of the pelvis was weak from the babies and the pelvis had gradually cracked.

She was unsure of her future, as her heart wanted to be back in Congo despite continued unrest there. As a planner and organizer, she was unsure of what she was

The boys at Three Hills, Alberta.

preparing for; life back in the Congo or in Canada.[131] Whatever her destiny, Ione kept herself and the family busy as she shared with her sister in law, Florence:

.....We keep well, and the boys active. Hector has been dismantling an old binder for [his wheat farmer friend] *Bert Cullum, whenever they could sneak away from the gardening! I caught them all just in time yesterday to get beans and peas picked so that I could can them! The boys love to help Hector and*

---

[131] Readers might wonder why Ione and Hector would risk going back to Congo with the children given the existing political uncertainties there. One reason might be that they had invested a better part of their adult lives passionately devoted to missionary work in Congo and did not see an alternative plan. Feeling responsible for what they had been tasked with might be another reason. Above all, they appear to have found ample security that God would provide protection for them.

they do not mind the gardening either, but weeding and snipping beans does get tiresome. We have beets to do next. We are putting away whatever food we can get hold of, just in case we are to stay here. But we do not actually know yet. When Hector took the boys to camp a couple weeks ago, he stopped at a farm and the same man who gave us a cow in '50 gave us pig! So, we are enjoying this good meat and have it in packages in the locker downtown.

We still would like to make a short trip to Alaska to visit my sister, but we have to keep putting it off until we know our future and that of the two children with us. And school starts Aug. 31st! So, the summer will soon be gone.

Early August 1961, Ione received a letter from her sister Doris and Bob[132], who lived and worked in Soldotna, Alaska. They were interested in having the family up for the summer and offered to pay for gas, car repairs, etc. along the way on the Alaskan-Canadian Highway.

Eventually, the Nicholls children left the care of Ione and Hector and joined another missionary, Olive Bjerkseth, who took them to Toronto. From there, Olive accompanied them to Philadelphia and then onto the Congo to be reunited with their parents. This enabled the McMillans to set off for Alaska.

Back "home" at Three Hills, details of the family holiday are shared with Hector's sister Irene on the 3rd of September. Ione wrote:

.....It was a very unusual trip to Alaska, with breath-taking heights and cold in the glaciers and mountains. The wild-life was abundant, 5,000 moose on the peninsula where my sister lives. They killed one in their yard the morning we arrived. Hector enjoyed helping with the butchering. The children helped 'pick' salmon from the nets, and watched seals trying to get the fish; also, a killer whale [Beluga whale, more likely] *which went sailing by. They just love it, and we did not mind the cold, even when we cooked our meals on wind-swept rocks. We were well-dressed. It was 5 days each way from here, and 10 days staying there, not too tiring; had to load up enough food for all that time, as the prices were terribly high on the Alaskan Highway. One sign read, "It's high, but it's here!" Two eggs fried for 85¢; a hamburger for $1, cup of cocoa 20¢, all pops 25¢, etc.*

The big decision of returning to Congo had to be made immediate upon our return because of giving up the house to Bible school students. So, although Hector has been in bed most of the week with cold and fever, we keep pushing at the new plans, packing, writing etc. Pictures can be taken now, and a prayer card made, a new letter, etc. We are making an itinerary for meetings covering the states of Washington, Idaho, Montana, South Dakota, Nebraska, Illinois, Ohio, until we get to Michigan October 16, the Lord willing. There we expect to put the children into a school for 6 weeks while we contact the supporters of the three children and myself, take speaking engagements, etc. Hector will be able to leave me with the children and go to Toronto and even down home perhaps.

---

[132] Bob Schmidt, Doris' new husband, was a commercial fisherman on the shores of Cook Inlet, Alaska.

We are leaving here September 29, in order to free this house for students coming in soon. The children will have had just three weeks in school here when we take them out. The correspondence course which we are arranging will follow this work through the entire year.

In November, Ione learned that the mission would rather Hector travel alone to the Congo and that Ione stay home until June. Whatever the reasons for the change in plans, the McMillans agreed but Hector preferred the family be back at Avonmore. They left Drayton Plains, Michigan on the 18th of December where they had been for a few weeks. They arrived in Avonmore on the 22nd, having stopped along the way to visit family. Ione was able to rent a house near the school in Avonmore. Hector's planned departure was for the 12th of January and the change of plans meant Ione did not get to see her mother for Christmas Day. However, they met before their departure back to Canada. Ione described events in a letter to her mother on the 26th of December:

.....We had a nice supper and breakfast at Alice's [Hector's sister]. The next morning, we called at two places in Hamilton and Burlington, and went on to Toronto. I was pretty miserable by that time with a bad cold which I had had for two weeks. As soon as we arrived in Toronto, we stopped at People's Church and found their Women's Prayer Meeting in session. They asked us to bring the boys back at ten to 4 for singing at the close of their prayer time. So, we went back. It was just two blocks from the home; you know the UFM has a lovely new home there now. When the boys sang the women shouted and prayed and cried through it all. They were really touched. And as they went out, they left an offering for them which amounted to $25. Then they were asked to sing at the Sunday school Christmas program that evening. So that was our introduction to Dr Oswald Smith's church. He was there and gave us some encouragement in his greetings.

.....I felt quite ill during the trip from Toronto here on Friday, and had to lay down. That night I couldn't go to the Bible study at Finch but went to bed. I was feverish then. The next day I went to the doctor and he gave me a shot of penicillin, and eardrops, gargle, throat pills. I had trouble in the night with my ear, and he said if I wasn't careful, I would have mastoid trouble. So, I kept it medicated and covered and stayed in bed as much as I could. I went out last night for the first time, and the shot seems to have knocked it out of me. The cold is better, and aside from the headaches I feel all right.

This afternoon, a man is coming to talk about renting a furnished house in town, much nicer than the one we were first thinking about. It is on the main street, a big white house, with oil heat and all plumbing. The school is just a few houses away. We talked to the principal, and made arrangements for the children to start January 3rd. Hector wants to take some meetings in the Maritime Provinces, as there are some good contacts in New Brunswick, etc. But that will not be too soon. He will help us get moved in, and will only take short meetings away as yet.

.....The children just love it here. They were out early this morning at the barn, helping Archie, and putting the train together. I wish Mrs. Dickinson [the train's donor] *could see their pleasure in it, and excitement, even after six years. They are now able to recondition it themselves.*

Christmas here was very simple, but I think satisfying to the children. The big thing was the turkey, mince pie, and the sacks of apples, nuts, oranges, candy, etc.

We are going to Florence's for New Year's only we will go on Saturday. Pray for our testimony here, that we may not appear smug and self-satisfied, but that we can radiate a light that will draw these folk to the Lord. We had a nice time around the Word with old Uncle Neal, the only one left of the old McMillan family. He is 89, and makes you feel just a little breath of heaven to be near him. He and his son live up the road. That's where we went last evening.

Paul is working a jig-saw puzzle, with Auntie Jean's occasional help. Stephen and Kenny and John took grain to town with Uncle Archie on the sleigh. The rest are working on the train. I hope you have a nice Christmas. We want to hear about it. Wish you had been here.

Lovingly, Ione

And, thus ends another dizzyingly busy year. The problems and issues may have changed from those experienced in Congo but Ione tackled them all with her usual organizational style. The letters were mainly to family as she and Hector spoke at many meetings and they kept in touch with their supporters by seeing them in person.

Chapter 21
CHANGING PLANS

The family was back in Avonmore, waiting for permission to go back to Africa. As usual, at the beginning of most years, Ione wrote to family and friends thanking them for their support and to her mother with birthday greetings. The first letter of 1962 was to sister Lucille:

.....Thanks for your note. We'll be looking for that package from Esther [Lucille's daughter]! We're so sorry we missed the fellowship with you all at Christmas time. We had a nice time here with Jean and Archie. They had a tree, and special little sacks of goodies for the boys. We have a furnished house on Main Street in Avonmore, oil heater in living room, coal range in dining room, electric stove in kitchen, and another stove in the utility room, plus a couple of electric heaters! Oh, yes, and an electric blanket. So, we are warm! It has been cold here, too, but we are cosy. We do not have Hector's departure date yet. But the transport money has started to come in!! We'll wait until ours is all in. Hector goes to Founder's Week at Moody in February.

Love, Ione

On the 23rd of January Ione wrote to her mother:

.....The package arrived while we were at Jean and Archie's just after Christmas. I was especially glad you sent the little stockings as they had not put up any stockings this year. I saw Jean and Archie had prepared large plastic sacks of fruit, etc. and thought that it would be better not to put up stockings. So, your

Eleanor. Alice, Jean, Irene, Florence, Hector and Archie McMillan – 1962. This may have been the last time the Avonmore McMillan siblings were all together.

thoughtfulness gave them the stockings after all, and they were so glad. They have made them last a long time. And I noticed that when Kenny finished his candy, he filled his sock with some good things (left-over pancakes, etc.!) for the chick-a-dees out in the tree in back. He puts out special things for the woodpeckers and nut-hatches, too.

.....The boys are all taking piano now from a lady who is doing it for only $2 for all per week. The boys are singing a lot here, and are keeping real busy. They love skating best of all.

We spent last week-end at Toronto, where Hector's church had a farewell for him. It was quite a touching service. Although he has no departure date, they wanted to have it when it was convenient for them. They surely love the

452

boys there. Did I tell you they sang for Dr Oswald Smith in a service on our way
to Avonmore? Kenny and I are working on a new duet, "He Giveth More Grace
When the Burdens are Greater."

There have been quite a number of large gifts, of $100, some of them,
designated passage, and this brings our passage money that is in up to ¼ of what
is needed. Support yet needed is $60 a month. Quite a bit. Hector will not leave
till all this is in. We have had letters from the field and headquarters, and all
seem to indicate going ahead. There is no trouble in our area. Hector will go to
Founder's Week February 5-12 and take some meetings on the way. I think he
will be stopping at Lucille's. Much love, Ione

Settling the boys into a new school for the third time that school year must have
occupied a great deal of Ione's time during February, especially as Hector was away
taking meetings and trying to drum up the financial support required to get them all
to Africa. As stated in the letter above, they were still some way to their required
support target.

As mentioned in previous letters, the family periodically experienced fresh
outbursts of malaria. On March 4th, Ione, again writing to her mother reported:

.....Timmy is sitting beside me in a rocking chair, and the others have gone to do
chores at Jean and Archie's. Timmy's temperature is normal now and he has
started eating, but he was vomiting this morning. He responded to malaria
treatment, so guess that is what it was.

We had a letter from Al Larson, which says there will be no missionary
children's school in Stanleyville now. It was voted down by the Field Council.
Reasons will be given in the minutes which will be coming. They have
recommended Rethy Academy, the Africa Inland Mission School. This, Mother,
is where I've always wanted our children to go, as it is such a wonderful school.
But whenever I brought it up, it was voted against by the others who thought it
was too far away and too expensive. And now that they have recommended it, it
means that they have faith enough to believe that the money will be forthcoming.
It is right near the border of Congo, the safest place, and in the mountains, a
healthy climate, and very good food. The only hard part is the separation for 3
months. But there are planes that run between Bunia, which is near Rethy, and
Stanleyville, and we can have them for 1 month after each term of 3 months.
Isobelle Jones is stationed there, and for the time being, working right in the
school.

The Field Council have sent money to buy a 2-ton truck, probably in
Philadelphia, and Hector is to take it by boat around north Africa, down the east
coast to Mombasa, Kenya, and drive it inland to the Congo. He passes right
through Rethy on his way. Money will be given for the cost of the transport of
the truck. And when he gets it to Congo, he is to be stationed at <u>Bongondza</u>, and
have it for the construction of a medical unit there for the doctor. He is to work
along with the native church, and they seem to think he is just the one to fit into

that situation. That is where Viola Walker is, as well as Dr and Mrs Sharpe, from England, and their 3 small children.

And in another letter, Ione wrote:

.....We received the tape and game and are working on the tape. We have about ten numbers already recorded. Hector wants to put some interesting bird songs on, too, and some of the children's piano numbers. Timmy and I have a little duet. He is doing quite well in his piano. They are all taking piano from the organist of the Presbyterian Church.

We had hoped to visit you for Easter, but Archie is having trouble with his heart and Hector must not be away. Archie is supposed to stay in bed but gets up some. I wanted to go to Pontiac, too, for their Conference, but if I am gone it would be too hard on Jean who is not well, either.

.....Well, our plans will depend upon Archie's condition. Hector is needed here right now. And I have 8 meetings lined up for myself and the boys for the next month, right here in this community.

We are having spring weather but this week end brought 6 inches of snow. The robins are walking gingerly about looking wistful.

It was not easy while Hector was away, but we got along all right. I think the weekends were the hardest as there was no chance of getting rested up in between bouts with discipline, getting jobs done, etc. And the fires were a bit complicated, as I didn't want to get the wood fire too high for fear of a chimney fire. We had an extinguisher handy, however, and a box of soda!! Now it is not so cold, although the therm. said 8 above even this morning. And the children still wear their winter underwear and flannel shirts.

.....Yes, Timmy got over his sick spell; it was just for a day or so. All have kept very well, and I think only T has missed a day of school. I am getting real fat and am wondering how to keep from losing my figure entirely! If I wear a garment, I get that irritation that was bothering me when I went to Washington. It is a fungus that needs more fresh air!! I am getting shots (Vitamin B12) for my blood and nerves; the doctor here is giving free a series of ten. He says my blood count is OK. I feel in good enough condition to go back to the field, and this has been verified by the doctor. Hector and I are getting polio shots as well as the children. There have been polio cases on two of our stations. Enough about health. We'll get typhus shots yet and then we're thru.

Ione's optimism over her health issues was ill founded. On the 23rd of April, she informed her sister Lucille that she had been admitted to hospital as an emergency following a hemorrhage. The doctor she had seen previously thought Ione had fibroids in the uterus, and advised that there was no need for an operation as fibroids shrink with the onset of menopause. However, it would seem that the growths were uterine tumors and not benign fibroids.

On the 24th, she wrote to her mother:

.....Now I know the operation is to be tomorrow and I will start this hoping that Hector will add the fact that I am out of the anaesthetic O.K. The doctor made

another examination today to be sure and he will make the incision in the same place as my previous operations! Too bad there's no zipper!

I can see now why Hector was not allowed to go ahead to Congo. The Lord knew he would be needed now with the boys.

I had stopped flowing the first of February and thought it was the beginning of change of life. For nearly 2 years I had been having a period between 11 & 21 days. I didn't realize that when it stopped it was all going into tumour. So last Thursday when I started with a bang, I lost quite a bit and still thinking it was just a big period, I didn't tell the doctor. By Saturday morning I was too faint & weak & poor Hector couldn't get the ambulance there fast enough. They got me stopped so that I could get strength for the operation & till the cold was better.

Now a space for Hector –

Folks are good to us. Ione was still under anaesthetic. She went in about 8 a.m. & came back from recovery room about 1 p.m. They had an intravenous going.
Love, Hector

How Hector coped while Ione is hospitalized is revealed in a letter to his sister Florence on the 1st of May:

.....The children are off to school and the house is quiet now. I got the washing done yesterday and all put away. Dorthea (Mrs. John D. Dunbar) asked if she could wash and iron the white shirts, and Glenn McIntyre's wife wants to do any other ironing. Mary Belle sent a lovely cake yesterday afternoon; in fact, so many folks have been so helpful to us. Ione has received so many nice cards and quite a few visitors. I was up yesterday and took Orma along with me from Chesterville. On the way back, I had an opportunity to talk about spiritual things. Ione was feeling quite well but still had a little chest congestion. I hope she will be able to be home by this week-end. She phoned her mother in Washington D.C., as well as the chairman of her mission board of her home church in Pontiac.

And Hector reiterated the events leading up to Ione's operation, adding:

.....Now concerning the operation. She knew that she had a tumor in the uterus but a doctor in Alberta thought that it would shrink away. But about ten days ago she began to hemorrhage and on Saturday she felt so faint that she just about passed out. I got the ambulance to take her to the hospital in Winchester. When the doctor examined her, he said she would have to have a complete hysterectomy but that he would wait until she had the operation. She won't be able to do much for at least two months, so we may be delayed a month or more in our departure for Congo.

We have had an invitation to go to Rethy to help in supervising the dormitory. We have sent word that we are willing if our UFM field council thinks it advisable. So, we await further news.

I have been having the morning services in the United Church in Apple Hill the past two Sundays and have one more. The folks seem to appreciate the TRUTH. We will be at Finch Presbyterian this coming Sunday evening and Maxville next Tuesday night. It takes a lot of study but it is good for my own soul.

Just a day or so ago I read this to the children from a book by A.W. Tozer, "Pursuit of God", "Only as children get older and sin begins to stir within their hearts do jealousy and envy appear. Then they are unable to enjoy what they have if someone else has something larger or better. At that early age the galling burden comes down upon their tender souls, and it (pride) never leaves them till Jesus sets them free."

.....We should try to get down to see you some week-end, but we will have to plan that after Ione is better. Trust all goes well with you.

> *Love and prayer, Hector*

Ione's progress was chronicled in a series of letters to her mother; the first being on the 2nd of May when she was able to sit out of bed for a while:

.....I'll write until I have to lay down again, but it feels good to sit up straight for a while. A week ago, today I was in the operating room. The doctor marvels that I got over the "patch" of pneumonia so well, but I know the Lord gave me strength to keep spitting up the phlegm and drinking a lot. I've had unusual opportunities to witness & give tracts. My verse for today is Psa. 149: 5,6 as the verse says, I am "upon my bed", but with a "two-edged sword in my hand." May the Lord help me to use it at the right time.

.....I've an invitation to go to a friend's house until I am stronger, but there is a woman we can get to do housework and Hector can keep on cooking for a while. Friends keep sending in roasted meat, macaroni & cheese, soups, and all kinds of buns & desserts. I laughed at Hector yesterday for he said he didn't leave enough time to cook the potatoes & carrots for noon so he went down the street & bought a pressure cooker!

When I go home, I will just do correspondence for a while (& my 2 correspondence courses which I am behind in!). I will sleep upstairs, but stay down all day on the davenport. The bathroom is on the main floor.

I love my new clothes & will wear them home when I go (don't know when yet). The hat is perfect on me. I tried it.

> *Love, Ione*

It appeared that the doctor would not take a cent for his services! Hector had deposited payments for the 1st week at the hospital but they wrote off the rest of the 18 days.

About two weeks later, Ione again wrote to her mother. She was back home with the family and recorded her progress thus:

.....Tuesday Hector took me to see the doctor. He had asked me to come in 2 weeks after leaving the hospital. After examination he said everything was healed remarkably well. He muttered, "Must be the church you belong to". I must go back once more in a month's time. He gave me a letter which states that I can "resume former employment" after July!

And about her 'former employment':

> *We have had 2 letters from the field from Al Larson & Viola Walker. The missionaries on the field as well as natives think we should go to Bongondza.*

But if Rethy will accept UFM children only by our joining their dormitory staff, there will be no choice. [However] apparently, no senior missionaries are available for Bongondza & Viola is the only non-medical worker there. They are very keen for us to go there. Pray about it. – Ione

Ione was not the only one experiencing medical problems, her sister Lucille was also unwell, apparently with a low blood count and wanted to delay treatment. And Ione, herself, had a setback and wrote on the 11th of June:

.....A little "chastening for the present" appears to be our lot, you and I; I am to go back to the hospital at any time soon for a hernia operation. I had it when I went to Dr Westcott, but it was not so noticeable and he said it was nothing. Now it is more evident, and must be taken care of. 5 days in hospital & 3 weeks rest! We'll delay our visit with Mother until the middle of July; I think her holiday is the 15th now (I talked to her last night). Maybe she'll come here and then see you. We had a letter making it definite that we would take out the 2-ton Bongondza truck, so plan to go to Congo by boat and overland (that means leaving sooner, but I don't know what the mission will say now!). Mother said she read a letter from an AIM missionary saying we were going to Rethy, but we've had no such word. Lucille, please don't wait for your trip to hospital. I'm worried about you.

Love, Ione

Four days later, on the 23rd of June, Ione was able to report to Lucille that her operation on the hernia went without any problems and she was now recovering. She expressed concern that Lucille had yet to set a date for her hospital appointment, she wrote:

.....Please don't wait too long, Lucille. You are too precious.

As part of her preparations for returning to African, Ione and Hector had to be sure that they kept their supporters up to date. On July 15, Ione wrote a letter that was distributed widely:

Dear Friends,

This may be our last letter from this country. We expect to leave around the middle of August. Because we are taking out a 2-ton truck we will be going by boat. This will be fun for the six boys now ages 8 through 15 years, and they will be thrilled with the sights they will see between New York and Mombasa, Kenya, East Africa.

The month-long journey will take us the length of the Mediterranean Sea, through the Suez Canal and down the African coast. When the cargo boat reaches Mombasa, the truck will be assembled and adapted for family travel across the plains to the Congo. After a week's journey, we will leave the boys at Rethy Academy and go on three days more to Bongondza where the truck will be used for the completion of a medical unit.

It sounds good, but we do not have enough money yet to start the trip. The round-about way is costing more than we had anticipated. We were surprised to learn last week that we need $2,000 more! A shorter way into the Congo by the *west coast and up the Congo River would be cheaper. But that way is not possible just now. So once again we are "expecting great things of God and attempting great things for God." Won't you join us in prayer about this need?*

.....We want to thank you for all you have done for us. If you know Jesus Christ as your personal Saviour, you will understand what we mean when we say we are trusting the Lord, "which maketh a way in the sea, and a path in the mighty waters." Isa. 43:16. We are trusting Him to begin in mercy a new work of love with us and through us to needy Congolese.

Lovingly in Him, Hector and Ione McMillan

Once again, Ione's optimism was misplaced and there were yet more hiccups for the family, as Ione explained to her mother and sister Lucille on the 26th of July:

.....It is afternoon and we have all had a good rest. The children are playing in the barn while Hector and Archie see a man about selling his horses [Molly and Nelly]. Just a few hours ago Mother was still here and now she has gone and we find a big empty spot in our hearts as well as in the house. It was so nice having you here, but all too short. Thank you so much for coming all that way. And thank you for all your words of counsel, given in love.[133] Thanks, too, for the lovely gifts you gave to us all. As I think over everything you gave it makes a big total for such a big family. You might find this American $5 useful in purchases you will make while at Lucille's. I hope you can get your coat and some other things you can only get in Michigan.

.....Our visa forms still have not come, even after phoning twice to Washington. And we can't send them in until we get them! And after that the processing will take one month! Well, it is a good time to relax and let the sting wear away from the incision. Do you still find yourself sore, Lucille?

Mother, you surely gave us a nice evening last night and by the looks on the people's faces, everyone else was satisfied, too. I just hope you will not be too tired for that long journey. You must try to rest as much as you can while at Lucille's. We will let you know just as soon as we have more news.

Mother, be sure and tell Lucille about the help First Baptist church will give with passage money and also two months allowance in advance when we go. Also, we must make a date to see her when we come to Pontiac. It will probably be the last of August.

Will you pray that the Lord will send in the $1150 yet lacking for passage? Thanks so much for coming, Mother. We hope to see you the last of August, if not before.   Lovingly, Ione

In the end, Hector had to make a personal trip to the Embassy in Washington to fill out application forms for their visas; unfortunately, it did not leave him time to visit his mother in law; he needed to go to Philadelphia to pick up the truck they were taking back to Congo.

---

[133] This sounds like Ione was on the receiving end of advice-giving for a change.

Despite not having visas, the family prepared for departure and took services at supporting churches. Once again, plans changed, and the decision was made for Hector to travel by sea with the truck and the bulk of the family possessions. Ione would fly with the six boys, taking just hand luggage. The family got to Montreal, the truck and possessions were loaded on the *Thorsriver*, but still no visas. Hector cannot go with the ship, nor can the family fly. Hector was stuck! The family could always take a later plane, but the *Thorsriver* was the only ship sailing. It transpired that the ship had to sail 1000 miles up the St Lawrence river before setting out to sea and Hector was able to make the arrangements to fly to Fort Alfred in Quebec, so he could catch his ship.

Hector stayed with his sister and Ione and the boys go back to Avonmore to stay with Hector's cousins for five days. The visas arrived and the family set off, Hector to his ship at the end of August and Ione and boys to Africa five days later by air. One setback was that the family luggage was overweight for the plane and they had to leave behind four packages, which no doubt the family back home would send on to them.

Hector described some of his trip in a letter to his sister Florence on the 4th September:

> While waiting for breakfast I'll get a letter off to you. I was a bit sea sick crossing the Gulf so it is nice to be in port again. I'll be thinking about all you folks getting Ione and the boys off today. I know the Lord will give extra strength.
>
> Thank you again for all you did for me. It was the best visit we had of our whole furlough. There are so many things to pray about so we all need to be in close fellowship in the Lord.
>
> There are only 8 passengers on board......I've talked to one, a Salvation Army officer, and I believe he knows the Lord.
>
> We will be here until Thursday morning loading newsprint. By the way this place has the largest output of paper in the world. Just this morning a boat came in to the dock. I was talking with one of the superintendents and he said it was coming from Texas and had a load of 12,000 tons of sulphur – enough to last for 12 months. They burn sulphur and limestone rocks together and the acid produced is fed into tanks of wooden chips. This breaks down the wood fibre and prepares it for the paper process. I was up about 6 A.M. and had a nice long quiet time with the Lord. I found a "life principle" as Uncle Fergus Kirk says. Psalm 116:6 "The Lord preserveth the simple". We, in our pride, tend to make life complicated but we need to be brought low so that we can "look up".
>
> .....Well, bye for now. Love and Prayer, Hector.

Ione's journey was not without incident. She told her mother the story in a letter written on the 18th of September:

> .....Through some mistake we had no hotel reservations in Léopoldville, and the mission home was filled up there with Belgian [and other nationalities] people coming out to teach school. And they said the plane the next morning to Stanleyville was filled and we could get nothing for 3 weeks. It was a shock, but

the Lord sustained us as we found a quiet part of the big airport lobby to spend the night. The benches were long and it was dark enough to stretch out without being observed by the hundreds of soldiers outside. A kind Congolese policeman slept on a bench nearby. Toward morning he told us that if we stand near the Air Cargo desk when they were calling the names for the plane, we might get a place. We did that, and once more, the Lord performed a miracle. The names of a number of people were called and they didn't answer, so we were given their places. We were on the plane by 6:30 A.M. Then they served us a nice Congolese breakfast.

We arrived in Stanleyville on the 5th at 11:30 A.M. and Al [Larson] *was there to meet us. Because the ride was a bumpy one, we were all a bit sick, but it didn't take long to be feeling better after landing. We all had to have vaccination for smallpox. It is required every year now. We had no trouble with Customs, etc. At the Home we were thrilled to find our house helper, Malenza & wife. He made us a nice dinner.*

Ione was supposed to go from Stanleyville to Bunia by plane to get the boys into school but once again plans changed as Ione explained to Florence:

.....[Al] told us that the plane we should take to the school at Rethy via Bunia was booked up for 3 weeks and he could drive us there if he could get another missionary to share the driving. He took us to a nearby station, Banjwadi, for the week-end and arranged for the 3-day trip (water, gas, bread, etc.) from Stan to Rethy.

It was an exciting ride on very bumpy roads, many road barriers but the soldiers were friendly to missionaries. Two times we saw baboons on the road and several snakes, and we went right through pygmy territory. Six tires were changed, and once we were pushed up the side of a slippery rainy mountain by Africans who noisily demanded 400 francs. They even wanted more, but settled for this amount ($3). They can't do anything without shouts and chants and their leader sat in the front seat of the car directing them. It was all in good humor and we were thankful for their help.

From these letters, we learned that the journey took three days and David Grant shared the driving with Al Larson. They stopped off at mission stations along the way. Finally, they arrived at Rethy and Ione helped the boys settle into their new school.

.....Kenny, Paul, David and John are allocated to a dormitory where the house parents are the Sigg family (Dick and Mimi) who were at Kilometre 8 and had looked after them in 1960. Stephen and Timmy are to share a room in the younger boys' dormitory.

Ione writes to Hector's sister:

.....The boys like it real well at Rethy Academy and the cost was less than I expected. We pay $75 a term (3 months) for the two older boys and $65 for the 4 younger. That's cheaper than I thought.

The Congolese franc was relatively unstable so fees were paid in US dollars, which Ione arranged mission headquarters to pay. This meant Ione could spend her traveler's cheques locally. She also made a three hour trip over the border to Arua in Uganda to buy supplies that were not available in Congo, such as oatmeal, various kinds of canned meats, fruits, cookies in tins, corn syrup, candles, lamp mantles, etc..

Ione left the boys in school and headed back to Banjwadi where she stayed three days before heading on to Bongondza where she and Hector hoped to work again. On the 25th of September, she wrote:

I am at Bongondza now and living in the house where we expect to be for the next five years. It seems big and empty right now, but I hope to welcome Hector in about three weeks' time. Then at Christmas the walls will ring with boyish voices! I found a warm welcome here and much to do. I have one helper whom I knew as a lad, and a gardener who is a hospital patient. I expect to be teaching the Bible School from 8 to 10 each morning; their wives from 2-3 three times a week; all women in the area two afternoons a week. Since Hector isn't here I have been asked to speak already twice to the African congregation. This afternoon I will give a little talk to the women and tomorrow night to our 'white people'. The Bongondza white folk consist of Doctor and Mrs. Sharpe and three children (from England); Miss Viola Walker, whose place I will be taking when she leaves in two weeks; Miss Ruby Gray from Ireland, a nurse; David Wilmshurst, male nurse from England; and Bill Gilvear, a male nurse from Scotland.

You would be interested to know that when we were having so much trouble getting away, and had just missed both plane and boat, Hector sat down beside me and said quietly, "Only faith has the courage to fail." That has been a real encouragement to me during these days of adjustment.

Love, Ione

All the while, Hector was still in transit on board the ship, *Thorsriver*. From Port Elizabeth in South Africa, Hector wrote to his family in Canada on the 26th:

Dear Jean and Archie:

I have time to get a letter off before the ship leaves here this afternoon.

In Cape Town I got a letter that Ione had written that last Sunday she was in Avonmore. She said the boys helped with the threshing, and that you had one last picnic on the hill.

I was just up on deck talking to the captain. By the way he was telling the passengers the other day that on this boat's maiden voyage they loaded up in South Africa and sailed to Montreal. They had 6,000 tons of raw sugar for Toronto so they started up the newly-opened (St. Lawrence) seaway. When they got to Snell and Eisenhauer locks, they raised the ship 43 feet in five minutes. It was rubbing against the side, scrapping the paint off, and the sparks were flying. .....My! The cargo we have on board here. It has a capacity of ½ a million cubic feet. Big rolls of newsprint weighing up to 1700 lbs – loaded at Three Rivers,

Chicoutimi, and Corner Brook, Newfoundland; probably about 3,000 tons of the stuff. We haven't started unloading the wheat yet. I guess that is for a port farther along. We are putting into drydock at Durban so we will be there four or five days. The captain suggested October 20th for our arrival at Mombasa. Ione's letter was sent there but the shipping company knows where all the boats are so it was forwarded to Cape Town.

I was a bit sea-sick just out of Newfoundland for several days and then the water calmed down as we got into the tropics. I must have gotten a sun stroke as I was down sick again for five days. One evening when I was especially bad, the retired Salvation Army officer came into my room and had a reading and prayer with me. He really knows the Lord. He and his wife were in Rhodesia for 35 years doing missionary work. They are coming over for a short visit and are going back to Montreal on this same boat. I gave him Florence's address and phone number so he may call her up when they get back some time in November.

I had a lovely Sunday afternoon in Cape Town. I went for a walk and after a while asked a man where there was a Baptist church. When he found out that I was 'on foot' he very kindly took me in his car to a little church where they were just going in for three o'clock Sunday School. The elderly man in charge welcomed me so warmly and asked me to take the opening prayer. While we were waiting on the platform, he told me that he had been led to the Lord by George Mueller. He has been in South Africa for over sixty years and is the only man alive who worked with saintly Andrew Murray. I showed him the picture of our family and he was more than delighted and showed it to the Sunday School. After the classes he and I went for a walk, spent at least two hours over eggs on toast with a cup of tea, went to a street meeting, visited two cathedrals to see the architecture on our way back to the little church where we had a grand message from the pastor.

Well, I must close. I hope to be getting some mail in Durban. Trusting all is well with you. Love and prayer,

– Hector

On October 13th, Ione wrote to her mother from Stanleyville. She had travelled there with the Larsons and reported:

.....The Larson's, our field leaders, now have a darling baby [Carol] after being married 12 years.

When Larson's were ready to come back to Stanleyville, I came with them, and am enjoying the life at the Stanleyville Home. I am "in charge" of the cooking, so I feel that I am helping a little while waiting for Hector.

In another letter written in November, Ione explained how she sorted through all that she had left behind in Stanleyville in 1960 and wrote:

.....I left a set of household utensils, etc. for guest house equipment; also, silverware for 36 to be used for Conferences, as well as some enamel serving bowls and large double boiler, jug for powdered milk and large cookers. Very little of our stuff was stolen in that line. All the cups were gone, however and

some bedding and all the good pillows. I didn't find any clothes I had left behind of the boys. But we are thankful to have the use of a good many things yet, and added to what we have brought out it makes an abundance.

Yesterday I did some ironing and baking. In between jobs I am sorting bedding, dishes, etc. getting things lined up for Hector to take to Bongondza when he comes. He will probably be here next week.

.....I am downtown shopping just now, buying things for the station. It is surprising how many things one CAN get, but there are many empty shelves. I bought small cans of powdered milk, cooking fat, soap, spaghetti, canned soup, sardines, canned beef, so we'll not do too badly. I just got a letter from Kenny, Paul & John. They are real happy there, no one has been sick, not even homesick!

Much love, Ione

A few days later, she wrote from KM 8:

.....Letters from the boys sound good. I am waiting at Stan, where I have been for 10 days. [Hector] may arrive any day now.

.....But many people in Stanleyville are hungry and turn to stealing; there are bands of robbers that keep going around. While we were away from Bongondza just recently, they carried away the motor that pumps water. But we got it back (by paying 500 francs!).[134]

I am happy to be back, and am anxious to get going at Bongondza. I will be busy every morning from 8 – 10:30; every afternoon and every evening except Friday. I can take village meetings early in the morning or late in the afternoon. Hector is a long-waited foreman here. So many "jobs". But he will be happy to be so needed. Wide open doors for the gospel, and what stories we are hearing of the Lord's undertakings.

Love, Ione

Little is known of Hector's trip inland from Mombasa, Kenya, but he apparently arrived safely at Bongondza. Ione was very happy to be doing the work she felt she had been called by God to do however, it was now very different in many ways from the Africa she knew before. On the 24th of November she wrote to her sister Lucille:

Writing by lamp-light is not so much fun as it used to be. I guess that's why the letters coming from here are few and far between! I find my days filled right up until bed-time and it is hard to sit by lamp for very long. Hector will probably get the lights going soon, but he has only been here for six days altogether since he arrived November 6th. He is away now at Ekoko and has to make a side trip from there before returning. They have only one small car there and are needing heavy supplies.

When I first came here in September, they were pretty short on food supplies and a cheer went up when I presented them with a small bottle of ketchup! I was able to share some things I got in Uganda when I went there while at Rethy. But

---

[134] Indications that changes have occurred and life is not as secure as it was before.

lately there have been more trips to Stanleyville and more things available there. Our station has a cooler which can carry meat from Stanleyville, as well as butter when it is available there. When Hector came last Tuesday, he brought a basket of potatoes and some carrots, cabbage and leeks. He stayed only two hours, long enough to unload and load again. I surely miss him, but hope that when he comes early next week, I hope, that he can stay awhile. He has had men cutting big poles to use for stringing up light wires. That is done now and they are ready to drop the poles into the holes made.

I have three sewing classes and do you know how many needles I have to spare? Only three. I don't know what I will do if any more come. Do you think you could get a flat package of needles in an airmail letter, Lucille? There are none in town, so far as I could see.

Yes, we have a bath-tub here. The water system needs overhauling, and ever since a snake was killed in the cistern, I have not been brushing my teeth with that water! We have two seasons in Congo, dry and wet. Water becomes a precious commodity during the dry season. But when Hector comes back, he will clean and drain and patch up the cistern, and get a larger place to store water. I haven't been needing the treatments I had to have at home. Strange that the ailments I have at home I do not have out here, but the old Congo ailments come back!

.....The boys need trousers quite badly and Hector has bought some khaki which we'll try to have made up for them when they come home (in two weeks!). You asked about things to send. They'll probably soon need things like toothbrushes and underwear. They are supposed to have 12 of most everything, and I don't think they even have 6!!

When they write they often ask for candy. One time someone went over into Uganda and they sent money and got chocolate bars.

I think it is better to send packages here, except special gifts for the children, because the African Inland Mission sort of hinted that they couldn't handle too many of the packages for our mission.

Those packages of soup would be real welcome. The doctor from England who lives here gets a little envelope every month with a couple in. Baking powder is still not available. I have shared what I brought in several directions and have one can left. The necessary things are now available such as flour (OK when strained three times!), sugar, powdered milk, cooking fat. Dish cloths would be welcome. Any bits of cloth for my sewing classes. Baby clothes are always welcome for our Bible school families. Embroidery floss is very hard to get. I noticed that green goes faster than anything.

Ione wrote again on the 27th of November. Despite the distance, Ione was still mindful of her family and kept them informed. She mentioned that Ken was quite sure that after he finished high school, he wanted to return to Congo as a missionary. Hector returned from Ekoko and it was especially nice that this day was their 17th

Anniversary. Hector brought Ione a wooden antelope (18" tall) made of redwood, nicely polished, with little ebony horns.

She said the Siggs would bring the boys all the way to Bongondza at the end of the school term and visit for a few days. Ione had heard indirectly that the Siggs were pleased with the boys and that their singing had inspired the other boys to want a boys' choir. Up till then most of the school boys had thought it sissy.

Ione tried to get letters caught up before the boys came, as she'd have to make them all new pants. Hector bought a 20-yard bolt of khaki and Ione was able to buy some socks for Christmas in Stanleyville.

Hector had lots of jobs planned for the boys and some crafts like learning to weave grass mats, etc.

On the 14th of December, a very happy Ione wrote to her mother:

.....We have the boys with us now, and it surely is a good feeling. They came with the Siggs to Stanleyville on the 6th, and Hector and I were there to meet them! I think if they hadn't come when they did, we would have started out to meet them. They had a very good trip and were all so excited. Siggs had brought 200 eggs along with 11 kids! Only the bottom layer of the eggs was broken, and the kids were all in good condition!!

We had fun shopping in Stanleyville; bought the new bikes, six machetes and knives and some running shoes. The boys have enjoyed just laying around reading or painting or building with the mechano set. They don't have to help with even dishes until Sunday when the house helpers are off. Next week Kenny will start painting around the house windows and doors, a pale brick colour to match the reddish bricks of our house. We have a galvanized iron roof.

This week is busy for me at my school as we are giving exams, but that will soon be finished and then I can start in on the boys' clothes. We will have to make some pants out of khaki material (no zippers, tho!) and perhaps some shirts.

.....We have electric lights tonight for the first time. Hector didn't take long to get the wires strung up and the motor going again. It had a rat's nest in it; that's why it did not run. We have white ants in our attic and will have to get busy on them. [White ants eat through wood and if not treated would destroy the timber framework of the house]. *The tape recorder is going now. I guess next it will be movies, perhaps tomorrow night. This is so exciting for the boys and for the natives who are always nearby.*

I guess I was too excited about the boys' coming; I got sick on the way home and they had to wait at Banjwadi until I was able again to travel. It was first a cold and then went into malaria. I had missed taking Nivaquine for only two days. That shows how quick one can get it. From now on I'll not miss any time for taking anti-malarial drugs. It's no fun having malaria, and it leaves you so faint. But we have very good medicines here and I got over it quickly. By the time I reached home I was already much better. And now I am OK except for a slight cold.

.....I must quit now as Hector is starting family worship.

We bought two antelopes last night and they skinned and butchered them in our kitchen. They are in the fridge now ready for a Christmas party next Monday; we'll have about 30 here, the primary school teachers and wives. The following Saturday we'll have the hospital staff; then the night before Christmas the whole Bible school (about 15) and their families. Christmas day we will have the missionaries here.

During Post-Independence, there was far more emphasis on a shared working relationship with the Congolese Christians. Although it had always been the case of partnership working, it was not always made explicit in letters as it is at this point.

This year, Ione gets to write thank you letters before Christmas! To Lucille, she wrote on December 23rd:

Your letter and the needles were received yesterday. My, I was glad to see both! It shows me how quickly mail can come now. I will be able to start my work after the holidays with the right equipment.

We are enjoying the children and they are having a good rest and doing things they like. We were able to get two bikes in Stanleyville and they love to ride them. When you can get things out here, they are quite cheap as the exchange is now almost double the value of the American dollar.

.....The boys will leave again around the 13th of January. We are expecting the Siggs to visit us before they start back. It is a long hard journey and I'll be glad when this can be done by plane.

Mother writes that she is flying to you and I hope she has had a good trip. She is pretty brave and I am wondering what she will try next. Perhaps a trip out here!! I think the insects would bother her, though. Almost always I am itching somewhere, and I can seldom find the reason why. "C'est le Congo!" is the explanation in French (It's the Congo).

Bongondza is much damper than Stanleyville and life a little closer to African life and we eat more and more native things. However, just now we have some special treats which were available when we were in Stanleyville to get the boys. Cans of American chicken and even applesauce are on our shelves (just a few, though). I have had two big native dinners this week, one for 43 and one for 46, a big undertaking and along with giving of examinations and having the boys here, I feel a bit overwhelmed. But vacation starts for me tomorrow. Tomorrow night the Bible School will come here for supper: chicken, native sombi (like spinach with palm fat), fried cooking banana, pineapple and cake, coffee or tea. They will cook most of it and I have a house helper that makes a delicious 'pai pai' cake (he follows English recipes now). There will be 25 here.

Souls are being saved at the hospital nearly every week. The wives of the Bible school men have started reading classes in the TB (tuberculosis) section and in the general kitchen quarters of the relatives who cook the meals of the patients. Every patient has a relative who cares for him.[135] *These have listened well to the Gospel messages given by our women. And it is good experience for them. I have just finished helping about 25 little girls make petticoats to wear on Christmas Day. I meet with them on Saturday.*

I love the work here and am so thankful to be able to give so much time to it. I know it is going to be nice to look back on these days, so filled with doing just what I love to do and knowing that it is pleasing to the Lord.

.....I must get supper as this is the day we have no house help. I surely appreciate having someone go ahead and cook, even though' there are failures now and then.

.....Thanks so much for the needles. I have enough for a few months now. Packaged soups would be appreciated sometime, just a couple in an envelope. Love, Ione

P.S. I need cotton under pants. The nylon ones have been eaten by insects. 3 have already gone to shreds! But I could make some if I had elastic!

It seemed to have been a difficult year for Ione in many ways. She had health issues, plans that constantly changed, but in the end, she was back in the country she loved. Bongondza was the first mission station she went to as a novice missionary and again as a new bride and new mother. In previous years, there were always compromises to be made on the nature of her work. These last few months, she had been able to engage in mission work that she perceived as being 'mission work'; it does mean she missed the children but she knew they were safe and living in a healthier climate than the one she was living in.

Ione had times this year when Hector is not at her side, although she missed him, she managed to organize, maintain and steer the family onwards.

---

[135] Indigenous family members had quarters in the hospital compound as they usually travelled a distance to get medical help, but some slept under the patients' beds.

Chapter 22
POST-INDEPENDENCE MISSION WORK

Ione started the new year at Bongondza with the boys home from their boarding school 800 miles away. The first letter written on the 18th of January, 1963 was her letter to supporters:

Dear Friends:

Our last circular informed you of our need for passage money to the Congo. We are glad to report that this need was met. We are now in the heart of Africa, rejoicing at the Lord's goodness in permitting us to return.

.....People [here] are very friendly and appreciative of our great effort to get back. A visit out into the deeper part of the forest gave us some new believers and there was a request for a full-time native evangelist. We are training such in our Bible School.

Ione is teaching each morning; afternoons are alternated between village women and Bible school students' wives. On Saturday she meets with 23 girls called 'Lumieres'. Hector is in charge of the various building projects, the chief one being the completion of a medical unit.

Living conditions are not yet back to normal, but it is possible to get along with a minimum of household items. Our forest people will never suffer from starvation, and while they have manioc roots, greens and occasional eggs they will not let the missionaries lack! We are seeing a few cans of American meat and vegetables on the store shelves, in most cases rationed five to a customer. A can of peaches brought down from the mountains with our children, was too precious to use, so we saved it for a hospitality gift on another station!

Some missionaries receive frequent packages containing soups, cake mixes and puddings. These give a lift to an otherwise drab diet. Parcels seem to be coming safely now, as well as letters.

We want to thank you for your interest and help in our coming out. We are happy and are keeping fairly well in health. We are trusting the Lord to make us fruitful in this place. Our promise, from Psalm 1: "His leaf also shall not wither". Praise His matchless Name!

Lovingly, Hector and Ione McMillan

Time with the boys must have flown by and Ione kept very busy as her next letter was written at Bongondza on the 2nd of February:

Dearest Mother,

Again, I am rushed, but want to get a note off to you before the mail lad goes off on his bike. I have a few pictures to send, though they are not very enlightening! It at least shows you I am on my feet and that the truck is working.

I don't know whether you received in time the tiny package which Kenny and I got ready for your birthday. It was prepared with much love. Did you have a nice birthday?

We had a real nice Christmas with Congolese as well as missionaries. Viola Walker is here in readiness to go to the Babinza Tribe, but since the pontoon at the river there is broken down, she must wait here. While she is waiting, she will take my classes so that I can help in Stanleyville. I always enjoy going there and it is a break from the teaching which I find takes a lot out of me. It's not like teaching children and there are no discipline problems, but they [Bible School adult students] *are of varying intelligence and you can't give them all the same work; for instance, two cannot even read or write. Pray for these men and their wives who seem to really love the Lord.*

We did get out a form letter but I am still behind in my thank-yous for gifts sent out with our allowances. Pontiac church has increased my allowance $700 more a year. I must write and thank them. I don't have to do much housework as the cook we have goes right ahead and even makes out the menu. But we are still not all unpacked as there were many books, etc. in Stanleyville. And just now Hector has to keep shop things in the office until he gets his shop finished. We have electric lights and it is a real help.

The boys seemed to have a good time at home [during Christmas break], *and we have had one letter since they went back* (to Rethy). *They saw two elephants on their way back to school and some baboons. Their car broke down, but since there were two missionary cars taking the children, they all squeezed into the one and left their baggage in the other and the missionary stayed with it and got it fixed. They got their baggage late, but got to school on time. They like it really well there.*

.....My dresses are wearing out faster than I thought. The two lightweight ones we bought that last trip are very comfortable as it has been hot. And the two drip-dry ones that young Mrs. Ward Sly made at Lake Orion. I think I will write and ask if she would make two more of the same pattern. My socks are wearing out, too.

All for now. The man is waiting. We are well and happy here.

Much love, Ione

Ione got the opportunity at KM 8 to write to her mother again on the 25th of February:

.....Altogether, I've had three bouts with bladder infection, but have some real good pills now in case another spell comes on. I have had malaria once, but other than that, we keep well. A letter from the boys this morning says, "We are getting along fine in school. We received 6 books and 2 subscriptions from the Fenton Bible Church. In the Bible we are studying about the bridge of Salvation which spans over the chasm of sin. The 4 arches in the bridge are Incarnation, Crucifixion, Resurrection and Ascension." That from Kenneth. John says he can

play many songs on the ukulele and that they are praying much about Uncle Archie (he has had more trouble with his heart).

.....I have been thanking the Lord for the many people who help us out here. We have been receiving so many letters and gifts and we do hope that folk will not be disappointed as we represent them in this strategic spot. A statement in Power *caught my eye just now as I was resting. A Chaplain in Antarctica said he was happy "to be able to be a minister to men in definite need at a high hour in their lives". That sort of gives you the picture of what people do to make it possible for us to carry on here. Our mission is just now preparing to enter into a new territory among the Babinza tribe. Hector will be the one to carry the missionaries and their belongings in with the truck. Right now, they are held up because a ferry motor is broken and they can't get across a river.*

.....We are getting real nice things to eat while here in Stanleyville. And one store just got a number of cases of peaches, fruit cocktail, corned beef hash and powdered soap. There are fresh meats here, too, just now and vegetables.

.....Thanks so much for all you are doing, Mother. I have just received a letter from Lucille telling that you are resigning from the church. I hope you can take a little vacation and have enough rest to get you feeling better.

Much love, Ione

Ione's next letter to her mother was written on the 17th of March, David's birthday. It illustrates the freedom she now had without the children to accommodate:

I am writing this from Ekoko, not far from Marcellyn's old house which is still there. After nearly 1 month in Stanleyville helping with the big all-mission conference, Hector and I returned to Bongondza. I could have stayed there and taken on my teaching job again, but as Hector had another trip to Ekoko I thought I would like to visit Pearl Hiles. I had not been to Ekoko for 10 years (when Stephen was born). And I knew that Viola Walker would not be able to take my place much longer as she will be soon going into the new area known as the Babinzas. Hector was scheduled to take a new missionary to Ekoko and make several hauling trips while there with the truck. I'm so glad I came because it was suddenly decided here to take the first load of stuff into the Babinzas and I was allowed to go along.

.....Lovingly, Ione

Finally, at the end of March, the Christmas packages arrived at Bongondza which caused much rejoicing. Ione wrote to her mother that most items came in good condition except for some candy that was mouse-eaten. Ione shared two cans of ham with station guests and they enjoyed bacon for breakfast – a real treat.

She wrote that Hector was to leave and stop in Stanleyville to load the truck with supplies for AIM, then take a load of delegates for a UFM/AIM board meeting at Rethy. He was to arrive two days before the boys got out of boarding school then load up all the 11 children plus the delegates and start the return trip on April 10th. Hector had made comfortable seats with foam rubber cushion and backs, a canopy over the top and a windshield to keep out the rain.

Ione wrote again to Lucille and Maurice on the 27th of April:

.....This is a hasty letter as I am in the midst of school preparations and must start to teach on Monday even while the boys are here. And Kenny is sick in bed but better today. He had a low fever with vomiting. Doctor Sharpe thought it was his [bad] ear, but after taking out the wax he saw nothing very seriously wrong; and Kenny's dizziness continued after that. Two shots of penicillin have started him getting better and today he has some appetite. He is feeling good enough this afternoon to work on his model plane. The other boys are 'road grading' with their Daddy. He was able to get a road grading blade somewhere and has it weighted at the back of the truck; I say, weighted for five boys are sitting on the frame that contains it. It doesn't look too dangerous.

We are expecting Al Larson any time and he is to bring the man who will see if we can have M.A.F. [Missionary Aviation Fellowship] planes out here.[136] Do keep praying about this.

Of her activities as station host, she continued:

.....With the use of fresh lemons, egg powder and some fresh eggs we have made enough lemon pie for the 17 people (4 Sharpes, Bill Gilvear, David Wilmshurst, the two male nurses, and Ruby Gray, the Irish nurse) plus ourselves and two (possibly three) visitors. Potatoes that Hector bought are just finishing so we will extend our starches with some mashed manioc. The roast is not nearly big enough so we have some cans of chicken which we will fry. There are 3 cans of carrots. Then a salad of bananas with ground peanuts over. We do not have staff on Sunday so we have a few things made up ahead for tomorrow, like ice cream and some jello made with unflavoured gelatine (I found a can in Stanleyville), cool-aid for flavour, sugar, and some canned fruit salad which we were very fortunate to find in Stanleyville. We have lots of cans of chicken just now so will probably have that on Sunday. And the cook's chocolate cake was a flop so we'll have it as steam pudding with a mock whipped cream on top. You see we don't do too badly on food here. We use the juice of the chicken (those whole ones whenever we want to make soup, and have spaghetti to put in).

.....Kenny is up, but still [with] a slight temperature - the infection is from his ear [the one on the right which he can't hear with]. *He may have to go to Kampala, Uganda to a specialist,* [a day's journey beyond] *Rethy. We'll see the Rethy doctor first. Our mission doctor is going with the kids this time.*

Tonight, Dr Sharpe put Hector's left knee in a cast from thigh to ankle. It keeps going out of joint with pain. He thinks he can drive though.

II Cor. 1:12 – I want simplicity and godly sincerity, not with fleshly wisdom – an uncluttered life.

---

[136] Given the seasonal use of the roads, many mission stations elsewhere had airstrips built nearby to better serve the needs of those stations.

It would seem that Hector had not stopped since arriving in Africa. But even he had to stop when his knee injury slowed him down. Enforced rest meant he got a letter written to his sister and brother. On the 19th of May, he wrote:

Dear Jean and Archie,

.....I've been rather laid up for a week or ten days. My right knee had to be put in a cast but was taken off 5 days later because it got too loose after the swelling went down. I keep it bandaged now as it "goes out" so easily. Then I've had internal complaints - probably filaria in the blood. I don't seem to have any reserve energy. I may take a course of medicine to get rid of them.

There are two extra couples here now for a week to help us with preparation for conference for U.F.M. in July. An unknown number of missionaries and younger children (not Rethy group) and about 30 African delegates from the various stations are expected. They will be here at Bongondza for 10 days so it means a lot of food preparation.

Perhaps the last photo of the McMillan family with Hector – Bongondza, 1963

.....How did you like living in town? It must be nice to wake up in the morning with no thought of cows and pigs to feed!! Edythe and Archie McLean will be good company for you when they visit you from time to time. Do you still have the V.W.?

The boys had a nice holiday over Easter. As you can see, they are still growing. The three older boys are learning to drive. They were a big help around the mission station with its more than 14 buildings.

.....Well I better close for now. Write and tell us about your neighbours etc. Yours as ever, Hector & Ione

It would seem that, due to illnesses, Jean and Archie had finally given up on the farm and moved into more suitable accommodations.

This next letter to her mother demonstrates some of the pressures Ione was facing; it was written from Banalia, where one has to wait for a ferry to get across the river. Ione was not one to sit idly watching the river flow by, so she wrote on the 28th of May:

.....The children went back to school May 6. We went with them as far as Stanleyville. Kenny spent about half of his vacation in bed. He started getting dizzy, and Dr Sharpe traced it to the ear that has given trouble before. He was running a low temperature for a while, but penicillin shots helped this.

.....A message from Rethy came by short-wave to our station at Banjwadi about him, and as we cannot get this yet at Bongondza, I am on my way to Banjwadi to hear it the next time it comes over. Banjwadi sent a runner to the next station [Bopepe – just the other side of Banalia] and he arrived there the 3rd day after.

Mary Baker [the only resident missionary at Bopepe] *drove to Bongondza as soon as she got the message. It spoke of urgent surgery. Our doctor and wife are with him, but I am prepared to fly to Kampala* [Uganda] *when I get to Stanleyville.*

.....I'll let you know as soon as I get news. I was thinking of you and praying for your Mother's Day.   Love, Ione

As in many letters, Ione shared more detail of incidents with her sister Lucille, so we learn that Ione and Mary were marooned on the jungle road when the car broke down.[137] They ate buffalo meat and watched the monkeys leap from tree to tree not 15 feet away.

Finally, at Banjwadi, Ione got the news she had been waiting for and on May 31st, was able to write to Lucille:

I have just heard by radio that Kenny was operated on yesterday at Kampala, Uganda, for mastoid. I am just leaving Banjwadi for Stanleyville where I hope to get a plane to Kampala.

It is a round-about way, but I am trusting the Lord to get me to him in good time. I need my passport and health papers which are in Léopoldville just now [visa difficulty]. *So perhaps I can get an authorization to travel from the American Consul in Stanleyville. I need other papers, too, to get out of Congo.* [Nothing seems straight forward!]

.....We don't know how Kenny is since the operation, but they said he was in good spirits just before.

I'll try to let you know soon.   Love, Ione   P.S. His grace is sufficient

Ione had been under tremendous pressure, her husband was ill at Bongondza, her boys were hundreds of miles away and one had an operation that was considered urgent enough not to wait for parental consent. However, she got to Kampala and on the 6th of June, wrote to her sister Lucille:

.....My journey here was hectic and I arrived almost too sick to see Kenny. But I'm gradually getting hold of myself and can eat again. It is good to see him so cheerful with that huge bandage on his head. The Sharpes have stayed right with him and given him a lovely model boat and he's putting it together nicely. He is eating O.K.

.....I'll be able to see the other boys when we take Kenny back to Rethy. Sharpes are willing to wait for us and they are seeing a specialist about their little son's legs which are abnormal.

Praise the Lord that Kenny is out of danger.

Love, Ione

On the 9th of June, both Ione and Kenny wrote to Lucille and Leone:

Dear Lucille and Mother,

---

[137] Mary Baker was an indomitable lady, with years of experience who originally came from rural Virginia, so spending a night in the middle of the jungle on the road would not have fazed her!

I am sitting beside Kenny's bed on a Sunday morning. He looks nice and clean with fresh pyjamas on. The bandage is off his head and only a tiny scar shows behind his ear. When I came in just now, he was reading, "How I Found Livingstone", by Stanley. It is 10 days since the operation, and in 10 days more he will have his 16th birthday. Kenny will write a note now:

I am enjoying my stay in the hospital. For about a week after my operation, I had a bit of pain in my ear but now I am feeling fine. This is my first operation and the first time I have been in a hospital so it was strange at first, but now I am used to it. I am on the sixth floor of the hospital and in a room with 3 other men. The missionary family that brought me here bought me a plastic model boat to assemble, so I am kept busy. I like going to school at Rethy and most of my brothers do too. We often spend Saturdays climbing small mountains or taking hikes in the hills. The climate is very healthy up there and we seldom get malaria.

Since Daddy's bad knee makes it hard for him to work, we are glad for vacation time, when we can help him with his work on the station. I am glad that Mummy is with me now even though she was not here for the operation.

Love, Kenneth

The children's next vacation starts July 24 and they will have 7 weeks. Kenny and I are going to read and pray together now. I'll come in again this afternoon.

Much love, Ione

A much calmer Ione wrote on June 14th:

Dear Lucille and Mother,

At last I have gotten a little rested up and can see things in a little better perspective. I was at the end of my strength when I arrived here, and anxiety made me sick. I know how Mother has felt many times for us!

Now Kenny is out of the hospital and just about rested up enough to start the second journey to Rethy. We'll take it in easy stages and in a comfortable car. We may go through a wonderful park area [Murchison Falls National Park] *and see giraffes (Kenny saw some when he came).*

I was able to get hold of enough money to buy some things that we never see in Stanleyville; baking powder, mustard, cocoa, instant coffee, brown and icing sugar, raisins & canned meat. Also, a strainer, some scouring powder and detergent. And some chocolate bars that will not melt on the way. I got some matchbox toys to take the place of the ones the boys had to leave behind in Montreal [in 1962] *because of* [being] *overweight.*

.....I hate to leave this wonderful cool climate for the steamy Congo, but where the Lord wants us holds a real attraction.

Pray for our Conference July 7 to 17.

Lovingly, Ione

Ione's letter of the 23rd to Lucille completed the story of Kenny's emergency surgery:

Just to tell you that I left Kenny OK at Rethy. The doctor said he should recuperate in the mountains and the healthiest spot was Rethy. He felt good enough and wanted to finish his term. He has had straight A's, so will have no trouble in passing. He will not play ball or do sports until the end of the term (July 24).

.....P.S. They told me at Rethy our kids should have more new clothes. I can make pyjamas but can't get jeans here. I'll write again about this.

The planned-for conference occupied all Ione's attention and she did not get to letter writing again until the beginning of August. On the 5th of August she wrote:

.....I got back from Rethy just ten days before the Conference began. Already Bob and Alma McAllister were on the job, and the men were transforming a workshop into a big dining room. There were lots of native tomatoes on hand and onions and I immediately put Gaston Tele, our cook, to work making chili sauce (this is so good with native meats), and jar after jar of jam, made from a concentrate which we got from England, raspberry and apricot. Our former staff member, now in Stanleyville has agreed to have his wife make two huge jars of peanut butter and Al Larson was to bring the mayonnaise. Each missionary brought about 250 cookies, and for about two-thirds of the time we had bread

UFM Missionary Conference at Bongondza, July 7–17, 1963
Front Row (L-R): Allison Sharpe, David Muchmore, Brian Miesel (?), Susan Harms, Allen Muchmore, Marilyn Carper, a Scholten boy, Cathy Snyder, Sharon Harms, a Scholten, Ike Scholten.
Second Row: John Arton, John Miesel, Jan Miesel, Elsi Gscheidle, Volker Gscheidle, speaker (who was Margaret Hayes' pastor in England), Ma Kerrigan, Thelma Southard, Lois Carper.
Third Row: Marshall Southard, Mina Esrkine, Olive McCarten, Jean Sweet, Pearl Hiles, Ruby Grey, Betty O'Neill, Jean Larson, Olive Bjerkseth, Bill Gilvear (holding Ruthie Snyder), Nora Parry, Del Carper, George Kerrigan.
Fourth Row: Ian Sharpe, Audrey Sharpe, Herb Harms, Grace Harms, Mary Baker, Hector McMillan, Ione McMillan, Betty Arton, Bob McAllister, Dennis Parry.
Fifth Row (and behind): Charles Mann (holding Steven), Carol Snyder, Bill Snyder, Sonia Grant, Don Muchmore, Dave Grant, Eleanor Muchmore, Joan Pengilly, Jean Raddon, Viola Walker, Sue Schmidt, Dick Sigg, Dave Wilmshurst, Margaret Hayes, Bill Scholten, Alma McAllister, Stephanie Mann, Dottie Scholten (holding one of hers), Mary Rutt.

from Stanleyville, when there was a trip. The days we baked bread here some kitchen staff members made 9 and 10 loaves each.

We put some good missionary cooks in charge of evening meals which were as we called it European (American style, really), and the noon meal was entirely Congolese, prepared and served by the station and village women. The last night we ran out of bread as everyone was making up sandwiches for their journeys, so three of us stayed up until midnight making muffins, which were a treat the last morning.

......Just two days after all the missionaries had left (and we had a really good Conference with not any troubles like in '61 when there was general feeling between white and black; only little petty things which seemed to fall on my lot to settle in little private 'conferences' when personalities clashed), we went to get our children. They are all in good health and you should see how Kenny eats now since his operation! He is so much better and has a good colour. And the thing that made us all praise the Lord for especially was that he doesn't have to go way off to Kijabe [Kenya] in September, for two fine teachers at Rethy just couldn't rest until they had done their best for him, and finally arranged to give him 10th grade there under private tutoring. He will have one class with grade 9 which is a required subject for graduation and the rest he will do on his own in the library or in his room (they hope to give him a private room), and these two teachers will share his supervision. Now we think that is pretty nice, and the boys are happy they can be together one more year.

Lots more to say but I want this to go today.

Love, Ione

With the conference over and the children on a school holiday, Ione and Hector had the opportunity to travel further afield to reach more people with the Gospel. They wrote a newsletter in August that would be sent to all their supporters:

The boys demonstrating a 'tepoi' carrying chair for Mother! Hector's truck is in the background.

Dear Friends,

We have written to some of you many times, telling of driver ants, snakes, tarantulas, scorpions, monkeys and elephants. So, you may not be surprised to know that we spent some time this month with the pygmies.[138]

We took our six boys and they enjoyed the rough life in the Bokopo area. We went about 35

---

[138] Pygmies are a nomadic people who live mainly in the Western corner of Congo. They are very short in stature, men have an average height of 4 feet 11 inches, but are not 'dwarf'. The term 'pygmy' is now regarded as pejorative and the Kongo term 'bambenga' is often used; otherwise the people are referred to according to their tribal

miles, as far as the truck could possibly go, over terrific roads which were stirred up by the elephants. Then we went on by foot and I sat in the tepoi, carried by the natives.

We slept three nights in a village called Bogbama. It was a unique location, between two WARRING groups of pygmies! We didn't sleep in pygmy houses, which were only four upright sticks supporting a handful of leaves. No walls, no doors. Two horizontal sticks on the ground marked the spot where one of these tiny Africans slept; two more sticks if he had a wife! Kenny, Paul, and David, as well as our missionary friend, Charlie Mann (another missionary from Aketi), chose the back of the truck. John, Stephen, Timothy, Mother and Daddy, slept in a mud house belonging to ordinary-sized people.

Rafting across the Longele.

We crossed the Longele River on a ridiculously small raft, made of bamboo. It was hooked loosely over a vine cable. Only three of us could go at one time, and even then, it sank a little, getting some feet wet! We met pygmies in nearly every village. They passed the word along and by the time we returned to the river the first afternoon, there were quite a few around.

The pygmies gave us a 'program' which they called their 'joy'. It consisted of singing, drum-beating and clapping of hands on their chests. The handsome little leader began to dance. Then, on sudden inspiration, he darted into the forest. Out he came again with some fresh leaves. These he stuck in his bark cloth, front and back. The singing was weird, in a complicated syncopation. There were three 'movements', and each stopped abruptly on an off-beat. The last was an imitation of a hunt with bow and arrow and the animation of a real 'kill'.

After politely thanking them for their 'joy', we asked our pygmy hosts if they would like to see OUR 'joy'. They agreed to come to a meeting which we would arrange and receive a gift of salt. But when they learned that it would be on the

status, for example: they are Aka, Mbuti, Twa etc. In the 1960's, they were still 'forest people', hunter gatherers who did not usually live in villages. They were nomadic and carried what they possessed and built shelters out of wood and leaves. Villagers would trade with them to obtain meat but they were hard to reach. They were very distrustful of strangers and moved silently and invisibly through the forest. At this time, they made up only 2% of the population, but were subjected to the ethnic cleansing that occurred during the ensuing civil wars predominant in this corner of Congo.

other side of the river, they balked. The reason: they had stolen a woman from over there, and if they crossed, there would be a battle with poisoned arrows. We were not anxious to get into tribal warfare. We hastily suggested that these pygmies come as far as the river, where Hector and the boys would meet them. An evangelist and Mother would meet with their enemies. This was done with success, and a good witness was made to both factions.

We were not to miss entirely their little war. The group at home base (Bogbama) gathered. Hector and the boys had already crossed the river, when we saw a trio of warriors slipping through our village. They said they were going after their stolen woman! As they filed toward the river, we wondered if our 'joy' on the other side would be disturbed. But Hector and boys came back about 1 o'clock with good reports. We had dinner (baboon liver) and a rest.

It was toward evening when the pygmies moved silently into the village with their woman. She had a string around her neck. They told us they had gotten her peaceably. The miniature headman seemed to want to talk, but while he was occupied with us, the woman ran into the forest. This started quite a commotion, with horn-blowing, and a scurry after her. So far as we could tell they had not found her by night. We were disturbed a little later when in the dark we heard the patter of feet across the compound. But there were no flying arrows, and we slept peacefully, hoping the wee lady would get back to the other tribe, which she seemed to prefer.

The boys on a forest trail with the pygmy headman.

In our conversations with the pygmies a few believers were found. They had accepted Christ when Viola Walker was working among them before Congo's Independence. One older woman named Selina has a very good testimony. Several years ago, the missionaries considered one group ready for baptism. But when they went out to hold the service, the little people were in such a state of war with one another that they were disqualified for baptism. We were impressed with the need for a full-time worker in this area.

Through the entire Bokopo area there is a need of help medically. By the time their sick ones are brought to the Bongondza hospital they are either dead or cured! We found one entire village of sick folk, lying around in various stages of serious illness. There were strings of wooden bit, bones hair and leaves in a corner of the shelter. When we asked what these might be, a toothless hag with an evil smirk, took a bow, and said, "These are my medicines and my patients". (Witch craft is still widely practised.) It made us feel sick ourselves. We left with a deep sense of shame for the many doctors and nurses in the homeland.

May the Lord help you friends to see these things through our eyes. As you consider Christ's claim upon your own lives, will you not consider Congo's need at the present time?

Lovingly in Him, Hector and Ione McMillan

Ione was also able to write to her mother in August with more details:

.....The boys will never forget the trip we just made. You can only do it with a good strong truck, a healthy family, and a carrying chair for the Mother! We left on Friday and came back today, Monday.

It is wonderful, Mother, to be so conscious of the Lord's presence in a very hard place. Separation, isolation, deprivation (but very little of that, as we just received a Liggett's order with even chocolate bars in it!) cannot compare to the joy of being in the place where precious souls can be won to Christ.

.....Hector and I were routed out of bed in the night with driver ants, but they did not bother the children as it was not a general raid, but our bed was in their path. We sat up at the table with a kerosene lantern out of their way until they had finished going through. We cozily munched on two Almond Joy chocolate bars; my, what a treat is chocolate away out here! We enjoyed more of the chocolate the next day when we penetrated the deeper forest on foot and in the chair.

It was absolutely impossible for the truck to go any farther, we could see why the natives had been so emphatic about this. As I began to get used to my tepoi means of travel, I had to duck frequently as the vines and jagged bamboos were very close to us. But on the whole the chair was comfortable and I had a place to rest my feet, though very near to the first of the two native carriers ahead of me. The two behind me set a great shout and my ears were deafened to anything else while they sang and yelled joyfully to keep up their teamwork.

.....Kenny was able to negotiate with the pygmy headman for the bow, two arrows which were not the poisonous kind, a wrist band[139] and a quiver for the arrows.

.....We need strong young missionaries to come out to this area AND KEEP COMING until these people are properly reached. It will be at least Christmas time before anyone here can get out again to them, and they are no more than 50 miles from Bongondza. I hope our boys will keep this great need in their hearts until the Lord can lead them out as missionaries. I don't see how young people can make all sorts of nice plans for easy Christian service when these pygmies are not getting a fair chance to hear the Gospel. Won't you pray with us about this?

Much much love, Ione X

On August 15th, Ione wrote to Hector's sister Florence:

---

[139] A pouch made of skin and filled with kapok fiber which is hit by the bow string just before the arrow is launched.

.....We hear from Jean and Archie and are glad they are well. They seem happy in their new home. The boys keep wondering about the farm, and cherish all the pictures they have of the tractor and places they played and worked.

Hector has been taking medicine for rheumatism and the pain in the knee has stopped. I notice he limped some recently on a long trek we made. He insisted on my riding in a chair, but I think he felt like riding at times. We took the boys and spent a long week-end among the pygmies. They are just 50 miles from Bongondza. We went as far as there was a road and set up sleeping and eating quarters. Then took two trips by day out across the river.

Just now Hector and John are in Stanleyville getting planed lumber from a yard there. We hope they will find flour as we are just about out. We heard there would be none for a number of months.

We do praise the Lord that our boys can be together for one more year....We hope Kenny can get into the Rift Valley Academy by '64. Failing that, there is an English-speaking high school at Léopoldville.   Ione

Ken was indeed accepted for RVA in Kenya, but earlier in September 1963. On the 15th of September, he wrote to Leone Reed:

Dear Grandma,   How are you? Mummy, Daddy, and I had a nice trip from Congo to a high school named Rift Valley Academy. It is not far from Nairobi. We came by train part of the way, and also by car through a national park where we saw elephants, deer, buffalo, and a big group of giraffes.

We just spent Monday and Tuesday in Nairobi to do some shopping, and today I am being registered here at RVA and I am getting settled into the dormitory. Tomorrow I will start school. Every child must wear a khaki uniform to school. There are lots of sports here, too. There are 66 missionaries on this station, and there will be over 200 children here this year. 80 of them are new. I will be going into 10th grade with 31 other students. There is a good climate here, like at Rethy, but it is windier and colder here [at 7,000 ft altitude]. *The surrounding scenes are made up of beautiful hills and valleys. This school is about 1000 miles from our station, so I'll have to fly home part of the way. I am praying for you. May God bless you. Love, Kenneth*

Back at Rethy, the other five boys had letter writing day on September 30th as Ione and Hector were sent the following:

Dear Mommy and Daddy,   We are getting along alright here. School seems a little bit harder but with the Lord's help it doesn't seem too hard. On Thursday, the 3rd Mr. Larry Brown will start some evangelistic meetings here. In Bible we are studying about Saul and David. We learned the 2 Bible verses: I Sam 15:22 and I Cor. 10:4. They are very good verses to hide in my heart. I am praying for you and Kenneth every day. Love, Paul

Dear Daddy and Mommy,   I am writing in my bed because it is time to go to bed. I like Mrs. Pontier as a teacher. 6 grade is quite hard for me. I pray for you and Kenny every day. Bye-by. Love, John

Dear Mommy and Daddy, How was your trip home? We had films last Saturday night. It isn't too hard in the 7th grade except we get a lot of homework. We are praying for you and Kenny. Every Friday night we have clubs. By for now. Love, David

The photo below is of the UFM children residing at the school at Rethy, with Dick and Mimi Sigg who were house parents. Grace and Andrew Parry and two Sharpe children – Alisson and Jillian, were killed at Banalia in 1964.

Congo Missionary Kids, Rethy Academy, Congo c1963.
Back Row (L-R): Suzanne Sigg, Dorm parents Dick & Mimi Sigg, David McMillan, Paul McMillan
Middle Row: Marilyn Carper, Grace Parry, Steve McMillan, Cathy Snyder, Allen Muchmore, David Muchmore, Andrew Parry, Billy McAllister, David McAllister, John McMillan, Tim McMillan (in front of John)
Front Row: Miriam Snyder, Sammy Sigg, Ike Scholten, Alisson Sharpe, Jillian Sharpe
(Four of these children were killed in the Simba Rebellion a year or so after this photo was taken.)

It took Ione and Hector a month to drive the boys up to school and back in September. Ione wrote to her mother on the 8th of October:

Dearest Mother,

We arrived back at Bongondza last week after being off the station for nearly a month. We had a good trip. It is a long way to Kijabe, Kenya, but it is worth the time and expense of going. We were able to make proper arrangements for Ken and met everyone, including some former Moody classmates of mine. They will be very good to him, and take a personal interest in him. The school meets our expectations and more. We were able to make arrangements for him to fly to Stanleyville at Christmas time. He gets out of school December 9. The other boys get out December 5, so will have left Rethy by the time Kenny gets there. But some A.I.M. folk will take him to their home to sleep and then about 15 kilometres to Bunia where he can get another plane to Stanleyville. We will be waiting for him there. He is 16 now, and can take quite a bit of responsibility, but we want to help him all we can. Kenny is in a dormitory with 36 boys, five in his room. Real high Christian standards. Paul will have a chance now to be the big brother to the others. He is very tall now and takes life quite seriously. David is somewhat of a clown, always making dry remarks. John is loveable and friendly. Stephen is really developing into a nice boy. You are still very special to him. Timmy, they say, has a sparkle, but he does not out-sparkle Stephen. Speaking of sparkles, I bought some sparklers in Kampala and we'll celebrate at Christmas time with them. We also have marshmallows and hot dogs (from the Leggett's order).

.....May the Lord bless you. Much love, Ione

With the boys settled at school, Ione and Hector were able to engage in their mission work and head back 35 miles east of where they are based at Bongondza; Ione wrote to her mother on the 12th of October:

.....We came back yesterday to the pygmy area. We are at a brick government house in a village called Bokopo. In answer to prayer we are having a dispensary (this only for today) and a permanent school established. Bill Gilvear, has a real burden to do full-time medical work here. Pray that the Doctor at Bongondza will be able to spare him to come out here regularly.

The road is terrible and the people who walk it are not interested in making a road possible for a car. We had to stop and cut away branches and remove logs, and went over dangerous bridges and mud holes. Most of the trees and branches that were in the way were thrown there by elephants whose tracks we could plainly see. It took us two and a half hours to go 35 miles! There are about 80 children to start school, which will be held in the house where we're living. Two native men will teach. We brought out materials and have had some good meetings. We plugged up the places where bats came in and had a peaceful night. We'll return to Bongondza tomorrow. On the way back we'll pick up the Bible school students we dropped off in various villages.

The same day, Ione wrote a letter to Hector's sister Irene. In it, she shared that besides Bill, their other travelling companions were Congolese student evangelists and a pastor. They dropped off the students at various points along the way to undertake services and witness to the villagers. She wrote that most of the people had some skin disease and said:

.....Some have gotten into line three times as they did not want to mention all their ailments at one time! The phonograph is playing a record in their tribal tongue, and some who can read have found the books and tracts at the end of the porch. The Congolese would deem it impolite to take up a person's time with all their complaints at the expense of the person next in line, so re-joining the queue is 'best' behaviour.

Since Independence we find ourselves filling more and more the capacity of Counsellor. We have trained teachers, nurses and pastors. But they want our advice and help, our medicines, books, transport, etc. They are a friendly people and many have become strong Christian leaders.

Ione's next letter to her mother was written on the 18ᵗʰ of October:

Dearest Mother,

Just a little note before we eat dinner (potatoes, sardines, carrots, cabbage salad, cake), to send with these letters from Kenny and Timmy. This is Kenny's second letter since school started.

.....Our children have real special love for you, and so do I! I hope you are not sick, nor discouraged. We are trusting the Lord that your needs will be met. I believe He is able.

I have decided that I will send all the letters we got this week, as I know you will enjoy them as much as we. I'll try to keep you better informed about the children, and if you are not working too much maybe you will have more time to write them. How about that book you promised to write?[140] Whenever you are ready for it, I will have the notes hunted out from our stuff at Three Hills!!

I must close now. Have women's class this afternoon and am starting on a correspondence course with them in Bangala from Emmaus Bible Institute (Chicago); we get the lessons from Mr. Deans' mission at Nyankunde. We will also do hemstitching and embroidery work. Tomorrow we have the girls' club. The Bible school is still going on, but one fellow had to be dismissed as it was discovered he had two wives! Pray for the remaining ones. Some seem fine Christians and enter into all discussions. They have a burden to get out among their own people. They have been out in several directions this week and four people accepted Christ.

Much love, Ione

Ione was habituated into keeping letters short as they are sent airmail and weight is limited. Unsurprisingly, there are sometimes omissions, as in this case where Ione followed up the last letter with another on the 22ⁿᵈ of October:

This is just a note, as I realize I didn't thank you for the birthday gift which you sent, the lovely card and the Moody History. Thanks very much for remembering me. Also, I don't think I thanked you for the tape which came. It was so cute and the boys will enjoy listening to it when they come home.

I have had several good weeks with the Bible school students and girls and now the women are starting to come back. They have been unable to leave their gardens while it is daylight, as first the baboons and then the birds, kept coming to take their things. They know of no way except to stand and chase them away! We had a good meeting today, the second lesson in a correspondence course from Emmaus (printed in Bangala here at Nyankunde, Congo).

.....This week our students led 4 to the Lord in little meetings outside of class. On Wednesday the old chief sent for him (one of the evangelists named

---

[140] Ione was keen to have someone amalgamate all her letters and write a book of her story!

Cornelius) and asked him to preach to his wives and the villagers. There were three saved there, and since then Cornelius has been back twice and one more was saved. They say the chief's wives, two of them, are real keen Christians. But the old chief has not accepted Christ as yet. Nor has his son, the young chief who now is at Kole.

.....We heard on the radio that the Congo Capital, Léopoldville, is under martial law for six months. We don't know what this will mean, but as yet it means nothing. We carry on as usual, enjoying wonderful opportunities to witness and perfect freedom to go anywhere with the Gospel. Hector and I are well. Much love, Ione

Congo covers a vast landscape, so unrest in one area does not necessarily transmit across the whole country. The rich province of Katanga continued to be problematic for the administration based in Léopoldville. For a variety of reasons teachers were not paid, nor the police or public servants and these people began protesting. In addition, corruption was rife. The United Nations had a peace keeping force but it became increasingly difficult to maintain peace – hence martial law. Being a long way from a major city, and in the forest surrounded by people grateful to the missionaries, Ione and Hector would not feel any repercussions, but this did not last long. On November 13th, Ione wrote to Leone:

.....Yesterday Hector bought a spool of thread (one of the scarce things) for about 75¢. He just returned from Stanleyville where he had quite an experience.

He parked the truck in a parking enclosure of a friend of his, where no one else had access, but when he came back an hour later, the truck was gone. He was able to locate it several hours later with the help of Nigerian soldiers. Everything removable except tyres were taken, including the spare tyre. He found it in one of the five native cities.[141] He was able to buy a new tarpaulin and has collected a few tools from other missionaries. The local police were not much help and nothing will be done to find the thief, but we are thankful to have the car. In ways such as this we feel the political instability. But for the most part we enjoy peace and quiet. Hector saw lots of milk and soap in Stan, but very little of anything else.

.....As yet I don't know anything about where you live and what you are doing. I'm so glad that Lucille went to Washington with you. I just envy her the joy of being with you. I am looking forward to being with you a long time when we come home again.

.....Perhaps we can plan something together and then you and I can get busy on that book! I have more documentary material out here and lots of things from this term. It looks like there will be a lot more, too, the way things are going!

Ione provided Hector's sister, Irene, an explanation for the political unrest. On November 24th, she wrote:

---

[141] Stanleyville had five surrounding townships; the central town having been occupied by whites before Independence.

.....We heard the other night of a Communist plot to overthrow the Léopoldville government. It was instigated by Gizenga,[142] the same man who put our missionaries under house arrest in '61. He has been a prisoner in Léopoldville (because of his association with Soviet Union, China and Egypt), but made arrangements with some Russians across the River in Brazzaville to bring in arms and arrange a revolt. It was discovered and the Russians deported. Léopoldville is still under Marshal law, but this has not affected us.

The two hardships we face at the moment are shortages on some supplies as there are no imports at the moment. And the roads are almost impossible just now because of rains. The only way Hector can get out to the main road is by hauling gravel and taking men along to fix it up as he goes along. Today we had a visit from an Administrator (former student of mine!), and he expressed his appreciation to Hector for fixing up the road. Hector laughed and said it was a case of either fixing it or just never getting off the station! He goes to get sand for his building projects and takes a load of gravel from our hill so that he has a load both trips.

Some stores are closing up because they have nothing to sell. But at the moment we have ahead a sack of flour, two of sugar, and there are nearly always rice and peanuts. We are going to have a week-end out for meetings this week, and spend one day in a town called Buta, where we hope to get some kind of fat, either margarine or peanut oil. We are well and happy.

A few days later, Ione and Hector were out again, this time on the Basali Trail, as Ione explained in a letter dated the 1st of December:

.....We are out for a long week-end. This enables us to take some meetings and also do some shopping at Buta. We go to Kole, and instead of going Stanleyville way (which would have been a left turn), you turn the other way (right – it is effectively a T junction) toward Ekoko. The first biggish town is Buta. There you turn off on the Basali Trail.

We have bought quite a lot of things in Buta; cooking fat, margarine, milk, sardines, tomato paste, a piece of bacon, potatoes, carrots, cabbage, cauliflower and even some withered celery! Our Christmas presents will be: a shirt each for the boys and for the stockings some toothpaste and a comb! But there are several packages on the way, and Lake Orion church had deposited $110 in our Kampala, Uganda bank account specially labelled for Christmas. The next trip

---

[142] Antoine Gizenga was a compatriot of Patrice Lumumba. Like Lumumba, he had been educated in a Catholic mission school and believed in a pan African state. At the time of Independence, he was given the role of Deputy Prime Minister but this was short lived, especially as Western Countries supported the leadership that originated from the Leopoldville area.

there we'll get some toys and candy, games and clothes. I have a can of popcorn, some marshmallows and can make fudge and peanut brittle.

Later in the month she wrote:

.....The boys are ALL home, and we are so thankful to get them together again after such a separation. Dick Sigg brought the five down from Rethy. Hector was near Stanleyville at a Conference, and waited over a couple days till Kenny's plane came in. Another missionary brought the other five home here, so that they would not have to wait so many days in Stanleyville for Kenny. So, I had the five from Tuesday until Saturday, and then there was a great reunion when Daddy and Kenny arrived. All of them are well, and we all listened eagerly to Ken's report of Kijabe. He likes it there and it does seem to be where the Lord wants him and possibly his brothers when the time comes.

Although this Christmas will be our poorest for a long while, we are real happy to be together. And with making a few gifts and buying such things as are available in Buta and Stanleyville, we can give something to each (socks, hankies, shirts, toothpaste, comb, etc.). Hector found some crude native candy which seems to be clean as it is wrapped in plastic. We will have a big Christmas celebration in our out-districts and then bring all the 11 out-station preachers in to Bongondza with their wives and families. Mr. and Mrs. Jenkinson will come to Bongondza for Christmas here and it will be a time of refreshing for all those in the Lord's service.

The boys have their sleeping bags which we were able to buy for them in Nairobi, so trekking and travelling is not such a problem as it used to be. Although one cannot put a sleeping bag on the floor of native houses.

Now the truck is leaving, but I wanted to let you know that I love you and do hope that you have a happy Christmas. May the Lord bless you and use you to the salvation of many more souls. Just yesterday I had the joy of leading two Congolese women to the Lord. You may be sure it is worthwhile you giving your daughters for His service.

And so, 1963 drew to a close. In many ways, this had been a fulfilling year for Ione, now able to do the work she had always longed for - to preach the gospel and share her love for God with people in the Congo.

It had also been a difficult year, the boys were a long way from her and Ione had to trust others to guide, teach and care for them – which was not easy for someone who had always seemed to be in control of these matters herself. She and Hector had to spend time apart – so they could best combine the needs of the work and those of the family and meet these needs.

Ione and Hector came back to Africa with hope that they might continue in the work they felt called to, but the responsibility of the children weighed heavily. This was a time of increasing challenges and Post-Independence Congo did not seem a safe place to be and to work.

Chapter 23
TESTING THE LOVE

By the 16th of January 1964, the boys were back at school and Hector and Ione were at Bongondza. While most of the letter was written with a positive spin, there is an indication that both Hector and Ione were aware of possible troubles ahead: Ione wrote to her mother:

> .....*We are thinking of going up to the mountains for the children's next vacation which is April 1 to 30. We may take a cottage and have some time just as a family, then go over the border for some shopping in Kampala.*
>
> *Don't feel sorry about not doing anything for Christmas. I would have felt bad if you had, for I know this has been the hardest Christmas yet. I believe the Lord is preparing us for something special, as He seems to want us to be more and more dependent upon Him.*
>
> .....*The boys went off to school this time in another missionary's truck which he has fixed up with a closed-in body and they call it the "Ark". This was a very short vacation, made especially short because of a field council meeting at the beginning and the children had to wait several days in Stanleyville for their trip home.*
>
> .....*The report for Paul was especially good this time. Mrs Sigg said that he had proven that he was able to take Kenny's place at Rethy. He is taller than I am now and is getting quite nice looking. He trusts the Lord continually for help in his school work and gives the Lord credit. At Kenny's school they do not give a special time for the high school children's private devotions, and it seems quite an effort to have a quiet time. Kenny has five boys in his room, all missionary children, and not one of them gets up early enough to have devotions (they have breakfast at 6:15!). Will you pray especially for this as Kenny has been used to reading and praying regularly even when he was in the hospital. He wants to, but I am wondering if he will be tempted to skip it as his schedule is so full.*

Ione wrote to her mother again on the 27th. The news had more substance now as there were radio reports from West Congo where some people had been killed with machetes. Ione took comfort in that these atrocities happened a long way from where she and Hector were. She wrote:

> .....*But be sure that should this sort of thing come our way, the Lord would give grace for such a trial. We have been enjoying such wonderful liberties in preaching and leading souls to Christ that I would not wonder if the enemy of the soul would stir up trouble of this sort.*

Ione wrote that Dr. Sharpe preached a wonderful message on being born again, and a number of school boys accepted the Lord. He had moved with his family to

Bongondza in 1961 to rebuild the hospital Dr Wescott originally built. His wife, Audrey, was a qualified nurse and they made a powerful team.

Dr. Ian Sharpe family at Bongondza – c1963

Ever practical, Ione continued in a lighter vein:

.....I will be excited to know what you get with the money. But if you have debts you should use it for that first. I am about 33 in the waist now. Do you think I should wear those stocking socks that fit into the shoes and don't show? The younger missionaries think these socks with cuffs on are old-fashioned!! And it's too hot for stockings that are long or even knee-length. They say this will be the hottest hot season in 4 years as it is leap year!

We are well and happy, and can always have a good laugh. We planted some rose bushes all along the front of the house today. They need to be watered a lot during this season. I got them from an old Christian down the road, the only one around here who has roses. I wish you could come to our lovely station, smelling of jasmine and gardenias. Many things were cut down after Independence when the Africans lived in the houses, but much of the beauty is coming back. And the most beautiful part of the station anyway is the lovely spirit between the whites and blacks.

Don't get discouraged. Pray especially for the new events which are stirring our Congolese people once more. The Lord said, "I will build my church." He did not say just how He would do it.

Much love, Ione X

In a letter to Hector's sister Florence, written on the 9th of February, Ione explained why the McMillans had two bank accounts, one in Stanleyville for purchases they needed to make there and another in Kampala, Uganda, across the border from Congo. The exchange rate was better in Uganda and Ione shopped more there when taking the boys to school. She wrote:

.....Our life here is simple, and we do not have the problem of choosing what we will eat or wear, as there is no choice! Our biggest problem, as in the homeland, is always ourselves, and our own wicked ways. II Corinthians 9:11 – "Being enriched in everything to all bountifulness, which causeth through us thanksgiving to God".

But there were also hardships:

.....Mail service is very poor, but we have heard from the children twice since they left.

Hector's project right now is re-roofing the hospital. This has not been done for twenty years, so is a real job. And it has to be done in the hot, dry season, which makes it more exhausting. But he has some helpers and has his materials on hand.

.....Hector is quite heavy just now, I think, too heavy, as it slows him down. He is going to have a check-up soon. Nothing special seems to be wrong, just gets tired fast and has to stop now and then. I seem to be OK and have gotten over the operations all right.

Whatever the situation Ione found herself in, her concerns seemed to be for others. She wrote to her sister Lucille and husband Maurice on the 22nd of February:

The packages with the wintergreens arrived and were eagerly swallowed. Thanks very much.

Mother's letter of January 21 sounded a little sad. Is she thinking of moving nearer to you? And if so, where would that be? I have been wondering what your plans for the future are. I have been praying especially about that, as well as for Larry's future. I love him so much and want to see him happy and where God wants him.

I received a picture of Esther and family with her Christmas letter, and it was so good to see them all. I had not seen the baby. They are just darling children, and look so happy and contented and well-cared for.

This week Hector and I are going to Aketi, not far from Ekoko, where Marcellyn used to work. There is to be a Pastor's Conference and Dr. Henry Brandt is coming to speak. We are taking native pastors from here and from Bopepe, Mary Baker's station.

Mary moved to a village called Bopepe in the mid 1950's. For a long time, she lived there on her own supported by Congolese pastors Asani Benedictu and his twin brother Bo Martin. Asani was the elder and usually pulled rank on his very patient brother. Twins were considered unlucky in Congolese's families, usually one or both would be left in the forest to die, but these two survived because their parents were Christians. As they were identical, their mother gave them different facial tribal markings so she could tell them apart. They became very adept at surviving. The twins, Asani and Bo were committed Christians and ensured Mary was safe and well cared for at Bopepe.

Mary always kept an open house and, as it was en-route from Stanleyville to Bongondza and other stations beyond, she had many visitors. Mary was adventurous in more ways than one. She ate insects just as the Congolese did. She was a great favorite with visitors and it was always a pleasure to stop off and visit with her. By the early 1960's, Mary was joined by the English Nurse, Margaret Hayes. Ione continued:

Mary is going along to translate for Dr. Brandt. Hector and I will help with the meals and coordinating the affairs.

We had a sad accident here the first of the month, when a little girl was electrocuted. There had been a storm and a wire was hanging down unnoticed. When the Doctor started up the motor, she was touching the wire. It was a main wire, direct from the plant, and she died instantly. She was the oldest daughter of one of our finest evangelists. We remembered that the Lord was a man of grief and acquainted with sorrows, and we got better acquainted with sorrow through this incident. The people took it real well, and the parents accepted it as from the Lord. We watched to see if there was any resentment or race feeling or that we had been careless, but we did not see anything but sorrow.

Because we had heard so many bad reports of western Congo, we were naturally wondering how we stood here. This seemed to be a confirmation that everything was all right in our part of Congo.

There has been some dissension in the church at our station, Maganga. The five missionaries there were about to resign, when it was decided by the UFM Executive Committee that they should go to other stations for the time being, to see if things would get better. Pray for this station. It may be that this is the Lord's way of making them more indigenous. It will be proved whether they can carry on perhaps better without the missionaries. We are trying as much as possible to stay out of responsible jobs, just to give them a chance.

This was a major shift in emphasis and control that the mission had in Congolese churches. The missions in Congo did not exist in a vacuum but were part of the social world of their time. Ever since the country had gained independence there had been dissension and dividing factions that wrestled for power. The country needed unifying in some way, hence the setting up of a Congo Protestant Council. There was a degree of satisfaction that Pastor Asani had a leading role, however, he made it clear he was not a puppet but had views and ideologies of his own, as Ione wrote on February 22, 1964 to her sister Lucille:

.....This week the Congo Protestant Council comes under question by some of the more evangelistic missions on the issue of entering the World Council of Churches. Up till now this has not been a major issue. But we need much prayer at this time when the Congolese themselves will be deciding on the WCC. Just now the president of CPC is our own Asani, who is really on fire for the Lord. But as president, he will not get a vote. We have a Congolese delegate and a missionary representing us at this gathering at Elizabethville, Katanga.

The boys are OK, rejoicing over their jeans. Thanks so much for sending them.

Much love, Ione

Ione wrote to her mother on the 25th of March. She and Hector were preparing to travel to Stanleyville to meet up with the boys for their Easter holiday and she wanted to post her letter as soon as they reached the town. Ione warned of the unsettled times they were facing:

.....Pray for us in these coming weeks, as there will be elections beginning April first in some parts of Congo (in fact, in the area we have to pass thru when we get the children!).

.....Hector and I keep quite well. Hector has to take pills for a type of arthritic condition in his knees. Neither of us feel very peppy but you don't in this climate.

So, we do just a little bit less, and save strength for the big jobs. He is roofing the hospital now, the first time since Dr Westcott was here.

All for now. We are so happy to have intercommunications with nearly all of our UFM stations. We can hear AIM, but cannot talk to them. As yet, we haven't heard whether they are getting us. Yesterday we heard who was going to meet Kenny at Arua [just over the border in Uganda].

Much, much love,   Ione

The Easter vacation unexpectedly extended and Ione wrote from Stanleyville on April 26th to Lucille:

Dearest Sister,

We brought our boys here to send them on their journey to school, and when we arrived, we learned that school was postponed for one week. Instead of April 30 it is May 7, that it starts. The announcement was made on the radio. The first announcement said that it was because the dining room roof was not finished; the second radio broadcast said that it was because there had been some local demonstrations because of Congo elections. They wanted the children to wait "until the dust settled." Our roads are too muddy to make the 11-hour journey back to Bongondza to wait (it is the rainy season). Not much "dust" here, either politically speaking, or climatically. The Congo River is rising and nearly up to Second Street.

So, we are waiting in Stanleyville with several other families. We thought we could make a visit to another station in another direction, but their river is flooded, too. In fact, they are keeping their car on this side, so that when they bring their children they can connect up with canoes.

On May 5th, the boys finally left for school and Ione, writing to her mother, said:

..... we have sent them off knowing that the Lord will be with them. Four cars went up this time, as there are quite a few children. We are happy to have them in such a good school. Kenny got off OK for Kijabe, part way by car and part by plane. All are well. We have heard there is a possibility of an American school in Stanleyville soon (perhaps in September) If this comes, we may be able to have a children's home again.

......Archie has been in the hospital again and Jean started having pain in her other side of the jaw. This is the second or third time in hospital for Archie. His heart is bad.

We are happy here and feeding on the Lord's faithfulness day by day. We recently received another food order from Leggett's Wholesale. Your package has not come yet. Pray for its safety. So many thieves. Our David had a 1000-franc bill snatched right out of his hand. Love, Ione

In a letter to Lucille written on May 9th, Ione gave more information on how they filled their vacation time with the boys and an indication of the changes that were occurring in town:

.....We 'camped' in the old hangar which used to be the Children's Home and had some nice days together. Hector and the boys started a garage for Mr

Carper's truck[143] and dismantled the old Jeep to make a run-about out of it. Since there were three families of children there it was a bit complicated, with other houseguests and a nearby conference going on, but I took charge of drinking water and cookies and felt I had helped a little. Eventually the children got off. This gave the boys an extra week with Ken which was nice. Ken left before they did, on the first car that went up to Rethy. They had tamed a little squirrel and Ken took it to Rethy as his car was not so crowded. They will take care of it there.

All of us are well. We had several escapades with thieves in Stanleyville, but the Lord always gives a time and place to calm down and rest a little. The government does so little to thieves that are many, and when local people catch them, they are merciless, often beating them to death. Mrs Parry, the mother of two Rethy Children was standing beside me in a shop and her nylon shopping bag was slit with a razor; the man was ready to reach into it when she noticed and got out of the shop quick. These men are dangerous and we do not resist but get out of the way. One family was robbed while they were asleep after being sprayed with a fluid that put them to sleep. The thieves got 40,000 francs and many valuable possessions. The family was so frightened that they have come to headquarters for a while to recover.

.....If you hear of trouble in the Kivu Province or Bukavu, you will know that it is two days away from us. There was some evacuation of missionaries there when the youth terrorists surrounded mission stations. We have had none of this sort of thing. But there are some very bad youth groups called Jeunesse, trained to start revolutions. I hope they stay away from here. We have a loyal group who would put up a big fuss if anyone like that came around.

The Jeunesse (youth) movement developed in the early 1960's post-independence. The north east of the Congo supported Patrice Lumumba and his political party Partie Nationale Populaire (PNP). Lumumba became Zaire's first elected leader in 1960[144] but was murdered in January, 1961. His ideologies were largely socialist and he had a great deal of support from communist countries.

Lumumba was considered one of the elite middle class or 'evolue'; in 1958 he published a manuscript setting out his vision for Congo wherein he was looking for prison reform, abolishment of prostitution and for a strong central government that would not be partisan to tribal influences. The manuscript was only published after his death. In 1960, prior to the declaration of Independence, Lumumba's party won most seats in the legislature, power was divided between the west and eastern regions. Unfortunately, tribal loyalties came into play especially in the army where soldiers would not accept a promoted officer if he came from an inferior tribe.

The parties from Léopoldville were supported by the West; eventually Moise Tshombe came to power with support from America and Europe; his power base

---

[143] Del Carper is the new Deputy Secretary of the UFM in Congo.
[144] In the 1960's Independence, the state's name was changed from Belgian Congo to Zaire.

was mainly around Léopoldville. In Stanleyville, the 'Rebels', made up largely of the Jeunesse and led by Gibenye, began to command more power over everyone in their territory. Anyone in the north east who had previously been in opposition to the PNP were eliminated; it is reported that over 2000 Congolese were killed in Stanleyville's town Square in front of the statue of Lumumba.

Although Tshombe had American support, he had limited cash, so took on mercenaries to help clear up problems with provinces that were wanting to split away and set up their own independent states. These areas were copper and mineral rich and much needed for the country's economy and a split was untenable. This is an oversimplification of the political situation but hopefully will demonstrate the complexity of some of the issues that were influencing feelings at that time. Ione continued:

.....If there is any trouble it will be about elections and be between dissenting parties. Our local chief is being deposed and there may be something over this at Kole. The story is going around that there will be one day of retributions [the Congolese wanted to avenge the many years of misrule – mainly by 'white' people but really any injustice harbored was enough]*; I hope we find out which day and can stay very quiet until it is over. Pray for us in July, which seems to be the critical time. But the UN officers are staying in Congo, (plus 20 thousand troops from 34 nations) and recently Belgian leaders have come to Stanleyville to help with the Congo army once more. They dress like soldiers but are very helpful in maintaining discipline, under the commanding Congolese officers* [the UN were present in a peace keeping role and would not intervene to settle disputes]*. We are in touch with other stations by radio now, every noon, and also Stanleyville. We hear Rethy but cannot talk to them.*

Much love, Ione

On the 25th of May she wrote to her mother:

.....This week a curfew has been on in Léopoldville because of some bombs being set off there. We are not in a very quiet place Mother, but all over the world is unrest, and I would rather have Congo and its particular kind of difficulties than to be anywhere else in the world. We do believe the Lord brought us here and will take care of us as long as we are to stay. We have no assurance that we will finish our term, but go on day by day, doing just what He shows us to do. We have every courtesy among our local folk and feel quite secure on our station. We have no thieving, even though our house is insecure (from the standpoint of ant-eaten doors & woodwork).

We took a truckload of Congolese women to a Woman's Conference and they had a wonderful time, singing hymns all the way. It was lovely to see 50 women taking leadership in the meetings, giving messages homelitically prepared, discussing matters in a business-like way. And just a few years ago, they had to be shown even how to sit and stand on the platform. It is a thrill to hear them pray and they are teaching their children the things of the Lord. It is worthwhile being here just for them. Each of these women took a head of cooking bananas which is their 'bread'. And the women who were the hostesses even washed the clothes of their visitors. There were about 12 of us missionary ladies there, but we just sat by and let them go ahead. Of course, it was planned by one of the missionaries and some of the missionaries spoke and lead out in discussions. But a few more times like this and I think they could go ahead and do the whole thing themselves.

This week-end we were out on the Basali Trail. The road was worst ever and cracked the windshield because the tree branches were too close. Sometimes there was no vision ahead, just grass and jungle but we know there was a road there as we had been there before. Hector says the next trip will have to be on foot. Hector baptized 13 believers.

.....Much love, Ione

Ione finally received news that her mother was with Lucille and was comforted in the knowledge that they were able to support each other, she wrote:

.....it is a relief to me to know that you are together. You need each other just now, until you are both better. How I wish I could be there, too! Think of all the good jokes and laughs I am missing! I suppose you are well informed of all the crazy elephant stories we are hearing from folks who have just been home. Example: How can you get six elephants in a Volkswagen? Answer: 3 in the front and 3 in the back. I didn't think that one was even funny, but others have gone into gales of laughter!!

However, as the tensions built, Ione and Hector gave some consideration to their situation and Ione wrote to her mother and Lucille on the 30th of May from Bongondza:

.....We are thinking seriously of applying for a 4-year term this time, because the extra strains of missionary life out here just now seem to justify it. I am sure our churches would not object. We have not approached the subject yet to the mission, but be praying about it, and don't make it public until we write them. That would be just two years more, and we could go home at the time Ken finishes high school.

.....The rebels that were in Stanleyville have been arrested, so we may not be bothered for a while. Albertville was taken over by them for a while but the government troops have control now. Some are fighting in the Kivu district and this group, if they continue on, might get into our territory. But they will have a pretty close check on any strangers who come around.

Ione wrote on the 8th of June:

.....At last the package has arrived! And it is in perfect conditions!! The Lord has again fulfilled His promise to "supply every need." I did need these things and He brought every one of them to me, and the candy as well! I am enjoying the peppermints as I write this. And the nice smell of Old Spice talcum comes up to my nose when I jiggle the front of my dress! Your ability as a personal shopper has more than met my expectations, Mother. The daintiness of the nightdresses

is all my heart could desire. Everything is just right and of such nice material. Thank you very much for the time and expense you put into this package.

.....I may be needing some dental attention soon, some fillings, etc. We can go to the AIM dentist who looks after the children's teeth. Or some friends of ours from Mid-Missions just over the border in French Congo. I have heard that shopping is possible near where they live, so we might try to go there.

We are just not sure of the political temperature these days. I think there is supposed to be elections this month or next. There are many parties and among them the strong group which was active at the time of Independence. The Burks who have come back to the field recently say that it is pretty much like it was just after Independence.[145] They stayed all through those difficult days and do not hold much hope for matters to be improved.

Thread has been so scarce that it has become a burden for me to pass out thread in my sewing classes. They are so keen to get it that there is a struggle among the Christians women to not be greedy. I was just about out of any kind of thread when a parcel came last week from Mrs John D. Dunbar, with 24 spools of various kinds. But this will not last long. I have been rationing out a few yards at a time and they wind it around their woolly heads.

We have not had butter for some time, but cans of Blueband margarine are available usually. And they do keep well. We have flour and sugar and just now some whole wheat we brought from Rethy, for cereal. Doctor Sharpe and wife and little Andrew (their two daughters are at school with the other UFM children) have just returned from the mountains and have brought some fresh meat from Stanleyville. They carried it in a cooler that is kept cool for a day by means of four tins of special stuff.

.....Missionaries have to be judges sometimes. Two big school boys wanted to earn money so when Hector was ready to go to Stanleyville and I knew there would be room in the truck for wood, I asked these boys to cut wood for us to send to the headquarters in Stan for their woodstove. This is always a help to them. You would think there would be no end of places in this big forest where they could cut wood without getting into trouble. But they decided to cut it in a garden that belonged to one of the student evangelists. I have paid the boys for cutting it and the boys have probably spent the money. How would you judge the case? It is important to set it right because the principal of stealing is involved. Fortunately, I can have the help of the station Pastor for settling this.

My heart is being blessed daily by the scriptures. I am learning how to pray more and more and have learned a good many verses which help to combat the evil forces which are ever near. But the Lord has His host around us and he that toucheth you toucheth the "apple of His eye." Pray especially for my letter-writing, that it may be consistent and effective.

---

[145] This is probably why so many remained where they were during this current period of uncertainty as some felt they had departed with too much haste in 1960 and could have stayed.

Lovingly, Ione

On July 3rd, Ione and Hector carefully composed the following letter to supporters and friends at home. They did not wish to be alarmist yet they wanted to be honest. Neither did they want to deter any soon-to-be missionary, so they passed their letter to the Acting Field Leader, Del Carper, to read and advise them. He approved the wording:

Dear Friends:

"If it takes trial to make our hearts burn for Jesus, then, Lord, send us trial."

This prayer was made a few days ago by Machini Philip, the pastor from Bongondza. Just what sort of trials might come to the Congolese Church is hard to predict.

Reports of people being shot with arrows and skewered with spears may be true, and we don't say that could not happen here. But for the present time, the situation in our particular area does not seem to indicate immediate trouble.

It does not appear that the change of the Congo government should bring about as great an upheaval as their Independence four years ago. It may not greatly affect the missionary efforts. We expect to carry on as we have been unless there is evidence that we are not wanted.

Just now there are 52 missionaries working in Congo under the UFM. National workers number over 350, making up a team of ordained pastors, evangelists, qualified nurses and subsidized teachers. These are leaders of 250 congregations, 8 dispensaries and 95 schools.

Our mission is calling for reinforcements in the Congo. This means that qualified persons even at this present time can apply. Especially needed are teachers for secondary schools, teachers' training and seminary.

Your fellowship with us in this adventure is necessary for the full achievement of our hopes for the Congo. Our supporters have not let us down as yet. The money gets through – always – somehow. Letters of encouragement are being received. Some airmail letters include much-needed sewing needles! Periodicals keep coming, and parcels often contain just the items which are unobtainable here.

Prayer can always get through for us, if offered by a sincere heart of one who truly loves the Lord. Some are praying for the Lord to remove the danger. We would like you to pray that the Lord's people here may have grace to go through danger, and prove that God cares for His own.

We have daily communications by radio with the other UFM stations. We also have contact with the AIM where our children attend school. There is an American Consul in Stanleyville who will advise us if it is necessary to leave the country.

Whatever trials may be brought to bear upon these people through government changes, there will be some Christians who will be strong in the Lord. Men like Machini Philip with hearts burning for Jesus, will go on serving Him no matter what happens.

At this writing we are enjoying quietness. On our way to Stanleyville this week we were stopped several times and searched. There is a curfew enforced so we must always be clear of this. Any moves we make must be planned carefully and sometimes authorities notified. It takes time and patience, but the work goes on.

Be assured that we are well and happy, lovingly yours,

Hector and Ione McMillan

Ione remained in a positive mood when next writing to her mother on the 5th of July:

Dearest Mother,

Hector and I are in Stanleyville helping with the building project. The large building which we never got finished when we were in charge of the children's home is being made into apartments and guest rooms. It is a peaceful occupation for so many reports that you may have been hearing.

In spite of bad reports, we are all right, and have no reason to feel we should get ready to leave the country. The change of government may have reactions, but as far as we know we are still in favor.

There are ever so many soldiers around, but all are friendly. We try to stay away from them when they are drunk. Of course, it is noticeable here in Stanleyville more than at Bongondza. In a way we are safer at Bongondza as it is isolated. But somehow, I feel safer here in Stanleyville in spite of so much military activity. Here we have a way to get out if need be, and the American Consul is here.[146]

Yesterday we were invited with other Americans (I still count myself as such!) to the Consulate for Fourth of July Celebrations. For a while everyone wondered if it would be possible as there was bound to be suspicion whenever a group of people gather anywhere. But we did go about 3 and come back before curfew.

They had grilled frankfurters and buns, potato salad, lemonade and it was thrilling to sing the National songs with salutes, etc. Some children of University of Stanleyville acted out several cute skits and sang. There are half a dozen lovely well-trained American children. Some of them go to school in Léopoldville.

Although soldiers were with us constantly yesterday from daylight (all night in fact along the road in their trucks) until 2 P.M. they use the front yard to collect people whose papers are not in order, and to rest and to drill, etc. Although one can't be too sure of them, we felt no great fear of them as they were polite.

One nice-looking young man asked me if I had a song-book in Lingala. He and his friend accepted one each as a gift, and they sat down to try to sing from them. Others were reading Bibles and tracts. My job yesterday was transferring belongings from two stations over to the new building. I had a staff member to help me. I wondered if the soldiers would want to see everything, but they didn't.

---

[146] This is a prophetic observation from Ione.

Last Monday when we came from Bongondza, they searched even my purse for guns.

.....No one knew exactly what would happen when Congo's Independence was celebrated but all went off quietly. And now the coming of an exiled man, Tshombe, to Léopoldville, brings speculations of trouble. Some pro-Lumumba folk say they will not support him. And Stanleyville is pretty much the former. We cannot follow politics too well, but we listen to the radio several times a day and can at least know when it will affect us. The American Consul gave a nice talk yesterday saying that everyone of us (there were about 20 there) were under careful consideration and he admired us all greatly for our carrying on in these times.

Hector and I are well. We will go for the boys on July 20. Kenny arrives in Congo again the 30th, and will be met by another missionary and brought by car to Stanleyville.

We have often wondered where we would go if we were evacuated again. Rethy would take the children over the border as they are so close. If there is a choice, I would like them to go to Kijabe where Kenny is. We carry on our usual work, with some restrictions depending upon military activities. Today one missionary arrived from Boyulu to work with Hector and he went through 8 barriers of soldiers. So, they must be expecting trouble.

"In times like these we need an anchor," and we surely have One who not only called us to Congo but will keep us here until our work is finished.

Much love,   Ione

And Hector wrote to his family on the 10th of July:

Dear Jean & Archie,

It's easy to let weeks go by without writing. There are so many jobs to do especially since we are spending a month here at headquarters in Stanleyville reconstructing a building into an apartment & guest rooms.

We will be having a Mission Council meeting next week for several days & then the trip up for the children. Their school finishes Thursday July 23 and opens again September 9th. We may have to wait for Kenneth either at Rethy or some place along the line. It depends on the other children we have with us. Two families are going on furlough at the end of the month so we have to be sure to get them here to Stan with us on time. If either of the other two cars can take them we might wait until July 30th for Kenneth to fly from Nairobi to Arua.

.....Things are quiet around the area. Our missionary work is expanding & we have many unfilled positions. We were out in a district this morning (Sunday) for a service & the folks wanted a <u>sure promise</u> that we would come again <u>soon</u>. At the Council meeting we will have to move missionaries to fill in the gaps, since several are going on furlough & we must keep staff on each of our mission stations.

The truck is still doing well. I changed the mud grip tires around several weeks ago. They are getting worn down now but still good.

– Love Hector & Ione

"Turn thou to thy God, keep mercy & judgement." Hosea 12:6

The next part of Ione and Hector's story has been drafted from notes made by Ione and augmented by other records made at the time. Much of this material was shared by Ione in speeches and interviews in the years ahead.

Stanleyville fell to the insurgents and the family would begin what would become nearly four months of house arrest at the hands of the rebels. Ione wrote:

.....In July when we left Bongondza station in our two-ton truck, Hector and I were going to meet our sons who had finished their school year. We were to collect the five younger boys along with other missionary children, at Rethy Academy in northeast Congo, and bring them down from the mountains to Stanleyville. There we would wait several days for the sixth son, our oldest, Kenneth, to come from Rift Valley Academy, Kijabe, Kenya.

The dark blue Chevrolet truck was fitted with foam-rubber seats and canopy so that the mission children could travel in comfort from school to their stations. It resembled pretty much a ship of state as it sailed proudly into African Inland Mission's Rethy station.

School was out and it was a happy and busy time of loading into the truck the small cases and sleeping bags of the children assigned to us. Space was saved for baskets of vegetables, plentiful at Rethy, and much needed down on the UFM forest stations. Space was also reserved for the Chuck Davis family, to be added to the group when we stopped at Linga.

We did not linger long at Linga, but were able to get considerable baggage of the Davis' into the truck. This AIM family, in Congo only since April, were already assigned to the UFM station Banjwadi, where they would work on a loan basis in the joint mission project at the Banjwadi Theological Seminary.

Charles and Muriel Davis were good travellers, as were also the little four-year-old Stevie and chubby 1-1/2 year-old Beth Ann. This complacent blue-eyed baby ate sandwiches and drank water like the bigger children and did not require special baby food or milk.

A calmness and acceptance of each new travel situation on the part of this precious new missionary family, as well as in the more seasoned group of children (by now filling every part of the truck), made it a good journey.

Three days and two nights it took, first through mountains, then grass, then forest, stopping only at the Brethren station of Lolwa and our own

Chuck Davis family

mission's station of Boyulu.

.....We stayed at the Hobson home [an American family who recently arrived to teach at the new Protestant University] *for one week while waiting for Ken to*

arrive from his school. John Arton was to meet his Nairobi-Kampala-Arua plane and drive him overland in order to catch up with us. Ken's school was finished a few days later than that of the other five boys.

Thus, the end of July found us in the center of Stanleyville, enjoying the comforts of a lovely city dwelling and looking about town for sacks of coarse salt and yard goods the Bongondza Congolese had paid us in advance for - items which we could bring on the truck to them.

Meanwhile, on August 1st, the state's name changed once again, from Zaire to Democratic Republic of the Congo (DRC).

Hector and Paul took a load of lumber to Boyulu where Ken would arrive at the beginning of August and the plan was for them to return with Ken to Stanleyville. While they were away, Ione wrote:

.....On Tuesday afternoon, August 5th, at ten minutes before 3 o'clock, Al Larson and Bob McAllister arrived at Hobsons' house in Bob's Land rover.

We were told, "the rebels are on the edge of town; curfew at 3! We're moving you out to Kilometre Eight before the curfew falls."

Packing was quickly done as we hadn't much. By 3 o'clock we were travelling along in the Land Rover, leaving Stanleyville on the north side. We saw many people rushing to get into their homes. The crowd surged, like a tide, toward Belge I, the nearest native residential sector.

As we bumped along over the Ancienne Route de Buta toward Kilometre Eight, the rebels were already marching on the streets of Stanleyville at the east side.

We passed the KM. 8 post and turned left into the mission compound.

It was 3:30 when the four boys were installed with me in an unfinished room in the big building to the left of the Home.

At 4:30 two carloads of missionaries drove in from Route des Elephants, the road coming from the east which forked into our road.

.....It did not take the soldiers long to find us. The next day they drove into the broad mission entrance and introduced themselves as the People's Army of Liberation.

I took a good look as several of the dark-skinned soldiers passed through the house from front to back. Battle dress seemed to mean no shirt, rough pants, palm fronds fastened around the head almost like a bird cage. Pieces of fur on arms or other places; a black smear on forehead and chest, which I learned later was the congealed blood of their victims.

As one burly fellow came near to the back door where I was standing, I had a desire to befriend him, so put out my hand to shake his.

He drew back his own hand and shook his head. With a stern expression in his eyes he put one finger on his lips to show me he was not to talk to me. As he went out the door he muttered, "Our boss, Mulele, is a man of much 'matata' (trouble).

I sensed that he had been pressured into this hostile attitude. It was not like the usual friendly Congolese manner. This was the "systematized terrorization" which we learned more about later.

Less than one month after our circular [newsletter] *went out, the rebel army was in Stanleyville; they had reached Kilometer Eight. We were under house arrest, later to be used as hostages against mercenary and paratrooper attack. .....My heart was sick, but I did not realize then how sick one's heart can be. We later saw them loot and set up guard quarters in the* [Bonte] *house across the road.*

The Simbas [the Swahili term for lion and what the rebels called themselves], *sometimes crazed from drink or narcotics, often visited Kilometer 8. They threatened, cursed, shot off their guns, and commandeered our possessions.* Sometime later, Ione wrote:

.....Hector found Ken at Boyulu and the boys helped him to unload the lumber. They did some trucking jobs for Chester and then turned the vehicle toward Stanleyville. They did not get very far, for the road was already blocked by rebels. Hector and the two boys returned to Boyulu, where they were put under house arrest with the eleven other missionaries.

The political situation in the Congo was complicated. It was not just a case of dissension between political parties but included different tribal and regional issues. The 'rebels' referred to here were under the leadership of General Gibenye who was a trade unionist and vice president of the Confederation of Free Trade Unions of the Congo in the late 1950's. He was a supporter of Patrice Lumumba, who appointed Gibenye as Minister for the Interior but his political activities, tied as they were to Lumumba's fate, meant he fell out of power. When President Kasa Vubu dismissed Lumumba, Gibenye went too. Unlike Lumumba, Gibenye survived and enjoyed popularity in the Stanleyville area. Unrest in the Léopoldville area meant there was opportunity for Gibenye to oppose the government in power in the Léopoldville area. With funding from the Soviet Union, he set up his Rebel force. Although the United Nations sent soldiers to Stanleyville to maintain law and order it was difficult. The missionaries had to contend with poorly or unpaid soldiers, dissatisfied with their lot, and a Rebel army, who were gaining prominence.

.....For about two weeks we were able to communicate with them [Hector and the two boys] *by means of the radio transmitter. Even on my birthday, August 17, they were able to sing Happy Birthday and quote some verses from Proverbs 31. But when we discovered a few days later that they were no longer on the air, we knew the rebels had confiscated their transmitter. And very shortly after that, we lost our own in the same way.*

During the next few weeks, we had no communication, and I didn't know that Hector was sick with pneumonia until one night in early September the rebels delivered him [by special permission of the rebel government] *to our front door, along with the two boys, and Thelma and little Larry Southard. Hector was able to walk but was rather weak as he had lost forty pounds. The remains of his lunch gave me some idea of the quality of food he had been having. The bread was sour and made with wormy flour.*

Ken and Paul didn't say much, but I had the impression that the soldiers (rebel soldiers or Simbas) had given them a rough time at Boyulu. They said that one day at noon the rebels came and ate up all their dinner. "But Maurice, the cook, made us some more," they were quick to add.

Ken said one night he had a bad dream and was awakened by the terrible feeling that the rebels were coming to kill them. He called his Daddy, who lit a candle. Ken said the candle was a real comfort, as he could see by the light of it that his Daddy was not far away.

Of the group of twenty-eight at the (KM 8) mission headquarters, half were youths and children.[147]

Bob and Alma McAllister arrived in Congo in the 1950s with their three small children. Beginning in 1962 they were based at Ponthierville and the children went to school in Rethy along with the McMillan boys. Like the McAllisters, Al and Jean Larson, Del and Lois Carper and Marshall and Thelma Southard had been working with the UFM since the 1950s.

Ione recorded:

.....Nine of the fourteen children should have, by this time, been back at school in one of the other two African Inland Mission schools for missionary children. Rift Valley Academy in Kijabe, Kenya where our Ken was enrolled, had already started. Rethy Academy in northeast Congo near the Uganda border, where the remainder of school-age children should have been, was already evacuated and now continuing in a safer spot over the border.

Ione would have liked to see the children returned to Rethy, but the journey was far too hazardous. She was even prepared to meet with General Olenga, commander of

Mina Erskine, Viola Walker and Olive Bjerkseth

the rebel troops to plead her case. Fortunately, she was overruled as he was violent and ruthless and is believed to have said, "We will make fetishes out of the hearts of Americans and Belgians and we will dress ourselves in their skins."

So, life under house arrest required some structure. Lois Carper and Viola Walker set up classes for the smaller children to

---

147 The party at Kilometer 8 was made up of Hector and Ione McMillan and the six boys; Bob and Alma McAllister and their three children, Bill , David and Ruthie, Al and Jean Larson and their daughter Carol, the Davis family and their two children, Thelma Southard and her son Larry, Lois and Del Carper and daughter Marilyn, Mina Erskine, Viola Walker and Olive Bjerkseth.

keep them occupied in the mornings and Olive Bjerkseth gave French lessons in the afternoon.

Local people soon realized that there were now two midwives at Kilometer 8, Alma McAllister and Mina Erskine. They were called out six times to help with deliveries, reaching the expectant mothers by bicycle. The missionaries extended their work to leading meetings and worship for the women.

On one occasion, an official from the United Nations invited the children to his home a mile and a half away where they could inspect his model train set up. The boys came away with several model kits and soon started building them. They built a whole model village under the guidance of Ken. The McMillan construction and inventive skills had indeed been passed on to the boys.

Saturday evenings were game nights: they had table football, Snakes and Ladders, Sorry and Chinese Checkers, as well as quizzes mainly devised by Hector. Ione recalled:

.....Kilometer 8 was, of all the 10 stations in the UFM area, the one place where our children loved most to stay. Speaking for my own sons, that is, they remembered it as the Children's Home from 1955 to 60. During those years they attended the Belgian school in Stanleyville, and the three main buildings, and their surrounding yard and forest which later became the mission headquarters, were just where they liked best to be.

None of the children felt as limited as did their mothers. For it was the mothers who knew the substitutions which were made in the kitchen, when basic foods diminished and became non-existent.

Can you imagine nine women in one small kitchen?

It was evident that someone needed to be in charge, and the logical one was Jean Larson. Her aim, in planning menus for 28 people, was that the food should have an inviting, individual flavor.

"Sardines and rice could be served institution style," she remarked as she rolled up her eyes about the crowded kitchen, "but how about 'sardine pizzas'? Now, doesn't that sound better, and let's divide into three teams. Lois, see what you can do about it tonight with Ione and Alma to help."

"Alma makes a delicious English 'trifle'. Do we have the ingredients?" The preparations were made with jokes and laughter. Alma's merry laugh being the loudest.

The making of the bread fell to my lot, as there was no one else brave or foolish enough to try baking with flour that had to be sifted three times and then was heavy. Later Muriel Davis of AIM lent a hand in this, and it became a pleasure to work together over the bread or buns or coffee cake.

In addition to baking bread, I was in charge of the preparation of the breakfast cereal. Now wheat is not a common grain in our part of the Congo. But just before the rebels came, there were several tons of cracked wheat called Bulgar, sent out from the US by the Congo Protestant Relief Association.

A number of sacks of this Bulgar were available, and one job was to spread it in the sun on pieces of 4 x 8 feet metal roofing. When the roofing became hot from the sun the black weevils crawled out and over to the underside of the roofing and with some tapping, they fell to the ground. We picked out the creatures that couldn't walk then gathered the wheat on trays and sterilized it in the oven until it was toasty brown.

The boys and Hector enjoyed grinding the wheat. They had rigged up a V-belt on a gasoline motor which also served to run the washing machine. The days we did the washing we could not grind cereal.

.....Actually, we had enough food, and could have held out until December if necessary. But there was just such a scarcity as to give me a healthy respect for a loaf of bread.

Being blessed with a good appetite, and a sense of humor, is an asset to any missionary. And conditions at Kilometer 8 between August and November of 1964 were such as to make good use of both!

.....But the bulk items such as flour, rice, sugar, fat, must be obtained the hard way. That was, to brave

The Del Carper family

the rebels and by some conveyance arrive in Stanleyville where the merchants gladly would open a back door and give whatever they had free of charge. Our 'providers' were fathers and husbands of our flock, who suffered many indignities to do this for us. Bicycle, motor bike, the back of a pick-up truck driven by a rebel, all were among the means of our survival.

It was usually around 2 P.M. each day when we gathered to hear how the men made out, and just what they were able to bring to us. We always thanked the Lord that they returned safely. They were always hot and weary, and sometimes empty-handed. On one such occasion, Bob McAllister wiped away perspiration as he told his story.

"They took the bicycle out from under me. After they arrested me the second

time, I was able to get away, and that, only by the gift of talking my way out."

Talking his way out was easy for Bobbie. He was well known at roadblocks for greeting any soldier with the term, "Commander, how are you this fine day?", which most often was considered a compliment and broke the tension since most were mere privates or with no rank at all; thereby increasing his chances of getting

McAllister family, c1964

through the roadblock trouble-free.

It would seem that not long after everyone was corralled at Kilometer 8, that there was a degree of freedom to move about. Ione wrote:

>.....*One day when the guns were fired as the soldiers left our compound, we discovered some of our boys and the McAllister's; going along behind them, picking up the empty shells for souvenirs. We had to stop the children from this dangerous project.*

On another occasion, Ione found John engaged in conversation with a young gun-toting Simba about his age, who he had befriended prior to the rebellion. They were discussing why the boy had joined the Simbas. He answered that it was the "thing" to do at that time and was proud of his new status.

The Simbas often arrived looking for food; on one visit they were looking for meat to go with their rice; Bob McAllister quipped, "You have rice!! I only wish we had rice!!" the men departed empty handed.

Then they wanted a chicken and Bob claimed they had no chickens, at which point a scrawny bird came around the corner. "Ah" said Bob "it's not my chicken". At this time, the Simba's had a code which forebode them to steal, however, they could accept gifts. Having chased and caught the chicken, they did not wish to appear to steal it so they gave the bird to Bill McAlister (aged 12) who had witnessed the exchanges and decided to calmly walk across the compound and put the chicken in the waiting truck while the adults looked on in horror. There were rumors that white children were being forced to join the rebel cause and they were sure Bill would be ordered into the truck. He wasn't.

Ione continued recalling:

>.....*When the pressure of the rebel occupation began to be felt in earnest, this lively group of white children must nevermore be seen playing at the front of the house. They could play at the back behind the buildings, but seldom could we allow them to venture on the dirt road between us and our 'guards'.*
>
>*Reports of young white boys being taken to the army camp frightened us enough to keep our children out of sight as much as possible.*
>
>*If Saturday nights were games nights, Sunday nights were for praise. We sang loud and long, and put everything we had into it. I was so much blessed in my soul that I thought I would burst for sheer joy. Such liberty we had, and the numbers we sang were the most difficult, rousing selections with many parts and high sopranos. Songs like "He Giveth More Grace", "I Wandered Down a Lonely Road", "Follow Me", "All Your Anxiety", "Where No One Stands Alone", and "According to Thy Loving Kindness".*
>
>*Not only was there group singing, but duets, trios, and solos. One duet I sang with Alma McAllister was, "O My Soul, Bless Thou Jehovah!" And how my heart beat as I listened to Alma's sweet, free birdlike tones. I tried to blend so thoroughly with her that my voice would only be noticed as a shadow of the angel wings on which she flew.*

Bill Scholten and family.

Al Larson had the boys blowing horns by this time, and there were some really splendid hymns played on the trumpet and trombone. Nobody was sleepy. We almost forgot that we were in a dimly lighted room where we might have been whispering for fear of the rebels. The Lord gave us an especially happy time that night as He knew we needed it.

Two days later, they heard fellow missionary Bill Scholten had died at Ekoko. Ione recalled that they all experienced a time of great sadness. She wrote:

.....Bad news came frequently after that. It was accompanied by discouragement. But it was then that we worked harder, deliberately kept normal, and held to as rigid a schedule as we could. And we tried to think of humorous stories to relieve the tension. In this Hector excelled.

Our 11-year old Stephen, once jokingly said, "They told me to cheer up, it may get worse. So I cheered up – and it got worse!"

The children, too, entered into this spirit of blaming nobody, and went into each new phase of restrictions knowing the Lord Himself had commanded it.

When violence came our way, it was necessary to surrender our desire for immunity from suffering. There had to be some sort of understanding between us and the Lord concerning our safely. We surrendered to an unsafe circumstance.

The Simbas arrived at Kilometer 8 several times a day demanding food, using threatening behavior. Ione wrote:

.....They slept. They ate. They came and went. They inspected sometimes as many as five times during one day or night. Each time they came, they were fierce and bold. Each time the missionaries faced their guns, we hoped it would be the last.

But the Simbas then decided to take the men prisoners. Al Larson, Del Carper and Chuck Davis, being American, were imprisoned at Hotel des Chutes in Stanleyville along with Dr Paul Carlson. Bob McAllister with his usual pugnacious wit made representation that he and Hector be allowed their freedom as they were not Americans. He found a map of North America but it showed Canada and the United States as one color. It took him a while to persuade the largely uninformed Simbas where Britain and Canada were in relation to America and Belgium but he eventually won the day.

Once the rebel soldiers had commandeered radios, they then turned their attention to vehicles. At Boyulu, Chester Burk frequently repaired their trucks but eventually they took all the vehicles on the mission station. The missionaries tried to disable their cars and trucks by removing parts or hiding them in the forest at the edge of the mission compound. Viola Walker's Opel car had no radiator so it was towed away into the forest. Bob McAllister took the piston rings out of his Land Rover. He eventually replaced them when news was heard that relief was on its way, however the Simbas arrived and took it.

After Independence in 1960, the Kinsos set up a book shop in the middle of Stanleyville, from which they distributed Bibles, tracts, Christian texts and hymnals. They had living quarters in the shop's compound which they shared with Mary Rutt who helped manage the accounts and stock taking. It was an interdenominational

project called Librarie Evangelique au Congo (LECO). They had a Bedford bus (shown in photo) which became a travelling shop. Having lived in Congo since the 1920's, Kinso and Ma Kinso were well known and well respected and allowed to remain in their home which was opposite the prison. The bookshop remained open at all times and there were accounts of Rebels

The Kinsos (Mr and Mrs Jenkinson) and their LECO bus.

purchasing books, even General Olinge's wife.

Once the Kinsos heard that other missionaries were imprisoned across the road, Ma Kinso cooked and delivered food to the detainees. Those detained would send back clothes for laundering along with the empty food trays. Although they lost their bus, the Kinsos continued to work and take services in the various churches in the town and were largely left unharmed.

Ione wrote:

.....By the first week in November feeling was very strong against Americans due to the reports of Americans being among the mercenary group which by this time was actually headed toward Stanleyville.

For forty-eight hours we did not know where the men were taken. When the staff member came back from searching the town the next day, he said,

"The first place I looked was under the statue of Lumumba. I saw no fresh blood there, so I knew the men must be still alive."

He was right. They were still alive. And before many more hours had passed a messenger came with a note telling us they were at Hotel des Chutes, along with Doctor Paul Carlson, American Consul Mike Hoyt and four of his aides; also, the two Pax fellows from the University.

With the help of Peter Rombaut, the British acting Vice Consul, Hector and Bob McAllister were released November 8, after one week in the hotel, as Hector was Canadian and Bob was Irish. The Americans were then moved to the Victoria Residence.

Ione reflected on events at this time:

.....Hector was fully aware of the danger. We could see it in the tenseness of his face. But it was evident also that he had no hope or desire of saving his own

body.[148] *He had long ago consigned his old body to the worms of the earth. He often said, "Never give one small thought for what happens to my body". This was a comfort when we were unable to give him a proper burial.*

Combing his hair, I said [to Hector], *"Smarten up! These boys are growing up and when they leave home I don't want to be left with an untidy old man! Then I want you to be like my boyfriend once more as we'll just have each other". But he only smiled as though he knew something I didn't know, and went on with uncombed hair.*

His abandonment of the body was only exceeded by his anticipation of glory. His evident longing to be with the Lord increased as the days moved on toward the final assault which took his life so suddenly.

He ate and drank normally, especially enjoying a cool drink of water. Sometimes he drank cup after cup before his thirst was quenched. Then he would give a shout, and say,

"When I get to the River of Life, I'm going to drink and drink and drink."

During the last few days, the other missionaries noticed and remarked about a happy other-worldly expression upon Hector's face, which never left, even after his spirit was gone.

Ione then recalled the life-changing events of Tuesday, November 24th, 1964:

.....The McMillan's were beginning their 112th day of house arrest under the rebel government. Our sleeping quarters were in the 'hangar'.

My Canadian husband looked up lovingly at me from where he was sitting on one of the two camp cots, which belonged to Ken, aged 17, and Paul, aged 16. Hector's long, now quite thin, legs were neatly folded back so as not to have his feet trodden upon by the troop around him. A cluster of boyish legs in khaki shorts filled the tiny aisle between us.

I breathed deeply, feeling the fresh tropically-warmed breeze through the louvered glass windows, and then sat down carefully on the sunny side of the tucked-in blanket of 13-year-old John's bed. His cot fitted squarely into the head of 15-year-old David's. They liked to sleep with their heads together.

Hector was checking his little notebook which contained the Bible verses claimed each day for his six sons. He observed with satisfaction that the total of verses for the past three years was now up to 6,000. His leather-bound Bible was lying in his lap. Familiarly adjacent was an over-sized worn copy of Martin Luther's, "Reformation", its quotations having been the highlight for several weeks in our family worship. Especially pre-eminent was the great reformer's prayer on the night before his trial: "Do Thou, my God, stand by me against all the world's wisdom and reason. Oh, do it! Stand by me, Thou true, eternal God!"

Hector was opening the Bible as I considered our family of boys. From Tim, aged 10, to Stephen, almost 12, around the cluster of legs and eager faces.

---

[148] Hector was the only one who refused to pack a bag for an emergency departure.

Genesis 42:11 came to mind – "We are all one man's sons; we are true men," and I prayed that they might become six true men of God.

The Lord had sent us six little men in the midst of a 20-year missionary career. When it was evident that ours were all boys, Hector decided that this was because of the shortage of men on the mission field. Like the two famous missionary brothers, Doctors Don and Dick Hillis, ours would be "reared", as well as "called" to be missionaries.

"Perhaps the Lord wants us to raise missionary men," Hector suggested, and then set about to do just that. His tools were the "rod" and the "book", the rod being the short stout strap which was never far away from the book, which was God's own Holy Word.

"You can never have too many well-behaved children," a friend had written comfortingly upon receiving the announcement of the sixth. So, I decided that they must be well-behaved. And I stood with Hector in his plan for "on the spot" obedience.

Such obedience was paying off in time of stress. The discipline required by our captors was of the "obey first, question later" type, and although the rebels' unreasonableness extended beyond what we had taught the boys to expect, the result was an alertness and a genuine trust that the Lord would never make it too hard.

Hector sensed my thoughts concerning the boys and his warm hazel-brown eyes were misty as he confidently opened the Bible. But before he could read the first word, we hear the sound of the airplanes.

"A plane!" Ken whispered, remembering the rebels across the road. Hector laid his Bible on the bed as we moved quietly in a group through the door, and then through the unfinished middle of the 'hangar', to the back exit. There we saw Muriel Davis and her two little ones, Stevie, aged four, and Beth Ann, nearly two, coming out of their room. At the same time Lois Carper and daughter Marilyn, aged 11, appeared from the other side of the bathroom.

Stepping out into the sunlight, we saw auburn-haired Jean Larson and happy little two-year-old Carol on the back porch of the main building next to us, along with Mina Erskine, Olive Bjerkseth and Viola Walker. The McAllister's were looking skyward as they came from under the overhanging roof of their low, three-roomed brick "staff quarters" behind the main building of Kilometer Eight. Lastly, we saw Mrs Thelma Southard coming with an excited little son Larry, aged four, behind the single ladies. Twenty-five pairs of eyes were gazing up. The boys counted the planes – one, two, three, four, flying over Stanleyville.

"They will be looking up, too," Jean Larson reminded us of our captors, guards of the People's Army of Liberation, across the road in the house that formerly belonged to Charles Bonte.

We sought to regain our composure and went back to finish family worship.

After family worship, everyone sat down to breakfast and listened to the World News, the BBC news correspondent revealed that a rescue mission was underway. Ione wrote:

.....We knew the world was concerned about us. But it takes water to wash dishes, and when the water supply stopped, it was our third son, David, who was dispatched to the motor house, to turn the crank which started the diesel motor pumping water from the well to the kitchen.

The hum of the pumping could be heard along with the noise of the planes which continued overhead. As Hector turned off the world news, he glanced out the front door and saw rebel soldiers running toward the well. He hurried out and met them halfway, noticing how extremely agitated they were.

"Stop it!" they screamed at Hector first, and then at Bobbie, who came swiftly alongside.

"Stop what?" the men inquired.

"Stop that 'machinie' with which you are signalling to the planes!"

The missionaries quickly stopped the 'machinie' and returned to their captors for further orders. It was then they saw other soldiers coming.

One carried a rifle, another a pistol.

"Cause everyone to line up in the back yard!" came the order in Swahili.

I wiped my hands on a towel and crossed the kitchen and back porch.

A rebel soldier was by this time inside and he swept everyone ahead of him as we made for the door.

"Hurry!" he shouted, and emphasized his words by tipping over a table and breaking a bottle. He pushed Muriel Davis, and I caught her before she tumbled down the steps.

Nine women and fourteen children lined up in the back yard of Kilometer Eight. Hector and Bobbie were roughly hustled off toward the road and a waiting vehicle. The rest of us were waved back into the house. Our feet seemed heavy as we climbed the back steps and filed through the dining room into the living room of the main building. The man with the pistol followed us.

As we sat down wherever we could, we watched the young rebel who looked about 30 years old. His eyes were fierce with a glassy brightness. He went into the bedroom, emptied a suitcase and filled it with sardines from the hall cupboard. These he handed to his helper. He came very close to me as he seized the radio and passed it on to his aide.

Then, pacing nervously back and forth like the 'lion' that he was, the young man began to fire his pistol.

"They must be blanks," I reasoned, as I counted four shots.

But the bullets were flying, and we were falling to the floor as we were told to do in such times, mothers covering their tiny children with their own bodies. I don't know where all of my sons were just then. Ken and Paul were in chairs around the dining room table near to the soldier. Later, when I asked which ones were sitting and which were on the floor, Stephen said emphatically to me, "Mother, I was flat out!"

We remained still on the floor until the Simba went out the back door. Alma McAllister looked from one to the other. Sixteen-year-old Paul opened his eyes and saw his older brother, Ken was contorted with pain. "Kenny's been shot," Paul said. He felt a trickle on his own cheek, brushed it with his hand, and discovered that he too, had been hit. A quick but silent inventory determined that the two boys were the only victims of the Simba's close-range shooting. Alma quietly moved over beside them and assessed that while Paul's injury was slight, Ken's was more serious. He had been struck in the hip by a bullet that had gone through the aluminum table and bounced off the floor. Alma quickly stopped the flow of blood.

We heard shots fired outside. Hector clutched his leg. Bobbie shouted, "You've shot my friend!" then ran as fast as he could toward Hector. The gun was turned on him and fired. The bullet left a red welt as it grazed his forehead. He threw himself on his face and remained as he fell.

Hector, still holding his leg, turned toward the house, as he heard us crying. At this time the final bullet was sent into the back of his left shoulder. It passed through his chest and out his right upper arm. He died instantly.

Alma cleaned up Paul's bleeding cheek and put a bandage over it. A longer time was required to stop the bleeding at Ken's hip. As soon as this was accomplished, Alma joined Thelma Southard by the window and they observed that the rebel car was gone.

I lifted up my eyes above the window ledge in the living room in time to see a second car coming from town. It hesitated, then stopped, the rebel occupants peering out toward the path leading to the house.

One said, "Look, the white people are already dead. Let's go on to the next place." They drove on.

Bob McAllister was lying on the path near the road, face down. I couldn't see Hector at first. As I crept out on the screened porch, Alma and Thelma went out the back door and around the outside of the house.

I looked through the bamboo blinds and discovered Hector very near the front steps, on his back under the nearest mango tree. There was blood on the sleeve of his light-yellow shirt. The two missionary women approached cautiously, and spoke to Hector.

"If he answers, I'll know he's not dead," I assured myself, but I could tell by the white face and its expression that Hector was already gone. He did not answer the ladies when they called his name. They looked from him to Alma's husband.

Slowly Bob lifted his head from where he was lying on his face. His arms and legs moved into position as he raised himself. As he stood, I saw the red welt on his head. He came silently toward them and stooped to help the ladies carry Hector's body into the house.

Hector McMillan 1915-1964

I met them at the back door and opened it. As I shared the load, Thelma turned to the others and said mournfully,

"He's gone!"

I searched Alma's face.

"Alma, has he gone?"

She replied, "Ione, he's with the Lord,"

Job's words came to me so I said quietly,

"The Lord hath given and the Lord hath taken away – blessed be the Name of the Lord."

We carried our precious load past Ken and put it on the bed in Larson's room. I called the boys around him, except for Ken, who was lying on a mattress on the floor in the hall. We examined Hector's wounds and I asked Alma if there was any way to revive him. She shook her head.

So, I said to the boys, "You see your Daddy here this way, and there is nothing we can do to save his life. Now, you can cry if you wish, but I don't think I will, because I am so proud of him, and so glad that he could give his life for Jesus."

Stephen wiped his tears. Tim didn't cry but felt sick. He walked into the bathroom and vomited, then came back and lay on little Carol Ann's bed nearby.

Paul, David and John came as near as they could and sat down. The other missionaries gathered in the hall, some in the office at the end of the hall.

We talked together for a little while and then, because we all felt that more rebels would be coming, it was decided that six of the women should take the tiny children down into the forest to hide. The McAllister's and Viola Walker stayed with me.

Feeling that we might be there for some time, Alma tried to remove the bullet from Ken's hip. I left Hector's body and went to help. She had only a razor blade.[149] And the slug was deeply lodged, so she eventually gave it up. She stopped and made tea in the kitchen. Viola served cool aid to the McAllister children and ours.

During this time the youngest son Timothy, now feeling better, sat down beside us on the floor and began in his high, 10-year-old voice to quote Psalm 124:

"If it had not been the Lord who was on our side, when men rose up against us; then they had swallowed us up quick, when their wrath was kindled against us. Then the waters had overwhelmed us, the stream had gone over our soul. Blessed be the Lord, who hath not given us as a prey to their teeth. Our soul is

---

[149] John remembers bravely running across the opening between the two buildings to get the razor blade he knew was in Ken's small suitcase.

escaped as a bird out of the snare of the fowlers; the snare is broken, and we are escaped. Our help is in the Name of the Lord, who made heaven and earth."

Ken was lying quietly, but lifted his head once and asked me,

"Mother, will you come back to Congo?"

I said, "Yes, if you boys are willing."

At this point six or seven local friendly Congolese came into the house. I arose to greet them and showed them Hector's body. One tall man was a local leader. Several I did not know, but I was sure they were not rebels. One couple I knew well. It was old Ndule, and his wife, Terese. Toothless Ndule was the mission gardener. Faithful for many years, he now came to pay his last respects to the man who led him to the Lord. Terese put her small arms about me and said timidly, "O, Mama!" I appreciated their bravery in identifying themselves with us.

One of these friendly folk went over to the workshop at the back of the hangar and watched Bob McAllister as he tried to make a coffin. There were boards the right length, but he could not nail them because the noise of pounding might attract the rebels. He decided to lay the two bottom boards in the hole, then the sides, then Hector's body, then the two top boards. Now to get the hole dug. He turned to the Congolese who was watching him and asked in Swahili,

"Would you be able to dig a hole for the white Bwana's body?"

The Congolese shook his head.

"The rebels have a strong law," he apologized.

Then he added quietly, "But what we can't do in the daytime we will try to do at night."

Just then a motor was heard and all the friendly natives fled. It was not the rebels as we feared, but mercenaries[150] shown the way by Al Larson, coming from Stanleyville to deliver us.

Al had escaped harm during a mass killing in a residential side street near the Hotel des Chutes in Stanleyville where they had been held captive during the past month. He and several others had been moved to a house where they were under arrest. About 7 a.m., when the rebel soldiers heard the planes overhead, they made everyone line up by threes and march about 300 yards from the hotel and sit on the ground. As soon as an armored car arrived on the scene with paratroopers, the rebels opened fire with machine-guns. Al, Del, Chuck and Paul, who were outside the house where they had been staying, raced for a garden wall and threw themselves over the wall; Doctor Paul Carson didn't reach safety in time and was shot in the back. Chuck was holding his hand at the time in an attempt to pull him over the wall.

The rebels, realizing they were beaten, fled. About 15 men, women and children were killed and 40 were wounded.

Once Al was safe, his main objective was to get to Kilometer 8 which was outside Stanleyville. He first approached some Belgian paratroopers who said they didn't

---

[150] Cuban exiles, we were told, under an American Major.

have the equipment to make the dangerous trip outside of town where Simbas were still present. He then ran over to a group of Cuban mercenaries sitting idly in their vehicles loaded with guns and ammo. The Cubans had fought in the Bay of Pigs against Castro's regime and ended up in Miami where they were hired by the CIA to rescue US diplomatic personnel in Stanleyville. Given the situation, no such rescue was required. However, they had come all the way to the center of Africa anxious to fight communism where ever it had spread so they gladly took up the challenge to make the risky journey if Al accompanied them to show the way to Kilometer 8.

Al Larson with injured Ken and others rescued from KM8 awaiting the flight out of Stanleyville.

So, they made the dangerous journey to Kilometer 8, firing their loud guns the entire way to scare off any Simba sniper attackers. After their arrival they hastily got everyone into the back of the pickup truck, jeep and trailer. No one was allowed any luggage not even handbags and there was no time for a burial for Hector; Ione could only hope that the Congolese faithful to the mission would undertake this for her. As they moved off, rebels fired at the vehicles and once again the women shielded their children. Only one mercenary was wounded. He struggled to get his ammunition off his shoulder so his companion could use the bullets, Ione came to his assistance for which he was very grateful.

Once inside Stanleyville's borders, the shooting stopped and the trucks headed

KM 8 Missionaries entering C-130 with Ken on stretcher.

straight for the airport. A stretcher was found for Ken and they all boarded a C-130 plane to Léopoldville. As the plane left the ground, a Simba bullet penetrated one of the fuel tanks but the pilot felt they had enough spare fuel to reach their destination.

Ione wrote:

.....*Before I boarded the plane, a Catholic priest thrust into my hands a loaf of bread. Having not one other possession, I accepted the bread gratefully. I took it with me as I sat with my back against the side of the plane. Ken with the bullet still in his hip, lay beside me. Paul, a piece of bullet in his cheek, sat with his brothers and fellow missionaries across the plane, which was crowded. Greeks, Indians, and Belgians were sitting on the floor or lying on stretchers.*

I examined the bread, and thought, "This lovely crusty loaf is large enough to feed my six boys."

But rations were being handed out, and a cup of water was going around. I did not need to divide my bread, so I looked for a wrapper with which to cover it and give it a little dignity. Scarcities at Kilometer 8 had given me a healthy respect for a loaf of bread.

There was nothing at hand with which to cover it, but as I turned my head, I saw a plastic sack folded behind me on the wall. I took it out and read its label, "For sickness." It had not been used, so I unfolded it and put my bread inside.

I tucked my precious loaf of wrapped bread under my arm, and was just beginning to enjoy a feeling of security, when someone shouted, "Stephen's sick!" So, I took out the bread and handed the sack to my son. The unwrapped loaf went back under my arm again.

When we arrived in Léopoldville the bread went with me and Ken into the ambulance and to the hospital and on up to the operating room. The other five boys were with friends at the Union Mission House. Paul didn't need hospitalization. The bullet (fragment) was taken from his face a few days later. I stayed with Ken, but was not allowed to go into the operating room.

I stood by the door of the emergency operating area, with the bread still under my arm.

I was thinking, "Now if I had a cup of coffee, I would have some of this bread."

Just then a Flemish lady stepped up to me and said in French:

"S'il vous plait, Madame, would you like a cup of coffee?"

I answered her in my poor French, "Oui, merci beaucoup, Madame, I would like to have a cup of coffee, but I do not wish to go far, for my boy is in this room."

She assured me that her house was just a short distance down the road, and that she would bring me right back. So, I went with her. As we were walking up the steps of her lovely home, she turned to me again.

"And now, Madame, while I am preparing the coffee, you shall have a hot bath."

I was a bit alarmed at this announcement, and afraid that she would keep me from getting back to Kenneth. Then the thought came to me, "I wonder whatever made this dear lady think that I needed a bath!"

For the first time that day I looked down at myself. I saw that my dress was torn and dirty and there were spots of blood on it.

I agreed to have the bath, and found the lady had put out fresh clothing for me. Even a folded pocket handkerchief! I drank her coffee, and ate some of her bread. Then, picking up my loaf, I went back to the hospital.

I tucked the bread in Ken's closet, but he didn't need it, as they provided bread for him in the hospital. He finally gave it to the maid to carry out. "They give us bread here, Mother," he explained. We never needed that loaf, but I believe the Lord let me carry it all that while in order to show me that He would never deprive us of our daily bread. Nor has He.

.....From the plane, Mrs McAllister had taken our five younger boys along with her three children to the Union Mission House (UMH). Her husband went with me in the ambulance with Ken to the Danish Red Cross Hospital. And it was Bob who waited near Ken during the time I was being refreshed at the home of the Flemish lady. When I returned to the hospital, I noticed the dried blood on Bobbie's white shirt and suggested that he, too, go and wash. He shook his head. "I'm not ashamed of Hector's blood," he said stoutly, and went to obtain transport for us to the UMH.

It was after nine o'clock at night when Bob's wife and other ladies met us at the door and we partook of the warm food saved for us. Then Alma and Bob and I tip-toed into a large room where eight children were sleeping; five McMillan's and three McAllister's.

I expressed surprise at finding McAllister's' little Ruthie dressed in a nightgown, as we had left Stanleyville with no baggage.

Alma reminded me that our youngest son Tim had put his small suitcase in just the right place at Kilometer 8 for a mercenary to see and bring it to the Stanleyville airport. Tim had claimed and guarded it until arrival at the UMH, when he opened the case and finding his pajamas inside, he offered the top piece to Ruthie. "Tim's top is Ruth's nightgown," Alma twinkled. "Tim is wearing the bottom! The other fellows weren't so fortunate!"

There are many stories of detainments, brutality and killings that occurred during the last week of November, 1964. Unfortunately, space does not permit detailed accounts here. A brief listing of some of the missionaries Ione has spoken of in her letters is provided below. Those who died or were killed are listed in bold letters under the location where they died. The station where they served is listed in parenthesis.

Ekoko (missionaries were taken to Aketi):
Bill Scholten, his wife Dotti and 5 children
Pearl Hiles
Betty O'Neill

Banalia:
Dr Ian Sharpe, Audrey and 3 children (Bongondza)
Dennis & Nora Parry, Grace and Andrew (Bodela)
Mary Baker (Bopepe)
Ruby Gray (Bongondza)
Margaret Hayes (She had been taken away to provide medical care to the Simbas but survived this ordeal and would be discovered months later, alive.)

Boyulu (missionaries were taken to nearby Bafwasende):
Olive McCarten
Luis Rimmer

Chester Burk and wife Dolena
John & Betty Arton and daughter Heather
Jean Sweet
Laurel McCullum

<u>Stanleyville</u> (and Kilometer 8):
Mr and Mrs Jenkinson
David and Sonia Grant (Banjwadi)
Chuck and Muriel Davis and 2 children (Banjwadi)
Del and Lois Carper and daughter, Marilyn (Basoko, near Ekoko)
Hector McMillan, Ione and 6 boys (Bongondza)
Bob and Alma McAllister and 3 children (Pontierville, now Ubundu)
Olive Bjerseth (Basoko)
Mina Erskine (Boyulu)
Al and Jean Larson and daughter, Carol (KM 8)
Thelma Southard and son Larry (Banjwadi, husband Marshall was in Léopoldville)
Viola Walker (Basoko)

As the survivors arrived and congregated in Léopoldville, they slowly pieced together their stories and experiences. The deaths of Paul Carlson and Hector McMillan were the first reported in the news. The massacre at Banalia did not make worldwide news until it was uncovered in December.

Ione met up with Dolena Burk, her Matron of Honour when she married Hector; they had both lost their husbands. Chester, Dolena and Hector all attended the same Bible school in Three Hills, Alberta. They had shared so much – joy and sorrow.

Ione wrote that in Léopoldville they stayed first at the Canadian Ambassador's residence, then at the Union Mission House. Various missionary families in the area invited them into their homes for meals and fellowship:

.....*After dinner in a Congo Inland Mission home, a Congolese pastor joined the group. His kind, dark eyes brimmed with tears as he heard us tell in Bangala what happened at Kilometer Eight. Then he spoke,*

"Madame, you have my utmost sympathy. Young men, I am sorry for the loss of your father. And I trust the son in the hospital will soon recover. I shall never be the same again after hearing your story. It is evident that Christ is sufficient for you in this trial. And this has kindled a great fire in my heart. I shall go forth now with a strong message. The light will shine and the fire will burn, as I go to my countrymen. I'll tell them that truly Christ is real, and sufficient for every need. Truly, Madame, the flame in my heart burns hot and I want to go to my people and tell."

As I left that home there was a warm satisfaction in my heart and assurance that other Congolese would be enkindled to shine for Jesus during the dark years ahead.

On Sunday the 29th of November, a memorial service was held in one of the churches. Alma McAllister gathered all the children who had been living in Kilometer 8 to sing a hymn they had often sung – *Onward and Upward*, written by EE Hewitt, which was their contribution to the service.

The family stayed in Léopoldville two weeks, waiting for Ken's wound to heal sufficiently for the journey to the States. Ione wrote:

.....I kept on feeling that it would have been easier to die for the Lord than to live for Him and face up to the reality of heading up a family of six boys. But before I became anything else to those boys' I needed to be the one to lead their family worship. I asked Tim if I might borrow his Bible again.

"I don't mind lending it, Mother, but you know there are seven of us trying to read from one Bible, and it would take less time if we had a few more Bibles."

So, John and Stephen and I went across the street to the Bible Society, where Mrs Martinsen (who had been a missionary in China and had fled the Communists), received us cordially.

She was sympathetic, but could not promise Bibles for all, as they were very scarce just then. She could give us three.

Besides sitting at Ken's bedside, the family visited the Congo Protestant Relief Association looking for clothes. They didn't find much that was suitable, however, the American Consulate helped them shop for suits and raincoats. Ione wrote:

.....Collecting toothbrushes, combs, and simple medicines seemed to require a maximum of effort, and the matter of inoculations and replacement of passports would have been out of the question for our tired brains, had not we been so wonderfully cared for by our mission leader, Mr Ralph Odman.

Each day the missionaries and helping friends met for prayer for those still missing. There was not really much time for retrospection, nor for thoughts of the future. But as I sat with Ken at the hospital and watched his progress, I was aware of my feeling that this thing was not a catastrophe, but was planned of God.... I was confident that no matter what happened in the future, right now it was worthwhile.

On the 28th of November, Leone Reed wrote:

Dearest Ione, Kenny, Paul, David, John, Stephen, and Timmy:

It was so very wonderful to hear your voice this morning. And Timmie's too. I was sorry to get you out of bed, though. I tried to get you in the night here, and talked with the operator at two a.m. this morning. But the lines were held up and were not free until 8:30 a.m. this morning. I didn't know where you were staying, so told the overseas operator to try the three places: UFM Mission Home (if there was one there), the American Embassy or the Canadian. I am glad they persisted until you were reached.

We have been shocked and filled with sorrow over all that has happened. But we do know the Lord is over all and must have a purpose. I can understand your bereavement at this time, but I will never know what my darlings have endured and suffered. This old world is getting towards the end of time and Congo's troubles may invade the United States at any time. Communists are everywhere, and because of them being in many places in the US there is a real downward trend. The command for the Belgian paratroopers to land [using a convoy of US military C-130s] *came from the President of the United States. Many churches wired the President to intervene, and Pastor Bob Shelton and Agnes also sent one from the First Baptist Church. I was thankful for President Johnson's interest and help. He provided the planes, most of them, and equipment for the paratroopers.*

We have prayed for you all for months as well as the whole church in Pontiac and thousands of people in many churches all over the country. And I feel it was the same in Canada. I can't help but feel that Hector's ministry is not ended. His influence will continue and bring many more missionaries into His blessed service. You, Ione, were called to be a missionary because of John and Betty Stam's martyrdom, remember?

There was so much more I wanted to ask you over the phone, but time did not permit.

I am sorry that Kenny has had to have more surgery. I do hope he can be able to leave Congo in a week. Did David get hurt, too? What happened to Paul?

.....Irene Pierce in West Palm Beach has been interviewed twice on TV, Florence said. Also, folks have taken up a collection for you there. I have been interviewed by three newspaper men. Your family picture was on the front page of the Pontiac Press. I was interviewed by the Associated Press men of Detroit.

I have been worried about clothing that is warm for you all. It is cold in Canada and the States in this section. Can you get some things in Léopoldville? Love and prayers to my precious ones,

Mother and Grandmother

Eventually, Ione got to write to her sister Lucille on the 8th of December, with plans for her home coming:

.....We leave Léopoldville December 10, go to New York, then Philadelphia where Ken will be in another hospital for a few days 'check-up' (on his mastoid which has caused a little trouble) & other check-ups. Then Montreal, Ottawa, Toronto, and finally Detroit. Will wire you the dates. Ken's wound is in the seat, quite deep but not in the bone. He had stitches taken out today. An ambulance will take him from hospital to plane & he'll have a wheel chair in New York. He is weak but cheerful & out of danger. Paul had a piece of bullet taken out of his cheek. We will have to catch up on all the news when we see you. We have enough clothes to get to Philadelphia & they have more there. We came away from Stanleyville with only what we wore! Love, Ione

On the day before the family were due to fly home, Hector's brother Archie, aged 58 years, died in a hospital near Avonmore, Ontario. It is not known if Archie knew of his brother's death before he died.

Ione and her six boys arrived home on the 11th of December.

Reflecting back on her experiences, she wrote:

.....I let my mind journey right back to the days when as a young girl I felt just like a princess inside. The happy comfortable sensation of being someone special to somebody! Mary Baker had it, too. I remember one time she said that when she went visiting, she always felt inside that her friends would be glad to see her. And they always were! And I found that I could recapture still that thrill of "being someone special". Mother used to tell me, "Walk like a princess; lift up your head!"

And then as the Lord took hold of my life, I became a princess for Him. My Saviour led me into His service and to the Congo as a missionary. He gave me a precious husband who encouraged me to just go right on feeling like a princess inside. His earlier letters testified to his acceptance of this status.

I felt like a princess inside when I fingered the lovely wedding dress as it hung in the center of the cabin of the barge on the River Nile on the way to our wedding in Juba. Temporary dismay came when I discovered that the netting of the finger-tip veil was eaten by insects and required a multitude of mending's. But eventually rosettes and lover's knots covered neatly each mending place and the wedding was performed November 27, 1945.

The wedding dress was laid away in the same trunk out of which came the layette for the first baby and six times we prepared for a girl and received a boy!

By the last time the last little boy was born in 1954, we were wondering what our children thought of our continual service to the Lord in Congo. It was well and good for us to go so far, but what about the poor children? Did they really want to go back in 1955, as we proposed to do?

I had approached the older 7-year-old, Kenneth, and reminded him, "You must remember, Ken, that when we live in the Congo, we seldom have ice cream cones. No cornflakes; powdered milk instead of fresh. Do you really want to go?"

His answer was a rebuke to me. "But Mother, didn't the Lord call us?"

Then the Lord was leading the children, too. And whatever might come could be accepted by them as not strange. The bullet in Paul's cheek, Ken lying so pale and quiet on the bed brought this verse to me that morning in Kinshasa. In the UMH bedroom that very day, Paul had said confidently, "See this, I Peter 4:12 – Beloved, think it not strange concerning the fiery trial which is to try you, as though some strange thing happened to you."

"Thinking it not strange" really started at Kilometer Eight. But at Kinshasa I was sure that the boys were putting it into practice.

And when the General Secretary visited Ken in the hospital, I was not surprised to hear my oldest son say, "When I finish high school next year, I want to go to Bible School and then medical college. After that I will come back to Congo."

Twenty-three years [since her first arrival in Congo] seemed a long time to get ready for one day when our Daddy would become a martyr. But the martyrdom would not be the end, only the beginning of the harvest which would come in the Congo.

I could say with Samuel that, "hitherto hath the Lord helped us," and go from the help of the past to the hope for the future.

From those first few days in August occupation until the day of liberation on November 24, I often thought of that verse in Psalms 37, "I have seen the wicked in great power and spreading himself like a green bay tree." The rebels were like the Chaldeans about whom Habakkuk prophesied. They marched through the breadth of the land, to possess the dwelling places that were not theirs, to catch men in their nets and gather them in their drag.

It was in the perfect wisdom of God we arrived in Stanleyville just a few days before the town fell to the rebel forces, and experienced some of the horrors and fears of the organized take-over and the annihilation of many of the capable Congolese in the area.

Many people see only the acts that took place, but some will see in my account the ways of the Lord. Psalms 103:7 says, "He made known His ways unto Moses, His acts unto the children of Israel." And we as a family look at it as a reasonable thing planned of God, for the fulfilment of His will.

I remember feeling that it was fearful enough to make a good story. And the thought also came that perhaps none might live to tell it. But of our group, all survived except my husband, and Hector became the martyr of Kilometer Eight.

As a martyr's widow, one of the many now, I am glad to tell what it was like to me at the time Hector was killed.

"Many widows were in Israel in the days of Elias, when the heaven was shut up three years and six months, when great famine was throughout all the land; but unto none of them was Elias sent, save unto Sarepta, a city of Sidon, unto a woman who was a widow" (Luke 4:25, 26).

Like Elijah's widow woman, I feel singled out of the Lord to write about this significant occasion, and how our family was prepared for it, and affected by it.

When we left the homeland to become missionaries, we were never guaranteed safety from physical harm. When we offered our lives to go so far for Jesus, there was no limit as to how far we might have to go. If suffering and death were included in His call, then we would surrender any desire for immunity from this.

All that last week, Hector was aware of our desperate circumstances and pled with the Lord for deliverance, but never for himself. He behaved himself as one consigned to death, and yet in his manner was a great anticipation of the glory that awaited him. We all in a sense surrendered ourselves for whatever might come. We counted our lives not dear. And having submitted to this yoke of restraint and subjection, we found it padded with grace and love.

There came the moment of yielding to Divine Sovereignty when death and wounds came to our family. At this time, we began to see the personal implications of the Lordship of Christ, and restfully submit ourselves to the sovereign will of God.

How far can we go in claiming the protection of God because we are His people? Are we to be excused from involvement in the present world disorder, and should we not be prepared to surrender our own imagined immunity to suffering for the greater glory of God?

We must be agreeable to be involved in the long-term purpose of God, while recognizing the short-term powers of the devil.

So, on November 24, when the rebels came with violence, I found it possible as in Habakkuk 3:16, to be "resting in the day of trouble". When the shooting was over and two sons were wounded and Hector lay dead, it was Psalm 124, quoted by Tim, that comforted.

How far shall we go? Is a question which has come to me in recent months. How far should we go in our effort to win people to Christ? To me, it was never a question of whether or not I should go as a missionary, but HOW FAR CAN I GO? Just how far can I go in my lifetime, with the strength of my body for Jesus? He said, "Go ye into all the world and preach the Gospel to every creature."

When I offered my life to the Lord for missionary service, I felt that I should go just as far as I could with the Gospel. I tried to get to China first. When John and Betty Stam were martyred, I offered my life to take their place. But the door to China was closed. Then a call came through my church, First Baptist, in Pontiac, Michigan, from a missionary doctor in Congo. He wired, "Send us a nurse and a helper." Our pastor's wife, Mrs. H.H. Savage, came to me and said, "Since you can't go to China, why don't you consider Africa? We have found the nurse, Miss Pearl Hiles; now we need the helper."

I went to the Bible for guidance and found in the Acts the verse, "Come over into Macedonia and help us." Then I offered my life and became the helper that the Westcott's were needing. I helped the doctor's invalid wife and 3 children for 3 years and then on the next furlough became officially engaged to Hector McMillan.

We were newly married in the Congo, and as our family increased, we were faced each furlough with the big problem of going so far to our field. It is always an effort to go a long way and every time we were getting ready to go to Congo it was a tremendous job.

Adjustment to pioneer work in the heart of Africa came harder to me than to Pearl Hiles. I thought it was because I was from the city and she was from the country. It was a challenge to me, but it seemed the hardest jobs always lasted the longest.

Whenever I went to the Jenkinson's (Kinso's) for encouragement (and I never failed to receive it from this dear couple!), they always warned me to not set my heart on my trials being soon over. "These things last a long time," they cautioned. So, I set my heart to endure.

Later, I applied the same principle of endurance to marriage, to raising children, to restrictions imposed by the rebels, and when at last in the homeland, to being detained in comfortable America when I longed to return to Congo!

I remember when in 1955 we were going out with our six children and there was a good deal of packing yet to do. And furthermore, we did not even know to which station we would be assigned. Hector sighed, and said, "I feel just like Abraham, who "went out not knowing whither he went." I sighed, too. Then eyeing the work yet to be done, I added, "And we have a Lot, too!"

We decided then that if churches were willing to send out such a big family as ours, and to such a far-away place as the Congo, then we as missionaries should not mind going as far as we can in giving of ourselves and all that we possess in His glad service.

How much should a missionary give in his glad service for Christ? Paul's words in II Corinthians 11:23 indicates he felt danger to be part and parcel of the command to GO YE. He said, "Are they ministers of Christ? (I speak as a fool) I am more. In labors more abundant, in stripes above measure, in prisons more frequent, in deaths oft," He said in effect, "I have something to be proud of." Proud of what? Proud that Christ counted him worthy of suffering for the Gospel's sake.

Some of the things we do may seem foolhardy, but we are not asked to be foolhardy, but simply HARDY...Ready to go where and when He sends.

But I didn't think the rebels would go as far as they did.

When they tipped a table – we went ahead of them.

When they pushed Muriel Davis, I held her up.

When they smashed a bottle – I got out of the way.

When the young man with the pistol fired – we went to the floor.

But you never know how far you can go until you have tried.

It's not far to the altar of consecration; it's not far these days to go to a Bible school; it's not far to a mission board; and some mission fields are not far away. But just how far would you go for Jesus? And there's no turning back. "If any man draw back My soul shall have no pleasure in him." Hebrews 10:38 "If thou faint in the day of adversity, thy strength is small." Proverbs 24:10

"Some men die in battle, some men die in flames,

Others die by inches, playing their little games."[151]

An excerpt from a December 11, news article in the Canadian *Standard-Free Holder* stated:

Clad only in borrowed summer clothes, the six McMillan boys and their 51-year old mother returned to Canada yesterday from the Congo. The boys' missionary father was slain by Congo rebels 18 days ago.

---

[151] Ione quotes a loose interpretation of an excerpt from a poem written in 1938 by Robert D. Abrahams entitled, *The Night They Burned Shanghai.*

Grinning shyly, the boys embraced their grandmother, Mrs Leone Reed of Pontiac, Michigan, and then left by car with other relatives and friends for their father's former home at Avonmore, Ontario.

Ione and the boys, upon arrival in Montreal.

The boys range in age from 10 to 17. Their father, Rev. Hector McMillan, a missionary with the Unevangelized Fields Mission, was killed when Belgian paratroopers attacked rebel-held Stanleyville.

Mrs McMillan declined to talk about the political situation in the Congo.

She said she regards the death of her husband as a price to be paid in establishing Christianity in the Congo.

"It's a high price, but it's worth the cost," she said calmly.

She said she had no regrets about the 23 years she spent as a missionary in the Congo.

"I hope sometime to go back."

Two of her sons – Kenneth, 17, who still limps from a bullet wound suffered when his father died, and Paul, 16 - plan to be missionaries as well and are prepared to return to Congo.

Mrs McMillan, a white-haired woman who gave birth to four of her sons in the Congo, said she has no immediate plans except to visit Avonmore, then go to Philadelphia, where the Unevangelized Fields Mission has its headquarters, for Christmas.

They will attend a community memorial service tomorrow at Avonmore in tribute to Mr McMillan. People of the area have contributed more than $2,000 to assist the family and have collected clothing for the boys.

When they disembarked from the aircraft, they smiled at awaiting relatives and patiently posed for photographers.

Inside the terminal, a waiting passenger glowered and muttered: "Why are they so happy? I wouldn't be happy if someone had just killed my father."

Mrs Reed, Ione's mother, turned to the bystander and said softly:

"When they're killed in the name of the Lord, it's different. He's not gone, he's with the Lord."

Epilogue
IONE'S LIFE AFTER 1964

After Hector's memorial in Ontario, Ione and the boys had a short visit with Hector's relatives then headed to Drayton Plains, Michigan. All underwent a check-up with Dr George Westcott in Ypsilanti and he found everyone well including Ken, whose wound had completely healed. Within a few months, a lovely home on 1 acre of land with fruit trees in Pontiac was obtained with gifts from churches and friends. The boys were enrolled in the Emmanuel Christian School in Pontiac, Michigan.

Dolena Burk, Ione McMillan and Dotti Scholten – three widows of the 1964 Congo Rebellion. This may have been at a UFM Conference in Pennsylvania in 1965.

Ione took on many speaking engagements at this time. In August 1965, she published a newsletter for all her supporters, the first since her newsletter in June 1964. In it she expressed her thanks to all who sent letters and money to her family since the loss of her husband and the boys' father in Congo.

She also mentioned that, of the group of 68 UFM missionaries (including children) in the Congo at the time of the rebel invasion in August, 19 were dead. The Congo area of the UFM at this time was still controlled by rebel leaders, but the main part of Stanleyville was free. Some missionaries aspired to return to reoccupy their stations. Merchants and Catholic priests were going back. Ione stated:

.....*the servants of the Lord need to be there, too. The Psalmist said, in Psalm 132:4,5, "I will not give sleep to mine eyes, or slumber to mine eyelids, until I find out a place for the Lord, a habitation for the mighty God of Jacob". There is work to do yet for us in the Congo, and since we are now, more than ever, sure of a harvest (John 12:24), it is only normal for our family to want to have a part in that harvest.*

Ione hoped that by September of 1966, Kenneth would be ready for Bible School in the US and the rest of the family would go back to Congo. She felt that if Rethy reopened, she might help with the missionary children there or at another AIM station until the UFM area reopened. Her yearning to go back to Congo was shared with Al Larson at Mission Headquarters who supported her return in July 1966. This would also facilitate the boys being enrolled at Rethy Academy in Congo or Rift Valley Academy in Kenya - both being Christian boarding schools operated by

African Inland Mission (AIM). American and British school curriculum was followed as well as a British calendar schedule whereby each term was 3 months long, separated by a month of holiday time when the missionary kids returned to their respective stations and families.

A letter written to Ione by fellow UFM missionary, Bill Snyder, on September 28th, 1965 brought news of Congo. KM 8 was in ruins. Both the hangar and the

The McMillan boys (L) and Ione with Eleanor Muchmore and Carol Snyder (R) singing at the UFM Conference -1965

house were completely burned. Apparently, the mercenaries had come back and retrieved Hector's body and took it to Stanleyville. Al Larson told Ione that the Mission Council agreed in principle to her returning to mission work in September 1966.

As 1965 slipped into 1966, in June, Ken graduated from Emmanuel Christian School in Pontiac. Later in the month, the family traveled to Alaska where they joined Ione's younger sister, Doris. Her husband, Bob Schmidt ran a commercial salmon set-net business 12 miles from Soldotna. Ken started a three-year course at Moody Bible Institute in Chicago in September while the other boys continued with another school year in Pontiac.

By 1967 Ione was once again preparing for Africa and Congo in particular. Having lost everything she had, it was back to collecting table, chairs, ironing board, rugs, sheets, towels etc. By May, she had only one third of the support she needed. Support was much harder to get in the 1960s than it was in the 1930s and 40s when traveling to the heart of Africa was daring and novel.

Ione continued to raise funds for her next venture and for a 1967 Dodge crew-cab truck that became available. The plan was for Paul to complete his schooling in the US and stay with Grandmother Reed when Ione and four younger boys returned to Congo. Ken would continue at Moody Bible Institute. Letters asking for support went out far and wide. One reached an airman who was posted on the bleak coast of the Atlantic where he and Hector served at an air force radar station. He wrote an article that was published in the Toronto Daily Star on December 22. Excerpts are as follows:

.....We called him, affectionately, Hector the Rector and with good reason.

Hector endured the rigors of service life, uncomplainingly. His mood was consistently cheerful and optimistic. He habitually violated one of the airmen's basic principles – namely, under normal circumstances, never volunteer for anything. Hector volunteered for everything.

No job was too dreary or too hazardous. He was always going out of his way to make the lives of his bunkmates easier, more pleasant.

Not surprisingly, newcomers to our small station at first regarded Hector with suspicion. What strange breed of soldier was this? But in time, like the rest of us, they grew to admire and respect him. His sincerity was unquestionable. He had no ulterior motives.

I can see him now, sitting at the side of the bunk, deeply immersed in his Bible. It was a worn volume; on every page there were passages underlined with green, blue or red ink.

One morning, I was about to climb a tower to check on a recalcitrant aerial, when Hector hailed me from a distance. As he approached, I noticed that he was waving a telegram.

He explained to me that he was in love with a girl who was 1,000 miles away. Her name was Ione Reed. They had met at theological school and they both wanted to become missionaries. Last week, he had cabled a proposal of marriage and, at last, here was her terse reply: "See Ruth, Chapter 1, Verse 16."

Never did a woman commit herself more beautifully or poignantly to share her life with the man she loved.

The last time I saw Hector McMillan alive was a few days before Christmas, 1963. He was scheduled to resume his missionary post in Africa shortly after the New Year.

We sat in front of a roaring fire in my living room on a cold winter night, I sipping on wine, Hector drinking a glass of milk.

Since our air force days, he had spent most of his time in the Congo. He spoke proudly of his wife, Ione, and his sons. The talk got around to his imminent return to Africa. I asked: "Isn't it dangerous to be a white missionary in a black country in the throes of a revolution?"

Rethy Academy (one end of the station – July 1969) School and Chapel are in the upper left. In the foreground (L-R) is the 'Biggie' Dorm, Intermediate Dorm, Dining Hall and Kitchen, and 'Tichy' Dorm where Ione served as dorm mother during her last years in Congo.

Hector replied quietly: "If you walk in God's way, you are never afraid." His answer was final and left no room for further discussion.

Hector McMillan, the man, died near Stanleyville three years ago. But the spirit of Hector McMillan, the missionary, lives on, vitally and triumphantly.

On the 2nd of March 1968, Ione, David, John, Stephen and Tim flew from Kennedy airport to

Uganda via Senegal. Ione's luggage was overweight for the flight but she managed to get her typewriter on board the plane, stowed under her legs.

They reached Rethy, at 7,000 feet in northeastern Congo where Ione was posted as dorm mother for the younger kids at school there. She was given the Junior Dorm, more affectionately called the 'Tichy' Dorm[152]. Tim started school straight away but David, John and Stephen had to wait for a new term to start in April at the Rift Valley Academy (RVA) at Kijabe, Kenya. While Ione adjusted to the school schedule and routines of the dormitory, the boys helped out with a few jobs, such as working on a new airstrip. One project took them to another mission station 30 miles away at Kasengu to re-roof a house. Shortly after John got out of the car, his legs felt odd. The next day he found he couldn't stand and didn't walk for four days. Two doctors arrived, one being Dr Becker and the other, a visiting neurologist from the US. Neither of them could come up with a diagnosis but since John did not have fever, polio or a viral infection was ruled out. Later it was determined that he contracted Guillain Barre Syndrome and that he'd have a 50% chance of recovery. John built up his leg muscles with work-outs on the treadle sewing machine. Steve helped him set up the bicycle in one room on its stand for him to peddle in-situ. The bicycle light – powered by a small generator on the rear tire – was an additional strength-building measure and the light's intensity on the wall was his visible means of gaging his work out level. John lost 17 pounds from the illness but was finally able to walk without help and with a limp, he headed off to RVA with the others. He eventually recovered his strength after two years of strenuous, self-induced therapy.

Ione found life at Rethy rewarding what with visitors like the McAlister family, the activities with the kids, and planning meals as she had done for so many years. The Rethy school term started on May 1st and Ione had 10 girls and 11 boys in her dorm. Just after John's illness, Ione came down with malaria and was laid up for two days. She wrote:

.....We have real good meals here, meat once a day, fresh apples and strawberries just now, fresh milk and butter, homemade bread. And for the first time in 25 years I feel energetic in Congo, due to the high altitude and cool climate. The hottest it gets is around 70 and in mornings and evenings we have a fire in the fireplace. It is a new experience for me but I do enjoy it, and everything is done so nicely here and in good taste.

McMillans and the McAllisters at Ione's dorm at Rethy – 1968

In late July, Ione's goods arrived at Rethy. By that time, David, John and

---

[152] Tichy is an informal British word for small.

Steve had arrived back from RVA and were able to help with all the unpacking. While attending Rethy in the early '60s, John had noticed an abundance of bee swarms in the area so he was anxious to set up a bee hive using materials he had included in the shipment to Rethy.

Ione took the boys' holiday as an opportunity to take a 3-day trip to Stanleyville in the Dodge truck. They arrived August 1st and stayed in the UFM compound in Stanleyville which was surrounded by a high cement wall and metal gates. It comprised several apartments joined together. In spite of 3 guards on duty, thieving was prevalent. On a visit to KM 8 the next day, the guard there told Ione that Simbas fought among themselves for possession of the place and its belongings, and they finally burned it down. The grounds were terribly overgrown and damage was everywhere. This was the family's first visit to what had been their home in 1964 and where Hector was killed.

Malenza, who ended up being a house helper to a UFM missionary in Stanleyville, told of being captured by the Simbas and imprisoned in the soap factory (across from KM 9). He was not able to bury Hector. The guard who saw Hector's body being taken away by a mercenary verified that it was taken to Stanleyville. The fellow who killed Hector was still somewhere around but no longer a rebel. They all knew who he was. But Ione made it plain that if she met him, she would forgive him and didn't want revenge.

Ione McMillan and Alma McAllister being greeted with gifts in front of Kinso's House at Bongondza – 1968.

The family then spent 6 days in the Bongondza area and met a wonderful welcome everywhere. Ione wrote about the trip:

.....*It was a real joy, on that first trip back since Hector was killed, to join with the Christian Congolese who suffered so much but are still going on with the Lord. A highlight on this trip was a visit to Kilometer 8 where Hector was killed. The buildings were demolished, having been burned in a terrific fire or explosion. We were able to pick up bits of melted glass as we climbed thru waist-high weeds. There were no houses, but a church had been established since the rebellion, where Congolese from 4 tribes attended. The pastor hobbled over on feet permanently crippled. While he was a prisoner of the Simbas, his feet had been staked to the ground. Rags soaked in oil were tied to them. Then a fire was lighted. He eventually got away, but not before his ear was cut off and his teeth knocked in, all because he would not give up the Lord. His name is Samson. He gave me 2 eggs. He said, "I don't ask anything from the church as they are too poor. When my wife and 7 children and I have no more money, we go into the forest and cut down trees and sell firewood to get money. We look to the Lord and not to people.*

In a letter to Ken written on October 6th, Ione said that if the Moody Press folk asked about her book, to tell them she had not given up on them, nor on any other publisher and that she was just too busy making history to write it down! She continued to monitor the lives of Ken and Paul, their school assignments and schedules and especially their interactions with girls.

Ione, of course, found time for music. On October 14th, 1968, she wrote to her mother:

.....I sang in a trio yesterday, too, at the 3:45pm missionary church. I sang "So Send I You", the low part, with Mrs. Crossman and Mrs. Buyse. It went well and when Mr. Miller got up to speak, he said he felt as though he had already had the message thru that song. Tim sang in a mixed ensemble led by Mrs. Buyse. They did well, and looked so nice in dark suits and the girls in decent-lengthened black skirts and white blouses.[153]

Ione (in blue suit) with one of her Christmas choirs at Rethy Academy - 1968

As 1968 drew to a close, it had been eventful for Ione and the family - probably harder than she would care to admit. Being a dorm parent at Rethy was so very different from running the Children's Home at Kilometer 8. In the past, the lack of contact with the Congolese concerned her, she did not feel she was doing 'missionary' work; yet this does not get mentioned – her focus was on the children in her care – her little bees.

As 1969 started, Ione had two children in America, one child with her at Rethy and three attending school in Kenya at RVA. Financial worries seemed to be ever

---

[153] Skirt lengths become a major concern for Ione, unused to the fashion trends of the late 1960's!

present, both on the field and on the home front in Pontiac. As Hector used to do, Ione continued to claim verses from the Bible for the boys. In one sent to Ken she wrote that the verses she's found for him also spoke to her of conflict, yet she gained complete victory with the Lord's strength.

In the summer of 1969, Ione wrote for her home church magazine, *Gospel Echos*:

.....I am glad I am still out here in Congo, as I enjoy my work, and am thrilled to stay long enough to see what God is doing at Bongondza. Doctor Westcott's hospital has now a new look, repaired and gleaming white paint everywhere. The medical unit my husband put up in 1963 is now being used as a pharmacy. A team of wood-cutters, water-carriers, carpenters, masons, and nurses are on the job.

Back to my lively life as dorm parent, I never cease to delight in these small children, though I often get tired. But the Lord never lets it get too hard. And a good laugh helps to relax. After a jigger and its eggs were removed from a small toe (using a sterilised needle), we burned it in the fireplace, and listened to the tiny explosion when the eggs burst. While the children were standing around rather awed at the funny sound, little Julie, the Congolese girl of our group, said, "My Daddy took a jigger out of my toe and it was so big that it spit at him!" Can't you just see that jigger, no bigger than a flea, standing there spitting at Mr. Babili?!!

Leone Reed and Maurice and Lucille witnessed Ken's graduation from Moody Bible Institute - 1969

Ione heard news of Ken's graduation from Moody Bible Institute and that her mother and sister Lucille and her husband, Maurice were there to witness it.

At the end of July, she and the boys spent some holiday time at the Kenya coast just south of Mombasa – about 300 miles from RVA. She wrote her mother telling that David would not be coming home yet but would try to do so after helping out with building maintenance at Rethy. Ione also told of her feelings and concerns about the conditions at RVA, indicating much of her difficulty with long-distant parenting:

.....I don't think David has gotten into trouble, but both he & John were dropped off the Honour Society for the end of year & I can't find out why. It may be a mistake, as their picture was on the NHS page in the Annual but did not appear on the list on the end of school activities. I'm not too happy about their dormitory supervision, as they will be having 80 boys in one long dorm (4 per room) grades 10-12, and only one couple in charge. I guess I was just too tired when I arrived at Kijabe as everything seemed wrong. And David had started keeping company with a girl the last 3 wks. Not too serious, and he will probably not see her again.

By 1970, David had flown to the US for college and Ione was back at Rethy and left with only 3 boys now. Her trust in the boys' careers at school at Kijabe had been dented but she relied on her faith and belief that God would not let her down but meet all her needs. She had no control over the world that her boys (her six big horses) live in so she invested in guiding and directing them to see life through her eyes and steel themselves against other influences. A quote she used was 'Hector has gone on ahead and left me to tie up the loose horses'!

Paul and David were at Moody in the Foreign Missions course. At the beginning of July, Paul and David wrote to their mother. They were planning to go to Alaska and spend the summer with their Aunt Doris, presumably helping the family pick fish and process salmon. Ione worried that the boys would not keep Sunday as the Lord's day. Added to her concerns at this point was news that her mother had not been well. Ione worried that the boys were not helping her sufficiently.

Ken was a pre-med student at Oakland University, 10 miles from Pontiac, Michigan. He lived at the McMillan's home in Pontiac with Leone Reed who was still active with her ministry of speaking, teaching and playing her bells. She had been an active part of the 3-generation gospel team for the previous 5 years and was caring for the home. She also looked after all home affairs and the boys who remained in the States.

Tim, Steve and John were at Rethy on vacation from RVA. John had still not made an application anywhere, and expected to graduate in July. Ione stated that she didn't mind if he stayed on at Rethy a few months longer, like David did. He asked his mother for permission to attend Ontario Bible College (OBC) since his grandmother would not permit his attending Seattle University where he wanted to pursue art. At the time, OBC was a small college in Toronto that offered a one-year Missions course, as he only wanted one year to comply with UFM's requirement for applying for mission work, should that be in his future plans. Ione agreed and was pleased with his plans.

While at RVA, Ione gave her mother an update. She bought an inexpensive ticket for John to New York on August 21st. She also shared her experience at RVA with regard to John's behavior:

> .....John has been playing the drums here. I heard him tonight on the Senior night program. 3 numbers, one was, "When the Saints Go Marching In." Another - a drum & flute accompaniment to the Choir. And another with the pipe organ – a number something like the Sailor's Hymn they played at Kennedy's funeral. The devil's voice was not in any of these. But in the yearbook, it said the school was relaxing its views of some music, so I have this feeling John may have been playing some that the devil's voice was in. I talked to him about it & asked if he was compromising. He admitted he was, but Timmy said, "Mommy, you don't know how many times John has refused to do questionable things." I am not sure, but he seems ready for Bible school and says he does not expect to continue with RVA's standards of music at Ontario Bible College. But he is frail

Ione, Tim and Steve at Entebbe to see John off for New York - 1970

physically. He needs vitamins and good food. The food here is not so good or as plentiful as at Rethy. Well, God is still on the throne. Hallelujah.

Tying up the loose horses has proved problematic, especially as Ione's sons were in different countries and most of the communication was done through letters. Ione used her mother and sister Lucille to help out, which they did diligently. However, Ione found it challenging when the boarding school did not adhere to and share the same principles and viewpoints as she did.

It was also challenging for her sons, who for the most part conformed and fulfilled her wishes, in a changing and dynamic world. But it is natural for teenagers to question and think for themselves, just as Congo questioned its ideologies and practices.

At the start of 1971, it was a reflective time. The younger boys were back at school and Ione made a trip to her favorite mission station, Bongondza and was once again planning and arranging. Letter writing now required extra hours. Ione told Ken:

.....Today I tried getting up at 3 am instead of 4 to get more supporters thanked. I love to write letters but do not like the cold, hasty way which only thanks but puts no interest & life into it. And this takes time & a clear mind. I want the dew of heaven to be in my letters as well as my life.

The beginning of April found her at Oicha (Ken's birthplace), having a well-earned rest and doing some letter writing while the boys climbed Mt. Ruwenzori. Twice during her stay when the clouds lifted, she caught sight of the beautiful peaks covered with snow. The mountains are about 50 kilometers from Oicha. Ruwenzori is over 16,000 ft and there are cabins at each station where they slept nights. The pygmies were all around Oicha, and Ione helped to take care of pygmy twins (who are extremely tiny and frail) whose mother had died. As she thought of coming home, she was reminded that her dedication was to the Lord and not to a task. She said:

.....When we go as far as we can for Him, we must not complain if He calls us back for a little while. I count the next step as another adventure for the Lord and do trust Him to guide in all that I am to do.

Ione, once again, was able to visit Bongondza, the place where she and Hector began their missionary work together. She wrote that they left on the 6th in the 2-ton Dodge and slept at the usual stations along the way. But the roads were awful. The truck broke down 23 kilometers outside of Kisangani (the new official name for Stanleyville). Not just an axle broken, but the whole rear end fell off. After a

Bongondza church members gather for an outdoor meeting.

miserable night, they arrived in Kisangani at 4:30 AM. She stated that the conference was wonderful and it was worth everything to see the Congolese Christians in action at their conference, deciding peaceably the important issues of the church. There were 67 African delegates from all stations, and 20 missionaries and children. Along with her friend, Isobel Bray, she slept in the house where she and Hector last lived together. Every matter that came up in their meetings was checked with the Scriptures and discussed long and earnestly. The work at Bongondza was really being blessed of the Lord. She was thrilled to see her old station no longer abandoned and fine medical and educational work going on. It made her long to go back and help to get the Bible School started again.

After seeing Stephen graduate from high school at RVA, the 28th of July saw Ione in Nairobi on her way home with Steve and Tim. Later, Steve wrote that they were in Ireland spending a week with the McAllisters. They arrived back in the states on August 10th, 1971.

She was reunited in Pontiac with her mother and her sons Ken and David. On August 20 Paul and John came from Alaska with three huge frozen red salmon, edible trophies of their commercial fishing with their Aunt Doris. Ione was five days altogether with the 6 boys and then Paul left for LeTourneau College.

In early September, David and Steve went off to Moody. John stayed home 3 months and worked, but left for LeTourneau on January 1st when Paul went back for his second semester. Tim applied for Moody to enter next September after he graduated from high school. Ken was to receive his BA degree from Oakland University in June. He hoped by the following September to be either in medical school or to be taking graduate medical studies.

Between Christmas 1971 and New Year's Day, the six boys and Ione visited McMillan relatives in Canada and had meetings and contacts with supporters. She wrote:

.....Jeremiah 15:19 was the verse the Lord gave me before I left Congo/ Zaire the last of July. It says, "If thou return, then will I bring thee again, and thou shalt stand before me: and if thou take forth the precious from the vile, thou shalt be as My Mouth." I am hoping to return to Zaire after a normal one-year furlough. And I trust while I'm in this country that I may take forth the precious from the vile and be as the Lord's mouth.

In Him, Ione

As Ione was living with her mother, letters detailing her activities are few. Her mother still had the flu bug but was up most of the time. Ione didn't have meetings for a while but was expecting to be called for Doctor Westcott to take her to see his wife. Ellen (who Ione cared for when she first went to Africa in 1942) was dying of cancer and had asked for Ione to come over once more. Anne, Ellen's daughter, was there also.

Al Larson (now the director of UFM in the states) visited Ione in Pontiac in

McMillans c1972 - (L-R, back row) David, John, Ione, Stephen
(front row) Tim, Ken, Paul.

March of 1972. He seemed cheerful enough but explained the new crisis in Zaire (Congo was renamed Zaire as of June, 1971) concerning the legal status of missions in the country. It was hoped that Zaire's president would take a kindlier view of missions and churches who had not felt they could cooperate with the ecumenical leanings in the one group which represented all before the government. Two representative bodies were bidding for legal acceptance. UFM settled for one and AIM for the other. Al was hopeful that after talking with AIM leaders, they could figure out how the two missions could stand together with the present set up.

Ione told her sister, Lucille of receiving a letter from David's girlfriend at Moody and spoke of plans to spend some time at Moody in Chicago to see Becky. Becky Williams was her name and Ione was pleased to find out that her dad was the director of the Bible Witness Camp near St. Anne, Illinois. It was a camp for African Americans in that area and a work of faith. Ione was satisfied that Becky was the right girl. The couple were glad she approved. All they wanted was to be good friends and keep on with their schooling. A future in foreign missions was on their minds but they were not clear yet what that meant.

Ione took many meetings in churches and at conferences to spread the word about the work she was doing with an aim of garnering in increased support for her next trip back to Zaire, especially financial support. Besides the Christian message, Ione tried to include something which would engage her audience. She had a story about a snake.

.....THE LOADED SNAKE. Miss Walker was sitting one evening in the living room of her mud house, next door to mine, reading by the light of a small kerosene lantern. Her half-grown cat was beside her. And she heard a noise out in back, toward the School Girls' compound. "Dear me!" she said, "Those little girls are not settling down as they should. I must go out and see what is wrong". So, she picked up her lantern, and stepped out the back door down into the path.

*The little cat followed her. Then she saw the snake. She shouted, "Nyoka".
That's the word for snake. If you see an animal you shout, "Nyama". One time
another missionary saw a cockroach and she shouted, "Nyama", and a band of
Africans came running to her aid with spears, and she had a hard time living
that down. Miss Walker shouted, "Nyoka", and her helper, Patrice Likali came
running with a machete and with one stroke he cut the snake in two halves. And
out from one half, of all things, jumped a live mouse. Patrice Likali was
surprised. And so was Miss Walker. And so was the mouse! The mouse looked
himself over, and he had his tail, and his ears, and his legs, and he said, "I'd
better get going." He started to run. Then what do you suppose happened? The
cat got him!*

*So, you see, everyone is born the first time into a family, and everyone faces
death two times - the first time is when this body dies but the second death is
when we face God's judgment and face spiritual death. The mouse was born
once and had to die twice - first by the snake and then finally by the cat. People
who are born again into God's family are born twice and only die once when
their body dies. They will never die the second death but live forever with
God. If you're born only once, you die twice. But those born twice die only
once.*

In November, 1972, on her way back to Zaire, Ione visited the McAllisters in
Ireland, this time to appear at venues and meetings that were not included in the
previous year's visit. She flew back to London and visited the Jenkinsons and
seemed to jet-set around with no apparent difficulties, stopping in Brussels and then
on to Kinshasa. A UFM missionary there helped her get onto the next flight to
Kisangani. Ione stayed with Isobel Bray at the UFM compound and met with pastor
Asani and other church leaders. She was glad to hear Asani say the whole field was
open to her decision, and that she could go where she liked. But he felt in order for
Ione to more broadly engage in women's work on all stations, she needed to live in
a more centralized location such as Kisangani instead of Bongondza. Ione moved
into the apartment where she and the boys stayed in August, 1968. It already had
some furnishings and she hoped to get her things from Rethy by the end of
December.

Ione was grateful to be able to get right out in the villages so soon after her
arrival. Traveling with Ione were Del Carper, Betty O'Neill, Machini and Asani and
some others. There were some bad mud spots and rain, but they got along OK.

Ione kept well, gradually getting used to the extreme heat which was 120 degrees
a good deal of the time as they went into the December hot season. But it made the
roads more passable when they were dry.

She wrote that having bars on the windows and doors was an absolute necessity
in Kisangani:

*.....I had a thief the other night and he couldn't get in, so [he] reached through
the open window, separated the screen where it was joined. I heard the screen
being separated and saw from my bed his shape which filled half of the window.*

He was standing on a tiny ledge about 4 foot from the ground. His hand was inside the screen, but he remained motionless when I got out of bed. I picked up my torch and approached him [and] I [didn't] scream. Instead I spoke to the man and urged him to leave. I spoke first in Swahili, then Bangala and he just stood there. I flashed my torch in his face, and he angrily grabbed his own torch and flashed it in my eyes. When I saw that I was challenged I thought I'd better get out and shout in the back for the guard, which I did. He did not succeed [and finally left]. I have kept the glass window closed since that night. I wondered why so few people around here have curtains at their windows, and now I know why! It is easier to get rid of a snake!

Ione's women's sewing class had doubled in numbers. She figured in the big city, there would be many more. She got a calling list from Machini with names and addresses of women as well as the new converts from recent meetings. In her spare time, she worked on the little songbook, *Tasali Lembo* and she got the sol-fa written out so that there would be a music copy. But it took a lot of time. The choir leader at the church wanted help with putting some songs in the sol-fa so that he could teach them by syllable. He also wanted her to help with the costumes for the Christmas 'drama'.

Ione, the Carpers and Isobel Bray went to the cemetery to see Hector's grave. The birthdate had never been put on the memorial, so they took a small can of white enamel and a brush and added the date. The cemetery did not get regular landscaping care. The two larger bushes had grown to a tremendous size; the red-leafed one was loaded with bright red blossoms. Del had to chop down some of the shrubbery to even get close to the marker. They picked up the flowers and made a beautiful big bouquet for the English church service. Ione stated,

.....One doesn't usually take flowers away from the cemetery! But I think Hector would enjoy being different and supplying the flowers from his grave!

Her work was a combination of three jobs; Women's work, six teen-age children of pastors who came to her for help in their Bible study, and the Lingala translation work. She was learning Lingala as she wrote hymns and revised the book of songs. The old Bangala was being changed rapidly. She led 4 to the Lord in the women's section of the Kisangani Prison.

Always anxious to check out the mission work in progress, she planned to take a trek with Dr and Mrs Kyle and the Carpers in March all around the Bongondza area and to the pygmies nearby. Steve would get to go there when he came and Ione looked forward to this.

Ione wrote in her newsletter to supporters in August 1973, that she had the privilege to go to several remote places in Zaire including the Longele river beyond Bongondza, and to Ekoko where she found a wonderful active church. During the last session of the conference she was taken ill with bacillary dysentery which was later complicated with malaria. She was flown by MAF plane to the large Evangelical Medical Center at Nyankunde (a four-hour flight). It was there that Steve joined her as he had come out to spend the summer in Zaire. Steve was a real help in looking after her. The dysentery and malaria stopped, but after a month she was still being fed intravenously. The field leader thought it advisable for her to come home. Steve and a missionary nurse flew to the United States with her. She was put in a hospital in Michigan where she stayed two weeks before being allowed to go home to Pontiac. Her weight and health slowly came back but she found she needed rest for several weeks. She thanked all her supporters for the many cards, letters and assurances of prayers for her needs. She stated that God's purposes are sometimes more than we can understand, but we needed to be faithful in all things. As strength permitted her, she planned to complete the revision of the Lingala hymnbook *Njembo na Bomoi* (Hymns of Life).

As of August 1973, Ione's weight was 118 lbs and she stated that she had more eating to do but the Lord would not let it last too long. The illness certainly had taken a toll on Ione. In a formal letter to supporters written in 1974, she explained what happened:

.....*Some of you will remember that I came home from Zaire in June, 1973, ill with bacillary dysentery and malaria. Anemia persisted, and it was two months before I felt well again. In September, I began to accept speaking engagements again and had a good winter and spring. During the month of March 1974, I spoke 23 times. I felt good when I went in April to get medical clearance for return to Zaire in August.*

I was disappointed to learn that the anemia still persisted, and I would need a better blood report before I could go back to my work in Africa. Then followed many tests during May and part of the summer in an effort to find out whether the failure to manufacture blood was caused from multiple myeloma or from a hypo-plastic condition in the bone marrow. In the meantime, I contracted hepatitis from blood transfusions, and that set me back about six weeks. Now I feel well, and have learned how to carry on normal activities, including meetings, even with a low blood count. I do not have any symptoms of bone cancer in the form of aches or pains or weakness. So, I am thankful to be active and looking forward to conferences and travel in the fall and winter. If I can produce a better blood report by spring, I will try again to qualify for return to Zaire.

In Ione's letter in May, she wrote that she was given 2 pints of blood and had much pep and felt "great". She wrote some letters to the Nyankunde hospital to cable the names of the drugs she received there last summer so that the doctors in the states could have the entire picture as her doctors thought the drugs might have started the bone cancer. She said they had not given yet the prognosis nor filled out the UFM medical form for clearance and she wondered what would appear there. She also asked if she might continue medication in Zaire if she was near a medical center for monthly check-ups. At the time, this request was not answered. She wrote,

.....*So, you see I'm on the brink of a great career just waiting for someone to push me off! There is lots to do – here or there and feeling THIS good will help if I need to change my thinking & plans.....Much love, Ione*

She saw the doctor who was pleased that her blood count was up quite a bit – from 6.2 to 9.7. He took another type of blood test and said the blood was better but the bones were not.

In a newsletter to supporters and friends dated August 1975, she wrote that during a medical check-up leading up to her hopeful return to Zaire, the doctor found that she still had hepatitis and X-rays revealed five bone fractures. She was in bed some of the time but was ever thankful for gifts and support coming in.

And, so ended Ione's time in Africa, 31 years dedicated to preaching the gospel, living in faith that God would supply her every need. There were times when she struggled with managing the family finances and as her family grew and lived away from her, this became more and more complex.

Ione was always mindful that money donated by supporters for God's work ended up being used for that, which was always a further complication to her bookkeeping! Ione relied on the love and support from her mother and her sisters, they shopped, wrote letters, sent parcels and took on the care of her sons so she could fulfil what she had been asked of God to do. For a great deal of the time she had the love and support of Hector, and although she did not dwell on it, he was

The Reed Family, 1975
(L-R) Marcelyn, Ione, Lucille, Leone (mother) and Doris.

sorely missed. However, his legacy continued with their six sons who seemed to have inherited much of his passion for fixing things as he had done.

What follows are some excerpts of a letter sent out by Lucille on the 1st of September 1975:

Dear loved ones,

I am spending the day here & will have time to write between doing things for Ione.

Doris spent all day here yesterday. Ione is better but she wants someone with her. So, I am here when she feels the need of it and to do things that she would have to call the nurse for. It seems to help her to relax to know someone is here.

I'm enclosing a Polaroid picture taken Saturday evening. Please take good care of it for me. We knelt on the floor beside her. Several were taken but this is the only one I have. We four had not been together for so many years so Doris and Marcellyn wanted pictures.

If the Doctor comes in today, I'm all set to talk to him and find out what his opinion is about her condition. He said she can't leave the hospital until her lungs are clear of pneumonia. Both lungs have been pretty full & not responding to antibiotics. Doctor said it's a virus and is harder to treat. She still needs oxygen and intravenous feeding, etc.

The September 1975 family Newsletter was written by Ken:

Dear Ones:

My Mother, Mrs. Ione McMillan, is not well enough to write at this time, so perhaps I can fill the gap by supplying you with the important family news items of the last several months.

Last year ended with hopeful prospects of Mother's reinvolvement in missionary work in Zaire. And since January 1975 she has held 37 speaking engagements including missionary conferences and women's meetings in Canada and United States. However, the last two months have been rough on her. It has been a difficult experience dealing with one complication after another of the multiple myeloma and having to be in bed most of the time, in the hospital twice. She is now beginning to climb on top of a persistent pneumonia.

At home at 1205 Merry Road, Pontiac, Mich., Ione (center) enjoying her first grandchild, Karen McMillan, first born of David and Becky. Ken is to the right of David, John is in the foreground. Back row (L-R) is Grandmother Reed, Steve, Tim with Paul and Linda in front of them - 1975.

Through these trials she feels God is definitely closing the door of return to Zaire. The future hides special surprises I'm sure, but she would like me to convey to you that Zaire is "out" as an option. She leans on Psalm 18:30 – "As for God, His way is perfect."

For those of you who have not heard yet, Tim was accepted by the Moody Missionary Aviation training program in Tennessee and will be there two years. Paul is engaged to be married to Linda Hoffman. Both Linda and Paul are accepted at Grace College and Seminary in Indiana. Also, Mother's first grandchild was born on March 15, 1975. Karen Dawn McMillan is her name; David and Becky are her happy parents. Steve is home and attends Oakland Community College, after spending 8 months in Zaire. John spent all summer working in Alaska. Undecided as yet are his plans. Grandmother Reed is still part of our team in many capacities.

Mother says, "Thank You" to each of you who have sent cards, letters, flowers, and food, and to each who has lovingly supported her with finances and believing prayer.

Yours on behalf of Mother,

Kenneth McMillan – (Senior medical student)

Ione recovered enough to write to her sister Lucille on 30th December 1975:

.....Here I am in bed again with the "wheezers" having caught a "flu" germ from one of our visitors. Mother will write soon but is still bogged down with washing. The last of the visitors left Sunday afternoon. We had a real nice time. It was a lot of work for Mother to cook for 11 people but she got along OK. She

had two bells' engagements, too. Pray that this cold I have now will not go into pneumonia. The boys have the humidifier going and I have the oxygen tank still. Thanks for the $5 you sent.

I hope you are feeling OK these days.

We had a nice Christmas with 11 stockings on the mantle piece. A living Christmas tree. The boys are planting it today as 3 boys are here and the weather is warmer. We are trying to get together some gifts for Steve's birthday tomorrow.

The basement looks nice now. We had the plumber come back and put a vent through Mother's cupboard in the breezeway (all of her stuff is still out) and the toilet and shower are in. The shower was my Christmas gift to the boys. I'll have the boys draw a diagram. Pole shelves are real handy and places for visitors' towels. There were 5 boys slept down there. We were thankful for the roll-away bed. Mother may add to this so I'll close. Love, Ione

Ione had her first meeting since her illness and she and Steve presented the work in Zaire via slides and tapes. He concluded the presentation with recordings of singing in the Zaire churches (full of people) showing the worthwhileness of it all. Ione led the discussion afterward.

Ione and her mother and Ken when he received his MD at Wayne State University Medical School - May, 1976.

At this stage, Ione was well enough to write another newsletter, her last one, in March, 1976:

The last letter written from us was done by my son, Kenneth, as I was too sick to write then. Now I am better health wise. I have been out to church services a number of times and have begun to accept speaking engagements for the Spring.

The truth of the verse in Psalm 18:30 has proved true – "as for God, His way is perfect." It seems to be God's perfect way to heal me from the very serious illness through which I have come: double pneumonia, persistent hepatitis, and multiple myeloma. Then on January 28, just as I was making a real good return to health, I fell on the tiled basement floor and hurt my hip. But this handicap, too, seems to be passing away. I was on crutches for three weeks and am at present still limping, but carrying on normally.

I wanted the people interested in us to know that life is going on as planned by our

Ione and her Mother on Mother's Day – 1976.

Heavenly Father and some big events in the boys' lives are soon to be coming to pass. The first accomplishment will take place May 16 when Paul receives his Master's Degree of Divinity from Grace Seminary at Winona Lake, Indiana. At that time Paul's fiancée, Linda Hoffman, will graduate from Grace College at Winona Lake. Paul and Linda will be married May 28th in Eugene, Oregon. They are accepted candidates for missionary service in Zaire under U.F.M. On May 23 Kenneth will receive his MD from Wayne State University Medical School. Then the first part of June, David will receive his BA from Illinois University in Chicago. During the month of June, David and Becky and infant daughter, Karen, will be at our Unevangelized Fields Mission Candidate School in Bala Cynwyd, Pa. At which time decision will probably be made as to which overseas UFM field David and Becky will go.

John is thinking of taking a trip to East Africa after his summer of fishing in Alaska. Stephen will continue in his course of study at Oakland Community College through two more years, while living at home. And Tim has another year or so at Moody Flight School in Tennessee.

I marvel at the faithfulness of friends who have continued to support us, even though I have not been on the field for so long. The need is great in Zaire, and as another missionary wrote just before leaving for Bongondza, "The situation on the field is that I am needed very much."

So, the need is there, the supporters still give, and it remains to be seen what God will do so far as my medical clearance will be to go back. Will you continue to pray for us all, including my Mother? She is still part of our team: helping prepare our letters as well as caring for her own ministries: Thank you so very much.

Lovingly, Ione McMillan

The last letter was from Ken written on September 1976:

Dear Friends:

A few months have passed since my mother wrote to you. She is now in the presence of Jesus Christ.

In her March 1976 letter Mother told of the Lord's goodness in raising her up to a measure of physical health in spite of the multiple myeloma (bone marrow cancer). She then was able to enjoy each of those important events she wrote about – Paul's graduation from Grace Seminary, his marriage to Linda Hoffman on May 28 in Eugene, Oregon, my graduation from medical school in May and Dave's and Becky's acceptance as candidates for the Republic of Zaire under the Unevangelized Fields Mission. But she began to fail steadily after that and was confined much of the time to her bed at home.

On September 19, 1976 Mother was taken to be with her Lord. She did very much wish to be in Zaire the last years of her life and be buried near her husband, our father; however, she relinquished this desire earlier this year when it looked quite impossible. My brothers and I along with her mother, Mrs. Leone Reed, her sisters and her relatives can join with many of you and with her African friends in testifying of her great faith and love, gentleness of spirit and unquenchable humor. She expressed these qualities best in her roles as mother, daughter, sister, missionary of the Gospel, wife and public speaker. It is impossible to recall all the happy moments that came from having her around, but we will try in the months ahead [more like 44 years!] *to put together a biography of our parent's lives. Any personal anecdotes you can contribute toward this are welcome.*

As for the future I would appreciate very much if the following were done: if you wish to continue receiving an annual news letter from me covering us six boys and Grandmother, please mail the enclosed card with your current name and address. You may also want a prayer letter from individual family members. Paul and David are both appointed to Zaire mission work under UFM and are raising support. In either case I will be waiting for a response to indicate your desire to stay on the mailing list.

My brothers, Grandmother and I want to convey our deep personal gratitude to you for years of prayer and financial assistance. Our desire now is to seek "not to be ministered unto but to minister."

In His love, Ken McMillan M.D.

Leone Reed wrote:

.....Ione has been a very precious daughter, mother, sister, relative and friend, as well as a faithful servant of our Lord Jesus Christ. Her presence is greatly missed by everyone she has blessed. But earth's loss is heaven's gain. Her love for each one will linger on to keep us closer to Jesus Christ until He comes again.

Steve was at Ione's side during her last days and said:

.....She had such a vibrant ministry speaking everywhere up until just months before her death. The last word she was saying as she passed away was, "sufficient".

AFTERWORD

Ken, Paul, David, John, Steve and Tim McMillan, Aug. 2019

Hector and Ione McMillan left a legacy in their sons.

Ken kept his promise to become a doctor and obtained certification under the American Board of Surgery, and a Diploma of Tropical Medicine and Hygiene from the University of London in 1982 before proceeding to DR Congo. He met Ginny Stone, a missionary nurse in DR Congo and they married in 1983. Their two children were born to them while working in DR Congo. During his 15 years of service there he was Medical Director and Surgeon of Rethy Hospital and served as Public Health Officer for the surrounding 265,000 villagers. He founded and directed Rethy Nursing School, and was Flying Doctor to other rural hospitals without doctors. He trained seven nurses from those hospitals in major surgery, and taught three Congolese physicians in surgical procedures. Dr McMillan and his family had to evacuate DR Congo in 1996 due to civil war. In 1999 Ken settled with his family in Minnesota, finding a medical niche at the American Indian Community Development Corporation (AICDC) in Minneapolis.

Paul applied to UFM with plans to serve the Lord in missions. He was accepted and advised to pursue further ministerial studies at a theological seminary. He graduated in 1976 from Grace Theological Seminary in Indiana where he met his wife, Linda. They spent nine months studying Spanish in Texas and in the summer of 1978 left to serve the Lord in the Dominican Republic. In 1985, he began a ministry as one of the pastors of a new Church in the DR. Three years later they purchased a piece of property in Northern Santo Domingo where they now live. While raising a family of 3 children there, they established a school which has grown to 400 students and a church which now has close to 100 members. They also operate a small goat farm and host mission teams that visit from the US to work on projects in the DR.

David met his wife, Becky while at Moody and they were married in 1974 at her parents' church/camp south of Chicago. They joined the UFM team in France but after their first term, realized they needed to return to the US and put down roots. The growing family returned to Illinois near Becky's parents where David found work for 8 years at a pork slaughter house and later enjoyed 15 years of self-employed home repair. In 2002 they were asked by Becky's dying father to move to the family's church/camp (Bible Witness Camp) and replace him as pastor/director. BWC, where David and Becky reside, is a ministry in a rural African-American community, providing after-school Bible clubs, Sunday School and Church, summer camps and various other events. Support comes from churches and friends. David and Becky have six children of their own but since 2011 they have trained for foster care and have welcomed several additional children into their home.

John attended Ontario Bible College in Toronto for a one-year special missions program then spent 10 summers helping his Aunt Doris' commercial set net salmon fishing and seafood processing in Kenai, Alaska. He freelanced in art and design and later worked in Alaska's north slope oil patch where he supervised the design and installation of a pipe inspection facility for a Kenai oil service company. Keen to follow his own path and utilize his inherited design and inventive skills, he moved to Seattle where he began working on a toggle release invention inspired by a primitive one seen earlier in set net fishing. He graduated in 1992 from the Art Institute of Seattle with an AA degree in Industrial Design Technology and taught himself AutoCAD between work doing home repair. A year later he met Mary Manning while bird watching in Seattle. John traveled to Zaire in 1995 to help dedicate the Hector McMillan Chapel at KM 8 which he designed. He moved to Gig Harbor, Washington in 1996 where he continues to share a house on 4 acres with his partner Mary, a professional violinist/violist. After reading his parents letters it became apparent that his love of music (piano and accordion), and his mechanical and inventive insight are some of the main characteristics he attributes directly to them (which could be said of all his brothers). Of the 6 patents that he obtained, his toggle release invention, called the Sea Catch, has become a successful business venture selling over 131 models of quick release hooks to over 43 countries. John also volunteers at a restored boat yard on the Gig Harbor waterfront and shares his skills with the design and installation of a dual 70-ton marine railway carriage system.

Steve's commitment to missions led him to Rethy in DR Congo where he served as station manager between 1980 and 1997, responsible for electrical and water systems, vehicle upkeep and building maintenance (just like his father). He met his wife, Melinda, at Rethy and raised 4 children there prior to having to evacuate the country in 1996. The family moved to Kijabe, Kenya where Steve assumed the duties of technical manager for Kijabe Hospital which included oversight of the hospital biomed equipment, vehicles, busses, ambulances, and 4WD land cruisers used for bush clinics. He was also responsible for the station's backup generator system, water supply and upgrades including installing a large $80,000 pipeline to a spring 5 miles up the valley. Melinda served as physical therapist in the hospital. From 2008 to 2015 Steve was the maintenance supervisor for Rift Valley Academy, a K-12 boarding school with 500 students, also located at Kijabe. He was responsible for 120 residences, 15 admin buildings, and all the building, electrical and hot water system upgrades from electrical tank heaters to solar units. He maintained a complex water system and supervised over 2 dozen workers doing electrical, plumbing, building, and carpentry work for this large institution. Melinda headed up the school Physical Therapy Department treating injured students and helping others with post-op therapy. He and Melinda then moved to Malewa Community near Naivasha, Kenya in 2016 primarily for outreach with the Jesus Film to Dorobo, Masai, Kalenjin and Kikuyu tribes.

Tim began training in the fall of 1972 for Moody's Missionary Aviation Flight School in Tennessee then completed the course with a Commercial and Instrument Pilot's License as well as an A&P Mechanics License. He was then accepted by the Mission Aviation Fellowship (MAF) and with his wife Judy, he served briefly in Zaire and Sudan. Shortly it became apparent that the stress of all the challenges were too great and they asked to leave MAF in 1980. The Air Traffic Controller's strike in 1981 provided an opportunity for a different career. Tim began working as a radar controller at New York Center on Long Island, NY, in 1982. A transfer to Washington Center in Leesburg, VA, was made in 1988. Air Traffic Control provided a good match for Tim's problem-solving abilities – something he attributes to his father's well-loved talent. Creative woodworking also developed into a practical avenue for his skills. Tim retired from controlling air traffic in 2005, but continued to work for a Government Contractor as an ATC Instructor for an additional ten years. Tim and Judy have two children. Becoming care-givers for three grandchildren made the transition to being fully retired an easy decision in 2015.

In 2014, two return trips to Congo took place for 50-year commemoration events. In February, Tim along with brothers Ken and David returned for memorial events of Hector McMillan's death in 1964. They were accompanied by Ken's daughter, Jane; David's daughter, Amy; and Paul's daughter, Carol. The group was joined by Bob McAllister, sons Bill and David as well as David's wife Sabine. The historic eight-day visit was marked by a very warm welcome at many of the mission stations where these two families had invested their lives. The second trip was due to an invitation by the Governor for the missionaries to attend some November 24th events in Congo – 50 years to the day of liberation. This one was attended by Bob

McAllister, sons Bill and David and daughter Ruth, Steve McMillan, his wife, Melinda, his daughter Michelle and son Daniel, as well as Ken's son, Tom McMillan. There were grand celebrations at Bafwasende, Boyulu, Kisangani, KM 8 and other locations. The visitors also paid tribute to Hector McMillan at his grave site in Kisangani and at KM 8 where he was killed.

Hector McMillan Chapel completed in 1995 (shown here in 2014) at the site of his martyrdom.

Chronology of the Hector & Ione McMillan Story

1913: Ione was born August 17 in Grand Rapids, Michigan to Arthur and Leone Reed.

1915: Hector was born July 16 in Avonmore, Ontario, Canada to Dan L. and Jane (McElheran) McMillan.

1917: Ione's family moved to Wash. DC

1919: Ione's family moved to Pontiac, Mich.

1920: Hector's mother died of TB in October.

1921: Hector attended the Avonmore Public Schools.

1923: Ione accepted Christ as her savior and was baptized.

1930: Ione graduated from Pontiac Central High School.

1934: Ione was called to missionary service in China after hearing of the martyrdom of missionaries, John and Betty Stam but war conditions prevented her service there.

1935: Ione graduated from Moody Bible Institute, Chicago, then sang with the Sunshine Gospel Trio for 5 years in 33 states.

1936: Hector graduated from Avonmore Public High School and enrolled in the Prairie Bible Institute, Three Hills Alberta.

1938: Ione's father, Arthur Reed, died on October 20.

1940: Hector graduated from PBI and sought to serve as a missionary to Brazil with Unevangelized Fields Mission. For one year he attended a Missionary Medical School in Toronto while spending time at the UFM HQ in Toronto. He enlisted in the Canadian Air Force in order to speed up the time he could be free to serve as a missionary. The Sunshine Gospel Trio disbanded in the summer.

1941: Hector and Ione met in Toronto at the Unevangelized Fields Mission headquarters where Ione was sent for the candidate period for mission work in Congo. They were together for 3 weeks. Ione then traveled to UFM headquarters in Philadelphia prior to sailing with Pearl Hiles to Congo in December. Hector completed his medical course and was transferred to Toronto to take military drill.

1942: Ione was posted at Bongondza assisting the Westcott family. In October Hector still expected to go to Brazil with UFM but began to consider Congo instead. While waiting for the Brazil door to open, he was asked to help repair/remodel the new UFM mission home in Philadelphia. Hector returned to Toronto after his passport time elapsed and enlisted in the Canadian Air Force.

1943: Hector's Air Force service took him to New Brunswick and several other Maritime Provinces as a radar mechanic. Hector and Ione were engaged to be married (by mail) on May 12th. In July, Ione finally was able to go on trek with Viola Walker along the Basali Trail.

1944: Hector left the RCAF in July and was ordained in the High Park Baptist Church, Toronto on April 14. Hector went to UFM in Philadelphia in anticipation of sailing to Africa. By September Ione was heading back from Congo with the Westcotts for furlough to the US after her 3-year term in Congo. After a long wait at the coast, they sailed from Matadi on November 17th. Hector made plans to take the same boat back to Congo. Ione arrived in New York in December. They had one month together and became officially engaged at the UFM HQ in Philadelphia before Hector sailed to Congo alone.

1945: Hector sailed for Congo on January 14th. About 9 months later, after visiting Hector's sisters in Canada, Ione sailed on October 16th from New Jersey to Naples and

Port Said, Egypt, then traveled by rail and river steamer up the Nile River. Hector and Ione were married on November 27th in Juba, Sudan, and began missionary service together at Bongondza station after their honeymoon in the mountains of eastern Congo.

1946: At Bongondza, Ione had a miscarriage and lost a baby girl, on May 25th,

1947: Kenneth Reed McMillan was born June 19th at Oicha, Belgian Congo. Hector and Ione spent most of December and part of January, '48 working on a building project at Ekoko.

1948: Paul Daniel McMillan was born July 14th at Yakusu, Belgian Congo.

1949: The McMillan family left Congo by boat in March for furlough in Canada.

1950: David Lynn McMillan was born March 17th at Three Hills, Alberta, Canada. In July the family sailed on the SS *Stavelot* from New York to Congo and took the same river boat up the Congo River to Stanleyville.

1951: John Howard McMillan was born October 18th at Banda, Belgian Congo.

1952: Stephen Arthur McMillan was born December 31 at Aketi, Belgian Congo.

1953: Ione had a heart attack on July 11th. She flew home to Fenton, Michigan for medical care and recovery. Hector and the boys (along with Marcellyn), flew back to the US. The family stayed both in Fenton, Michigan and Newington, Ontario.

1954: Timothy George McMillan was born February 6th at Ypsilanti, Michigan. In November Ione lost her US citizenship on November 8th, by voting in Newington, Ontario, Canada while Hector was absent.

1955: Ione was fully recovered and the McMillan's flew back to Congo in August. They accepted a post in Stanleyville at a large rented house to care for UFM children while they attended the Belgian school in town. Around December 1st a larger home was found at Kilometer 9, north of Stanleyville. All the children were bused to Stanleyville's Athénée Royale Catholic school.

1956: The Children's Home was moved to Kilometer 8 in the fall.

1957: The family spent Christmas at Katwa, eastern Congo. Hector's father died July 18th.

1958: KM 8

1959: KM 8

1960: Riots, strikes, and race troubles, occurred in Congo's major towns. Congo gained independence from Belgium on June 30. Due to unsafe conditions, and furlough hastened by evacuation, the family flew to Montreal on July 8. Hector was reunited with his family six weeks later and they traveled to Three Hills, Alberta.

1961: Their furlough year ended on July 1st and the family drove to Alaska to visit Ione's sister, Doris and her family, in late summer and returned to Three Hills. They left in September for meetings throughout the States and Canada and the children attended Emmanuel Christian School in Pontiac, Michigan till December when the family moved to Avonmore, Ontario.

1962: At a hospital near Avonmore, in May Ione underwent a complete hysterectomy for a tumor in the uterus. Hector left by boat from New York (via Newfoundland) with a 2-ton truck and Ione and the boys left by plane from New York September 4th. The children attended school at Rethy Academy, northeast Congo and Ione traveled onward to Bongondza Station for a 5-year term of missionary service with Hector. Hector sailed via Durban, then to Mombasa, Kenya and drove the truck overland via Rethy and Stanleyville to arrive at Bongondza on November 6th.

1963: Hector and Ione were mainly at Bongondza Station. The children alternated school & vacation schedule with 3 months at school and one month off. Ken was taken to Kampala, Uganda for mastoid surgery. Ione flew to Kampala to be with Ken. The family took a pygmy trek to Bakopo for several days. 5 of the boys attended Rethy again and Ione took Ken, via road and rail to enroll him at the Rift Valley Academy in Kenya. In November, the Congo capital, Léopoldville went under martial law for six months. Ken flew to Stanleyville from Kenya and the others were driven from Rethy to Stanleyville and all were taken to Bongondza for their last Christmas together as a complete family.

1964: In August the 5 Rethy-schooled McMillan boys were driven from Rethy to Stanleyville. Hector took Paul with him in the truck to deliver lumber from Stanleyville to Boyulu Station where they collected Ken on his return from his school in Kenya. The family was to go onward to Bongondza, but In August, Hector and the two boys and Boyulu station staff were put under house arrest. A curfew fell on Stanleyville and Ione and the 4 younger boys were taken from Stanleyville to KM 8 along with several other missionaries and their families while Simba Rebels marched in to town. Hector (with Ken and Paul) was later brought in to KM 8 by special permission of the rebel government. All 25 missionaries and children at KM 8 were under house arrest for 4 months. November 24th rescue came by way of paratroopers descending on Stanleyville to secure the airport and mercenaries who entered town by road. Hector was killed on that day and Bob McAllister, Ken and Paul were injured. Al Larson engaged the help of anti-Castro Cuban exiles in a road rescue of those still alive at KM 8. Hector's body was left at KM 8. A flight was arranged to Léopoldville where Ken was sent to a hospital to recover for two weeks. The family then flew to Montreal and eventually to Pontiac, Michigan.

1965: Ione applied to regain her US citizenship. She took meetings in Canada. She was approved to return to Congo in September 1966 with the four younger boys. The family spent several weeks in August at Three Hills, Alberta.

1966: The family went to Alaska in June for the summer to assist with Doris' commercial fishing/processing operation.

1967: A double-cab Dodge pick-up truck was acquired for use by Ione and the boys upon their return to Congo. Ione got her US citizenship reinstated in September.

1968: Ione and four boys left February 2 for Congo. Ione was posted at Rethy Academy in the northeast of Congo and the 3 older boys attended the Rift Valley Academy at Kijabe, Kenya.

1969: David graduated from RVA in July. In August Ken graduated from Moody Bible Institute.

1970: John graduated from RVA in July.

1971: Steve graduated from RVA and in August, Ione, Steve, and Tim flew back to the US via Ireland.

1972: Ione was in Pontiac, Michigan and traveled around for meetings. November 12 Ione returned to Congo and was posted in Kisangani to work with women as well as on other projects.

1973: Ione did some trekking to outposts near Bongondza. Steve went to Zaire for the summer. Ione became ill at Ekoko and was flown to Nyankunde Medical Center then she flew with Steve to the US and was hospitalized near Pontiac.

1974: Ione was permitted to return to the home in Pontiac and awaited better health reports that would allow her return to Zaire.

1975: In the summer, Ione was hospitalized again near Pontiac with complications, including pneumonia, and was put on respirator, oxygen, and intravenous feeding. On September 16, she was permitted to return home but she still required care.

1976: In March, Ione took a few meetings but the double pneumonia, persistent hepatitis, and multiple myeloma took their toll. Then on January 28, while making a real good return to health, she fell on the tiled basement floor and hurt her hip. She was on crutches for three weeks and with some limping, carried on normally and still made plans for her future activities. Her health deteriorated and she passed on to Glory on September 19th.

1987: Leone Reed, Ione's mother, passed away on April 15th. She loved Ione so much that she selected the grave site next to Ione's rather than that of her husband, Arthur Stuart Reed.

Fast-forward to the Cuban connection: A meeting in the Miami airport in September, 2011 occurred of some living members of the anti-Castro Cuban group who were conscripted by the CIA to help with the rescue operation in Stanleyville - and who went 8 kilometers beyond the call of duty to rescue 25 missionaries and children in November of 1964. Hector had been killed just a few hours prior to this rescue effort. At the Miami meeting these Cubans received a booklet that John had prepared. This memento contained current family photos and comments from all the living survivors of KM 8. Three McMillans, Paul, David and Tim as well as Al Larson and his wife, Jean, were present at this tearful gathering (see photo below). It was wonderful to be able to say thank you to each of them, over 47 years after it happened.

Appendix A

MAP OF BONGONDZA

Appendix B

MAP OF CONGO AREA / MAP OF KM 8

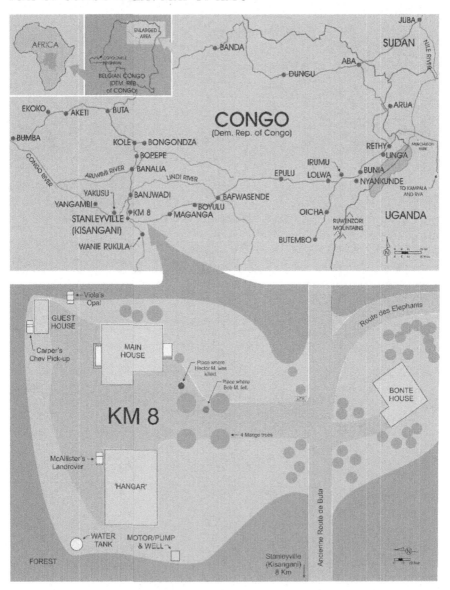

Made in the USA
Coppell, TX
10 May 2021

55405970R00312